STUDIES IN MATHEMATICAL
ECONOMICS

MAA STUDIES IN MATHEMATICS

Published by
THE MATHEMATICAL ASSOCIATION OF AMERICA

———

Studies in Mathematics

Gerard Debreu
University of California, Berkeley

Leonid Hurwicz
University of Minnesota

Harold W. Kuhn
Princeton University

Andreu Mas-Colell
Mathematical Sciences Research Institute

Roger B. Myerson
Northwestern University

Roy Radner
Bell Laboratory

Stanley Reiter
Northwestern University

Carl Simon
University of Michigan

Studies in Mathematics

Volume 25

STUDIES IN MATHEMATICAL ECONOMICS

Stanley Reiter, *editor*
Northwestern University

Published and distributed by
The Mathematical Association of America

©1986 by
The Mathematical Association of America (Incorporated)
Library of Congress Catalog Card Number 85-063770

Complete Set ISBN 0-88385-100-8
Vol 25 ISBN 0-88385-127-x

Printed in the United States of America

Current printing (last digit):
10 9 8 7 6 5 4 3 2 1

PREFACE

Mathematics has been used in a significant way in economics for at least a century. In recent times, mathematics has played an essential role in economic theory, especially in microeconomic theory. The specialty known as mathematical economics is now practically coextensive with microeconomic theory. The variety of mathematical ideas and techniques used in economics has increased dramatically in the past few decades, and so has its depth. These developments have been accompanied by an increase in interest in economics on the part of professional mathematicians. Many of the papers in this volume either constitute, or are related to, contributions made to economics by distinguished mathematicians. Yet the mathematicians who have worked in economics or who are familiar with mathematical economics still constitute only a small portion of the mathematics community.

The role of mathematics in economic theory is basically the same as its role in other subjects. Economics involves complex and subtle relationships among relatively large numbers of variables. Mathematics is the natural way of ensuring the precise, clear, and definite formulation of ideas, and provides a way of checking the logical truth of statements. Some applications of mathematics are made to systems involving relationships depending on a small number of rather precisely observable parameters. In many of the important areas of economics this is not the case. Important parameters, such as those describing preferences, are difficult to observe. For this reason economists are often interested in statements that are true for a large class of parameter values, and, of course, that also say something important about the way economic institutions function. Most of the theorems in this volume are of this kind. For example, competitive equilibrium is shown to exist for all economies with certain qualitative properties, such as convex preferences and production sets, without quantitative specification of those sets. Similarly, the theorems which, by relating competitive equilibria and Pareto optimal allocations, assert that the equilibria of the competitive economic organization have a certain efficiency property, depend only on broad qualitative properties of the underlying economy. While this type of result is more characteristic of economics than is the precise formula permitting numerical calculation, such things also appear. The methods for computing a general competitive equilibrium are an example.

This study is part of a series addressed primarily to students of mathematics and their teachers. The technical level has been chosen to make the study accessible to that audience. It is not intended to be an encyclopedic survey either of economic theory or of mathematics used in economics. The papers present a number of applications of mathematics in economics which are valuable as economics and have genuine mathematical interest. But a number of interesting and important subjects are not represented here, e.g., game theory applied to economics, experimental economics, and dynamics, among others. I hope that students of mathematics will find in what is here a basis for a deeper interest in, and understanding of, mathematical economics. I suspect that graduate students of economics will find much here that is useful. Perhaps professional mathematicians will also.

The volume consists of eight chapters, in addition to the Introduction. Though related to one another, they can be read independently. The first paper, by Roger Myerson, is an introduction to game theory presenting a unified development of the important fundamental ideas of game theory, and the decision theoretic foundations on which game theory rests. This paper discusses sophisticated ideas without making high technical demands on the reader. The next two chapters deal with differential methods in the study of general equilibrium. The first of these chapters, by Carl

Simon, gives a self-contained treatment of multivariable calculus methods, especially, the study of constrained vector maximization from the viewpoint of mathematical programming. These methods are widely used in economic theory. This paper provides a unified presentation of them, and shows their application to important problems of economic theory. While the results are not basically new, some of them are given in a sharper form than can be found elsewhere. It should be possible for anyone who has two years of calculus to read this paper. Its clarity and sophistication make it an excellent way of acquainting students and teachers of mathematics with the uses of calculus in economic theory. It will, in all likelihood, also prove useful to students of economics.

The second paper of this group, Chapter III, by Andreu Mas-Colell, studies the theory of competitive equilibrium from the differentiable point of view. It applies the methods of differential topology to a carefully formulated model of the competitive, or Walrasian, organization of economic activity in order to analyze the set of competitive equilibria and to study its variation as the underlying economic data change. Sard's Theorem is one of the fundamental mathematical tools. This paper presents, at a suitable technical level, the theory of regular economies referred to by Debreu in the last chapter. The combination of technical and economic sophistication and careful, clear exposition makes this an excellent introduction to the subject.

In about 1967, H. Scarf introduced algorithms for computing general competitive equilibria. These methods, which are methods for computing fixed points of maps, use Sperner's Lemma and related notions from combinatorial topology. H. Kuhn's paper, which is Chapter IV of this study, provides an excellent elementary introduction to this line of research. A very active literature has developed in this area since 1975, and those wishing to pursue it will find Kuhn's paper an excellent beginning.

Chapters II and III of this study have in common a concern with one aspect or another of the competitive model of economic organization. The next three chapters depart from this focus in different ways. A new approach to welfare economics, pioneered by Hurwicz, considers organization of economic activity itself to be the variable studied. Systems other than the competitive one are admitted as possibilities. The paper by S. Reiter, Chapter V, gives a brief exposition of the "mechanism" approach to welfare economics and of a part of the literature which sprang from it, presenting the main ideas and some of the methods used. This serves as an introduction to Chapter VI, by L. Hurwicz, which surveys work on the informational properties of decentralized mechanisms. This paper presents in a unified framework the methods and results of a substantial and rather technical literature. Hurwicz has extracted the essence of the contributions to this subject and presents the various theorems and proofs with particular clarity. This paper should make a difficult literature accessible to those not yet acquainted with it.

In the standard models of economic theory, including the competitive model and those of game theory, individual behavior is based on "optimal" choice. Economic agents are supposed to be able to find solutions to what may be very complex constrained maximization problems, or to strategic problems. Critics of these models, especially H. Simon, have pointed out that economic agents have limited capacity to solve such problems, even with the aid of computers. As Simon put it, rationality is bounded. In Chapter VII, Radner examines an alternative to optimizing behavior in a stochastic setting and studies the long run consequences of it. The methods used are those of discrete probability theory, at the level of Feller's book, Vol. I. This paper represents an as yet small but growing branch of economic theory. Perhaps readers will find that its clarity of thought and exposition opens windows into new areas of economics and mathematics.

The final chapter by Gerard Debreu discusses four lines of mathematics used in the study of general competitive, or Walrasian, equilibrium. The themes of this paper, existence of equilibrium, regular economies, computation of equilibrium and core equivalence, lead from those treated in some of the papers in this volume to some important topics in the large areas of economic theory not represented here.

S. REITER
Evanston, IL
September 1985

CONTENTS

AN INTRODUCTION TO GAME THEORY*

Roger B. Myerson

Abstract

Game theory is the study of mathematical models of conflict and cooperation between intelligent rational decision makers. This paper is an introduction to game theory for economists and other social scientists. No attempt is made to survey all major results in the literature. Instead, the goal is to present a unified development of the important fundamental ideas of game theory. Topics include: decision-theoretic foundations of game theory, basic models of games, Nash equilibria, extensions and refinements of the equilibrium concept, the Nash bargaining solution, cooperative games with and without transferable utility, and cooperative games with incomplete information.

1. THE DECISION-THEORETIC FOUNDATIONS OF GAME THEORY

To understand the fundamental ideas of game theory, one should begin with a review of decision theory. Decision theory is con-

---

*An earlier version of this paper was presented at the North American meeting of the Econometric Society on June 22, 1983, in Evanston, Illinois.

1

cerned with the problem of one individual who has to choose among various risky options, which may be called "lotteries." Each lottery would give the individual a randomly determined outcome or "prize," possibly depending upon some unknown factors which we may call the "state" (or "state of the world"). Using remarkably weak assumptions about how a rational decision maker should behave, it has been shown that such a decision maker should be able to assess *subjective probability* numbers $p(s)$ for every possible state s, and *utility* numbers $u(x)$ for every possible price x, such that he always prefers to choose the lottery that has the highest subjective expected utility. The *subjective expected utility* of a lottery is defined by the formula

$$\sum_x \sum_s p(s)f(x|s)u(x),$$

where $f(x|s)$ denotes the objective probability that the lottery would give prize x if s were the true state of the world. (Classic and seminal presentations of this result are in von Neumann and Morgenstern [48], Savage [60], and Raiffa [53]. See also Luce and Raiffa [31, chapter 2] and Myerson [36].)

This result assures us that the behavior of a rational decision maker can be described mathematically, for both theoretical and practical purposes, if these probability and utility functions can be assessed. However, suppose that one of the factors that is unknown to some given individual (#1) is the action of some other individual (#2). To assess a subjective probability distribution over 2's possible actions, individual 1 may try to imagine himself in individual 2's position. But in this thought experiment, he may realize that 2 is trying to solve a rational decision-making problem of his own, and that problem involves assessing a subjective probability distribution over 1's possible actions. Thus, the rational solution to each individual's decision problem depends on the solution to the other individual's problem, and neither can be solved without the other. So when rational individuals interact, their decision problems must be analyzed together, like a system of equations. Such analysis is the subject of game theory.

Game theory can be defined as the study of mathematical models of conflict and cooperation between intelligent rational decision makers. By "rational" we mean that each individual's decision-making behavior would be consistent with the maximization of subjective expected utility, if the other individuals' decisions were specified. By "intelligent" we mean that each individual understands everything about the structure of the situation that we theorists understand, including the fact that all other individuals are intelligent rational decision makers. Thus, if we develop a theory that describes how the players in some game should behave, then we must assume that each player in the game will also understand this theory and its predictions.

It may be useful to compare game theory to price theory, for example. In the general equilibrium model of price theory, it is assumed that every individual is a rational utility-maximizing decision maker, but it is not assumed that individuals understand the whole structure of the economic model that the price theorist is studying. In price-theoretic models, individuals only perceive and respond to some intermediating market signals. In game theory, we assume that all individuals perceive and respond to each other directly. Thus, game theory may be better than price theory for describing markets with relatively few participants, as in oligopolistic competition or union-management relations. On the other hand, game theory is generally worse than price theory for describing the macroeconomy, in which even the assumption that individuals know all the prices may be too strong.

Of course, the game theorist's assumption that all individuals are perfectly rational and intelligent (in the above sense) may never be satisfied in any real life situation. But on the other hand, we should be suspicious of theories and predictions that are not consistent with this assumption. That is, if a theory predicts that some individuals will be systematically fooled or led into mistakes that hurt themselves, then this theory will tend to lose its validity when these individuals learn to better understand the situation. The importance of game theory in the social sciences is derived from this fact.

2. BASIC MODELS OF GAME THEORY

The most general models used to describe games are *dynamic models*, which describe all the sequences of actions or moves that could be made by the players over time during the play of the game. Kuhn [29] developed the formal definition of the *extensive form*, which is now the standard dynamic model in the literature on game theory. (See Luce and Raiffa [31, chapter 3], Owen [51, chapter 1], Shubik [67, chapter 3], and Kreps and Wilson [28]). For our purposes here, however, it will suffice to discuss a somewhat simpler *multistage form* (used in Myerson [42]).

To describe a game in multistage form, we must first specify the set of sequentially numbered *stages* ($\{1, 2, \ldots, K\}$) and the set of *players* in the game. We let $N = \{1, 2, \ldots, n\}$ denote the set of players, with i denoting a member of N. For each stage k and for each player i, we must specify the set of possible *signals* (or new information) that player i could get at the beginning of stage k, and the set of possible *actions* (or moves) that player i could choose at the end of stage k. An *information state* for player i in stage k is any possible sequence of signals that he might have gotten in the first k stages and of actions that he might have taken in the first $k - 1$ stages. If we assume that each player has perfect recall, then such an information state would characterize what player i knows at the beginning of stage k. For any stage k before the last, and for any possible combination of the players' information states and actions at stage k, we must specify the probability of each possible combination of new signals for the players at the beginning of the next stage $k + 1$. For stage 1, we must specify the probability of each possible combination of signals for the players at the beginning of the first stage. The set of *outcomes* of the game is the set of all possible sequences of signals and actions for all players at all the stages of the game. For every player, we must specify a *payoff function*, which assigns a utility value to each outcome of the game. These payoff functions describe the players' preferences, and complete our specification of the multistage game.

A game in *strategic form* is a special case of the multistage form in which there is only one stage and each player has only one possible information state. That is, to define a game in strategic form, we need to specify a set of players ($N = \{1, 2, \ldots, n\}$), and, for each player i, we must specify a set of possible actions or strategies (C_i) and a payoff function (u_i). Here, each player's payoff function is a map from the set of possible combinations of actions for all the players $(C_1 \times \cdots \times C_n)$ into the set of real numbers. That is, $u_i(c_1, \ldots, c_n)$ denotes the utility value, for player i, of the outcome of the game when $(c_1, \ldots, c_n)$ is the combination of players' actions (each player j using c_j).

Von Neumann and Morgenstern [48] argued that there may be no loss of generality in restricting our theoretical attention to these conceptually simpler games in strategic form. Given any multistage game, they showed how to construct an equivalent game in strategic form (which is also called the *normal form* of the multistage game). A *strategy* for a player in a multistage game is any function that specifies a feasible action for the player, at every stage and every possible information state. That is, a strategy for player i is a complete plan of action for player i, at all stages and all possible information states in the multistage game. The set of actions for any player in the equivalent strategic-form game is defined to be his set of strategies in the given multistage game. For any combination of strategies $(s_1, \ldots, s_n)$, the payoff $u_i(s_1, \ldots, s_n)$ to any player i in the strategic-form game is defined to be his expected payoff in the multistage game when all players plan to use their given strategies (each player j using his strategy s_j).

Thus, when we reduce a multistage game to strategic form, we suppress its dynamic structure and condense all decision making into one stage. This is a major simplification in the conceptual structure of our model. However, the set of strategies is sometimes so large that it may be more practical to study the dynamic model than the strategic form. (For example, the set of all possible strategies for each player in chess is a finite but astronomically large set.)

When we theoretically analyze a multistage game, we are trying, before the game begins, to predict what each player should do at each stage and each possible information state. If each player is as intelligent as we are, then he should also be able, before the game, to analyze the game and rationally plan all of his actions in all possible events. But if all players choose their strategies in advance (at stage "0") then the equivalent strategic form is a precise description of their decision problems. That is, when players plan their actions in advance, they are taking their decision-making process outside of the dynamic structure of the game. This strongly suggests that there may be no theoretical loss in reducing multistage games to the conceptually simpler strategic form.

This insight is very important in game theory, even though its limitations are now being reexamined in the literature (Selten [61], Kreps and Wilson [28], Kohlberg and Mertens [27], and Myerson [42]). For example, sometimes a theorist may try to defend a general solution concept for strategic-form games by arguing that players would converge to it in a game that has been repeated many times. But such an argument would ignore the fact that a repeated game is just a kind of multistage game, and so it can be reduced to one large strategic-form game itself. If the general solution concept is valid then it should be applied to this overall game, not to the repeated stages separately.

The argument for reducing a game to strategic form relied on the assumption that each player could plan his actions before getting any private information or signals. However, some parts of a player's private information may be so basic to his identity that it is not meaningful to talk about him planning his actions before learning this information (e.g., what is the player's gender, native language, and level of risk aversion). Harsanyi [17] called such initial information the *type* of a player. If the players have any uncertainty about each others' types, then it may not be possible to completely reduce a game to strategic form. Instead, we must use a somewhat more general class of models, which Harsanyi called *Bayesian games*.

To define a Bayesian game, we must specify a set of players ($N = \{1, 2, \ldots, n\}$), and for each player i we must specify a set of possible *actions* (C_i), a set of possible *types* or information states (T_i), a *probability function* (p_i), and a *payoff function* (u_i). For every possible type t_i of player i, the probability function p_i must specify a probability distribution $p_i(\cdot|t_i)$ over the set of all possible combinations of other players' types ($T_{-i} = T_1 \times \cdots \times T_{i-1} \times T_{i+1} \times \cdots \times T_n$), which represents what player i would believe about the other players' types if his type were t_i. That is, $p_i(t_1, \ldots, t_{i-1}, t_{i+1}, \ldots, t_n|t_i)$ (or $p_i(t_{-i}|t_i)$) denotes the subjective probability that i would assign to the event that player 1's type is t_1, 2's type is t_2, etc., when i knows that his own type is t_i. The payoff function for player i must specify a numerical utility value $u_i(c_1, \ldots, c_n, t_1, \ldots, t_n)$ to every possible combination of players' actions $(c_1, \ldots, c_n)$ and every possible combination of players' types $(t_1, \ldots, t_n)$.

When we study a Bayesian game, we assume that the sets and functions specified above are *common knowledge* among the players (that is, every player knows these structures, every player knows that every player knows them, etc.; see Aumann [2]). In addition, each player knows his own actual type. Thus, the type of player i is defined to be a variable that represents all of his initial information (about preferences and endowments and other players' beliefs) that may be unknown to other players and to us theorists. Mertens and Zamir [32] showed that, in principle, it should always be possible to mathematically construct type-sets that are large enough to subsume all possible states of each player's initial private information, so that the Bayesian game model has complete theoretical generality among nondynamic models. In some applications, of course, these type sets may be too large for tractable analysis, which may limit the practical applicability of the Bayesian game model. On the other hand, if each player has only one possible type, then the Bayesian game reduces to a game in strategic form. If there is at least one player who has more than one possible type, then the game is said to be a game with *incomplete information*.

Harsanyi [17], following a suggestion by R. Selten, discussed a formal way of reducing any Bayesian game to a game in strategic form, using what he called the *Selten model*. In the Selten model, there is one player for every possible type of every player in the original Bayesian game. Thus, for a Bayesian game with three players, each of whom has five possible types, there are fifteen players in the Selten model. The set of actions for each player in the Selten model is the same as the set of possible actions for that player in the original game for whom the Selten-model player represents one possible type. The payoffs to players in the Selten model are defined to be the expected payoffs for the corresponding types of players in the original Bayesian game. That is, if we let $\gamma_j(t_j)$ denote the action selected by the Selten-model player for each type t_j of each player j in the Bayesian game, then the corresponding payoff to the Selten-model player for any type t_i of any i would be

$$\sum_{t_{-i}} p_i(t_{-i}|t_i) u_i(\gamma_1(t_1), \ldots, \gamma_n(t_n), t_1, \ldots, t_n).$$

For a more detailed introduction to the analysis of Bayesian games, see Myerson [43].

3. NASH EQUILIBRIA

Nash's [46] definition of equilibrium is probably the most important concept in game theory. Given a strategic-form game, a combination of actions or strategies for the players is a Nash equilibrium if each player's action maximizes his expected utility, given the actions of the other players.

To prove existence of equilibria, it is necessary to allow players to randomize. A *randomized strategy* for player i is any probability distribution over the set of possible actions for player i. If σ_i is a randomized strategy for player i, then $\sigma_i(c_i)$ denotes the probability that player i will select the action c_i in the randomized strategy σ_i. The players are assumed to randomize independently in a game without communication, so that player i's expected payoff would be

$$u_i(\sigma_1, \ldots, \sigma_n) = \sum_{(c_1, \ldots, c_n)} \left(\prod_{j=1}^n \sigma_j(c_j) \right) u_i(c_1, \ldots, c_n),$$

when the players used the randomized strategies $(\sigma_1, \ldots, \sigma_n)$. (Here $\prod$ represents the multiplicative product.) A combination of randomized strategies $(\sigma_1, \ldots, \sigma_n)$ is a (*Nash*) *equilibrium* if, for every player i and every randomized strategy $\hat{\sigma}_i$,

$$u_i(\sigma_1, \ldots, \sigma_n) \geqslant u_i(\sigma_1, \ldots, \sigma_{i-1}, \hat{\sigma}_i, \sigma_{i+1}, \ldots, \sigma_n).$$

That is, each player i cannot increase his expected payoff by using any other randomized strategy $\hat{\sigma}_i$ instead of σ_i, when every other player j is using σ_j. Nash proved that, for any strategic-form game in which the set of players and the sets of possible actions are all finite, there exists at least one equilibrium in randomized strategies. It is appropriate to call this existence theorem the fundamental theorem of game theory.

For a Bayesian game with incomplete information, Harsanyi [17] defined *Bayesian equilibria* to be the Nash equilibria of the equivalent Selten-model game in strategic form. That is, a Bayesian equilibrium specifies an action or randomized strategy for each type of each player, so that each type of each player would be maximizing his own expected utility, over all his possible actions, when he knows his own type but does not know the other players' types. Notice that, in a Bayesian equilibrium, a player's action can depend on his own type, but not on the types of the other players. (By definition, a player's type is supposed to subsume all of his private information at the beginning of the game, when he chooses his action or strategy.) We need to specify what every type of every player would do, not just the actual types, because otherwise we could not define the expected payoff for a player who does not know the other players' actual types.

The importance of Nash (and Bayesian) equilibria comes from the following argument. Suppose that we are acting either as theorists, trying to predict the players' behavior in a given game, or as social planners, trying to prescribe the players' behavior. If we specify what strategies should be used by the players, and if the players understand this specification also (recall that they know everything that we know about the game), then we must either specify an equilibrium or impute irrational behavior to some players. If we are not specifying an equilibrium, then some player could gain by changing his strategy. Thus, a nonequilibrium specification would be a self-denying prophecy if the players all believed it.

This argument uses the assumption that the players in a strategic form game are choosing their actions or strategies independently, so that one player's change of strategy cannot cause a change by any other player. In a sense, this independence assumption is without loss of generality. If there are rounds of communication between the players, then the set of strategies for each player in the strategic-form game can be redefined to include all plans for what to say in these rounds of communication and what actions to choose, depending on the previously received messages. That is, a game with preplay communication can be viewed as an extensive or multistage game, and can be reduced to an equivalent strategic-form game as described in Section 2. (On the other hand, we will see that it is often more convenient to omit such possibilities for communication from the structure of the game and to build them into the solution concept instead, which will take us to the concept of *correlated equilibrium* in Section 5.)

Aumann and Maschler [6] reexamined the argument for Nash equilibrium as a solution for games like the following example (in strategic form):

Player 2

		L	R
	T	0, 0	0, −1
Player 1	B	1, 0	−1, 3

EXAMPLE 1

(Here $C_1 = \{T, B\}$, $C_2 = \{L, R\}$ and the numbers in each box are the utility payoffs (u_1, u_2)). The unique equilibrium for this game is the pair of randomized strategies (σ_1, σ_2), where $\sigma_1(T) = 3/4$, $\sigma_1(B) = 1/4$, $\sigma_2(L) = 1/2$ and $\sigma_2(R) = 1/2$. However, Aumann and Maschler suggest that player 1 might prefer to choose T and player 2 might prefer to choose L (each with probability one), because these actions are optimal responses to the equilibrium strategies and guarantee each player his expected equilibrium payoff of zero. But if such behavior were correctly anticipated then player 1 would be irrational not to choose B, because it is his unique best response to L. Thus, a theory that predicts the actions T and L in this game would destroy its own validity, because (T, L) is not a Nash equilibrium.

Notice that we have not given any direct argument as to why intelligent rational players must use equilibrium strategies in a game. When someone asks why players in a game should behave as in some Nash equilibrium, this author's favorite response is to ask "why not?" and to let the challenger specify what he thinks the players should do. If this specification is not a Nash equilibrium, then (as above) we can show that it would destroy its own validity if the players believe it to be an accurate description of each others' behavior. It may be better to think of Nash equilibrium as a "presolution concept," rather than as a solution concept, because being a Nash equilibrium is only a necessary condition, not a sufficient condition, for being a good prediction of rational players' behavior. That is, every outcome that is not an equilibrium will necessarily be an unreasonable prediction of how intelligent rational decision makers would behave. Thus, the concept of Nash equilibrium imposes a constraint on social planners and theorists, in that they cannot predict nonequilibrium behavior.

Equilibria in randomized strategies sometimes seem difficult to interpret. It is easy to check (by examining the four possibilities) that there is no equilibrium without randomization in Example 1. But the necessity for player 1 to randomly choose among T and B with probabilities $3/4$ and $1/4$, respectively, might not seem to coincide with any compulsion that people experience in real life. Of course, if player 1 thinks that player 2 is equally likely to choose L or R then player 1 is willing to randomize in any way between T and B. But what could make player 1 actually want to use the precise probabilities $3/4$ and $1/4$?

Harsanyi [18] showed that Nash equilibria that involve randomized strategies can be interpreted as limits of equilibria in which each player is (almost) always choosing his uniquely optimal action. Harsanyi's basic idea is to modify the game so that each player has slightly different information about the payoffs. (See also Milgrom and Weber [33].) For example, suppose that Example 1 were modified slightly, to the following game with incomplete information:

Player 2

		L	R
	T	$\varepsilon\tilde{\alpha}, \varepsilon\tilde{\beta}$	$\varepsilon\tilde{\alpha}, -1$
Player 1	B	$1, \varepsilon\tilde{\beta}$	$-1, 3$

EXAMPLE 1a

Here $0 < \varepsilon < 1$, and $\tilde{\alpha}$ and $\tilde{\beta}$ are independent and identically distributed, each with a uniform distribution over the interval from

0 to 1. When the game is played, player 1 knows the value of $\tilde{\alpha}$ but not $\tilde{\beta}$, and player 2 knows the value of $\tilde{\beta}$ but not $\tilde{\alpha}$. If ε is zero then Example 1a becomes exactly the same as Example 1, so let us think of ε as a very small positive number (say, 10^{-9}). Then $\tilde{\alpha}$ and $\tilde{\beta}$ can be interpreted as minor factors that have a very small influence on the players' payoffs when T or L is chosen.

Given ε, there is a unique Bayesian equilibrium for Example 1a. Player 1 chooses T if he observes $\tilde{\alpha}$ greater than $(2 + \varepsilon)/(8 + \varepsilon^2)$, and he chooses B otherwise. Player 2 chooses L if he observes $\tilde{\beta}$ greater than $(4 - \varepsilon)/(8 + \varepsilon^2)$, and he chooses R otherwise. In these equilibrium strategies, each player always gets strictly higher utility from the action that he is choosing than he would get from the other action (except in the zero-probability event that $\tilde{\alpha} = (2 + \varepsilon)/(8 + \varepsilon^2)$ or $\tilde{\beta} = (4 - \varepsilon)/(8 + \varepsilon^2)$). That is, each player's expected behavior makes the other player almost indifferent between his two actions, so that the minor factor that he observes independently can determine a unique optimal action for him. Notice that, as ε goes to zero, this equilibrium converges to the unique equilibrium of Example 1, in which player 1 chooses T with probability $3/4$ and player 2 chooses L with probability $1/2$.

Thus, in general, when we study an equilibrium involving randomized strategies, we may interpret each player's randomization as depending on minor factors that have been omitted from the description of the game. Or, to put it another way, when a game has no nonrandom equilibria, we should expect that a player's optimal action may be determined by some minor factors that he observes independently of the other players.

The general observations about Nash equilibria are now in order. Nash equilibria may be *nonunique*; and Nash equilibria may be *inefficient*.

For an example of inefficiency, consider the following game, known as the "Prisoner's Dilemma":

Player 2

		L	R
Player 1	T	5, 5	0, 6
	B	6, 0	1, 1

EXAMPLE 2

In this game, (B, R) is the unique Nash equilibrium, but it is also the only outcome of the game that is not Pareto efficient. (See Luce and Raiffa [31] for the story behind the names of this and the next example.)

For an example of nonuniqueness, consider the following game, known as the "Battle of the Sexes":

Player 2

		L	R
Player 1	T	2, 1	0, 0
	B	0, 0	1, 2

EXAMPLE 3

There are three equilibria of this game: (T, L), which player 1 prefers; (B, R), which player 2 prefers; and a randomized equilibrium $(2/3[T] + 1/3[B], 1/3[L] + 2/3[R])$, which gives each player an expected utility of $2/3$. The third equilibrium is also an example of inefficiency, since both players would prefer (T, L) or (B, R).

For games with multiple equilibria, anything (in the structure of the game or in the commonly observed environment in which it is played) that focuses the players' attentions on one particular equilibrium may create a situation in which all players expect this equilibrium and thus actually implement it. Schelling [62] called this the *focal-point effect*. For example, if the players learned the Battle of the Sexes game from a book in which the payoff "1, 2" was printed in red ink, all else being in black ink, then the (B, R) equilibrium would be much more likely to be played. Alternatively, suppose that player 1 is a woman and player 2 is a man in this game, and suppose that the players come from a culture in which women have traditionally deferred to men. Then, even though this cultural tradition has no binding force on the players, it probably will cause both players to have the self-verifying expectation that player 2 will choose R and player 1 will choose B.

Another way that the players could become focused on one equilibrium, and so induced to implement it, is if some authoritative individual suggests it. If one player in the game has such authority or power of suggestion, so that he can select the equilibrium that all players will implement, then he may be called the *principal* of the game. (This definition is consistent with the usage of the term in most of the literature on principal-agent analysis.) An *arbitrator* is an outside individual, different from the players, who has power of suggestion to select the equilibrium.

4. REFINEMENTS OF THE NASH EQUILIBRIUM CONCEPT

In some games with multiple equilibria, there may be some equilibria that seem intrinsically unreasonable for the players to implement, even if a principal or arbitrator tried to persuade the players to do so. For example, consider the following game:

Player 2

		L	R
	T	1, 9	1, 9
Player 1	B	0, 0	2, 1

EXAMPLE 4

There are two equilibria (T, L) and (B, R); but it may be unreasonable to expect the players to implement (T, L). Player 2 can only gain by choosing R instead of L. (Remember that the players choose independently, so player 2 should not expect a switch from L to R to affect player 1's choice.) Then, if player 1 expects player 2 to choose R, B must be player 1's rational choice.

To identify and eliminate such unreasonable equilibria from our solution concepts, many refinements of the Nash equilibrium concept have been proposed. Three general criteria have been used to develop such refinements: (i) elimination of unreasonable actions; (ii) sequential rationality; and, (iii) stability against small perturbations of the game. Let us begin by considering some ways of eliminating unreasonable actions.

Given a strategic-form game, we say that an action c_i for player i is *strongly dominated* if there exists some randomized strategy σ_i

such that player i would always get a strictly higher expected payoff from σ_i than from c_i, no matter what actions are used by the other players; that is, for every $(c_1, \ldots, c_{i-1}, c_{i+1}, \ldots, c_n)$,

$$u_i(c_1, \ldots, c_i, \ldots, c_n) < \sum_{d_i} \sigma_i(d_i) u_i(c_1, \ldots, d_i, \ldots, c_n).$$

An action c_i is *weakly dominated* if there exists some randomized strategy σ_i such that player i would never get a strictly lower expected payoff from σ_i than from c_i, and could possibly get a strictly higher expected payoff from σ_i than from c_i, depending on what actions are used by the other players.

It seems unreasonable to suggest that a player should use an action that is strongly dominated, since he can surely expect better with the dominating strategy. Similarly, equilibria that involve weakly dominated actions may be considered unreasonable. For example, consider Example 4 above and Example 5 below:

Player 2

		L	R
	T	5, 5	0, 5
Player 1	B	5, 0	1, 1

EXAMPLE 5

In each of these examples, there are two equilibria ((T, L) and (B, R)), but the action L is weakly dominated by R. So, by the criterion of elimination of dominated actions, (B, R) is the only reasonable equilibrium in both examples. Notice that, in Example 5, the "more reasonable" equilibrium is actually worse for both players.

After the (weakly or strongly) dominated actions have been eliminated from a game, the smaller game that remains may have new dominated actions. Luce and Raiffa [31] suggest we should continue to eliminate dominated actions iteratively until there are no dominated actions in the game that remains. For example, iterative elimination of weakly dominated actions leaves only the equilibrium at (z_1, z_2) in the following game:

Player 2

	x_2	y_2	z_2
x_1	3, 3	0, 3	0, 0
y_1	3, 0	2, 2	0, 2
z_1	0, 0	2, 0	1, 1

Player 1 labels x_1, y_1, z_1 rows.

EXAMPLE 6

(The order of elimination is x_1 and x_2 first, then y_1 and y_2.)

Several related criteria for identifying unreasonable actions have been suggested. Harsanyi [19] proposed a concept of *inferior* actions, Bernheim [9] and Pearce [52] proposed a concept of *unrationalizable* actions, and Myerson [41] proposed a concept of *codominated* actions. Each of these concepts includes all of the weakly dominated actions. One might argue that an equilibrium should be considered "unreasonable" if it uses actions that can be eliminated (or iteratively eliminated) by any of these concepts.

Concepts of sequential rationality are applied to dynamic games, in extensive or multistage form. As discussed in Section 2, any dynamic game can be reduced to an equivalent strategic-form game. The Nash equilibria of a game in extensive or multistage form are defined to be the Nash equilibria of the equivalent strategic-form game. Unfortunately this definition admits too many equilibria, including some that are clearly irrational.

When a decision maker chooses his plan of action in advance, the maximization of expected utility (as viewed ex ante) does not impose any restrictions on what he should plan to do after observing an event that has probability zero. Thus, when we compute the Nash equilibria from the strategic-form reduction of a dynamic game, we abandon all rational restrictions on players' behavior in events that have probability zero. This might not sound like a serious problem, since a zero-probability event should (almost) never occur. However, in game theory (unlike probability theory), the zero-probability events are determined endogenously by the plans or strategies of the players, so we cannot simply ignore such events *a priori*. An event that has probability zero in one equilibrium may have positive probability in another. So we want to identify the equilibria in which every player is behaving rationally in all events, not just in the positive-probability events. To do so, we must analyze dynamic games directly in extensive or multistage form, not just in the strategic-form reduction.

For such analysis, Kreps and Wilson [28] proposed a concept of *sequential equilibrium*, which refined Selten's [61] earlier definition of *subgame-perfect equilibrium*. To characterize a sequential equilibrium, we must specify, not only the action or randomized strategy that each player would use at each stage in each of his possible information states, but also the beliefs that he would have at each stage in each of his information states (including states with probability zero). In every information state, the designated strategies should be *rational*, in the sense that they maximize the player's conditionally expected payoff given his beliefs (about the other players and chance events) at this information state. The designated beliefs at the various information states should be *consistent* with each other and with the designated strategies, according to the rule of Bayesian inference from probability theory. A *sequential equi-*

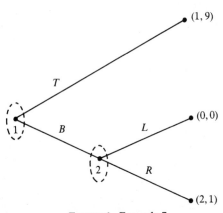

FIGURE 1. Example 7.

librium is any such rational and consistent designation of strategies and beliefs for all players in all information states. (See Kreps and Wilson [28] for a more precise definition.)

Consider Example 7, which is shown in extensive form in Figure 1. In this game, player 1 first chooses between T and B. If player 1 chooses T, then the payoffs (u_1, u_2) are $(1, 9)$ independent of any actions by player 2. If player 1 chooses B then player 2 is informed of this fact and must choose between L and R. The payoffs (u_1, u_2) are $(0, 0)$ after B and L, and are $(2, 1)$ after B and R. The equivalent strategic-form game is just Example 4, which has two Nash equilibria: (T, L) and (B, R). Let us consider the (T, L) equilibrium. Player 1 would prefer T if he expected player 2 to choose L after B; and, at the beginning of the game, player 2 would be willing to plan to choose L after B if he were sure that player 1 would choose T (since the plan would never have to be used). Thus, (T, L) is a Nash equilibrium. But if player 2 cannot actually precommit himself to the L-if-B plan at the beginning of the game, then we must ask what player 2 would rationally choose if he were in the position of choosing between L and R after observing B. In such a circumstance, player 2 should certainly choose R (giving him a payoff of 1) rather than L (giving 0). Thus, (T, L) is not a sequential equilibrium of Example 7. The unique sequential equilibrium is (B, R).

Of course, elimination of dominated actions already excluded (T, L) from the set of reasonable equilibria of Example 4. However, more complicated games, such as Example 8 (shown in Figure 2), may have Nash equilibria that are not sequential equilibria, even though there are no dominated actions.

In Example 8, player 1 first chooses among x_1, y_1, and z_1. If he chooses x_1 or y_1, then player 2 must choose between x_2 and y_2, and player 3 must choose between x_3 and y_3. The dotted curves indicate that, when players 2 and 3 make these choices, they do not observe each others' choices, and they do not observe whether x_1 or y_1 was chosen by player 1, but they do know that player 1 has not chosen z_1. If player 1 chooses z_1, then the final payoffs (u_1, u_2, u_3) will be $(1, 4, 4)$ without players 2 and 3 making any choices at all. Otherwise, the three players' payoffs (u_1, u_2, u_3) depend on the actions of all three players, as indicated at the right ends of the tree.

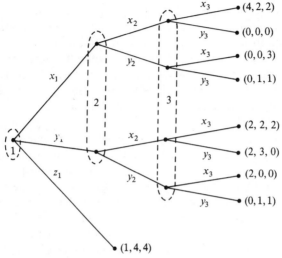

FIGURE 2. Example 8.

There are two nonrandom Nash equilibria of this game, (x_1, x_2, x_3) and (z_1, y_2, y_3); but only (x_1, x_2, x_3) is a sequential equilibrium. To try to justify (z_1, y_2, y_3) as a sequential equilibrium, we would have to specify what players 2 and 3 should believe about player 1's choice (x_1 or y_1) if they observed that he did not choose z_1 as expected. If player 2 would believe x_1 and player 3 would believe y_1 under such circumstances then their actions would be rational, but such beliefs would obviously not be consistent. It can be shown that, for any probability distribution over x_1 and y_1, either player 2 or player 3 could expect to gain by deviating from (y_2, y_3). Thus, (z_1, y_2, y_3) is not a sequential equilibrium.

On the other hand, suppose that we revise Example 8 by setting $u_2(y_1, x_2, y_3)$ and $u_3(x_1, y_2, x_3)$ both equal to some number α, where $\alpha \leqslant 2$. (In Figure 2, we had $\alpha = 3$.) Then (z_1, y_2, y_3) can be supported as a sequential equilibrium, by specifying that players 2 and 3 would both assign probability $1/2$ to x_1 and probability $1/2$ to y_1 if they unexpectedly learned that z_1 was not chosen.

The concept of sequential equilibrium gives us a stronger characterization of rational behavior in dynamic games than Nash equilibrium does. However, we pay an analytical price for changing our solution concept to sequential equilibrium, because we can no longer restrict our attention to the strategic form. Two dynamic games that both reduce to the same equivalent game in strategic form may have different sets of sequential equilibria.

Nevertheless, there is still strong interest in studying refinements of the Nash equilibrium concept for games in strategic form. One desirable property that we might want such a refinement to satisfy is that any equilibrium that it accepts should correspond to a sequential equilibrium in every dynamic game that can be reduced to the given strategic-form game. This property has been proven by Selten [61] for his concept of *perfect equilibrium*, by Kohlberg and Mertens [27] for their concept of *stable equilibria*, and by Van Damme [14] for Myerson's [34] concept of *proper equilibrium*. (Selten [61] does not use the normal reduction to strategic form, however. He represents each of a player's information states in each stage by a different "agent" in his strategic-form reduction.)

The definitions (omitted here) of perfect, proper, and stable equilibria are all motivated by the general idea that a reasonable equilibrium ought to be stable (in some sense) when the game is slightly altered by introducing small probabilities of players' mistakes or small perturbations of the payoffs. Kalai and Samet [25] defined a concept of *persistent equilibrium*, which is also derived from a concern for such stability.

Harsanyi and Selten [20] have considered ways to try to identify one equilibrium that would be most rational, in some sense, for every finite game in strategic form. However, they have also shown that it is impossible to select a unique equilibrium for every game in a way that depends continuously on the payoffs. This result casts doubt on whether we could ever hope for a truly satisfactory general solution to the problem of multiple equilibria.

5. EXTENSIONS OF THE EQUILIBRIUM SET

There are many games, like the Prisoner's Dilemma (Example 2), in which the Nash equilibria yield very low payoffs for the players, relative to other nonequilibrium outcomes. In such situations, the players would want to transform the game, if possible, so as to extend the set of equilibria to include better outcomes. We consider here th.ᵉe such ways that a game might be transformed: with contracts, repetition, and communication.

Joint contracts are the simplest way to extend the equilibrium set. For example, in the Prisoner's Dilemma (Example 2), the players might consider signing a contract that says: "We, the undersigned, promise to choose actions T and L, unless this contract is signed by only one player, in which case he will choose B or R." The option to sign this contract may be introduced into the game description (as action "S"); and then the transformed game

Player 2

		L	R	S
	T	5, 5	0, 6	0, 6
Player 1	B	6, 0	1, 1	1, 1
	S	6, 0	1, 1	5, 5

has an equilibrium at (S, S), which gives a payoff of 5 to each player.

In general, given any strategic-form game, a *correlated strategy* for a set of players is any probability distribution over the set of all possible combinations of actions that they might choose. The *minimax value* (or *security level*) for a player i is the best expected payoff that he could get against the worst (for him) correlated strategy that the other $(n-1)$ players could use. That is, the minimax value for player 1 would be

$$\text{minimum}_\sigma \left(\text{maximum}_{c_1} \sum_{(c_2,\dots,c_n)} \sigma(c_2,\dots,c_n) u_1(c_1, c_2, \dots, c_n) \right)$$

where σ ranges over the set of all probability distributions on $C_2 \times \cdots \times C_n$. The correlated strategy that achieves this minimum is called the *minimax strategy* against player 1.

Let μ be a correlated strategy for all of the players. The expected payoff to i from μ is

$$U_i(\mu) = \sum_{(c_1,\dots,c_n)} \mu(c_1,\dots,c_n) u_i(c_1,\dots,c_n),$$

Roger B. Myerson

where $\mu(c_1, \ldots, c_n)$ denotes the probability assigned to the combination of actions $(c_1, \ldots, c_n)$ by the correlated strategy μ. To implement μ, the players might use a trustworthy mediator (or a computer with a random number generator) to randomly designate a combination of actions in $C_1 \times \cdots \times C_n$ according to these probabilities. Our basic question is, under what circumstances might the players all voluntarily sign a contract that commits them to implement μ? Obviously, no player would sign if his expected payoff from μ were less than his minimax value (since he can always get at least his minimax value, whatever the other players might do). Conversely, suppose that each player's expected payoff from μ is greater than or equal to his minimax value; then it would be a Nash equilibrium for every player to sign a contract that says: "We the undersigned agree to choose the actions designated for us randomly according to the correlated strategy μ, unless this contract is signed by all but one player, in which case we will implement the minimax strategy against that player." (We assume in this argument that each player signs independently, without knowing which other players have signed.) Thus, if players' actions can be regulated by joint contracts, any correlated strategy that gives every player at least his minimax value can be implemented by a Nash equilibrium of the transformed game with contract-signing.

Of course, there are many situations in which the players cannot commit themselves to binding contracts. The players' actions might be unobservable to the legal enforcers of contracts; or sanctions to guarantee compliance with contracts might be inadequate; or some players' actions might be inalienable rights (such as the right to quit a job).

The effect of repeating a game is very similar to the effect of allowing binding contracts. Any correlated strategy that gives each player a higher expected payoff than his minimax value can be enforced in an equilibrium of an infinitely repeated game, if each player's objective is to maximize his long-run average payoff per round. The essential idea is that, if any one player diverged from his role in the correlated strategy then the others would punish him with the minimax strategy against him for many rounds of the game, and any player who diverged from his designated role in punishing another player would similarly be liable for such punishment, so the punishment process is self-enforcing. This idea was rigorously formulated and proven by Rubinstein [57]. For a general introduction to the study of repeated games, see Aumann [3].

The effect of allowing players to communicate in a strategic-form game, without binding contracts and without repetition, was first studied by Aumann [1], who defined the concept of *correlated equilibrium* for such games. To understand this concept, let us begin by considering Example 9.

Player 2

		L	R
	T	5, 1	0, 0
Player 1	B	4, 4	1, 5

EXAMPLE 9

There are three equilibria of this game: (T, L), giving payoffs $(u_1, u_2) = (5, 1)$; (B, R), giving payoffs $(1, 5)$; and a randomized equilibrium giving expected payoffs $(2.5, 2.5)$. The best symmetric payoffs $(4, 4)$ cannot be achieved by the players without binding contracts, because (B, L) is not an equilibrium. (Player 1 would choose T if he expected player 2 to choose L.) The expected payoff $(3, 3)$ can be achieved by the players, with communication but without binding contracts, by tossing a coin and planning to choose (T, L) if heads and (B, R) if tails. Such a plan is self-enforcing, even though the coin has no binding force on the players, because neither player could gain by unilaterally diverging from the plan.

Even better, $(3\frac{1}{3}, 3\frac{1}{3})$ can be achieved in this game, with the help of a mediator. Suppose that a mediator randomly recommends actions to the two players in such a way that each of the pairs (T, L), (B, L), and (B, R) may be recommended with probability $1/3$. Suppose also that each player hears only his own recommended action from the mediator. Then, even though the mediator's recommendation has no binding force, it is a Nash equilibrium (of the transformed game with such mediated communication) for both players to plan to obey the mediator's recommendations. If player 1 hears a recommendation "B," then he thinks that player 2 may have been told to do L or R with equal probability, in which case his expected payoff from B (2.5) is as good as from T. If player 1 hears "T" then he knows that player 2 was told to do L, in which case T is player 1's best action. So player 1 is willing to obey the mediator if he expects player 2 to obey, and a similar argument applies to player 2. Randomizing equally between (T, L), (B, L) and (B, R) with equal probability gives expected payoffs $(3\frac{1}{3}, 3\frac{1}{3})$.

More generally, for any strategic-form game (as in Section 2), Aumann [1] defined a correlated equilibrium to be any correlated strategy that can be achieved as an equilibrium with the help of such a mediator. Formally, a *correlated equilibrium* is any probability distribution μ over $C_1 \times \cdots \times C_n$ such that, for every player i and every function δ_i that maps C_i into C_i,

$$U_i(\mu) \geqslant \sum_{(c_1, \ldots, c_n)} \mu(c_1, \ldots, c_n) u_i(c_1, \ldots, \delta_i(c_i), \ldots, c_n).$$

That is, no player i should expect to gain from disobeying the mediator's recommendations by any rule δ_i (doing $\delta_i(c_i)$ when told to do c_i), if the mediator's recommendations are randomly selected according to the probability distribution μ and every other player is expected to obey his recommendations. (Player i's prospective disobedience $\delta_i(c_i)$ can depend only on c_i, the recommended action for player i, because i does not hear the mediator's recommendations to the other players.) These inequalities are called *strategic incentive constraints* (or *moral-hazard* constraints), because they constrain the set of correlated strategies that a mediator could implement without giving any player an incentive to disobey. By analyzing these incentive constraints, we can characterize the set of all correlated equilibria for a game. For example, it is straightforward to show that $(3\frac{1}{3}, 3\frac{1}{3})$ is the best symmetric payoff allocation that can be achieved by any correlated equilibrium for Example 9. (See Myerson [43].)

For Bayesian games with incomplete information, communication would allow the players' actions to depend on each others' types, as well as on extraneous random variables like coin tosses. Formally, μ is a (*direct*) *communication mechanism* (or a generalized correlated strategy) for the players in a Bayesian game if, for every possible combination of types $(t_1, \ldots, t_n)$, μ specifies aprobability distribution, denoted $\mu(\cdot | t_1, \ldots, t_n)$, over the set of possible combinations of actions $(C_1 \times \cdots \times C_n)$. We let $\mu(c_1, \ldots, c_n | t_1, \ldots, t_n)$ denote the probability that each player i should be told to do c_i, if every player j reported his type to be t_j, in the communication mechanism μ. We let $U_i(\mu | t_i)$ denote the expected payoff to player i from the communication mechanism μ when his type is t_i; that is

$$U_i(\mu | t_i) = \sum_{t_{-i}} p_i(t_{-i} | t_i) \sum_c \mu(c|t) u_i(c, t).$$

(We use here the notation $t_{-i} = (t_1, \ldots, t_{i-1}, t_{i+1}, \ldots, t_n)$, $c = (c_1, \ldots, c_n)$, and $t = (t_1, \ldots, t_n)$.)

Suppose that a mediator were to help the players implement a communication mechanism μ in a Bayesian game. Suppose also that the mediator can communicate confidentially with each player, receiving type reports and sending action recommendations; but he cannot force the players to report honestly or to act obediently. Then honest reporting and obedient action by all players would be a Bayesian equilibrium if and only if μ satisfies the following general *incentive constraints*, for every player i, every pair of possible types t_i and s_i, and every function δ_i from C_i into C_i:

$$U_i(\mu | t_i) \geqslant \sum_{t_{-i}} p_i(t_{-i} | t_i) \sum_c \mu(c|t_{-i}, s_i) u_i((c_{-i}, \delta_i(c_i)), t).$$

(Here we use the notation $(t_{-i}, s_i) = (t_1, \ldots, t_{i-1}, s_i, t_{i+1}, \ldots, t_n)$, and $(c_{-i}, \delta_i(c_i)) = (c_1, \ldots, c_{i-1}, \delta_i(c_i), c_{i+1}, \ldots, c_n)$.) That is, no player i should expect to gain, when his type is t_i, by reporting type s_i and then disobeying according to δ_i, when the mediator chooses his recommendations (as a random function of the player's reports) according to μ and when all other players are expected to be honest and obedient. Any communication mechanism that satisfies these incentive constraints may be called a *communication equilibrium* (or a *generalized correlated equilibrium*, or an *incentive-compatible mechanism*) for the players in the Bayesian game.

The above definition of communication equilibria was motivated by considering what can be achieved by a mediator with a fully centralized communication system. However, the class of communication equilibria defined above actually characterizes what can be achieved by any kind of communication system, in the following sense. Any communication system effectively transforms any given Bayesian game into a new Bayesian game, in which each player's "action" is a communication strategy (that is, a specification of what messages he will send and how we will choose his action in the originally given game as a function of the messages that he receives). For any communication system and any Bayesian equilibrium of the transformed game with communication, we can construct an equivalent communication equilibrium μ (as above) by letting $\mu(c_1, \ldots, c_n | t_i, \ldots, t_n)$ be the probability that $(c_1, \ldots, c_n)$ would be the actions chosen in the original game if $(t_i, \ldots, t_n)$ were the players' types, when the players use their equilibrium communication strategies. It is straightforward to show (see Myerson [37]) that this μ must satisfy the incentive constraints from the preceding paragraph. This result is called the *revelation principle*, since it shows that there is no loss of generality in only considering communication systems in which all players reveal all their information to a central mediator.

By the revelation principle, for any social welfare function, the problem of designing an optimal communication system can be solved as a mathematical optimization problem, where the incentive constraints define the feasible set. These constraints are linear in μ, so this optimization problem can often be explicitly solved by well-known techniques. In fact, it is sometimes easier to characterize the set of communication equilibria of a game than the set of Bayesian equilibria of the same game without communication, even though the communication equilibria include the Bayesian equilibria. The set of Bayesian equilibria has no simple geometrical structure, but the set of communication equilibria is a convex polyhedron.

At this point, it may be helpful to distinguish between the terms *mediator* and *arbitrator* as they have been used in this paper. Both terms refer to an outside individual who intervenes in a game to help the players in some way. A mediator acts as a communication channel between the players, thereby transforming the game and enlarging the set of equilibria. An arbitrator (as described at the end of Section 3) helps to determine which equilibrium should be implemented by the players in a game with multiple equilibria. In short, a mediator is an outside individual who communicates with the players in order to enlarge the set of equilibria, whereas an arbitrator is an outside individual who uses his authority or power of suggestion to help the players select among multiple equilibria. Of course, there are many situations in which an individual may serve both as a mediator and as an arbitrator in a game, but these two functions are logically distinct.

To appreciate this distinction, suppose that the players in some game are in communication with many different mediators, each of whom uses a different incentive-compatible mechanism for determining his recommendations. There are many equilibria of this transformed game with communication. For example, the players could simply babble to all the mediators and implement some Bayesian (or Nash) equilibrium of the original game without communication. (We may say that a player babbles to a mediator if the player's report to the mediator is chosen independently of the player's type and the player's action is chosen independently of the mediator's recommendation. We may suppose that a babbling player simply randomizes uniformly over the set of possible type-reports.) It is also an equilibrium for the players to be honest and obedient to one particular mediator and babble to all the others. An arbitrator could designate any one of the mediators as the one whom the players should obey.

In some situations, a mediator may also have the power to act as an auditor or as a regulator of the players in a game. A *regulator* is an individual who can directly control the players' actions, so that they cannot disobey him. (When we considered the effect of binding contracts, we implicitly assumed the existence of a regulator.) If a mediator is also a regulator, then he can implement any communication mechanism that satisfies the following *informational incentive constraints* (or *self-selection* constraints) for every player i and every pair of possible types t_i and s_i:

$$U_i(\mu|t_i) \geq \sum_{t_{-i}} p_i(t_{-i}|t_i) \sum_c \mu(c|t_{-i}, s_i) u_i(c, t).$$

(That is, the mediator only needs to guarantee that no player could expect to gain by lying about his type.) An *auditor* is an individual who can directly observe and verify the players' types, so that they cannot lie to him. A mediator who can both regulate and audit the players can implement any communication mechanism, without regard for incentive constraints.

Dynamic multistage games with communication have been studied by Myerson [42]. The set of communication equilibria for such games is defined by incentive constraints that are similar to those for strategic-form and Bayesian games. Unfortunately, the set of communication equilibria of a multistage game *cannot* be identified with the set of correlated equilibria of the "equivalent" strategic-form game (as in Section 2), because opportunities for the players to communicate after the beginning of the game would be suppressed in the reduction to strategic form. To characterize sequential rationality in multistage games with communication, a concept of *sequentially rational communication equilibria* has also been defined. Myerson [42] showed that a communication equilibrium of a multistage game is sequentially rational if and only if it never involves the use of certain *sequentially codominated* actions, which include dominated actions. Thus, two approaches to the refinement of the Nash equilibrium concept (sequential rationality and elimination of unreasonable actions) can be unified in the context of multistage games with communication.

6. THE NASH BARGAINING SOLUTION

We have seen that the problem of multiple equilibria can create the role of an *arbitrator*, an outside individual who can, by his authority or power of suggestion, determine which equilibrium will be implemented. If there is no arbitrator and no other external determinant of a focal equilibrium, then one prestigious player (called the *principal*) might have a similar authority to select among the equilibria. But another possibility is that the players may jointly determine the equilibrium to be implemented, by some process of preplay bargaining or negotiation. That is, the focal equilibrium could be determined by a consensus among all the players, where the consensus is reached through negotiations in which every player has an opportunity to participate. The fundamental problem of *cooperative game theory* is to predict the negotiated focal equilibria that might be selected by such a process. The second half of this paper (Sections 6–9) is an introduction to the ideas of cooperative game theory.

Let us begin by considering Example 10, the "Divide the Dollars" game. In this game, there are two players who can divide $100 between themselves, provided that they can both agree on the division; otherwise they each get nothing. To be specific, let us suppose that each player simultaneously chooses a demand, which is any number between 0 and 100. If the sum of their demands is less than or equal to 100, then each player gets a payoff equal to his demand. If the sum of the demands is greater than 100, then each player gets a payoff of zero. (This example is a special case of the demand games studied by Nash [47]. In this case we are identifying utility with money.)

This game has multiple equilibria. For any number x such that $0 < x < 100$, there is an equilibrium in which player 1 demands x and player 2 demands $100 - x$; so every efficient allocation is achievable in an equilibrium. There are also inefficient randomized equilibria. For example, there is an equilibrium in which each player (independently) randomizes between demanding 1, with probability $1/99$, and demanding 99, with probability $98/99$, so that the probability that both get nothing is almost 98%.

In Section 3, we argued that the outcome of such a game with multiple equilibria is likely to be a focal equilibrium which may be designated by an arbitrator or other environmental factors. Since "environmental factors" are not included in the given mathematical description of the game, analysis of such focal equilibria may be beyond the scope of mathematical game theory. For example, if player 1 is male and player 2 is female, and if there has been a tradition that males take 75% of mutually feasible gains in the players' society, then the $(75, 25)$ equilibrium is the focal and most likely outcome of this game. On the other hand, if the selection of a focal point depends on an arbitrator, rather than on some exogenous social tradition, and if we assume that an arbitrator's judgement should depend only on the given mathematical description of the game, then we can hope to apply the methods of mathematical game theory to predict the outcome of the game. To do so, we must develop a theory of arbitration in games.

For the Divide the Dollars game, it seems clear that an impartial arbitrator should recommend the equilibrium in which each player gets 50. We should expect that an impartial arbitrator would recommend a symmetric allocation, because players 1 and 2 are completely symmetric in the mathematical description of the game. The $(50, 50)$ equilibrium is the only symmetric equilibrium in which the players are sure to divide all the available money. Thus, the $(50, 50)$ equilibrium is likely to be recommended by an arbitrator because it is the unique outcome that is both equitable and efficient.

Once $(50, 50)$ has been identified as the impartially arbitrated solution, it is not really necessary to have an arbitrator actually present when the game is played. The two players, being intelligent, can predict arbitrated settlements as well as we theorists can. Thus, it should be common knowledge among the players that an impartial arbitrator would recommend the $(50, 50)$ equilibrium, and this fact gives the $(50, 50)$ equilibrium an intrinsic focal property, even when no arbitrator is present. That is, *properties of equity and efficiency can determine a focal equilibrium in a game, as well as social or environmental factors.* Thus, in the Divide the Dollars game, unless there is some strong social tradition pointing to some other outcome, the $(50, 50)$ equilibrium is the most likely outcome to be chosen by the players, even when there is no actual arbitrator.

To extend this analysis to other games, we need a general theory of fair arbitrated settlements in games. The first and most compelling of such theories in the literature (see Roth [54]) is the bargaining solution of Nash [45, 47].

The Nash bargaining solution can be defined as a function of a *feasible set* (F) and a *disagreement point* (v), which in turn depend on the strategic form of the game. The *feasible set* of an n-player game is a closed and convex subset of $\mathbb{R}^n$, representing the set of all allocations of expected utility that the players can jointly achieve. If the players can make jointly binding contracts to regulate their actions, then we may define the feasible set F to be the set of all vectors $(U_1(\mu), \ldots, U_n(\mu))$ such that μ is any correlated strategy. If the players cannot make jointly binding contracts, then we may define the feasible set F to be the set of all vectors $(U_1(\mu), \ldots, U_n(\mu))$ such that μ is any correlated equilibrium, satisfying the strategic incentive constraints.

The *disagreement point* of an n-player game is a vector in $\mathbb{R}^n$ that represents the utility payoff that each player could guarantee himself if he did not coordinate with the other players. One way to formalize this idea is to define the disagreement point to be the vector $v = (v_1, \ldots, v_n)$ where each v_i is the minimax value for the player i. An alternative suggestion is to let v be the vector of expected utility payoffs that the players would get in some focal Nash equilibrium. A third suggestion, developed by Nash [47] is to define v to be the vector of expected utility payoffs that the players would get if each carried out some (endogenously determined) optimal threat. (The distinction between these definitions corresponds to different assumptions about whether the players can commit themselves before arbitration to offensive and defensive threats that would be implemented if some player subsequently refused to accept the arbitrated settlement.)

Once a feasible set and a disagreement point have been specified, it seems reasonable that one should be able to define an equitable and efficient payoff allocation as a function of these two structures, without further reference to the underlying strategic-form game. The efficient payoff allocations, in the sense of Pareto, are precisely the points on the upper boundary of the feasible set. That is $(x_1, \ldots, x_n)$ is *efficient* if it is in the feasible set and there is no other vector $(y_1, \ldots, y_n)$ in the feasible set such that $y_i \geqslant x_i$ for all i, with at least one strict inequality. The definition of equitable allocations is more problematic, but equity is supposed to mean that each player's gains from the arbitrated settlement are in some sense commensurate with every other player's gains. Once the disagreement point is specified, to represent the consequences of rejecting arbitration, the utility gains from arbitration can be computed for each player at each feasible payoff allocation.

Let us assume henceforth that there is a point in the feasible set in which every player does strictly better than in the disagreement point, so that no player would want to force disagreement.

Nash [45] listed several axioms that an impartial arbitration procedure should satisfy. If the players are symmetric, as in the Divide the Dollars game, then they should get equal payoffs. The payoff allocation selected by the procedure should be on the efficient boundary of the feasible set, and should give each player a higher payoff than he gets at the disagreement point. If a game is changed in such a way that the feasible set is made smaller, but the disagreement point is unchanged and the old arbitrated settlement is still feasible, then the new arbitrated settlement should be the same as the old (because the lost utility allocations would not have been used anyway, so they are irrelevant). If a game is changed by multiplying one player's utility function by a positive constant or by adding a constant, then his payoff in the settlement should be changed by the same multiplicative or additive constant, and all other players' payoffs should remain the same. (This is because multiplying by a positive constant or adding a constant does not change any of the decision-theoretic properties of a utility function. Thus, a player's utility function can only be defined up to such linear transformations.) Nash's remarkable result is that these properties are satisfied by only one arbitration rule: choose the utility allocation $(x_1, \ldots, x_n)$ that maximizes

$$\prod_{i=1}^{n} (x_i - v_i),$$

the multiplicative product of the players' gains over the disagreement point $(v_1, \ldots, v_n)$, subject to the constraints that $(x_1, \ldots, x_n)$ is in the feasible set and $x_i \geq v_i$ for every i. This allocation is the *Nash bargaining solution* of the game.

An alternative characterization of the Nash bargaining solution may clarify in what sense it is equitable. We use here the fact that no decision-theoretic properties are affected by multiplying a player's utility function by a positive constant. Thus, any weighted-utility functions $\lambda_i u_i$, where $\lambda_i > 0$, can represent player i's preferences as well as the given utility function u_i. This fact creates a problem for the arbitrator who wants to treat the players equitably in his recommended settlement. Since there is no decision-theoretic basis for distinguishing between the different weighted-utility functions as representations of a given player's preferences, which functions should be used in making the interpersonal comparisons that equity requires?

There are actually two kinds of interpersonal comparisons of utility that people often try to make in games: utilitarian comparisons and egalitarian comparisons. Utilitarian comparisons are implicit in the sentence: "You should do this for me because it will help me more than it hurts you." A utilitarian optimum is a feasible outcome that maximizes the sum of all players' utilities. Egalitarian comparisons are made implicit in the sentence: "You should do this for me because I am doing more for you." An egalitarian optimum is an outcome in which all players gain equally over the disagreement point. In general, there may be nothing that is optimal in both senses at once. Furthermore, if we make comparisons in *weighted* utility scales, the sets of optimal outcomes change as the λ_i weights are changed. However, there always exists some vector of weights $(\lambda_1, \ldots, \lambda_n)$ such that, when we make interpersonal comparisons in terms of weighted utilities, the utilitarian optima and the egalitarian optima intersect; and this intersection is exactly the Nash bargaining solution. That is, given the feasible set F and the disagreement point $(v_1, \ldots, v_n)$, an allocation $(x_1, \ldots, x_n)$ in F is the Nash bargaining solution if and only if there exists some vector of positive weights $(\lambda_1, \ldots, \lambda_n)$ such that

$$\sum_{i=1}^{n} \lambda_i x_i = \underset{y \text{ in } F}{\text{maximum}} \sum_{i=1}^{n} \lambda_i y_i$$

(where $y = (y_1, \ldots, y_n)$) and

$$\lambda_1 x_1 - \lambda_1 v_1 = \lambda_2 x_2 - \lambda_2 v_2 = \cdots = \lambda_n x_n - \lambda_n v_n.$$

We may refer to the λ_i that satisfy these conditions as the *natural utility weights* for the given game. Thus, the Nash bargaining solution gives the players equal gains over the disagreement point, in terms of the naturally weighted utility scales for the game.

Nash [45] stated that his bargaining solution was intended to predict the outcome of bargaining, without an arbitrator, between two players who have equal ability to bargain and who can jointly select any feasible correlated strategy for the given game. ("Feasible" here may mean either subject to incentive constraints or not, depending on whether binding contracts are possible.) As in the Divide the Dollars game, we can make the logical transition from the theory of arbitration to the theory of unarbitrated bargaining by invoking the focal-point effect. Thus, for any two-person bargaining problem, we may predict that the equity and efficiency properties of the Nash bargaining solution will lead the players to select it in their bargaining process, unless some other environmental factor or tradition focuses more strongly on some other outcome.

There may be situations in which players have unequal bargaining ability. To describe such situations, nonsymmetric versions of the Nash bargaining solution have been proposed. Nonsymmetric bargaining solutions may also be applied in arbitration, when the arbitrator feels that one player's welfare deserves relatively more weight, because of the player's intrinsic personal characteristics. For example, if player 1 is single and player 2 represents a family of four people, then an arbitrator in the Divide the Dollars game might recommend the 20–80 division, to equalize per capita gains.

In general, a *nonsymmetric Nash bargaining solution* may be defined as any solution function (mapping feasible sets with disagreement points into payoff allocations) that satisfies all of Nash's axioms except the axiom of symmetry. It can be shown (see Kalai [24]) that a nonsymmetric Nash bargaining solution always maximizes some product of the players' gains raised to various powers; that is, it maximizes

$$\prod_{i=1}^{n} (x_i - v_i)^{\alpha_i}$$

subject to $(x_1, \ldots, x_n)$ being in the feasible set F and satisfying $x_i \geq v_i$ for all i. Here the exponents $(\alpha_1, \ldots, \alpha_n)$ are some nonnegative parameters (not all zero) that represent the players' relative weight in arbitration or relative bargaining ability.

The above discussion has followed the cooperative approach to the theory of bargaining. There is an alternative *noncooperative* approach to the theory of bargaining, which was originally advocated by Nash [46] himself in his seminal paper on equilibria. (So it is also called *Nash's program*.)

The noncooperative approach to bargaining is to try to explicitly describe the sequence of decisions and actions that individual players can make during the bargaining process. Each player's role in the process of "jointly selecting a correlated strategy" must be made through some sequence of actions that he controls individually (actions of making threats and offers, and accepting or rejecting others' offers). Since the outcome of this process is the selection of a feasible correlated strategy to be used in a given game, and since the expected payoffs from this correlated strategy can be computed (as was discussed in Section 5), the bargaining process itself can (in principle) be modelled as a multistage game. Thus, Nash [46] argued, we should try to predict the outcome of the bargaining process by modelling this game and analyzing its Nash equilibria.

There are difficulties with the noncooperative approach to bargaining. Bargaining between individuals who can communicate face to face in a sophisticated language such as English is obviously a much more complex process than the simple bargaining models which theorists can study. Any tractable model must make some simplifications which may seem arbitrary or ad hoc. Furthermore, even in a simple bargaining model, the set of equilibria may be very large, especially if players can make bargaining decisions simultaneously, or if there is incomplete information on the game. From the perspective of Section 5, we could even say that an ideal bargaining process would transform the game so that all of the feasible correlated strategies of the original game would become alternative equilibrium outcomes. (See Crawford [13] for a comprehensive development of this idea.) In such a bargaining process, there remains a problem of equilibrium selection, where each equilibrium corresponds to an allocation in the feasible set. This selection problem leads us back to cooperative game theory and concepts such as the Nash bargaining solution.

On the other hand, the Nash bargaining solution is limited as a solution concept by the fact that its relevance to equilibrium selection is based on the focal-point effect. Experimental evidence (see Roth and Shoumaker [56]) suggests that factors from the sociological environment often have much stronger focal effect than the theoretical properties of the Nash bargaining solution. Furthermore, the nonsymmetric Nash bargaining solutions involve a concept of "relative bargaining ability," which begs deeper explanation or analysis. Thus, there has been a growing interest in exploring the noncooperative approach to bargaining.

The noncooperative models of bargaining studied by Rubinstein [58] give significant insights into what might determine a player's "relative bargaining ability." In these models, there are two players who can alternately make offers to each other. For a specific example, suppose that the two players (beginning with player 1) alternately offer payoff allocations in the feasible set F, either until one player accepts the other's most recent offer, or until the bargaining terminates in disagreement. Each time that player 2 makes an offer instead of accepting 1's most recent offer, there is an exogenous probability p_1 that the bargaining process will terminate in disagreement. (Actually we only need to assume that player 2 gets his disagreement payoff in this event.) Similarly, after the first offer, each time that player 1 makes an offer instead of accepting player 2's most recent offer, there is an exogenous probability p_2 that the bargaining will terminate in disagreement (so that player 1 gets his disagreement payoff). Otherwise, when an offer is accepted, both players get the payoffs specified in the offer. Using the methods of Rubinstein [58], it can be shown that this game has a unique sequential equilibrium, provided that at least one of the given probabilities (p_1 or p_2) is positive. In this unique sequential equilibrium, player 1's first offer is always accepted by player 2. Furthermore, as Binmore [10] shows, if we let $p_1 = \varepsilon \alpha_1$ and $p_2 = \varepsilon \alpha_2$ and we then take the limit as ε goes to zero, the accepted equilibrium offer converges to the nonsymmetric Nash bargaining solution with parameters α_1 and α_2.

Thus, the parameter α_i, which measures player i's relative bargaining ability in the nonsymmetric Nash solution, can be interpreted as player i's relative ability to make a credible threat to terminate bargaining if his offer is rejected. The rationale for considering very small exogenous probabilities of such termination is that, in these sequential equilibria, both players would lose if termination actually occurred, so that no one would want to enforce the termination ex post. Player i's bargaining ability thus derives from this ability to introduce at least some infinitesimal doubt in the other player's mind as to whether player i might "irrationally" terminate bargaining if his most recent offer were rejected.

7. COOPERATIVE GAMES WITH TRANSFERABLE UTILITY

The preceding section discussed the Nash bargaining solution in the context of bargaining games with any number of players. In fact, the Nash bargaining solution was originally advocated by John Nash only for the analysis of two-player games, and this limitation seems appropriate. The essential problem is that the Nash bargaining solution, as defined in the preceding section, ignores the possibility that the players might form any effective coalitions among themselves other than the *grand coalition* that contains all the players together.

To illustrate, let us compare Examples 11 and 12, each a game among three players. In Example 11, the players get payoffs of \$0 unless all three agree on how to divide \$300 among themselves. In Example 12, the rules are the same except that only players 1 and 2 need to agree, to implement the division of the \$300. (Let us equate utility payoffs with dollar payoffs here.) In both games, the disagreement point is $(0, 0, 0)$, and the feasible set for the grand coalition ($\{1, 2, 3\}$) is the set of all allocation vectors (x_1, x_2, x_3) such that $x_1 + x_2 + x_3 \leqslant 300$. The difference is that, in Example 11 no coalition of two players could achieve any payoffs other than zero, whereas in Example 12 the coalition $\{1, 2\}$ can achieve any allocation vector (x_1, x_2) such that $x_1 + x_2 \leqslant 300$. In Example 11, the Nash bargaining solution $(100, 100, 100)$ seems reasonable, but it does not seem reasonable in Example 12. When we take account of the fact that players 1 and 2 do not need player 3, the allocation $(150, 150, 0)$ seems like a much more reasonable outcome for Example 12.

Before we completely dismiss $(100, 100, 100)$ as an unreasonable prediction for Example 12, let us carefully examine the assumptions implicit in this rejection. To be more explicit, let us suppose that the strategic rules for the second game are that, after nonbinding preplay communication, players 1 and 2 simultaneously propose an allocation vector (x_1, x_2, x_3) such that $x_1 + x_2 + x_3 \leqslant 300$; if the proposed vectors are equal then they are implemented; otherwise all three players get zero. For players 1 and 2 to both propose $(100, 100, 100)$ is an equilibrium of this game, just as $(150, 150, 0)$ is also an equilibrium. Even if preplay communication is made an explicit part of the extensive or multistage characterization of the game, there is still an equilibrium in which each of the players 1 and 2 ignores anything that the other player might say (including: "Let's cut out player 3 and both choose $(150, 150, 0)$," because each interprets the other's speech as meaningless babble rather than as English), and then both choose $(100, 100, 100)$. If player 3 has any influence in such matters, he would certainly want to promote such mutual misunderstanding between players 1 and 2. Thus, the key assumption that we need, to dismiss $(100, 100, 100)$ as unreasonable, is that players 1 and 2 can *negotiate effectively* during their preplay communication opportunities.

In general, when we say that the members of a coalition can *negotiate effectively*, we mean that, if there were a feasible joint change in the coalition-members' strategies that would benefit them all, then they would actually agree to make such a change unless it contradicted agreements that some members might have made with other (nonmember) players in the context of some other equally effective coalition. The key assumption that distinguishes cooperative game theory from noncooperative game theory may be the assumption that players can negotiate effectively. In our discussion of the Nash bargaining solution, we implicitly assumed that only the grand coalition of all players can negotiate effectively together. In this section we now assume that any coalition or subset of the players can also negotiate effectively.

Because the interactions between $2^n - 1$ different coalitions in an n-player game can be so complex, a simplifying assumption of *transferable utility* is often used in cooperative game theory. That is, there is assumed to be a commodity, called money, that players can freely transfer among themselves, such that any player's utility payoff increases one unit for every unit of money that he gets.

With transferable utility, the cooperative possibilities of a game can be described by a *characteristic function* v that assigns a number $v(S)$ to every coalition S. Here $v(S)$ is called the *worth* of coalition S and represents the total amount of transferable utility that the members of S could earn together without any help from the other players outside of S. For Example 11, discussed above, the characteristic function is $v(\{1, 2, 3\}) = 300$, $v(\{1, 2\}) = v(\{1, 3\}) = v(\{2, 3\}) = 0$, and $v(\{1\}) = v(\{2\}) = v(\{3\}) = 0$. The characteristic function for Example 12 differs from this only in that $v(\{1, 2\}) = 300$. (In any characteristic function v, we let $v(\varnothing) = 0$ where $\varnothing$ is the empty set.)

Given a game in strategic form, von Neumann and Morgenstern [48] suggested that the characteristic function should be defined by

$$v(S) = \underset{\sigma_{N-S}}{\text{minimum}} \; \underset{\sigma_S}{\text{maximum}} \left(\sum_{i \text{ in } S} u_i(\sigma_S, \sigma_{N-S}) \right)$$

where σ_S is any correlated strategy for the coalition S, $N - S$ is the set of all players not in S, σ_{N-S} is any correlated strategy for $N - S$, and $u_i(\sigma_S, \sigma_{N-S})$ is player i's expected utility payoff, before transfers of money, when these correlated strategies are independently implemented. That is $v(S)$ is the maximum sum of utility payoffs that the members of S can guarantee themselves against the best offensive threat for the complementary coalition $N - S$. It can be shown that such a "minimax" characteristic function is always *superadditive*, in the sense that $v(S \cup T) \geqslant v(S) + v(T)$ for any two coalitions S and T such that $S \cap T = \varnothing$. Harsanyi [16] recommended an alternative way of deriving the characteristic function from the strategic form, such that

$$v(S) - v(N - S)$$
$$= \underset{\sigma_{N-S}}{\min} \; \underset{\sigma_S}{\max} \left(\sum_{i \text{ in } S} u_i(\sigma_S, \sigma_{N-S}) - \sum_{j \text{ in } N-S} u_j(\sigma_S, \sigma_{N-S}) \right).$$

(See also Myerson [35] for more on threats and the characteristic function.)

Once the characteristic function of a game has been specified, we can try to predict the outcome of bargaining among the players. Such analysis is based on the assumption, discussed in the preceding section, that the focal bargaining equilibrium will depend on the power structure, rather than on the details of how bargaining proceeds. A player's *power* is his ability to help or hurt other players by agreeing to cooperate with them or refusing to do so. Thus, the characteristic function is a representation of the power structure in a game.

Let v be any characteristic function of an n-player game with transferable utility. (As usual $N = \{1, 2, \ldots, n\}$ denotes the set of all players.) We may say that a coalition S can *object* to a payoff allocation $x = (x_1, \ldots, x_n)$ if

$$v(S) > \sum_{i \text{ in } S} x_i,$$

so that the members of S could get more together than they get in the allocation x. An allocation x is the *core* of v if no coalition can object to x and

$$\sum_{i=1}^{n} x_i = v(N),$$

so that x is feasible for the grand coalition N.

The core is a very attractive solution concept, in view of our assumption that any coalition can negotiate effectively. Unfortunately, the core may be empty. Consider Example 13, which differs from Example 11 in that an allocation that is proposed by any two of the three players will be implemented. The characteristic function of this game is $v(\{1\}) = v(\{2\}) = v(\{3\}) = 0$, $v(\{1, 2\}) = v(\{1, 3\}) = v(\{2, 3\}) = 300 = v(\{1, 2, 3\})$. If player i gets a positive payoff, then the other two players must get less than the \$300, which they can get by themselves, so they can object. Thus, the core of this game is empty. On the other hand, there are some games in which the core is very large. In Example 11, any allocation of the available \$300 is in the core (as long as no player's share is negative).

Shapley [65] considered the problem of how to select a unique allocation or *value* for every game represented by a characteristic function. He proposed several natural properties that such a value function should have (linearity, efficiency, symmetric treatment of symmetric players, and zero payoff allocation for powerless "dummy" players), and he showed remarkably that only one value function satisfies these axioms. In this *Shapley value*, the value assigned to player i in the n-player game represented by v is

$$\phi_i(v) = \sum_{S \subseteq N - i} \frac{|S|!(n - |S| - 1)!}{n!} \left(v(S \cup \{i\}) - v(S) \right).$$

(Here $|S|$ is the number of players in S, $n! = 1 \cdot 2 \cdot 3 \cdots n$, and $N - i$ is the set of players other than i.) A generalization of the Shapley value to games with infinitely many players has been developed by Aumann and Shapley [7].

To understand the Shapley value, observe first that it is a linear function from the set of all characteristic functions (which, for n-player games, is a vector space with $2^n - 1$ dimensions) into the set of payoff allocations (n-dimensional vectors). Linearity is composed of two properties:

$$\phi_i(\mathbf{0}) = 0, \tag{1}$$

$$\phi_i(\lambda v + (1 - \lambda)w) = \lambda \phi_i(v) + (1 - \lambda)\phi_i(w), \tag{2}$$

for any two characteristic functions v and w and any number λ between 0 and 1. ($\mathbf{0}$ is the characteristic function that assigns worth zero to every coalition; and $\lambda v + (1 - \lambda)w$ is the characteristic function that assigns worth $\lambda v(S) + (1 - \lambda)w(S)$ to each coalition S.) Equation (1) asserts that, if every coalition can only get zero, then each player should get zero. To interpret equation (2), suppose that the players will play tomorrow either a game represented by v, with probability λ, or a game represented by w, with probability $1 - \lambda$. The expected Shapley value to player i is $\lambda \phi_i(v) + (1 - \lambda)\phi_i(w)$, if the players plan to bargain tomorrow. On the other hand, if the players actually bargain today, planning their strategies in advance, then they are playing a game represented by $\lambda v + (1 - \lambda)w$, because today any coalition S can make plans that earn the expected worth $\lambda v(S) + (1 - \lambda)w(S)$. So the value to player i from bargaining today should be $\phi_i(\lambda v + (1 - \lambda)w)$. Equation (2) asserts that it should not matter whether players bargain today (before the resolution of uncertainty) or tomorrow (after the resolution of uncertainty).

Now, let R be any coalition and consider the game w_R defined by

$$w_R(S) = \begin{cases} 1 & \text{if } S \supseteq R, \\ 0 & \text{otherwise.} \end{cases}$$

That is, a coalition that contains all members of R can get a total of one unit of transferable utility; and a coalition that lacks any member of R gets zero. (This game is called the *carrier game* for R.) In this game, the members of R all make equally essential contributions to earning the unit of payoff, whereas the other players have nothing to contribute to any coalition. Thus, by the same argument that led us to predict the $(50, 50)$ allocation in the Divide the Dollars game, the reasonable outcome of this game is to divide the available utility equally among the members of R, giving nothing to the dummy players outside of R; that is,

$$\phi_i(w_R) = \begin{cases} 1/|R| & \text{if } i \text{ is in } R, \\ 0 & \text{if } i \text{ is not in } R. \end{cases} \tag{3}$$

Using basic results of linear algebra it is straightforward to show that there is a unique value function $\phi = (\phi_1, \ldots, \phi_n)$ that satisfies (1), (2), and (3) above, and this is the Shapley value. Thus, the Shapley value can be understood as the natural linear extension of the equitable solution concept that we applied in the Divide the Dollars game. (Nonsymmetric values have been studied by Kalai and Samet [26].)

A variety of other solution concepts have been defined for cooperative games in characteristic function form. Broadly speaking, these solution concepts can be divided into two categories: *equitable solutions* and *unobjectionable solutions*. The unobjectionable solutions include the *core*, the *stable sets* or *solutions* of von Neumann and Morgenstern [48], the *bargaining set* (Aumann and Maschler [5]), and *aspiration levels* (Bennett [8]). (See Lucas [30], Shubik [67], and Owen [51] for more about these concepts.) Each of these "unobjectionable" solution concepts tries to identify the set of payoff allocations that are stable, in some sense, against each coalition's ability to make a demand for some reallocations that it can enforce. The equitable solution concepts include the Shapley value, the Nash bargaining solution, and the nucleolus (Schmeidler [63]). These "equitable" solution concepts try to identify a reasonable compromise or equitable balance between the various players and coalitions, so that each player's gains from cooperation should be commensurate (in some sense) with what his cooperation contributes to other players.

The simplest way to distinguish between these two categories is by considering the two-player Divide the Dollars game. Each unobjectionable concept identifies the entire set of efficient allocations, from $(100, 0)$ to $(0, 100)$, as the set of solutions. Every equitable concept identifies the equal division $(50, 50)$ as the unique solution to this game.

In Section 6 we discussed Nash's [46] argument that cooperative games should be analyzed by computing the equilibria of a fully specified model of the bargaining process. As a criticism of the existing literature in cooperative game theory, this argument is more relevant to the unobjectionable solution concepts than to the equitable solution concepts. The unobjectionable solutions are supposed to include all the payoff allocations that the players would accept without forming coalitions to demand reallocation, so it does seem reasonable to ask for a full description of the strategic process by which players form coalitions and make such demands. (Whatever this process is, it always has some equilibria, by the general existence theorem; so the core cannot be identified with the set of equilibria of a bargaining process.)

On the other hand, the equitable solutions can be defended against Nash's argument. As with the Nash bargaining solution, we can interpret the Shapley value and other equitable solution concepts as arbitration guidelines and as determinants of focal equilibria in unarbitrated bargaining, when all coalitions can negotiate effectively. We only need to assume that the unspecified bargaining process has a sufficiently large set of equilibria, and that the focal equilibrium will be determined by its properties of efficiency and equity, which can be computed from the characteristic function.

The core of a game tends to be much more sensitive to changes in the worths of some coalitions (typically those with larger worths) than others. That is, the core and other unobjectionable solution concepts implicitly identify some coalitions as being more important than others. On the other hand, all worths of coalitions with the same number of members enter into the Shapley-value formula with the same coefficient. Thus, the Shapley value has been criticized for failing to account for the possibility that some coalitions might be more active and important in bargaining than other coalitions of similar size. For example, coalitions that can object to the value might be more active than those with no objections. Some players might have an incentive to make restrictive covenants that prevent them from negotiating separately with other players. For some exogenous reasons (cultural identity, perhaps), some players might be better able to negotiate effectively with each other than with others. To account for such factors, Owen [50] and Hart and Kurz [22] have generalized the Shapley value to games with an additional *cooperation structure* that specifies which coalitions are more active than others.

In the Owen-Hart-Kurz theory, the given cooperation structure consists of a list of certain active coalitions or *unions*. We let $S_k(i)$ denote the kth largest active union to which player i belongs, and we assume that

$$N \supset S_1(i) \supset S_2(i) \supset \cdots \supseteq \{i\},$$

for every player i. That is, we assume that the unions are *nested*. If player j is in $S_k(i)$ then $S_l(j) = S_l(i)$ for every $l \leqslant k$, since the k largest unions that contain i must also contain j.

Given such a cooperation structure, let us define a *permissible ordering* of the players to be any strict ordering such that, for any three players h, i, and j, if there is some number k such that $S_k(i) = S_k(j) \neq S_k(h)$, then either i and j both come before h in the ordering or i and j both come after h in the ordering. (That is, a player cannot come in between two members of a union to which he does not belong.) Now suppose that we will randomly select among all the permissible orderings, so that each permissible ordering has equal probability of being selected. Let $\tilde{Q}(i)$ denote the random set of players who come before player i in this randomly selected ordering. The *Owen-Hart-Kurz* (*OHK*) *value* for player i, in a game with characteristic function v and the given cooperation structure (denoted by $(S_1(\cdot), S_2(\cdot), \ldots)$), is defined to be

$$\phi_i(v|S_1, S_2, \ldots) = E(v(\tilde{Q}(i) \cup \{i\}) - v(\tilde{Q}(i)))$$

(where E denotes the expected value). So the OHK value for i is his expected marginal contribution to the random coalition that precedes him.

If $S_1(i) = \{i\}$ for every player i, so that there are no multi-player unions, then every ordering of the players is permissible. In this case, the OHK value is equal to the Shapley value.

With the OHK value as our solution concept, we may try to analyze games to predict which unions of players are most likely to become active. In the three-player majority game (Example 13, above), players 1 and 2 can gain by forming the union $\{1, 2\}$, since it would increase each of their values from 100 (the Shapley value) to 150. On the other hand, in the three-player unanimity game (Example 11, above), players 1 and 2 would lose by forming the union $\{1, 2\}$, since it would decrease each of their payoffs from 100 to 75. In general, the development of a plausible model of endogenous determination of cooperation structures remains an important unsolved problem in game theory. A theory of bargaining that is based on a value for games with cooperation structure and on a plausible model of endogenous union formation, could combine the best properties of the equitable and unobjectionable solution theories.

8. COOPERATIVE GAMES WITHOUT TRANSFERABLE UTILITY

To extend the Shapley value (and other solution concepts similarly) to games without transferable utility, Shapley [66] suggested the following "λ-transfer" theory. Given a strategic-form game

$$\Gamma = (C_1, \ldots, C_n, u_1, \ldots, u_n)$$

as in Section 2, and given any vector $\lambda = (\lambda_1, \ldots, \lambda_n)$ such that all $\lambda_i > 0$, let the λ-*rescaled version* of Γ be

$$\lambda * \Gamma = (C_1, \ldots, C_n, \lambda_1 u_1, \ldots, \lambda_n u_n).$$

That is, $\lambda * \Gamma$ differs from Γ only in that the utility function of each player i is multiplied by λ_i. Without transferable utility, there is no decision-theoretically testable distinction between these two games. So let us consider any such rescaled version $\lambda * \Gamma$ and analyze it as if the λ-weighted utilities were freely transferable, computing its characteristic function v^λ and its Shapley value $\phi(v^\lambda) = (\phi_1(v^\lambda), \ldots, \phi_n(v^\lambda))$. Let x_i^λ be the payoff for player i in the original utility scales of Γ that corresponds to the payoff $\phi_i(v^\lambda)$ in the λ-weighted utility scales of $\lambda*\Gamma$; that is

$$x_i^\lambda = \frac{1}{\lambda_i}\phi_i(v^\lambda).$$

In general, the allocation $x^\lambda = (x_1^\lambda, \ldots, x_n^\lambda)$ would be feasible in Γ if λ-weighted utilities were transferable; but x^λ is usually not feasible without such transfers. However, if x^λ actually is feasible in Γ, without any transfers of utility, then we say that x^λ is a *Shapley NTU value* (or a *λ-transfer value*) for Γ, and λ is a vector of *natural utility weights* for Γ. (Here NTU stands for "nontransferable utility.") The existence of a Shapley NTU value can be guaranteed (see Shapley [66] and Myerson [40]) if we allow any vector λ in which all components are nonnegative. (For vectors in which some λ_i are zero, we may define x^λ as any limit of a sequence of $x^{\lambda(k)}$ allocations, such that all components of each vector $\lambda(k)$ are positive and the vectors $\lambda(k)$ converge to λ as k goes to infinity.)

Alternative definitions of NTU values have been suggested by Harsanyi [16] and Owen [49]. Axiomatic derivations of the Shapley NTU value and the Harsanyi NTU value have recently been developed by Aumann [4] and Hart [21]. (See also Samet [59].) In the case of games with two players, all three of these NTU values are equal to the Nash bargaining solution, with the same natural utility weights as in Section 6. For games with transferable utility, these three NTU values all equal the Shapley value.

Roth [55] and Shafer [64] have shown examples in which the Shapley NTU value selects outcomes that seem intuitively to be very unreasonable. The Harsanyi NTU value seems somewhat more reasonable for Roth's examples. (The Owen NTU value seems too complicated to compute.) On the other hand, Myerson [40] has been able to define a natural extension of the Shapley NTU value to games with incomplete information, but not the more complicated and nonlinear Harsanyi NTU value. Thus, the Shapley NTU value stands as the most broadly defined natural extension of our two most compelling solution concepts: the Shapley value (for games with transferable utility) and the Nash bargaining solution (for games with two players). Furthermore, there is reason to hope that some modification of the Shapley NTU value, perhaps based on the OHK value with endogenously determined cooperation structures, could provide a satisfactory analysis of all examples. Thus it is important to try to understand the logic behind the Shapley NTU value.

Consider the Banker Game from Owen [49]. In this three-player game, the coalition $\{1,2\}$ can achieve any nonnegative utility allocation (y_1, y_2) such that $y_1 + 4y_2 \leqslant 100$. The grand coalition $\{1,2,3\}$ can achieve any nonnegative utility allocation (y_1, y_2, y_3) such that $y_1 + y_2 + y_3 \leqslant 100$. Every other coalition can only get zero for its members. The idea is that player 1 can get \$100 with the help of player 2. To reward player 2 for his help, player 1 can try to send him money; but without player 3, there is a 75% chance of losing the money that is sent. Player 3 is a banker who can prevent such loss in transactions. How much should player 1 pay to player 2 for his help and to player 3 for his banking services?

The unique Shapley NTU value for this game is $(50,50,0)$, supported by the natural utility weights $\lambda = (1,1,1)$. With these weights, $v^\lambda(\{1,2\}) = 100$, because the maximum λ-weighted sum of utilities that coalition $\{1,2\}$ can get is 100, at $(y_1, y_2) = (100,0)$. Also, $v^\lambda(\{1,2,3\}) = 100$, and every other coalition S gets $v^\lambda(S) = 0$. The Shapley value of this v^λ is $(50,50,0)$.

Owen [49] argued that player 1 should get more than player 2, and that player 3 should get some positive fee for his banking services; but there is a rationale to this Shapley NTU value. Getting zero, player 3 is indifferent between accepting this NTU-value outcome or not, so it is not unreasonable to assume that he probably will accept it. (Think of his NTU-value payoff as positive but infinitesimal, while his cost of providing banking services is zero.) So suppose that there is only some small probability q that player 3 will refuse to accept his NTU-value allocation and will break up the grand coalition. As long as $q \leqslant 1/2$, players 1 and 2 can accommodate this possibility with no loss of expected utility. They simply plan to choose $(100,0)$ if 3 rejects the grand coalition (no transfer of money without the banker), and plan to choose $(100 - 50/(1 - q), 50/(1 - q), 0)$ if 3 agrees to cooperate (a transfer of $50/(1 - q)$ using the banker).

Now let i equal 1 or 2; and suppose instead that there were a small probability q that player i would reject the NTU-value outcome, even though it is better for him than the zero that he gets alone. In this case, the expected payoffs to the other two players could not sum to more than $50(1 - q)$ without reducing player i's allocation in the case of agreement. Thus, a low-probability threat of rejection by either player 1 or 2 would cause real losses in the expected payoffs of the other players, and in a symmetrical manner; but such a threat by player 3 would have no effect on expected payoffs if it were anticipated correctly. In this sense, players 1 and 2 have equal power and player 3 has none, so that $(50, 50, 0)$ is a reasonable bargaining solution.

In general, let x be an efficient payoff allocation for the grand coalition in a given game. Let λ be a vector of utility weights such that x maximizes the sum of λ-weighted utilities $(\lambda_1 x_1 + \cdots + \lambda_n x_n)$ over all payoff allocations that are feasible for the grand coalition. Suppose that the efficient frontier is differentiable or smooth at x. Then, to a first-order approximation, small transfers of λ-weighted utility are feasible near x for players in the grand coalition. That is, for any sufficiently small δ, if player i reduced his utility payoff from x_i to $x_i - \delta/\lambda_i$ (sacrificing δ units of λ-weighted utility) then, without changing any other players' payoffs from what they get in the allocation x, player j could increase his utility payoff from x_j to $x_j + \delta/\lambda_j$, minus some "transactions cost" that is small in proportion to δ.

Now suppose that the players are expected to unanimously accept the allocation x almost surely, except that, with some small probability, a smaller coalition S might have to choose something feasible for themselves. In this situation, a small transfer of λ-weighted utility in the event that everyone accepts x would have the same effect on expected payoffs as a large transfer of λ-weighted utility in the event that coalition S acts alone. Thus, when the members of coalition S plan what to do if they must act alone, they can effectively transfer λ-weighted utility among themselves, where the coin of transfer is a promise to make a small feasible real-location around x in the much more likely event that x is accepted. (The players outside S would not object to such reallocation because it does not affect their payoffs. We are assuming that these coalitional plans are made before it is learned whether the coalition must act alone or not.) So it is appropriate to analyze this bargaining game as if λ-weighted utility really were transferable for any such coalition S. The results of this analysis (when we compute the Shapley value of the λ-rescaled version of the game, and then convert this value back into the original utility scales) will coincide with the originally hypothesized allocation x if and only if x is a Shapley NTU value. In this sense, the Shapley NTU values are the plausible cooperative solutions of the game.

9.   COOPERATIVE GAMES WITH INCOMPLETE INFORMATION

In a cooperative game with incomplete information, the players already know their private information or "type" when they bargain over which communication mechanism to implement. Recall that a communication mechanism for a Bayesian game with incomplete information is a rule for determining the actions of all players as a (possibly random) function of reports that the players submit to some mediator. Let us suppose that the players can make binding commitments to regulate their actions but cannot verifiably audit each others' types. Thus, a communication mechanism μ is *feasible* for the players together only if it satisfies the informational incentive constraints discussed near the end of Section 5.

If player i's actual type is t_i, then his objective in bargaining is to maximize his conditionally expected payoff $U_i(\mu|t_i)$ given his actual type. His conditionally expected payoff given any other possible type, and his ex ante expected payoff before his type was learned, would be completely irrelevant to his welfare, since he already knows his actual type. However, an outside arbitrator, who does not know any player's actual type, can be sure that all players would want to make some change in their communication mechanism only if the change increased the conditionally expected payoffs $U_i(\mu|t_i)$ for every type t_i of every player i. From such an outsider's viewpoint, if there are three players and if there are five possible types or information states for each player, then a change is an unambiguous welfare improvement only if it increases (or at least does not decrease) each of the fifteen conditionally expected payoffs for the various possible types of players. In general, we may say a communication mechanism μ is *efficient* if it is feasible and there does not exist any other feasible communication mechanism ν such that

$$U_i(\nu|t_i) \geq U_i(\mu|t_i)$$

for every possible type t_i of every player i, with at least one strict inequality. (For a comprehensive discussion of efficiency with incomplete information, see Holmstrom and Myerson [23]. We are here defining efficiency to mean *interim incentive-efficiency*, in the terminology of Holmstrom and Myerson.)

In bargaining without an arbitrator, the expected payoffs for all possible types of a player may still be relevant to the bargaining process, because the other players do not know his actual type and he may wish to conceal it. If a player were expected to demand the feasible communication mechanism that maximizes his conditionally expected utility given his actual type, then his demand could reveal his type-information to the other players, and they might be able to use this information against him. Thus, a player's optimal bargaining strategy should represent some kind of inscrutable compromise between his actual preferences and the preferences that he would have had if his informational type had been different. Therefore, a cooperative bargaining solution should be an equitable compromise, in some sense, not only between all the different players, but also between all the different possible types of each player.

Based on such considerations of efficiency and equity, Myerson [38, 39, 40] has defined *neutral bargaining solutions*, which generalize the Nash bargaining solution and the Shapley NTU value to games with incomplete information. These neutral bargaining solutions satisfy equity and efficiency properties that can be described in terms of certain *virtual-utility* functions. Without giving a formal definition here, we may say that a player's virtual utility differs from his real utility by taking into account the costs of satisfying his informational incentive constraints. (In a sense, the definition of virtual utility is an application of one of the most basic ideas of economic theory: that efficient social plans could be decentralized if the constraints facing society were multiplied by some appropriate shadow prices and added into the individual's payoff functions. The only difference is that here we are considering incentive constraints, instead of resource constraints. For a full basic explanation of virtual utility see Myerson [43].) The essential idea of these neutral bargaining solutions is to apply the Shapley value (in each information state) to a transformed game in which the players get transferable virtual-utility payoffs, in the same way that the Shapley NTU value applies the Shapley value to a transformed game in which the players get transferable weighted-utility payoffs. If the resulting allocation of virtual utility corresponds to an allocation of real utility that can actually be achieved by a feasible communication mechanism then that mechanism is a neutral bargaining solution.

It is best to introduce these ideas in the context of a simple two-player example. Let player 1 be a (monopolistic) seller and let player 2 be a (monopsonistic) buyer of some commodity. The seller has a supply of one unit of the commodity, and he knows whether it is good quality (type "1a") or bad quality (type "1b"). If it is good quality then it is worth \$40 per unit to the seller and \$50 per unit to the buyer. If it is bad quality then it is worth \$20 per unit to the seller and \$30 per unit to the buyer. The buyer thinks that the probability of good quality is 0.2. We assume that the buyer cannot verifiably audit the seller's information, and the seller cannot offer any enforceable warranties. They must simply negotiate a price and quantity to be traded, possibly depending on what the seller claims about his information.

To describe a *trading mechanism* that the players might use, let x_a and q_a denote, respectively, the amount of money that the buyer will pay to the seller and the quantity of the commodity that the seller will give to the buyer if the seller claims that the quality is good; and let x_b and q_b denote corresponding quantities if the seller claims that the quality is bad. If the seller is honest in such a trading mechanism then his expected payoff is

$$U_{1a} = x_a - 40q_a \quad \text{if a commodity is good, and}$$
$$U_{1b} = x_b - 20q_b \quad \text{if the commodity is bad.}$$

The buyer, who does not know the quality, gets the expected payoff

$$U_2 = (.2)(50q_a - x_a) + (.8)(30q_b - x_b).$$

To be feasible, a trading mechanism must satisfy the following two informational incentive constraints

$$U_{1a} \geq x_b - 40q_b, \qquad U_{1b} \geq x_a - 20q_a,$$

so that the seller cannot gain by lying about his information. Also, since each player has the option to not trade at all (which gives him a payoff of zero) a feasible trading mechanism must also satisfy the following three *minimum-payoff constraints* (often called *individual-rationality* constraints)

$$U_{1a} \geq 0, \qquad U_{1b} \geq 0, \qquad U_2 \geq 0.$$

In addition, we must have $0 \leq q_a \leq 1$ and $0 \leq q_b \leq 1$, since there is only one unit to trade.

Notice that the commodity is always worth $10 more to the buyer than to the seller. However, there is no feasible trading mechanism in which the buyer always gets all of the seller's supply. Such a mechanism would have $q_a = q_b = 1$; but then the incentive constraints would imply that $x_a = x_b$, so that either $U_{1a} < 0$ or $U_2 < 0$. Thus, by the revelation principle (see Section 5), in any equilibrium of any bargaining process applied to this game, there must be some positive probability that the seller will end up owning some of the commodity, even though it should be worth more to the buyer. The problem is that the good-type seller (1a) cannot convincingly demonstrate that he really needs and deserves a price above $40, unless he implements a threat to withold some of his supply. Without such a demonstration, the buyer would be unwilling to pay more than $34 = (.8)(30) + (.2)(50).

There are many trading mechanisms that do satisfy all of the feasibility constraints, however. Analysis of these constraints shows that, for any numbers q_a and q_b such that $0 \leq q_a \leq (4/7)q_b$ and $q_b \leq 1$, there exist some x_a and x_b that make a feasible trading mechanism. (See Proposition 3 in Myerson [44].) In general, the good-type seller always sells strictly less than the bad type, but at a higher price per unit.

To determine which trading mechanisms are efficient, we must characterize the set of all allocations of expected utility (U_{1a}, U_{1b}, U_2) to the two types of seller and the buyer that can be achieved using a feasible trading mechanism. It can be shown, by mathematical analysis of the feasibility constraints, that an allocation (U_{1a}, U_{1b}, U_2) can be achieved if and only if it satisfies the following five inequalities:

$$.3U_{1a} + .7U_{1b} + U_2 \leqslant 8, \qquad U_{1a} \leqslant U_{1b},$$
$$U_{1a} \geqslant 0, \qquad U_{1b} \geqslant 0, \quad \text{and} \quad U_2 \geqslant 0.$$

Thus, any feasible mechanism that satisfies

$$.3U_{1a} + .7U_{1b} + U_2 = 8$$

must be efficient, in the sense that there is no other feasible trading mechanism that would be surely preferred by the seller (of either type) and by the buyer.

The best feasible mechanism for the buyer is

$$q_a = 0, \qquad x_a = 0, \qquad q_b = 1, \qquad x_b = 20, \tag{4}$$

which gives expected payoffs

$$U_{1a} = 0, \qquad U_{1b} = 0, \qquad U_2 = 8.$$

This mechanism is implemented by letting the buyer make a nonnegotiable first-and-final offer to buy the seller's unit of supply for \$20, accepting the 20% chance that the seller might refuse to trade because he is a good type. To increase q_a above zero, it would be necessary to offer a higher price to the bad-type seller, which would reduce the buyer's expected payoff.

The best feasible mechanism for the seller depends on his type. For the good type (1a) the best feasible mechanism is

$$q_a = 0, \qquad x_a = 8, \qquad q_b = 1, \qquad x_b = 28 \tag{5}$$

which gives

$$U_{1a} = 8, \qquad U_{1b} = 8, \qquad U_2 = 0.$$

This mechanism differs from the buyer' best (4) in that the buyer first has to pay a nonrefundable fee of $8, to buy the right to then make a final offer of $20 for the commodity. The good-type seller would take the $8 fee and then refuse to sell for $20. In expected value, the buyer is compensated for his potential losses to the good type by his $2 gains from the more likely bad type. On the other hand, the best feasible mechanism for the bad type (1b) is

$$q_a = \tfrac{4}{7}, \qquad x_a = 22\tfrac{6}{7}, \qquad q_b = 1, \qquad x_b = 31\tfrac{3}{7}, \qquad (6)$$

which gives

$$U_{1a} = 0, \qquad U_{1b} = 11\tfrac{3}{7}, \qquad U_2 = 0.$$

In this mechanism, the buyer buys $4/7$ units from the good type at a price per unit of $x_a/q_a = 40$. So his gains from the good type compensate, in expected value, for his losses when he pays a price above $30 to the bad type.

Under the assumption that the buyer and seller have equal bargaining ability, the neutral bargaining solution selects the trading mechanism

$$q_a = \tfrac{1}{6}, \qquad x_a = \tfrac{50}{6}, \qquad q_b = 1, \qquad x_b = 25 \qquad (7)$$

which gives

$$U_{1a} = 1\tfrac{2}{3}, \qquad U_{1b} = 5, \qquad U_2 = 4.$$

(Notice that $.3(10/6) + .7(5) + 4 = 8$, so this is efficient.) In this mechanism, the seller can either sell his entire supply for $25, or he can sell $1/6$ of his supply for a price per unit of $50 = x_a/q_a$; the bad type chooses the former and the good type chooses the latter. The price of $25 seems clearly equitable for the bad type of seller (averaging the seller's valuation of $20 and the buyer's valuation of $30), but the $50 price for the good type fully exploits the buyer.

However, it can be shown (see Myerson [43]) that if the costs of the incentive constraints were internalized using the hypothetical construction of virtual utility, the good-type seller's virtual valuation would become $50 instead of $40, so the $50 price satisfies the property of "virtual equity" for the good type. The intuitive idea behind the virtual-utility hypothesis is that the good type of seller is jeopardized by the bad type (that is, type 1a needs to prove to the buyer that he is not type 1b), so that the good type might tend to distort his effective preferences and act as if the commodity was worth $50 to him rather than $40, to exaggerate his difference from the bad type. These exaggerated virtual preferences could also justify the outcome that only a fraction of the good seller's supply is sold, since his virtual valuation equals the buyer's valuation for the commodity.

To understand the rationale behind the neutral bargaining solution more rigorously, it is necessary to face the issue of inscrutable compromise between two types of the seller. The buyer's expected payoff $U_2 = 4$ seems equitable, in that it is halfway between the best ($U_2 = 8$) and worst ($U_2 = 0$) that he could expect in any feasible trading mechanism. There are many possible allocations for the different types of seller (from $(U_{1a}, U_{1b}) = (4, 4)$ to $(U_{1a}, U_{1b}) = (0, 5\frac{5}{7})$) that are all achievable with feasible trading mechanisms in which the buyer's expected payoff is 4, but only if both types of seller are expected to use the same mechanism (so that the choice of mechanism does not alter the buyer's beliefs). What is special about the allocation $(U_{1a}, U_{1b}) = (1\frac{2}{3}, 5)$ that makes it the most reasonable or inscrutable compromise between the conflicting interests of the two types of seller (so that the buyer should not infer anything about the seller's type from the fact that he is willing to settle for a mechanism that gives this allocation)?

Consider first the simpler case in which the seller has all of the bargaining ability (or the seller is a *principal* in the sense discussed at the end of Section 3). In this case, the seller does not need to compromise with the buyer, who will presumably accept any trading mechanism that gives him a nonnegative expected payoff. However, the seller must still make some compromise between his actual type and the other possible type, to avoid conveying information to the buyer by the mechanism selection itself. That is, the seller cannot simply demand the feasible mechanism that he likes best given his actual type, because the buyer would reject mechanism (5) when he realizes that only the good type would want to implement it, and the buyer would reject (6) when he realizes that only the bad type would implement it. (The buyer would expect to lose \$8 to the good type in (5) and lose \$1$\frac{3}{7}$ to the bad type in (6).) The most inscrutable compromise for the informed seller would be

$$q_a = \tfrac{1}{3}, \qquad x_a = \tfrac{50}{3}, \qquad q_b = 1, \qquad x_b = 30. \qquad (8)$$

In this feasible mechanism, the bad type sells his entire supply for \$30 and the good type sells $1/3$ of his supply for \$50 per unit. The buyer's payoff is zero with either type of seller, so the buyer would be willing to participate in this mechanism no matter what he inferred about the seller's type from the fact that the seller proposed it. Furthermore, this mechanism is efficient and gives $U_2 = 0$, so there is no feasible mechanism that makes both types of the seller better off. These properties make mechanism (8) a *strong optimum* for the seller, in the sense of Myerson [38]. It can be shown that, for any alternative feasible mechanism that is better for one type of the seller, the buyer would expect negative payoff in this alternative mechanism if he inferred that the seller's type is the one that prefers it. So any other proposal by the seller would be rejected by the buyer, on the basis of the information revealed by the proposal itself.

The expected payoffs from the seller's optimum (8) are

$$U_{1a} = 3\tfrac{1}{3}, \qquad U_{1b} = 10, \qquad U_2 = 0.$$

The averages of these payoffs with those of the buyer's optimum (4) are exactly equal to the expected payoffs of the neutral bargaining solution (7). That is, the neutral bargaining solution is equivalent to a randomization between the buyer's optimum (4) and the seller's optimum (8), in which each mechanism gets equal probability. This *random-dictatorship* property is in fact one of the two axioms (the other being an analogue of Nash's axiom of *independence of irrelevant alternatives*) from which the neutral bargaining solution was first derived by Myerson [39].

It can also be instructive to analyze this game by the noncooperative approach to bargaining, characterizing the equilibria of a specific bargaining process. Similar games have been analyzed in this way by many authors, including Fudenberg and Tirole [15], Cramton [12], Sobel and Takahashi [68], Rubinstein [58], and Chatterjee and Samuelson [11]. By the revelation principle, any equilibrium of any such bargaining process will be equivalent to some feasible mechanism as described above. Unfortunately, many natural bargaining processes turn out to have multiple equilibria.

For example, consider the bargaining process in which the seller first sets a price per unit, and then the buyer decides what quantity to purchase. There are infinitely many sequential equilibria of this game. For any price y between 40 and 50, there is a sequential equilibrium in which the good type of the seller sets a price of y. The bad type randomizes between setting a price of 30, with probability $(5y - 170)/(4y - 120)$, and a price of y, with probability $(50 - y)/(4y - 120)$. When the bad type randomizes in this way, the buyer would rationally believe, after getting a price of y, that the commodity should be worth $\$y$ per unit to him, because

$$y = \frac{(30)(.8)(50 - y)/(4y - 120) + (50)(.2)}{(.8)(50 - y)/(4y - 120) + .2}.$$

So the buyer's demand can be rationally set at $10/(y - 30)$ units of the commodity after getting a price of y, and at one unit after getting a price of 30. For any price above 30 other than y, we may suppose that the buyer would demand no units of the commodity, because he might infer that the unexpected price quote came from the bad type of seller. Notice that the bad type of seller is indifferent between setting the price at 30 or at y, as is necessary to induce him to randomize.

All of these equilibria correspond to efficient trading mechanisms, and all give the same expected payoff to the bad type of seller. The difference is that the buyer prefers the equilibria with lower y and the good type of seller prefers the equilibria with higher y. (There are other, inefficient equilibria of this game which are worse for both the buyer and the good type of seller than the equilibria described above.) Thus, if we add the assumption that the seller not only sets the price but also has the persuasive power of a principal to determine the equilibrium (that is, he can explain which sequential equilibrium he is implementing when he sets his price, and the buyer will accept his explanation), then we should expect that the sequential equilibrium with $y = 50$ will be implemented. This equilibrium is equivalent to the seller's neutral optimum (trading mechanism (8)) which we discussed above.

ACKNOWLEDGEMENTS

The author is deeply indebted to Ehud Kalai and Robert Weber for many long discussions about game theory. Support by the John Simon Guggenheim Memorial Foundation and the Alfred P. Sloan Foundation is gratefully acknowledged.

REFERENCES

1. R. J. Aumann, "Subjectivity and correlation in randomized strategies," *Journal of Mathematical Economics* **1** (1974), 67–96.
2. ———, "Agreeing to disagree," *Annals of Statistics* **4** (1976), 1236–1239.
3. ———, "Survey of repeated games," in *Essays in Game Theory and Mathematical Economics*, by R. J. Aumann et al., Zurich: Bibliographisches Institut, 11–42, 1981.
4. ———, "An axiomatization of the non-transferable utility value," *Econometrica* **53** (1985), 599–612.
5. R. J. Aumann and M. Maschler, "The bargaining set for cooperation games," in *Advances in Game Theory*, ed. by M. Dresher, L. S. Shapley, and A. W. Tucker, Princeton University Press, Princeton, 1964, pp. 443–447.
6. R. J. Aumann and M. Maschler, "Some thoughts on the minimax principle," *Management Science* **18** (1972), P54–P63.
7. R. J. Aumann and L. S. Shapley, *Values of Non-Atomic Games*, Princeton University Press, Princeton, 1974.
8. E. Bennett, "The aspiration approach to predicting coalition formation and payoff distribution in sidepayment games," *International Journal of Game Theory* **12** (1983), 1–28.
9. B. D. Bernheim, "Rationalizable strategic behavior," *Econometrica* **52** (1984), 1007–1028.
10. K. Binmore, "Nash bargaining theory II," discussion paper, London School of Economics, 1981.
11. K. Chatterjee and W. Samuelson, "Bargaining under incomplete information," *Operations Research* **31** (1983), 835–851.

12. P. Cramton, "The role of time and information in bargaining," discussion paper, Graduate School of Business, Stanford University, 1984.

13. V. Crawford, "Efficient and durable decision rules: a reformulation," *Econometrica* **53** (1985), 817–835.

14. E. van Damme, "A relation between perfect equilibria in extensive games and proper equilibria in normal form games," *International Journal of Game Theory* **13** (1984), 1–13.

15. D. Fudenberg and J. Tirole, "Sequential bargaining with incomplete information," *Review of Economic Studies* **50** (1983), 221–247.

16. J. C. Harsanyi, "A simplified bargaining model for the *n*-person cooperative game," *International Economic Review* **4** (1963), 194–220.

17. ———, "Games with incomplete information played by 'Bayesian' players," *Management Science* **14** (1967–8), 159–182, 320–334, 486–502.

18. ———, "Games with randomly disturbed payoffs: a new rationale for mixed-strategy equilibrium points," *International Journal of Game Theory* **2** (1973), 1–23.

19. ———, "The tracing procedure: a Bayesian approach to defining a solution for *n*-person games," *International Journal of Game Theory* **4** (1975), 61–94.

20. J. C. Harsanyi and R. Selten, *A General Theory of Equilibrium Selection in Games*, forthcoming 1985. (Available in discussion papers of the Institute for Mathematical Economics of the University of Bielefeld.)

21. S. Hart, "An axiomatization of Harsanyi's non-transferable utility solution," *Econometrica* **53** (1985), 1295–1313.

22. S. Hart and M. Kurz, "Endogenous formation of coalitions," *Econometrica* **51** (1983), 1799–1819.

23. B. Holmstrom and R. B. Myerson, "Efficient and durable decision rules with incomplete information," *Econometrica* **51** (1983), 1799–1819.

24. K. Kalai, "Nonsymmetric Nash solutions and replications of two-person bargaining," *International Journal of Game Theory* **6** (1977), 129–133.

25. E. Kalai and D. Samet, "Persistent equilibria in strategic games," *International Journal of Game Theory* **13** (1984), 129–144.

26. E. Kalai and D. Samet, "On weighted Shapley values," discussion paper, Northwestern University, 1984.

27. E. Kohlberg and J. F. Mertens, "On the strategic stability of equilibria," CORE discussion paper No. 8248, Université Catholique de Louvain, 1983.

28. D. Kreps and R. Wilson, "Sequential equilibria," *Econometrica* **50** (1982), 863–894.

29. H. W. Kuhn, "Extensive games and problems of information," in *Contributions to The Theory of Games II*, edited by H. W. Kuhn and A. W. Tucker, Princeton University Press, Princeton, 1953, pp. 193–216.

30. W. F. Lucas, "An overview of the mathematical theory of games," *Management Science* **18** (1972), P3–P19.

31. R. D. Luce and H. Raiffa, *Games and Decisions*, John Wiley and Sons, New York, 1957.

32. J. R. Mertens and S. Zamir, "Formulation of Bayesian analysis for games with incomplete information," *International Journal of Game Theory* **14** (1985), 1–29.

33. P. R. Milgrom and R. J. Weber, "Distributional strategies for games with incomplete information," *Mathematics of Operations Research* **10** (1985), 619–632.

34. R. B. Myerson, "Refinements of the Nash equilibrium concept," *International Journal of Game Theory* **7** (1978), 73–80.

35. ———, "Threat equilibria and fair settlements in cooperative games," *Mathematics of Operations Research* **3** (1978), 265–274.

36. ———, "An axiomatic derivation of subjective probability, utility, and evaluation functions," *Theory and Decision* **11** (1979), 339–352.

37. ———, "Optimal coordination mechanisms in generalized principal-agent problems," *Journal of Mathematical Economics* **10** (1982), 67–81.

38. ———, "Mechanism design by an informed principal," *Econometrica* **51** (1983), 1767–1797.

39. ———, "Two-person bargaining problems with incomplete information," *Econometrica* **52** (1984), 461–487.

40. ———, "Cooperative games with incomplete information," *International Journal of Game Theory* **13** (1984), 69–96.

41. ———, "Acceptable and predominant correlated equilibria," discussion paper, Northwestern University, to appear in *International Journal of Game Theory*, 1986.

42. ———, "Multistage games with communication," discussion paper, Northwestern University, to appear in *Econometrica*, 1986.

43. ———, "Bayesian equilibrium and incentive compatibility: an introduction," in *Social Goals and Social Organization*, edited by L. Hurwicz, D. Schmeidler, and H. Sonnenschein, Cambridge University Press, 1985, pp. 229–259.

44. ———, "Analysis of two bargaining problems with incomplete information," in *Game Theoretic Models of Bargaining*, edited by A. E. Roth, Cambridge University Press, 1985, pp. 115–147.

45. J. F. Nash, "The bargaining problem," *Econometrica* **18** (1950), 155–162.

46. ———, "Noncooperative games," *Annals of Mathematics* **54** (1951), 289–295.

47. ———, "Two-person cooperative games," *Econometrica* **21** (1953), 128–140.

48. J. von Neumann and O. Morgenstern, *Theory of Games and Economic Behavior*, Princeton University Press, Princeton, 1944.

49. G. Owen, "Values of games without sidepayments," *International Journal of Game Theory* **1** (1972), 94–109.

50. ———, "Values of games with a priori unions," in *Essays in Mathematical Economics and Game Theory*, edited by R. Hein and O. Moeschlin, Springer-Verlag, Berlin, 1977, pp. 76–88.

51. ———, *Game Theory* (2nd edition), Academic Press, New York, 1982.

52. D. G. Pearce, "Rationalizable strategic behavior and the problem of perfection," *Econometrica* **52** (1984), 1029–1050.

53. H. Raiffa, *Decision Analysis*, Addison-Wesley, Reading, Massachusetts, 1968.

54. A. E. Roth, *Axiomatic Models of Bargaining*, Springer-Verlag, Berlin, 1979.

55. ———, "Values for games without side payments: some difficulties with current concepts,"*Econometrica* **48** (1980), 457–465.

56. A. E. Roth and F. Schoumaker, "Expectations and reputations in bargaining," *American Economic Review* **73** (1983), 362–372.

57. A. Rubinstein, "Equilibrium in supergames with the overtaking criterion," *Journal of Economic Theory* **21** (1979), 1–9.

58. ———, "Perfect equilibrium in a bargaining model," *Econometrica* **50** (1982), 97–109.

59. D. Samet, "An axiomatization of the egalitarian solutions," to appear in *Mathematical Social Sciences*, 1984.

60. L. J. Savage, *The Foundations of Statistics*, John Wiley and Sons, New York, 1954.

61. R. Selten, "Reexamination of the perfectness concept for equilibrium points in extensive games," *International Journal of Game Theory* **4** (1975), 25–55.

62. T. C. Schelling, *The Strategy of Conflict*, Oxford University Press, London, 1960.

63. D. Schmeidler, "The nucleolus of a characteristic function game," *SIAM Journal of Applied Mathematics* **17** (1969), 1163–1170.

64. W. Shafer, "On the existence and interpretation of value allocations," *Econometrica* **48** (1980), 467–477.

65. L. S. Shapley, "A value for *n*-person games," in *Contributions to the Theory of Games* **2**, edited by H. Kuhn and A. W. Tucker, Princeton University Press, Princeton, 1953, pp. 307–317.

66. ———, "Utility comparison and the theory of games," in *La Decision*, Editions du CNRS, Paris, 1969, pp. 251–263.

67. M. Shubik, *Game Theory in the Social Sciences*, MIT Press, Cambridge, 1982.

68. J. Sobel and I. Takahashi, "A multistage model of bargaining," *Review of Economic Studies* **50** (1983), 411–426.

SCALAR AND VECTOR MAXIMIZATION: CALCULUS TECHNIQUES WITH ECONOMICS APPLICATIONS*

Carl P. Simon

The main purpose of this paper is to present a thorough and systematic study of the necessary and sufficient conditions for a smooth nonlinear mapping $u: \mathbb{R}^n \to \mathbb{R}^a$ to have a vector maximum (or Pareto optimum) on some (constraint) subset of $\mathbb{R}^n$, and to apply this study to some of the basic problems in microeconomics. The principal technique in this study will be to equate any given constrained vector maximization problem with a system of constrained scalar maximization problems, that is, problems of mathematical programming. This approach seems much simpler and more rewarding than the usual ad-hoc methods used in vector maximization problems. (See Theorem 7.1 and the remarks in Section 7.1.)

Consequently, we also need to present a thorough introduction to the theory of mathematical programming. We begin this presentation in Section 2 by recalling the first- and second-order conditions involved in unconstrained maximization problems. In Section 3, we

---

*Supported in part by NSF Grant MCS 79-00933

use these results to study constrained maximization problems where the constraint set is a smooth manifold, i.e., the derivative of the mapping which defines the constraints has maximal rank near the proposed solution. We also derive very general second-order sufficient conditions for a constrained maximum in this section.

In Section 4, the strong nondegeneracy assumptions on the constraint set are replaced by the more general "constraint qualifications" of Kuhn-Tucker, Arrow-Hurwicz-Uzawa, and Slater. An attempt is made to keep the presentation of these different cases as unified, yet as simple as possible. The first-order necessary conditions of Section 4 are the basic ingredients of the general theorems on vector maximization presented in Section 7.

In Section 5, we examine the situation where the first-order necessary conditions are also sufficient—the economically important case of concave and almost concave objective and constraint functions. This section also includes a brief introduction to saddle-point theorems and to duality.

Section 6 brings together the theory of the previous four sections by using programming theorems to introduce the basic concepts and norms of the economic theories of the consumer and of the firm. We first derive the classical necessary (and often sufficient) conditions that describe a consumer's choice of a most preferred commodity vector from a set of feasible and affordable commodity vectors. We then turn to a similar study of a firm trying to choose the level of production that will maximize profits or revenues. This study includes an introduction to the activity analysis of production.

In Section 7, all the theory developed for scalar maximization problems is applied to vector maximization problems. This includes both necessary conditions and sufficient conditions, first-order and rather strong second-order conditions. We discuss both the "proper" solutions of Kuhn-Tucker and Geoffrion and the saddle point approach to vector maximization problems. We end this section by reviewing some of the insights into vector maxima that Smale and others have achieved by using techniques of differential topology.

Finally, the eighth section extends the applications of Section 6 to the case where a number of consumers interact in an economy. Special properties of the utility mappings that arise in these situations are related to the hypotheses of theorems in Section 7. Then, results of Sections 5 and 7 are used to prove the Fundamental Theorems of Welfare Economics, which relate the concepts of Pareto optimum and competitive equilibrium. The section closes with an application of vector maximization to the choice of an efficient portfolio of securities.

The author hopes that after reading this paper the general reader will develop an understanding of and an intuition for some of the more basic concepts and techniques of mathematical economics and, as a result, will be adequately prepared to examine the more advanced topics in mathematical economics that are presented in this book.

With the exception of a few references to elementary facts about matrices, the only mathematical tools used are the basic theorems of multidimensional calculus, e.g., the Chain Rule, Taylor's Theorem, the Mean Value Theorem, and the Implicit Function Theorem. Consequently, this paper should be accessible to any reader who has taken the basic two-year sequence of differential calculus. To refresh the reader's familiarity with these theorems and to introduce the convenient coordinate-free notation which will be used throughout this paper, the author presents a minicourse in advanced calculus—without proofs—in the first part of Section 1. This section also contains an introduction—with proofs—to the properties of concave functions and their generalizations which are important in programming problems.

This paper contains no really new results in scalar and vector maximization, although a number of theorems in the last three sections are presented with weaker hypotheses or stronger conclusions than the author has found in the literature. The emphasis has been on presenting a very thorough description of the theory of nonlinear vector maximization and as unified and as simple an approach as possible to the problems of scalar and vector maximization.*

I am grateful for comments and suggestions by L. Blume, J. Tolle, and H. Varian on an earlier draft of this paper.

1. MATHEMATICAL BACKGROUND

1.1. Derivatives. In this section, we will summarize some of the important results from differential calculus which will be needed in later sections. No proofs will be given. To facilitate later expositions, we will try to stay with a coordinate-free notation. See Courant [11], Fleming [24], and Edwards [19], for example, for complete proofs and further discussions.

Let $\mathbb{R}^n$ denote the usual linear space of n-vectors $\{\underline{x} = (x_1, \ldots, x_n) | x_i$ is a real number$\}$. Let $\mathbb{R}^n_+$ denote the positive orthant of $\mathbb{R}^n$, i.e., $\{\underline{x} \in \mathbb{R}^n | x_i \geq 0$ for $i = 1, \ldots, n\}$. If $\underline{x}$ and $\underline{y}$ are in $\mathbb{R}^n$, we will write $\underline{x} \leq \underline{y}$ if $x_i \leq y_i$ for $i = 1, \ldots, n$, and $\underline{x} < \underline{y}$ if $x_i < y_i$ for all i. We will denote the standard inner product between $\underline{x}$ and $\underline{y}$ as

$$\underline{x} \cdot \underline{y} = \sum_{i=1}^{n} x_i y_i$$

and the norm or length of $\underline{x}$ as

$$|\underline{x}| = \sqrt{\underline{x} \cdot \underline{x}}$$

On $\mathbb{R}^1$, write $[a, b]$ for $\{t \in \mathbb{R} | a \leq t \leq b\}$ and (a, b) for $\{t \in \mathbb{R} | a < t < b\}$, where a and $b \in \mathbb{R}^1$.

Let $f: \mathbb{R}^n \to \mathbb{R}^m$ be a continuous mapping. Then, f has a derivative at $\underline{x}^0 \in \mathbb{R}^n$ (or f is differentiable at $\underline{x}^0$) if there is a linear mapping $L: \mathbb{R}^n \to \mathbb{R}^m$ such that

$$\lim_{\underline{h} \to 0} \frac{f(\underline{x}^0 + \underline{h}) - f(\underline{x}^0) - L(\underline{h})}{|\underline{h}|}$$

exists and is $\underline{0}$. In this case, L is called the *first derivative of f* at $\underline{x}^0$ and written as $Df(\underline{x}^0)$. Since $Df(\underline{x}^0)$ is a linear map from $\mathbb{R}^n$ to $\mathbb{R}^m$, it has an $(m \times n)$ matrix representation in the standard basis of $\mathbb{R}^n$—the usual *Jacobian* matrix

$$\begin{pmatrix} \dfrac{\partial f_1}{\partial x_1}(\underline{x}^0) & \cdots\cdots & \dfrac{\partial f_1}{\partial x_n}(\underline{x}^0) \\[2em] \vdots & & \vdots \\[2em] \dfrac{\partial f_m}{\partial x_1}(\underline{x}^0) & \cdots\cdots & \dfrac{\partial f_m}{\partial x_n}(\underline{x}^0) \end{pmatrix}$$

where $f_1, \ldots, f_m$ are the components of f. More precisely, if the linear map $Df(\underline{x}^0)$ exists, then all the first-order partial derivatives $\partial f_i / \partial x_j$ of f exist at $\underline{x}^0$ and the above Jacobian matrix represents $Df(\underline{x}^0)$. Conversely, if all the partial derivatives $\partial f_i / \partial x_j$ exist and are continuous on a neighborhood U of $\underline{x}^0$, then f is differentiable with derivative as above. In this case, we say f is continuously differentiable or C^1 on U since its derivative changes continuously as $\underline{x}$ varies in U, i.e., the mapping

$$Df: U \to L(\mathbb{R}^n, \mathbb{R}^m)$$

is continuous where $L(\mathbb{R}^n, \mathbb{R}^m)$ is the vector space of linear maps from $\mathbb{R}^n$ to $\mathbb{R}^m$ (or equivalently, the $m \cdot n$-dimensional vector space of $m \times n$ matrices).

One can now go on to define the higher order derivatives of f. If f is C^1, one can ask whether the continuous map $Df: U \to L(\mathbb{R}^n, \mathbb{R}^m)$ has a derivative at $\underline{x}^0$. If it does, one writes $D(Df)(\underline{x}^0)$ or $D^2 f(\underline{x}^0)$ for its derivative, a linear map from $\mathbb{R}^n$ to $L(\mathbb{R}^n, \mathbb{R}^m)$, or equivalently a bilinear map from $\mathbb{R}^n \times \mathbb{R}^n$ to $\mathbb{R}^m$. One usually takes the latter point of view and writes $D^2 f(\underline{x}^0)(\underline{v}, \underline{w})$ instead of $(D(Df)(\underline{x}^0)(\underline{v}))(\underline{w})$.

What is the bilinear map $D^2 f(\underline{x}^0)$ in coordinates? If $f: \mathbb{R}^n \to \mathbb{R}^1$ is C^1, then $Df: \mathbb{R}^n \to L(\mathbb{R}^n, \mathbb{R}^1)$ is the map

$$\underline{x} \mapsto \left(\frac{\partial f}{\partial x_1}(\underline{x}), \frac{\partial f}{\partial x_2}(\underline{x}), \ldots, \frac{\partial f}{\partial x_n}(\underline{x}) \right). \tag{1}$$

Then, the matrix representation of $D^2f(\underline{x}^0)$, the derivative of Df, is the Jacobian matrix of (1), i.e., the matrix $[[\partial^2 f/\partial x_j \partial x_i(\underline{x}^0)]]_{ij}$. This matrix is usually called the *Hessian* matrix of f at $\underline{x}^0$. If $\underline{v}$ and $\underline{w}$ are in $\mathbb{R}^n$, one checks easily that

$$D^2f(\underline{x}^0)(\underline{v}, \underline{w}) = \sum_{i,j} \frac{\partial^2 f}{\partial x_i \partial x_j}(\underline{x}^0) v_i w_j$$

$$= (v_1 \ldots v_n) \begin{pmatrix} \dfrac{\partial^2 f}{\partial x_1^2}(\underline{x}^0) & \cdots & \dfrac{\partial^2 f}{\partial x_1 \partial x_n}(\underline{x}^0) \\ \vdots & & \\ \dfrac{\partial^2 f}{\partial x_n \partial x_1}(\underline{x}^0) & \cdots & \dfrac{\partial^2 f}{\partial x_n^2}(\underline{x}^0) \end{pmatrix} \begin{pmatrix} w_1 \\ w_2 \\ \vdots \\ w_n \end{pmatrix}.$$

Some authors write $\underline{v}^t D^2 f_{\underline{x}^0} \underline{w}$ for $D^2f(\underline{x}^0)(\underline{v}, \underline{w})$. If $f = (f_1, \ldots, f_m)$: $\mathbb{R}^n \to \mathbb{R}^m$, then

$$D^2f(\underline{x})(\underline{v}, \underline{w}) = \left(D^2f_1(\underline{x})(\underline{v}, \underline{w}), \ldots, D^2f_m(\underline{x})(\underline{v}, \underline{w}) \right).$$

Again, if the bilinear map $D^2f(\underline{x}^0)$, or equivalently all the second-order partial derivatives $(\partial^2 f/\partial x_i \partial x_j)(\underline{x}^0)$, depend continuously on $\underline{x}^0$ in U, then f is called C^2 on U.

One can continue this process and define the third derivative of f and $\underline{x}^0$ as the derivative of the map $\underline{x} \mapsto D^2f(\underline{x})$ from $\mathbb{R}^n$ to the space of bilinear maps on $\mathbb{R}^n$. The third derivative is a trilinear mapping from $\mathbb{R}^n \times \mathbb{R}^n \times \mathbb{R}^n$ to $\mathbb{R}^m$ and is written $D^3f(\underline{x}^0)(\underline{u}, \underline{v}, \underline{w})$. If it is continuous in $\underline{x}^0$, i.e., if all the partial derivatives of f of order 3 exist and are continuous, we say f is C^3; and so on to define C^k. A central fact about these derivatives is that they are all *symmetric* multilinear maps. In particular for the second derivative, this symmetry means that $D^2f(\underline{x}^0)(\underline{v}, \underline{w}) = D^2f(\underline{x}^0)(\underline{w}, \underline{v})$ for all $\underline{v}$ and $\underline{w}$. In coordinates, this symmetry means that the Hessian is a symmetric matrix and the appropriate mixed partial derivatives are equal $(\partial^2 f/\partial x_i \partial x_j = \partial^2 f/\partial x_j \partial x_i)$.

In our coordinate-free notation, the Chain Rule and Taylor's Theorem have particularly elegant formulations. The reader is encouraged to write these formulae in coordinates. Theorem 1.2.b is a form of the Mean Value Theorem.

THEOREM 1.1 (Chain Rule for First and Second Derivatives.)   *If* $f: \mathbb{R}^n \to \mathbb{R}^m$ *and* $g: \mathbb{R}^m \to \mathbb{R}^p$ *are* C^r *maps, then* $g \circ f: \mathbb{R}^n \to \mathbb{R}^p$ *is* C^r*. If* $r \geq 1$,

$$D(g \circ f)(\underline{x}^0)\underline{h} = Dg(f(\underline{x}^0)) \circ Df(\underline{x}^0)\underline{h}.$$

So, the Jacobian matrix of the composition $g \circ f$ is the matrix product of the Jacobian matrix of g at $f(\underline{x}^0)$ and the Jacobian matrix of f at $\underline{x}^0$. If $r \geq 2$ and $y^0 = f(x^0)$ in $\mathbb{R}^m$,

$$D^2(g \circ f)(\underline{x}^0)(\underline{h}, \underline{k}) = D^2g(\underline{y}^0)(Df(\underline{x}^0)\underline{h}, Df(\underline{x}^0)\underline{k})$$
$$+ Dg(\underline{y}^0)(D^2f(\underline{x}^0)(\underline{h}, \underline{k})).$$

THEOREM 1.2 (Taylor's Theorem of order two).   *Suppose that* f: $\mathbb{R}^n \to \mathbb{R}^m$ *is a* C^2 *mapping on a convex neighborhood* U *of* $\underline{x}^0 \in \mathbb{R}^n$.
   a) *Then, there is a* C^2 *map* $S: \mathbb{R}^n \to \mathbb{R}^m$ *(depending continuously on* $\underline{x}^0$*) such that for all* $\underline{h} \in \mathbb{R}^n$ *with* $\underline{x}^0 + \underline{h} \in U$

$$f(\underline{x}^0 + \underline{h}) = f(\underline{x}^0) + Df(\underline{x}^0)\underline{h} + \frac{1}{2!}D^2f(\underline{x}^0)(\underline{h}, \underline{h}) + S(\underline{h})$$

where $\dfrac{S(\underline{h})}{|h|^2} \to 0$ *as* $|h| \to 0$.
   b) *Let* $m = 1$ *and let* f, $\underline{x}^0$, *and* h *be as in* a). *There are* $\underline{x}'$, $\underline{x}''$ *on the line segment between* x^0 *and* $\underline{x}^0 + \underline{h}$ *such that*

$$f(\underline{x}^0 + \underline{h}) = f(\underline{x}^0) + Df(\underline{x}')\underline{h} \text{ and}$$
$$f(\underline{x}^0 + \underline{h}) = f(\underline{x}^0) + Df(\underline{x}^0)\underline{h} + \tfrac{1}{2}D^2f(\underline{x}'')(\underline{h}, \underline{h}).$$

As an illustration of the chain rule, let $f: \mathbb{R}^n \to \mathbb{R}^1$ and α: $\mathbb{R}^1 \to \mathbb{R}^n$ be C^2 maps with $\alpha(0) = \underline{x}^0$ and $\alpha'(0) \equiv D\alpha(0)1 = \underline{v} \in \mathbb{R}^n$. One says that α is a C^2 curve at $\underline{x}^0$ with tangent (or velocity) vector $\underline{v}$. The rate of change of f at $\underline{x}^0$ along α is

$$\frac{d}{dt}(f \circ \alpha)(0) = D(f \circ \alpha)(0)(1)$$

$$= Df(\alpha(0)) \cdot D\alpha(0)1$$

$$= Df(\underline{x}^0)\underline{v},$$

which is called the *directional derivative* of f at $\underline{x}^0$ in the direction $\underline{v}$. Similarly, one computes that

$$\frac{d^2}{dt^2}(f \circ \alpha)(0) = D^2f(\underline{x}^0)(\underline{v}, \underline{v}) + Df(\underline{x}^0)(\alpha''(0)),$$

where $\alpha''(0) = D^2\alpha(0)(1, 1)$.

Putting together the definition of $Df(\underline{x}^0)$ and the above paragraph, one notes that

$$Df(\underline{x}^0)\underline{v} = \lim_{t \to 0^+} \frac{f(\underline{x}^0 + t\underline{v}) - f(\underline{x}^0)}{t}.$$

Let U be a subset of $\mathbb{R}^n$ with $\underline{x}^0 \in U$. The set of all tangent vectors at $\underline{x}^0$ to C^1 curves which remain in U is called the *tangent space* to U at $\underline{x}^0$ and denoted by $T_{\underline{x}^0}U$. In other words,

$$T_{\underline{x}^0}U = \{ v = \alpha'(0) \in \mathbb{R}^n | \alpha: [0, \varepsilon) \to \mathbb{R}^n \text{ is a } C^1 \text{ curve}$$

$$\text{with } \alpha(0) = \underline{x}^0 \text{ and } \alpha(t) \in U \text{ for all } t \}.$$

Thus, if U is an open subset of $\underline{x}^0$ in $\mathbb{R}^n$, $T_{\underline{x}^0}U$ is $T_{\underline{x}^0}\mathbb{R}^n$, which is just $\mathbb{R}^n$ with the origin pictured at $\underline{x}^0$.

There is one more interpretation of the derivative of a C^1 $f: \mathbb{R}^n \to \mathbb{R}^1$. Instead of working with the $1 \times n$ matrix

$$\left(\frac{\partial f}{\partial x_1}(\underline{x}^0) \cdots \frac{\partial f}{\partial x_n}(\underline{x}^0) \right)$$

which represents $Df(\underline{x}^0)$ as a linear map, one often thinks of the column vector

$$\nabla f(\underline{x}^0) = \begin{pmatrix} \dfrac{\partial f}{\partial x_1}(\underline{x}^0) \\ \vdots \\ \dfrac{\partial f}{\partial x_n}(\underline{x}^0) \end{pmatrix} \in \mathbb{R}^n$$

as a vector in $T_{\underline{x}^0}\mathbb{R}^n$, i.e., a geometric vector with its tail at $\underline{x}^0$. One notices easily that

$$Df(\underline{x}^0)\underline{v} = \nabla f(\underline{x}^0) \cdot \underline{v}$$

and that $\nabla f(\underline{x}^0)$, if nonzero, points into the direction in which f increases most rapidly at $\underline{x}^0$ and is perpendicular to the level set of f at $\underline{x}^0$, $\{\underline{x} | f(\underline{x}) = f(\underline{x}^0)\} = f^{-1}(f(\underline{x}^0))$.

As the linear approximation to a C^1 function $f: \mathbb{R}^n \to \mathbb{R}^m$ at $\underline{x}^0$, the derivative not only tells us much about f at $\underline{x}^0$ but can also yield important information about the behavior of f in a whole neighborhood of $\underline{x}^0$. The outstanding example of this phenomenon is the implicit function theorem—a result which will play an important role in later sections of this paper.

Recall that an $m \times n$ matrix has maximal rank if either all its rows or all its columns are linearly independent or equivalently it contains a $p \times p$ nonsingular square matrix where $p = \min\{m, n\}$.

THEOREM 1.3 (Implicit Function Theorem). Suppose that $f: \mathbb{R}^n \to \mathbb{R}^m$ is a C^r mapping with $r \geq 1$ and that $\underline{x}^0 \in \mathbb{R}^n$. Suppose that $Df(x^0)$ has maximal rank $p = \min\{m, n\}$.

a) If $n \leq m$, $p = n$ and $Df(\underline{x}^0)$ is a 1-1 linear map. Then, f itself is 1-1 on a neighborhood of $\underline{x}^0$, i.e., there is an open neighborhood U of $\underline{x}^0$ such that for each y in $f(U)$, the equation $f(x) = y$ has *at most* one solution x in $\underline{U}$.

b) If $m \leq n$, $p = m$ and $Df(\underline{x}^0)$ is surjective. Then, there are neighborhoods U of $\underline{x}^0$ in $\mathbb{R}^n$ and V of $f(\underline{x}^0)$ in $\mathbb{R}^m$ such that f maps U onto V, i.e., for each y in V, there is *at least* one $\underline{x}$ in U such that $f(\underline{x}) = \underline{y}$. In addition, the (local) level set of f through $\underline{x}^0$

$$f^{-1}\left(f\left(\underline{x}^0\right)\right) \cap U = \left\{\underline{x} \in U | f(\underline{x}) = f\left(\underline{x}^0\right)\right\}$$

is a $C^r(n - m)$-dimensional submanifold of $\mathbb{R}^n$. This means that it sits in U like a smooth (nonlinear) $(n - m)$-dimensional slice or graph; one can find coordinates $y_1, \ldots, y_n$ on U in which $\underline{x}^0$ corresponds to the origin and the level set through $\underline{x}^0$ is the $y_{m+1}, \ldots, y_n$ coordinate plane ($y_1 = \cdots = y_m = 0$) in the new coordinate system. Furthermore, the set of tangent vectors to the level set at $\underline{x}^0$, $T_{\underline{x}^0}[f^{-1}(f(\underline{x}^0)) \cap U]$, is the nullspace of $Df(\underline{x}^0)$, $\{\underline{v}|Df(x^0)v = 0\}$.

c) In particular, if $m = 1$ in b) and if $Df(x^0)$ (or $\nabla f(x^0)$) is nonzero, say $\dfrac{\partial f}{\partial x_1}(\underline{x}^0) \neq 0$, then the level set of f through $\underline{x}^0$ is the graph of a smooth function $x_1 = g(x_2, \ldots, x_n)$ around $\underline{x}^0$ and the set of tangent vectors to the level set is precisely $\{\underline{v}|\nabla f(x^0) \cdot \underline{v} = 0\}$.

d) Furthermore, if $m < n$, if we write $\mathbb{R}^n$ as $\mathbb{R}^m \times \mathbb{R}^{n-m} = \{(x_1, x_2)|x_1 \in \mathbb{R}^m, x_2 \in \mathbb{R}^{n-m}\}$, if $f(x_1^0, x_2^0) = 0$ and the square matrix $D_{x_1}f(x_1^0, x_2^0)$ has maximal rank m, then there is a neighborhood U of x_2^0 in $\mathbb{R}^{n-m}$ and a unique C^r map g: $U \to \mathbb{R}^m$ such that $g(x_2^0) = x_1^0$ and $f(g(x_2), x_2) = 0$ for all x_2 in U. (For each fixed x_2 near x_2^0, $x_1 = g(x_2)$ is the solution of $f(x_1, x_2) = 0$. In other words, $f(x_1, x_2) = 0$ defines x_1 as an (implicit) function of x_2.)

1.2. Definite symmetric bilinear maps. If $f: \mathbb{R}^n \to \mathbb{R}^1$ is a C^2 function, the second derivative of f at $\underline{x}^0$, $D^2f(\underline{x}^0)$, is a symmetric bilinear map $\mathbb{R}^n \times \mathbb{R}^n \to \mathbb{R}^1$, as indicated above, and can be represented by the $n \times n$ (symmetric) Hessian matrix

$$\left(\left(\frac{\partial^2 f}{\partial x_i \partial x_j}(\underline{x}^0)\right)\right).$$

In studying second-order tests for optimality, we will need to work with symmetric maps which are definite.

Let $L: \mathbb{R}^n \times \mathbb{R}^n \to \mathbb{R}$ be a symmetric bilinear map. Then, L is *negative definite* if $L(\underline{v}, \underline{v}) < 0$ for all $\underline{v} \neq \underline{0}$; L is *negative semidefinite* if $L(\underline{v}, \underline{v}) \leq 0$ for all $\underline{v} \in \mathbb{R}^n$; L is *positive definite* if $L(\underline{v}, \underline{v}) > 0$ for all $\underline{v} \neq \underline{0}$; L is *positive semidefinite* if $L(\underline{v}, \underline{v}) \geq 0$ for all $\underline{v} \in \mathbb{R}^n$.

If L is symmetric and bilinear and if $\underline{e}^1, \ldots, \underline{e}^n$ is a basis of $\mathbb{R}^n$, then the matrix of L with respect to this basis is $(L(\underline{e}^i, \underline{e}^j))_{i,j}$ since

$$L\left(\sum_i a_i \underline{e}^i, \sum_j b_j \underline{e}^j\right) = \sum_{i,j} L(\underline{e}^i, \underline{e}^j) a_i b_j.$$

Conversely, if A is a symmetric matrix, then $L(\underline{v}, \underline{w}) = \underline{v}^t A \underline{w}$ is its corresponding symmetric bilinear map. The most straightforward test for the positive or negative definiteness of L uses the leading principal minors of A.

The $k \times k$ square submatrix of A obtained by deleting $(n - k)$ rows and *the same* $(n - k)$ columns from A is called a kth order *principal submatrix* of A. If this $k \times k$ submatrix is formed by deleting the *last* $(n - k)$ rows and columns from A, it is called the kth *leading principal submatrix of A*. The determinant of a (leading) principal submatrix is called a (leading) *principal minor*. The following important result relates the definiteness of L to the eigenvalues and principal minors of A.

THEOREM 1.4. *Let $L: \mathbb{R}^n \times \mathbb{R}^n \to \mathbb{R}$ be a bilinear, symmetric map with matrix $A = ((L(e^i, e^j)))_{i,j}$. Then, all the eigenvalues of A are real and A has a complete set of eigenvectors, i.e., A is diagonalizable. Furthermore, the following three statements are equivalent:*

   a)   *L is positive definite;*
   b)   *all the eigenvalues of A are positive;*
   c)   *the n leading principal minors of A are positive.*

If one is testing for negative-definiteness, then the corresponding three equivalent statements are:

   a′)   *L is negative definite;*
   b′)   *all the eigenvalues of A are negative;*
   c′)   *the kth leading principal minor of A has the same sign as $(-1)^k$ for $k = 1, 2, \ldots, n$.*

There are corresponding results for semidefiniteness. For example, L is *negative semidefinite* if and only if all the eigenvalues of A are nonpositive if and only if each of the nonzero kth order principal minors of A has the same sign as $(-1)^k$ for $k = 1, \ldots, n$. Note that to check for definiteness, one only checks the sign of n *leading* principal minors; but to check for semidefiniteness, one must check the sign of all $2^n - 1$ principal minors. The proofs of these results can be found in most linear algebra books and in Bellman [8] and Debreu [15].

In our necessary and sufficient conditions for constrained optimization problems, we will need to check whether the *restriction* of a symmetric bilinear map to some linear subspace of $\mathbb{R}^n$ is definite or not. The following theorem provides a sufficient condition for this phenomenon.

THEOREM 1.5. *Let $L(\underline{v}, \underline{w}) = v^t A \underline{w}$ be a symmetric bilinear map on $\mathbb{R}^n$. Let B be an $m \times n$ submatrix with m linearly independent rows, $m < n$. Let S be the $(n - m)$-dimensional nullspace of B, $\{ \underline{x} \in \mathbb{R}^n | B\underline{x} = \underline{0} \}$. Form the bordered $(n + m) \times (n + m)$ matrix $C = \begin{pmatrix} 0 & B \\ B^t & A \end{pmatrix}$. If each of the last $(n - m)$ leading principal minors of C (i.e., the ones of order $2m + 1, \ldots, m + n$) has the same sign as $(-1)^m$, then $L(\underline{x}, \underline{x}) > 0$ for all nonzero $\underline{x}$ such that $B\underline{x} = \underline{0}$. On the other hand, if the last $(n - m)$ leading principal minors of C alternate in sign the with determinant of C having the same sign as $(-1)^n$, then $L(\underline{x}, \underline{x}) < 0$ for all nonzero $\underline{x}$ such that $B\underline{x} = \underline{0}$.*

The proof of this theorem is fairly intricate. See Debreu [15] or Bellman [8].

1.3. Concave and convex functions. As we will see in Sections 6 and 8, concave functions arise naturally in problems of economics and concavity is a common and useful hypothesis in many theorems of maximization. In this section, we will survey some of the important properties of concave and almost concave functions. For further reading and more complete proofs, see Fenchel [21], Karlin [37], Gale [25], and Mangasarian [48]. Many of the ideas and proofs of this section are adopted from the excellent presentation of Mangasarian [48].

DEFINITIONS. Let $\underline{x}$ and $\underline{y}$ lie in $\mathbb{R}^n$. We will denote the line segment from $\underline{x}$ to $\underline{y}$ by $l(\underline{x}, \underline{y})$, i.e.,

$$l(\underline{x}, \underline{y}) = \left\{ t\underline{y} + (1 - t)\underline{x} | 0 \leq t \leq 1 \right\}.$$

A subset U of $\mathbb{R}^n$ is *convex* if whenever $\underline{x}, \underline{y} \in U$, then $l(\underline{x}, \underline{y}) \subset U$. Let $f: U \rightarrow \mathbb{R}^1$ be a function on the convex subset U of $\mathbb{R}^n$. Then, f is *concave* (*convex*) on U if for all $\underline{x}, \underline{y} \in U$ and $t \in [0, 1]$.

$$f\left(t\underline{y} + (1 - t)\underline{x} \right) \geq tf(\underline{y}) + (1 - t)f(\underline{x})$$
$$\left(f\left(t\underline{y} + (1 - t)\underline{x} \right) \leq tf(\underline{y}) + (1 - t)f(\underline{x}) \right).$$

If, for all $\underline{x}, \underline{y} \in U$ and for all $t \in (0, 1)$, the above inequalities can be written as strict inequalities, then we say that f is *strictly concave* (or *strictly convex*) on U. Note that linear maps are concave and convex. Fleming [24] gives a proof that any function which is convex or concave on an *open* subset of $\mathbb{R}^n$ is continuous.

IMPORTANT REMARK. Note that f is convex if and only if $-f$ is concave. Since minimizing f is equivalent to maximizing $-f$, all the results of this paper on maximization can be written as results on minimization. In this case, one naturally changes hypotheses about concave functions to hypotheses about convex functions.

If f is C^1 or C^2, there are some powerful criteria from calculus for concavity, as summarized in the following theorem.

THEOREM 1.6. *Let* $f: U \rightarrow \mathbb{R}^1$ *be a* C^1 *function on a convex open subset* U *of* $\mathbb{R}^n$. *Then, the following are equivalent:*
   a) f *is concave on* U,
   b) $f(\underline{y}) - f(\underline{x}) \leq Df(\underline{x})(\underline{y} - \underline{x})$ *for all* $\underline{x}, \underline{y} \in U$,
   c) $[D\overline{f}(\underline{y}) - Df(\underline{x})](\underline{y} - \underline{x}) \leq 0$ *for all* $\underline{x}, \underline{y} \in U$.
If f *is* C^2, a), b) *and* c) *are equivalent to*
   d) $D^2f(\underline{x})(\underline{v}, \underline{v}) \leq 0$ *for all* $x \in U$ *and all nonzero* $\underline{v} \in \mathbb{R}^n$ (*i.e.*, $D^2f(\underline{x})$ *is negative semidefinite on* U).

REMARK. Theorem 1.6 is true if one changes "concave" to "convex" in a) and reverses the inequalities in b), c) and d). If one changes "concave" to "strictly concave" in a) and make the inequalities strict in b), c) and d), then

$$d) \Rightarrow a) \Leftrightarrow b) \Leftrightarrow c),$$

with $f(x) = -x^4$ a counterexample to a) $\Leftrightarrow$ d) in the strict case.

Proof. Throughout this proof, $\underline{x}$ and $\underline{y}$ will denote arbitrary elements in U with $t \in [0, 1]$.

a) $\Rightarrow$ b): Since f is concave,

$$tf(\underline{y}) + (1 - t)f(\underline{x}) \le f(t\underline{y} + (1 - t)\underline{x}); \quad \text{or}$$
$$f(\underline{y}) - f(\underline{x}) \le \frac{f(\underline{x} + t(\underline{y} - \underline{x})) - f(\underline{x})}{t}$$

Taking the limit as $t \to 0$ and using the remarks under Theorem 1.2, we see that $f(\underline{y}) - f(\underline{x}) \le Df(\underline{x})(\underline{y} - \underline{x})$.

b) $\Rightarrow$ c): Add the two inequalities:

$$f(\underline{y}) - f(\underline{x}) - Df(\underline{x})(\underline{y} - \underline{x}) \le 0$$

and

$$f(\underline{x}) - f(\underline{y}) - Df(\underline{y})(\underline{x} - \underline{y}) \le 0.$$

c) $\Rightarrow$ b): By Theorem 1.2b (Mean Value Theorem),

$$f(\underline{y}) - f(\underline{x}) = Df(\underline{y} + t_0(\underline{x} - \underline{y}))(\underline{y} - \underline{x})$$
$$\text{for some } t_0 \in (0, 1).$$

By c),

$$\left[Df(\underline{y} + t_0(\underline{x} - \underline{y})) - Df(\underline{x}) \right](1 - t_0)(\underline{y} - \underline{x}) \le 0, \quad \text{or}$$
$$Df(\underline{y} + t_0(\underline{x} - \underline{y}))(\underline{y} - \underline{x}) \le Df(\underline{x})(\underline{y} - \underline{x}).$$

Thus,

$$f(\underline{y}) - f(\underline{x}) \le Df(\underline{x})(\underline{y} - \underline{x}).$$

b) $\Rightarrow$ a): By b),

$$f(\underline{x}) - f((1 - t)\underline{x} + t\underline{y}) \le -tDf((1 - t)\underline{x} + t\underline{y})(\underline{y} - \underline{x})$$

and

$$f(\underline{y}) - f((1 - t)\underline{x} + t\underline{y}) \le (1 - t)Df((1 - t)\underline{x} + t\underline{y})(\underline{y} - \underline{x}).$$

Now, a) follows immediately after one multiplies the first inequality by $(1 - t)$ and the second by t and then adds the two inequalities.

d) $\Rightarrow$ b): By Theorem 1.2b,

$$f(\underline{y}) - f(\underline{x}) = Df(\underline{x})(\underline{y} - \underline{x}) + \tfrac{1}{2}D^2f(\underline{z})(\underline{y} - \underline{x}, \underline{y} - \underline{x})$$

for some $\underline{z} \in l(\underline{x}, \underline{y})$. Since the last term is nonpositive, b) follows.

b) $\Rightarrow$ d): Suppose there are $\underline{x}^0 \in U$ and $\underline{v} \in \mathbb{R}^n$ such that $D^2f(\underline{x}^0)(\underline{v}, \underline{v}) > 0$. Since f is C^2, there is a convex neighborhood W of $\underline{x}^0$ in U such that $D^2f(\underline{x})(\underline{v}, \underline{v}) > 0$ for all $\underline{x} \in W$. Also, $D^2f(\underline{x})(t\underline{v}, t\underline{v}) = t^2D^2f(\underline{x})(\underline{v}, \underline{v}) > 0$ for all $\underline{x} \in W$ and for all t.

Choose $t_0 > 0$ and small enough so that $\underline{x}^0 + t_0\underline{v} \in W$. By Theorem 1.2.b,

$$\begin{aligned} f(\underline{x}^0 + t_0\underline{v}) - f(\underline{x}^0) &= Df(\underline{x}^0)(t_0\underline{v}) + \tfrac{1}{2}D^2f(\underline{x}^0 + t_1\underline{v})(t_0\underline{v}, t_0\underline{v}) \\ &> Df(\underline{x}^0)(t_0\underline{v}) \end{aligned}$$

for some $t_1 \in [0, t_0]$—a contradiction to b). Note that the last two paragraphs, show that d) $\Rightarrow$ b) in the strict convexity case. ∎

In some problems that arise in economics, concavity is a little too strong as an hypothesis. Since many important maximization theorems hold with weaker forms of concavity, we will discuss some of these modifications now. One important property of a concave function is that its level sets bound a convex set, i.e., if f is concave, $\{\underline{x} | f(\underline{x}) \ge a\}$ is convex. Since any monotone function from $\mathbb{R}^1$ to $\mathbb{R}^1$ (e.g., $f(\underline{x}) = \underline{x}^3$) also has this property, it does not characterize concave functions. So, if $f: U \to \mathbb{R}$ is a function on a convex U of $\mathbb{R}^n$, it is natural to call f *quasi-concave* on U if $\{ \underline{x} \in U | f(\underline{x}) \geq a \}$ is convex for all $a \in \mathbb{R}$. Similarly, f is *quasi-convex* on U if $\{ \underline{x} \in U | f(\underline{x}) \leq a \}$ is convex for all $a \in \mathbb{R}$. Fortunately, there is a useful calculus criterion for quasi-concavity.

THEOREM 1.7. *Suppose that $f: U \to \mathbb{R}$ is a C^1 function on an open convex subset U of $\mathbb{R}^n$. Then, f is quasi-concave on U if and only if $f(\underline{y}) \geq f(\underline{x})$ implies that $Df(\underline{x})(\underline{y} - \underline{x}) \geq 0$.*

Proof. Suppose f is quasi-concave on U and that $f(y) \geq f(x)$ for some $x, y \in U$. Then, for all $\mu \in [0,1]$,

$$f(x + \mu(y - x)) \geq f(x).$$

Since

$$\frac{f(\underline{x} + \mu(\underline{y} - \underline{x})) - f(\underline{x})}{\mu} \geq 0$$

for all $\mu \in (0,1)$,

$$Df(\underline{x})(\underline{y} - \underline{x}) \geq 0, \qquad \text{letting } \mu \to 0.$$

To prove the converse, choose $\underline{x}^0$ and $\underline{x}^1 \in U$ with $\underline{x}^0 \neq \underline{x}^1$ and $f(\underline{x}^1) \geq f(\underline{x}^0)$. Let $\underline{x}^\mu \equiv \underline{x}^0 + \mu(\underline{x}^1 - \underline{x}^0)$. We will prove that $f(\underline{x}^\mu) \geq f(\underline{x}^0)$ for all $\mu \in [0,1]$.

To reach a contradiction, suppose there is a $\mu^* \in (0,1)$ with $f(\underline{x}^{\mu^*}) < f(\underline{x}^0) \leq f(\underline{x}^1)$. Let $J = [\mu^1, \mu^2]$ be a (connected) interval in $(0,1)$ with $\mu^* \in J$, $f(\underline{x}^\mu) \leq f(\underline{x}^0)$ for all $\mu \in J$, and $f(\underline{x}^{\mu^1}) = f(\underline{x}^{\mu^2}) = f(\underline{x}^0)$. We first claim that $Df(\underline{x}^\mu)(\underline{x}^1 - \underline{x}^0) = 0$ for all $\mu \in J$. If $\mu \in J$, $f(\underline{x}^\mu) \leq f(\underline{x}^0) \leq f(\underline{x}^1)$. By hypothesis,

$$Df(\underline{x}^\mu)(\underline{x}^0 - \underline{x}^\mu) \geq 0 \quad \text{and} \quad Df(\underline{x}^\mu)(\underline{x}^1 - \underline{x}^\mu) \geq 0.$$

Since $\underline{x}^0 - \underline{x}^\mu = -\mu(\underline{x}^1 - \underline{x}^0)$ and $\underline{x}^1 - \underline{x}^\mu = (1 - \mu)(\underline{x}^1 - \underline{x}^0)$, we have

$$-\mu Df(\underline{x}^\mu)(\underline{x}^1 - \underline{x}^0) \geq 0 \quad \text{and} \quad (1 - \mu)Df(\underline{x}^\mu)(\underline{x}^1 - \underline{x}^0) \geq 0.$$

Since μ and $1 - \mu$ are positive, $Df(\underline{x}^\mu)(\underline{x}^1 - \underline{x}^0) = 0$.

On the other hand,

$$0 < f\left(\underline{x}^0\right) - f\left(\underline{x}^{\mu^*}\right) = f\left(\underline{x}^{\mu^1}\right) - f\left(\underline{x}^{\mu^*}\right)$$
$$= Df\left(\underline{x}^{\mu^3}\right)\left(\underline{x}^{\mu^1} - \underline{x}^{\mu^*}\right) \quad \text{(by Theorem 1.2b, } \mu^3 \in J)$$
$$= \left(\mu^* - \mu^1\right) Df\left(\underline{x}^{\mu^3}\right)\left(\underline{x}^1 - \underline{x}^0\right),$$

since $x^{\mu^1} - x^{\mu^*} = (\mu^* - \mu^1)(x^1 - x^0)$—a contradiction to the last paragraph.

REMARK.   Of course, there is an analogous result for quasi-convexity. One can also define and work with strict quasi-concave functions and strict quasi-convex functions.

Quasi-concave functions share with concave functions the property that local maxima are global maxima. However, there is an important difference. Because a) ↔ b) in Theorem 1.6, a critical point of a concave function is a local (and therefore) global maximum. But $f(x) = x^3$ shows that quasi-concave functions do not have this property. To fill this gap, Mangasarian [46] introduced the concept of a pseudoconcave function.

DEFINITION.   A C^1 function $f: \mathbb{R}^n \to \mathbb{R}$ is *pseudoconcave* at $\underline{x}^0 \in \mathbb{R}^n$ if whenever $Df(\underline{x}^0)(\underline{y} - \underline{x}^0) \le 0$, $f(\underline{y}) \le f(\underline{x}^0)$. One defines a pseudoconvex function similarly.

THEOREM 1.8.   *Let* $f: U \to \mathbb{R}$ *be a* C^1 *pseudoconcave function at all* $\underline{x}$ *in the convex subset* U *of* $\mathbb{R}^n$. *Then,*

a) $\underline{x}^0$ *maximizes* f *on* U *if and only if* $Df(\underline{x}^0)(\underline{x} - \underline{x}^0) \le 0$ *for all* $x \in U$;

b)   *if* U *is open,* $\underline{x}^0$ *maximizes* f *on* U *if and only if* $Df(\underline{x}^0) = \underline{0}$.

The, "only if" parts of a) and b) hold for all C^1 functions f.

Proof.   a) If $\underline{x}^0$ maximizes f on U, $f(\underline{x}^0 + t(\underline{x} - \underline{x}^0)) - f(\underline{x}^0) \le 0$ for all $\underline{x} \in U$ and all $t \in [0, 1]$. Dividing by t and letting t tend to 0 yields $Df(\underline{x}^0)(\underline{x} - \underline{x}^0) \le 0$. The converse is immediate from the definition of a pseudoconcave function.

b) That a maximizer on an open set is a critical point is a classical result (see Theorem 2.1) and also follows from a), since the openness of U implies that $Df(\underline{x}^0)\underline{v} \le 0$ for all $\underline{v} \in T_{\underline{x}^0}\mathbb{R}^n$. The converse also follows from a).

Pseudoconcavity is a less geometric concept than quasi-concavity, although it is an important analytical one. But notice that the definition of pseudoconcavity is a slight strengthening of the contrapositive of the analytical characterization of quasi-concavity in Theorem 1.7. Part b) of Theorem 1.9 describes the mild conditions under which the two concepts are equivalent, namely f is C^2 and ∇f is nonzero on a "solid convex" set. Part a) of Theorem 1.9 summarizes the hierarchy of concavity for C^1 functions, while part c) summarizes the principal-minor conditions which can easily be used to test a C^2 function for concavity or quasi-concavity.

THEOREM 1.9. Let U be a convex of $\mathbb{R}^n$. Let $f: U \to \mathbb{R}$ be a C^1 function. Then,

a) f is strictly concave on $u \Rightarrow f$ is concave on U

$\Rightarrow f$ is pseudoconcave on U

$\Rightarrow f$ is strictly quasi-concave on U

$\Rightarrow$ is quasi-concave on U.

Furthermore, none of the implications can be reversed. (The C^1 hypothesis is made only to include pseudoconcave functions.)

b) If U has a nonempty interior, if f is C^2 on U, and if ∇f is never $\underline{0}$ on U, then f is pseudoconcave if and only if it is strictly quasi-concave if and only if it is quasi-concave.

c) Let $H(\underline{x})$ be the $n \times n$ Hessian matrix for $D^2f(\underline{x})$. Let $B(x)$ be the $(n + 1) \times (n + 1)$ bordered matrix

$$B(\underline{x}) = \begin{pmatrix} 0 & \nabla f(\underline{x})^t \\ \nabla f(\underline{x}) & H(\underline{x}) \end{pmatrix}.$$

If the kth leading principal minor of $H(\underline{x})$ has the same sign as $(-1)^k$ for $k = 1, \dots, n$ and for all $\underline{x}$ in U, then f is strictly concave on U. If every nonzero $k \times k$ principal minor of $H(\underline{x})$ has the same sign as $(-1)^k$ for $k = 1, \dots, n$ and for all x in U, then f is concave on U. If the kth *leading* principal minor of $B(\underline{x})$ has the same sign as $(-1)^{k-1}$ for $k =$

$3, 4, \ldots, n + 1$, then f is pseudoconcave (and hence quasi-concave) on U.

Proof. a) Most of these implications follow from the definition or from Theorem 1.6. See Mangasarian [48] for complete details. We will sketch a proof of the third implication here.

Suppose f is pseudoconcave but not strictly quasi-concave. Then, there are $\underline{x}^0, \underline{x}^1 \in U$ such that $f(\underline{x}^0) > f(\underline{x}^1)$ but for some $\mu \in (0, 1)$, $f(\underline{x}^\mu) \leq f(\underline{x}^1)$, where $\underline{x}^\mu = \underline{x}^0 + \mu(\underline{x}^1 - \underline{x}^0)$. Choose $\bar{\mu}$ so that $f(\underline{x}^{\bar{\mu}}) \leq f(\underline{x}^\mu)$ for all $\mu \in [0, 1]$. Since $\underline{x}^{\bar{\mu}}$ minimizes f on the line segment $l(\underline{x}^0, \underline{x}^1)$, $Df(\underline{x}^{\bar{\mu}})(\underline{x}^\mu - \underline{x}^{\bar{\mu}}) \geq 0$ for all $\mu \in [0, 1]$ by Theorem 1.8.a. By the method of proof of the claim in Theorem 1.7, $Df(\underline{x}^{\bar{\mu}})(\underline{x}^1 - \underline{x}^0) = 0$, since $\underline{x} - \underline{x}^{\bar{\mu}} = -\bar{\mu}(\underline{x}^1 - \underline{x}^0)$ and $\underline{x}^1 - \underline{x}^{\bar{\mu}} = (1 - \bar{\mu})(\underline{x}^1 - \underline{x}^0)$. Similarly, $Df(\underline{x}^{\bar{\mu}})(\underline{x}^1 - \underline{x}^{\bar{\mu}}) = 0$. But now, since f is pseudoconcave, $f(\underline{x}^1) \leq f(\underline{x}^{\bar{\mu}})$. Since $f(\underline{x}^0) < f(\underline{x}^1)$, we have a contradiction to the minimizing property of $\underline{x}^{\bar{\mu}}$.

b) See Ferland [22].

c) The first two sentences follow from Theorem 1.4, 1.5, and 1.6. Under the hypotheses of the last statement, Theorem 1.5 tells us that $D^2 f(\underline{x})$ is negative definite on the nullspace of $Df(x)$. By Theorem 3.4 below, each $\underline{x}$ in U maximizes f on the constraint set $\{ y | Df(\underline{x})\underline{y} - Df(\underline{x})\underline{x} \geq 0 \} = \{ y | Df(\underline{x})(\underline{x} - y) \leq 0 \}$. In other words, if $x, y \in U$ and $Df(x)(x - y) \leq 0$, then $f(x) \geq f(y)$. But this is the definition of pseudoconcavity on U. ∎

There is one important result, as described in the following theorem, which holds for concave functions but not for pseudoconcave or quasi-concave functions. This theorem is one reason why one cannot weaken the concavity hypotheses in some of the theorems of Section 7.

THEOREM 1.10. *Let $f_1, \ldots, f_a : U \to \mathbb{R}$ be concave functions on a convex subset U of $\mathbb{R}^n$. Let $\lambda_1, \ldots, \lambda_a$ be nonnegative numbers. Then, $\sum_i^a \lambda_i f_i : U \to \mathbb{R}$ is a concave function. This result is not true for pseudoconcave or quasi-concave functions.*

Proof. Since each $\lambda_i \geq 0$ and each f_i is concave.

$$\lambda_i f_i(x^0 + \mu(x' - x^0)) \geq \lambda_i f_i(\underline{x}^0) + \mu[\lambda_i f(\underline{x}') - \lambda_i f(x^0)].$$

The theorem follows by adding these inequalities. To see the last sentence, note that $f_1(x) = -2x$ and $f_2(x) = x^3 + x$ are both pseudoconcave, but $(f_1 + f_2)(x) = x^3 - x$ is not even quasi-concave. ∎

2. UNCONSTRAINED MAXIMA

2.1. Necessary conditions. Let C be some subset of $\mathbb{R}^n$. For example, C may be $\{\underline{x} \in \mathbb{R}^n | g_1(\underline{x}) \geq 0, \ldots, g_M(\underline{x}) \geq 0,\ h_1(\underline{x}) = 0, \ldots, h_N(\underline{x}) = 0\}$, where $g_1, \ldots, g_M, h_1, \ldots, h_N$ are functions from $\mathbb{R}^n$ to $\mathbb{R}^1$. Then, if $f: \mathbb{R}^n \to \mathbb{R}$ and if $\underline{x}^0 \in C$, f has a *local maximum* on C at $\underline{x}^0$ (or $\underline{x}^0$ locally maximizes f on C) provided $\underline{x}^0$ has a neighborhood U in $\mathbb{R}^n$ with $f(\underline{x}) \leq f(\underline{x}^0)$ for all $\underline{x} \in U \cap C$.

If one can take U to be $\mathbb{R}^n$, then f has a *global* maximum on C at $\underline{x}^0$. In this paper, "maximum" will always mean "local maximum" unless stated otherwise.

If one uses calculus techniques, then there are usually two steps in a maximization problem. First, look at effective necessary conditions for a point to be a maximum. This step should quickly narrow down the number of candidates for a maximum point—possibly to a finite set of points. Secondly, apply some effective method for checking out each of these points. Such methods will usually involve the local convexity of f or the negative-definiteness of some second derivative.

Let us first examine the simplest such problem, i.e., find the maxima of a C^1 $f: \mathbb{R}^n \to \mathbb{R}^1$ with no other constraints. (Equivalently, C is some *open* subset of $\mathbb{R}^n$.) We first list the classical necessary conditions.

THEOREM 2.1. *If $f: \mathbb{R}^n \to \mathbb{R}$ is C^2 and if x^0 is a (local) maximum point of f, then* a) $Df(\underline{x}^0) = 0$, *and* b) $D^2f(x_0)(v, v) \leq 0$ *for all $\underline{v}$.*

Proof. We will assume that the reader is familiar with this theorem for the case $n = 1$. Let $g(t) = f(\underline{x}^0 + t\underline{v})$ for some arbitrary $\underline{v} \in T_{\underline{x}^0}\mathbb{R}^n$. By hypothesis, $t = 0$ is a local maximum point of g. Therefore, by theorems of Calculus I, $g'(0) = 0$ and $g''(0) \leq 0$.

By the Chain Rule,

$$g'(0) = \frac{d}{dt} f\left(\underline{x}^0 + t\underline{v}\right)\bigg|_{t=0} = Df\left(\underline{x}^0\right)\underline{v} \quad \text{and}$$

$$g''(0) = \frac{d^2}{dt^2} f\left(\underline{x}^0 + t\underline{v}\right)\bigg|_{t=0} = D^2f\left(\underline{x}^0\right)(\underline{v}, \underline{v}). \qquad \blacksquare$$

2.2. Sufficient conditions. By Theorem 2.1, in searching for maxima one need only check out the critical points of f, i.e., $\{\underline{x}|Df(\underline{x}) = \underline{0}\}$. For most smooth functions, the critical points are isolated in $\mathbb{R}^n$. (See Section II.6 of Golubitsky-Guillemin [28].) The next theorem gives the classical sufficient condition for a critical point to be a local maximum. Its proof uses the basic fact that any sequence on a compact set has a convergent subsequence.

THEOREM 2.2. *Suppose that x^0 is a critical point of a C^2 f: $\mathbb{R}^n \to \mathbb{R}^1$. If $D^2f(\underline{x}^0)$ is negative definite, then $\underline{x}^0$ is a strict local maximum point of f.*

Proof. Suppose $\underline{x}^0$ is not a strict local maximum point of f. Then there is a sequence of distinct $\underline{x}^n$ approaching $\underline{x}^0$ with $f(\underline{x}^n) \geq f(\underline{x}^0)$. By the compactness of $\{\underline{v}\|\underline{v}| = 1\}$ in $\mathbb{R}^n$, we can choose $\{\underline{x}^n\}$ so that $\underline{v}^n \equiv (\underline{x}^n - x^0)/|\underline{x}^n - x^0|$ converges to some $\underline{v}^0$ with $|\underline{v}^0| = 1$. Using Taylor's Theorem,

$$0 \leq f\left(\underline{x}^n\right) - f\left(\underline{x}^0\right) = Df\left(\underline{x}^0\right)\left(\underline{x}^n - \underline{x}^0\right)$$
$$+ \tfrac{1}{2}D^2f\left(\underline{x}^0\right)\left(\underline{x}^n - \underline{x}^0, \underline{x}^n - \underline{x}^0\right) + R\left(\underline{x}^n\right),$$
$$\text{(A)}$$

where $Df(x^0)(x^n - x^0) = 0$ for all n and $R(\underline{y})/|\underline{y} - \underline{x}^0|^2 \to 0$ as $\underline{y} \to \underline{x}^0$. Divide (A) by $|\underline{x}^n - x^0|^2$:

$$0 \leq \frac{f\left(\underline{x}^n\right) - f\left(\underline{x}^0\right)}{|x^n - x^0|^2} = D^2f(x^0)(v^n, v^n)$$
$$+ \frac{R\left(\underline{x}^n\right)}{|x^n - x^0|^2}, \quad \text{for all } n. \quad \text{(B)}$$

Now, if $n \to \infty$ in (B), one finds $0 \le D^2 f(x^0)(v^0, v^0)$, contradicting the negative definiteness of $D^2 f(x^0)$.

For another proof, note that by Theorem 1.4.c, negative definiteness is an "open" property in $\mathbb{R}^n$. In other words, if $D^2 f(\underline{x}^0)$ is negative definite and f is C^2, $D^2 f(\underline{x})$ will also be negative definite for all $\underline{x}$ in an open ball V around $\underline{x}^0$. If $\underline{y} \in V$ and $\underline{y} \le x^0$,

$$f(\underline{y}) - f(\underline{x}^0) = Df(\underline{x}^0)(\underline{y} - \underline{x}^0)$$
$$+ \tfrac{1}{2} D^2 f(\underline{y}')(\underline{y} - \underline{x}^0, \underline{y} - \underline{x}^0) \qquad \text{(C)}$$

for some $\underline{y}'$ in V. Since $Df(\underline{x}^0) = 0$ and $\underline{y} - \underline{x}^0 \ne 0$ and $D^2 f(\underline{y}')$ is negative definite, the right-hand side of (C) is negative. So, $f(\underline{y}) < f(\underline{x}^0)$ for all $\underline{y}$ in V.

This proof even works in infinite-dimensional spaces provided one replaces "$D^2 f(\underline{x}^0)$ negative-definite" by "$D^2 f(\underline{x}^0)$ strictly negative definite" to make sure the condition is valid for an open set around $\underline{x}^0$. (One says that $D^2 f(\underline{x}^0)$ is strictly negative definite if there is a positive number c such that $D^2 f(\underline{x}^0)(\underline{v}, \underline{v}) \le -c|\underline{v}|^2$ for all $\underline{v}$, or equivalently such that the eigenvalues of $D^2 f(\underline{x}^0)$ are strictly less than $-c$. This concept is the same as negative-definiteness in the finite dimensional case.)

For concave functions, the first-order necessary conditions are also sufficient and yield *global* maxima. Theorem 2.3 is a restatement of Theorem 1.8 and is included here for completeness.

THEOREM 2.3. *Suppose $f: \mathbb{R}^n \to \mathbb{R}^1$ is C^1 and concave (or even pseudoconcave). Then f has a global maximum at $\underline{x}^0$ if and only if $Df(\underline{x}^0) = \underline{0}$*

3. PROBLEMS WITH NONDEGENERATE CONSTRAINTS

3.1. The nonlinear programming problem. In most maximization problems arising in economics and engineering, there are constraints on the set of feasible states, i.e., the set C of Section 2.1 is not an open subset of $\mathbb{R}^n$. In the next sections, we will discuss the following problem, often called "the classical problem of nonlinear programming":

Maximize $f: \mathbb{R}^n \to \mathbb{R}$ on the set C, where

$$C = \left\{ \underline{x} \in \mathbb{R}^n | g_i(\underline{x}) \geq 0, \, i = 1, \ldots, M; \, h_j(\underline{x}) = 0, \, j = 1, \ldots, N \right\}$$

and g_i's and h_j's are smooth functions $\mathbb{R}^n \to \mathbb{R}$.   (D)

If $f(\underline{x}) = \underline{c} \cdot \underline{x}$, $g_i(\underline{x}) = \underline{A}_i \cdot \underline{x} + a_i$, and $h_j(\underline{x}) = \underline{B}_j \underline{x} + b_j$ for some vectors $\underline{A}_1, \ldots, \underline{A}_M, \underline{B}_1, \ldots, \underline{B}_N$, and $\underline{c}$ in $\mathbb{R}^n$, and scalars $a_1, \ldots, a_M, b_1, \ldots, b_N$, the problem (D) is the usual linear programming problem. Since the constraint set C for the linear problem is a polyhedral set and f is linear, the solution of this problem, if it exists, lies at a vertex of C (or sometimes at a complete bounding face of C). There are simple, but beautiful algorithms for solving the linear problem, which we will not discuss here. See (for example) Karlin [37], Hadley [31], Dantzig [13], Intrilligator [35], or Varaiya [71] for further details and examples.

Returning to the nonlinear problem, in this section we will first discuss conditions for maximization where the constraint set C is a "manifold" or the smooth boundary of a manifold. Analytically, this means that the Jacobian matrix of the constraint functions has maximal rank at the proposed solution. We'll call such constraints "nondegenerate." In this situation, it is convenient to consider first the case of equality constraints, i.e., $M = 0$ in (D).

3.2. Nondegenerate equality constraints. The following theorem gives the classical necessary conditions of Lagrange for $\underline{x}^0$ to maximize a function on a submanifold of $\mathbb{R}^n$. We write $h_1 = 0, \ldots, h_N = 0$ as $h \equiv (h_1, \ldots, h_N) = 0$.

THEOREM 3.1. *Suppose that x^0 maximizes $f: \mathbb{R}^n \to \mathbb{R}$ on the set $M_h = \{ \underline{x} \in \mathbb{R}^n | h(\underline{x}) = 0$ where $h: \mathbb{R}^n \to \mathbb{R}^N, \, N < n \}$. Suppose further that f and h are C^1 and that $Dh(\underline{x}^0)$ has maximal rank. a) Then, there exists a unique $(\mu_1^0, \ldots, \mu_N^0) \in \mathbb{R}^N$ such that $Df(\underline{x}^0) + \sum_1^N \mu_i^0 Dh_i(\underline{x}^0) = \underline{0}$. b) If f and h are C^2, then*

$$D^2 \left[f + \sum_1^N \mu_i^0 h_i \right] (\underline{x}^0)(\underline{v}, \underline{v}) \leq 0, \text{ for all } \underline{v}$$

for which $Dh(\underline{x}^0)\underline{v} = 0$, i.e., all $v \in T_{\underline{x}^0} M_h$.

Proof. We will work with the function (f, h): $\mathbb{R}^n \to \mathbb{R}^1 \times \mathbb{R}^N$ $\cong \mathbb{R}^{N+1}$. We first claim that $D(f, h)(\underline{x}^0)$: $\mathbb{R}^n \to \mathbb{R}^{N+1}$ does not have maximal rank. For, if it does, then by the implicit function theorem (Theorem 1.3.b) (f, h) is locally onto, i.e., there is a neighborhood U of $\underline{x}^0$ in $\mathbb{R}^n$ and a neighborhood V of $(f(\underline{x}^0), h(\underline{x}^0))$ in $\mathbb{R}^{N+1}$ so that f maps U onto V. So, we can choose $\underline{x}^1 \in U$ with $(f(\underline{x}^1), h(\underline{x}^1)) = (f(\underline{x}^0) + \varepsilon, h(\underline{x}^0))$ in V for some $\varepsilon > 0$. Then $f(\underline{x}^1) > f(\underline{x}^0)$ and $h(\underline{x}^1) = h(\underline{x}^0) = \underline{0}$, contradicting the fact that $\underline{x}^0$ maximizes f on M_h.

Since $D(f, h)(\underline{x}^0)$ is not of maximal rank, its rows are linearly dependent, i.e., there exists nonzero $(\lambda_0, \ldots, \lambda_N) \in \mathbb{R}^{N+1}$ such that $\lambda_0 Df(\underline{x}^0) + \Sigma_1^N \lambda_i Dh_i(\underline{x}^0) = \underline{0}$. If $\lambda_0 = 0$, then $\Sigma_1^N \lambda_i Dh_i(\underline{x}^0) = 0$ for some nonzero $(\lambda_1, \ldots, \lambda_N)$, contradicting the maximal rank of $Dh(\underline{x}^0)$. So, let $\mu_i^0 = \lambda_i/\lambda_0$. If there is another $(\mu_1^1, \ldots, \mu_N^1)$ with $Df(\underline{x}^0) + \Sigma_1^N \mu_i^1 Dh_i(\underline{x}^0) = 0$, we can subtract one equation from the other to obtain $\Sigma_1^N (\mu_i^1 - \mu_1^0) Dh_i(\underline{x}^0) = \underline{0}$. Again, the nondegeneracy of $Dh(\underline{x}^0)$ implies that $\mu_i^1 - \mu_i^0 = 0$ for all i.

To see part b), let $\underline{v} \in \ker Dh(\underline{x}^0) = T_{\underline{x}^0} M_h$. Again, by the implicit function Theorem (1.3.b), there is a C^2 curve $a: [0, \varepsilon) \to \mathbb{R}^n$ with $a(0) = \underline{x}^0$, $a'(0) = \underline{v}$, and $h(a(t)) = 0$ for all t. By hypothesis, $f \circ a: [0, \varepsilon) \to \mathbb{R}^1$ has a maximum at 0. By results of Calculus I,

$$0 \geq \frac{d^2}{dt^2}(f \circ a)\bigg|_{t=0} = \frac{d^2}{dt^2}\left[f \circ a + \sum_i \mu_i^0(h_i \circ a)\right]\bigg|_{t=0} \quad (h_i \circ a = 0)$$

$$= \frac{d}{dt}\left[Df(a(t))a'(t) + \sum_i \mu_i^0 Dh_i(a(t))a'(t)\right]\bigg|_{t=0} \quad \text{(chain rule)}$$

$$= D^2f(a(0))(a'(0), a'(0)) + Df(a(0))(a''(0))$$
$$+ \sum_i \mu_i^0 D^2h_i(a(0))(a'(0), a'(0)) + \sum_i \mu_i^0 Dh_i(a(0))a''(0)$$

$$= D^2f(\underline{x}^0)(\underline{v}, \underline{v}) + \sum_i \mu_i^0 D^2h_i(\underline{x}^0)(\underline{v}, \underline{v}),$$

since $Df(\underline{x}^0) + \sum_i \mu_i^0 Dh(\underline{x}^0) = \underline{0}$. ∎

The geometric interpretation of Theorem 3.1 is simple since the maximal rank of $Dh(\underline{x}^0)$ implies that $M_h \equiv h^{-1}(\underline{0})$ is a submanifold around $\underline{x}^0$. Recall that $Dg(\underline{x}^0)v = \underline{v} \cdot \nabla g(\underline{x}^0)$ where $\nabla g(\underline{x}^0)$ is the gradient (column) vector of g at $\underline{x}^0$. Then, 3.1.a says that $\nabla f(\underline{x}^0)$ is a linear combination of $\nabla h_1(\underline{x}^0), \ldots, \nabla h_N(\underline{x}^0)$. Since each $\nabla h_i(\underline{x}^0)$ is perpendicular to $T_{\underline{x}^0} M_h$, so is $\nabla f(\underline{x}^0)$. This means that the projection of $\nabla f(\underline{x}^0)$ on $T_{\underline{x}^0} M_h$ is zero, i.e., that $f|M_h$ has a critical point. If one now uses coordinates that give M_h as a hyperplane of $\mathbb{R}^n$ around $\underline{x}^0$, then Theorem 2.1.b becomes Theorem 3.1.b in these coordinates.

However, one does not need nondegenerate constraint equations to derive second-order sufficient conditions, i.e., the analogue of Theorem 2.2. We will even use the more general first-order condition of Section 4.

THEOREM 3.2 (Second-order sufficient condition). *Suppose that* $f, h_1, \ldots, h_N$ *are* C^2 *functions on* $\mathbb{R}^n$. *Suppose* $h(\underline{x}^0) \equiv (h_1(\underline{x}^0), \ldots, h_N(\underline{x}^0)) = 0$. *Suppose there is a nonzero* $(\mu_0, \ldots, \mu_N)$ *such that* $\mu_0 \geq 0$, $D(\mu_0 f + \Sigma \mu_i h_i)(\underline{x}^0) = 0$, *and* $D^2(\mu_0 f + \Sigma \mu_i h_i)(\underline{x}^0)(\underline{v}, \underline{v}) < 0$ *for all* $\underline{v}$ *with* $Dh(\underline{x}^0)\underline{v} = 0$, $\underline{v} \neq 0$. *Then,* $\underline{x}^0$ *is a strict local maximum point of* f *on* $h^{-1}(\underline{0})$.

Proof. Let $M_h = h^{-1}(\underline{0})$ and let $F \equiv \mu_0 f + \Sigma \mu_i h_i \colon \mathbb{R}^n \to \mathbb{R}^1$. Now, just imitate the proof of Theorem 2.2, using F. That is, suppose there is $x^n \to x^0$ such that $x^n \neq \mathrm{b}x^0$ for all n, $h(\underline{x}^n) = \underline{0}$, $f(x^n) \geq f(\underline{x}^0)$, and $\underline{v}^n \equiv \dfrac{x^n - x^0}{|x^n - x^0|} \to v^0$. Since $\mu_0 \geq 0$, $0 \leq F(\underline{x}^n) - F(\underline{x}^0)$ for all n. As in the proof of Theorem 2.2, one finds that $D^2 F(\underline{x}^0)(\underline{v}^0, \underline{v}^0) \geq 0$ using Taylor's series. Since $|\underline{v}^0| = 1 \neq 0$, we need only show that $Dh(\underline{x}^0)\underline{v}^0 = \underline{0}$ to find a contradiction. But, for each $i = 1, \ldots, N$ and for each n,

$$0 = \frac{h_i(\underline{x}^n) - h_i(\underline{x}^0)}{|\underline{x}^n - \underline{x}^0|} = Dh_i(\underline{x}^{n,i})\underline{v}^n$$

for some $\underline{x}^{n,i}$ on the line between $\underline{x}^n$ and $\underline{x}^0$. As $n \to \infty$, $\underline{x}^n \to \underline{x}^0$, $\underline{x}^{n,i} \to \underline{x}^0$, and $\underline{v}^n \to \underline{v}^0$. Since each h_i is C^1, $Dh_i(\underline{x}^0)v^0 = 0$. ∎

3.3. Nondegenerate inequality constraints. The next step is to generalize the problem by allowing inequality constraints, $g_i(\underline{x}) \geq$

0, $i = 1, \ldots, M$, as in statement (D). We will still focus on the situation where the "effective" constraints are nondegenerate.

Let $x^0 \in \mathbb{R}^n$ with $h(\underline{x}^0) = \underline{0}$ and $g(\underline{x}^0) = (g_1, \ldots, g_m)(x^0) \geq 0$. Let $E \equiv \{i | g_i(x^0) = 0\}$ and $I \equiv \{j | g_j(x^0) > 0\}$. Reparameterize so that $E = \{1, \ldots, \kappa\}$ and $I = \{\kappa + 1, \ldots, M\}$ for some κ and $g = (g_E, g_I): \mathbb{R}^n \to \mathbb{R}^E \times \mathbb{R}^I \cong \mathbb{R}^M$. The mapping $(g_E, h): \mathbb{R}^n \to \mathbb{R}^E \times \mathbb{R}^N$ represents the *effective constraints* at $\underline{x}^0$. The next theorem states the necessary first- and second-order conditions for a maximum under nondegenerate constraints. The first such theorems were proved by Karush [38] and Pennisi [55].

THEOREM 3.3. *Suppose that* $\underline{x}^0$ *is a local maximum of* f *on* $C_{g,h} \equiv \{\underline{x} \in \mathbb{R}^n | g(x) \geq 0, h(\underline{x}) = \underline{0}\}$. *Suppose that* f, g, *and* h *are* C^2 *and that* $D(g_E, h)(\underline{x}^0)$ *has maximal rank. Then, there is a unique* $(\lambda_1, \ldots, \lambda_M, \mu_1, \ldots, \mu_N)$ *such that*

i) $$D_x\left[f + \sum_1^M \lambda_i g_i + \sum_1^N \mu_j h_j\right](\underline{x}^0) \equiv DL(\underline{x}^0) = \underline{0},$$

ii) $$\lambda_j \geq 0 \quad \text{for} \quad j = 1, \ldots, M,$$

and

iii) $$\lambda_j g_j(\underline{x}^0) = 0 \text{ for } j = 1, \ldots, M, \left(\text{i.e., } \underline{\lambda} \cdot g(\underline{x}^0) = 0\right).$$

Furthermore,

iv) $$D^2L(\underline{x}^0)(\underline{v}, \underline{v}) \leq 0 \quad \text{for all } \underline{v} \text{ such that}$$
$$Dg_E(\underline{x}^0)\underline{v} = \underline{0} \quad \text{and} \quad Dh(\underline{x}^0)\underline{v} = \underline{0}.$$

Proof. If I is nonempty, let U denote the *open* set $\{\underline{x} \in \mathbb{R}^n | g_I(\underline{x}) > \underline{0}\}$. If I is empty, let U denote $\mathbb{R}^n$. Then, i), iii), and iv) follow immediately if one notices that $\underline{x}^0$ maximizes f on the set $\{\underline{x} \in U | g_E(\underline{x}) = \underline{0}, h(\underline{x}) = \underline{0}\}$ and then applies Theorem 3.2, setting $\lambda_j = 0$ for $j \notin E$, i.e., when $g_j(\underline{x}^0) \neq 0$. To prove the important statement ii), let $j \in E$. Without loss of generality, we will take j to be 1. Since $(Dg_E(\underline{x}^0), Dh(\underline{x}^0))$ has maximal rank, there is a vector $\underline{v}$ with

$$Dg_1(\underline{x}^0)\underline{v} > 0, \ Dg_2(\underline{x}^0)\underline{v} = \cdots = Dg_\kappa(\underline{x}^0)\underline{v} = 0,$$

and

$$Dh(\underline{x}^0)\underline{v} = \underline{0}. \qquad (E)$$

By the implicit function theorem (Theorem 1.3.b) applied to $(g_2, \ldots, g_\kappa, h) = \underline{0}$, there is a smooth curve $c: [0, \varepsilon) \to \mathbb{R}^n$ such that $c(0) = \underline{x}^0$, $c'(0) = \underline{v}$, $g_2(c(t)) = \cdots = g_\kappa(c(t)) = 0$ and $h(c(t)) = \underline{0}$ for all t. Since $Dg_1(\underline{x}^0)\underline{v} > 0$, $g_1(c(t)) > 0$ for $t \in (0, \varepsilon_1)$ for some $\varepsilon_1 > 0$, i.e., $c(t) \in C_{g,h}$ for $t \in [0, \varepsilon_1)$. Since $c(0) = \underline{x}^0$ maximizes f on $C_{g,h}$, $f(c(t)) \le f(x^0)$ for t small and

$$Df(\underline{x}^0)\underline{v} = (f \circ c)'(0) \le 0.$$

By i) and (E), $Df(\underline{x}^0)\underline{v} + \lambda_1 Dg_1(\underline{x}^0)\underline{v} = 0$. Since $Df(\underline{x}^0) \le 0$ and $Dg_1(\underline{x}^0)\underline{v} > 0$, $\lambda_1 \ge 0$. One argues similarly for $\lambda_2, \ldots, \lambda_\kappa$. ∎

Finally, we consider second-order sufficient conditions for a constrained maximum. Hestenes [32], McCormick [51], and Fiacco-McCormick [23] seem to be the first ones to prove a strong second-order sufficiency result for inequality-equality constraints without any nondegeneracy assumptions on the constraint set. Their proofs are basically similar to the one described below.

THEOREM 3.4.   *Suppose $f, g_1, \ldots, g_M, h_1, \ldots, h_N$ are C^2 functions on $\mathbb{R}^n$. Suppose $g(\underline{x}^0) \ge \underline{0}$ and $h(\underline{x}^0) = \underline{0}$. Suppose there exist $\lambda_0, \lambda_1, \ldots, \lambda_M, \mu_1, \ldots, \mu_N$ so that*

i) $$\lambda_i \ge 0 \quad \text{for} \quad i = 0, \ldots, M,$$

ii) $$\lambda_i g_i(\underline{x}^0) = 0 \quad \text{for} \quad i = 1, \ldots, M,$$

iii) $$D\left[\lambda_0 f + \sum_1^M \lambda_i g_i + \sum_1^N \mu_j h_j\right](\underline{x}^0) = \underline{0},$$

and

iv) $$D^2\left[\lambda_0 f + \sum_1^M \lambda_i g_i + \sum_1^N \mu_j h_j\right](\underline{x}^0)(\underline{v}, \underline{v}) < 0$$

for all nonzero $\underline{v}$ satisfying $\lambda_0 Df(\underline{x}^0)\underline{v} \equiv 0$, $\lambda_i Dg_i(\underline{x}^0)\underline{v} = 0$, $i = 1, \ldots, M$, and $Dh(\underline{x}^0)\underline{v} = \underline{0}$. Then, there is a neighborhood U of $\underline{x}^0$ such that $f(\underline{x}) < f(\underline{x}^0)$ for all $\underline{x} \neq \underline{x}^0$ in $U \cap C_{g,h}$.

REMARK. One can further restrict $\underline{v}$ in iv) to those for which $Dg_i(\underline{x}^0)\underline{v} \geq 0$ for i such that $\lambda_i > 0$ and $Df(\underline{x}^0)\underline{v} \geq 0$.

Proof. First, choose a neighborhood V of $\underline{x}^0$ so that $g_i(\underline{x}) > 0$ for $i \in I$ and $\underline{x} \in V$. Working within V, our constraints are now $g_E \geq \underline{0}$ and $h = \underline{0}$ and our Lagrangian is

$$L' \equiv \lambda_0 f + \sum_{i \in E} \lambda_i g_i + \sum_1^N \mu_j h_j = \lambda_0 f + \sum_1^M \lambda_i g_i + \sum_1^N \mu_j h_j \equiv L.$$

Arguing by contradiction as in Theorem 3.2, suppose there exist $\underline{x}^n \to \underline{x}^0$ such that $x^n \in C_{g,h}$, $f(\underline{x}^n) \geq f(\underline{x}^0)$, and $\underline{x}^n \neq \underline{x}^0$ for each n. As before, choose $\underline{x}^n$ so that $\underline{v}^n = (\underline{x}^n - \underline{x}^0)/|\underline{x}^n - \underline{x}^0|$ converges to some unit vector $\underline{v}^0$.

Next, we show that $\underline{v}^0$ satisfies the conditions of hypothesis iv). Arguing as in Theorem 3.2, one proves easily via the Mean Value Theorem that

$$Df(\underline{x}^0)\underline{v}^0 \geq 0, \ Dh(\underline{x}^0)\underline{v}^0 = \underline{0}, \quad \text{and} \quad Dg_i(\underline{x}^0)\underline{v}^0 \geq 0$$

$$\text{for each} \quad i \in E \quad \text{(F)}$$

Furthermore, $\lambda_i Dg_i(\underline{x}^0)\underline{v}^0 = 0$ for each i. Otherwise, there exists a j such that $\lambda_j Dg_j(\underline{x}^0)\underline{v}^0 > 0$ and then by (F) and i)

$$DL(\underline{x}^0)\underline{v}^0 = \lambda_0 Df(\underline{x}^0)\underline{v}^0 + \sum_{i \in E} \lambda_i Dg_i(\underline{x}^0)\underline{v}^0 > 0,$$

which contradicts hypothesis iii). Similarly, $\lambda_0 Df(\underline{x}^0)\underline{v}^0 = 0$.

Finally, by Taylor's Theorem (Theorem 1.2a), there exist C^2 functions R, S, and T such that for each n

$$0 \le f(\underline{x}^n) - f(\underline{x}^0)$$
$$= Df(\underline{x}^0)(\underline{x}^n - \underline{x}^0)$$
$$+ \frac{1}{2!} D^2 f(\underline{x}^0)(\underline{x}^n - \underline{x}^0, \underline{x}^n - \underline{x}^0) + R(\underline{x}^n);$$

$$0 \le g_i(\underline{x}^n) - g_i(\underline{x}^0)$$
$$= Dg_i(\underline{x}^0)(\underline{x}^n - \underline{x}^0)$$
$$+ \frac{1}{2!} D^2 g_i(\underline{x}^0)(\underline{x}^n - \underline{x}^0, \underline{x}^n - \underline{x}^0) + S_i(\underline{x}^n), \qquad i \in E; \qquad \text{(F')}$$

$$0 = h_j(\underline{x}^n) - h_j(\underline{x}^0)$$
$$= Dh_j(\underline{x}^0)(\underline{x}^n - \underline{x}^0)$$
$$+ \frac{1}{2!} D^2 h_j(\underline{x}^0)(\underline{x}^n - \underline{x}^0, \underline{x}^n - \underline{x}^0) + T_j(\underline{x}^n),$$

where $R(\underline{x}^n)/|\underline{x}^n - \underline{x}^0|^2$, $S_i(\underline{x}^n)/|\underline{x}^n - \underline{x}^0|^2$, and

$$T_j(\underline{x}^n)/|\underline{x}^n - \underline{x}^0|^2$$

all tend to zero as $\underline{x}^n \to \underline{x}^0$. Divide each expression in (F') by $|\underline{x}^n - \underline{x}^0|^2$, multiply through by the corresponding Lagrange multiplier, and add the expressions to obtain

$$0 \le \frac{DL(\underline{x}^0)(\underline{x}^n - \underline{x}^0)}{|\underline{x}^n - \underline{x}^0|^2} + \frac{1}{2!} D^2 L(\underline{x}^0)(\underline{v}^n, \underline{v}^n) + \frac{Q(\underline{x}^n)}{|\underline{x}^n - \underline{x}^0|^2},$$

where the last term tends to zero as $\underline{x}^n \to \underline{x}^0$. Using $DL(\underline{x}^0) = \underline{0}$ and then letting $\underline{x}^n \to \underline{x}$, one finds that $0 \le D^2 L(\underline{x}^0)(\underline{v}^0, \underline{v}^0)$. Since $\underline{v}^0$ satisfies the conditions of iv), we have a contradiction to iv) and $\underline{x}^0$ must be a strict local maximum of f on $C_{g,h}$. ∎

REMARK. Condition iv), the second-order condition, in Theorem 3.4 is difficult to check as it is written. However, by Theorem 1.5, one can replace iv) by the following much more easily checked condition:

iv)′: Let H be the bordered matrix

$$\begin{pmatrix} 0 & 0 & A \\ 0 & 0 & B \\ A^t & B^t & C \end{pmatrix}$$

where

$$A = \left(\left(\lambda_i \frac{\partial g_i(\underline{x}^0)}{\partial x_k} \right) \right) \quad \text{for } k = 1, \ldots, n$$

and for i such that $\lambda_i \neq 0$,

$$B = \left(\left(\frac{\partial h_j(\underline{x}^0)}{\partial x_k} \right) \right) \quad \text{for } k = 1, \ldots, n \quad \text{and} \quad j = 1, \ldots, N,$$

$$C = \left(\left(\frac{\partial^2 L}{\partial x_i \partial x_j}(\underline{x}^0) \right) \right) \quad \text{for } i, j = 1, \ldots, n.$$

We require H to satisfy the conditions of Theorem 1.5, namely determinant H has the same sign as $(-1)^n$ and the last $(n - m)$ leading principal minors of H alternate in sign, where $m =$ number of rows of $A +$ numbers of rows of $B = \#\{i | \lambda_i > 0, \ i = 1, \ldots, M\} + N$.

Some authors, e.g., McShane [52], Weinberger [76] and Ben-tal [9], have noticed that one can find an even stronger sufficiency test than that of Theorems 3.2 and 3.4. For, in the proofs of these results, one can easily allow the Lagrange multipliers to depend on the vector $\underline{v}$ being tested and thus prove the following result.

THEOREM 3.5. *Suppose that* $f, g_1, \ldots, g_M, h_1, \ldots, h_N$ *are* C^2 *functions on* $\mathbb{R}^n$. *Suppose that* $g(\underline{x}^0) \geq \underline{0}$ *and* $h(\underline{x}^0) = \underline{0}$. *Suppose that for each nonzero* $\underline{v}$ *such that* $Df(\underline{x}^0)\underline{v} \geq \underline{0}$, $Dg_E(\underline{x}^0)\underline{v} \geq \underline{0}$, *and* $Dh(\underline{x}^0)\underline{v} = \underline{0}$, *there exists* $\lambda_0, \lambda_1, \ldots, \lambda_M, \mu_1, \ldots, \mu_N$ *so that* i), ii), *and* iii) *of Theorem 3.4 are satisfied and*

$$D^2\left[\lambda_0 f + \sum_1^M \lambda_i g_i + \sum_1^N \mu_j h_j\right](\underline{x}^0)(\underline{v}, \underline{v}) < 0.$$

Then, there exists a neighborhood U *of* $\underline{x}^0$ *such that* $f(\underline{x}) < f(\underline{x}^0)$ *for all* $x \neq \underline{x}^0$ *in* U *satisfying* $g(\underline{x}) \geq 0$, $h(\underline{x}) = \underline{0}$.

As we will see later, an important variant of problem (D) is the following:

Maximize $f: \mathbb{R}^n \to \mathbb{R}$ on the set $\{x | G_i(x) \geq 0, i = 1, \ldots, M;$

$$x_j \geq 0, \; j = 1, \ldots, n\}. \quad (G)$$

We state without proof the application of Theorems 3.3 and 3.4 to this special problem.

COROLLARY 3.6. *Suppose* $f, G_1, \ldots, G_M$ *are* C^2 *functions on* $\mathbb{R}^n$.

a) *If* $\underline{x}^0$ *is a solution of* (G) *and if* $(\partial G_E / \partial x_B)(\underline{x}^0)$ *has maximal rank where* $E = \{i | G_i(\underline{x}^0) = 0\}$ *and* $B = \{j | x_j^0 > 0\}$, *then there exists unique* $\underline{\lambda}^0 = (\lambda_1^0, \ldots, \lambda_N^0)$ *such that*

(i) $\qquad\qquad \lambda_i^0 \geq 0 \quad$ *for all* i,

(ii) $\qquad$ *if* $L(x, \lambda) \equiv f(x) + \sum_1^M \lambda_i G_i(x),$

then

$$\frac{\partial L}{\partial \underline{x}}(\underline{x}^0, \underline{\lambda}^0) \leq 0 \quad \text{and} \quad \underline{x}^0 \cdot \frac{\partial L}{\partial \underline{x}}(\underline{x}^0, \underline{\lambda}^0) = 0,$$

$$\frac{\partial L}{\partial \underline{\lambda}}(\underline{x}^0, \underline{\lambda}^0) = G(\underline{x}^0) \geq 0 \quad \text{and} \quad \underline{\lambda}^0 \cdot \frac{\partial L}{\partial \underline{\lambda}}(\underline{x}^0, \underline{\lambda}^0) = 0.$$

(iii) $\quad D_x^2 L\left(\underline{x}^0, \underline{\mu}^0\right)(\underline{v}, \underline{v}) \leq 0 \quad$ for all nonzero $\underline{v}$ with

$$DG_E\left(\underline{x}^0\right)\underline{v} = 0 \quad \text{and} \quad v_i = 0 \quad \text{for} \quad i \notin B.$$

b) Conversely, suppose that $G(\underline{x}^0) \geq 0$ and $\underline{x}^0 > 0$. Suppose further that there is $\underline{\lambda}^0 = (\lambda_1^0, \ldots, \lambda_N^0) \geq 0$ such that L satisfies (ii) and (iii) at $(\underline{x}^0, \underline{\lambda}^0)$ with " < " replacing " $\leq$ " in (iii), then $\underline{x}^0$ is a strict local maximum of f on $\{\underline{x}|G(\underline{x}) \geq 0,$ $\underline{x} \geq 0\}$.

Conditions i), ii), and iii) of Theorem 3.3 are usually called the Kuhn-Tucker conditions for problem (D). Conditions (i) and (ii) of Corollary 3.6 are called the Kuhn-Tucker conditions for problem (G).

El-Hodiri [20] and Milleron [53] both have complete, yet concise, discussions of the nonlinear programming problem with nondegenerate constraints. El-Hodiri also adds some interesting historical comments.

3.4. Lagrange multipliers as sensitivity indicators. Consider the problem of maximizing $f: \mathbb{R}^n \to \mathbb{R}$ subject to the equality constraint $h(\underline{x}) = \underline{b}$, where $h: \mathbb{R}^n \to \mathbb{R}^M$ and $\underline{b}$ is viewed as a parameter. A natural and important question is: how does the optimal value of f change as $\underline{b}$ is allowed to vary. The following theorem shows that the Lagrange multipliers themselves measure the sensitivity of the optimal value of f to changes in the constraint $\underline{b}$. We will see a number of economic applications of this fact in Section 6.

THEOREM 3.7. *Let $f, h_1, \ldots, h_N: \mathbb{R}^n \to \mathbb{R}$ be C^2 functions with $\underline{x}^0 \in \mathbb{R}^n$ and $h(\underline{x}^0) = \underline{b}^0$. Suppose that the following sufficient conditions for a maximum of f on $h^{-1}(\underline{b}^0)$ are satisfied at $\underline{x}^0$:*
  i) *There exist $\lambda_1^0, \ldots, \lambda_N^0$ such that $DL(\underline{x}^0) = \underline{0}$, where*

$$L(\underline{x}) \equiv f(x) + \sum_1^N \lambda_i^0 \left(b_i^0 - h_i(\underline{x})\right).$$

  ii) $\quad D^2 L(\underline{x}^0)(\underline{v}, \underline{v}) < 0$ *for all nonzero $\underline{v}$ in the kernel of $Dh(\underline{x}^0)$;*
  iii) $\quad Dh(\underline{x}^0)$ *has maximal rank.*

Then, there is a neighborhood W of $\underline{b}^0$ in $\mathbb{R}^N$ and C^1 functions

$$\xi: W \to \mathbb{R}^n, \qquad \lambda: W \to \mathbb{R}^N$$

such that $\xi(\underline{b}^0) = \underline{x}^0$, $\lambda(\underline{b}^0) = \underline{\lambda}^0$, and for all $\underline{b} \in W$, $\xi(b)$ maximizes f on $h^{-1}(\underline{b})$ with Lagrange multipliers $\lambda_1(b), \ldots, \lambda_N(b)$. Furthermore, $\lambda_i(\underline{b}) = \dfrac{\partial}{\partial b_i}(f \circ \xi)(\underline{b})$.

Proof. Define $M = (M_1, M_2): \mathbb{R}^n \times \mathbb{R}^N \times \mathbb{R}^N \to \mathbb{R}^n \times \mathbb{R}^N$ by $M(\underline{x}, \underline{\lambda}, \underline{b}) = (\nabla f(\underline{x}) - \lambda \cdot \nabla h(\underline{x}), \; \underline{b} - h(\underline{x}))$. Then $M(\underline{x}^0, \underline{\lambda}^0, \underline{b}^0) = (\underline{0}, \underline{0})$ and

$$D_{(x,\lambda)}M\left(\underline{x}^0, \underline{\lambda}^0, \underline{b}^0\right) = \begin{pmatrix} D^2L\left(\underline{x}^0\right) & -Dh\left(\underline{x}^0\right)^T \\ -Dh\left(\underline{x}^0\right) & \underline{0} \end{pmatrix}$$

Here, $D^2L(\underline{x}^0)$ denotes the Hessian matrix of L at $\underline{x}^0$. To solve $M = 0$ for $\underline{x}$ and $\underline{\lambda}$ as functions of $\underline{b}$, we will use the implicit function theorem, of course. We need only show that the above $(n + N) \times (n + N)$ matrix is one-to-one and therefore nonsingular by Theorem 1.3.d.

Suppose $D_{(x,\lambda)}M(\underline{x}^0, \underline{\lambda}^0, \underline{b}^0)(\underline{v}, \underline{w}) = (\underline{0}, \underline{0})$. Then,

$$D^2L\left(\underline{x}^0\right)\underline{v} - Dh\left(\underline{x}^0\right)^T\underline{w} = \underline{0} \quad \text{and} \qquad (+)$$

$$-Dh\left(\underline{x}^0\right)\underline{v} = 0. \qquad (++)$$

Take the inner product of equation $(+)$ with $\underline{v}$. Since $\underline{v} \cdot Dh(\underline{x}^0)^T = \underline{0}$ by $(++)$, $(+)$ becomes $v \cdot D^2L(\underline{x}^0)\underline{v} = D^2L(\underline{x}^0)(\underline{v}, \underline{v}) = 0$. By hypothesis ii), $\underline{v}$ must be zero and $(+)$ becomes $-Dh(\underline{x}^0)^T\underline{w} = \underline{0}$. By hypothesis iii), $Dh(\underline{x}^0)^T$ is injective and $\underline{w}$ is zero also.

Since our partial derivative is nonsingular, the Implicit Function Theorem (Theorem 1.3.d) tells us that there is a neighborhood W of $\underline{b}^0$ in $\mathbb{R}^N$ and C^1 functions $\xi: W \to \mathbb{R}^n$, $\lambda: W \to \mathbb{R}^N$ such that $M(\xi(\underline{b}), \lambda(\underline{b}), \underline{b}) = (\underline{0}, \underline{0})$ for all $\underline{b} \in W$ with $\xi(\underline{b}^0) = \underline{x}^0$ and $\lambda(\underline{b}^0) = \underline{\lambda}^0$. Choose W small enough so that hypotheses ii) and iii) hold for all $\underline{b} \in W$ and $x \in \xi(W)$. (Conditions ii) and iii) define open sets since they can be expressed by the nonvanishing of certain determinants.) By Theorem 3.4, each $\xi(b)$ maximizes f on $h^{-1}(\underline{b})$.

To see that $\lambda_i(\underline{b}) = (\partial/\partial b_i)(f \circ \xi)(\underline{b})$, note that

$$f(\xi(\underline{b})) = f(\xi(\underline{b})) + \sum_1^N \lambda_i(\underline{b})(b_i - h_i(\xi(\underline{b})) \text{ since } h(\xi(\underline{b})) = \underline{b}$$

$$\equiv L(\xi(\underline{b}), \lambda(\underline{b}), \underline{b}).$$

Thus,

$$D_b(f \circ \xi)(b)\underline{v} = D_x f(\xi(b)) \circ D\xi(\underline{b})\underline{v}$$

$$+ \sum_i (D\lambda_i(\underline{b})\underline{v})(b_i - h_i(\xi(\underline{b}))$$

$$+ \lambda(b) \cdot (I - Dh(\xi(b)) \cdot D\xi(b))\underline{v},$$

by Theorem 1.1,

$$= \lambda(b) + [D_x f(\xi(b)) - \lambda(\underline{b}) \cdot Dh(\xi(b))] D\xi(b)$$

$$\cdot v \quad (\text{since } b_i - h_i(\xi(b)) = 0)$$

$$= \lambda(\underline{b}),$$

since $M_1(\xi(\underline{b}), \lambda(\underline{b}), \underline{b}) = \underline{0}$. ∎

REMARK 1. Note that hypotheses ii) and iii) hold for most functions f and for most constraint values $b \in \mathbb{R}^N$. The latter part follows from Sard's Lemma and the former from the fact that most functions on a manifold are "Morse functions," functions with only nondegenerate critical points. See Golubitsky-Guillemin [28] for proofs of these results and Dierker [17] and Mas-Collel (this book) for further applications of these results to economics. The word "most" is used in the sense of an open-dense subset or second-category subset of the set of all constraint-values and of the set of all objective functions.

REMARK 2. Lagrange multipliers yielded the same sensitivity analysis when the constraints involve *inequalities* such as $g(\underline{x}) \geq \underline{a}$,

$h(\underline{x}) = \underline{b}$. Let $I = \{i | g_i(\underline{x}^0) > a_i^0\}$. For $i \in I$, the Lagrange multiplier λ_i^0 must be zero. On the other hand, since these g_i give ineffective constraints, the optimal value of f does not change as one varies a_i for $i \in I$. Thus, for $i \in I$,

$$0 = \lambda_i^0 = \frac{\partial(f \circ \xi)}{\partial a_i}(\underline{a}, \underline{b})$$

One is then led to the problem of maximizing f subject to $g_E(\underline{x}) = a_E$, $h(\underline{x}) = \underline{b}$; and one can argue as in Theorem 3.7.

REMARK 3.   Condition (iii) can be relaxed, though at some cost. See Gauvin and Tolle [26] for results in this direction.

REMARK 4.   Theorem 3.7 is a special case of the "envelope theorem," a theorem which has begun to play a large role in comparative statistics. In Theorem 3.8, we state the unconstrained and constrained versions of the envelope theorem. Their proofs are essentially the same as that of Theorem 3.7. Note that 3.8.a states that the change in the objective function adjusting x optimally is equal to the change in the objective function when one does not adjust x.

THEOREM 3.8.   a) Let $f: \mathbb{R}^n \times \mathbb{R}^1 \to \mathbb{R}$ be a C^1 function $f(x_1, \ldots, x_n; a)$ with parameter a. Let $x = \xi(a)$ be the maximizing value of x and let $M(a) = f(\xi(a))$. (M is called the *indirect* objective function.) If $\xi(a)$ is a C^1 function, e.g., if $D_x^2 f(\xi(a), a)$ is nondegenerate, then

$$\frac{dM}{da}(a) = \frac{\partial f}{\partial a}(\xi(a), a).$$

b) Let $f, h_1, \ldots, h_N$ be C^1 functions on $\mathbb{R}^n \times \mathbb{R}^1$ where the last variable is a parameter b. Let $\underline{x} = \xi(b)$ be the maximizer of $f(x; b)$ on the constraint set

$$C_b = \{\underline{x} | h_i(\underline{x}; b) = 0, \, i = 1, \ldots, N\}.$$

Let $M(b) = f(\xi(b), b)$. Suppose $\xi(b)$ is a C^1 function of b, e.g., (f, h) satisfies hypotheses similar to those of Theorem 3.7. Then

$$\frac{dM}{db}(b) = \frac{\partial}{\partial b}L(\xi(b), b),$$

where $L(x, b) = f(x; b) + \sum_{i=1}^{N} \lambda_i h_i(x; b).$

4. CONSTRAINT QUALIFICATIONS

4.1. Fritz John's first-order necessary conditions. In the last section, we discussed necessary and sufficient conditions for constrained maxima under the condition that the Jacobian matrix of the effective constraint functions be of maximal rank. However, such a condition is too stringent for some applications and too difficult to check for others. In this section, we will examine much weaker and more geometric hypotheses on the constraint set. Since we will impose conditions only on the constraint set and not on the function to be maximized, such conditions are called "constraint qualifications." The most famous early paper on constraint qualifications is that of Kuhn and Tucker [43]. One can also find excellent surveys in Arrow-Hurwicz-Uzawa [4] and Mangasarian [48].

In contrast to the approach for nondegenerate constraints, one usually proves theorems about *inequality* constraints first, when working with constraint qualifications. Then, one can often handle equality constraints, like $h(x) = 0$, by writing them as the set of inequality constraints: $h(x) \geq 0$, $-h(x) \geq 0$.

The following result of Fritz John [36] is the broadest first-order necessary condition. Condition (H) is usually called the *Fritz John Condition*.

THEOREM 4.1. *Let $f, g_1, \ldots, g_M, h_1, \ldots, h_N$ be C^1 functions on $\mathbb{R}^n$ and let $\underline{x}^0$ be a local maximum of f on the set $C_{g,h} = \{x \in \mathbb{R}^n \mid g(\underline{x}) \geq 0, \ h(\underline{x}) = 0\}$. Then, there exists $(\lambda_0, \lambda_1, \ldots, \lambda_M, \mu_1, \ldots, \mu_N)$ such that $\lambda_i \geq 0$, $\lambda_i g_i(\underline{x}^0) = 0$ for all*

$i \leq M$, *and*

$$\lambda_0 Df\left(\underline{x}^0\right) + \sum_1^M \lambda_i Dg_i\left(\underline{x}^0\right) + \sum_1^M \mu_j Dh_j\left(\underline{x}^0\right) = 0. \qquad (H)$$

Proof. We will first assume there are no equality constraints, i.e., that $N = 0$. We'll need the following important lemma, usually attributed to Gordan [29].

LEMMA. *The following statements are equivalent for vectors $\underline{a}^1, \ldots, \underline{a}^m$ in $\mathbb{R}^n$: a) There exists no $\underline{v} \in \mathbb{R}^n$ such that $\underline{a}^i \cdot \underline{v} > 0$ for all i; b) There exists nonzero $(\lambda_1, \ldots, \lambda_m) \geq \underline{0}$ in $\mathbb{R}^m$ such that $\sum_1^m \lambda_i \underline{a}^i = \underline{0}$.*

Proof of Lemma. b) $\Rightarrow$ a): Suppose b) with $\lambda_k > 0$ and suppose there exists $\underline{v}$ with $\underline{a}^i \cdot \underline{v} > 0$ for all i. Then,

$$\underline{a}^k \cdot \underline{v} = -\lambda_k^{-1}\left(\sum_{i \neq k} \lambda_i \underline{a}_i \cdot \underline{v} \right) \leq 0,$$

a contradiction.

a) $\Rightarrow$ b): Let $X \subseteq \mathbb{R}^m$ be the linear subspace $\{(\underline{a}^1 \cdot \underline{b}, \ldots, \underline{a}^m \cdot \underline{b}) \in \mathbb{R}^m | \underline{b} \in \mathbb{R}^n\}$. By a), $X \cap P = \phi$, where $P \equiv \{\underline{x} \in \mathbb{R}^m | x_i > 0$ for all $i\}$. So, there is a nonzero $(\lambda_1, \ldots, \lambda_m) \in \overline{P}$ so that $(\lambda_1, \ldots, \lambda_m)$ is perpendicular to X. But then, $\sum_1^m \lambda_i \underline{a}^i \cdot \underline{b} = 0$ for all $\underline{b} \in \mathbb{R}^n$, which implies that $\sum_1^m \lambda_i \underline{a}^i = \underline{0}$.

Returning to the proof of Theorem 4.1, we claim that there is no $\underline{v} \in \mathbb{R}^n$ so that $Df(\underline{x}^0)\underline{v} > 0$ and $Dg_i(\underline{x}^0)\underline{v} > 0$ for all $i \in E \equiv \{ j | g_j(\underline{x}^0) = 0 \}$. For, if there were such a $\underline{v}$, f and each g_i for $i \in E$ would be increasing on the curve $t \to \underline{x}^0 + t\underline{v}$ for small enough t. Since $g_i(\underline{x}^0 + t\underline{v})$ would still be positive for $i \notin E$ and t small, $\underline{x}^0$ would not maximize f on $g \geq 0$.

We can now apply Gordan's Lemma with $\underline{a}^0 = \nabla f(\underline{x}^0)$ and $\underline{a}^i = \nabla g_i(\underline{x}^0)$ for $i \in E$. So, there is a nonzero $(\lambda_0, \ldots, \lambda_M)$ with $\lambda_i = 0$ for $i \notin E$, $\lambda_j \geq 0$ for all j, and $\lambda_0 \nabla f(\underline{x}^0) + \sum_1^M \lambda_i \nabla g_i(\underline{x}^0) = \underline{0}$.

230433

If one now includes the equality constraints: $h_1 = \cdots = h_N = 0$, the proof becomes a bit more complicated. We will outline the basic ideas and leave the details to the reader. If $\nabla h_1(\underline{x}^0), \ldots, \nabla h_N(\underline{x}^0)$ are linearly dependent, there is a nonzero $(\mu_1, \ldots, \mu_N)$ such that $\sum_1^N \mu_j \nabla h_j(\underline{x}^0) = 0$. In this case, take $\lambda_0 = \lambda_1 = \cdots = \lambda_M = 0$.

On the other hand, if $Dh(\underline{x}^0)$ has maximal rank N, $h^{-1}(\underline{0})$ is an $(n - M)$-dimensional submanifold around $\underline{x}^0$. In particular, by the implicit function theorem, there are coordinates $y_1, \ldots, y_N, z_1, \ldots, z_{n-N}$ on a neighborhood U of $\underline{x}^0$ such that in U:

i) $\qquad\qquad \underline{h} = \underline{0}$ if and only if $\underline{y} = \underline{0}$,

ii) $\qquad\qquad z_1, \ldots, z_{n-N}$ coordinatize $U \cap h^{-1}(\underline{0})$,

iii) $\qquad\qquad \dfrac{\partial h_i}{\partial z_j}(\underline{x}^0) = 0$ for all i and j,

and

iv) $\qquad\qquad \dfrac{\partial h_i}{\partial y_j}(\underline{x}^0)$ is 1 if $i = j$ and 0 if $i \neq j$.

Work first on $h^{-1}(\underline{0}) \cap U$ and apply the above arguments to find a nonzero $(\lambda_0, \ldots, \lambda_M)$ such that $\lambda_i \geq 0$ and $\lambda_i g_i(\underline{x}^0) = 0$ for each i and

$$\lambda_0 \frac{\partial f}{\partial z_k}(\underline{x}^0) + \sum_{i=1}^M \lambda_i \frac{\partial g_i}{\partial z_k}(\underline{x}^0) = 0, \quad \text{for } k = 1, \ldots, n - N.$$

Let $\mu_k = -\dfrac{\partial}{\partial y_k}[\lambda_0 f + \sum_1^M \lambda_i g_i](\underline{x}^0)$ for $k = 1, \ldots, N$. By iii) and iv),

$$\frac{\partial}{\partial z_k}\left[\lambda_0 f + \sum_1^M \lambda_i g_i + \sum_1^N \mu_j h_j\right](\underline{x}^0) = 0, \qquad k = 1, \ldots, n - N$$

$$\frac{\partial}{\partial y_h}\left[\lambda_0 f + \sum_1^M \lambda_i g_i + \sum_1^N \mu_j h_j\right](\underline{x}^0) = 0, \qquad h = 1, \ldots, N.$$

Therefore, the gradient of this Lagrangian is zero at x^0 in any smooth coordinate system (Theorem 1.3). ∎

John's statement of this result dealt only with inequality constraints. See Mangasarian and Fromowitz [47] for the first proof involving both inequality and equality constraints.

4.2. Constraint qualifications. The following simple example illustrates the difference between Theorem 3.1.a and Theorem 4.1. Let $f(x, y) = x$ and let $g(x, y) = y^2 + x^3$. Then, $g^{-1}(0)$ is the standard "cusp" in the left half-plane of $\mathbb{R}^2$; and $(0, 0)$ is a global maximum of f on $g = 0$ and on $(-g) \geq 0$. Since $Df(0, 0) = (1, 0)$ and $Dg(0, 0) = (0, 0)$, $\lambda_0 Df(\underline{0}) + \lambda_1 Dg(\underline{0}) = \underline{0}$ implies that $\lambda_0 = 0$ and λ_1 is arbitrary.

In situations like this where $\lambda_0 = 0$, the Fritz John Necessary Condition (H) says nothing about the maximization problem since it does not involve the function f at all. Thus, it is very important to introduce some conditions on g and h that will guarantee the existence of a nonzero λ_0 in (H). These are the above-mentioned "constraint qualifications." Roughly speaking, we need to eliminate the case where the constraint set C has a cusp at the point in question, i.e., we want C to satisfy some weak convexity assumption.

Let us write C_g for our constraint set $\{x \in \mathbb{R}^n | g_i(x) \geq 0, i = 1, \ldots, M\}$. As before, if $\underline{x}^0 \in C_g$, $E(\underline{x}^0) \equiv E = \{i | g_i(\underline{x}^0) = 0\}$ and $I = \{j | g_j(\underline{x}^0) > 0\}$. A *constrained path from $\underline{x}^0$ in direction $\underline{v}$* is a smooth arc $a: [0, \varepsilon) \to \mathbb{R}^n$ so that $a(0) = \underline{x}^0$, $a'(0) = \underline{v}$, and $a(t) \in C_g$ for all t. For such $\underline{v}$, it follows immediately that $Dg_E(\underline{x}_0)\underline{v} \geq \underline{0}$.

DEFINITION. The mapping g satisfies the *Karush-Kuhn-Tucker constraint qualification* (KKT) at $\underline{x}^0 \in C_g$, if for each $\underline{v}$ with $Dg_E(\underline{x}^0)\underline{v} \geq 0$ ("*constrained direction*") there is a constrained path from $\underline{x}^0$ in direction $\underline{v}$. See Karush [38], Kuhn and Tucker [43], and Kuhn [42].

It is easy to see that the above example does not satisfy (KKT) at $(0, 0)$ and that (KKT) rules out such cusp-like constraint sets. A slightly weaker constraint qualification is due to Arrow, Hurwicz and Uzawa [4].

DEFINITION. The mapping g satisfies the *Kuhn-Tucker weak constraint qualification* (w-K-T) at $\underline{x}^0 \in C_g$ if every constrained direction at $\underline{x}_0$ lies in the smallest closed convex cone containing $\{a'(0) | a$ is a constrained path from $\underline{x}^0\}$, i.e., if $Dg_E(\underline{x}^0)\underline{v} \geq 0$ implies that there are nonnegative $\lambda_1, \ldots, \lambda_k$ and smooth a_i: $[0, \varepsilon) \to C_g$ for $i = 1, \ldots, k$ with $a_i(0) = \underline{x}^0$ and $\underline{v} = \sum_i \lambda_i a_i'(0)$.

It is easy to see that $g_1 = x_1$, $g_2 = x_2$, $g_3 = -x_1 x_2$ satisfies (w-K-T) at $(0, 0)$ but not (KKT). See Arrow-Hurwicz-Uzawa [4].

The following algebraic lemma is the key step in many optimization theorems where the constraints may be degenerate.

FARKAS' LEMMA. *Let A be an $(n \times m)$ matrix and let $\underline{b}$ be a fixed vector in $\mathbb{R}^m$. If $\underline{b} \cdot \underline{v} \geq 0$ for all $\underline{v}$ in $\mathbb{R}^m$ such that $A\underline{v} \geq \underline{0}$, then there exist $\lambda_1, \ldots, \lambda_n$ all ≥ 0 such that*

$$A^T \begin{pmatrix} \lambda_1 \\ \vdots \\ \lambda_n \end{pmatrix} = b, \quad i.e., \quad \sum_{i=1}^n \lambda_i \underline{a}_i = \underline{b}$$

where the $\underline{a}_i$ are the columns of A.

Proof. We first recall some simple properties of convex cones from Fenchel [21] or Gale [25]. If B is a set of vectors, let $B' = \{\underline{u} | \underline{u} \cdot \underline{x} \geq 0 \text{ for } \underline{x} \in B\}$. Then, B' is a closed, convex cone, called the *polar cone* of B. If $B_1 \subset B_2$, then $B_2' \subset B_1'$; and if B is a closed convex cone, $B = (B')'$.

Let $L = \{\underline{v} | A\underline{v} \geq 0\}$. Let $B = \{\sum \lambda_i \underline{a}_i | \lambda_i \geq 0\}$, a closed convex cone. To see that $B' \subset L$, let $\underline{v} \in B'$, i.e.,

$$\sum_i \lambda_i \underline{a}_i \underline{v} \geq 0 \qquad \text{for all} \quad \lambda_i \geq 0.$$

Thus, $A\underline{v} \geq 0$ (taking $\lambda_j = (0, \ldots, 0, 1, 0, \ldots,)$); and $\underline{v} \in L$. Finally, $B' \subset L$ implies that $L' \subset B'' = B$. ∎

The fundamental result on constraint qualifications is the following theorem.

THEOREM 4.2.   *Suppose that* $g: \mathbb{R}^n \to \mathbb{R}^M$ *satisfies* (KKT) *or* $(w\text{-}K\text{-}T)$ *at* $\underline{x}^0$ *and that* $\underline{x}^0$ *maximizes* f *on* C_g. *Then, there exist nonnegative* $\lambda_1, \ldots, \lambda_N$ *such that*

$$Df(\underline{x}^0) + \sum_1^N \lambda_i Dg_i(\underline{x}^0) = \underline{0} \quad and \quad \lambda_i g_i(\underline{x}^0) = 0 \quad for\ all\ i.$$

Proof.   [Arrow-Hurwicz-Uzawa [4]].   Since (KKT) implies (w-K-T), we will assume (w-K-T) at $\underline{x}^0$ and apply Farkas' Lemma with $A = Dg_E(\underline{x}^0)$ and $\underline{b} = -\nabla f(\underline{x}^0)$. To see that $-\nabla f(\underline{x}^0) \in L'$, choose $\underline{v} \in L$, i.e., $Dg_E(\underline{x}^0)\underline{v} \geq 0$. By (w-K-T), there are constrained paths $a_1, \ldots, a_k$ from $\underline{x}^0$ and nonnegative $\mu_1, \ldots, \mu_k$ with

$$\underline{v} = \sum \mu_i a_i'(0).$$

Then,

$$
\begin{aligned}
\underline{v} \cdot \left(-\nabla f(\underline{x}^0)\right) &= -Df(\underline{x}^0)\underline{v} \\
&= -Df(\underline{x}^0)\left(\sum \mu_i a_i'(0)\right) \\
&= -\sum \mu_i \frac{d}{dt} f(a_i(t))\Big|_{t=0} \\
&\geq 0,
\end{aligned}
$$

since f is nonincreasing along each a_i.

Applying Farkas' Lemma, there exist nonnegative $\lambda_1, \ldots, \lambda_N$, with $\lambda_i = 0$ for $i \notin E$, such that

$$-Df(\underline{x}^0) = \sum_1^N \lambda_i Dg_i(\underline{x}^0). \qquad \blacksquare$$

We are now in a position to describe some other successful constraint qualifications—all of which guarantee some sort of convexity or concavity for the constraint set. Condition d) below is the nondegeneracy condition of Section 3. Here, we see how it implies the weaker constraint qualifications of this section.

THEOREM 4.3. *Let $f, g_1, \ldots, g_M$ be C^1 functions on $\mathbb{R}^n$. Suppose that $\underline{x}^0$ maximizes f on C_g. Suppose g satisfies one of the following constraint qualifications at $\underline{x}^0$:*

a) [Arrow-Hurwicz-Uzawa [4]] *There is a vector $\underline{v}$ with $Dg_{E_1}(\underline{x}^0)\underline{v} \geq 0$ and $Dg_{E_2}(\underline{x}^0)\underline{v} > \underline{0}$, with $E_1 = \{i \in E | g_i$ is pseudo-convex around $\underline{x}^0\}$ and $E_2 = E - E_1$;*

b) [Slater [62]] *There is a convex neighborhood U of $\underline{x}^0$ such that g is concave on U and $g(x') > 0$ for some $x' \in U$;*

c) *g is convex (e.g., linear);*

d) *$Dg_E(\underline{x}^0)$ has maximal rank.*

Then, there exist $\lambda_1, \ldots, \lambda_N \geq 0$ with $\lambda_i g_i(\underline{x}^0) = 0$ for all i and

$$D\left[f + \sum \lambda_i g_i \right](\underline{x}^0) = \underline{0}.$$

Proof. Following Arrow-Hurwicz-Uzawa [4], one shows that a) implies condition (w-K-T) and that b), c), and d) each imply a). To see that a) implies (w-K-T), let $\underline{w}$ be a constrained direction. For $\varepsilon > 0$, let $\phi^\varepsilon(t) = \underline{x}^0 + t(\underline{w} + \varepsilon\underline{v})$, where $\underline{v}$ is as in qualification a).

We first show that $\phi^\varepsilon(t)$ is a constrained path. For $i \in E$,
$\frac{d}{dt} g_i \circ \phi^\varepsilon(t)|_{t=0} = Dg_i(\underline{x}^0)(\underline{w} + \varepsilon\underline{v}) \geq \underline{0} + \varepsilon Dg_i(\underline{x}^0)\underline{v} \geq 0$. If $i \in E_2$, $\frac{d}{dt}(g_i \circ \phi^\varepsilon)(0) > 0$ and so $0 = g_i(x^0) = g_i(\phi^\varepsilon(0)) < g_i(\phi^\varepsilon(t))$ for t small. If $i \in E_1$, $g_i \circ \phi^\varepsilon$ is pseudo-convex; and so $\frac{d}{dt}(g_i \circ \phi^\varepsilon)(0) \geq 0$ implies that $0 = g_i(\phi^\varepsilon(0)) \leq g_i(\phi^\varepsilon(t))$ for t small. If $i \notin E$, then $g_i(\phi^\varepsilon(t))$ will be positive for t small. So ϕ^ε is a constrained path. Thus,

$$\underline{w} = (\phi^0)'(0) = \lim_{\varepsilon \to 0} (\phi^\varepsilon)'(0)$$

lies in the closure of $\{a'(0) | a(t)$ is a constrained path from $\underline{x}^0\}$; and constraint qualification (w-K-T) is satisfied.

b) $\Rightarrow$ a): Since g_j is concave, $Dg_j(\underline{x}^0)(\underline{x}' - \underline{x}^0) \geq g_j(\underline{x}') - g_j(\underline{x}^0) = g_j(x') > 0$ for any $j \in E$. (See Theorem 1.6.) Take $\underline{v} = \underline{x}' - \underline{x}^0$ in a).

c) $\Rightarrow$ a): Here E_2 is empty. So, take $\underline{v} = \underline{0}$.

d) $\Rightarrow$ a): Let $\underline{b}$ be a positive vector in $\mathbb{R}^E$. Since $Dg_E(\underline{x}^0)$: $T_{\underline{x}^0}\mathbb{R}^n \to \mathbb{R}^E$ has maximal rank, it is onto and there is a $\underline{v} \in T_{\underline{x}^0}\mathbb{R}^n$ with $Dg_E(\underline{x}^0)\underline{v} = \underline{b} > \underline{0}$. ∎

One can now add equality constraints $h_1(\underline{x}) = \cdots = h_N(\underline{x}) = 0$ to the inequality constraints $g(\underline{x}) \geq \underline{0}$. In this case, the standard device to replace the equality $h_j(\underline{x}) = 0$ by the two inequalities $h_j(\underline{x}) \geq 0$, $-h_j(\underline{x}) \geq 0$. Parts i), ii), and iii) of the following proposition then follow immediately from Theorems 4.2 and 4.3. See Mangasarian-Fromowitz [47] or Mangasarian [48] for a proof of part iv), or use the techniques described in the last paragraph of our proof of Theorem 4.1.

THEOREM 4.4. *Suppose that* $f, g_1, \ldots, g_M, h_1, \ldots, h_N$ *are* C^1 *functions on* $\mathbb{R}^n$. *Suppose* $\underline{x}^0$ *maximizes* f *on* $\{\underline{x}|g_i(\underline{x}) \geq 0, i = 1, \ldots, M; h_j(\underline{x}) = 0, j = 1, \ldots, N\}$. *Suppose any one of the following constraint qualifications hold:*

   i) *If* $Dg_E(\underline{x}^0)\underline{v} \geq 0$ *and* $Dh(\underline{x}^0)\underline{v} = \underline{0}$, *then there is a* C^1 *path* $a: [0, \varepsilon] \to \mathbb{R}^n$ *with* $a(0) = \underline{x}^0$, $a'(0) = \underline{v}$, $g(a(t)) \geq 0$, *and* $h(a(t)) = \underline{0}$;

   ii) h *is pseudoconcave and pseudoconvex (e.g., linear) and there is a* $\underline{v} \in T_{\underline{x}^0}\mathbb{R}^n$ *such that* $Dg_{E_1}(\underline{x}^0)\underline{v} \geq 0$, $Dg_{E_2}(\underline{x}^0)\underline{v} > 0$, *and* $Dh(\underline{x}^0)\underline{v} = \underline{0}$, *with* E_1 *and* E_2 *as in Theorem 4.3a;*

   iii) g *is convex and* h *is linear;*

   iv) $Dh(\underline{x}^0)$ *has maximal rank and* $Dg_E(\underline{x}^0)\underline{v} > \underline{0}$, $Dh(\underline{x}^0) = \underline{0}$ *for some* $\underline{v} \in T_{\underline{x}^0}\mathbb{R}^n$.

For a more complete discussion of constraint qualifications and their intrinsic geometry, see Mangasarian [48] and Gould-Tolle [30].

4.3. Second order conditions. Since Theorems 3.2 and 3.5 do not make nondegeneracy assumptions on $\{x|g(x) \geq 0, h(\underline{x}) = 0\}$, they are just about the most effective second-order sufficient conditions around. (However, stronger sufficient conditions using constraint qualifications are required for theoretical convergence of many algorithms for solving nonlinear problems.) We now stop for a second to consider second-order necessary conditions. Since one would think that some second derivative would have to be negative

semidefinite at a maximum, it is surprising that the nondegeneracy
of the constraint set is not an easy hypothesis to remove in looking
for second-order necessary conditions. Consider the following example of McCormick [51]:

Maximize $f(x, y) = -y$, subject to $g_1(x, y) \equiv -x^9 + y^3 \geq 0$,

$g_2(x, y) \equiv x^9 + y^3 \geq 0$, and $g_3(x, y) \equiv x^2 + (y + 1)^2 - 1 \geq 0$.

It is easy to see that $(0,0)$ is such a maximum and that constraint
qualification (KKT) is satisfied at $(0,0)$. The Lagrangian is

$$L = f + \lambda_1 g_1 + \lambda_2 g_2 + \tfrac{1}{2} g_3,$$

where λ_1 and λ_2 are arbitrary. But $D^2 L(0,0)$ is

$$\begin{bmatrix} 1 & 0 \\ 0 & 1 \end{bmatrix},$$

a positive definite matrix.

McCormick [51] also proves the following second-order necessary
condition.

THEOREM 4.5. *Suppose $f, g_1, \ldots, g_M, h_1, \ldots, h_N$ are C^2 func-
tions on $\mathbb{R}^n$ and x^0 maximizes f subject to $g(\underline{x}) \geq 0$ and $h(\underline{x}) = \underline{0}$.
Suppose further that (g, h) satisfies (KKT) and the following con-
straint qualification: for any $\underline{v} \in T_{x^0}\mathbb{R}^n$ such that $DG_E(\underline{x}^0)\underline{v} = 0$
and $Dh(\underline{x}^0)\underline{v} = 0$ there is a C^2 arc $a: [0,1] \to \mathbb{R}^n$ such that $a(0) =
\underline{x}^0$, $a'(0) = \underline{v}$, $g(a(t)) \equiv \underline{0}$ and $h(a(t)) \equiv \underline{0}$. Then, there exist
$\lambda_1, \ldots, \lambda_M$ nonnegative and $\mu_1, \ldots, \mu_N$ such that*

$$D\left[f + \sum_1^M \lambda_i g_i + \sum_1^N \mu_j h_j \right](\underline{x}^0) = \underline{0},$$

$$\underline{\lambda} \geq \underline{0}, \; \lambda_i g_i(\underline{x}^0) = 0,$$

and

$$D^2\left[f + \sum \lambda_i g_i + \sum \mu_j h_j \right](\underline{x}^0)(\underline{v}, \underline{v}) \leq 0$$

for all $\underline{v}$ with $Dg_E(\underline{x}^0)\underline{v} = 0$ and $Dh(\underline{x}^0)\underline{v} = \underline{0}$.

The proof of this theorem is very similar to that of Theorem 3.1.b and will be omitted. McCormick [51] also shows that the above second-order constraint qualification holds if $(Dg_E(\underline{x}^0),\ Dh(\underline{x}^0))$ has maximal rank.

See Kuhn [42] for an interesting historical survey of the theorems of this chapter. He describes the various applied problems which motivated the papers of Karush [38], John [36] and Kuhn-Tucker [43].

5. CONCAVE PROGRAMMING

5.1. First-order necessary conditions. In many optimization problems, one finds conditions that lead naturally to concave constraint and objective functions. Fortunately, for these situations one never has to use second order tests since, as in Theorem 2.3, the first-order necessary conditions are also sufficient. While discussing these results, we will first assume that there are only inequality constraints.

THEOREM 5.1. *Suppose that* $f, g_1, \ldots, g_m$ *are differentiable concave functions on* $\mathbb{R}^n$ *and that* $\underline{x}^0 \in C_g \equiv \{\underline{x} \in \mathbb{R}^n | g(\underline{x}) \geq \underline{0}\}$. *If there exist nonnegative* $\lambda_1, \ldots, \lambda_m$ *such that*

$$Df(\underline{x}^0) + \sum \lambda_i Dg_i(\underline{x}^0) = \underline{0} \quad and \quad \lambda_i g_i(\underline{x}^0) = 0 \quad for\ all\ i,$$

then $\underline{x}^0$ *maximizes* f *(globally) on* C_g. *Furthermore, the set of all such maximizers is convex.*

Proof. Note that $L(\underline{x}) = f(\underline{x}) + \sum \lambda_i g_i(\underline{x})$ is a nonnegative linear combination of concave functions and thus is concave. Since the g_i are concave, C_g is convex. By Theorem 2.3, $\underline{x}^0$ is a global maximizer of L since $DL(\underline{x}^0) = \underline{0}$. If $\underline{x}' \in C_g$ and $f(\underline{x}') > f(\underline{x}^0)$, then

$$L(\underline{x}') = f(\underline{x}') + \sum \lambda_i g_i(\underline{x}') \geq f(\underline{x}')$$
$$> f(\underline{x}^0) = f(\underline{x}^0) + \sum \lambda_i g(\underline{x}^0) = L(\underline{x}^0),$$

a contradiction. So, $\underline{x}^0$ maximizes u on C_g.

If $\underline{x}'$ and $\underline{x}^2$ maximize f on C_g, then $t\underline{x}' + (1 - t)\underline{x}^2 \in C_g$ and $f(t\underline{x}' + (1 - t)\underline{x}^2) \geq tf(\underline{x}') + (1 - t)f(\underline{x}^2) = f(\underline{x}')$ (or $f(\underline{x}^2)$). So, $t\underline{x}' + (1 - t)\underline{x}^2$ is also a maximizer.

The converse of Theorem 5.1 is true provided there is an $\underline{x}'$ with $g(\underline{x}') > 0$ by Theorem 4.3.b. One can add equality constraints $\{h_1 = \cdots = h_N = 0\}$ to the hypothesis of Theorem 5.1 provided the h_i are affine functions, i.e., $h_i(\underline{x}) = A_i\underline{x} + \underline{b}_i$. For then, $-h$ and h are concave and, as in Section 4, one replaces the N equality constraints $h = 0$ by the $2N$ inequality constraints $h \geq \underline{0}$, $-h \geq \underline{0}$.

Theorem 5.1 appears in Kuhn-Tucker [43]. Arrow-Enthoven [2] and Mangasarian [48] prove the following generalizations of Theorem 5.1, relaxing the concavity hypotheses. ∎

THEOREM 5.2. *Suppose that* $f, g_1, \ldots, g_M$ *are* C^1 *functions on* $\mathbb{R}^n$, *that* f *is pseudoconcave, and that the* g_i *are quasi-concave. Suppose that* $g(\underline{x}^0) \geq \underline{0}$ *and that there are nonnegative* $\lambda_1, \ldots, \lambda_M$ *with* $\lambda_i g_i(\underline{x}^0) = 0$ *for all* i

$$and\ D\Big[f + \sum \lambda_i g_i\Big]\big(\underline{x} - \underline{x}^0\big) \leq 0\ for\ all\ \underline{x} \in C_g. \qquad \text{(I)}$$

(*For example,* $D[f + \Sigma\lambda_i g_i](\underline{x}^0) = \underline{0}$.) *Then,* $\underline{x}^0$ *maximizes* f (*globally*) *on* C_g.

REMARK. One can now include more general equality constraints, i.e., h_i that are both pseudoconcave and pseudoconvex.

Proof. Let $\underline{x} \in C_g$. Then, $g_E(x) \geq 0 = g_E(\underline{x}^0)$. Since g_E is quasi-concave, $Dg_E(\underline{x}^0)(\underline{x} - \underline{x}^0) \geq \underline{0}$. Since $\lambda_I = \underline{0}$ and $\lambda_E \geq 0$, $\Sigma\lambda_i Dg_i(\underline{x}^0)(\underline{x} - \underline{x}^0) \geq 0$. By (I), $Df(\underline{x}^0)(\underline{x} - \underline{x}^0) \leq 0$. Since f is pseudoconcave, $f(\underline{x}) \leq f(\underline{x}^0)$. ∎

Note that we really only need g_E to be quasi-concave.

Finally, we note that for concave problems, not only is the solution set convex but the optimal value function is a convex function of the parameters.

THEOREM 5.3. a) *Suppose that* $f, g_1, \ldots, g_m$ *are concave functions on* $\mathbb{R}^n \times \mathbb{R}^p$, *where the last* p *variables are treated as parame-*

ters. Let $C_b = \{\underline{x} \in \mathbb{R}^n | g(\underline{x}, \underline{b}) \geq 0\}$ *and let* $\xi(b)$ *be the set of maximizers of* $f(\cdot, b)$ *on* C_b. *Finally, let* $v(\underline{b}) = f(\xi(\underline{b}), \underline{b})$. *Then,* $v(\underline{b})$ *is a concave function of* $\underline{b}$.

b) *Now drop the dependence of g on the parameter b and the concavity assumption on g. Suppose only that* $f(\underline{x}, \underline{b})$ *is convex as a function of* $\underline{b}$. *Then,* $v(\underline{b})$, *the maximum value of* $f(x, \underline{b})$ *subject to the constraint* $g(x) \geq 0$, *is also a convex function.*

Proof.   a) Let $\underline{b}_1$ and $\underline{b}_2$ be two parameter values. Let $\underline{x}_i = \xi(\underline{b}_i)$, $i = 1, 2$; so $g(\underline{x}_i, \underline{b}_i) \geq 0$ for $i = 1, 2$. Consider the convex combination $b_3 = \lambda \underline{b}_1 + (1 - \lambda)\underline{b}_2$ for some λ in $[0, 1]$. Since g is concave in $(\underline{x}, \underline{b})$,

$$g(\lambda \underline{x}_1 + (1 - \lambda)\underline{x}_2, \lambda \underline{b}_1 + (1 - \lambda)\underline{b}_2) \geq \lambda g(\underline{x}_1, b_1)$$
$$+ (1 - \lambda)g(\underline{x}_2, \underline{b}_2)$$
$$\geq 0.$$

Therefore, $\lambda x_1 + (1 - \lambda)x_2$ is in C_{b_3}. Now by the definition of v and the concavity of f,

$$v(\lambda \underline{b}_1 + (1 - \lambda)\underline{b}_2) \geq f(\lambda \underline{x}_1 + (1 - \lambda)\underline{x}_2, \lambda \underline{b}_1 + (1 - \lambda)\underline{b}_2)$$
$$\geq \lambda f(\underline{x}_1, \underline{b}_1) + (1 - \lambda)f(\underline{x}_2, \underline{b}_2)$$
$$= \lambda v(\underline{b}_1) + (1 - \lambda)v(\underline{b}_2).$$

b) Using the same notation as in a), let $\underline{x}_3$ denote $\xi(\underline{b}_3)$, where $\underline{b}_3 = \lambda \underline{b}_1 + (1 - \lambda)\underline{b}_2$. Note that $g(\underline{x}_i) \geq 0$ for $i = 1, 2, 3$; in particular $\underline{x}_3$ is in the constraint set when $\underline{x}_1$ and $\underline{x}_2$ were chosen. This implies

$$f(\underline{x}_3, \underline{b}_1) \leq f(\underline{x}_1, \underline{b}_1) \equiv v(\underline{b}_1)$$

and

$$f(\underline{x}_3, \underline{b}_2) \leq f(\underline{x}_2, \underline{b}_2) \equiv v(\underline{b}_2).$$

Therefore,

$$v(\lambda \underline{b}_1 + (1 - \lambda)\underline{b}_2) = f(\underline{x}_3, \lambda \underline{b}_1 + (1 - \lambda)\underline{b}_2)$$
$$\leq \lambda f(\underline{x}_3, \underline{b}_1) + (1 - \lambda)f(\underline{x}_3, \underline{b}_2)$$
$$\text{by the convexity of } f \text{ in } b$$
$$\leq \lambda v(\underline{b}_1) + (1 - \lambda)v(\underline{b}_2),$$

and v is convex in $\underline{b}$. ∎

Let $v(\underline{b})$ denote the maximum value function for the problem of maximizing $f(\underline{x})$ subject to the constraints $g(\underline{x}) \geqslant \underline{b}$, where $f, g_1, \ldots, g_m$ are concave functions. Let $\lambda(\underline{b})$ denote the corresponding multiplier. Theorem 3.7 showed that in the smooth, nondegenerate case $\lambda_i(\underline{b}) = \dfrac{\partial v}{\partial b_i}(b)$. One can use Theorem 5.3 and some basic theory about concave functions to show that when one replaces "smooth, nondegenerate" by "concave":

$$\lim_{h \to 0^+} \frac{v(\underline{b} + h\underline{e}_i) - v(\underline{b})}{h} \leq \lambda_i(b) \leq \lim_{h \to 0^-} \frac{v(\underline{b} + h\underline{e}_i) - v(\underline{b})}{h}.$$

See Dixit [18] for further discussion.

5.2. Saddle-point conditions. In order to *compute* maxima of f under constraints, one often considers the corresponding "saddle-point problem," especially when the functions involved are concave.

DEFINITION. Let $f, g_1, \ldots, g_M$ be continuous functions on $\mathbb{R}^n$. Consider the Lagrangian $L(\underline{x}, \lambda_1, \ldots, \lambda_M) = f(\underline{x}) + \Sigma \lambda_i g_i(\underline{x})$ as a function of $\underline{x}$ and $\underline{\lambda}$. Then, $(\underline{x}, \underline{\lambda})$ is a (nonnegative) *saddle point* of L if

$$L(\underline{x}, \lambda^0) \leq L(\underline{x}^0, \underline{\lambda}^0) \leq L(\underline{x}^0, \underline{\lambda}) \tag{J}$$

for all $\underline{\lambda} \geq \underline{0}$ in $\mathbb{R}^M$ and all $\underline{x} \in \mathbb{R}^n$ (and all $\underline{x} \geq \underline{0}$ in $\mathbb{R}^n$, where $\underline{x}^0 \geq \underline{0}$.)

THEOREM 5.4.   *If $(\underline{x}^0, \underline{\lambda}^0)$ is a (nonnegative) saddle point for L as above, then $\underline{x}^0$ maximizes f subject to $g \geq \underline{0}$ (and $\underline{x} \geq 0$).*

Proof. First, show $g(x^0) \geq 0$. The right side of (J) means that $\sum_i(\lambda_i - \lambda_i^0)g_i(\underline{x}^0) \geq 0$ for all $\lambda_i \geq 0$. For any fixed K, plug in $\lambda_K = \lambda_K^0 + 1 \geq 0$ and $\lambda_j = \lambda_j^0$ for $j \neq K$. Then, $g_K(\underline{x}^0) \geq 0$ and $\Sigma \lambda_i^0 g_i(\underline{x}^0) \geq 0$.

Setting $\underline{\lambda} = 0$ in (J) yields, $\Sigma\lambda_i^0 g_i(\underline{x}^0) \leq 0$. So, $\Sigma\lambda_i^0 g_i(\underline{x}^0) = 0$ and thus each $\lambda_i^0 g_i(\underline{x}^0) = 0$. If $g(\underline{x}) \geq 0$ (and $\underline{x} \geq \underline{0}$),

$$f(\underline{x}) \leq f(\underline{x}) + \sum\lambda_i^0 g_i(\underline{x}), \qquad \text{since each } \lambda_i^0 g_i(\underline{x}) \geq 0,$$
$$\leq f(\underline{x}^0) + \sum\lambda_i^0 g_i(\underline{x}^0), \qquad \text{by (J)},$$
$$= f(\underline{x}^0). \quad \blacksquare$$

In concave programming, solutions to the saddle-point problem are more or less equivalent to solutions of the programming problem, as Kuhn and Tucker [43] pointed out:

THEOREM 5.5. *Suppose that $f, g_1, \ldots, g_M$ are C^1 concave functions and that $\underline{x}^0$ maximizes f subject to $g \geq 0$ (and $\underline{x} \geq 0$). Suppose further that $g(\underline{x}') > \underline{0}$ for some $\underline{x}'$ (constraint qualification 4.3.b) or that g is linear. Then, there exists $\underline{\lambda}^0 \geq \underline{0}$ such that $(\underline{x}^0, \underline{\lambda}^0)$ is a (nonnegative) saddle point of*

$$L(\underline{x}, \underline{\lambda}) = f(\underline{x}) + \lambda \cdot \underline{g}(\underline{x}).$$

Proof. By Theorem 4.3, the Kuhn-Tucker conditions are satisfied, i.e., there exists $\underline{\lambda}^0 \geq \underline{0}$ with $\underline{\lambda}^0 \cdot g(\underline{x}^0) = 0$ and

$$Df(\underline{x}^0) + \sum\lambda_i^0 Dg_i(\underline{x}^0) = \underline{0}. \tag{K}$$

Since $L(\underline{x}, \underline{\lambda}^0)$ is a concave function of $\underline{x}$, for any $\underline{x} \in C_g$

$$L(\underline{x}, \underline{\lambda}^0) - L(\underline{x}^0, \underline{\lambda}^0) \leq \frac{\partial L}{\partial \underline{x}}(\underline{x}^0, \underline{\lambda}^0)(\underline{x} - \underline{x}^0) = \underline{0}$$

by (K) and Theorem 1.6, On the other hand, for any $\underline{\lambda} \geq \underline{0}$ in $\mathbb{R}^M$,

$$L(\underline{x}^0, \underline{\lambda}^0) = f(\underline{x}^0) + \underline{\lambda}^0 \cdot g(\underline{x}^0) \qquad (\text{since } \underline{\lambda}^0 \cdot g(\underline{x}^0) = 0)$$
$$= f(\underline{x}^0) \leq f(\underline{x}^0) + \underline{\lambda} \cdot \underline{g}(\underline{x}^0)$$
$$= L(\underline{x}^0, \underline{\lambda}). \quad \blacksquare$$

We will see in Section 6 that the saddle-point approach has certain advantages in economic problems. Furthermore, as we mentioned earlier, one can use this approach to compute solutions of concave programming problems and their corresponding multipliers.

5.3. Duality in linear programming. An important special case of concave programming is linear programming; and one of the most powerful tools in the theory of linear programming is the existence of a dual problem to every linear problem. If the original (or *primal*) problem arises from an economics question, the dual problem usually is filled with economic significance. An illustration of this fact will be discussed in Section 6.3. Consider the linear problem of maximizing

$$f(\underline{x}) = \underline{c} \cdot \underline{x}, \quad \text{subject to the constraints}$$

$$A\underline{x} \leq \underline{b} \text{ in } \mathbb{R}^M \quad \text{and} \quad \underline{x} \geq \underline{0} \text{ in } \mathbb{R}^n. \tag{L}$$

Then, the *dual problem* is that of minimizing

$$F(\underline{y}) = \underline{y} \cdot \underline{b}, \quad \text{subject to the constraints}$$

$$\underline{y}A \geq \underline{c} \text{ in } \mathbb{R}^n \quad \text{and} \quad \underline{y} \geq 0 \text{ in } \mathbb{R}^M. \tag{M}$$

If the jth inequality in the constraint $A\underline{x} \leq \underline{b}$ in (L) becomes an equality constraint, then the constraint $y_j \geq 0$ is dropped in (M).

We will use the above saddle-point theorems to give simple proofs of the basic facts on duality.

THEOREM 5.6. *Let* $\underline{c} \in \mathbb{R}^n$, $\underline{b} \in \mathbb{R}^M$, *and let* $A: \mathbb{R}^n \to \mathbb{R}^M$ *be a linear map. Let* (L) *denote the above primal problem and let* (M) *denote its dual. Then,*

i) $\underline{x} \in \mathbb{R}^n$ *solves* (L) *if and only if there is a* $y \in \mathbb{R}^M_+$ *such that* $(\underline{x}, y)$ *is a saddle point of* $L(\underline{x}, y) \equiv f(\underline{x}) + y \cdot (\underline{b} - A\underline{x})$;

ii) *if* $x \in \mathbb{R}^n$ *solves* (L), *then there exists a* $y \in \mathbb{R}^M$ *which solves* (M), *and conversely. Furthermore,* $\underline{c} \cdot \underline{x} = y \cdot \underline{b}$.

iii) *if the constraint sets of* (L) *and of* (M) *are nonempty, then both problems have solutions.*

iv) *if $\underline{x}'$ is in the constraint set of* (L) *and y' is in the constraint set of* (M) *such that $\underline{c} \cdot \underline{x}' = \underline{b} \cdot y'$, then $\underline{x}'$ solves* (L) *and y' solves* (M).

Proof. Part i) follows directly from Theorems 5.4 and 5.5. The Lagrangian for (M) is $M(y, \underline{x}) = -\underline{b} \cdot y + (yA - \underline{c}) \cdot \underline{x}$. Note that $M(y, \underline{x}) = -L(\underline{x}, y)$. By i), if $\underline{x}$ solves (L), there is a y such that $(\underline{x}, y)$ is a saddle point of L, i.e., $(y, \underline{x})$ is a saddle point for $-M$. By i) again, y solves (M). Since $y \cdot (\underline{b} - A\underline{x}) = 0$ and $(yA - \underline{c}) \cdot \underline{x} = 0$ for the optimal $\underline{x}$ and y by Theorem 4.3, $y \cdot \underline{b} = y \cdot (A\underline{x}) = (yA) \cdot \underline{x} = \underline{c} \cdot \underline{x}$, and ii) follows.

To prove iii), let y^0 lie in the constraint set of (M) and $\underline{x}^0$ in the constraint set of (L). Then,

$$\underline{c} \cdot \underline{x}^0 \le y^0 A \cdot \underline{x}^0 = y^0 \cdot A\underline{x}^0 \le y^0 \cdot \underline{b}. \qquad (N)$$

Thus, the linear function f is bounded on the closed constraint set of Problem (L). Consequently, f achieves its maximum on this set. One argues similarly for (M).

To prove iv), let $\underline{x}'$ and y' be as in the hypothesis and let $\underline{x}^0$ be any vector in the constraint set of (L). By (N),

$$\underline{c} \cdot \underline{x}^0 \le y' \cdot \underline{b} = \underline{c} \cdot \underline{x}'$$

i.e., $\underline{x}'$ maximizes $\underline{c} \cdot \underline{x}$ on the constraint set for (L). ∎

Note that by Theorem 5.3, the maximum value function $v(\underline{c}, \underline{b})$ of problem (L) is a concave function of $(\underline{c}, \underline{b})$.

Karlin [37], Mangasarian [48], and Intrilligator [35] have excellent discussions of duality theory. Mangasarian [48] also gives an introduction to the study of nonlinear duality. Kuhn [42] discusses the origins of duality in mathematical programming.

6. APPLICATIONS OF MATHEMATICAL
    PROGRAMMING TO ECONOMICS

Since one of the basic problems of economics is the allocation of scarce resources among competing groups, it is natural that much of mathematical economics deals with constrained maximization problems. In this section, we will examine some of the important programming problems that arise in economics, and we will try to use the theory of the last four sections to gain some insights into these problems. Most theoretical books on mathematical economics study these and related problems. The reader should refer to Debreu [14], Karlin [37], Baumol [6], Kuhn [41], Intrilligator [35], Malinvaud [45], Silberberg [60], and Varian [72], for further discussion of such problems. Kuhn [41] and Intrilligator [35] base their entire presentations on programming methods.

6.1. Theory of the consumer of household. We first examine an individual consumer's (or family's) consumption decision. We suppose that there are n commodities with $1 < n < \infty$ and with $x_i \in \mathbb{R}$ denoting the amount of the ith commodity. A *consumption vector* or *commodity vector* is an $\underline{x} = (x_1, \ldots, x_n)$ in $\mathbb{R}^n$, listing the amount of each commodity to be consumed. To develop our theory, we make the following assumptions about our consumer and the set of available commodity vectors.

We assume that each commodity is perfectly divisible so that any nonnegative quantity can be purchased. Thus, the *commodity space*, or space of all feasible commodity vectors, is

$$C = \left\{ \underline{x} \in \mathbb{R}^n | x_i \geq 0 \right\}.$$

We need not assume a bound on the availability of any commodity since budget restrictions will give us natural bounds.

We further assume that the tastes or preferences of the consumer are summarized by a complete preordering $\prec$ on C. The consumer prefers commodity vector y to commodity vector x (or finds them equally preferable) if and only if $\underline{x} \prec \underline{y}$. We assume that this preordering is continuous in that, for each $\underline{x} \in C$, $\{ y \in C | \underline{x} \prec \underline{y} \}$ and $\{ y \in C | y \prec \underline{x} \}$ are both closed sets. By a theorem of Debreu [14], there is a continuous function $u: C \to \mathbb{R}$ such that $\underline{x} \prec \underline{y}$ if and only if $u(\underline{x}) \leq u(\underline{y})$. The function u is called a utility function. (Note that infinitely many utility functions can represent the same preference ordering.)

We assume a fixed price vector $\underline{p} = (p_1, \ldots, p_n) \in \mathbb{R}^n$ with each p_i a positive number giving the unit price of the ith commodity. The consumer has an initial wealth w in $\mathbb{R}_+$. In some problems, he has an initial commodity vector $\underline{x}^0 \in C$, in which case his initial wealth is $w = \underline{p} \cdot \underline{x}^0$.

Finally, the consumer's goal is to select the commodity vector $\underline{x} \in C$ which is affordable yet maximizes his preference ordering among all affordable vectors in C. Mathematically, his problem is to find $\underline{x} \in \mathbb{R}^n$ such that $\underline{x}$ maximizes u subject to the constraints

$$0 \le x_i, \quad \text{for } i = 1, \ldots, n; \qquad \underline{p} \cdot \underline{x} \le w. \qquad (O)$$

Note that since the constraint set is closed and bounded and u is continuous, problem (O) has a solution for each $\underline{p}$ and w.

Our first application of programming theory to this problem is to derive the norm that an interior optimal allocation, the marginal rate of substitution of good i with respect to good j, equals p_i/p_j. At commodity vector $\underline{x}^0 \in C$, the *marginal rate of substitution* (MRS) of good j with respect to good i is

$$\frac{\partial u}{\partial x_i}(\underline{x}^0) \bigg/ \frac{\partial u}{\partial x_j}(\underline{x}^0).$$

It measures (at the infinitesimal level) the additional quantity of good j which would compensate the consumer for a one-unit loss of good i while keeping the consumer's utility constant. To see this, fix x_k^0 for $k \ne i, j$ and write

$$u\left(x_1^0, \ldots, x_i, x_{i+1}^0, \ldots, x_j(x_i), \ldots, x_n^0\right) = u\left(\underline{x}^0\right)$$

to indicate how a change in x_i brings about a change in x_j at the same utility level. Taking the derivatives with respect to x_i and evaluating $\underline{x}^0$ yields

$$\frac{\partial u}{\partial x_i}(\underline{x}^0) + \frac{\partial u}{\partial x_j}(\underline{x}^0)\frac{dx_j}{dx_i}(\underline{x}^0) = 0$$

or

$$\frac{dx_j}{dx_i} = -\frac{\partial u}{\partial x_i}(\underline{x}^0) \bigg/ \frac{\partial u}{\partial x_j}(\underline{x}^0).$$

The MRS is the slope of the consumer's indifference set, $\{y | u(y) = u(\underline{x}^0)\}$, at $\underline{x}^0$ in the $i - j$ direction and measures the consumer's relative internal valuation of goods i and j. The optimality condition states that this internal valuation should equal the market's valuation, p_i/p_j.

THEOREM 6.1. *Suppose that* $u: C \to \mathbb{R}$ *is a* C^1 *utility function with the property that for each* $\underline{x} \in C$ *there is an* i *such that* $\dfrac{\partial u}{\partial x_i}(\underline{x}) > 0$. *Suppose that* $\underline{p}$ *is a positive price vector and that* $\underline{x}^0 \in C$ *is a solution to problem* (O) *above. Then, there is an* $\eta > 0$ *in* $\mathbb{R}$ *such that*

i) $\dfrac{1}{p_i}\dfrac{\partial u}{\partial x_i}(\underline{x}^0) \le \eta$ *for* $i = 1, \ldots, n$ *with equality for those* i

with

$x_i^0 \ne 0$,

ii) *thus, if* $\underline{x}^0$ *lies in the interior of* C, $\dfrac{\partial u}{\partial x_i}(\underline{x}^0) > 0$ *for all* i *and*

$\nabla u(\underline{x}^0) = \eta \underline{p}$,

iii) *if* x_i^0 *and* x_j^0 *are nonzero, then* $\dfrac{\partial u}{\partial x_j}(\underline{x}^0) > 0$,

$$\frac{1}{p_i}\frac{\partial u}{\partial x_i}(\underline{x}^0) = \frac{1}{p_j}\frac{\partial u}{\partial x_j}(\underline{x}^0), \text{ and } \frac{\partial u}{\partial x_i}(\underline{x}^0) \bigg/ \frac{\partial u}{\partial x_j}(\underline{x}^0) = \frac{p_i}{p_j},$$

iv) $\underline{p} \cdot \underline{x}^0 = w$ *(all income is spent)*.

Conversely, if u is C^1 and pseudoconcave (e.g., u is C^2 and quasi-concave) and some $\dfrac{\partial u}{\partial x_i}$ is positive at each $\underline{x}$ and if $\underline{x}^0$ satisfies i) and iv) for some $\eta > 0$, then $\underline{x}^0$ is a global solution of problem (O).

Figure 1 below illustrates Theorem 6.1 for an interior solution $\underline{x}^0$ of problem (O) when $n = 2$. The straight line through $\left(\dfrac{w}{p_1}, 0\right)$ and $\left(0, \dfrac{w}{p_2}\right)$ is the price line $p_1 x_1 + p_2 x_2 = w$, which is perpendicular to the (dotted) price vector (p_1, p_2). The curved lines are the level sets of u with u increasing as x_1 and x_2 go to $+\infty$. Note that at the maximizer $\underline{x}^0$, $\nabla u(\underline{x}^0)$ is perpendicular to the price line and therefore parallel to (p_1, p_2) as ii) indicates.

Proof. One merely applies the Kuhn-Tucker conditions of Theorem 4.3 to problem (O). Since the constraints are defined by linear

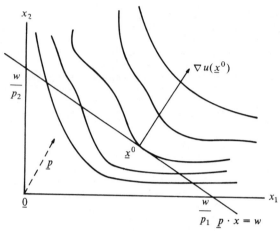

FIGURE 1

functions, constraint qualifications KKT and (4.3.c) hold automatically. By Theorem 4.3, there are nonnegative Lagrange multipliers $\lambda_1, \ldots, \lambda_n, \eta$ such that for each i

$$\frac{\partial u}{\partial x_i}(\underline{x}^0) + \lambda_i - \eta p_i = 0$$

where $\lambda_i x_i^0 = \eta(w - \underline{p} \cdot \underline{x}^0) = 0$. Since

$$\frac{1}{p_i} \frac{\partial u}{\partial x_i}(\underline{x}^0) - \eta = -\frac{\lambda_i}{p_i} \leq 0$$

and $\lambda_i x_i^0 = 0$, i), ii) and iii) follow. Since

$$\frac{\partial u}{\partial x_i}(\underline{x}^0) > 0$$

for some i and $p_i > 0$, $\eta > 0$ by i). Since

$$\eta\left(w - \underline{p} \cdot \underline{x}^0\right) = 0,$$

$w = \underline{p} \cdot \underline{x}^0$ as in iv).
The converse follows from Theorem 5.2. ∎

The correspondence which sends each price vector $\underline{p}$ and each initial wealth w to the corresponding optimal commodity vector or vectors (i.e., solutions of problem (O)) is called the *demand correspondence* and will be written as

$$(\underline{p}, w) \mapsto \xi(\underline{p}, w) \in C.$$

If u is *strictly* concave, then ξ is a single valued function. Furthermore, if one makes the slightly stronger assumptions that u is C^2 and that $D^2 u(\underline{x})$ is negative definite on C, then ξ is a C^1 function when it takes on values in the interior of C. One can use the Kuhn-Tucker equations (i) in Theorem 6.1 to compute the derivatives of ξ.

THEOREM 6.2.   *Suppose that u is a C^2 utility function on C with ξ the corresponding demand correspondence. Suppose that for some $\underline{x}^0$ in the interior of C, some price vector p^0 and some wealth $w^0 = p^0 \cdot \underline{x}^0$, $\underline{x}^0 = \xi(\underline{p}^0, w^0)$. Suppose that $(\partial u / \partial x_i)(\underline{x}^0) > 0$ for some i and $D^2 u(\underline{x}^0)(\underline{v}, \underline{v}) < 0$ for all nonzero $\underline{v}$ such that $\underline{p}^0 \cdot \underline{v} = 0$. (For example, $D^2 u(x^0)$ may be negative definite).*

Then, there are neighborhoods U of $\underline{x}^0$, V of $\underline{p}^0$, and W of $\underline{w}^0$ such that $\xi: V \times W \to U$ is a C^1 mapping. Furthermore, the multiplier η in Theorem 6.1 also equals $\partial u(\xi(p, w)) / \partial w$ and therefore measures the sensitivity of the optimal value of u to change in the initial wealth w. (It is often called the marginal utility of money.)

Proof. Choose a neighborhood U_1 of $\underline{x}^0$ such that for all $\underline{x} \in U_1$, $x_i > 0$ for all i and $\dfrac{\partial u}{\partial x_j}(\underline{x}) > 0$ for some j. Now apply Theorem 3.7 to the problem of maximizing u under the constraints $\underline{x} \in U_1$ and $\underline{x} \cdot \underline{p} = w$. ∎

One can use some further optimization theory to derive more properties of ξ and its derivatives. Consider first the related problem of choosing the commodity bundle which achieves a fixed level of utility at minimum expenditure, i.e.,

$$\text{Minimize } \underline{p} \cdot \underline{x} \text{ subject to } u(\underline{x}) \geq u \text{ and } \underline{x} \geq \underline{0}. \qquad (O')$$

Let $z(p, u)$ be the minimizer of (O'); z is called the *compensated* (or Hicksian) *demand function* since in its construction, income changes compensate for price changes to keep the consumer at a fixed level of utility.

In addition, consider the optimal value functions for problems (O) and (O'). The function $v(\underline{p}, w) = u(\xi(\underline{p}, w))$ is called the consumer's *indirect utility function* and $M(\underline{p}, u) = \underline{p} \cdot z(\underline{p}, u)$ is called the consumer's *expenditure function*. Note that M is a concave function of $\underline{p}$ by Theorem 5.3.b. These functions play a central role in modern consumer theory. We first list some elementary facts about them. The nonlinear programming problems (O) and (O') are dual to each other in a natural way. Statements 4) and 5) in Theorem 6.3 are nonlinear analogues of Theorem 5.5.

THEOREM 6.3.   *Let ξ, z, v, and M be as in the above paragraph. Then*
1) $\xi(\lambda \underline{p}, \lambda w) = \xi(\underline{p}, w)$ *for all* $\lambda > 0$ (*homogeneity*)
2) $z(\underline{p}, u) = \xi(\underline{p}, M(\underline{p}, u))$
3) $\xi(\underline{p}, w) = z(\underline{p}, v(\underline{p}, w))$
4) $u = v(\underline{p}, M(\underline{p}, u))$
5) $w = M(\underline{p}, v(\underline{p}, w))$.

Proof.   1) follows from the fact that $\underline{p} \cdot \underline{x} = w$ and $(\lambda \underline{p}) \cdot \underline{x} = (\lambda w)$ are equivalent constraints. To prove 3), we show that if $\underline{x}^*$ solves (O), then it solves (O') with $u = u(\underline{x}^*)$. By the Saddle-Point Theorem 5.5,

$$u(\underline{x}) + \lambda^*(w - \underline{p} \cdot \underline{x}) \leq u(\underline{x}^*) + \lambda^*(w - \underline{p} \cdot \underline{x}^*) \qquad (*)$$

for all $\underline{x} \geq 0$ where λ^* is the multiplier in (O) corresponding to $\underline{x}^*$.

Let $\underline{x}'$ be an arbitrary bundle in the constraint set of (O'), i.e.,

$$u(\underline{x}') \geq u(\underline{x}^*) \quad \text{and} \quad \underline{x}' \geq 0. \tag{**}$$

Then,

$$u(\underline{x}^*) + \lambda^*(w - \underline{p} \cdot x') \leq u(\underline{x}') + \lambda^*(w - \underline{p} \cdot x')$$
$$\leq u(x^*) + \lambda^*(w - \underline{p} \cdot x^*)$$

by (**) and (*). These imply that $\underline{p} \cdot x' \geq \underline{p} \cdot \underline{x}^*$, and so $\underline{x}^*$ is a solution of (O').

The proof of 2) is similar; 4) and 5) follow directly from 2) and 3) by evaluation. ∎

We can now compute some properties of ξ and its derivatives.

THEOREM 6.4. *Assume that ξ, z, v, and M are C^1 functions. (See, for example, the hypotheses of Theorem 6.2.) Then,*

1) $\xi_i(\underline{p}, w) = -\dfrac{\partial v(\underline{p}, w)}{\partial p_i} \bigg/ \dfrac{\partial v(\underline{p}, w)}{\partial w}$ *(Roy's Identity)*

2) $\dfrac{\partial \xi_j}{\partial p_i}(\underline{p}, w) = \dfrac{\partial z_j(p, v(p, w))}{\partial p_i} - \dfrac{\partial \xi_j(p, w)}{\partial w} \cdot \xi_i$

                                              (Slutsky Equation)

3) *The matrix of "substitution terms"*

$$\left(\left(\dfrac{\partial z_j(p, u)}{\partial p_i}\right)\right) = \left(\left(\dfrac{\partial \xi_j}{\partial p_i}(p, w) + \xi_i \dfrac{\partial \xi_j}{\partial w}(p, w)\right)\right)$$

is a symmetric, negative semidefinite matrix.

  4) *In particular,*

$$\dfrac{\partial z_i}{\partial p_i}(p, u) \leq 0$$

and

$$\frac{\partial \xi_i}{\partial p_i} + \xi_i \frac{\partial \xi_i}{\partial w} \le 0.$$

Proof. 1) follows from differentiating 4) in the statement of Theorem 6.3 with respect to p_i:

$$0 = \frac{\partial v}{\partial p_i} + \frac{\partial v}{\partial w} \cdot \frac{\partial M}{\partial p_i}.$$

But $(\partial M/\partial p_i)(p, u) = \xi_i$, since by the Envelope Theorem 3.8.b,

$$\frac{\partial M(p, u)}{\partial p_i} = \frac{\partial}{\partial p_i} \left[\underline{x} \cdot \underline{p} + \mu(u(\underline{x}) - u(\underline{x}^*)) \right]$$
$$= x_i^* = z_i(\underline{p}, u) = \xi_i(\underline{p}, M(\underline{p}, u)). \qquad (***)$$

Conclusion 2) follows from differentiating equation 2) in Theorem 6.3 with respect to p_i:

$$\frac{\partial z_j}{\partial p_i}(p, u) = \frac{\partial \xi_j}{\partial p_i}(\underline{p}, w) + \frac{\partial \xi_j}{\partial w}(\underline{p}, w) \cdot \frac{\partial M}{\partial p_i}(p, u).$$

Then, apply (***) and rearrange terms. To prove the symmetry in 3), recall from (***) that

$$\frac{\partial M}{\partial p_i}(\underline{p}, u) = z_i(\underline{p}, u).$$

So,

$$\frac{\partial z_i}{\partial p_j} = \frac{\partial^2 M}{\partial p_j \partial p_i} = \frac{\partial^2 M}{\partial p_i \partial p_j} = \frac{\partial z_j}{\partial p_i}.$$

Since M is concave by Theorem 5.3.b, its Hessian is negative-semi-definite. Finally 4) follows from the fact that the 1×1 principal minors of a negative semidefinite matrix must be nonpositive. ∎

The Slutsky equation in 2) of Theorem 6.4 is an important relationship between the two demand functions ξ and z. If we write this equation as

$$\Delta x_j \cong \frac{\partial \xi_j}{\partial p_i} \Delta p_i = \frac{\partial z_j}{\partial p_i}(p, u) \cdot \Delta p_i - \frac{\partial \xi_j}{\partial w} \cdot x_i \cdot \Delta p_i,$$

we see that the change in demand Δx_j due to a change in price Δp_i decomposes into two separate effects: the *substitution effect* $(\partial z_j / \partial p_i)(p, u) \cdot \Delta p_i$, during which utility is held constant, and the *income effect* $(\partial \xi_j / \partial w) \cdot x_i \cdot \Delta p_i$, in which $x_i \Delta p_i$ represents the change in income.

It turns out that conclusion 3) in Theorem 6.4 provides a necessary and sufficient condition for an observed demand function $\xi(p, w)$ to arise from utility maximization. See Samuelson [58] and Hurwicz and Uzawa [34].

6.2. Theory of the firm or producer. We turn now to an analysis of the economic behavior of a firm. A firm uses inputs such as materials, labor, and land to produce outputs which it sells to households or other firms. Given the price and supply of each input, the price and demand of each output, and the technological relations between input and output, the firm must decide how much to produce and how much input to use in this production in order to meet its economic objectives.

Suppose that the firm in question produces a single commodity from n inputs. Let x_i denote the quantity of the ith input, $\underline{x} = (x_1, \ldots, x_n)$ the resulting *input vector*, and $y \in \mathbb{R}$ the amount of output produced. We assume that there is a *production function* $f: \mathbb{R}^n \to \mathbb{R}$, where $f(\underline{x})$ denotes the maximum output for each input vector $\underline{x}$.

In order to examine the most general situations, let $p_1(y)$ and $p_2(\underline{x})$ denote the inverse demand functions for output and input, respectively, i.e., $p_1(y)$ is the unit price a firm can charge if its level of output is y and $p_2(\underline{x}) \in \mathbb{R}^n_+$ is the input price vector which the firm will pay if it needs input vector $\underline{x}$. For a firm in *perfect competition*, p_1 and p_2 are constant; for a *monopolist* firm, p_2 is constant but p_1 is not and the firm can control the price of its product by varying production amounts; for a *monopsonistic* firm, p_1 is constant but p_2 is not and the firm can influence the price of an input by varying its purchases of the input.

Let us assume first that our firm wants to maximize its profit, $\Pi = p_1(y)y - p_2(\underline{x}) \cdot \underline{x}$, where $y = f(\underline{x})$. We can use the results of chapter two to find a necessary condition for such a maximum, namely that the marginal revenue product equals the marginal cost of each input. The *marginal cost* of input k is, of course, $(\partial/\partial x_k)p_2(\underline{x}) \cdot \underline{x}$. The *marginal revenue product* of input k is the marginal revenue,

$$\left.\frac{dp_1(y)y}{dy}\right|_{y=f(\underline{x})},$$

times the marginal product of input k, $(\partial f/\partial x_k)(\underline{x})$. To derive this norm, one merely sets the first derivative of Π with respect to x_k equal to zero.

If one considers the case of a firm in perfect competition where $p_1 = p$ and $\underline{p}_2 = w$ are constant, the above norm becomes

$$p\nabla f(\underline{x}^0) = \underline{w}. \tag{P}$$

If one assumes further that the production function is concave, then one learns from Theorem 2.3 that (P) is also a sufficient condition for $\underline{x}^0$ to be an input which maximizes profit. In this case, the firm is operating at the optimal input level if an additional unit of output will bring in as much revenue as it costs to produce. Furthermore, as in Section 6.1, one can define $\chi(p, \underline{w}) = \underline{x}^0$ to be the solution of (P) for a fixed p and w. This correspondence is called the *input demand correspondence*. If f is strictly concave, χ is a single-valued function, which is homogeneous of degree zero. If f is C^2 and $D^2 f(x)$ is negative definite for all x, then χ is C^1. The function $F(p, \underline{w}) = f(\chi(p, \underline{w}))$ is called the *output supply function*, a component in the usual demand/supply analysis.

One can derive conditions on the derivatives of these functions by using techniques similar to those in Theorems 6.3 and 6.4 of the previous section. Let $\pi^*(p, \underline{w}) = \pi(\chi(p, \underline{w}))$ be the optimal profit function. By the Envelope Theorem 3.8.a;

$$\frac{\partial \pi^*(p, \underline{w})}{\partial p} = y = F(p, \underline{w})$$

and

$$\frac{\partial \pi^*(p, \underline{w})}{\partial w_i} = -x_i = -\chi_i(p, \underline{w}). \qquad (*)$$

The latter leads to the *reciprocity condition*:

$$\frac{\partial \chi_j}{\partial w_i}(p, \underline{w}) = -\frac{\partial^2 \pi^*}{\partial w_i \partial w_j} = -\frac{\partial^2 \pi^*}{\partial w_j \partial w_i} = \frac{\partial \chi_i}{\partial w_j}(p, \underline{w}),$$

i.e., the effect of a change in the wage of the ith input on the demand for the jth input is the same as the effect of a change in the wage of the jth input on the demand for the ith input. The first equation in (1) leads to:

$$\frac{\partial \chi_i}{\partial p}(p, \underline{w}) = -\frac{\partial^2 \pi^*}{\partial p \partial w_i} = -\frac{\partial^2 \pi^*}{\partial w_i \partial p} = -\frac{\partial F}{\partial w_i}(p, \underline{w});$$

so an increase in the output price raises the demand for input i if and only if an increase in the wage of input i reduces the optimal output. Finally, by Theorem 5.3.b, $\pi^*(p, w)$ is a convex function, and so its Hessian is positive semidefinite. In particular, this means that $\partial \chi_i / \partial w_i = -\dfrac{\partial^2 \pi^*}{\partial w_i^2}$ must be negative for all i; an increase in the wage of an input always leads to a reduction in its demand. See Varian [72] and Silberberg [60] for further discussion.

Let us now change the problem a little. Suppose that the firm in question has its policy determined by a manager whose objective is to maximize sales, i.e., revenue, without letting the profit drop below some fixed level. (See Baumol [6] for a complete discussion of such firms and Kuhn [41] for the following mathematical analysis.) To make things even more interesting, let us add an advertising cost $a \in \mathbb{R}_+$ to this problem. Let $R(y, a)$ denote the firm's revenue when the level of production is $y \in \mathbb{R}_+$ and the advertising cost is

$a \in \mathbb{R}_+$. Let $C(y)$ denote the cost of manufacturing y units of output. We will assume not only that C and R are C^1 functions but also that $C'(y) > 0$ (increased production implies increased costs) and $\partial R / \partial a > 0$ (increased advertising brings in increased revenues). Our programming problem is to maximize $R(y, a)$ subject to the constraints $y \geq 0$, $a \geq 0$, and

$$\Pi \equiv R(y, a) - C(y) - a \geq m.$$

Assume that (y^0, a^0) is an optimal solution with $y^0 > 0$. In addition, assume that some constraint qualification is valid at (y^0, a^0), e.g., R may be concave and C convex. Then, there are nonnegative multipliers μ^0 and $v^{\underline{0}}$ such that the Lagrangian

$$L(y, a) = R(y, a) + \mu^0 a + v^{\underline{0}}[R(y, a) - C(y) - a - m]$$

has a critical point at (y^0, a^0). In other words,

$$\frac{\partial L}{\partial y}(y^0, a^0, \lambda^0, \mu^0, v^{\underline{0}}) = (1 + v^{\underline{0}})\frac{\partial R}{\partial y} - v^{\underline{0}}C'(y^0) = 0 \quad \text{(Q)}$$

and

$$\frac{\partial L}{\partial a}(y^0, a^0, \lambda^0, \mu^0, v^{\underline{0}}) = (1 + v^{\underline{0}})\frac{\partial R}{\partial a} + \mu^0 - v^{\underline{0}} = 0. \quad \text{(R)}$$

Since $\partial R / \partial a > 0$ and $v^{\underline{0}} \geq 0$, $\mu^0 - v^{\underline{0}} < 0$ in (R). Since $\mu^0 \geq 0$, $v^{\underline{0}}$ must be strictly positive. Therefore, $\Pi(y^0, a^0) = m$; the profit realized is the minimal profit allowed. Since $v^{\underline{0}} > 0$ and $C'(y^0) > 0$ in (Q), $(\partial R / \partial y)(y^0, a^0) > 0$ and marginal revenue is positive at the optimum level. On the other hand, the marginal profit, $\partial \Pi / \partial y$, is negative at (y^0, a^0) since

$$(1 + v^{\underline{0}})\frac{\partial \Pi}{\partial y}(y^0, a^0) = \frac{\partial L}{\partial y}(y^0, a^0) - C'(y^0)$$

$$= 0 - C'(y^0) < 0.$$

Consequently, output y^0 is greater than the output in the profit-maximizing situation. Finally, by Theorem 3.7, the multiplier $v^{\underline{0}}$ can be interpreted as the marginal loss in maximal revenue with respect to the limit on profit.

Just as we added advertising cost to our study of a sales maximizing firm, so the economist can use programming principles to determine the effect of such items as sales taxes and regulatory constraints on the optimal behavior of a firm. For example, see Averch and Johnson [5] for an analysis of how a "fair rate of return" regulatory constraint would alter the behavior of a monopolist firm.

6.3. Activity analysis. In this section, we will apply the linear duality theory, discussed at the end of Section 5, to the important problem of the activity analysis of production. In this model, a firm in a competitive economy produces k different outputs from m different resources or inputs. Furthermore, different combinations of inputs can be used to produce the same combination of outputs, but these transformations are organized into n processes or *activities*, where $1 \leq n < \infty$. The jth activity, for example, combines the k inputs in fixed proportions into the m outputs in fixed proportions at some nonnegative level or intensity, $z_j \geq 0$.

The firm's technology is then described by an $m \times n$ matrix $A = ((a_{ij}))$ and a $k \times n$ matrix $B = ((b_{ij}))$, where $a_{ij} > 0$ is the amount of the jth input used in operating the jth activity at unit intensity and $b_{ij} > 0$ is the amount of the ith output produced when process j runs at unit intensity. If the firm conducts all its activities at the same time with the jth activity at level $z_j \geq 0$ for $j = 1, \ldots, n$, then it transforms the input vector $\underline{x} = A\underline{z} \in \mathbb{R}_+^m$ into the output vector $\underline{y} = B\underline{z} \in \mathbb{R}_+^k$.

Let $p_i > 0$ denote the fixed market price for the ith output, $i = 1, \ldots, k$: and let $q_i > 0$ denote the fixed market price for the ith input, $i = 1, \ldots, m$. Thus, $\underline{p} = (p_1, \ldots, p_k)$ and $\underline{q} = (q_1, \ldots, q_m)$ are the corresponding price vectors in an economy of perfect competition. Let b_i denote the available stock of the ith resource or input, with $\underline{b} = (b_1, \ldots, b_k)$.

If the firm's director wants to maximize profits, he must solve the following linear programming problem:

Find an activity vector $\underline{z}$ in $\mathbb{R}^m$ such that $\underline{z}$ maximizes $\underline{p} \cdot \underline{y} - \underline{q} \cdot \underline{x}$ subject to

$$\underline{x} = A\underline{z}, \quad \underline{y} = B\underline{z}, \quad \underline{x} \leq \underline{b}, \quad \underline{z} \geq \underline{0}.$$

If we substitute the equality constraints into the profit function, the problem becomes:

Find $z \in \mathbb{R}^n$ such that z maximizes

$$p \cdot Bz - q \cdot Az$$

subject to $Az \leq b$ and $z \geq 0$.

Finally, if we let $r = B^t p - A^t q$ in $\mathbb{R}^n$, r_j denotes the value or profit of the output achieved by operating the jth activity at unit level. We then want to choose z to

$$\text{maximize} \quad r \cdot z \quad \text{subject to} \quad Az \leq b \quad \text{and} \quad z \geq 0. \quad \text{(S)}$$

One can, of course, use the simplex algorithm to solve this linear programming problem; but let us see what we can learn about the problem and its solution from our programming theory. The Lagrangian is

$$L(z, \lambda) = r \cdot z + \lambda \cdot (b - Az).$$

The Kuhn-Tucker necessary and sufficient conditions for a solution are that we find a $\lambda \geq 0$ in $\mathbb{R}^m$ and a $z \geq 0$ in $\mathbb{R}^n$ such that

$$r - A^t \lambda \leq 0, \qquad z \cdot (r - A^t \lambda) = 0, \qquad \lambda \cdot (b - Az) = 0.$$

If we have such a λ, then by Theorem 3.9, λ_i can be regarded as the infinitesimal change in maximal profit as the amount of the ith resource that is available increases. It can, therefore, be interpreted as the firm's internal valuation of the ith resource and is usually called the firm's imputed or *shadow price* of this input.

This naturally leads us to consider the dual problem, as discussed in Section 5. The dual problem to (S) is to

$$\text{find } \lambda \geq 0 \text{ in } \mathbb{R}^m \text{ such that } \lambda \text{ minimizes } \lambda \cdot b$$
$$\text{subject to the constraints } \lambda A \geq r. \quad \text{(S')}$$

If λ is the shadow price vector described above, $\lambda \cdot b$ is the total value which the firm sets on its resources in stock (in its internal price system). Examining the constraint in (S′), one notices that the jth component of $\lambda A = A^t\lambda$ is the total value of the output as a result of operating activity j at unit intensity in the internal price system λ and that r_j is the actual value of this output (in the external price system). Therefore, in solving (S′), the firm tries to determine a valuation or internal price system on its resources so that the value of its resources will be minimized under the constraint that when the firm operates any activity at unit level the total value of the resulting output in the internal valuation must be at least as large as its total value in the market's price system. Karlin [37] summarizes this constraint by stating that "internal prices cannot be set to get more value from a product than you put into it."

Let $z^* \in \mathbb{R}^n_+$ be the activity vector which solves (S) and let λ^* be the shadow price vector which solves (S′). By Theorem 5.5, $z^* \cdot r = \lambda^* \cdot b$, i.e., the optimal total profit in the activity analysis problem equals the minimal total (internal) value of the resources in stock. This equation is closely related to the macroeconomic norm that the value of the final goods produced (national product) must equal the cost of the primary factors of production (national income).

An alternate but related interpretation of the dual problem is the viewpoint of a competitor who wants to buy the resources of the producer (possibly believing that he can use them more efficiently). He offers to pay the producer the amount λ_i for each unit of resource i. The constraint $\lambda A \geq r$ assures the original producer that "the amount offered is at least as much as he could obtain from any production schedule." (Gale [25]) The competitor tries to minimize the total cost of his purchase subject to the above assurance to the producer. By (N), the producer has nothing to lose and may even gain if his competitor misses the optimal buy-out price.

In programming problems where the primal problem describes the search for the best joint strategy in a decentralized economic system, the dual problem often can be interpreted as a central planner's viewpoint of the same system.

Finally, we can use the activity analysis model to gain further insight into the economists' enthusiasm for the saddle-point approach to concave programming. Generalizing (S), consider the problem of maximizing $f(\underline{x})$ subject to $\underline{x} \geq 0$ and $g(\underline{x}) \leq \underline{b}$. Assume that $\underline{x} \geq \underline{0}$ represents the activity level of a firm's operations, f is a C^1 concave function representing the value of the firm's output for any given activity level, $\underline{b}$ is a constant vector which measures the amount of primary resources that are available, and $g(\underline{x})$ is a measure of the amount of these resources used when the activity vector is $\underline{x}$.

The Lagrangian function for this problem is $L(\underline{x}, \underline{\lambda}) = f(\underline{x}) + \underline{\lambda}[\underline{b} - g(\underline{x})]$, and, as mentioned above, $\underline{\lambda}$ can be viewed as the vector of shadow prices for the primary resources. Thus, L is the combined value of the firm's outputs and the unused balance of primary resources. Suppose there is an $\underline{x}' \geq 0$ with $g(\underline{x}') < \underline{b}$, and that $\underline{x}^0$ maximizes f subject to $g(\underline{x}) \leq \underline{b}$ and $\underline{x} \geq \underline{0}$. Then, by Theorem 5.5, there is a $\underline{\lambda}^0 \geq \underline{0}$ such that L has a saddle point at $(\underline{x}^0, \underline{\lambda}^0)$, i.e.,

$$L(\underline{x}, \underline{\lambda}^0) \leq L(\underline{x}^0, \underline{\lambda}^0) \leq L(\underline{x}^0, \underline{\lambda}) \quad \text{for all} \quad \underline{x} \geq 0, \underline{\lambda} \geq 0.$$

(By Theorem 5.4, $\underline{x}^0$ solves problem (S) if $(\underline{x}^0, \underline{\lambda}^0)$ is a saddle point of L.) The existence of $(\underline{x}^0, \underline{\lambda}^0)$ expresses an equilibrium between the value of the output and the prices of the available resources and is a basic step in the theory of equilibria for production economics.

For further discussion on the activity analysis problem the reader is referred to Koopmans [40], Karlin [37], Charnes-Cooper [10], Varaiya [71], and Silberberg [60].

7. VECTOR MAXIMIZATION

7.1. Preliminaries. In the applications of Section 6, we studied an individual consumer trying to maximize his utility function under budgetary constraints and a single firm striving to maximize its profits or sales while producing a single output from a stock of available resources. The next step is to examine economies where a number of consumers compete among themselves for goods and services and where firms producing a number of products decide on optimal output *vectors*. To treat such problems as a large number of independent maximization problems would be to ignore not only the boundedness of the stock of available goods and resources but also the interactions between the various components of the economy. More importantly, such a treatment will usually lead to a mathematical problem with an empty solution set. We therefore introduce the more natural notion of a vector maximum or Pareto optimum for situations where a number of different participants are trying to meet their independent objectives.

DEFINITION. Let C be a subset of $\mathbb{R}^n$. Let $u_1, \ldots, u_a$ be real-valued functions on C. Then, $u = (u_1, \ldots, u_a)$ has a *vector maximum* or *Pareto optimum* at $\underline{x}^0 \in C$ if there is no $\underline{x} \in C$ such that $u_i(\underline{x}^0) \leq u_i(\underline{x})$ for all i and $u_j(\underline{x}^0) < u_j(\underline{x})$ for some j, i.e., such that $u(\underline{x}^0) \leq u(\underline{x})$ but $u(\underline{x}^0) \neq u(\underline{x})$ in the usual partial ordering on $\mathbb{R}^a$.

A number of recent papers have proven necessary conditions and sufficient conditions for vector maximization on constrained sets without using any of the nonlinear programming results surveyed in Sections 3, 4, and 5. In this section, we will show how many of these vector maximization theorems do indeed follow easily from the scalar maximization theorems we have studied. The following theorem is the key step in this process.

THEOREM 7.1. *Let C be a subset of $\mathbb{R}^n$. A necessary and sufficient condition that $\underline{u}: \mathbb{R}^n \to \mathbb{R}^a$ have a Pareto optimum at $\underline{x}^0$ on C is that $\underline{x}^0$ maximizes each u_i on the constraint set $C_i \equiv \{\underline{x} \in C | u_j(\underline{x}) - u_j(\underline{x}^0) \geq 0; \ j = 1, \ldots, a; \ j \neq i\}$.*

Proof. Suppose that u has a Pareto optimum on C at $\underline{x}^0$. If $\underline{x}$ does not maximize u_k on C_k, then there is an $\underline{x} \in C$ such that $u_j(\underline{x}) \geq u_j(\underline{x}^0)$ for all $j \neq k$ and $u_k(\underline{x}) > u_k(\underline{x}^0)$, contradicting the Pareto optimality of $\underline{x}^0$.

Conversely, suppose that $\underline{x}^0$ maximizes each u_k on C_k. If $\underline{x}^0$ is not a Pareto optimum on C, there is an $\underline{x} \in C$ and a k such that $u_i(\underline{x}) \geq u_i(\underline{x}^0)$ for all i and $u_k(\underline{x}) > u_k(\underline{x}^0)$, contradicting the maximality of $\underline{x}^0$ for u_k on C_k. ∎

Although this result is probably well known to many who work in this area, I have not found an explicit statement of it in the literature. Some authors, such as El-Hodiri [20] and Wan [74], have noted and used parts of this theorem in their work.

7.2. Necessary conditions for optimality. In this section, we'll use the results of Sections 3 and 4 to derive necessary conditions for $\underline{x}^0 \in \mathbb{R}^n$ to be a Pareto optimum. Throughout this section, $C_{g,h}$ will denote the constraint set $\{ \underline{x} \in \mathbb{R}^n | g_i(\underline{x}) \geq 0, \ i = 1, \dots, M; \ h_j(\underline{x}) = \underline{0}, \ j = 1, \dots, N \}$.

THEOREM 7.2. *Suppose that* $u_1, \dots, u_a, g_1, \dots, g_M, h_1, \dots, h_N$ *are* C^1 *functions on* $\mathbb{R}^n$. *Suppose that* $\underline{x}^0 \in C_{g,h}$ *is a Pareto optimum for* $u = (u_1, \dots, u_a)$ *on* $C_{g,h}$. *Then, there exist scalars* $\alpha_1, \dots, \alpha_a, \lambda_1, \dots, \lambda_M, \mu_1, \dots, \mu_N$ *such that*

$$\left(\underline{\alpha}, \underline{\lambda}, \underline{\mu} \right) \neq \underline{0};$$

$$\alpha_i \geq 0, \quad i = 1, \dots, a; \quad \lambda_j \geq 0, \quad j = 1, \dots, M;$$

$$\lambda_j g_j \left(\underline{x}^0 \right) = 0, \quad j = 1, \dots, M;$$

$$\sum_1^a \alpha_i Du_i \left(\underline{x}^0 \right) + \sum_1^M \lambda_j Dg_j \left(\underline{x}^0 \right) + \sum_1^N \mu_k Dh_k \left(\underline{x}^0 \right) = \underline{0}. \quad \text{(T)}$$

Proof. Since $\underline{x}^0$ is a Pareto optimum of u on $C_{g,h}$, $\underline{x}^0$ maximizes u_1 on the set $\{ \underline{x}^0 \in C_{g,h} | u_j(x) - u_j(\underline{x}^0) \geq 0, \ j = 2, \dots, a \}$. By F. John's result (Theorem 4.1), there exist $\alpha_1 \geq 0$; $\alpha_2, \dots, \alpha_a, \lambda_1, \dots, \lambda_M$ nonnegative; and $\mu_1, \dots, \mu_N$ such that $(\underline{\alpha}, \underline{\lambda}, \underline{\mu}) \neq 0$ in $\mathbb{R}^{a+M+N}$, $\lambda_i g_i(\underline{x}^0) = 0$, and

$$\alpha_1 Du_1 \left(\underline{x}^0 \right) + \sum_2^a \alpha_i D \left[u_i - u_i \left(\underline{x}^0 \right) \right] \left(\underline{x}^0 \right)$$

$$+ \sum_1^M \lambda_j Dg_j \left(\underline{x}^0 \right) + \sum_1^N \mu_k Dh_k \left(\underline{x}^0 \right) = \underline{0}.$$

But $D[u_i - u_i(\underline{x}^0)](\underline{x}^0) = Du_i(\underline{x}^0)$. ∎

Another proof of Theorem 7.2 may be found in DaCunha and Polak [12]. As before, Theorem 7.2 says very little unless one can guarantee that all of the α_i are nonzero. Thus, we need to make some assumptions on u, g, and h so that we can apply our theorems on constraint qualifications.

THEOREM 7.3. Suppose that $u_1, \ldots, u_a$, $g_1, \ldots, g_M$, $h_1, \ldots, h_N$ are C^1 functions on $\mathbb{R}^n$. Suppose that $\underline{x}^0 \in C_{g,h}$ and that u has a Pareto optimum on $C_{g,h}$ at $\underline{x}^0$. Suppose that u, g, and h satisfy *one* of the following hypotheses, where $u^{(i)} \equiv (u_1, \ldots, u_{i-1}, u_{i+1}, \ldots, u_a) : \mathbb{R}^n \to \mathbb{R}^{a-1}$:

a) $D(u^{(i)}, g_E, h)(\underline{x}^0)$ has maximal rank for each $i = 1, \ldots, a$.

b) Let $A_1 = \{i | u_i$ is pseudoconvex in some neighborhood of $\underline{x}^0\}$, $A_2 = \{1, \ldots, a\} - A_1$, $E_1 = \{j \in E | g_j$ is pseudoconvex in some neighborhood of $\underline{x}^0\}$, and $E_2 = E - E_1$. Suppose that h is linear and there is a $\underline{v} \in T_{\underline{x}^0}\mathbb{R}^n$ such that $Du_{A_1}(\underline{x}^0)\underline{v} \geq 0$, $Du_{A_2}(\underline{x}^0)\underline{v} > 0$, $Dg_{E_1}(\underline{x}^0)\underline{v} \geq 0$, $Dg_{E_2}(\underline{x}^0)\underline{v} > \underline{0}$, and $Dh(\underline{x}^0)\underline{v} = 0$.

c) u and g are pseudoconvex and h is linear,

d) h is affine; u and g are concave on some convex neighborhood U of $\underline{x}^0$; and for each $i \in \{1, \ldots, a\}$ there is an $\underline{x}^i \in \mathbb{R}^n$ such that $u^{(i)}(\underline{x}^i) > u^{(i)}(\underline{x}^0)$ and $g(\underline{x}^i) > \underline{0}$, $h(\underline{x}^i) = 0$.

e) Suppose whenever $Du^{(i)}(\underline{x}^0)\underline{v} \geq 0$, $Dg_E(\underline{x}^0)\underline{v} \geq 0$, and $Dh(\underline{x}^0)\underline{v} = 0$ for some i and some $\underline{v} \in T_{\underline{x}^0}\mathbb{R}^n$, there is a C^1 path $a: [0, \varepsilon) \to \mathbb{R}^n$ with $a(0) = \underline{x}^0$, $a'(0) = \underline{v}$, $u^{(i)}(a(t)) \geq u^{(i)}(\underline{x}^0)$, $g(a(t)) \geq \underline{0}$, and $h(a(t)) = \underline{0}$.

f) (Kuhn-Tucker [43]): For each $i = 1, 2, \ldots, a$, there is no vector $\underline{v}$ such that

$$Du_i(\underline{x}^0)\underline{v} > 0$$
$$Du_j(\underline{x}^0)\underline{v} \geq 0, \quad \text{for all} \quad j \neq i$$
$$Dg_E(\underline{x}^0)\underline{v} \geq \underline{0},$$
$$Dh(\underline{x}^0)\underline{v} = \underline{0}.$$

g) (Geoffrion [27]): There exists a scalar M such that, for each i, we have

$$\frac{u_i(\underline{x}) - u_i(\underline{x}^0)}{u_j(\underline{x}^0) - u_j(\underline{x})} \le M$$

for some j such that $u_j(\underline{x}) < u_j(\underline{x}^0)$ whenever $\underline{x} \in C_{g,h}$ and $u_i(\underline{x}) > u_i(\underline{x}^0)$.

Then, there are scalars $\alpha_1, \ldots, \alpha_a, \lambda_1, \ldots, \lambda_M, \mu_1, \ldots, \mu_N$ such that (T) of Theorem 7.2 holds, where the α_i are all strictly positive.

Proof. For hypotheses a) through e), fix $i \in \{1, \ldots, a\}$. By Theorems 3.3, 4.3, and 4.4, there are $\beta_1^i, \ldots, \beta_a^i, \lambda_1^i, \ldots, \lambda_M^i, \mu_1^i, \ldots, \mu_N^i$ such that

$$\beta_j^i \ge 0 \quad \text{for all} \quad j = 1, \ldots, a; \beta_i^i = 1;$$

$$\lambda_j^i \ge 0 \quad \text{and} \quad \lambda_j^i g_j(\underline{x}^0) = 0 \quad \text{for all} \quad j = 1, \ldots, M_j$$

and

$$\sum_{j=1}^{a} \beta_j^i Du_j(\underline{x}^0) + \sum_{m=1}^{M} \lambda_m^i Dg_m(\underline{x}^0) + \sum_{k=1}^{N} \mu_k^i Dh^k(\underline{x}^0) = 0.$$

Let

$$\alpha_j = \sum_{i=1}^{a} \beta_j^i \ge 1, \qquad \lambda_m = \sum_{i=1}^{a} \lambda_m^i \ge 0, \quad \text{and} \quad \mu_k = \sum_{i=1}^{a} \mu_k^i.$$

For hypothesis f), apply Farkas' Lemma (see Section 4.2) for each i with $A = (Du^{(i)}(\underline{x}^0), Dg_E(\underline{x}^0), Dh(\underline{x}^0), -Dh(\underline{x}^0))$. By hypothesis f), whenever $A\underline{v} \ge \underline{0}, -Du_i(\underline{x}^0)\underline{v} \ge 0$. So, there exist $\beta_1^i, \ldots, \lambda_1^i, \ldots, \mu_1^i, \ldots, \mu_N^i$ as in the preceding paragraph.

For hypothesis g), see Geoffrion [27]. ∎

Kuhn and Tucker call a vector maximum which satisfies hypothesis f) in Theorem 7.3 a *proper* solution of the vector maximum problem. Geoffrion [27] calls a vector maximum which satisfies hypothesis g) a *properly efficient solution* of the vector maximum problem. Both of these papers indicate that at a Pareto optimum which is not proper one can find paths which allow first-order gains for some of the u_i's and only second-order losses for the other u_i's. See also Klinger [39].

We will use some of the hypotheses of Theorem 7.3 when we study some more economics applications in Section 8.

7.3. Second-order sufficient conditions. One can now easily combine Theorem 7.1 and the results of Section 3 to prove the following strong second-order sufficiency condition for Pareto optimization. Weinberger [76], Smale [67], Wan [74], and de Melo [16] have proven similar results using other methods.

THEOREM 7.4.   *Let* $u_1, \ldots, u_a, g_1, \ldots, g_M, h_1, \ldots, h_N \colon \mathbb{R}^n \to \mathbb{R}^1$ *be* C^2 *functions. Suppose that* $\underline{x}^0 \in C_{g,h} \equiv \{ \underline{x} \in \mathbb{R}^n | g(\underline{x}) \geq \underline{0},$ $h(\underline{x}) = \underline{0} \}$. *Suppose there exist multipliers* $\underline{\alpha} \geq \underline{0}$ *in* $\mathbb{R}^a$, $\underline{\lambda} \geq \underline{0}$ *in* $\mathbb{R}^M$, *and* $\underline{\mu} \in \mathbb{R}^N$ *such that* $\lambda_i g_i(\underline{x}^0) = 0$ *for all i and if*

$$L \equiv \sum_1^a \alpha_i u_i + \sum_1^M \lambda_j g_j + \sum_1^N \mu_k h_k$$

then $DL(\underline{x}^0) = \underline{0}$ *and* $D^2 L(\underline{x}^0)(\underline{v}, \underline{v}) < 0$ *for all nonzero* $\underline{v}$ *such that* $\alpha_i Du_i(\underline{x}^0)\underline{v} = 0$ *and* $Du_i(\underline{x}^0)\underline{v} \geq 0$ *for* $i = 1, \ldots, M$; $\lambda^i Dg_i(\underline{x}^0)\underline{v}$ $= 0$ *and* $Dg_i(\underline{x}^0)\underline{v} \geq 0$ *for each* $i \in E$; *and* $Dh(\underline{x}^0)\underline{v} = 0$. *Then,* $\underline{x}^0$ *is a strict local Pareto optimum for* $\underline{u}$ *in* $C_{g,h}$.

Proof.   By Theorem 7.1, we need only show that $\underline{x}^0$ maximizes each u_i on $u^{(i)} - u^{(i)}(\underline{x}^0) \geq \underline{0}$, $g \geq \underline{0}$, $h = \underline{0}$. We will work with $i = 1$ for simplicity of notation and use Theorem 3.4. Of course, we choose the $\alpha_1, (\alpha_2, \ldots, \alpha_a), \underline{\lambda}, \underline{\mu}$ of our hypothesis for the multipliers in our scalar maximization problem.

Letting

$$L' = \alpha_1 u_1 + \sum_2^a \alpha_i \big(u_i - u_i(\underline{x}^0) \big) + \sum_1^M \lambda_j g_j + \sum_1^N \mu_k h_k,$$

we see that $DL'(\underline{x}^0) = DL(\underline{x}^0) = \underline{0}$. Now, choose nonzero $\underline{v}$ so that $Du_1(x^0)\underline{v} \geq 0$, so that $\alpha_i D(u_i - u_i(\underline{x}^0))(\underline{x}^0)\underline{v} = 0$ and $D(u_i - u_i(\underline{x}^0))(\underline{x}^0)\underline{v} \geq 0$ for $i = 2, \ldots, a$, so that $\lambda_i Dg_i(\underline{x}^0)\underline{v} = 0$ and $Dg_i(\underline{x}^0)\underline{v} \geq 0$ for each $i \in E$, and so that $Dh(\underline{x}^0)\underline{v} = 0$. Since $DL(\underline{x}^0) = 0$,

$$-\alpha_1 Du_1(\underline{x}^0)\underline{v} = \sum_{2}^{a} \alpha_i Du_i(\underline{x}^0)\underline{v} + \sum_{1}^{M} \lambda_j Dg_j(\underline{x}^0)\underline{v}$$

$$+ \sum_{1}^{N} \mu_k Dh_k(\underline{x}^0)\underline{v} = 0.$$

By hypothesis, $D^2L'(\underline{x}^0)(\underline{v}, \underline{v}) = D^2L(\underline{x}^0)(\underline{v}, \underline{v}) < 0$. By Theorem 3.4, u_1 restricted to $\{u^{(1)} \geq u^{(1)}(\underline{x}^0), g \geq \underline{0}, h = \underline{0}\}$ has a strict local maximum at $\underline{x}^0$. Since this is clearly true for all $i > 1$ also, $\underline{u}$ restricted to $g \geq \underline{0}$, $h = \underline{0}$ has a strict local Pareto optimum at $\underline{x}^0$ by Theorem 7.1. ∎

As before, one can strengthen the sufficiency test of Theorem 7.4 by allowing the multipliers to depend on the vector $\underline{v}$ to be tested. See Ben-Tal [9] and Weinberger [76].

See example 1 after Theorem 7.6 below for a calculation of a Pareto optimum based on Theorem 7.4.

7.4. First-order sufficient conditions. In many applications in economics, the u_i's, g_j's, and h_k's which arise naturally are concave or convex. For example, let $u(x_1, x_2)$ denote a consumer's utility function in an economy with two commodities. If commodities one and two are desirable ones and about equally so, then the natural assumption that the consumer would prefer to have some of each commodity rather than lots of one commodity and little or none of the other leads to the usual hypothesis that the u_j's are concave or at least quasi-concave functions. In fact, the desire of consumers to achieve balanced distributions of the goods in question—hopefully, by trading with other consumers—is a concept at the core of the theory of microeconomics.

In this section, we use Theorem 7.1 and the results of Section 5 to describe sufficient conditions for optimality when the functions involved are concave or almost concave.

THEOREM 7.5. *Suppose* $u_1, \ldots, u_a, g_1, \ldots, g_M, h_1, \ldots, h_N$: $\mathbb{R}^n \to \mathbb{R}^1$ *are* C^1 *functions with* $g(\underline{x}^0) \geq \underline{0}, h(\underline{x}^0) = \underline{0}$. *Suppose that*

i) *the* u_i's *are pseudoconcave at* $\underline{x}^0$, *e.g.,* $\nabla u_i(x^0) \neq 0$ *and* u_i *quasi-concave at* x_0.

ii) *the* g_j's *are quasi-concave at* $\underline{x}^0$, *and*

iii) *the* h_k's *are quasi-concave and quasi-convex at* $\underline{x}^0$ *(e.g., linear)*.

If there exist multipliers $\underline{\alpha} \geq 0$ *in* $\mathbb{R}^a, \underline{\lambda} \geq 0$ *in* $\mathbb{R}^M, \mu \in \mathbb{R}^N$ *such that* $\alpha_i > 0$ *for* $i = 1, \ldots, a,$

$$\lambda_j g_j(\underline{x}^0) = 0 \quad for \quad j = 1, \ldots, M,$$

and

$$D\left[\sum_1^a \alpha_i u_i + \sum_1^M \lambda_j g_j + \sum_1^N \mu_k h_k\right](\underline{x}^0) = 0,$$

then $\underline{u}$, *restricted to* $C_{g,h}$, *has a global Pareto optimum at* $\underline{x}^0$.

Proof. The proof of Theorem 7.5 is similar to that of Theorem 7.4. By Theorem 7.1, we need only show that each u_i attains its maximum at $\underline{x}^0$ when the constraint set is $u^{(i)} - u^{(i)}(\underline{x}^0) \geq 0$, $g \geq 0$, $h = 0$. To demonstrate this, one applies Theorem 5.2. ∎

In using Theorem 7.5, one should keep in mind the hierarchies of concavity as described in Theorem 1.9. One is tempted to try to generalize Theorem 7.5 to the case where the u_i's are quasi-concave. However, if $u_1(x_1, x_2) = x_1^3$ and $u_2(x_1, x_2) = x_2^3$, u_1 and u_2 are quasi-concave and

$$1 \cdot Du_1(0,0) + 1 \cdot Du_2(0,0) = \underline{0}.$$

But $(0, 0)$ is not a Pareto optimum for (u_1, u_2).

Nor can one generalize Theorem 7.5 to the case where some of the α_i's are zero. For, let $u_1(x_1, x_2) = x_1$, $u_2(x_1, x_2) = -x_1$, and $u_3(x_1, x_2) = x_2$. The u_i's are all linear and therefore concave. If one chooses multipliers $\alpha_1 = \alpha_2 = 1$ and $\alpha_3 = 0$, then the origin (in fact, any point) is a critical point of the corresponding Lagrangian. However, if $x_2' > x_2$, then (x_1, x_2') is superior to (x_1, x_2) for all x_1.

Thus, Theorem 7.5 is just about the strongest first-order sufficient condition possible. It is a bit stronger than some similar results in the literature, e.g., Kuhn and Tucker [43], Karlin [37], Geoffrion [27], and Smale [68].

There are two other aspects of concave Pareto optimization that should be mentioned because of their important place in the past and present theory of microeconomics. The first involves the classical treatment of Pareto optimization problems (e.g., see Section 8.3 and Samuelson [57]) whereby one tries to reduce such a problem to a single maximization problem by working with a weighted sum of the u_i's.

THEOREM 7.6.   *Suppose that* $u_1, \ldots, u_a, g_1, \ldots, g_M, h_1, \ldots, h_N$: $\mathbb{R}^n \to \mathbb{R}^1$ *are C^1 functions and that* $\underline{x}^0 \in C_{g,h}$, *i.e.,* $g(\underline{x}^0) \geq \underline{0}$, $h(\underline{x}^0) = \underline{0}$. *Suppose that the u_i's are concave, the g_j's are quasi-concave, and the h_k's are linear. If $\underline{u}$ restricted to $C_{g,h}$ has a local Pareto optimum at $\underline{x}^0$, then there exist multipliers* $\alpha_1, \ldots, \alpha_a \geq 0$, *not all zero, such that $\underline{x}^0$ maximizes $\sum_1^a \alpha_i u_i$ (globally) on $C_{g,h}$. If, in addition, u, g, and h satisfy one of hypotheses* a) *to* g) *of Theorem 7.3 at $\underline{x}^0$, then one can choose all the α_i's to be strictly positive.*

Proof.   Since $\underline{u}$ restricted to $C_{g,h}$ has a local Pareto optimum at $\underline{x}^0$, there exists nonzero $(\underline{\alpha}, \underline{\lambda}, \underline{\mu}) \in \mathbb{R}^a \times \mathbb{R}^M \times \mathbb{R}^N$ such that $\alpha_i \geq 0$ for all i, $\lambda_j \geq 0$ for all j, and

$$D\left[\sum_1^a \alpha_i u_i + \sum_1^M \lambda_j g_j + \sum_1^N \mu_k h_k\right](\underline{x}^0) = \underline{0}. \tag{U}$$

But $\sum \alpha_i u_i$ is concave. Applying Theorem 5.2, one sees that $\sum_1^a \alpha_i u_i$ must have a global maximum in $C_{g,h}$ at x^0.

If one of the hypotheses of Theorem 7.3 holds, then we can choose all the α_i's to be positive in (U) and therefore in the theorem. However, we still need to find a nonzero $\underline{\alpha}$ in the general case in order to give this theorem some content. To do this, we must use the fact that disjoint convex sets can be separated by a hyperplane. See Chapter 3 in Mangasarian [48] or Appendix B in Karlin [37].

Suppose that for all nonzero choices of $(\underline{\alpha}, \underline{\lambda}, \underline{\mu})$ as above, $\underline{\alpha} = \underline{0}$. It follows that 1) $D(\Sigma\lambda_j g_j + \Sigma\mu_k h_k)(\underline{x}^0) = \underline{0}$ for all such $(\underline{\alpha}, \underline{\lambda}, \underline{\mu})$, 2) there is no nonzero $\underline{\alpha} \geq 0$ with $\Sigma_i \alpha_i Du_i(\underline{x}^0) = \underline{0}$, and 3) $Du_i(\underline{x}^0) \neq 0$ for all i. Let $U = \{x \in \mathbb{R}^n | u_i(\underline{x}) > u_i(\underline{x}^0)$ for all $i\}$ and let $C_{g,h}$ denote the constraint set as usual. By Gordan's Lemma (see Section 4.1), 2) implies that there is a nonzero vector $\underline{v} \in T_{x_0}\mathbb{R}^n$ with $Du_i(\underline{x}^0)v > 0$ for all i. Thus, U is nonempty and $\underline{x}^0$ is in its closure. Also, since $\underline{x}^0$ is a Pareto optimum, $\underline{x}^0 + t\underline{v} \notin C_{g,h}$ for all $t > 0$ and $C_{g,h}$ does not contain an open neighborhood of $\underline{x}^0$.

Since $\underline{u}$ restricted to $C_{g,h}$ has a Pareto optimum at $\underline{x}^0$, U and $C_{g,h}$ are disjoint convex sets. By the above mentioned separation theorems, there exists a hyperplane H that separates U and $C_{g,h}$.

Suppose that $f: \mathbb{R}^n \to \mathbb{R}^1$ is a C^1 pseudoconcave function with $\nabla f(\underline{x}^0)$ perpendicular to H and lying in the half-space of U. We claim that f restricted to $C_{g,h}$ has a global maximum at $\underline{x}^0$. Let $\underline{x}' \in C_{g,h}$. Since $Df(\underline{x}^0)(\underline{x}' - \underline{x}^0) = \nabla f(\underline{x}^0) \cdot (\underline{x}' - \underline{x}^0) \leq 0$, and since f is pseudoconcave, $f(\underline{x}') \leq f(\underline{x}^0)$ and our claim is verified.

If $\nabla u_i(\underline{x}^0)$ were normal to H for some i, then u_i restricted to $C_{g,h}$ would have a maximum at $\underline{x}^0$ and we would be done. Thus, we can assume that each $\nabla u_i(\underline{x}^0)$ is nonzero and is not perpendicular to H. Let $P: T_{x_0}\mathbb{R}^n \to H$ be the standard projection along the perpendicular to H. We know that $P(\nabla u_i(\underline{x}^0))$ is not zero for all i. If there were a nonzero vector $\underline{w} \in T_{x_0}\mathbb{R}^n \cap H$ such that $P(\nabla u_i(\underline{x}^0)) \cdot \underline{w} > 0$ for all i, then $\nabla u_i(\underline{x}^0) \cdot \underline{w} > 0$ for all, i a contradiction to the fact that U lies on one side of H. Gordan's Lemma now implies that there exists a nonzero $(\alpha_1, \ldots, \alpha_a)$ with

$$\alpha_i \geq 0 \quad \text{for all} \quad i \quad \text{and} \quad \sum_1^a \alpha_i P\big(\nabla u_i(\underline{x}^0)\big) = \underline{0}.$$

The linearity of P gives $P(\Sigma_1^a \alpha_i \nabla u_i(\underline{x}^0)) = \underline{0}$, i.e., $\Sigma_1^a \alpha_i \nabla u_i(\underline{x}^0)$ is perpendicular to H. By the claim of the proceeding paragraph, $\sum_1^a \alpha_i u_i$ restricted to $C_{g,h}$ has a maximum at $\underline{x}^0$. ∎

EXAMPLE 1. Smale [66] gives an example to show that Theorem 7.6 is not true if the u_i are not concave. Let

$$u_1(x, y) = y - x^2 + y^3, \qquad u_2(x, y) = \frac{-y}{x^2 + 1}.$$

Since $Du_1(0,0) = (0,1)$ and $Du_2(0,0) = (0,-1)$, $D[\lambda_1 u_1 + \lambda_2 u_2](0,0) = \underline{0}$ if and only if $\lambda_1 = \lambda_2 = \lambda$. Since $D^2[\lambda u_1 + \lambda u_2](0,0) =$

$$\begin{bmatrix} -2\lambda & 0 \\ 0 & 0 \end{bmatrix},$$

which is negative definite on the kernel of $D(u_1, u_2)(0,0)$, Theorem 7.4 tells us that $(0,0)$ is a local Pareto optimum of (u_1, u_2). (Keep in mind that λ must be positive.) However,

$$\lambda(u_1 + u_2)(x, y) = \lambda\left[x^2\left(\frac{y}{x^2 + 1}\right) + y^3\right]$$

is a strictly increasing function on the line $x = 0$, and certainly does not have a maximum at $(0,0)$.

EXAMPLE 2. The following simple example shows that one cannot always expect to find all positive α_i's in Theorem 7.6. Let $u_1(x_1, x_2) = -x_1^2 - x_2^2$ and $u_2(x_1, x_2) = x_1$. Since u_1 has a global maximum at $(0,0)$, (u_1, u_2) has a Pareto optimum at $(0,0)$. But,

$$\alpha_1 Du_1(0,0) + \alpha_2 Du_2(0,0) = (\alpha_2, 0)$$

equals zero if and only if $\alpha_2 = 0$.

The converse to Theorem 7.6 is a classical result, whose simple proof we will leave to the reader. Note that no continuity or convexity assumptions are needed.

THEOREM 7.7. *Let $u_1, \ldots, u_a$: $\mathbb{R}^n \to \mathbb{R}$ be functions and let X be a subset of $\mathbb{R}^n$. If $\underline{x}^0 \in X$ and if there exist $\alpha_1, \ldots, \alpha_a$ all strictly positive such that $\sum \alpha_i u_i$ restricted to X has a local (global) maximum at $\underline{x}^0$, then $(u_1, \ldots, u_a)$ restricted to X has a local (global) Pareto optimum at $\underline{x}^0$. If $\underline{x}^0 \in X$ and if there exists a nonzero $(\alpha_1, \ldots, \alpha_a)$, with $\alpha_1 \geq 0$ for all i, such that $\sum_1^a \alpha_i u_i$ restricted to X has a strict (local) maximum at $\underline{x}^0$, then $(u_1, \ldots, u_a)$ has a strict (local) Pareto optimum at $\underline{x}^0$.*

7.5. Saddle-point formulations.

The other important approach to concave Pareto optimization is the saddle-point formulation. In trying to optimize $(u_1, \ldots, u_a)$: $\mathbb{R}^n \to \mathbb{R}^a$ over the constraint set $C_g \equiv \{\underline{x} \in \mathbb{R}^n | g_i(\underline{x}) \geq 0\}$, $i = 1, \ldots, M$ economists often go right to the Lagrangian L: $\mathbb{R}^n \times \mathbb{R}^a \times \mathbb{R}^M \to \mathbb{R}$; where

$$L(\underline{x}, \underline{\alpha}, \underline{\lambda}) = \sum_1^a \alpha_i u_i + \sum_1^M \lambda_j g_j.$$

A *saddle point* for L is an $(\underline{x}^0, \underline{\alpha}^0, \underline{\lambda}^0)$ such that $\underline{\alpha}^0 \geq \underline{0}$, $\underline{\alpha}^0 \neq \underline{0}$, $\underline{\lambda}^0 \geq \underline{0}$, and for all $\underline{x}$ and all $\underline{\lambda} \geq \underline{0}$

$$L(\underline{x}, \underline{\alpha}^0, \underline{\lambda}^0) \leq L(\underline{x}^0, \underline{\alpha}^0, \underline{\lambda}^0) \leq L(\underline{x}^0, \underline{\alpha}^0, \lambda).$$

If $(\underline{x}^0, \underline{\alpha}^0, \underline{\lambda}^0)$ is a saddle point with $\alpha_i^0 > 0$ for $i = 1, \ldots, a$, then it is called a *strong saddle point*.

The following theorem summarizes the relationship between strong saddle points and Pareto optima.

THEOREM 7.8. *Let $u_1, \ldots, u_a, g_1, \ldots, g_M$: $\mathbb{R}^n \to \mathbb{R}^1$ be C^1 functions. Let L: $\mathbb{R}^n \times \mathbb{R}^a \times \mathbb{R}^M$ be*

$$L(\underline{x}, \underline{\alpha}, \underline{\lambda}) = \sum_1^a \alpha_i u_i(\underline{x}) + \sum_1^M \lambda_j g_j(\underline{x}).$$

A) *If $(\underline{x}^0, \underline{\alpha}^0, \underline{\lambda}^0)$ is a strong saddle point for L, then u restricted to C_g has a Pareto optimum at $\underline{x}^0$.*

B) *If the u_i's and g_j's are concave, if $\underline{x}^0 \in C_g$, and if any of hypotheses a) to g) of Theorem 7.3 hold, then u restricted to C_g has a*

Pareto optimum at $\underline{x}^0$ if and only if there is an $(\underline{\alpha}^0, \underline{\lambda}^0) \in \mathbb{R}^a \times \mathbb{R}^M$ such that $(\underline{x}^0, \underline{\alpha}^0, \underline{\lambda}^0)$ is a strong saddle point for L.

Proof. By Theorem 5.4, hypothesis A) implies that $\underline{x}^0 \in C_g$ and that $\underline{x}^0$ maximizes $\sum_1^a \alpha_i^0 u_i$ on C_g. By Theorem 7.7, u restricted to C_g has a Pareto optimum at $\underline{x}^0$. To prove B), one combines Theorem 7.6 and Theorem 5.5. ∎

Of course, one would like to replace the phrase "strong saddle point" by the phrase "saddle point" in Theorem 7.8. It is easy to see that this is impossible for part A). However, following Bergstrom (notes), one can make the following modification to part B).

THEOREM 7.9. *Let $u_1, \ldots, u_a, g_1, \ldots, g_M: \mathbb{R}^n \to \mathbb{R}^1$ be C^1 concave functions. Let $L(\underline{x}, \underline{\alpha}, \underline{\lambda}) = \underline{\alpha} \cdot \underline{u} + \underline{\lambda} \cdot \underline{g}$ be the corresponding Lagrangian. Suppose that $\underline{x}^0 \in C_g$, that there is an $\underline{x}^*$ with $g(x^*) > \underline{0}$ and that there is a conflict of goals at $\underline{x}^0$, i.e., for each proper subset K of $\{1, \ldots, a\}$, there is an $\underline{x} \in C_g$ such that $\underline{u}_i(\underline{x}) \geq u_i(\underline{x}^0)$ for all $i \in K$ and $u_j(\underline{x}) > u_j(\underline{x}^0)$ for some $j \in K$. Then, u restricted to C_g has a Pareto optimum at $\underline{x}^0$ if and only if there is an $(\underline{\alpha}^0, \underline{\lambda}^0) \in \mathbb{R}^a \times \mathbb{R}^M$ such that $(\underline{x}^0, \underline{\alpha}^0, \underline{\lambda}^0)$ is a saddle point for L.*

Proof. One shows that when there is a conflict of goals, a saddle point is a strong saddle point. Suppose $(\underline{x}^0, \underline{\alpha}^0, \underline{\lambda}^0)$ is a saddle point, but not a strong one. Let $K = \{i | \alpha_i^0 > 0\}$, a proper subset of $\{1, \ldots, a\}$. But there is an $\underline{x}' \in C_g$ such that $u_i(\underline{x}') \geq u_i(\underline{x}^0)$ for all $i \in K$ and $u_j(\underline{x}') > u_j(\underline{x}^0)$ for some $j \in K$. Then, $L(\underline{x}', \underline{\alpha}^0, \underline{\lambda}^0) > L(\underline{x}^0, \underline{\alpha}^0, \underline{\lambda}^0)$, a contradiction which implies that $(\underline{x}^0, \underline{\alpha}^0, \underline{\lambda}^0)$ is a strong saddle point.

Part A) of Theorem 7.8 now yields half of Theorem 7.9. To prove the other half, suppose that $\underline{u}$ restricted to C_g has a Pareto optimum at $\underline{x}^0$. By Theorem 7.6, there is a nonzero $\underline{\alpha}^0 \geq \underline{0}$ such that $\underline{x}^0$ maximizes $\sum_1^a \alpha_i^0 u_i$ on C_g. By Theorem 5.5, there is a $\underline{\lambda}^0 \geq 0$ such that $(\underline{x}^0, \underline{\alpha}^0, \underline{\lambda}^0)$ is a saddle point, and, therefore, a strong saddle point, for L.

The basic references for saddle points in concave vector maximization problems are Kuhn-Tucker [43] in the finite-dimensional case and Hurwicz [33] in the infinite-dimensional case.

7.6. Pareto optima via differential topology. The field of differential topology has made important contributions to the qualitative, global study of critical points and maxima of scalar-valued functions under nondegenerate constraints, i.e., on manifolds. For example, see Milnor [54]. Smale [63], in a series of papers entitled *Global Analysis and Economics*, applied the techniques of differential topology and of singularity theory (e.g., Golubitsky and Guillemin [28]) to the study of vector maxima. Corresponding to the usual critical set of a real valued function, Smale [63], [65] defined the *critical Pareto* set Θ to be the set of feasible points which satisfy the first-order necessary conditions for optimality, i.e.,

$\Theta = \{\underline{x} \in C_{g,h} |$ there exists nonzero $(\underline{\alpha}, \underline{\lambda}, \underline{\mu}) \in \mathbb{R}^a \times \mathbb{R}^M \times \mathbb{R}^N$ such that $\underline{\alpha} \geq \underline{0}, \underline{\lambda} \geq \underline{0}, \lambda \cdot g(\underline{x}) = 0$ and

$$\sum_1^a \alpha_i Du_i(\underline{x}) + \sum_1^M \lambda_j Dg_j(\underline{x}) + \sum_1^N \mu_k Dh_k(\underline{k}) = \underline{0}\}$$

Working with constraint sets which are compact manifolds, i.e., bounded sets described by nondegenerate equality constraints in the sense of Section 3, Smale [63] argued that, for an open dense subset of the set $C(M, \mathbb{R}^a)$ of all smooth mappings from an m-dimensional manifold M into $\mathbb{R}^a$, $\Theta - \partial\Theta$ is an $(a-1)$-dimensional manifold and $\partial\Theta$, the boundary of Θ, is a finite union of lower dimensional manifolds. (There are some dimensional requirements on the magnitude of m relative to a—requirements that are always met in the economic applications.) The proof of this result was completed and extended by de Melo [16]. Wan [74] has shown that for most mappings the set of local Pareto optima sit in M in a similar way.

Let us see why it is natural for the set of Pareto optima of a mapping $u: \mathbb{R}^n \to \mathbb{R}^a$ to be an $(a-1)$-dimensional subset. We are assuming that our usual constraint space $C_{g,h}$ is (locally) $\mathbb{R}^n$. Suppose $\underline{x}^0$ is a nondegenerate Pareto optimum for u, i.e., $\sum_1^a \alpha_i^0 Du_i(\underline{x}^0) = \underline{0}$ for some positive $\alpha_1^0, \ldots, \alpha_a^0, \sum_1^a \alpha_i^0 D^2 u_i(\underline{x}^0)$ is negative definite on the nullspace of $Du(\underline{x}^0)$, $Du_i(\underline{x}^0) \neq \underline{0}$ for all i, and the rank of $Du(\underline{x}^0)$ is $(a-1)$. Choose a neighborhood U of $\underline{x}^0$ in $\mathbb{R}^n$ and a neighborhood V of α^0 in $\mathbb{R}_+^a$ such that for all

$(\underline{x}, \underline{\alpha}) \in U \times V$: i) rank $Du(x) \geq a - 1$, ii) each $Du_i(\underline{x}) \neq \underline{0}$, and $\Sigma_1^a \alpha_i D^2 u_i(x)$ is negative definite on the nullspace of $Du(x)$. By Theorem 7.4, $\underline{x}' \in U$ will be a local Pareto optimum for u if and only if rank $Du(\underline{x}') = a - 1$, i.e., if all the $a \times a$ minors of $Du(\underline{x}')$ have zero determinant. (It follows from i) and ii) that if $\underline{x}' \in U$ and rank $Du(\underline{x}') = a - 1$, there exist positive $\alpha_1', \ldots, \alpha_a'$ near $\alpha_1^0, \ldots, \alpha_a^0$ so that $\Sigma_1^a \alpha_1' Du_i(\underline{x}') = \underline{0}$.) Since there are $(r - a + 1)$ independent $(a \times a)$ minors in $Du(\underline{x})$, $x' \in V$ must be a zero of a system of $(r - a + 1)$ equations to be a local Pareto optimum. If these equations are independent at $\underline{x}^0$ (as they usually are), then the local Pareto set in V will have dimension $r - (r - a + 1) = a - 1$.

Under the classical monotonicity and strict concavity assumptions of welfare economics, the set of Pareto optima is homeomorphic to the standard $(a - 1)$-dimensional simplex. See Arrow-Hahn [3] or Smale [68]. However, even with all these concavity assumptions, the set of optima need not be convex if $a > 1$, as the example at the end of the next section shows. (See Figure 2.) Of course, this set is affine in the linear vector maximization problem. See Koopmans [40] and Charnes-Cooper [10].

Simon and Titus [61], also using tools of differential topology and working with nondegeneracy hypotheses that occur in economics problems, showed how to reduce a vector maximization problem to a *single* scalar maximization problem (in contrast to Theorem 7.1) where the functions involved are nonlinear but are not concave so that Theorem 7.5 cannot be applied. The following theorem summarizes their results in this direction.

THEOREM 7.10.   *Let* $u_1, \ldots, u_a, h_1, \ldots, h_N$: $\mathbb{R}^n \to \mathbb{R}^1$ *be* C^1 *functions with* $h(\underline{x}^0) = \underline{0}$. *Suppose that i)* $Dh(\underline{x}^0)$ *has maximal rank* $N \leq a$, *ii) for each i,* $D(u_i, h)(\underline{x}^0)$ *has maximal rank, and iii) rank* $D(u, h)(\underline{x}^0) \geq N + a - 1$. *Then the following are equivalent:*

a) u *restricted to* $h^{-1}(\underline{0})$ *has a local Pareto optimum at* $\underline{x}^0$;

b) $\underline{x}^0 \in \Theta$, *the critical Pareto set; and for* <u>*some*</u> $i \in \{1, \ldots, a\}$ $\underline{x}^0$ *maximizes* u_i *on the constraint set*

$$U_{\underline{x}^0}^i \equiv \left\{ \underline{x} \in \mathbb{R}^n | u_j(\underline{x}) = u_j(\underline{x}^0), \ j \neq i, \ and \ h(\underline{x}) = \underline{0} \right\},$$

an $(n + 1 - a - N)$-*dimensional submanifold of* $h^{-1}(\underline{0})$.

We omit the proof of Theorem 7.10 since it involves techniques of differential topology. In the hypotheses, condition i) implies that $h^{-1}(\underline{0})$ is a manifold around $\underline{x}^0$, condition ii) means that no $u_i|h^{-1}(\underline{0})$ has a critical point at $\underline{x}^0$, and condition iii) asserts that the corank of $Du(\underline{x}^0)$ on $h^{-1}(\underline{0})$ must be at most one. If $a = 2$, condition iii) holds for all $\underline{x}^0 \in h^{-1}(\underline{0})$ for an open dense set of mappings from $\mathbb{R}^n$ to $\mathbb{R}^2$. (See Golubitsky-Guillemin [28].) Saari and Simon [56] have shown that, if one searches for Pareto optima using Theorem 7.10, one finds large open subsets of mappings u for which *degenerate* maxima of $u_i|U^i$ arise naturally. More specifically, when $a \geq 3$, there are open sets of mappings $u: \mathbb{R}^n \to \mathbb{R}^a$ which have Pareto optima that do not pass the second-order sufficiency test of Theorem 7.4. This contrasts with the situation for scalar maximization where most mappings from $\mathbb{R}^n$ to $\mathbb{R}^1$ have only nondegenerate critical points (see Golubitsky-Guillemin [28]) and with the situation for $a = 2$ where, for most mappings from $\mathbb{R}^n$ to $\mathbb{R}^2$, all the Pareto optima fulfill the second-order conditions of Theorem 7.4 (see Wan [73] and Saari-Simon [56]).

O. Lange [44] carried out one of the earliest systematic studies of Pareto optima in economics using techniques of calculus. He defined a "maximum of total welfare" of a utility mapping $u: \mathbb{R}^n \to \mathbb{R}^a$ as an $\underline{x}^0 \in \mathbb{R}^n$ that maximizes each u_i subject to the $(a - 1)$ equality constraint $u_j = u_j(\underline{x}^0)$ for $j \neq i$. By taking all the u_j's to be equal, it is apparent that, in general, Lange's notion is different from that of the vector maxima in this chapter. However, in the next section, we will use Theorem 7.10 to show that Lange's notion is equivalent to the usual one in an economic setting with the classical monotonicity and concavity assumptions.

8. VECTOR MAXIMIZATION IN ECONOMICS

8.1. Pareto optima in welfare economics. In Section 6.1, we formalized the theory behind a consumer's desire to select a most preferred commodity vector from the set of all feasible and affordable commodity vectors. We now examine the situation where there are A consumers in an economy with n goods, $1 \leqslant A, n < \infty$. Assume that the kth consumer has a smooth utility function

$u^k : C \to \mathbb{R}$ and an initial commodity vector $\underline{z}^k \in C \equiv \{\underline{x} \in \mathbb{R}^n | \underline{x} \geqslant \underline{0}\}$. There is still a fixed positive price vector $\underline{p} \in \mathbb{R}^n_+$; and the initial wealth of the kth consumer is $w^k = \underline{p} \cdot \underline{z}^k$. (Note that superscripts are being used to index consumers, while subscripts are used to label commodities.)

Let $\xi^k(\underline{p}, \underline{z}^k)$ denote the kth consumer's demand correspondence, i.e., the solution set for the problem of maximizing $u^k(\underline{x})$ subject to $\underline{0} \leqslant \underline{x}$ in $\mathbb{R}^n$ and $\underline{p} \cdot \underline{x} \leqslant \underline{p} \cdot \underline{z}^k$. For simplicity of notation, we will assume that each ξ^k is a single-valued function. However, much of the theory of this section holds for demand correspondences as well as for demand functions, provided the reader substitutes set inclusion for equality in the relevant equations below.

Assume now that we are dealing with a closed economy in that the total amount of each commodity remains fixed during the consumers' interactions. Thus, if $\underline{b} = \Sigma_1^A \underline{z}^k$, our *state space* is

$$\Omega \equiv \left\{ \underline{X} = \left(\underline{x}^1, \ldots, \underline{x}^A\right) \in \left(\mathbb{R}^n_+\right)^A | \underline{x}^k \geqslant 0 \right.$$

$$\left. \text{for each} \quad k \quad \text{and} \quad \sum_1^A \underline{x}^k = \underline{b} \right\},$$

an $(nA - n)$-dimensional affine subspace of $(\mathbb{R}^n)^A$. We will call an element of Ω a *commodity bundle*. The A utility functions can be considered as functions on Ω by writing

$$U^k\left(\underline{x}^1, \ldots, \underline{x}^A\right) = u^k\left(\underline{x}^k\right), \quad \text{for} \quad k = 1, \ldots, A.$$

Finally, these A utility functions can be combined to form the *utility mapping*

$$U = \left(U^1, \ldots, U^A\right) : \Omega \to \mathbb{R}^A.$$

In this simple setting, an *economy* is an initial commodity bundle $(\underline{z}^1, \ldots, \underline{z}^A)$, a utility mapping U, and a price system $\underline{p}$.

There are a couple of natural ways of expressing an optimum or equilibrium in such an economy. There is, of course, the notion of a

Pareto optimum (PO) or Pareto-optimal bundle $\underline{X}$ in Ω for the utility mapping U, i.e., $\underline{X}$ is a PO for U if there is no $\underline{Y} \in \Omega$ such that $U(\underline{Y}) \geqslant U(\underline{X})$ and $U(\underline{Y}) \neq U(\underline{X})$ in $\mathbb{R}^A$. There is the similar concept of a local Pareto optimum (LPO).

Our first goal is to use the theorems of Section 7 to write necessary conditions and sufficient conditions for a commodity bundle to be an LPO. We would also like to know whether or not we can find strictly positive Lagrange multipliers and whether we can use Theorem 7.10 to find LPO's. Theorem 8.1 below collects the necessary conditions for an LPO, while Theorem 8.2 deals with the sufficient conditions.

THEOREM 8.1   Let $\underline{b}$ be a positive vector in $\mathbb{R}^n$ and let $\Omega \equiv \{ \underline{X} = (\underline{x}^1, \ldots, \underline{x}^A) \in (\mathbb{R}^n)^A |$ each $\underline{x}^k \geqslant \underline{0}$ and $\Sigma_1^A \underline{x}^k = \underline{b} \}$. Let $u^1, \ldots, u^A : \mathbb{R}_+^n \to \mathbb{R}$ be C^1 utility functions. Suppose that for each $k \in \{1, \ldots, A\}$ and for each $\underline{x}$ with $\underline{0} \leqslant \underline{x} \leqslant \underline{b}$, $(\partial u^k / \partial x_i)(\underline{x}) > 0$ for some i, and that whenever $x_j = 0$, $(\partial u^k / \partial x_j)(\underline{x}) > 0$.

a) Suppose that $Y = (\underline{y}^1, \ldots, \underline{y}^A) \in \Omega$ is an LPO for $U : \Omega \to \mathbb{R}^A$. Then, there exist nonnegative multipliers $\alpha^1, \ldots, \alpha^A$, not all zero, and a nonzero vector $\underline{\gamma} \in \mathbb{R}^n$ such that

$$\alpha^k \nabla u^k \left(\underline{y}^k \right) \leqslant \underline{\gamma}, \quad \text{for} \quad k = 1, \ldots, A$$

with   (V)

$$\alpha^k \frac{\partial u^k}{\partial x_j} \left(\underline{y}^k \right) = \gamma_j, \quad \text{whenever } y_j^k \neq 0.$$

b) Let $\underline{Y}$ be as in a) with the added hypothesis that no (vector) component $\underline{y}^k$ of $\underline{Y}$ is zero. Suppose $(\partial u^k / \partial x_j)(\underline{x}) > 0$ for all k and j and for all $\underline{x}$ with $\underline{0} \leqslant \underline{x} \leqslant \underline{b}$. Then, there exist $\alpha^1, \ldots, \alpha^A, \gamma_1, \ldots, \gamma_n$, all positive, such that (V) holds.

c) If $\underline{Y}$ is an LPO in the interior of Ω, then there are positive multipliers $\alpha^1, \ldots, \alpha^A$ and a nonzero vector $\underline{\gamma}$ in $\mathbb{R}$

such that
   i) $\alpha^k \nabla u^k(\underline{y}^k) = \gamma$, for $k = 1, \ldots, A$;

   ii) $\sum\limits_1^A \alpha^k DU^k(\underline{Y})\underline{V} = \underline{0}$, for all $\underline{V} = (\underline{v}^1, \ldots, \underline{v}^A) \in (\mathbb{R}^n)^A$

such that $\sum\limits_1^A \underline{v}^k = \underline{0}$, i.e., $\underline{V} \in T_{\underline{Y}}\Omega$;

   iii) at $\underline{Y}$, the marginal rate of substitution of good i for good j is the same for all consumers, i.e., if

$$\frac{\partial u^1}{\partial x_j}(\underline{y}^1) \neq 0,$$

$$\frac{\partial u^k}{\partial x_i}(\underline{y}^k) \bigg/ \frac{\partial u^k}{\partial x_j}(\underline{y}^k) = \frac{\partial u^m}{\partial x_i}(\underline{y}^m) \bigg/ \frac{\partial u^m}{\partial x_j}(\underline{y}^m)$$

for all $k, m \in \{1, \ldots, A\}$ and all $i, j \in \{1, \ldots, n\}$;

   iv) if α^1 is set equal to 1, the other α^k's are uniquely determined.

Proof. This theorem is a reasonably straightforward application of the results of Section 7 to our economic model. One simple method of handling $U: \Omega \to \mathbb{R}^A$ is to remove the equality constraint that defines Ω by letting $(\underline{x}^1, \ldots, \underline{x}^{A-1})$ be independent coordinates for Ω with $\underline{x}^A = \underline{b} - \sum_1^{A-1}\underline{x}^k$. This is the approach taken by Simon-Titus [61]. We will use an approach more in line with the techniques of earlier sections of this paper. See Smale [65], [68] for a similar approach.

The Lagrangian for this optimization problem is

$$L\left(\underline{x}^1, \ldots, \underline{x}^A, \alpha^1, \ldots, \alpha^A, \underline{\mu}^1, \ldots, \underline{\mu}^A, \underline{\gamma}\right)$$

$$= \sum_1^A \alpha^k U^k(\underline{X}) + \sum_1^A \underline{\mu}^k \cdot \underline{x}^k + \underline{\gamma} \cdot \left(\underline{b} - \sum_1^A \underline{x}^k\right).$$

Setting the derivatives of L with respect to $\underline{x}^k$ equal to zero and evaluating at $\underline{Y}$ yields

$$\alpha^k \nabla u^k(\underline{y}^k) + \underline{\mu}^k - \underline{\gamma} = \underline{0} \quad \text{in } \mathbb{R}^n. \tag{W}$$

If $\underline{Y}$ is an LPO, Theorem 7.2 states that there exists a nonzero $(\alpha^1, \ldots, \alpha^A, \mu^1, \ldots, \mu^A, \gamma)$ that solves (W) for $k = 1, \ldots, A$, where each α^k and μ^k is nonnegative and each $\mu_i^k y_i^k$ is 0. Now, (V) follows from (W) since each $\mu^k \geqslant \underline{0}$.

Suppose every α^k is zero. For any $i \in \{1, \ldots, n\}$, there is a $j \in \{1, \ldots, A\}$ such that $y_i^j \neq 0$ and, consequently,

$$0 = \alpha^j \frac{\partial u^j}{\partial x_i}(\underline{x}^j) = \gamma_i.$$

So, $\alpha^1 = \cdots = \alpha^A = 0$ implies $\gamma_1 = \cdots = \gamma_n = 0$, which in turn implies that each μ^k is $\underline{0}$ in (W). This contradiction to the fact that $(\underline{\alpha}, \mu^1, \ldots, \mu^A, \gamma) \neq \underline{0}$ shows that some α^k is positive.

To prove b), let $\underline{Y}$ be an LPO with each $y^k \neq \underline{0}$. By part a), some α^j is nonzero, say α^1. Since

$$\alpha^1 \frac{\partial u^1}{\partial x_j}(\underline{y}^1) \leqslant \gamma_j \quad \text{and} \quad \frac{\partial u^1}{\partial x_j}(\underline{y}^1) > 0 \quad \text{for all} \quad j,$$

$\gamma_j > 0$ for $j = 1, \ldots, n$. Let $k \in \{1, \ldots, A\}$. By hypothesis, some $y_i^k \neq 0$; and therefore $\alpha^k(\partial u^k/\partial x_i)(\underline{y}^k) = \gamma_i$. Since γ_i and $(\partial u^k/\partial x_i)(\underline{y}^k)$ are positive, so is α^k.

To prove c), note that i) follows from (W) since each μ^k is $\underline{0}$ for an interior LPO. If any α^k were 0, then γ would be $\underline{0}$. Since no $\nabla u^k(\underline{y}^k)$ is $\underline{0}$, $\gamma = 0$ implies that each $\alpha^k = 0$—a contradiction.

Suppose $(\partial u^1/\partial x_j)(\underline{y}^1)$ is positive. If one sets $\alpha^1 = 1$, then $\underline{\gamma} = \nabla u^1(\underline{y}^1)$ and

$$\alpha^k = \frac{\partial u^k}{\partial x_j}(\underline{y}^k) \left/ \frac{\partial u^1}{\partial x_j}(\underline{y}^k) \right.$$

for any j, i.e., each α^k is uniquely determined. If $(\partial u^1/\partial x_i)(\underline{y}^1) \neq 0$ also,

$$\frac{\alpha^k}{\alpha^m} = \frac{\partial u^k}{\partial x_j}(\underline{y}^k) \left/ \frac{\partial u^m}{\partial x_j}(\underline{y}^m) \right. = \frac{\partial u^k}{\partial x_i}(\underline{y}^k) \left/ \frac{\partial u^m}{\partial x_i}(\underline{y}^m) \right. ;$$

and part iii) in c) follows.

To prove ii), let $\underline{V} = (\underline{v}^1, \ldots, \underline{v}^A) \in (\mathbb{R}^n)^A$ with $\Sigma_1^A \underline{v}^k = \underline{0}$. Then,

$$\sum_1^A \alpha^k DU^k(Y)\underline{V} = \sum_1^A \alpha^k Du^k\left(\underline{y}^k\right)\underline{v}^k$$

$$= \sum_1^A \underline{\gamma} \cdot \underline{v}^k = \underline{\gamma} \cdot \sum_1^A \underline{v}^k$$

$$= \underline{0}. \quad \blacksquare$$

REMARK. The hypotheses that for each feasible $\underline{x}$ some $(\partial u^k/\partial x_j)(\underline{x}) > 0$ and that $(\partial u^k/\partial x_j)(\underline{x}) > 0$ whenever $x_j^k = 0$ are basic economics assumptions. They state that each consumer would always like to consume more of some commodity and that he would like to have at least a little of each commodity. Without some such mild desirability assumptions on the commodities in our economy, interaction among the consumers might not take place.

THEOREM 8.2 (Sufficient Conditions). Let $\underline{b}$, Ω, and $U: \Omega \to \mathbb{R}^A$ be as in Theorem 8.1. Assume again for each $\underline{X} \in \Omega$ and for each $k \in \{1, \ldots, A\}$ that some $(\partial u^k/\partial x_j)(\underline{x}^k) \neq 0$.

a) If $\underline{Y}$ is in the interior of Ω, then $\underline{Y}$ is an LPO if and only if i) there exists positive $\alpha^1, \ldots, \alpha^A$ and nonzero γ such that $\alpha^k \nabla u^k(\underline{y}^k) = \underline{\gamma}$ for $k = 1, \ldots, A$, and ii) $\underline{Y}$ maximizes some U^k on the submanifold $\{\underline{X} \in \Omega | U^j(\underline{X}) = U^j(\underline{Y}), j = 1, \ldots, A, j \neq k\}$.

b) Let $\underline{Y} \in \Omega$, and suppose $u^1, \ldots, u^A$ such that (V) holds (or if $\underline{Y}$ is in the interior of Ω, such that i), ii), or iii) of Theorem 8.1.c holds), then $\underline{Y}$ is a PO for U.

c) Let $Y \in \Omega$. If there exist nonnegative $\alpha^1, \ldots, \alpha^A$ such that (V) holds and such that

$$\sum_1^A \alpha^k D^2 U^k(Y)(\underline{V}, V) = \sum_1^A \alpha^k D^2 u^k\left(\underline{y}^k\right)\left(\underline{v}^k, \underline{v}^k\right) < 0$$

for all nonzero $V = (\underline{v}^1, \ldots, \underline{v}^A) \in (\mathbb{R}^n)^A$ such that $\Sigma_1^A \underline{v}^k = \underline{0}$ and $Du^k(\underline{y}^k)\underline{v}^k = \underline{0}, k = 1, \ldots, A$, then $\underline{Y}$ is a strict LPO for U.

Proof. Part a) follows directly from Theorem 7.10, part b) from Theorem 7.5, and part c) from Theorem 7.4. One computes easily that the hypotheses of Theorem 7.10 are satisfied with $h(\underline{X}) = \underline{b} - \sum_1^A \underline{x}^k$ and

$$
D(U, h)(\underline{X}) = \begin{pmatrix}
Du^1(\underline{x}^1) & 0 & \cdots & 0 \\
0 & Du^2(\underline{x}^2) & \cdots & 0 \\
\vdots & \vdots & & \vdots \\
0 & 0 & & Du^A(\underline{x}^A) \\
-I_n & -I_n & & -I_n
\end{pmatrix} \quad \blacksquare
$$

8.2. Pareto optima and price equilibria. The notion of a Pareto optimum, while natural in our economic model, ignores the economy's price system and the consumer's demand functions. A natural notion of equilibrium which includes these is the *competitive equilibrium*. Let $\underline{Y}$ be an initial commodity bundle in Ω, and let $\underline{p}$ be the prevailing price system. With these initial conditions, the kth consumer will demand commodity vector $\xi^k(\underline{p}, \underline{y}^k)$. The *total demand* of the A consumers is the vector

$$
\sum_{k=1}^A \xi^k(\underline{p}, \underline{y}^k) \in \mathbb{R}_+^n,
$$

and the commodity bundle demanded is

$$
\Xi(\underline{p}, \underline{Y}) = \left(\xi^1(\underline{p}, \underline{y}^1), \ldots, \xi^A(\underline{p}, \underline{y}^A) \right) \in (\mathbb{R}^n)^A.
$$

If $\Xi(\underline{p}, \underline{Y})$ is in Ω, i.e., if the total demand vector equals the total supply vector,

$$
\sum_1^A \xi^k(\underline{p}, \underline{y}^k) = \sum_1^A \underline{y}^k = \underline{b},
$$

then we say that $\underline{p}$ is an *equilibrium price* for $\underline{Y}$ and that $(\underline{p}, \Xi(\underline{p}, \underline{Y}))$ is a *competitive equilibrium* (with respect to $\underline{Y}$). Often, one defines the *excess demand vector*

$$Z\left(\underline{p}, \underline{Y}\right) = \sum_{1}^{A} \xi^{k}\left(\underline{p}, \underline{y}^{k}\right) - \sum_{1}^{A} \underline{y}^{k}$$

and notes that $\underline{p}$ is an equilibrium price for $\underline{Y}$ if and only if $Z(\underline{p}, \underline{Y}) = \underline{0}$ in $\mathbb{R}^{n}$. By Theorem 6.1.iv,

$$\underline{p} \cdot Z\left(\underline{p}, \underline{Y}\right) = 0 \quad \text{for all} \quad \underline{Y} \in \Omega$$

if U satisfies the usual monotonicity assumption. The equation is usually known as *Walras' Law*.

If $(\underline{p}, \Xi)$ is a competitive equilibrium, then Ξ represents a solution to A independent maximization problems—but a solution with economic relevance since $\Xi \in \Omega$. A natural question is: how does Ξ relate to the vector maximization problems we discussed in the previous section? Theorems 8.3 and 8.4 below, often called the *Fundamental Theorems of Welfare Economics*, answer this question by stating that a competitive equilibrium is always a Pareto optimum and that a Pareto optimum can always be realized as a competitive equilibrium for some price vector $\underline{p}$.

The latter statement solves a major dilemma. If $\underline{Y} \in \Omega$, there is usually a multidimensional set of LPO's which are Pareto-superior to $\underline{Y}$. The economist, who would like to have some natural way of choosing a meaningful LPO from this set, can proceed as follows. He first finds a price system $\underline{p}^{*}$ which is an equilibrium price for $\underline{Y}$. To prove the existence of such a $\underline{p}^{*}$ and also to compute it, economists use Walras' Law and the Brouwer or Kakutani fixed-point theorem to find a zero of $\underline{p} \mapsto Z(\underline{p}, \underline{Y})$. (See Debreu [14], Dierker [17], and Malinvaud [45], for example, for proofs of the existence of $\underline{p}^{*}$. See Scarf [59] and Smale [69] for methods of computing $\underline{p}^{*}$.) Theorem 8.3 then assures the economist that the corresponding competitive equilibrium $(\underline{p}^{*}, \Xi)$ with respect to $\underline{Y}$ lies in the set of PO's.

THEOREM 8.3.   *Let $\underline{b}$ be a positive vector in $\mathbb{R}^{n}$ and let $\Omega = \{ \underline{X} = (\underline{x}^{1}, \ldots, \underline{x}^{A}) \in (\mathbb{R}^{n})^{A} \mid$ each $\underline{x}^{k} \geqslant \underline{0}$ and $\sum_{1}^{A} \underline{x}^{k} = \underline{b} \}$. Let*

$u^1, \ldots, u^A : \mathbb{R}^n_+ \to \mathbb{R}$ *be C^1 utility mappings such that*

$$\frac{\partial u^k}{\partial x_j}(\underline{x}) > 0 \quad \text{for all} \quad k, \ j \quad \text{and all} \quad \underline{x}.$$

Let $\underline{p}$ be a positive price vector in $\mathbb{R}^n$ and let

$$\hat{Y} = \left(\xi^1\left(\underline{p}, \underline{y}^1\right), \ldots, \xi^A\left(\underline{p}, \underline{y}^A\right)\right).$$

If $\hat{\underline{Y}} \in \Omega$, i.e. $(\underline{p}, \hat{\underline{Y}})$ is a competitive equilibrium for $\underline{Y}$, then $\hat{\underline{Y}}$ is a PO for U, that is Pareto-superior to $\underline{Y}$.

Proof. Suppose that $\hat{\underline{Y}}$ is not a PO for U, i.e., that there exists $Z \in \Omega$ and a nonempty subset S_1 of $\{1, \ldots, A\}$ such that

$$U^k(Z) > U^k(\hat{Y}) \quad \text{for} \quad k \in S_1,$$
$$U^k(Z) = U^k(\hat{Y}) \quad \text{for} \quad k \in S_2 \equiv \{1, \ldots, A\} - S_1.$$

Since each $\hat{y}^k$ maximizes u^k on $\{\underline{x} \in \mathbb{R}^n_+ | \underline{p} \cdot \underline{x} \leqslant \underline{p} \cdot y^k\}$, it follows that $u^k(\hat{y}^k) \geqslant u^k(y^k)$ for each k and $\underline{p} \cdot \underline{z}^k > \underline{p} \cdot \underline{y}^k$ for $k \in S_1$.

We claim that $\underline{p} \cdot \underline{z}^k \geqslant \underline{p} \cdot \underline{y}^k$ for all $k \in S_2$. For, if $\underline{p} \cdot \underline{z}^m < \underline{p} \cdot \underline{y}^m$ for some $m \in S_2$, then $\underline{z}^m$ also maximizes u^m on $\{\underline{x} \in \mathbb{R}^n_+ | \underline{p} \cdot \underline{x} \leqslant \underline{p} \cdot \underline{y}^m\}$. This contradicts Theorem 6.2.iv which states that $\underline{p} \cdot \underline{z}^m = \underline{p} \cdot \underline{y}^m$ for all $\underline{z}^m$ in $\xi^m(\underline{p}, \underline{y}^m)$.

Consequently, $\Sigma_1^A \underline{p} \cdot \underline{z}^k > \Sigma \underline{p} \cdot \underline{y}^k$ or

$$\underline{p} \cdot \sum_1^A \underline{z}^k > \underline{p} \cdot \sum_1^A \underline{y}^k,$$

which contradicts $\Sigma_1^A \underline{y}^k = \Sigma_1^A \underline{z}^k = \underline{b}$. ∎

The above proof of Theorem 8.3 is adapted from Malinvaud [45]. Smale [65] proves this result by using Theorems 6.1 and 7.3 to show that when $(\underline{p}, \underline{Y})$ is a competitive equilibrium, $\underline{Y}$ is a critical Pareto point (as in Section 7.5). Then, concavity assumptions are needed to show that $\underline{Y}$ is a PO. Theorem 8.4 states the converse of Theorem 8.3.

THEOREM 8.4.   *Let $\underline{b}$, Ω, $\underline{p}$, and $u^1, \ldots, u^A$ be as in the hypothesis of Theorem 8.3. Suppose further that each u^k is quasi-concave and that $\underline{Y}$ is a PO for U. Then, there is a positive price vector $\underline{p}$ in $\mathbb{R}^n$ such that $(\underline{p}, \underline{Y})$ is a competitive equilibrium on Ω.*

Proof.   By Theorem 8.1.a, b, there is a positive vector $\underline{\gamma} \in \mathbb{R}^n$ and nonnegative $\alpha^1, \ldots, \alpha^A$ with

$$\alpha^k > 0, \quad \text{if} \quad \underline{y}^k \neq \underline{0},$$

and

$$\alpha^k \nabla u^k\left(\underline{y}^k\right) \leqslant \underline{\gamma}, \quad \text{for} \quad k = 1, \ldots, A.$$

Let $\underline{p}$ be the positive vector $\underline{\gamma}$. For each k such that $y^k \neq 0$, we have

$$\nabla u^k\left(\underline{y}^k\right) \leqslant \frac{1}{\alpha^k}\underline{p}$$

and

$$\frac{\partial u^k}{\partial x_j}\left(\underline{y}^k\right) = \frac{1}{\alpha^k}p_j, \quad \text{if} \quad y_j^k \neq 0.$$

For such k, $\underline{y}^k$ maximizes the pseudoconcave function u^k on $\{\underline{x} \in \mathbb{R}^n_+ | \underline{p} \cdot \underline{x} \leqslant \underline{p} \cdot \underline{y}^k\}$ by Theorem 6.1. But this statement holds trivially for those k with $y^k = \underline{0}$ since in this case, the constraint set $\{\underline{x} \in \mathbb{R}^n_+ | \underline{p} \cdot \underline{x} \leqslant \underline{p} \cdot \underline{y}^k\}$ contains only the zero vector. Therefore, $(\underline{p}, \underline{Y})$ is a competitive equilibrium. ∎

The model we have been describing in Section 8 is a simple one since it does not include firms, production, shares, etc. However, it is a straightforward matter to bring all these concepts into our model and to define Pareto optimum and competitive equilibrium in this more general framework. One then proves the same fundamental theorems relating these two types of optima, using the same techniques but keeping track of a few more constraints and multipliers. See the excellent presentations in Debreu [14], Karlin [37], Intrilligator [35], Malinvaud [45], and Smale [68].

There is another setting where theorems comparing Pareto-optimal situations with price equilibria are important—the activity analysis model introduced in Section 6.3. In this case, an output vector $y = (y_1, \ldots, y_m)$ is called *efficient* (instead of Pareto-optimal) if there is no feasible output vector $\underline{z}$ such that $\underline{z} \geqslant \underline{y}$ and $\underline{z} \neq \underline{y}$. The feasible output vectors are those which can be produced by some activity vector, i.e., $\{ \underline{y} \in \mathbb{R}^m | \underline{y} = B\underline{x}$ for some $\underline{x} \in \mathbb{R}^n_+ \}$. Using linear analysis similar to the marginal analysis of Theorems 8.3 and 8.4, one shows that the equilibrium outputs for the activity analysis problem of Section 6.3 are efficient and that every efficient, feasible output vector is an equilibrium solution for some price vector $\underline{p}$. For further readings in this area, see Koopmans [40], Karlin [37], and Charnes-Cooper [10].

8.3. Social welfare functions. As we discussed earlier, Theorem 8.3 provides an effective method for selecting an economically important element from the set of PO's that are Pareto superior to a given $\underline{Y} \in \Omega$. Another method that has classically been used for this selection process involves a *social welfare or social utility function*, i.e., a real valued function S on $\mathbb{R}^A$ (in an economy with A consumers) with the property that $S(\underline{a}^1) \geqslant S(\underline{a}^2)$ whenever $\underline{a}^1 \geqslant \underline{a}^2$. The function $\Sigma : \Omega \to \mathbb{R}$ defined by $\Sigma(\underline{X}) = S(U^1(\underline{X}), \ldots, U^A(\underline{X}))$ gives a complete ordering to the states in Ω in contrast to the partial ordering that $U : \Omega \to \mathbb{R}^A$ bestows on Ω. In principle, by maximizing Σ, one can now make a choice among the Pareto-optimal bundles.

For example, one can give the kth consumer a weight (or measure of importance) $c_k > 0$ and let

$$S(a_1, \ldots, a_A) = \sum_1^A c_k a_k.$$

By Theorem 7.7, a maximizer of Σ is a Pareto-optimal element of Ω. By Theorem 7.6, one can find all the PO's this way by proper choice of $c_1, \ldots, c_A$ if the u^k's are concave—but not if the u^k's are not concave, as Example 2 after Theorem 7.6 shows.

Thus, social welfare functions were often used to reduce concave vector maximization problems to more comfortable scalar maximization problems. Because they attach importance to the actual values of the utility functions and judge among the various consumer's gains in utility, social welfare functions are used less enthusiastically than they were thirty years ago. For further readings on social welfare functions, see Samuelson [57], Arrow [1], and Malinvaud [45].

8.4. Efficient portfolios. We close with a different but very interesting application of the theory of vector maximization in economics—an investor's selection of an optimal portfolio of securities. This problem is discussed in detail in Markowitz ([49], [50]) and summarized in Karlin [37].

Assume that an investor desires to select a portfolio of securities. If there are n different securities involved, let $x_i \geq 0$ denote the percentage of the investor's assets that will be invested in security i. The state space is $S = \{\underline{x} = (x_1, \ldots, x_n) \in \mathbb{R}^n | x_i \geq 0$ for all i and $\sum_1^n x_i = 1\}$.

The investor's first task is to appraise the future performances of the n securities. If he computes that r_{it} is the anticipated return at time t for each dollar invested in security i and d_{it} is the rate of return on security i at time t discounted back to the present, then he computes the discounted return of one unit of security i as

$$R_i = \sum_t r_{it} d_{it}.$$

In this case, the discounted anticipated return from security vector $\underline{x} \in S$ is $R(\underline{x}) = \sum_1^n R_i x_i$.

If the investor decided to maximize R on S, he would clearly select only the security (or securities) for which R_i is maximal. However, such a choice goes against the axiom that a wise investor should diversify his holdings to take into consideration the inaccuracies in his expectations and the fluctuations in the various sectors of the market.

To get around this dilemma, let us regard the R_i's as normal random variables and suppose that the investor computes some fixed probability beliefs $\{\mu_1, \ldots, \mu_n, \sigma_{11}, \sigma_{12}, \ldots, \sigma_{nn}\}$ concerning the expected returns. Here, μ_i is the mean return on the ith security and σ_{ij} is the covariance between R_i and R_j, i.e., the expected value of $(R_i - \mu_i)(R_j - \mu_j)$. Now, the mean return $E(\underline{x})$ for $\underline{x} \in S$ is

$$E(\underline{x}) = \sum_1^n \mu_i x_i,$$

and its variance is $V(\underline{x}) = \sum_{i,j} \sigma_{ij} x_i x_j$. Since $E(\underline{x})$ is a measure of the "return" of security vector $\underline{x}$ and $V(\underline{x})$ is a measure of the "risk" involved in choosing $\underline{x}$, the investor will want to maximize both E and $-V$ on S. It makes sense to define an *efficient portfolio* vector $\underline{x}$ as a PO of $(E, -V): S \to \mathbb{R}^2$.

If one assumes that V is positive definite, then there are a number of ways to compute efficient portfolios. Since E and $-V$ are both concave, the investor can give a positive weight a to E and another positive weight b to $-V$ and then maximize $aE - bV: S \to \mathbb{R}$. By Theorem 7.7, such maximizers in S will be efficient, and by Theorem 7.6 all efficient portfolios can be found this way. Alternatively, the investor can use Theorem 7.10 and maximize E on any level set of V or minimize V on the constant hyperplanes of E, provided that the gradient of E and the gradient of V point in the same direction at such solutions. By using this type of analysis, one can easily check that the set of efficient portfolio vectors is a

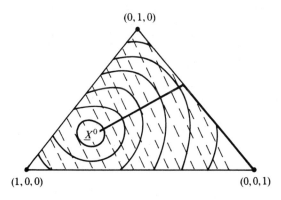

FIGURE 2

(possibly broken) line segment on S which runs from the minimizer of $V|S$ to the boundary of S and which can be parameterized by values of E.

In Figure 2, we have diagrammed an example for $n = 3$. The concentric ellipses are the level sets of $V|S$ and the dotted lines are the level sets of $E|S$. The vector $\underline{x}^0$ is a minimizer of $V|S$ and $(0, 0, 1)$ is a maximizer of $E|S$. The heavy solid line from $\underline{x}^0$ to $(0, 0, 1)$ is the set of efficient portfolios. For more details, we refer the reader to Markowitz ([49], [50]).

REFERENCES

1. K. Arrow, *Social Choice and Individual Values*, Yale University Press (1963 edition), New Haven, 1951.
2. K. Arrow and A. Enthoven, "Quasiconcave programming," *Econometrica* **29** (1961), 779–800.
3. K. Arrow and F. Hahn, *General Competitive Analysis*, Holden-Day, San Francisco, 1971.
4. K. Arrow, L. Hurwicz, and H. Uzawa, "Constraint qualification in maximization problems," *Naval Research Logistics Quarterly* **8** (1961), 175–191.
5. H. Averch and L. L. Johnson, "Behavior of the firm under regulatory constraint," *American Economic Review* **52** (1962), 1052–1069.
6. W. J. Baumol, *Economic Theory and Operations Analysis*, Prentice-Hall, Englewood Cliffs, N.J., 1961.
7. T. Bergstrom, "Notes on concave programming," Washington University Mimeographed Notes, St. Louis.
8. R. Bellman, *Introduction to Matrix Analysis*, McGraw-Hill, New York, 1960.
9. A. Ben-Tal, "Second order and related extremality conditions in non-linear programming," *Journal of Optimization Th. & Appl.* **31** (1980), 143–165.
10. A. Charnes and W. Cooper, *Management Models and Industrial Applications of Linear Programming*, vol. I, John Wiley, New York, 1961.
11. R. Courant, *Differential and Integral Calculus*, vol. II, Interscience, New York, 1947.
12. N. DaCunha and E. Polak, "Constrained minimization under vector-valued criteria in finite dimensional spaces," *Journal of Math. Analysis and Applications* **19** (1967), 103–124.
13. G. Dantzig, *Linear Programming and Extensions*, Princeton University Press, Princeton, N.J., 1963.
14. G. Debreu, *Theory of Value*, Wiley, New York, 1959.
15. G. Debreu, "Definite and semidefinite quadratic forms," *Econometrica* **20** (1952), 295–300.
16. W. de Melo, *On the Structure of the Pareto Set*, I.M.P.A., Rio de Janeiro, reprint, 1975.

17. E. Dierker, *Topological Methods in Walrasian Economics*, Springer, New York, 1974.
18. A. Dixit, *Optimization in Economic Theory*, Oxford University Press, 1976.
19. C. H. Edwards, *Advanced Calculus of Several Variables*, Academic Press, New York, 1973.
20. M. El-Hodiri, *Constrained Extrema: Introduction to the Differentiable Case with Economic Applications*, Springer, New York, 1971.
21. W. Fenchel, "Convex cones, sets, and functions," mimeographed lecture notes, Princeton University, 1953.
22. J. Ferland, "Mathematical programming problems with quasi-convex objective functions," *Mathematical Programming* **3** (1972), 296–301.
23. A. Fiacco and G. McCormick, *Non-linear Programming: Sequential Unconstrained Minimization Techniques*, John Wiley, New York, 1968.
24. W. Fleming, *Functions of Several Variables*, McGraw-Hill, New York, 1965.
25. D. Gale, *Theory of Linear Economic Models*, McGraw-Hill, New York, 1960.
26. J. Gauvin and J. Tolle, "Differential stability in non-linear programming," *S.I.A.M. Journal of Control and Optimization* **15** (1977), 294–311.
27. A. Geoffrion, "Proper efficiency and the theory of vector maximization," *Journal of Mathematical Analysis and Application* **22** (1968), 618–630.
28. M. Golubitsky and V. Guillemin, *Stable Mappings and their Singularities*, Springer, New York, 1973.
29. P. Gordan, "Über die Auflösungen linearer Gleichungen mit reelen coefficienten," *Mathematische Annalen* **6** (1873), 23–28.
30. F. J. Gould and J. Tolle, "Geometry of optimality conditions and constraint qualifications," *Mathematical Programming* **2** (1972), 1–18.
31. G. Hadley, *Linear Programming*, Addison Wesley, Reading, Mass., 1962.
32. M. Hestenes, *Calculus of Variations and Optimal Control Theory*, John Wiley, New York, 1966.
33. L. Hurwicz, "Programming in linear spaces," in Arrow, Hurwicz and Uzawa (eds.), *Studies in Linear and Non-Linear Programming*, Stanford University Press, Stanford, CA, 1958.
34. L. Hurwicz and H. Uzawa, "On the integrability of demand functions," in Chipman, Hurwitz, Richter, and Sonnenschein, (eds.), *Preferences, Utility, and Demand*, Harcourt Brace Jovanovich, New York, 1971.
35. M. Intrilligator, *Mathematical Optimization and Economic Theory*, Prentice-Hall, Englewood Cliffs, New Jersey, 1971.
36. F. John, "Extremum problems with inequalities as subsidiary conditions," in Friedrichs, Neugebauer, and Stoker, (eds.), *Studies and Essays: Courant Anniversary Volume*, Interscience, New York, 1948, pp. 187–204.
37. S. Karlin, *Mathematical Methods and Theory in Games, Programming and Economics*, vol. I, Addison-Wesley, Reading, Mass., 1959.
38. W. Karush, "Minima of functions of several variables with inequalities as side conditions," University of Chicago Master's Thesis, 1939.
39. A. Klinger, "Improper solutions of the vector maximum problem," *Operations Research* **15** (1967), 570–572.

40. T. Koopmans, "Analysis of production as an efficient combination of activities," in Koopmans, (ed.), *Activity Analysis of Production and Allocation*, John Wiley, New York, 1951.

41. H. Kuhn, "Lectures on mathematical economics," in G. Dantzig and A. Veinott (eds.), *Mathematics of the Decision Sciences*, Part 2, American Math. Soc. Lectures in Applied Math., vol. 12, Providence, Rhode Island, 1968, pp. 49–84.

42. ———, "Non-linear programming; a historical view," in R. Cottle and C. Lemke (eds.), *Nonlinear Programming*, SIAM-AMS Proceedings, volume IX Providence, Rhode Island, 1976.

43. H. Kuhn and A. Tucker, "Nonlinear programming," in J. Neuman (ed.), Proc. Second Berkeley Symposium on Math. Statistics and Probability, Univ. of California Press, Berkeley, CA, 1951.

44. O. Lange, "The foundations of welfare economics," *Econometrica* **10** (1942), 215–228.

45. E. Malinvaud, *Lectures on Microeconomic Theory*, North Holland/American Elsevier, New York, 1972.

46. O. Mangasarian, "Pseudo-convex functions," *Society for Industrial and Applied Mathematics Journal on Control* **3** (1965), 281–290.

47. O. Mangasarian and S. Fromowitz, "The Fritz John necessary optimality conditions in the presence of equality and inequality constraints," *J. Math. Analysis and Applications* **17** (1967), 37–47.

48. ———, *Nonlinear Programming*, McGraw-Hill, New York, 1969.

49. H. Markowitz, "Portfolio selection," *Journal of Finance* **7** (1952), 77–91.

50. ———, *Portfolio Selection*, John Wiley, New York, 1959.

51. G. McCormick, "Second order conditions for constrained minima," *Society for Industrial and Applied Math. Journal on Applied Mathematics* **15** (1967), 641–652.

52. E. J. McShane, "Sufficient conditions for a weak relative minima in the problem of Bolza," *Transactions of Amer. Math. Soc.* **52** (1942), 344–379.

53. J. C. Milleron, "The extrema of functions of several variables with or without constraints on the variables," Appendix to Malinvaud [45].

54. J. Milnor, *Morse Theory*, Princeton Univ. Press, Princeton, 1963.

55. L. Pennisi, "An indirect sufficiency proof for the problem of Lagrange with differential inequalities as added side conditions," *Transactions of the American Math. Society* **74** (1953), 177–198.

56. D. Saari and C. Simon, "Singularity theory of utility mappings I: degenerate maxima and Pareto optima," *Journal of Math. Economics* **4** (1977), 217–251.

57. P. Samuelson, *Foundations of Economic Analysis*, Atheneum, New York, 1974.

58. ———, "The problem of integrability in utility theory, *Econometrica* **17** (1950), 355–385.

59. H. Scarf with T. Hansen, *The Computation of Economic Equilibria* Yale University Press, New Haven, 1973.

60. E. Silberberg, *The Structure of Economics*, McGraw Hill, New York, 1973.

61. C. Simon and C. Titus, "Characterization of optima in smooth Pareto economic systems," *Journal of Math. Economics* **2** (1975), 297–330.

62. M. Slater, "Lagrange multipliers revisited: a contribution to nonlinear programming," Cowles Commission Discussion Paper, Mathematics 403, 1950.

63. S. Smale, "Global analysis and economics I, Pareto optimum and a generalization of Morse theory," in M. Peixoto (ed.), *Dynamical Systems*, Academic Press, New York, 1973.

64. ———, "Global analysis and economics III, Pareto optima and price equilibria, *Journal of Math. Economics* **1** (1974), 107–117.

65. ———, "Global analysis and economics V, Pareto theory with constraints, *Journal of Math. Economics* **1** (1974), 213–222.

66. ———, "Optimizing several functions," in A. Hattui (ed.), *Manifolds*, Tokyo 1973, University of Tokyo Press, 1975.

67. ———, "Sufficient conditions for an optimum," in A. Manning (ed.), *Dynamical Systems*, Warwick 1974, Springer, New York, 1975, pp. 287–292.

68. ———, "Global analysis and economics VI: geometric analysis of Pareto optima and price equilibria under classical hypotheses," *Journal of Math. Economics* **3** (1976), 1–14.

69. ———, "Convergent process of price adjustment and global Newton methods," *Journal of Math. Economics* **3** (1976), 107–120.

70. F. Valentine, "The problem of Lagrange with differential inequalities as added side conditions," in *Contributions to the Calculus of Variations 1933–37*, University of Chicago Press, 1937.

71. P. P. Varaiya, *Notes on Optimization*, Van Nostrand Reinhold, New York, 1972.

72. H. Varian, *Microeconomic Analysis*, Norton, New York, 1978.

73. Y. H. Wan, "Morse theory for two functions," *Topology* **14** (1975), 217–228.

74. ———, "On local Pareto optima," *Journal of Math. Economics* **2** (1975), 35–42.

75. ———, "On the algebraic criteria for local Pareto optima I," in R. Bednarek (ed.), *Dynamical Systems: Proceedings of a University of Florida International Symposium*, Academic Press, New York, 1977.

76. H. Weinberger, "Conditions for a local Pareto optimum," University of Minnesota preprint, 1974.

AN INTRODUCTION TO THE DIFFERENTIABLE APPROACH IN THE THEORY OF ECONOMIC EQUILIBRIUM*

Andreu Mas-Colell

1. INTRODUCTION

The purpose of this article is to give a synthetic treatment of the modern mathematical approach, characterized by the heavy use of

---

*A first version of this article was presented under the title "The Theory of Economic Equilibrium from the Differentiable Point of View" as a lecture at the A.M.S. Short Course on Mathematical Economics held at Toronto in August 1976. The present version has been prepared for the volume *Studies in Mathematical Economics* (MAA Studies in Mathematics series), edited by S. Reiter. It has been written in part at the Universität Bonn during my stay for the academic year 1976–77. I am indebted to C. Simon for a very careful reading of the manuscript and for many suggestions on how to improve it. It goes without saying that remaining obscurities are not his fault. Financial support of the Sonderforschungbereich 21 at the Universität Bonn and National Science Foundation Grants SOC76-19700 and SOC76-19700A01 to the University of California, Berkeley, is gratefully acknowledged.

Any opinions, findings, and conclusions or recommendations expressed in this publication are those of the author and do not necessarily reflect the views of the National Science Foundation. The last version of this paper was completed and submitted in January, 1978.

differential methods, to the theory of general economic equilibrium. The latter was founded slightly over a hundred years ago by Walras [51] and its modern versions have crystallized in works such as Debreu's *Theory of Value* [7] or Arrow and Hahn's *General Competitive Analysis* [2]. Although our exposition will be self-contained, there is no doubt that to develop a good intuition for the economic meaning of concepts and theorems, as well as for historical background, the reader will benefit from the consultation of these books.

Trained as they were in the nineteenth century, the classical mathematical economists (Walras [51], Pareto [39], Fisher [22]) who put together general equilibrium theory used calculus as their basic tool. Hicks' *Value and Capital* [25] and Samuelson's *Foundations of Economic Analysis* [41] represent the culmination of this classical line of work. After World War II there was a reversal. Under the combined impact of input-output analysis, linear programming and two-person zero-sum games, the differential methods were deemphasized and even fell into disrepute, in favour of topology and convexity theory. There were, undoubtedly, many valid reasons for this radical change of mathematical instruments. As one, especially relevant here, we could mention that the classical writers were quite often found guilty of settling the question of existence of solutions to the system of equations modelling an economy by a mechanical counting of equation and unknowns.

In the last ten years the differentiability techniques have come back in force. (It goes without saying that they were never completely lost; they were, for example, strongly relied upon in stability analysis, see Arrow and Hurwicz [1].) This renaissance has been due on the one hand to a purely mathematical development: the new vitality in the last two decades of the differential approach to topology, and on the other hand to the growing realization among general equilibrium theorists that equilibrium existence questions, while basic, did not exhaust the field of the determinateness of equilibrium problems (which would include matters such as uniqueness, local uniqueness, sensitivity, stability, etc.) and that in the broader context of this problem perhaps there was something valid in the counting of equations and unknowns of the old days. The seminal paper was by Debreu [8]. He and Smale (see, for example,

his recent article [48]) have been key figures in the new developments. The influence of Milnor's book *Topology from the Differentiable Viewpoint* [38] has also been considerable.

Since our primary aim is to illustrate how the new mathematical
techniques are put to use, we do not strive to present the most
general economic model but settle for one that, hopefully, strikes a
good balance between ease of manipulation and conceptual rich-
ness. Thus, we proceed by treating the consumption side of the
economy very succinctly by means of a so-called aggregated excess
demand function and the production side by means of Koopmans'
linear activity model.

Our presentation in Parts 2 to 5 builds towards the statement in
Part 4 of a fundamental result: a global index theorem for the
equilibrium set of an economy. Part 7 gives the proof which, with
an unknown degree of success, has been devised to be an instructive
one. The references are at the ends of parts and sections.

For the mathematics used, the books of Guillemin and Pollack
[24] and Hirsch [29] are recommended; but to read this article one
needs only some familiarity with the implicit function theorem and
with the notion of the derivative as a linear map. Survey papers on
the economic theory are Debreu [13] and Dierker [16]. The article
by Simon, Chapter 2, also testifies to the current interest in calculus
tools in economics.

2. DESCRIPTION OF AN ECONOMY. EQUILIBRIUM

We will deal with the situation where there are $l \geq 1$ perfectly
divisible *commodities*. In this context, a *price system p* is a vector
$(p^1, \ldots, p^l)$. We will only consider strictly positive price vectors,
i.e., $p \gg 0$ (meaning $p^i > 0$ for all i).

For the purposes at hand an *economy* shall be described by two
objects: the *excess demand function* and the *production activities*.
The excess demand function summarizes the (price-taking)
behaviour of the consumption side of the economy while the
production activities describe the technological possibilities of
transforming commodities into commodities, i.e., the feasible
input-output combinations.

2.1. Excess demand functions. Let $R^l_{++} = \{q \in R^l: q \gg 0\}$, $R^l_+ = \{q \in R^l: q \geqslant 0\}$. Formally, an excess demand function f is a *continuous* map from R^l_{++}, interpreted as the domain of prices, to R^l, interpreted as a set of net demands (positive components) and supplies (negative components), which satisfies:

H.1: (Homogeneity): For every $p \in R^l_{++}$ and $\lambda > 0$, $f(\lambda p) = f(p)$, i.e., only relative prices matter.

H.2: (Walras Law): For every $p \in R^l_{++}$, $p \cdot f(p) = 0$, i.e., intended expenditures in buying commodities equal the expected receipts of selling commodities.

H.3: (Boundedness below): There is a $\lambda \in R$ such that for all $p \in R^l_{++}$ and $1 \leqslant i \leqslant l$, $f^i(p) > \lambda$, i.e., it is not possible to supply an arbitrarily large amount of a commodity.

H.4: (Desirability): If $p_n \to p$, $p_n \gg 0$, $p \neq 0$ and $p^i = 0$ for some i, then $\|f(p_n)\| \to \infty$, where $\|\ \|$ is the usual Euclidean norm, i.e., if some, but not all, prices go to zero then the demand of some of the commodities with prices going to zero becomes infinite (assume that H.3 holds).

The concept of excess demand function as well as the set of hypotheses H.1–H.4 is entirely standard in economics (see, for example, Arrow and Hahn [2] Chs. 2, 4). An excess demand function fulfilling H.1–H.4 could, for example, be originated from more basic concepts as follows.

EXAMPLE 1. There are n consumers; each one of them, say the jth, has some initial endowments of commodities $\omega_j \in R^l_{++}$ and a continuous, strictly quasi-concave utility function $u_j: R^l_+ \to R$ such that if $x \geqslant y$, $x \neq y$, then $u_j(x) > u_j(y)$ (strong monotonicity). The individual excess demand function f_j is then defined by letting $f_j(p)$ be the vector obtained by subtracting ω_j (supply) for the unique maximizer of u_j on $\{x \in R^l_+: p\ x \leqslant p \cdot \omega_j\}$ (demand). Figure 1 illustrates $f_j(p)$ for $l = 2$. It is easily verified that f_j satisfies H.1–H.4. The excess demand function of the economy is

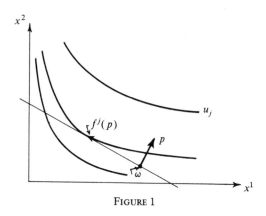

then $f = \sum_{j=1}^{n} f_j$ which, clearly, also satisfies H.1–H.4. It can be shown that essentially any excess demand function can be generated as in this example (see Sonnenschein [49], Mantel [34], Debreu [12], Mas-Colell [37]).

While hypotheses H.1–H.3 are in the nature of the concept of excess demand function, H.4 is quite restrictive in a production context, since it implies that every commodity will, at some prices, be demanded, i.e., every commodity is to some extent desirable and affordable for consumption purposes. Thus, in Example 1, it is because of H.4 that we have to impose the stringent and unnatural requirement of strong monotonicity of utility functions and strict monotonicity of initial endowments. Although the theory and results to be developed in this paper do not depend crucially on H.4, they become slightly more cumbersome to present without H.4. Since our purposes are mainly expository, we shall stick to H.4.

By H.1 only relative prices matter. Hence from now on we will regard $S = \{ p \in R_{++}^l : \|p\|^2 = (p^1)^2 + \cdots + (p^l)^2 = 1 \}$ as the price domain of the excess demand function. The advantage of $\|p\| = 1$ over other normalizations is that f becomes then a *tangent vector field* on S since, by H.2, for every $p \in S$, $f(p) \in T_p(S) = \{ v \in R^l : p \cdot v = 0 \}$, the tangent space to S at p; see Figure 2.

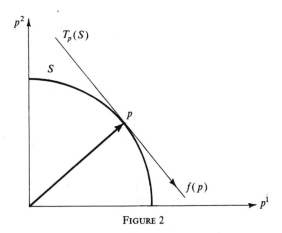

FIGURE 2

REFERENCES. For the concepts of this section see Arrow and Hahn [2] Chs. 2, 4, Debreu [7] Ch. 4, and Dierker [15].

2.2. Production activities. An *activity* is a vector $a \in R^l$. With the convention of giving outputs a positive sign and inputs a negative sign, any positive multiple of $a \in R^l$, designated as an activity, is interpreted as a feasible input-output combination. In other words, given any $\alpha > 0$ it is assumed that if, for every i, there was available the amount of commodity $\max\{0, -\alpha a^i\}$ it would be technically possible to produce the amounts $\max\{0, \alpha a^i\}$, $1 \leq i \leq l$, as outputs. The number α is called the *level of operation* of the activity a. For example, the activity vector $(-1, -2, 4)$ means that it is possible to produce 4α units of commodity 3 with α units of commodity 1 and 2α units of commodity 2.

We are given a *finite* set $\mathscr{A} \subset R^l$ of activities. The set $Y(\mathscr{A}) \subset R^l$ of feasible input-output combinations, called the *production set*, is then

$$Y(\mathscr{A}) = \left\{ \sum_{a \in \mathscr{A}} \alpha_a a : \alpha_a \geq 0 \quad \text{all } a \in \mathscr{A} \right\}.$$

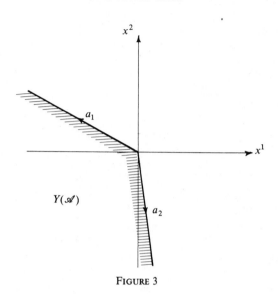

FIGURE 3

We assume

H.5: $Y(\mathscr{A})$ is a pointed cone containing the negative orthant. See Figure 3.

By definition $Y(\mathscr{A})$ is also convex and polyhedrical; H.5 embodies the economic assumptions of *constant returns to scale* (if $x \in Y(\mathscr{A})$ then $\alpha x \in Y(\mathscr{A})$ for all $\alpha \geq 0$), *impossibility of free production* ($Y(\mathscr{A}) \cap R_+^l = \{0\}$), *free disposal* ($-R_+^l \subset Y(\mathscr{A})$) and *irreversibility* (if $x \in Y(\mathscr{A})$ and $-x \in Y(\mathscr{A})$ then $x = 0$).

EXAMPLE 2. $\mathscr{A} = \{e_i : 1 \leq i \leq l\}$, where $e_i^j = 0$ if $j \neq i$ and $e_i^i = -1$. Then $Y(\mathscr{A}) = -R_+^l$. That is to say, the only conceivable productive activity is the disposal of already existing commodities.

REFERENCES.   The production model just described is Koopmans' linear activity analysis [33]. See, also, Debreu [7] Ch. 3.

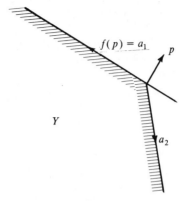

FIGURE 4

2.3. Equilibrium. An *economy* is, simply, the pair $(\mathscr{A}, f)$.

A price system $p \in S$ and activity levels $\{\bar{\alpha}_a: a \in \mathscr{A}\}, 0 \leqslant \bar{\alpha}_a < \infty$, are in *production equilibrium* if, for every $a \in \mathscr{A}$, the levels $\bar{\alpha}_a$ maximizes the profits of operation of the activity. Since profits at level α_a are $\alpha_a(p \cdot a)$, $\bar{\alpha}_a$ should maximize $\alpha_a(p \cdot a)$ on $\alpha_a \geqslant 0$. Clearly, if there exists such an $\bar{\alpha}_a$, $p \cdot a$ cannot be positive. In other words, $\{\bar{\alpha}_a: a \in \mathscr{A}\}$, $0 \leqslant \bar{\alpha}_A < \infty$, are in production equilibrium at prices p if and only if $p \cdot a \leqslant 0$ for all a and $p \cdot a = 0$ whenever $\alpha_a > 0$.

A price system p and activity levels $\{\bar{\alpha}_a: a \in \mathscr{A}\}$ constitute *an equilibrium for the economy* $(\mathscr{A}, f)$ if:

(i) there is production equilibrium,
(ii) $\sum_{a \in \mathscr{A}} \bar{\alpha}_a a = f(p)$, i.e., the net input-output vector equals the vector of supplies and demands.

We also say that a price vector p is an equilibrium price if there is a set of activity levels satisfying (i) and (ii) above. See Figure 4, where $\bar{\alpha}_2 = 0$ and $\bar{\alpha}_1 = 1$.

We will now introduce some concepts and reformulate the equilibrium condition in a manner convenient for later application.

Given any $A \subset \mathscr{A}$, let L_A, L_A^+ be, respectively, the subspace and the positive cone spanned by A (by convention, $L(\varnothing) = \{0\}$); $L_A^\perp$ is the orthogonal complement of L_A. Denote $S_A = S \cap L_A^\perp$ i.e., S_A is the set of prices at which the activities in A just break even, and let Π_A be the perpendicular projection map of R^l onto $L_A^\perp$. Define $f^A \colon S_A \to R^l$ by $f^A(p) = \Pi_A \circ f(p)$. Note that $p \cdot f^A(p) = 0$ for every $p \in S_A$ so that f^A is a tangent vector field on S_A.

For any $p \in S$ call $A(p) = \{a \in A \colon p \cdot a = 0\}$ the *base* of p. Of course $p \in L_{A(p)}^\perp$ and so $p \in S_{A(p)}$.

Then $p \in S$ is an equilibrium price system if, besides $p \cdot a \leqslant 0$ for all $a \in \mathscr{A}$, we have $f(p) \in L_{A(p)}^+$. Clearly, this latter condition implies $f^{A(p)}(p) = 0$.

REFERENCES. The (competitive) equilibrium notion described is the classical one of Walras [51]. See Arrow and Hahn [2] Chs. 2, 5 and Debreu [7] Ch. 5.

3.   A SPACE OF ECONOMIES

We will now introduce a parameterized set of economies.

We begin with a set $\mathscr{M}$ such that to every $m \in \mathscr{M}$ there is associated an economy $(\mathscr{A}_m, f_m)$. Since so general a setting could scarcely be useful we further postulate:

H.6: $\mathscr{M}$ is a compact metric space.

H.7: f is jointly continuous on p and m.

H.8:   H.3 holds uniformly on $\mathscr{M}$.

H.9:   H.4 holds uniformly on $\mathscr{M}$, i.e., if $m_n \to m$, $p_n \to p$, $p_n \in S$, $p \notin S$, then $\|f_{m_n}(p_n)\| \to \infty$.

H.10:   If $m_n \to m$ then, as sets, $\mathscr{A}_{m_n} \to \mathscr{A}_m$ (in, say, the Hausdorff distance for the nonempty, closed subsets of R^l).

Except for the convenience hypothesis H.9 (the same comment as in Part 2 applies here), the framework H.6–H.10 encompasses most of the specific situations one encounters in the economics literature.

For simplicity, in all the subsequent examples we have a fixed $\mathscr{A}$ and put $\mathscr{A}_m = \mathscr{A}$ for all $m \in \mathscr{M}$.

EXAMPLE 3. With reference to Example 1 and with utility functions fixed we could let $\mathcal{M}$ be a compact subset of R^{ln}_{++} and interpret every $m \in \mathcal{M}$ as a n-tuple of initial endowments (see Debreu [8]).

EXAMPLE 4. Again with reference to Example 1 but now keeping the initial endowments fixed (this is really immaterial) we could let $\mathcal{M}$ be a compact subset of $\mathcal{U}^m$ where $\mathcal{U}$ is a suitable topologized space of utility functions or, perhaps, of individual excess demand functions (see, respectively, Smale [45] and Dierker and Dierker [17]).

EXAMPLE 5. $\mathcal{M}$ is the set of measures on a compact metric space of agents characteristics (endowed with the topology of the weak convergence); see Hildenbrand [27].

Define

$$E = \{(m, p) \in \mathcal{M} \times S: p \text{ is an equilibrium price vector}$$
$$\text{for } (\mathcal{A}_m, f_m)\}.$$

We call E the equilibrium set. It would be more appropriate at this stage to include the equilibrium level of activities in the definition of E but this will become very soon (Part 4.1) unimportant and so, we shall save on notation.

THEOREM 1. E is a compact set.

Proof. Let $(m_n, p_n) \in E$, $m_n \to m$. We show first that $\{p_n\}$ has an accumulation point in S. Indeed, suppose $p_n \to p \notin S$. By H.9 $\|f_{m_n}(p_n)\| \to \infty$; by H.8 this means that, denoting $b_n = f_{m_n}(p_n)$, $b_n/\|b_n\|$ has an adherent point b in R^l_+. Since $A_{m_n} \to A_m$ and $b_n/\|b_n\| \in Y(A_{m_n})$ we have $b \in Y(A_m)$ which contradicts H.5. Therefore we can assume $(m_n, p_n) \to (m, p) \in \mathcal{M} \times S$. By H.7 and H.10 $f_{m_n}(p_n) \to f_m(p)$, $f_m(p) \in Y(A_m)$, and $x \in Y(A_m)$ implies $p \cdot x \leqslant 0$. Furthermore, $f_m(p) = \lim_n f_{m_n}(p_n) \in L^+_{A_m(p)}$, since each $f_{m_n}(p_n)$ lies in $L^+_{A_{m_n}}$ and $A_{m_n} \to A_m$. Hence, $(m, p) \in E$. ∎

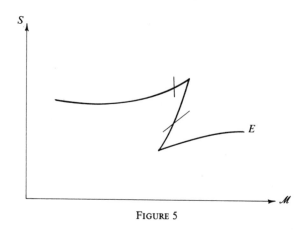

FIGURE 5

The attentive reader of the preceding proof can verify that if instead of H.6 we had just assumed that $\mathcal{M}$ is a separable metric space, then the projection of E on $\mathcal{M}$ would be a proper map. See Figure 5.

REFERENCES. The consideration of whole spaces of economies was initiated by Kannai [30] and Hildenbrand [27]. The need for such a study arose with the continuum approach to the Core Equivalence Theorem (see Aumann [3]) and has led to the heavy utilization of measure theoretical tools in economics.

4. REGULAR ECONOMIES

In this part we shall place the theory of Part 2 and 3 in a smoothness framework.

We consider first a single fixed economy $(\mathcal{A}, f)$ and postulate that, besides H.1–H.5, it satisfies:

H.11: f is a C^1 function.

This is a natural hypothesis and not difficult to justify in the context of Example 1 (see Debreu [9], [10], Mas-Colell [37]).

Smoothness allows us to speak meaningfully about "degenerate" and "nondegenerate" equilibria. Consider, for example, the zeros of

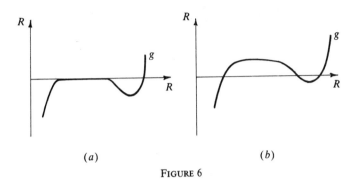

FIGURE 6

a C^1 function $g: R \to R$; it is intuitive that a situation such as Figure 6a is "degenerate" and that, consequently the set of zeros of the function is very "unstable"; on the contrary the situation of Figure 6b is nondegenerate, i.e., regular, and the zero set is "stable." What distinguishes the two cases? Clearly, an important difference is the fact that in the first case the derivative map at a zero of the function vanishes. With this hint we proceed to formulate a notion of regular economy.

4.1. Some definitions and a theorem. We begin by hypothesizing a general position condition on the activities $\mathscr{A}$.

H.12: If $A \subset \mathscr{A}$ and $\#A \leqslant l$ then A is a linearly independent collection of vectors.

Obviously, if $\mathscr{A}$ does not satisfy H.12, a small perturbation will. If H.12 holds then for any $p \in S$ the basis $A(p) = \{a \in \mathscr{A}: p \cdot a = 0\}$ is a linearly independent collection and so, if $p \in S$ is an equilibrium price vector the equilibrium activity levels $\{\alpha_a: a \in \mathscr{A}\}$ are uniquely determined (remember that at equilibrium $\alpha_a = 0$ if $a \notin A(p)$); they will be denoted $\alpha_a(p)$. Thus an equilibrium is unambiguously determined by the price vector.

Condition H.12 will be part of our definition of regularity. It will be assumed from now on.

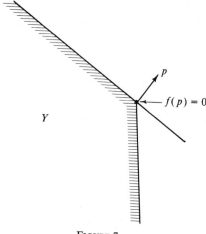

FIGURE 7

Next, we want to eliminate the possibility that at an equilibrium a basis vector not be in operation, i.e., if an activity does not operate it must be because it would make losses otherwise.

H.13: If $p \in S$ in an equilibrium, then $\alpha_a(p) > 0$ for every $a \in A(p)$ (geometrically, $f(p)$ belongs to the interior of the face $Y(\mathscr{A}) \cap \{v \in R: p \cdot v = 0\}$).

Figure 7 describes the situation ruled out.

A consequence of H.13 is that if p is an equilibrium price vector then there is no change in the base $A(p)$ over a sufficiently small neighbour of p on $S_{A(p)}(= \{q \in S: q \cdot a = 0 \text{ for all } a \in A(p)\})$.

Suppose that $\bar{p}$ is an equilibrium price vector satisfying H.12 and H.13.

Consider $S_{A(\bar{p})}$, the intersection of S with $L_{A(\bar{p})}^{\perp}$ in R^l. In Section 2.3, we defined

$$f^{A(\bar{p})}: L_{A(\bar{p})}^{\perp} \rightarrow L_{A(\bar{p})}^{\perp}$$

as $f^{A(\bar{p})} = \Pi_{A(\bar{p})} \circ f$, where $\Pi_{A(\bar{p})}$ is the projection of R^l onto

$L^{\perp}_{A(\bar{p})}$. As noted near the end of Section 2.3, $f^{A(\bar{p})}$ is a tangent vector field on $S_{A(\bar{p})}$ since, for all $p \in S_{A(\bar{p})}$, we have $f^{A(\bar{p})}(p) \in L^{\perp}_{A(\bar{p})}$ and $p \cdot f^{A(\bar{p})}(p) = 0$, that is to say,

$$f^{A(\bar{p})}(p) \in T_p\big(S_{A(\bar{p})}\big) = T_p(S) \cap L^{\perp}_{A(\bar{p})}$$
$$= \big\{ v \in L^{\perp}_{A(\bar{p})} : p \cdot v = 0 \big\}.$$

Since $\bar{p}$ is an equilibrium price vector, $f^{A(\bar{p})}(\bar{p}) = 0$ and we may conclude that $Df^{A(\bar{p})}(\bar{p})$ maps $T_{\bar{p}}(S_{A(\bar{p})})$ into $T_{\bar{p}}(S_{A(\bar{p})})$—indeed, differentiating $p \cdot f^{A(\bar{p})}(p) = 0$ at $\bar{p}$, we have

$$0 = \bar{p} \cdot Df^{A(\bar{p})}(\bar{p}) + f^{A(\bar{p})}(\bar{p}) = \bar{p} \cdot Df^{A(\bar{p})}(\bar{p}).$$

We shall add to our definition of regularity that this map be onto

H.14: Assume H.12 and H.13. At every equilibrium price vector p, $Df^{A(p)}(p)$ maps $T_p(S_{A(p)})$ onto $T_p(S_{A(p)})$ or, *equivalently*, rank $Df^{A(p)}(p) = l - 1 - \#A(p)$. By definition, $Df^{A(p)}(p) = \Pi_{A(p)} \cdot Df(p)$.

In spite of its apparent technicality, the meaning of H.14 is transparent: It says that infinitesimally there are as many nonredundant equations to determine the equilibrium price as there are unknowns.

DEFINITION. An economy $(\mathscr{A}, f)$ is regular if H.12, H.13, and H.14 are satisfied.

DEFINITION. Let $(\mathscr{A}, f)$ be regular and p be an equilibrium price vector. The index of p denoted $i(p)$ is defined to be $(-1)^{\#A(p)}$ times the sign of the determinant of the linear map $\Pi_{A(p)} \circ Df(p)$: $T_p(S_{A(p)}) \to T_p(S_{A(p)})$. If $\#A(p) = l - 1$ then $T_p(S_{A(p)}) = \{0\}$; by convention the determinant sign is then $+1$ (hence, if $\#A(p) = l - 1$, $i(p) = (-1)^{l-1}$).

EXAMPLE 6. Let $Y(\mathscr{A}) = -R^l_+$ as in Example 2. Then an economy is regular if whenever $f(p) = 0$, rank $Df(p) = l - 1$.

This is the situation studied by Debreu [8] and Dierker and Dierker [17].

For the purposes of demonstrating our main theorem it will be convenient, but not at all necessary, to strengthen somewhat conditions H.13 and H.14.

H.13′: If $p \in S$ is such that $f(p) = \sum_{a \in A(p)} \alpha_a a$, then $\alpha_a \neq 0$ for every $a \in A(p)$.

H.14′: Assume H.12 and H.13. For every $p \in S$, if $f(p) \in L_{A(p)}$ then $Df^{A(p)}(p)$ maps $T_p(S_{A(p)})$ onto $T_p(S_{A(p)})$ or, equivalently, rank $Df^{A(p)}(p) = l - 1 - \#A(p)$. By definition, $Df^{A(p)}(p) = \Pi_{A(p)} \circ Df(p)$.

Note that H.13′ and H.14′ are the same as H.13 and H.14 except we no longer require $p \cdot a \leqslant 0$ for every $a \in \mathscr{A}$.

From now on, we take H.12, H.13′, and H.14′ as our definition of a regular economy.

Let us reintroduce our space of economies $\mathscr{M}$ satisfying H.7–H.10 and impose an appropriate smoothness hypothesis. For the moment we postulate that there is a fixed $\mathscr{A}$ such that $\mathscr{A}_m = \mathscr{A}$ for all $m \in \mathscr{M}$. Hence, only f_m depends on m.

H.15: $Df_m(p)$ is jointly continuous in m and p.

The next theorem summarizes the sharp implications for equilibrium that lie in the concept of regularity. It justifies the name "regular economies." It shows that at regular economies the equilibrium set E_m is finite and "locally stable," i.e., as m in Figure 8.

THEOREM 2. *Let $\overline{m} \in \mathscr{M}$ be regular. Then there is a neighborhood of $\overline{m}$, $U \subset \mathscr{M}$ and continuous functions $\phi_1, \ldots, \phi_h \colon U \to S$ such that for every $m \in U$:*

(i) $$\phi_j(m) \neq \phi_{j'}(m) \quad \text{if } j \neq j', \quad \text{and}$$

(ii) $$\{ p \in S \colon (m, p) \in E \} = \bigcup_{j=1}^{h} \phi_j(m).$$

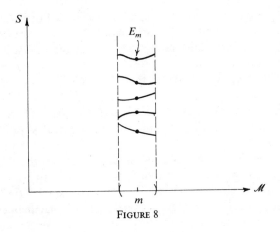

FIGURE 8

Proof. By Theorem 1 it suffices to show that if $\bar{p} \in E_{\bar{m}}$ then there are neighbourhoods $\bar{m} \in U \subset \mathcal{M}$, $\bar{p} \in Q \subset S$ and a continuous function $\phi: U \to S$ such that $(m, p) \in (U \times Q) \cap E$ if and only if $p = \phi(m)$.

By H.12 and H.13 there are neighborhoods $\bar{m} \in U \subset \mathcal{M}$ and $\bar{p} \in Q \subset S$ such that $(m, p) \in (U \times Q) \cap E$ if and only if $f_m^{A(\bar{p})}(p) = 0$.

The result will now be a consequence of the following version of the Implicit Function Theorem (L. Schwartz [43], pg. 278):

> *Let $\mathcal{M}$ be a topological space, $S \subset R^n$ an open set and $G: \mathcal{M} \times S \to R^n$ a function such that for all $(m, p) \in \mathcal{M} \times S$ $D_p g(m, p)$ exists and depends jointly continuously on m and p. Suppose that $g(\bar{m}, \bar{p}) = 0$ and rank $D_p g(\bar{m}, \bar{p}) = n$. Then there are open sets $\bar{m} \in U \subset \mathcal{M}$, $\bar{p} \in Q \subset S$ and a continuous function $\phi: U \to Q$ such that $(m, p) \in U \times Q$, $g(m, p) = 0$ if and only if $p = \phi(m)$.*

To get our result from the previous theorem we only have to perform a trivial normalization on $f^{A(\bar{p})}$. Take, without loss of generality, the case $A(\bar{p}) = \varnothing$ so that $f^{A(\bar{p})} = f$. We can identify S with its projection in the first $l - 1$ coordinates and regard therefore the price domain as an open subset of R^{l-1}. Further, letting g: $S \to R^{l-1}$ be the first $l - 1$ coordinates of f, we have because of H.2 that $g(p) = 0$ if and only if $f(p) = 0$ and rank $Df(\bar{p}) = l - 1$ if and only if rank $Dg(\bar{p}) = l - 1$. By putting $n = l - 1$ in the previous theorem we are done. ∎

4.2. A treatment of regularity via transversality. This section is in the nature of a detour and can be skipped without further consequence.

The theorem of the previous section hypothesized a space of economies $\mathscr{M}$ with a fixed production set $\mathscr{A}$. It was shown that if $(\mathscr{A}, f_m)$ is regular then the equilibrium set is "stable" (in the sense of Figure 7) if f_m is slightly perturbed. But, what happens if the perturbation is made on $\mathscr{A}$? The answer is that the equilibrium set is stable in this case as well. In fact, loosely speaking, at a regular economy there is stability against any (small, C^1) perturbation. This is not well seen from the phrasing chosen to define regularity. Hence in this section we will state an equivalent definition, based on the notion of transversality of smooth manifolds, which will make the stability property intuitively most plausible. We shall not give proofs nor be very rigorous here; everything stated however can be proved without much difficulty. The books of Guillemin and Pollack [24], and Hirsch [29] can be consulted for the mathematical concepts to be introduced.

Let Q be a C^1 manifold and $M, N \subset Q$ be two C^1 submanifolds. One says that M and N are transversal, denoted $M \pitchfork N$ if whenever $x \in M \cap N$ the sum $T_x(M) + T_x(N)$ equals $T_x(Q)$; in Figure 9a, M and N are transversal, in Figure 9b they are not. In particular, if dim M + dim N = dim Q and $M \pitchfork N$, then $M \cap N$ is a discrete set of points (see Figure 9a) and it is intuitive, and at any rate a consequence of the Implicit Function Theorem, that in bounded regions of Q the intersection set is stable against small, C^1 perturbations of M and N. If dim M + dim N < dim Q and $M \pitchfork N$, then $M \cap N = \varnothing$.

We want to show that the notion of regular economy can be expressed in terms of manifold transversality.

Let $T(S) = \{(p, x) \in S \times R^l : p \cdot x = 0\}$; $T(S)$ is a C^∞ manifold of dimension $2(l - 1)$ called the *tangent bundle* of S.

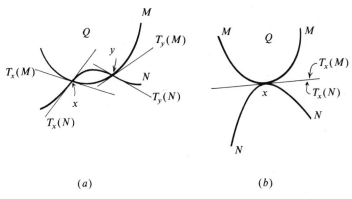

(a)   (b)

FIGURE 9

Given a C^1 excess demand function $f: S \to R^l$ its graph is Graph$(f) = \{(p, f(p)): p \in S\} \subset T(S)$. So, Graph$(f)$ is a $(l - 1)$ submanifold of $T(S)$.

Let a set of activities $\mathscr{A}$ be given. For every $A \subset \mathscr{A}$ and $A' \subset A$ put

$$J(A, A') = \left\{(p, x) \in S \times R^l: p \in L_A^\perp, x \in L_{A'}\right\} \subset T(S).$$

Then $J(A, A')$ is a submanifold of $T(S)$ of dimension $(l - 1) - \#(A \setminus A')$.

Observe that if $p \in S$ is an equilibrium price for $(\mathscr{A}, f)$ then $(p, f(p)) \in \text{Graph}(f) \cap J(A(p), A(p))$.

It is not hard to verify that conditions H.13′ and H.14′ are equivalent to the following condition:

H.16: $(\mathscr{A}, f)$ is regular if H.12 is verified and for every $A \subset \mathscr{A}$, $A' \subset A$, Graph$(f) \pitchfork J(A, A')$.

In words, $(\mathscr{A}, f)$ is regular if the "consumption side" of the economy is transversal to the "production side."

REFERENCES. The seminal paper in the theory of regular economies is Debreu's [8]. The concept of regular exchange economy was introduced there while, for the exchange case, the definition given here first appeared in Dierker and Dierker [17]. Again for the exchange case the index of an equilibrium was first recognized by Dierker [14]. Definitions of regular economies for more general models of production have been proposed in G. Fuchs [23], and Mas-Colell [36]. A theory of regular economies not centered on the concept of aggregate excess demand has been extensively studied (including production) by Smale [45], [46]. Except in a somewhat unsatisfactory manner in Mas-Colell [36] the linear activity model had not previously been studied. K. Hildenbrand [26] was first to call attention to the version of the Implicit Function Theorem used. For further references see Dierker [16] and Debreu [11], [13].

5.   GENERICITY OF REGULAR ECONOMIES

In this part we shall argue that, provided the parameterized set of economies $\mathcal{M}$ is rich enough, most economies will be regular. "Most" could mean open-dense if $\mathcal{M}$ is a general metric space and "of full Lebesgue" measure if $\mathcal{M}$ is, say, an open subset of an Euclidean space. Thus the situation is analogous to the one depicted in Figures 6a and b where 6a appears clearly pathological. In the mathematical literature, properties of this kind are referred to as *generic*.

Since the theory of general economic equilibrium is a static one, the genericity of regular economies provides justification for restricting our analysis to equilibria of regular economies. The "static" qualification must be emphasized. For the purposes of a *dynamic theory* the in-depth analysis of *critical* (i.e., nonregular) *economies* is most important since, in the first place, it is there that any qualitative change takes place and, second, they may unavoidably appear in the trajectory of a dynamic path.

We will give a very rough treatment of the genericity question. It is assumed that there is a fixed set of activities $\mathcal{A}$ and that $\mathcal{M}$ is an open subset of R^s for some $s > 0$. We write $f_m(p)$ in the form $f(p, m)$ and require:

H.17: $f: S \times \mathcal{M} \to R^l$ is a C^1 function.

H.18:   For any $p \in S$, $D_m f(p, m)$ has rank $l - 1$.

It is hypothesis H.18 that captures the "rich enough" requirement on $\mathcal{M}$; given any economy m it is possible to distort it in any direction.

EXAMPLE 7. Example 3 satisfies both H.17 and H.18.

There is an unpalatable aspect to the above treatment: It postulates the inexistence of purely intermediate commodities, i.e., produced commodities which only become valuable in the process of production but are neither final consumption goods nor non-produced original inputs supplied by consumers. While a satisfactory genericity treatment has to, and no doubt can, allow for intermediate goods there appears to be a gap in the literature which we shall not fill for the occasion. Given the illustrative purposes (of types of reasonings, tools and techniques) which dominate this presentation H.18 will be good enough.

An economy $m \in \mathcal{M}$ which is nonregular shall be called *critical*.

THEOREM 3. *The set of critical, i.e., nonregular, economies form a closed set of (Lebesgue) measure zero.*

The proof constitutes an (immediate) application of Sard's theorem, a recent (1942) but most important theorem of analysis. For the present version see, for example, Guillemin and Pollack [24] p. 68, where the phrasing is in terms of transversality but the translation is immediate; the usual version is on page 39. See also Spivak [50].

SARD'S THEOREM. *Let $U \subset R^s$, $V \subset R^t$ be open sets and g: $U \times V \to R^n$, $s \leqslant n$, a C^1 function. Suppose that g satisfies the condition: for every $(u, v) \in U \times V$ $Dg(u, v)$ has rank n, i.e., maps onto, then for almost every v $f(u, v) = 0$ implies rank $D_u f(u, v) = n$.*

Call a function g regular if it satisfies the conditions of Sard's theorem. If $s = n$ then by the usual version of the Implicit Function Theorem the set $\{u \in U: f(u, v) = 0\}$ must be discrete for every v satisfying the conclusion of the Theorem. If $s < n$ the only possibility is that $\{u \in V: f(u, v) = 0\}$ be empty.

Let us now apply Sard's theorem to our problem. Hypotheses H.13′ and H.14′ can be strengthened and written jointly as follows:

H.19: For any $A' \subset A \subset \mathcal{A}$, $\#A \leqslant l - 1$, if $f(p) \in L_{A'}$, $A = A(p)$, then $Df^A(p)$ maps $T_p(S_A)$ onto $T_p(S_{A'})$.

Clearly H.19 implies H.14'. To see that it also yields H.13' note that if $A' \subset A$ and $A' \neq A$ then dim $T_p(S_A) <$ dim $T_p(S_{A'})$. So, the conclusion can only be satisfied if $f(p) \in L_{A'}$, $A = A(p)$, is impossible. But this is precisely H.13'.

To deduce H.19 from H.17, H.18 and Sard's theorem, we need to "normalize" f, i.e., to work in a space of dimension $l - 1$ rather than l. The simplest and most standard (although not the most elegant) way to do this is to project all the spaces and functions on the $l - 1$ space spanned by the first $l - 1$ commodities; in other words, we drop from consideration the price and demand-supply of the lth commodity. With this understanding the measure zero property of critical economies follows from Sard's theorem if for every $A' \subset A \subset \mathscr{A}$, $\#A \leqslant l - 1$, we interpret $V = \mathscr{M}$, $U = S_A$, $g = f^{A'}$, and $R^n = T_p(S_{A'})$; note also there is only a finite number of $A' \subset A \subset \mathscr{A}$ combinations.

The closedness properties of critical economies is an immediate consequence of the definition, Theorem 1, and the continuity of determinant functions.

REFERENCES. The prototypical version of Theorem 3 was given first by Debreu [8] in the context of Example 7. Versions encompassing more general and complete situations than Debreu's have been offered by Dierker and Dierker [17], Smale [45], [46], Fuchs [23], Mas-Colell [36], Balasko [4], Dierker [18], Cheng [5], Hildenbrand [26], and others. See Debreu [13], for an extensive reference list.

6. THE MAIN THEOREM

For every economy $(\mathscr{A}, f)$ let $E(\mathscr{A}, f)$ be the set of its equilibrium prices. It is assumed that economies satisfy the hypotheses H.1–H.5 and H.11. Clearly, if an economy is regular then $\#E(\mathscr{A}, f) < \infty$.

MAIN THEOREM. *If the economy $(\mathscr{A}, f)$ is regular then*

$$\sum_{p \in E(\mathscr{A}, f)} i(p) = (-1)^{l-1}.$$

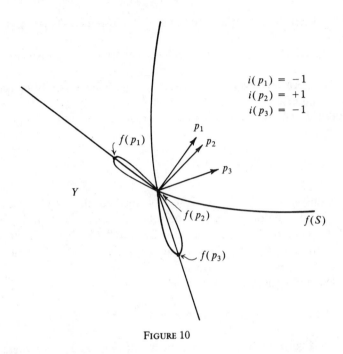

FIGURE 10

Some consequences of the theorem are:

(i) Since $i(p) = \pm 1$, $\#E(\mathscr{A}, f)$ is an odd number. In particular $\#E(\mathscr{A}, f) \neq 0$, i.e., a price equilibrium *exists*.

(ii) Suppose that a regular economy $(\mathscr{A}, f)$ is such that for every $p \in E(\mathscr{A}, f)$ there is a full set of activities in operation, i.e., $\#A(p) = l - 1$ for every $p \in E(\mathscr{A}, f)$. Since then $i(p) = (-1)^{(l-1)}$ for every $p \in E(\mathscr{A}, f)$ we conclude that the equilibrium is unique.

An illustration of the theorem is provided in Figure 10.

REFERENCES. For the case of Examples 2, 6, and 7, the so-called exchange economies, the index theorem was given by Dierker [14]. For the present linear activity case the theorem as well as consequence (ii) seem to be new. Both have been the object of simultaneous and independent finding by Timothy Kehoe [31] at Yale. The production equilibrium problem can be formally subsumed in the so-called "non-linear complementary problem." An index theory for the latter is implicitly contained in Saigal and Simon [40]. See also Eaves and Scarf [20].

7. PROOF OF THE MAIN THEOREM BY PATH-FOLLOWING

For all of this part a fixed *regular* economy $(\mathscr{A}, f)$ is given.

7.1. An auxiliary construction: one parameter family of economies. Let $e = (1, \ldots, 1) \in R^l$ and $\Delta = \{q \in R^l_{++}: q \cdot e = 1\}$. To every $q \in \Delta$, we associate an excess demand function

$$f_q(p) = (p \cdot e)\left(\frac{q^1}{p^1}, \ldots, \frac{q^l}{p^l}\right) - e.$$

Denote $\hat{q} = (1/\|q\|)q$. It is easily verified that $f_q(\hat{q}) = 0$ and $q \cdot f_q(p) > 0$ for $p \neq \hat{q}$. Furthermore, for any $q \in \Delta$ and $p \in S$, $D_q f_q(p)$ maps $T_q\Delta = \{w: w \cdot e = 0\}$ onto $T_p(S)$. This is clear since for any $w \in R^l$, $D_q f_q(p)w = (p \cdot e)(w^1/p^1, \ldots, w^l/p^l)$. Note also that $T_q(\Delta) = T_e(S)$ for any $q \in \Delta$.

We will choose $q \in \Delta$ satisfying:

H.20: $q \cdot y < 0$ for any nonzero $y \in Y(\mathscr{A})$.

See Figure 11. If there is a q in Δ satisfying H.20, then there is a whole open set of such q since the property will be preserved under small perturbations. The existence of one such q follows from the separating hyperplane theorem (see, for example, Debreu [7]) and H.5.

An economy $(\mathscr{A}, f_q)$ which satisfies H.20 has the unique equilibrium $\hat{q}$. Furthermore,

$$D_p f_q(p)w = (w \cdot e)\left(\frac{q^1}{p^1}, \ldots, \frac{q^l}{p^l}\right) - (p \cdot e)\left(\frac{q^1 w^1}{(p^1)^2}, \ldots, \frac{q^l w^l}{(p^l)^2}\right).$$

One checks easily that $D_p f_q(p)w = 0$ if and only if w is a multiple of p. Therefore, rank $D_p f_q(p)|T_p(S) = l - 1$ for all $p \in S$ and $(\mathscr{A}, f_q)$ is a regular economy.

To compute the index of the equilibrium q, we need to compute the sign of det $D_p f_q(\hat{q})$ on $T_{\hat{q}}(S)$, which will clearly

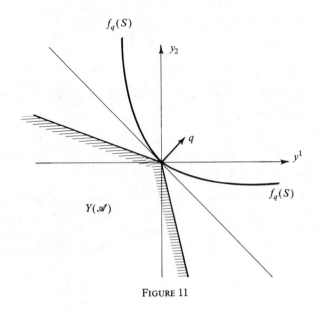

FIGURE 11

equal the sign of $\det D_p \hat{f}_q(q)$ on R^{l-1} where $\hat{f}_q(p) = (f_q^1(p), \ldots, f_q^{l-1}(p))$. But, $D_p f_q(q)$ has a negative diagonal matrix; hence, the sign of its determinant is $(-1)^{l-1}$. Thus, the index of $\hat{q}$ is $(-1)^{l-1}$.

For every $q \in \Delta$ we define a *one-parameter family of excess demand functions* as follows: for every $0 \le t \le 1$, let $f_{q,t} = tf + (1-t)f_q$. Of course, $f_{q,0} = f_q$ and $f_{q,1} = f$. We will also write $f_{q,t}(p)$ as $f_q(p, t)$. The *one-parameter family of economies* is then $(\mathscr{A}, f_{q,t})$, $0 \le t \le 1$. Note that the family satisfies H.3 and H.4 uniformly.

Relative to a fixed q, let

$$E = \left\{ (p, t) \in S \times [0,1] : p \text{ is an equilibrium for } (\mathscr{A}, f_{q,t}) \right\},$$

$E_t = \{ p \in S : (p, t) \in E \}$, and, for every $A \subset \mathscr{A}$ with $\#A \le l - 1$, put $I_A = \{(p, t) \in S_A \times [0,1] : f_q^A(p, t) \equiv \Pi_A \circ f_q(p, t) = 0\}$. Disregarding the nonnegativity requirement, I_A is a kind of equilibrium set relative to the activities in A. Of course,

$$E \subset \bigcup_{\substack{A \subset \mathscr{A} \\ \#A \leq l-1}} I_A.$$

The one-parameter family $(\mathscr{A}, f_{q,t})t \in [0, 1]$ will be called *regular* if it satisfies:

H.21:   For every $A \subset A' \subset \mathscr{A}$ with $\#A' \leq l - 1$ we have that if $p \in S_{A'}$ and $f_q^A(p, t) = 0$ i.e., $f_q(p, t) \in L_A$, then $D_{p,t} f_q^A(p, t)$ maps $T_p(S_{A'}) \times R$ onto $T_p(S_A)$.

The implications of the regularity property will be spelled out later on. The next section will be devoted to showing that by perturbing q slightly we can guarantee that the one-parameter family be regular. If the reader is willing to believe this, the section can be skipped.

7.2.   Genericity of regular one-parameter families.   We shall now use Sard's theorem in a manner entirely analogous to its use in Part 5.

Let $Q = \{ q \in \Delta \colon q$ satisfies H.20$\}$; Q is nonempty and open.

Consider two fixed $A \subset A' \subset \mathscr{A}$, $\#A' \leq l - 1$.

By construction at any $\bar{p} \in S_{A'}$, $\bar{t} \in [0, 1)$ and $\bar{q} \in Q$, $D_q f_{\bar{q}}^A(\bar{p}, \bar{t})$ maps $T_e(S)$ onto $T_{\bar{p}}(S_A)$. If $\bar{t} = 1$ and $f_{\bar{q}}^A(\bar{p}, 1) = 0$ then, by the regularity assumption on $f_{\bar{q},1}$, $D_p f_{\bar{q}}^A(\bar{p}, 1)$ maps $T_{\bar{p}}(S_{A'})$ onto $T_{\bar{p}}(S_A)$—if $A' = A$ this is true by H.14'; if $A' \neq A$ this is true vacuously because by H.13' $p \in S_{A'}$ and $f_{\bar{q}}^A(\bar{p}, 1) = 0$ cannot simultaneously hold. Hence, at any $\bar{p} \in S_{A'}$, $\bar{q} \in Q$ and $\bar{t} \in [0, 1]$ if $f_{\bar{q}}^A(\bar{p}, \bar{t}) = 0$ then $D_{q,p,t} f_{\bar{q}}^A(\bar{p}, \bar{t})$ maps $T_{\bar{p}}(S_{A'}) \times R \times T_e(S)$ onto $T_{\bar{p}}(S_A)$. Therefore, by Sard's theorem—see Part 5—almost every $q \in Q$ will be such that f_q satisfies H.21 with respect to A' and A. Since there is only a finite number of pairs $\{A, A'\}$, the proof of the existence of one $q \in Q$ fulfilling H.21 is concluded. Strictly speaking, to apply Sard's theorem we must normalize f_q in the usual manner; this is done, without difficulty, as in Part 5 (project $T_p(S_{A'})$, into the first $l - 1$ coordinates of R^l and drop from f_q the last coordinate function).

N.B.:   From now on, a fixed q making $(\mathscr{A}, f_{q,t})$, $t \in [0, 1]$, regular is retained. We drop reference to it.

7.3. The structure of I_A. We now consider a fixed $A \subset \mathscr{A}$, $\#A \leq l - 1$, with $S_A \neq \varnothing$ and study $I_A \subset S_A \times [0,1]$. Without loss of generality and merely for notational convenience we take $A = \varnothing$. Then, we replace S_A by S and $f_t^A: S_A \times R \to L_A^\perp$ by $f_t: S \times R \to R^l$. We also put $I_A = I$ and let z stand for (p, t).

By H.21, whenever $f(z) = 0$, $Df(z)$ maps $T_p(S) \times R$ onto $T_p(S)$. Hence, we can apply the following form of the Implicit Function Theorem (see Milnor [38] pg. 13 and Appendix):

> *Let M be an m dimensional smooth manifold with boundary. Let $f: M \to R^{m-1}$ be a C^1 function such that f and $f|\partial M$ have 0 as regular value (i.e., if $f(z) = 0$—resp. $(f|\partial M)(z) = 0$—then $Df(z)$—resp. $D(f|\partial M)(z)$—maps onto; ∂M denotes the boundary of M) then $f^{-1}(0)$ is a 1-dimensional manifold and $\partial f^{-1}(0) = f^{-1}(0) \cap \partial M$. Further, if $f^{-1}(0)$ is compact then it consists of a finite number of components each diffeomorphic to the unit circle or the unit interval*

(see Figure 12 or 13).

In our case, relying on the usual normalization of f (i.e., project S onto R^{l-1} and drop the last coordinate of f) we see that the conditions of the theorem are met with $M = S \times [0,1]$. Also, by

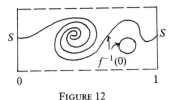

FIGURE 12

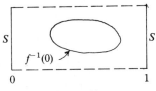

FIGURE 13

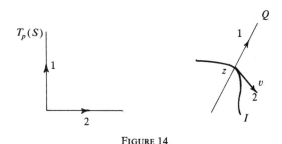

FIGURE 14

H.4, $f^{-1}(0)$ is compact (remember the proof of Theorem 1 and note that $S_A \neq \varnothing$ implies $L_A \cap R_+^l = \{0\}$). So, up to diffeomorphism, $f^{-1}(0)$ is composed of a finite number of pairwise disjoint segments and circles.

For each $p \in S$ we can choose a set of $(l-1)$ vectors $w_1(p), \ldots, w_{l-1}(p)$ tangent to S at p which form a basis of $T_p(S)$ and vary smoothly with p. Adding to the basis the positive unit vector of R, we have a smooth basis for $T_p(S) \times R$ for each p, which we will call the main basis of $T_p(S) \times R$.

Consider a point $z = (p, t) \in I$. Take a vector $v \neq 0$ tangent to the one-dimensional set I at z. Since I is defined as $f^{-1}(0)$, $Df(z)v = 0$. Supposing that $l > 1$, consider any $(l-1)$ dimensional subspace $Q \subset T_p(S) \times R$ which does not include v. Give Q an ordered basis in such a manner that by adding v to this basis as the lth vector, this new basis has the same orientation as our main basis of $T_p(S) \times R$ (i.e., the linear map which carries our new jth basis vector to the jth vector in the main basis has positive determinant). See Figure 14. Since rank $Df(z) = l - 1$ and since $Df(z)v = 0$, $Df(z): T_p(S) \times R \to T_p(S)$ maps Q onto $T_p(S)$ in a one-to-one manner and so $Df(z)|Q$ has a nonzero determinant. It is a simple argument (use the continuity of the determinant function) to verify the sign of this determinant is independent of the choice of Q and of the choice of ordered basis of Q and $T_p(S)$. We will call the sign of the determinant "sign v."

If $\#A = l - 1$, then S_A is a single point $p_A \in S$ and $I_A = \{p_A\} \times [0, 1]$. In this case if v is tangent to I_A and is not zero, sign v has the natural meaning.

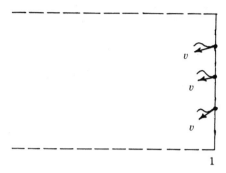

FIGURE 15

Define the index of z relative to A and v, written as $i(z, A, v)$, as $(-1)^{\#A} \cdot \text{sign } v$.

Of course, we always have $i(z, A, v) = -i(z, A, -v) \neq 0$.

Let $p \in S$ be an equilibrium price vector of our given economy $(\mathcal{A}, f_1)$. Then, $(p, 1) \in I_{A(p)}$. Denote $(p, 1)$ by z. For a tangent vector $v \in T_p(S_{A(p)}) \times R$ to $I_{A(p)}$ at z, let's study $i(z, A(p), v)$. Since $(\mathcal{A}, f)$ is regular, the last coordinate of v—denoted v_t—must be different from zero (see Figure 15). Suppose $v_t > 0$. Letting $Q = T_p(S)$, we can then take as basis for Q the main basis $w_1(p), \ldots, w_{l-1}(p)$, of $T_p(S)$. Hence, if $v_t > 0$,

$$i(z, A(p), v) = i(p) = (-1)^{\#A(p)} \times \text{sign det } Df_1^{A(p)}(p)$$

(with the convention that $\text{sign det } Df_1^{A(p)}(p) = 1$ if $\#A(p) = l - 1$). Of course, if $v_t < 0$, $i(z, A(p), v) = -i(p)$.

7.4. Fitting together different I_A. Let $V = \{z \in S \times [0,1] | z \in I_A \cap I_{A'}, \; A \neq A'\}$. For reasons to become clear in the next section, points of $\mathcal{V}$ shall be called *switch points*.

Let $z = (p, t) \in I_A$ for some $A \subset \mathcal{A}$ with $\#A \leq l - 1$. So, $f(p,t) \in L_A$. Then, $A \subset A(p) = \{a \in \mathcal{A}: \; p \cdot a = 0\}$ and $z \in I_{A(p)}$. Hence, we can write $f^{A(p)}(p, t) = \sum_{a \in A(p)} \alpha_a a$ in a unique manner, by our assumption H.12 on $\mathcal{A}$. Put $A'(p) = \{a \in A(p): \alpha_a \neq 0\}$. Then, $A'(p) \subset A$ and $z \in A'(p)$ also. Therefore, if

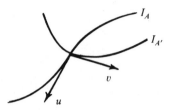

FIGURE 16

$z \in V$, we must have $A'(p) \neq A(p)$. Let $A' = A'(p)$ and $A = A(p)$. Since $A' \subset A$, $S_A \subset S_{A'}$ and $\#A' + 1 \leq \#A$. By the regularity hypothesis H.21, $Df^{A'}(z)$ maps $T_p(S_A) \times R$ onto $T_p(S_{A'})$. Therefore, $\dim[T_p(S_A) \times R] \geq \dim T_p(S_{A'})$, or $(l - 1) - \#A + 1 \geq (l - 1) - \#A'$, or $\#A' + 1 \geq \#A$. We conclude that $\#A' + 1 = \#A$ and that $A(p) = A'(p) \cup \{a\}$ for some $a \in \mathscr{A} \setminus A'(p)$. In words, the only way that (p, t) may belong to two distinct I_A, $I_{A'}$, is for one of $\{A, A'\}$ to be $A(p)$ and the other to be $A(p)$ with exactly one activity vector a removed.

Let $z = (p, t) \cup V$. Set $A' = A'(p)$ and $A = A(p)$ with $A = A' \cup \{a\}$. Take $v \neq 0$ (resp. $u \neq 0$) to be a vector tangent to $I_{A'}$ (resp. I_A) at z, i.e., $v \in T_p(S_{A'}) \times R$ and $Df^A(z)v = 0$ (resp., $u \in T_p(S_A) \times R$ and $Df^A(z)u = 0$). See Figure 16.

We claim that (i) $(a, 0) \cdot v \neq 0$, and (ii) $a \cdot Df^{A'}(z)u \neq 0$. Indeed,

(i) if $(a, 0) \cdot v = 0$, then $v \in T_p(S_A) \times R$ because $v \in T_p(S_{A'}) \times R$. However, $v \neq 0$ and $Df^{A'}(z)v = 0$. This contradicts the fact that $Df^{A'}(z)$ maps $T_p(S_A) \times R$ one-to-one and onto $T_p(S_{A'})$, (by H.21 and $\dim(T_p(S_A) \times R) = \dim T_p(S_{A'})$).

(ii) if $a \cdot Df^{A'}(z)u = 0$, then $Df^{A'}(z)u$ is perpendicular to a and lies in $T_p(S_A)$. Hence, $Df^A(z)u = Df^{A'}(z)u$. So, $Df^A(z)u = 0$, $u \in T_p(S_A) \times R$, and $u \neq 0$, which is impossible for the same reason as in (i).

Let us interpret (i) and (ii). At z the activity a breaks even and it is operated at zero level; (i) says that as we move along $I_{A'}$ in the v direction we pass from the region of positive (or negative) potential profits of the activity to the region of negative (or positive) poten-

FIGURE 17

tial profits without even infinitesimally dwelling in the region of zero profits. The interpretation of (ii) is entirely analogous with respect to the level of operation of the activity.

An implication of (i) and (ii) is that any two I_A, $I_{A'}$ cross at most a finite number of times. Hence, V is a finite set.

7.5. Defining some piecewise smooth paths. Pick any $z \in E \cap (\partial(S \times [0,1]))$ i.e., $z = (p, t) \in E$ and $t \in \{0, 1\}$. Then $z \in I_{A(p)}$ and $z \notin V$. Since z belongs to the boundary of $S \times [0,1]$, see Figure 17, the orientation of a tangent vector $v \in T_p(S_{A(p)}) \times R$ to $I_{A(p)}$ at z, which is required to point inwards, is well determined.

We begin now a path at z by following $I_{A(p)}$ in the v direction. We claim that if the rule of never leaving the E region is enforced there is a uniquely determined path beginning at z (i.e., there is never the possibility of bifurcation) and this path necessarily terminates at a point of the boundary of $S \times [0,1]$ *distinct* from z. Indeed, z is an endpoint of a component of $I_{A(p)}$ which is a segment, we now show that the other endpoint belongs also to the boundary of $S \times [0,1]$ (see Section 3). The path starting at z follows this segment "at a steady pace." Subject to the constraint of staying in E, only two things are possible: (i) a point of V is reached, (ii) the other endpoint of the segment is reached. In case (ii) we are done. Consider case (i).

Let $z' = (p', t') \in V$ be the point reached and take $v_{z'}^-$ to be the tangent vector to $I_{A(p)}$ in the direction of arrival (i.e., in the direction compatible with v); see Figure 18. At z', $A(p') = A(p)$ and $A'(p') = A(p') \setminus \{a\}$ for an activity $a \in \mathscr{A}$. Denoting $A =$

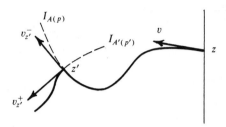

FIGURE 18

$A(p')$, $A' = A'(p')$, we saw in Section 4 that $a \cdot Df^{A'}(z')v_{z'}^- \neq 0$ which because we arrive from region E implies $a \cdot Df^{A'}(z')v_{z'}^- < 0$. So, if we keep to I_A we are led to a negative level of activity for a, i.e., we abandon region E. There is no choice but to switch from I_A to $I_{A'}$. In which direction? In Section 4, we saw that if u is tangent to $I_{A'}$ at z' then $(a, 0)u \neq 0$. So, there is only one direction leading to negative potential profits for a, i.e., we must choose $v_{z'}^+$, the exit direction from z', so that $(a, 0)v_{z'}^+ < 0$. We have now a new starting point and a new starting direction to follow. The ruling principle is always the same: if a switch point is reached, either a new activity enters and we join it to the basis and follow in the direction where the activity comes into operation, or an activity reaches zero level of operation and we drop it from the basis and follow in the direction where it would give potential losses. There are only a finite number of points in V and, subject to the constraint of staying in E, the path constructed never has bifurcations or crossroads, i.e., every point of V can be visited at most once. Therefore, the path must terminate and since it can only do so at the boundary of $S \times [0, 1]$ we obtain our conclusion. See Figure 19.

We shall prove in the next section:

INVARIANCE OF INDEX PROPERTY. *Let* $\bar{z} = (\bar{p}, \bar{t})$ *be the endpoint of the path started at* $z = (p, t)$ *in the direction* v. *Let* $\bar{v}$ *be the arrival direction at* $\bar{z}$ *(see Figure 19). Then*

$$i(z, A(p), v) = i(\bar{z}, A(\bar{p}), \bar{v}).$$

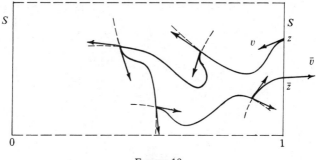

FIGURE 19

The invariance of index property yields the main theorem. Indeed, take first $z = (q, 0)$ as starting point of our path. Then, the corresponding ending point $\bar{z}$ must necessarily be of the form $(\bar{p}, 1)$—remember $E \cap \partial(S \times [0,1]) = (q, 0)$—i.e., $\bar{p}$ is an equilibrium of $(\mathscr{A}, f_1)$. Since v points inward, $\bar{v}$ must point outward, i.e., $v_t > 0$, $\bar{v}_t > 0$, see Figure 20. Therefore, $i(\bar{p}) = i(\bar{z}, A(\bar{p}), \bar{v})$ $= i(z, \varnothing, v) = (-1)^{l-1}$ because, given $v_t > 0$, $i(z, \varnothing, v)$ equals the index of q in the economy $(\mathscr{A}, f_0)$. Any path starting at $z \in S \times \{1\}$, $z \neq \bar{z}$, can only terminate at $S \times \{1\}$ (the endpoint $(q, 0)$ has already been preempted by $(\bar{p}, 1)$ and only one path begins, hence ends, at $(q, 0)$). So, letting aside $\bar{p}$, the equilibria of $(\mathscr{A}, f_1)$ are associated in pairs. Consider one of those pairs, say p' and p''; there is a path connecting $z' = (p', 1)$ and $z'' = (p'', 1)$. The exit

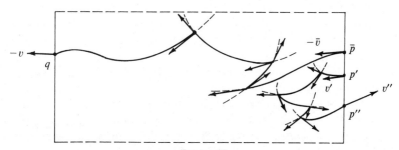

FIGURE 20

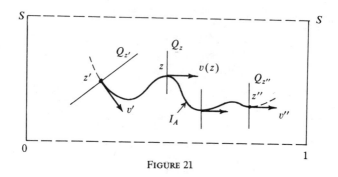

FIGURE 21

direction v' at z' points inwards, i.e., $v'_t < 0$, while the arrival direction at z'' points outwards, i.e., $v''_t > 0$. See Figure 20. So, $i(p') = -i(z', A(p'), v') = -i(z'', A(p''), v'') = -i(p'')$. Therefore,

$$\sum_{p \in E(\mathscr{A}, f)} i(p) = (-1)^{l-1}.$$

7.6. Proof of the invariance of index property. We first note that for any $A \subset \mathscr{A}$, $\#A \leq l - 1$, if two $z', z'' \in I_A$ belong to the same component of I_A and v', v'' are tangent vectors to I_A at z', z'', respectively, which are oriented in a compatible manner, then $i(z', A, v') = i(z'', A, v'')$. Indeed, there is a nonzero vector field $v(z)$ along the component of I_A having $v(z') = v'$, $v(z'') = v''$, see Figure 21. Hence, if for any $z = (p, t)$ we let Q_z be the orthogonal complement of $v(z)$ in $T_p(S_A) \times R$, the determinant of the map $Df(z) \colon Q_z \to T_p(S_A)$ moves continuously with z and cannot vanish. So, it cannot change signs, i.e., $i(z', A, v') = i(z'', A, v'')$.

Therefore, it is the behavior of the index at switch points which must occupy us.

Let $z = (p, t) \in V$ be reached along the path. Denote by A' (resp. A) the base associated with the incoming (resp. outgoing) paths and v^- (resp. v^+) the arrival (resp. exit) direction. We need to show that $i(z, A', v^-) = i(z, A, v^+)$.

Without loss of generality, we can take $A = A' \cup \{a\}$. Since $a \in T_p(S_A)$ we can assume that the main base of $T_p(S_A)$ is orthogonal and has, as the first coordinate, the vector a. For notational ease we put $T = T_p(S_{A'})$, $T_a = T_p(S_A) = \{u \in T: a \cdot u = 0\}$.

Set $h = \dim T = (l - 1) - \#A' \geq 1$. Let B be the $h \times (h + 1)$ matrix of the linear map $Df^{A'}(z): T \times R \to T$. We can write B as

$$ B = \begin{bmatrix} \beta & \eta & \xi \\ \gamma & \hat{B}_a & \theta \end{bmatrix}, $$

where β is a number, η is an $(h - 1)$ row vector, ξ is a number, $\hat{B}_a$ is a $(h - 1) \times (h - 1)$ matrix corresponding to T, and γ and θ are $(h - 1)$-column vectors.

Similarly, let B_a be the $(h - 1) \times h$ matrix of the linear map $Df^A(z): T_a(S^A) \times R \to T_a$. We can write B_a as

$$ B_a = \begin{bmatrix} \hat{B}_a & \theta \end{bmatrix}. $$

If $h = 1$ (i.e., T is one-dimensional), then $\hat{B}_a$, η, γ, and θ are empty symbols. Let $\hat{B} = \begin{bmatrix} \beta & \eta \\ \gamma & \hat{B}_a \end{bmatrix}$. The indices $i(z, A', v^-)$ and $i(z, A, v^+)$ are properties of the matrices B and B_a and of the vectors v^- and v^+. Since both indices are different from zero, they are invariant under a small perturbation of the matrices B and B_a.

Carrying out, if necessary, such a small perturbation, we can assume that $\hat{B}$ and, if $h > 1$, $\hat{B}_a$ are nonsingular. Since $B_a v^+ = 0$ and $\hat{B}_a$ is nonsingular, $v_t^+ \neq 0$. Since $Bv^- = 0$ and $\hat{B}$ is nonsingular, $v_t^- \neq 0$. Then, in order to compute the index, we can take as complementary space to v^- (resp. v^+) the space T (resp. T_a) itself. If $v_t^- > 0$ (resp. $v_t^+ > 0$), we can take as oriented basis in T (resp. T_a) the main basis itself. So, if we take into account that $i(z, A', v^-) = -i(z, A', -v^-)$ and $i(z, A, v^+) = -i(z, A, -v^+)$, we can conclude

$$ i(z, A', v^-) = (-1)^{\#A'} \text{sign}(v_t^-) |\hat{B}| $$

$$ i(z, A, v^+) = (-1)^{\#A} \text{sign}(v_t^+) |\hat{B}_a|, $$

where $|\ \ |$ denotes determinant. If $\hat{B}_a$ is an empty symbol (i.e., $h = 1$), then $|\hat{B}_a| = 1$.

Since $(-1)^{\#A} \cdot (-1)^{\#A'} = -1$, $i(z, A', v^-) \cdot i(z, A, v^+) = -\text{sign}[(v_t^-) \cdot (v_t^+) \cdot |\hat{B}| \cdot |\hat{B}_a|]$. To demonstrate $\text{sign}\, i(z, A', v^-) = \text{sign}\, i(z, A, v^+)$, we need only show that

$$\text{sign}(v_t^-)(v_t^+) = -\text{sign}\, |\hat{B}| \cdot |\hat{B}_a|.$$

Hence, the following Lemma concludes the proof.

LEMMA. $\text{sign}(v_t^-)(v_t^+) = -\text{sign}\, |\hat{B}| \cdot |\hat{B}_a|.$

Proof.   Recall that $(a, 0)$ is the first basis vector of $T \times R$. Since v^- is the direction coming from the region E of economic equilibria, on $I_{A'}$, the new activity a enters the picture at z (as argued in Section 7.5) and we must have $v_1^- > 0$. Similarly, v^+ is the direction going to E and we must have $(Bv^+)_1 > 0$, where $(Bv^+)_1$ is the first coordinate of Bv^+.

Put $\hat{v}^- = (\text{sign}\, v_t^-)v^-$ and $\hat{v}^+ = (\text{sign}\, v_t^+)v^+$. Then, $\hat{v}_t^- > 0$, $\hat{v}_t^+ > 0$, and $\text{sign}(\hat{v}_1^-)(B\hat{v}^+)_1 = \text{sign}(v_t^-)(v_t^+)$. We will show that $\text{sign}(\hat{v}_1^-)(B\hat{v}^+)_1 = -\text{sign}|\hat{B}||\hat{B}_a|.$

We can take $\hat{v}_t^- = \hat{v}_t^+ = 1$. Consider the equation

$$B\begin{bmatrix} u \\ y \end{bmatrix} = \begin{bmatrix} \beta & \eta & \xi \\ \gamma & \hat{B}_a & \theta \end{bmatrix}\begin{bmatrix} u \\ y \end{bmatrix} = \begin{bmatrix} w \\ 0 \end{bmatrix},$$

where u and w are scalars and y is an h-column vector. If $y_t = 1$, we have that

$$\hat{v}_1^- = u \qquad \text{when} \quad w = 0,$$
$$(B\hat{v}^+)_1 = w \qquad \text{when} \quad u = 0.$$

Let $\bar{w}$ be the solution of the equation with $u = 0$. Then $\bar{w} = -\eta \hat{B}_a^{-1}\theta + \xi$ (where if $h = 1$ an "empty" term of the sum such as $-\eta \hat{B}_a^{-1}\theta$ is taken to be zero. This comment applies as well to similar situations in the next paragraph).

Let $\bar{u}$ be the solution of the equation with $w = 0$. If we denote by (δ, ω)—δ being a number—the first row of $\hat{B}^{-1}$ then $\bar{u} =$

$-(\delta\xi + \Sigma_{i=2}^{h}\omega_i\theta_i)$. More explicitly:

$$\delta = \frac{|\hat{B}_a|}{|\hat{B}|}$$

and

$$\omega_i = \frac{(-1)^{i+1}}{|\hat{B}|}\left(\sum_{k=2}^{h}(-1)^k\eta_k|\hat{B}_{a(k,i)}^T|\right)$$

where $\hat{B}_a^T$ is the transpose of $\hat{B}_a$ and $\hat{B}_{a(k,i)}^T$ is the matrix obtained from $\hat{B}_a^T$ by deleting the kth row and ith column. Remember, also, that if $h = 1$ then $|\hat{B}_a| = 1$.

Therefore,

$$\bar{u} = -\frac{1}{|\hat{B}|}\left(|\hat{B}_a|\xi + \sum_{i=2}^{h}\sum_{k=2}^{h}(-1)^{i+k+1}\eta_k\theta_i|\hat{B}_{a(k,i)}^T|\right)$$

or, simply,

$$\bar{u} = -\frac{|\hat{B}_a|}{|\hat{B}|}\left(\xi - \eta\hat{B}_a^{-1}\theta\right).$$

We conclude that

$$\bar{u}\bar{w} = -\frac{|\hat{B}_a|}{|\hat{B}|}\left(\xi - \eta\hat{B}_a^{-1}\theta\right)^2$$

and so,

$$\text{sign}(\hat{v}_1^-)(B\hat{v}^+)_1 = -\text{sign}|\hat{B}_a||\hat{B}|. \qquad Q.E.D.$$

7.7. Final comment. The reader will have noticed that the previous proof has a constructive and computational flavor. In fact, the path constructed from $(q, 0)$ and arriving at an equilibrium of the given economy could be (approximately) followed either by complementarity pivot methods (Scarf [42], Eaves [19], Eaves-Scarf

[20]) or by numerical solution methods for differential equations (see Kellogg, Li and Yorke [32] and Smale [47]).

It should come as no surprise that we get an existence result without appealing to any fixed point theorems. It was shown by Hirsch [28] (see also Milnor [38] pg. 14) that Brouwer's fixed point theorem can be obtained via Sard's theorem.

REFERENCES. The path following procedure of the proof is well known. Mathematically, it is a quite standard homotopy argument. The same applies to the orientation arguments used. The interested reader may consult the book by Milnor [38] which has had a substantial influence in mathematical economics.

In the context of theoretic simplicial methods of computation, Eaves [19] pointed out the usefulness of adding a parameter and appealing to homotopy arguments. The technique has been further developed and applied to the computation of solutions of piecewise linear equations by Eaves and Scarf [20]; their paper also contains an analysis of the index.

Kellogg, Li and Yorke [32] and Smale [47] have proposed algorithms for differentiable functions based on differential equations but not relying on the addition of a parameter. The one-parameter trick seems to have the advantage that if we actually want to compute a solution then, a priori information on its approximate location can be exploited by appropriately choosing the function at $t = 0$.

Our problem is a mixture of differentiable and piecewise linear and this is reflected in the piecewise differentiable nature of our solution paths.

A simplicial type algorithm to compute equilibria of economies with linear activities was given by Scarf in his book [42], Ch. 5. Different algorithms for piecewise linear economies specified by production activities and utility functions (i.e., as Example 1) rather than excess demand functions have been recently proposed by Dantzig, Eaves and Gale [6], Wilson [56] and Elken [21]. The latter contains an extensive survey of path-following methods.

REFERENCES

1. K. Arrow and L. Hurwicz, "On the stability of the competitive equilibrium," *Econometrica* **26** (1958), 522–552.
2. K. Arrow and F. Hahn, *General Competitive Analysis*, Holden-Day, 1971.
3. R. Aumann, "Markets with a continuum of traders," *Econometrica* **32** (1964), 39–50.
4. Y. Balasko, "The graph of the Walras correspondence," *Econometrica* **43** (1975), 907–912.
5. H. Cheng, "Convergence of value and core allocations in a piecewise smooth model," Ph.D. Dissertation, University of California, Berkeley, 1977.
6. G. Dantzig, C. Eaves, and D. Gale, "An algorithm for a piecewise linear model of trade and production with negative prices and bankruptcy," mimeographed,

Department of Operations Research, Stanford University, 1976.

7. G. Debreu, *Theory of Value*, John Wiley, New York, 1959.

8. ———, "Economies with a finite set of equilibria," *Econometrica* **38** (1970), 387–392.

9. ———, "Smooth preferences," *Econometrica* **40** (1972), 603–615.

10. ———, "Corrigendum," *Econometrica* **44** (1975), 831–832.

11. ———, "Four aspects of the mathematical theory of economic equilibrium," Proceedings of the International Congress of Mathematicians, Vancouver, Canada, 1974, pp. 65–77.

12. ———, "Excess demand functions," *Journal of Mathematical Economics* **1** (1974), 15–23.

13. ———, "Regular differentiable economies," *American Economic Review* **66** (1976), Papers and Proceedings, 280–287.

14. E. Dierker, "Two remarks on the number of equilibria of an economy," *Econometrica* **40** (1972), 951–953.

15. ———, *Topological Methods in Walrasian Economics*, Lecture Notes on Economics and Mathematical Systems, 92, Springer-Verlag, Berlin, 1974.

16. ———, "Regular economies," In M. Intrilligator (ed.), *Frontiers in Quantitative Economics*, North-Holland, New York, 1976.

17. E. Dierker and H. Dierker, "The local uniqueness of equilibria," *Econometrica* **40** (1973), 867–881.

18. H. Dierker, "Smooth preferences and the regularity of equilibria," *Journal of Mathematical Economics* **2** (1975), 43–63.

19. E. Eaves, "Homotopies for computation of fixed points," *Mathematical Programming* **3** (1972), 1–22.

20. C. Eaves and H. Scarf, "The solution of systems of piecewise linear equations," *Mathematics of Operations Research* **1** (1976), 1–27.

21. T. Elken, "The computation of equilibria by path methods," Ph.D. Dissertation, Stanford University, 1977.

22. I. Fisher, *Mathematical Investigations in the Theory of Value and Prices*, (1892) reprinted by Augustus Kelley, New York, 1961.

23. G. Fuchs, "Private ownership economies with a finite number of equilibria," *Journal of Mathematical Economics* **1** (1974), 141–159.

24. V. Guilleman and A. Pollack, *Differential Topology*, Prentice-Hall, New Jersey, 1974.

25. J. Hicks, *Value and Capital*, Clarendon Press, Oxford, 1939.

26. K. Hildenbrand, "Continuity of the equilibrium—set correspondence," *Journal of Economic Theory* **5** (1972), 152–162.

27. W. Hildenbrand, *Core and Equilibria of a Large Economy*, Princeton University Press, Princeton, 1974.

28. M. Hirsch, "A proof of the non-retractability of a cell onto its boundary," *Proc. Amer. Math. Soc.* **14** (1963), 364–365.

29. ———, *Differential Topology*, Springer-Verlag, New York, 1976.

30. Y. Kannai, "Continuity properties of the core of a market," *Econometrica* **38** (1970), 791–815.

31. T. Kehoe, "An index theorem for a general equilibrium production," Cowles Discussion Paper, Yale, 1972.

32. R. Kellogg, T. Li, and J. Yorke, "A constant proof of the Brouwer fixed point theorem," *SIAM J. Numerical Analysis* **13** (1976), 473–483.

33. T. Koopmans, "Analysis of production as an efficient combination of activities," in T. Koopmans (ed.), *Activity Analysis of Production and Allocation*, John Wiley, New York, 1951, pp. 33–97.

34. R. Mantel, "On the characterization of aggregate excess demand," *Journal of Economic Theory*, **7** (1974).

35. A. Mas-Colell, "Continuous and smooth consumers: approximation theorems," *Journal of Economic Theory* **8** (1974), 305–336.

36. ———, "On the continuity of equilibrium prices in constant return production economies," *Journal of Mathematical Economics* **2** (1975), 21–33.

37. ———, "On the equilibrium price set of an exchange economy," *Journal of Mathematical Economics* **4** (1977), 117–126.

38. J. Milnor, *Topology from the Differentiable Viewpoint*, The University Press of Virginia, Charlottesville, 1965.

39. V. Pareto, *Manuel d'economie Politique*, Giard, Paris, 1909.

40. R. Saigal and C. Simon, "Generic properties of the complementarity problem," *Mathematical Programming* **4** (1973), 324–333.

41. P. Samuelson, *Foundations of Economic Analysis*, Harvard University Press, Cambridge, 1947.

42. H. Scarf with the collaboration of T. Hansen, *The Computation of Economic Equilibria*, Yale University Press, New Haven, 1973.

43. L. Schwartz, *Cours d'Analyse I*, Hermann, Paris, 1967.

44. C. Simon, "Scalar and vector maximization: calculus techniques with economic applications," Chapter 2 of this volume.

45. S. Smale, "Global analysis and economics IIA; extension of a theorem of Debreu," *Journal of Mathematical Economics* **1** (1974), 1–15.

46. ———, "Global analysis and economics IV; finiteness and stability of equilibria with general consumption sets and production," *Journal of Mathematical Economics* **1** (1974), 119–129.

47. ———, "A convergent process of price adjustment and global Newton methods," *Journal of Mathematical Economics* **3** (1976), 107–120.

48. ———, "Global analysis and economics," in K. Arrow and M. Intrilligator (eds.), *Handbook of Mathematical Economics*, North-Holland, 1977.

49. H. Sonnenschein, "Do Walras identity and continuity characterize the class of community excess demand functions?," *Journal of Economic Theory* **6** (1973), 345–354.

50. M. Spivak, *Calculus on Manifolds*, Benjamin, New York, 1965.

51. L. Walras, *Elements d'economie Politique Pure*, Corbaz Lausanne, 1874. Edition definitive, 1900, Librairie Generale de Droit et de Jurisprudence, Paris.

52. R. Wilson, "The bilinear complementarity problem and competitive equilibria of linear economic models," *Econometrica* **46** (1978), 87–103.

HOW TO COMPUTE
ECONOMIC EQUILIBRIA
BY PIVOTAL METHODS*

Harold W. Kuhn

1. INTRODUCTION

The object of this lecture is to give an introduction to, and an evaluation of, a class of algorithms which can be called "pivotal methods." The sole credit for the introduction of these methods for application to economics must be given to Herbert Scarf. His seminal work in this area, published in 1967, has been developed and extended by a number of other mathematicians and economists. We now have enough experience with the methods so that a

* This paper is a revision of a lecture delivered in Torun, Poland, July 8, 1974, to the Conference on Computing Equilibria: How and Why?, sponsored by the Computation Center of the Polish Academy of Sciences. The revised version was presented at the international meeting on Optimization Problems in Engineering and Economics, held in Naples, Italy on December 16–20, 1974 and sponsored by the Centro Studi di Economia applicata all'Ingegneria (CSEI), the Centro di Formazione e Studi per il Mezzogiorno (FORMEZ), and Rice University. The research of the author has been supported by the National Science Foundation under Grant GP-35698X.

tentative evaluation of their advantages and disadvantages can be given. With these considerations in mind and recognizing that the type of mathematics employed may be novel, this exposition will be organized as follows:

—A Simple Economic Model. The algorithms can be easily understood by means of a simple class of models of general economic equilibrium, in which the detail has been reduced to the basic abstractions of supply and demand. Although these models are simple, they are typical and general enough to allow the introduction of the basic mathematical tools.

—Labelling and Equilibrium. The basic tools are combinatorial and use the economic data to label the vertices of a subdivision of the price simplex. Using classical techniques from topology, these labels allow us to show the existence of an economic equilibrium. What is new is the idea that they can also be used for practical calculation.

—Applications: Types of Problems. Calculation is possible for what kinds of problems? The answer to this will be provided by a two-way classification listing first mathematical types, then economic applications. Of course, this diverse set of applications cannot be attacked by the direct use of the simple algorithm that has been used for motivation.

—Variants: Subdivision and Labelling. The extension of pivotal methods to a wider class of problems has come about through imaginative developments of the mathematical structure. These developments can be seen in terms of variations of the initial examples of subdivision and labelling. The success of these improvements can only be judged by actual evidence of computation.

—Computing Experience. Currently, a wide array of computational data is available. Although it varies according to the implementation of the original mathematical ideas, a survey of the principal issues will illustrate representative results.

—Conclusions. The object of this lecture is to present you with ideas and evidence from which you should be able to draw your own conclusions. In this final section, such conclusions are suggested.

(Since this text is primarily the record of the lecture as presented in a strictly limited time, it has been provided with a large number of references to a bibliography which will lead the interested reader to detailed information and argument for further study of these methods. Comments to guide the reader in this bibliography which were not part of the lecture are set off by parentheses; the references are numbered in square brackets.)

2. A SIMPLE ECONOMIC MODEL

Pivotal methods can be motivated by a classical model of equilibrium in an exchange economy. (This model is essentially the same as that used by Scarf in his report of the first successful computational results in 1967 [27]. It is also used as a first approach to economic equilibrium in the comprehensive treatment of general competitive analysis by Arrow and Hahn [1].) The economy trades n goods indexed by $k = 1, \ldots, n$ with prices $p_1, \ldots, p_n$. A price vector $p = (p_1, \ldots, p_n)$ generates supply and demand for each of these goods and their difference is called the excess demand function for good k and is denoted by $g_k(p)$. These n functions are assumed to be continuous and homogeneous of degree zero for nonnegative, nonzero prices. Also, the prices and excess demands are assumed to satisfy Walras' Law which says that expenditures equal revenues when summed over all goods, that is,

$$p_1 g_1(p) + \cdots + p_n g_n(p) = 0 \qquad \text{for all } p \geqq 0.$$

Equilibrium for such a model is a set of prices $\bar{p}$ that generate a supply that is not less than the demand for each good, that is such that $g_k(\bar{p}) \leqq 0$ for $k = 1, \ldots, n$. Of course, Walras' Law implies that the price $\bar{p}_k$ of any good with excess supply ($g_k(\bar{p}) < 0$) is zero.

The first mathematical trick is to normalize prices to the standard simplex where prices sum to one. This is possible due to the assumption of homogeneity of degree zero and, henceforth, we shall assume all $p_k \geqq 0$ and $p_1 + \cdots + p_n = 1$. Thus, for three goods, we shall work on the price triangle with barycentric coordinates (p_1, p_2, p_3) shown in Figure 1.

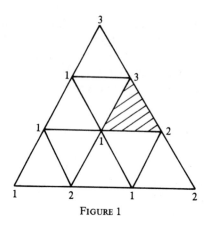

FIGURE 1

3. LABELLING AND EQUILIBRIUM

The algorithm starts from a subdivision of the simplex of prices and the labelling of its vertices. In Figure 2, we have subdivided the price triangle in a convenient and representative manner. (The efficient implementation of the algorithm on a computer depends on simple subdivisions of the simplex or cube in n-space. M. Todd [37] has given an illuminating history of such subdivisions referring

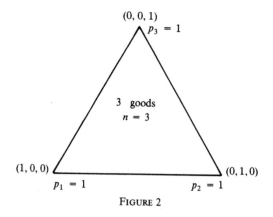

FIGURE 2

to discoveries and rediscoveries to be found in [5], [7], [8], [10], [12], [14], [15], [16], [18], [31], and [41].)

A vertex p of this subdivision is given the label k if the excess demand for good k is smallest among those goods with positive price. If several such achieve the minimum, choose the first. Of course, due to Walras' Law, if the label of p is k then $q_k(p) \leq 0$. Also, by the labelling rule,

$$\text{if the label of } p \text{ is } k \text{ then } p_k > 0. \qquad (*)$$

The property $(*)$ is exactly the hypothesis of Sperner's Lemma [36], which was proved in 1926 to simplify several topological results of Brouwer. (For the interested reader, [38] is an elementary exposition of some aspects of Sperner's Lemma and [2] contains an elegant proof in the spirit of the argument that follows.) For the triangle of Figure 2, which is labelled, the three corners carry the labels 1, 2, and 3, respectively, and the subdivision points in each side of the triangle contain one of the two labels at the end. Then Sperner's Lemma asserts the existence of (an odd number and hence) at least one small triangle with all three labels. In Figure 2, such a triangle is shaded.

This is enough to prove the existence of an equilibrium in general. We may call the subdivision of Figure 2 a subdivision of *degree* 3 since each edge has 3 subdivision points. For the general case, consider subdivisions of degree $d = 1, 2, \ldots$ (with smaller and smaller pieces) and find in each a completely labelled simplex with vertices $p^1(d), \ldots, p^n(d)$ with the label of $p^k(d)$ equal to k. Since each sequence $(p^k(1), p^k(2), \ldots, p^k(d), \ldots)$ lies in a compact set, we can choose one subsequence of degrees $d_1 < d_2 < \cdots < d_l < \cdots$ such that all of the sequences $(p^k(d_1), p^k(d_2), \ldots, p^k(d_l), \ldots)$ converge. Since the diameter of the subsimplices tends to zero, each of the sequences converges to the same point, which we call $\bar{p}$. We noted previously that $g_k(p^k(d)) \leq 0$ for all k and d. Hence, by the continuity of the g_k, $g_k(\bar{p}) \leq 0$ for all k. Then Walras' Law implies $g_k(\bar{p}) = 0$ for all k with $\bar{p}_k > 0$ and $\bar{p}$ is an equilibrium.

Although our proof has contained the nonconstructive step of choosing a convergent subsequence, with a little more effort it can be shown that *completely labelled simplices approximate equilibria for fine enough subdivisions*. Therefore, our problem has been reduced to finding completely labelled simplices. If we can do this efficiently for very fine subdivisions, then we will have solved our problem. Figure 3 illustrates the extremely simple method of search that is used. Incidentally, it also proves Sperner's Lemma in a constructive manner. Finally, the combinatorial nature of the search gives the name *pivotal method* to the algorithm by analogy with pivoting in linear programming.

In this figure, a subdivision of a two-dimensional simplex is shown. It has been labelled to conform to the condition that a point can only receive a label k if its kth coordinate is positive. The lower edge of the triangle is a one dimensional simplex with the same property. As we proceed from the left-hand 1 to the right-hand 2, it is clear that there must be exactly one more edge labelled (12) than there are edges (21). Let us label all of the edges labelled (12) as STARTS. Then the algorithm proceeds as follows. Each edge on the lower boundary labelled (12) can be completed in a unique manner to a triangle. If the third vertex is labelled 3 we are done,

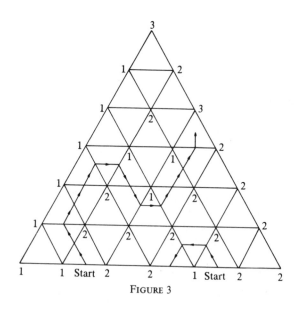

FIGURE 3

otherwise its label repeats exactly one label on the given edge. If we drop the corresponding vertex from the triangle we are in the same position as before with a new edge labelled (12) and a new vertex that completes it to a triangle. If we repeat this process only one of two things can happen. Either we find a label 3 and are successful, or our search leads us back out of the triangle through an edge on the lower boundary labelled (21). (Note that, since there is at most one way "into" a triangle through an edge labelled (12) in the usual positive orientation of the plane and at most one way "out" of a triangle through an edge labelled (21), the algorithm never examines the same triangle twice. Expressed differently, there are no loops in the path of triangles being examined.) These two possibilities are shown in the diagram. Since there is one more edge on the boundary labelled (12) than there are edges labelled (21), we must be successful when we try all of the STARTS.

The second disagreeable case where the path leads back to the boundary can be avoided by the device shown in Figure 4. Here we have added a border at the bottom of this figure and have given it an artificial labelling that provides *exactly* one START. We have

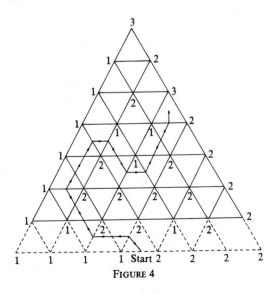

FIGURE 4

not created any new completely labelled triangles so this START must lead us, by pivoting, to our desired result.

4. APPLICATIONS: TYPES OF PROBLEMS

At this point you should be convinced that there is a combinatorial pivoting procedure that leads to an approximate equilibrium for a simple class of economic problems. A priori, there is no reason to believe that it is efficient or that it applies to a wider class of problems. Figure 5 gives an indication of some of the kinds of problems to which the method has been applied successfully.

First, a classification by mathematical type is given. Of course, economists will realize that the existence of a general equilibrium is closely related to fixed point problems. (A decisive result that establishes the connection was provided by Uzawa in 1962 [40].) In the simplest case (the Brouwer fixed point theorem), a continuous function mapping the simplex into itself is given and a point $\bar{x}$ is sought such that $f(\bar{x}) = \bar{x}$. In the more general case (the Kakutani fixed point theorem), an upper-semicontinuous correspondence is given, defined on a compact convex set with closed convex subsets

Applications: Types of Problems

Mathematical
  Fixed Point Problems   Brouwer   Kakutani
    $x \rightarrow f(x)$, find $\bar{x}$ such that $f(\bar{x}) = \bar{x}$ $\bar{x} \in f(\bar{x})$
  Nonlinear Equations
    $g(x)$, find $\bar{x}$ such that $g(\bar{x}) = 0$ $0 \in g(\bar{x})$
  Nonlinear Complementarity Problems
    $\varphi(x)$, find $\bar{x}$ such that $\varphi(\bar{x}) \geqq 0$ and $\bar{x} \cdot \varphi(\bar{x}) = 0$
  Nonlinear Programming

Economic
  Core of an n-person game.
  Equilibrium models with exchange, production, intermediate goods,
    international trade, taxes, etc.
  Urban economics.

FIGURE 5

as images and a point $\bar{x}$ is sought such that $\bar{x} \in f(\bar{x})$. Pivotal methods calculate approximations for both of these cases directly. (To see this for the Brouwer fixed point theorem, consider the following labelling rule [14]: label x with the first index k such that $f_k(x) \leq x_k \neq 0$. This rule satisfied the hypotheses of Sperner's Lemma and hence the pivotal methods apply. To convert our model of Section 3 into a fixed point problem, let relative prices be mapped into relative prices by the following transformation:

$$p'_k = \frac{p_k + \max(g_k(p), 0)}{1 + \Sigma_k \max(g_k(p), 0)}.$$

This is a reasonable type of "dynamics" since it increases the prices of those goods for which there is an excess demand. Fixed points of this transformation are equilibria and conversely. Finally, the labelling of Section 3 coincides with the fixed point labelling for this transformation.

The application of pivotal methods to the Kakutani fixed point theorem [5] is more complicated and uses vector labels, to be touched on in Section 5.)

Closely related to fixed point problems are systems of nonlinear equations $g(x) = 0$. Of course, the trivial transformation $f(x) = g(x) + x$ converts this problem formally into a fixed point problem. However, only in special circumstances will the hypotheses of the Brouwer and Kakutani theorems be fulfilled and this naive approach will be successful only for an extremely limited class of simultaneous nonlinear equations. (A variation of the method proves very successful for the solution of one polynomial equation in a complex variable with complex numbers as coefficients [16].) The classification of Figure 5 lists the case analogous to the Kakutani theorem. This asks for a solution to the equation $0 \in g(x)$, where g is a vector-valued correspondence.

Of more interest and more promise is the class of complementarity problems, both linear and nonlinear. Indeed, one of the ideas that influenced Scarf was the work of Lemke and Howson ([19], [20]) that produced a pivotal method for finding equilibrium points for bimatrix games and for linear complementarity problems. Figure 5 gives a statement of the nonlinear complementarity problem: Given an *n*-vector function φ of n variables x, find a nonnegative $\bar{x}$ that makes $\varphi(\bar{x})$ nonnegative and such that $\bar{x}$ and $\varphi(\bar{x})$ are orthogonal. Of course, this is the form of the necessary conditions for nonlinear programming [17]. Again there is a trivial transformation that converts the nonlinear complementarity problem into a fixed point problem, namely, $f(x) = \max(x - \varphi(x), 0)$. This suggests labellings which have solved some special nonlinear programs. (The application of the methods to nonlinear complementarity and programming problems is in an active stage of development. References [6], [9], [11], and [13] are typical of this research but do not exhaust it.)

Figure 5 also gives a partial listing of the economic applications of the algorithms. Scarf first developed the method to calculate the core of an *n*-person game with transferable utility [26]. He then applied it to models of exchange [27]. Since then, he and others have extended its application to equilibrium models with production [28], [29], [30], intermediate goods, international trade, taxes [33], [34], [35], etc. A somewhat separate application has been made to equilibria in urban economics [21]. (It must be emphasized that these references are representative of the literature to date and that one may expect a rapid expansion in the near future.)

5. VARIANTS: SUBDIVISION AND LABELLING

We shall now consider developments of the method which have made it more efficient. These will be illustrated in Figure 6 by the one variable problem: find a root of the function $g(x)$. We assume that we have an interval where $g(x)$ changes sign from negative to positive and we use the labelling rule: The label of x is 1 if $g(x)$ is nonpositive and is 2 if $g(x)$ is positive. Clearly this gives us the conditions of Sperner's Lemma for the interval as a 1-dimensional simplex and the subintervals which have both labels approximate a root.

The first methods used by Scarf and later by Scarf and Hansen may be called *fixed grid methods*. A fixed subdivision of the simplex is chosen and a completely labelled simplex is found as the

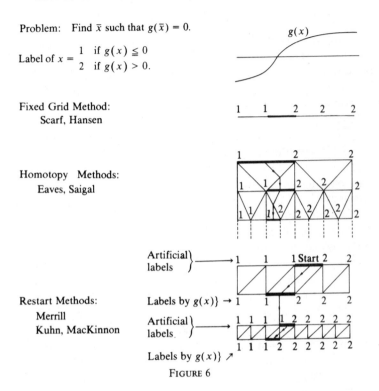

Problem: Find $\bar{x}$ such that $g(\bar{x}) = 0$.

Label of $x = \begin{cases} 1 & \text{if } g(x) \leqq 0 \\ 2 & \text{if } g(x) > 0. \end{cases}$

Fixed Grid Method:
   Scarf, Hansen

Homotopy Methods:
   Eaves, Saigal

Restart Methods:
   Merrill
   Kuhn, MacKinnon

FIGURE 6

approximation. The difficulty with this method is that if the grid is very fine then many pivots will be needed to reach the approximation while otherwise the error in the approximation may be unacceptable. For example, in an economy with 10 goods at least one good has a relative price less than or equal to 0.1. For a rather fine grid of, say, $d = 200$, a mistake of 1 in the approximation is a 5 per cent error in that price. The computational strategy used by Scarf and Hansen was to choose a subdivision that was fine enough to get an answer fairly close to the result, then refine the result by other methods such as a local linear approximation or Newton's Method. By these means, Scarf reported very good results on models of economic exchange with 5, 8, and 10 prices in his first paper on the computational aspects of the algorithm in 1967 [27]. Nevertheless, it is unaesthetic to combine two algorithms and also it is difficult to know whether the approximation is good enough to switch to, say, Newton's Method. Therefore, other methods to refine the approximation were sought. The first of these is called *homotopy* by Eaves who developed it in 1971 [7]. It can be illustrated as follows: A sequence of subdivisions of the interval is considered, with each twice as fine as the preceding. Each subdivision is labelled by the rule given above. The sequence is connected by a triangulation that coincides with the subdivision on each interval. The name "homotopy" is appropriate since the labelled set consisting of the Cartesian product of a simplex and an interval can be generated by successive linear approximations to g at the subdivision points. In this manner, the linear approximations deform homotopically to the true function g as the grid tends to zero.

Of course, the pivots are exactly the same as those described in Section 3. The vertex to go out is the vertex with a repeated label, while the vertex to come in is the unique vertex on the other side of those remaining that completes them to a simplex in the subdivision. Thus, in our example we are lead to the path shown in Figure 6. Note that the homotopy method coincides with the "method of bisection" for a function of one variable and that the completely labelled simplices found at successive levels are nested. This is not true with more variables and the algorithm can backtrack to coarser subdivisions before eventually reaching the level of approximation desired.

Alternative means for handling very fine subdivisions are the so-called *restart methods*. These were first used by Oren Merrill in his doctoral thesis in 1972 [34] and were discovered independently by James MacKinnon in the same year. Again we increase the dimension of the problem by one by taking the product of the given simplex and an interval with the *same subdivision* at each end of the interval. At one end of the interval an artificial labelling such as that described in Section 3 produces exactly one start near any given point. At the other end of the interval the true labelling induced by g is used. Clearly, the method of pivoting leads us to a completely labelled simplex labelled by g. This is used to create an artificial labelling on a refined subdivision and the process is repeated. Although no definitive choice can be made at present between homotopy and restart methods, it can be seen that the restart method has two potential advantages: (1) it can use a priori information concerning the answer; (2) it can refine the subdivision at any rate desired.

The limitations of time and space exclude an adequate exposition of another variant of pivotal methods that covers more general problems. The basic idea is to use vectors as labels on the subdivisions rather than integers. (In rudimentary form, this concept was used in [39] and [14] for the proofs of combinatorial lemmas and was utilized in the context of fixed points by Eaves in [4]. It played an essential rôle in the earliest research of Scarf on the core of an n-person game [26] and found a particularly elegant statement in Eaves' algorithm for the Kakutani fixed point theorem in [5].) Figure 7 summarizes some of the more obvious differences between the methods. First, it is clear that a vector can contain more information than one of its indices. In terms of our original example, the entire vector of excess demands is used instead of merely the index of the smallest excess demand. On the other hand, the test for which vector to throw out is more complicated than

Variants: Integer versus Vector Labels

"Partial" Information	"Full" Information
First *index* k that achieves $\min_j g_j(p)$ over j with $p_j > 0$.	Vector $(g_k(p))$.
Simple Pivot Step	Complicated Pivot Step
Vertex with repeated label out.	Linear programming change of basis.
Weak Approximation	Strong Approximation
Linear.	Quadratic.
Special Problems	General Problems
Functions, Brouwer fixed point theorem.	Correspondences, Kakutani fixed point theorem.

FIGURE 7

hunting for a repeated label. This test is essentially equivalent to one change of basis in an appropriate linear program. This extra work purchases better approximations. Saigal has recently shown a sense in which they are quadratic rather than linear [25]. Finally, as indicated earlier, vector labels are needed for the treatment of demand correspondences (as opposed to demand functions) and for applications of Kakutani's fixed point theorem.

6. COMPUTATIONAL EXPERIENCE

There is at present a considerable body of computational experience with pivotal methods. The data to be presented in this section has been largely computed by James MacKinnon using the restart method that is called the Sandwich Method. The results reported are consistent with the reports of others, notably Scarf and Hansen with fixed grid methods [30], Merrill with his restart methods [22], [23], [24], and Wilmuth with both homotopy and restart methods [42]. However, MacKinnon's work sheds special light on three aspects which seem to be important.

First, in any problem with physical or economic structure dealing with quantities that are measured in units with dimensions, the efficiency of the algorithm is very sensitive to the labelling rule used. This phenomenon, although not identical to, is analogous to "scaling" problems. For example, in the case of economic general equilibrium models, many different labelling rules can be used that have different economic motivation. A large-scale statistical experiment was performed to determine the relative performance of five different rules and the sensitivity of the cost of computation to the choice of rule. Recall that, in Section 3, a vertex p of the subdivision was given the label k if the *excess demand* g_k for good k was smallest among those with positive price. This is the first of the five rules studied. In the other four rules, the only change is the replacement of *excess demand* by other quantities. These were:

(1) Excess demand: g_k.
(2) Value of excess demand: $p_k g_k$.
(3) Excess demand deflated by supply: g_k/s_k.
(4) Value of excess demand deflated by supply: $p_k g_k/s_k$.
(5) Excess demand inflated by supply divided by price: $s_k g_k/p_k$.

Alternate Labelling Rules

	Rule 1	Rule 2	Rule 3	Rule 4	Rule 5
Exchange Model 1:					
Sample size 100					
$n = 5,\ d = 16 \times 3^8$					
Mean labellings	124	107	107	104	156
Median labellings	111	108	106	102	121
Exchange Model 2:					
Sample size 200					
$n = 4,\ d = 20 \times 3^8$					
Mean labellings	72	69	69	67	82
Median labellings	69	68	67	67	74
Production Model:					
Sample size 100					
$n = 5,\ d = 16 \times 3^8$					
Mean labellings	278	228	240	215	320
Median labellings	150	133	143	129	184
Taxation Model:					
Sample size 100					
$n = 6,\ d = 25 \times 3^8$					
Mean labellings	277	221	201	205	***
Median labellings	214	214	196	198	282

***Sample mean very large due to bad cases.

FIGURE 8

Obviously, the last rule was constructed to behave badly for commonsense economic reasons (and it did). The results of the experiment are shown in Figure 8. Statistical analysis of the samples confirms what can be read from the aggregate data. Rules 2, 3, and 4 are better than Rules 1 and 5, all on the average. Roughly speaking, if you are paying for the computation of a general equilibrium model of the type described in Section 3, the best bet is Rule 4.

Another fact is evident in the data. This is the happy discovery of Scarf that these myopic pivotal searches are quite efficient. The total number of simplices in the final subdivision is very large, precisely n^{d-1}, which is greater than $10^{70,000}$ for problems in the first sample. However, we have examined, on the average, only about 100 simplices on the path to a solution. This is reminiscent of empirical behavior of the Simplex Method of linear programming compared to theoretical upper bounds on the number of pivots.

A second computational consideration for restart methods is how to refine the subdivision at an optimal rate. Without giving details, a reasonable heuristic argument shows that, at each stage of the Sandwich Method, the degree d of the subdivision should be increased by a factor of 3 or more. (For several large classes of problems, an optimal factor of 4 or 5 is indicated.) This explains why the final subdivisions in Figure 8 are given in the form shown (for example, 16×3^8 means that the initial d was 16 and that it was increased by a factor of 3 eight times). Further experience has been that, if the current approximation can be improved by any means, then the factor of refinement can be raised considerably. For some cases, a factor of 1,000 has been used with good results. These observations contrast with the homotopy methods which are forced to use a factor of 2 at each stage with the geometry of subdivision currently in use.

Third, there has been a good deal of speculation concerning the cost of a solution as a function of the dimension of the problem. This clearly depends on two factors: (1) the number of labellings and (2) the cost of a labelling. Both factors depend on n. Without entering into the detail of the mass of computational experience

Tentative Estimates of Computation Time

n	Time (seconds)
5	1
10	25
25	150

Note: These figures are very conservative! Computation is carried to degree of accuracy required by n.

FIGURE 9

that is available, it may be summarized as follows, at least for general equilibrium models. Both factors seem proportional to $(n-1)^2$ with possible savings in the functional evaluation.

Figure 9 shows a very conservative estimate of computation time on a reasonably fast machine (such as the IBM 360/91 or 370/168). These figures are conservative because models of the type of Section 3 with simple excess demands actually require only about 2 seconds to compute. However, the conclusion should be clear: If the cost is really proportional to $(n-1)^4$, approach large problems with caution.

7. CONCLUSIONS

The conclusions to be drawn from this survey seem simple and self-evident. The advantages enjoyed by pivotal methods are of three kinds.

First, they have the advantage of simplicity, requiring only functional evaluations; no derivatives or matrix inversions are needed. Secondly, they have flexibility. With enough imagination, they apply to fixed points, complementarity problems, and optimization problems. Finally, they are competitively efficient for small problems. As vivid evidence of this, all of the Colville nonlinear programming test problems [3] have been solved using pivotal methods.

The disadvantages seem to fall into two types. First, they are inefficient for large problems. It is not clear where the crossover occurs; in one test of the method against a conjugate gradient method, pivotal methods were superior up to about 10 to 15 variables. Finally, there are equilibria that are not accessible and cannot be found from any start. This phenomenon has been known for the Lemke-Howson algorithm for the linear complementarity problem for some time (see, for example, Shapley's paper [32]) and is a fascinating research question to unravel in general.

The object of this survey has been to give an accurate picture of the state of research on pivotal methods, with particular emphasis on their use in the computation of economic equilibria. Although it is customary for anyone involved with an algorithm to attempt to sell it as the best in the world, perhaps this account has given a more balanced judgement of the strengths and weaknesses of pivotal methods as applied to economics and optimization.

REFERENCES

1. K. J. Arrow and F. H. Hahn, *General Competitive Analysis*, Holden-Day, 1971.
2. D. I. A. Cohen, "On the Sperner lemma," *Journal of Combinatorial Theory*, 2 (1967) 585–7.
3. A. R. Colville, "A comparative study of nonlinear programming codes," in *Proceedings of the Princeton Symposium on Mathematical Programming*, H. W. Kuhn, (ed.), Princeton University Press, Princeton, New Jersey, 1970.
4. B. C. Eaves, "An odd theorem," *Proceedings of the American Mathematical Society*, 26 (1970) 509–13.
5. ———, "Computing Kakutani fixed points," *S.I.A.M. Journal on Applied Mathematics*, 21 (1971) 236–44.
6. ———, "On the basic theorem of complementarity," *Mathematical Programming*, 1 (1971) 68–75.
7. ———, "Homotopies for computation of fixed points," *Mathematical Programming*, 3 (1972) 1–22.
8. B. C. Eaves and R. Saigal, "Homotopies for computation of fixed points on unbounded regions," *Mathematical Programming*, 3 (1972) 225–37.
9. M. L. Fisher and F. J. Gould, "A simplicial algorithm for the nonlinear complementarity problem," *Mathematical Programming*, 6 (1974) 281–300.
10. H. Freudenthal, "Simplizialzerlegungen von Beschränkter Flachheit," *Annals of Mathematics*, 43 (1942) 580–2.
11. C. B. Garcia, "The complementarity problem and its applications," Ph.D. Thesis, Rensselaer Polytechnic Institute, Troy, New York, 1973.
12. T. Hansen, "On the approximation of a competitive equilibrium," Ph.D. Thesis, Yale University, New Haven, Connecticut, 1968.
13. M. Kojima, "Computational methods for solving the nonlinear complementarity problem," *Keio Engineering Reports*, 27 (1974) 1–41.
14. H. W. Kuhn, "Some combinatorial lemmas in topology," *IBM Journal of Research and Development*, 4 (1960) 508–24.
15. ———, "Simplicial approximations of fixed points," *Proceedings of the National Academy of Sciences, USA*, 61 (1968) 1238–42.
16. ———, "A new proof of the fundamental theorem of algebra," in *Pivoting and Extensions*, Mathematical Programming Study 1, M. L. Balinski, (ed.), North-Holland, Amsterdam, 1974.
17. H. W. Kuhn and A. W. Tucker, "Nonlinear programming" in *Proceedings of the Second Berkeley Symposium on Mathematical Statistics and Probability*, J. Neyman, (ed.), University of California Press, Berkeley, California, 1951.
18. S. Lefschetz, *Introduction to Topology*, Princeton University Press, Princeton, New Jersey, 1949.

19. C. E. Lemke, "Bimatrix equilibrium points and mathematical programming," *Management Science*, **11** (1965) 681–9.

20. C. M. Lemke, and J. T. Howson, "Equilibrium points of bimatrix games," *Journal of the Society for Industrial and Applied Mathematics*, **12** (1964) 413–23.

21. J. G. MacKinnon, "Urban general equilibrium models and simplicial search algorithms," *Journal of Urban Economics*, **1** (1974) 161–183.

22. O. H. Merrill, "Applications and extensions of an algorithm that computes fixed points of certain non-empty convex upper semi-continuous point to set mappings," Technical Report 71-7, Dept. of Industrial Engineering, University of Michigan, 1971.

23. ———, "Applications and extensions of an algorithm that computes fixed points of certain upper semi-continuous point to set mappings." Ph.D. Thesis, University of Michigan, 1972.

24. ———, "A summary of techniques for computing fixed points of continuous mappings," in *Mathematical Topics in Economic Theory and Computation*, Society for Industrial and Applied Mathematics, Philadelphia, Pennsylvania, 1972.

25. R. Saigal, Private communication.

26. H. E. Scarf, "The core of an *N*-person game," **35** (1967) 50–69.

27. ———, "The approximation of fixed points of a continuous mapping," *SIAM Journal on Applied Mathematics*, **15** (1967) 1328–43.

28. ———, "On the computation of equilibrium prices," in *Ten Economic Studies in the Tradition of Irving Fisher*, John Wiley & Sons, New York, 1967.

29. ———, "An example of an Algorithm for Calculating General Equilibrium Prices," *American Economic Review*, **59** (1969) 669–77.

30. ———, with the collaboration of T. Hansen, *The Computation of Economic Equilibria*, Yale University Press, New Haven, Connecticut, 1973.

31. L. S. Shapley, "On balanced games without side payments," in *Mathematical Programming*, T. C. Hu and S. M. Robinson, eds., Academic Press, New York, 1973.

32. ———, "A note on the Lemke-Howson algorithm," in *Pivoting and Extensions*, Mathematical Programming Study 1, M. L. Balinski, (ed.), North-Holland, Amsterdam, 1974.

33. J. B. Shoven, "A proof of the existence of a general equilibrium with ad valorem commodity taxes," *Journal of Economic Theory*, **8** (1974) 1–25.

34. ——— and J. Whalley, "A general equilibrium calculation of the effects of differential taxation of income from capital in the U.S.," *Journal of Public Economics*, **1** (1972) 281–321.

35. J. B. Shoven and J. Whalley, "General equilibrium with taxes: a computational procedure and an existence proof," *Review of Economic Studies*, **40** (1973) 475–490.

36. E. Sperner, "Neuer Beweis für die Invarianz der Dimensionszahl und des Gebietes," *Abh. Math. Sem. Hamburg*, **6** (1928) 265–

37. M. J. Todd, "Union Jack triangulations," Technical Report No. 220, Department of Operations Research, Cornell University, June, 1974.

38. C. B. Tompkins, "Sperner's Lemma and some extensions," in *Applied Combinatorial Mathematics*, E. F. Beckenbach, ed., John Wiley & Sons, New York, 1964.
39. A. W. Tucker, "Some topological properties of disk and sphere," in *Proceedings of the First Canadian Mathematical Congress*, University of Toronto Press, Toronto, 1946.
40. H. Uzawa, "Walras' existence theorem and Brouwer's fixed point theorem," Technical Report No. 80, Institute for Mathematical Studies in the Social Sciences, Stanford University, 1960.
41. H. Whitney, *Geometric Integration Theory*, Princeton University Press, Princeton, New Jersey, 1957.
42. R. J. Wilmuth, "The computation of fixed points," Ph.D. Thesis, Stanford University, 1973.

INFORMATION INCENTIVE AND PERFORMANCE IN THE (NEW)^2 WELFARE ECONOMICS*

Stanley Reiter

The title refers to a distinction between the new welfare economics, (now not so new) and a newer welfare economics. The objective of the new welfare economics was to provide principles for evaluating and comparing alternative allocations in a given economy. The Pareto principle is as far as common agreement goes in this problem, and there are now dissenters even from that. Perhaps the main accomplishment of the new welfare economics was to derive conditions characterizing (Pareto) efficient production and exchange, and to show that in classical economies, (those in which preferences and production possibilities have suitable convexity and continuity properties) the equilibria of the competitive mechanism precisely meet the conditions characterizing Pareto optimal production and exchange. That is, in classical economies the competitive equilibrium allocations and the Pareto optimal allocations are two names for the same collection of allocations. These are, of

*I wish to thank Morton I. Kamien, Peter McCabe and D. John Roberts for helpful comments.

course, the classical welfare theorems of Arrow, Debreu and Koopmans.

However, during the period of the development of this line of theory there was also interest in nonclassical economies and in systems other than the competitive one. People sought to characterize Pareto-optimal allocations when there are indivisibilities, increasing returns, or externalities. The work of Hotelling provides examples, and Pigou and Marshall also discussed such problems. Marginal cost pricing proposals, and the organizational proposals of the Lange-Lerner-Taylor type, were attempts to design economic systems which would function satisfactorily in nonclassical situations, where the competitive system lacks optimal properties. These proposals constituted a shift of the focus of welfare economics to the system of economic organization. As might be expected, this shift of focus brought new subjects into the discussion. Questions of administrative feasibility and the costs of operating the system were raised in connection with the early controversies over central planning. Questions were raised about the extent to which private incentives are in conflict with the system, thereby creating a need for policing with its attendant costs, or divergences of the outcome produced by the system from the one it was designed to produce. These lines of thought lead to the central problem of the (new)^2 welfare economics.*

That problem is not merely one of evaluating alternative allocations in a given economy, but of comparing the functioning of alternative systems operating in a class of economic environments, such as the classical ones, or alternatively those with indivisibilities or other nonconvexities. In such a problem the allocations which are the outcome of the system are just one of the important aspects of its functioning, but others are also important, among them its administrative feasibility, the costs of operating the system itself, the extent to which private incentives are incompatible with the system. These considerations pertain to properties of the economic mechanism itself, not merely of its resulting allocations. All these

---

*I have called it "(new)^2" to suggest a difference by an order of magnitude from the "new" welfare economics.

properties of an economic system must be weighed in order to evaluate the system and compare it with alternatives. For this a theory is needed which encompasses these elements. This is the main objective of the (new)[2] welfare economics, to provide a normative theory of economic mechanisms.

It was with the publication of Hurwicz's paper "Informational Efficiency of Resource Allocation Mechanisms" (Hurwicz [23]) in 1960 that a formal structure for the comparative study of economic mechanisms appears in economics. The fifteen or so years since then have seen a substantial development of this field. New results, new questions and new methods have accumulated. It is by now a thriving industry perhaps just emerged from its infancy and entering the phase of exponential growth. I shall try here to give some picture of its methods, questions and results so far.

An economic system, insofar as it determines the allocation of resources, may be viewed as a kind of machine which accepts as inputs the basic data of an economy and produces as its output an allocation of commodities among the participants in the economy.

The basic data of an economy, briefly an *economy* or *economic environment*, consists of the list of agents $\{1, \ldots, n\}$, the list of commodities $\{1, \ldots, l\}$, and the *characteristics* of each agent. These typically are, for agent i, his preference relation $\precsim_i$, or its representation by a utility function u^i, his technology T^i, given, say, as a production possibilities set, and his initial endowment vector ω^i. Denote the characteristic of the ith agent by $e^i = (\precsim_i, T^i, \omega^i)$ for $i = 1, \ldots, n$. We assume the commodity space to be the l-dimensional Euclidean space $\mathbb{R}^l$, the same for all the economies we are considering, and that the list of participants is also the same for all economies. With these assumptions, a specified economic environment e determines the n-tuple of characteristics of n agents; thus, $e \mapsto (e^1, \ldots, e^n)$.

Note that this formulation does not exclude externalities. We will from now on identify the environment with the n-tuple of characteristics; thus $e = (e^1, \ldots, e^n)$.

Economic activity results in allocations which are representable by points in $\mathbb{R}^{nl}$. An economic system generally must deal with more than one set of economic data, just as a computational algorithm is designed to accept more than just one numerical problem. So the class E of economies to be accepted by the mechanism must be specified.

The allocations (or trades) which are *feasible* for the economy e are denoted $\mathcal{T}(e)$. Thus, $\mathcal{T}$ is a *correspondence* (a multi-valued function) which assigns to each economy e in the specified class E of economies the set of feasible allocations (trades) for e. For a two-person two-good pure exchange economy $\bar{e}$, the set of feasible allocations $\mathcal{T}(\bar{e})$ consists of those allocations which are (i) individually feasible for each agent and (ii) add up to a total which does not exceed the total endowment of commodities.

Similarly, the set of allocations (or trades) of e considered *desirable* is also represented by a correspondence $\not{p}$, which assigns to each economy e in E the subset $\not{p}(e)$ of the feasible allocations $\mathcal{T}(e)$ which are considered desirable. Frequently $\not{p}$ is taken to be the Pareto correspondence, in which case $\not{p}(e)$ is the set of Pareto optimal allocations (trades) for e.*

An initial distribution of knowledge about the economy is assumed. Each agent knows something, but generally not everything, about the economy he is in. We assume here, as is typical in this literature, that each agent i knows directly only his own characteristic e^i. Since to determine whether or not an allocation is feasible in an economy e, let alone Pareto-optimal, in general requires data from all of the characteristics (e.g., the total initial endowments $\omega = \sum_{i=1}^{n} \omega^i$), no agent by himself knows enough to figure out the feasible allocations. Optimal coordination of economic activity in general requires communication among the agents when knowledge about the economy is dispersed. We discuss next how the process of communication is modelled.

A resource allocation system is modelled in two closely related ways. The first, as an *adjustment process*, (Hurwicz [23]) and the second as a *mechanism* (Mount and Reiter [38] and [39]). There are two stages. In the spirit of tâtonnement agents first communicate; "real" economic action is taken only when "equilibrium" is reached. (Non-tâtonnement formulations can also be given.) Thus,

---

*A trade y is Pareto optimal in e if the allocation $x = \omega + y$, where ω is the initial allocation in c, is a Pareto optimal allocation in c.

in the first stage, the agents communicate with one another by sending formalized messages taken from a specified set of messages or *language*. After no further communication is worthwhile, or when this stage otherwise comes to an end, the final message is translated into action.

The adjustment process formulation models the iterative exchange of messages as follows. Agent i can emit a message $m^i(t)$ at time t which is drawn from his *language* M^i, $i = 1, \ldots, n$. He can select this message on the basis of what he knows at time t (just prior to the exchange of messages at t). His response at t is given by a function f^i according to the equation

$$m^i(t) = f^i\big(m(t-1), e^i\big) \qquad i = 1, \ldots, n$$

where $m^i(t)$ is an element of M^i and $m(t) = (m^1(t), \ldots, m^n(t))$ is an element of the message space $M = M^1 \times \cdots \times M^n$. Thus, the process of communication is modelled by a system of temporally homogeneous first order difference equations in the messages, with the individual characteristics as parameters.* That the message of i depends only on e^i and not on any other economic data expresses the idea that agent i initially knows only e^i, and that the only way he has of acquiring additional information is via the communication process. This property of the *response function f^i* Hurwicz called *privacy* (Hurwicz [26]). (It was defined in Hurwicz [23], but given another name.)

Using vector notation we may abbreviate the system $(*)$, to

$$m(t) = f\big(m(t-1), e\big) \qquad\qquad (**)$$

A joint message $\overline{m} = (\overline{m}^1, \ldots, \overline{m}^n)$ in M is a *stationary message for the economy e* and the response function f if and only if

$$\overline{m} = f(\overline{m}, e).$$

---

*This formulation covers the case of agents with finite memories, since a temporally homogeneous difference equation of finite order can be transformed into one of first order by making the message big enough. Instead of having two concepts of informational capacity, memory and message size, this formulation allows us to capture both in one.

We may assume that stationary messages exist for the economies and response functions we consider and that solutions of the difference equations converge to them.

Stationary messages are translated into *actions* or *outcomes* by the *outcome function h*; thus, if $\overline{m}$ is a stationary message for e, then $a = h(\overline{m})$ is an outcome or action determined by the mechanism for the economy e. If e is a pure exchange economy, then typically $h(\overline{m})$ would denote a vector of trades. Thus, an adjustment process is a triple (M, f, h) where M is the message space, f the (vector of) response functions(s), and h the outcome function of the process. An adjustment process whose response functions satisfy privacy is said to preserve privacy.

Such a mechanism can be represented in another somewhat more general way which is sometimes more convenient. Here we suppose communication takes place in one step, rather than iteratively, and that what is communicated is the collection of all joint messages "acceptable" to the agent. This can be thought of as a function which gives the message agent i would emit in response to the other components. To represent the process (M, f, h) in this way, we define the correspondence μ, called the (equilibrium) *message correspondence* by

$$\mu(e) = \{m \in M | f(m, e) - m = 0\}.$$

Thus, a message m belongs to the set $\mu(e)$ if and only if it is a stationary message of f at e. In order to give effect to the privacy requirement on f, the correspondence μ must have a special structure; it must be a *coordinate correspondence* (Mount-Reiter [38]). Namely, there must exist correspondences μ^i for $i = 1, \ldots, n$ defined only for characteristics of i, and such that $\mu(e) = \cap_{i=1}^{n} \mu^i(e^i)$. Given the privacy preserving process (M, f, h) if we take μ^i to be given by

$$\mu^i(e^i) = \{m \in M | f^i(m, e^i) - m^i = 0\},$$

then μ will also be privacy preserving. The privacy preserving process (M, f, h) can also be written in terms of the message correspondence as (M, μ, h).

The performance of such a mechanism can be represented in the following fundamental triangular diagram.

The message correspondence μ selects for each economy e in E a message (or messages) in M. These are translated by the outcome function h into outcomes in A. Application of the message correspondence μ to an economy followed by applying h to the messages $m = \mu(e)$, denoted $h \circ \mu$, associates the action(s) "computed" by the mechanism to the given economy e in E, and thus, can be considered to determine an arrow $h \circ \mu$ directly from E to A.

A process (M, μ, h) can be defined in two ways, one of which allows the composition $h \circ \mu$ to be a correspondence, the other restricts it to be a single-valued function.

In each case there is an appropriate definition of "$\not p$-satisfactoriness" technically different but expressing the same concept. It amounts to this: A mechanism is $\not p$-satisfactory on a class E of economies if and only if the outcomes produced by the mechanism exactly cover the correspondence $\not p$, i.e., for each economy e in the class E every outcome is $\not p$-optimal, and every $\not p$-optimum is a possible outcome. (See Hurwicz [23] and Mount-Reiter [38], [39].)

A criterion of performance commonly used for mechanisms is that the relation between outcomes in A and economies should be the same as the one given by the Pareto correspondence. A mechanism is *Pareto satisfactory* on E if this condition is met. The classical welfare theorems (together with existence theorems) of Arrow, Debreu and Koopmans assert that the competitive mechanism is Pareto satisfactory on a class of economies satisfying certain convexity and continuity conditions. A weaker property sometimes studied is that for each economy e in E the outcome be Pareto-optimal,* i.e.,

$$h(\mu(e)) \in \not p(e) \quad \text{for all } e \text{ in } E.$$

A mechanism with this property is called *nonwasteful* on E.

In terms of the diagram in Figure 1 we may ask whether there is a mechanism which for an arbitrary class of economies E, and an

---

*Here and in what follows we take the mechanism to be defined so as to make $h \circ \mu$ a function.

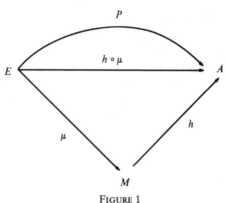

FIGURE 1

arbitrary performance criterion p is p-satisfactory (or p-nonwaste-ful) on E? Without additional conditions the answer would always be affirmative. One could take the identity mappings for each μ^i, taking M equal to E, and make h equal to p, or a suitable selection from it if $h \circ \mu$ is required to be single-valued. Such a mechanism provides enough "channel capacity" to permit each agent to communicate his entire characteristic to the others. Then any or all of them could calculate p-optimal outcomes.

One of the criticisms of such a mechanism, which is in an obvious sense "centralized", is that it is either infeasible for every agent to communicate fully his characteristic to a center and have the center calculate the outcome, or the resources used in communication and computation would be so large as to leave too little for direct economic use. This sort of consideration has been expressed in two related ways.

For a certain class of adjustment processes called "concrete" processes (characterized by the fact that the language used is one in which plans for the whole economy can be expressed (resource flow matrices), and the outcome function is the one given by consensus), Hurwicz restricted the extent to which one agent can plan for any other agent. In effect the messages an agent may send correspond to specifying net trades for himself vis à vis the rest of the economy in the aggregate. This concept is made the basis of a definition of *informational decentralization* for concrete processes, (Hurwicz [23]).

Hurwicz posed the question of whether there are informationally decentralized processes whose performance is Pareto satisfactory for all economies. The answer is in the negative. Economies with externalities do not admit such processes. On the other hand, if the question is confined to a subclass of economies excluding those with externalities but still admitting economies with indivisibilities, increasing returns or other nonconvexities which make the performance of the competitive process unsatisfactory, then the answer is in the affirmative. The "greed" process (Hurwicz [23]) is such a process. The greed process makes each agent's message at $t + 1$ consist of all resource flaws which he prefers to every proposal received at time t. Hence the term "greed". However this process is a) not stable and b) points of its message are subsets of the commodity space, rather complicated messages. The B-process (Hurwicz-Radner-Reiter [30]) is Pareto-satisfactory in a class of economies with divisible commodities but which admit increasing returns and other nonconvexities, or in a class in which all commodities are indivisible. This process uses simpler messages and is stochastic in nature. It is globally stable in a suitable stochastic sense. (From any initial position the process converges to the Pareto set with probability equal to unity.)

A second way of expressing the limitation of "channel capacity" is through the information-carrying capacity of the messages used by the process. One could restrict the message space M in an appropriate way, thereby allowing some information to pass but not necessarily all information. Such a restriction would act analogously to a limitation of the cross-sectional diameter of a pipe restricting the flow of fluid through that pipe. When the message variables take real values, a natural restriction is to limit the number of variables whose values can be communicated, i.e., to limit the dimension of the (Euclidean) message space. However, a technical difficulty arises due to the fact that it is possible to "smuggle" two variables by encoding them in the value of one variable and then recovering the two values at the other end. The same phenomenon exists even when the messages are allowed to have a more general qualitative nature than the values of real variables. "Smoothness" or regularity conditions must be imposed on the communication process in order to make restrictions of

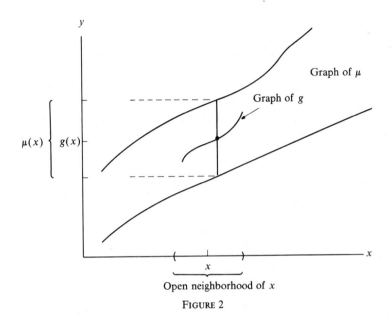

FIGURE 2

information-carrying capacity meaningful. Two types of conditions have been given: one by Hurwicz [26] applies to the case when the message space is Euclidean, the other, given by Mount-Reiter [38], [39], applies to topological message spaces.*

When such conditions are imposed on a mechanism its performance is thereby restricted. The question arises whether there are

---

*The Mount-Reiter condition requires that the message correspondence be *locally threaded*. A correspondence (from one topological space to another) is locally threaded if at every point of its domain there is an open neighborhood of the point on which a continuous function is defined whose graph is inside the graph of the correspondence. (By the graph of correspondence F with domain X and range Y is meant the subset of pairs of points (x, y) in $X \times Y$ such that y is in $F(x)$.) In the case of a correspondence from the real line to the real line a typical picture is as shown in Figure 2. The term "locally threaded" comes from the fact that the graph of the function g runs through the graph of the correspondence μ like a piece of thread through a cloth.

any mechanisms which meet the conditions and if so, for what class of economies are there Pareto satisfactory mechanisms of this type. This problem is analogous to the problem of characterizing the subset of classical economies for which competitive equilibrium exists. Mount and Reiter [39] have studied this problem. Their results are summarized next.

Using the definition of a process which makes the composition $h \circ \mu$ single-valued, they consider a collection of such processes, which they call a *mechanism*, all using the same message space and outcome function, and show that a mechanism whose message correspondences are locally threaded can be p-satisfactory on a class of environments E if and only if the correspondence p is a union of continuous functions (a completely threaded correspondence) on E.

These theorems identify a property (complete threading) which when applied to the Pareto correspondence gives a condition which is necessary and sufficient for the existence of a (decentralized) mechanism whose performance is Pareto-satisfactory. They then ask the question, "On what class of environments does the Pareto correspondence have that property?", i.e., on what class of environments is the Pareto correspondence completely threaded? Equivalently, on what class of environments can all Pareto optima be achieved by decentralized means? They show that, in the presence of certain rather standard conditions on economies, if preferences are strictly monotone, then the Pareto utility frontier correspondence (associating with each economy its Pareto frontier in the space of utility values of the participants) is completely threaded. Examples show that strict monotonicity is indispensable. If, further, the set of points (allocation or trades) which are Pareto equivalent to a given Pareto optimal point is a singleton, (Pointedness Assumption), then the "Contract Curve" correspondence is also completely threaded. (The contract curve correspondence associates to each economy the set of its Pareto optimal allocations.)

The classical welfare theorems establish the Pareto-satisfactoriness of the competitive mechanism on the class of convex environments. However, it is not known whether the competitive mechanism has a locally threaded message correspondence on the full class of environments on which the welfare theorems hold. It was established by Mount and Reiter [38] that the competitive mechanism does satisfy that regularity condition on the class of pure trade environments with Cobb-Douglas utilities. Furthermore, it is clear that when the competitive equilibrium is unique (and the Walras correspondence is upper hemi-continuous), the regularity condition (local threading) is also met. The case of multiple equilibria for environments which do not satisfy the assumptions of their theorems remains open. It should be pointed out that the competitive mechanism, as it is ordinarily specified, does not meet their requirements for a mechanism when it is applied to economies in which it has multiple equilibria. Mount and Reiter in effect require that a particular equilibrium be selected in a continuous fashion as the environment varies. Indeed, one interpretation of their results is that the conjunction of (i) the requirement that the economic mechanism make a selection of equilibria for cases in which there are multiple equilibria, (ii) the regularity condition on communication, and (iii) Pareto-satisfactoriness of performance, restricts the allowable environments to very classical ones.

Another class of questions posed by the (new)[2] welfare economists relates to the communication capacity (informational size of the message space) needed in order to have a mechanism that achieves specified performance on a given class of economies. Questions of this type were posed by Hurwicz for mechanisms that are restricted to Euclidean message spaces, (Hurwicz [27]). He considered the classical economies, for which the competitive mechanism is non-wasteful, and asked whether there is any other mechanism whose performance is nonwasteful on the same class of economies, but whose message space is of lower dimension than that of the competitive process. He showed that there can be no such process. (To exclude "smuggling" of information, Hurwicz uses the condition that the lower inverse of the message correspondence be *quasi-Lipschitzian*, i.e., have a selection which satisfies a uniform Lipschitz condition.) (See e.g., Apostol [3].)

Mount and Reiter [38], using their concept of informational size of message spaces and the (regularity) condition that the message correspondence be locally threaded, showed independently that there can be no other mechanism whose performance is the same as that of the competitive mechanism (e.g., whose outcomes are competitive equilibria) which uses a message space informationally smaller than that of the competitive mechanism.*

Walker [46], exploring the concept of informational size introduced by Mount and Reiter, gave definitions of some stronger related concepts. Osana [40], using one of these extended concepts of informational size and using the Mount-Reiter regularity condition (locally threaded message correspondence), showed that there can be no process which is non-wasteful in classical economies and whose message space is informationally smaller, in the modified sense, than that of the competitive process.**

These theorems establish the minimality (in an appropriate sense) of the competitive process in terms of the channel capacity required to achieve nonwasteful performance in classical economies.

The same questions are raised about mechanisms designed to work in nonclassical (nonconvex) economies. Are there informationally decentralized mechanisms whose performance is Pareto satisfactory in nonclassical economies? What are the informational requirements in terms of size of message space of mechanisms designed to perform nonwastefully in nonclassical economies?

We first note that environments having externalities, (nondecomposable environments) are fundamentally different from those having no externalities, (decomposable environments).

Hurwicz [26] and [27] has explored a certain class of economies with externalities via the analysis of examples. Without reporting on this work in detail, the result is that, for the class of economies Hurwicz considered, informational decentralization and Pareto-satisfactory performance are, in general, incompatible. More generally, to require Pareto-satisfactory performance in economies with

---

*Message spaces are required to be Hausdorff spaces. In Hausdorff space points may be separated from one another by a pair of nonoverlapping open neighborhoods, each containing one of the points.

**A related result is the characterization of the competitive mechanisms given by Sonnenschein [45].

externalities tends to increase the information requirements of the mechanism.

For the case of decomposable economies (no externalities) several Pareto satisfactory informationally decentralized processes are known.

The "greed' process (Hurwicz [23]) is, as we have already noted, Pareto-satisfactory for all decomposable environments and is informationally decentralized, although it lacks stability. It uses subsets of the commodity space as messages, which means that the message space of the greed process is large, much larger, for example, than that of the competitive process.

The *B*-process of Hurwicz, Radner and Reiter [30], which is Pareto satisfactory for the two important types of nonclassical environments described above, in the discrete case uses points of the commodity space as messages; in the continuous case subsets are used. As was already pointed out, the *B*-process is globally stable (in a stochastic sense) in economies with nonconvexities in preferences or production. It is also informationally decentralized. We may also mention Kanemitsu's revision of the greed process (Kanemitsu [31] and the Arrow-Hurwicz modified Lagrangian gradient process which converges for certain increasing returns environments.*

While there are informationally decentralized processes which perform satisfactorily in nonclassical economies, they have "large" message spaces. On the other hand, the competitive process, whose message space is "small", does not perform satisfactorily in nonconvex environments. The question arises, what is the smallest message space sufficient for a process which has satisfactory performance in nonconvex economies?

In response to this question, Hurwicz ([27], revised [29]) has given an example with two agents and two goods, one of them indivisible, for which no finite dimensional message space suffices.

---

*For other work in the same spirit see Aoki [2], Arrow and Hurwicz [6], Camacho [8], Dreze and De La Vallee Poussin [12], Heal [19], and Ledyard [34] and [35].

Calsamiglia [7] has shown that the message space of a mechanism which is nonwasteful in environments allowing increasing returns cannot be finite dimensional even in an economy with two agents. Calsamiglia also exhibits an informationally decentralized process (the C-process) which is nonwasteful in cases in which all firms have increasing returns. However, the dimension of the message space of the C-process is an exponential function of the number of inputs in the economy.

These explorations of Hurwicz and Calsamiglia show that the search for a "simple" resource allocation mechanism that "works" when there are increasing returns (or more broadly in nonconvex economies) cannot be successful. Something must give, whether it is by narrowing the class of economies on which nonwasteful performance can be assured, as in the work of Chipman [9] and Aoki [1], or by increasing the size of the message space, or by some degree of centralization; some retreat from the ambitions implicit in "marginal cost pricing" schemes must be made.

The possibility that the natural motivations of economic agents may be in conflict with the behavior called for by the mechanism has been recognized at least since Adam Smith's well-known comment about businessmen seizing any occasion of meeting to conspire to raise prices. When they do so they do not behave as price-takers, as the competitive mechanism requires. Hence if Adam Smith has correctly described natural motivations of businessmen he has made an argument that the competitive mechanism is not compatible with private incentives. Adam Smith's statement refers to a collusive group; the same issue has been given an analytical formulation insofar as individual behavior is concerned.

An individual agent has the opportunity to adopt behavior different from that called for by the mechanism whenever some component of his characteristic is not observable by others, e.g., his preferences. By "falsifying" his preferences, an agent may be able to move the outcome of the mechanism to one preferred by him over the outcome that would otherwise have resulted. This is the case, for example, in economies with public goods. A mechanism in which no agent has an incentive to deviate from the prescribed behavior, in some class of economies, is called (individually) incentive compatible for that class of economies. This concept has been formalized in terms of a noncooperative game derived from the given mechanism, using Nash equilibrium as the solution concept.*

Actually from a given mechanism one can derive two different games, leading to two different concepts of incentive-compatibility, one allowing more room for strategic behavior of agents than the other. A solution of one game, called the *parameter game* because in one version the strategy of each player is the parameter specifying his characteristics, is called *Manipulative Nash Equilibrium* (MNE) and a solution of the other, called the *message game* because the strategy variable of each player is his message, is called *Non-Manipulative Nash Equilibrium* (NNE). Without going into detail, the nature of results obtained in this area may be indicated roughly as follows.

There are no mechanisms whose MNE lead to individually rational Pareto-optimal outcomes** for a class of economies broad enough to include those with utility functions which are nonlinear in private goods.*** (Hurwicz [28]).

In particular, there is no mechanism which is Pareto satisfactory, individually rational, (and preserves privacy), including the competitive mechanism, incentive-compatible (in the MNE sense) in classical pure exchange economies (Hurwicz [26]).

There are mechanisms, for example, the Groves-Ledyard mechanism, whose NNE are Pareto-optimal in economies with both private and public goods**** (Groves and Ledyard [14]).

The requirement that the outcome of a mechanism correspond to a NNE of the message game derived from the mechanism may lead to an increased requirement for informational capacity. In fact, for

---

*A Nash Equilibrium of a game is an array of feasible strategies, one for each player such that no player can increase his payoff by changing to another of the strategies available to him, given that no other player changes his strategy.

**A mechanism (or game) is called individually rational if the outcome is at least as good for every player as his initial endowment.

***"Impossibility Theorems" of this kind are closely related to theorems on the impossibility of "strategy-proof" social welfare functions by Satterthwaite and Gibbard, (Satterthwaite [44] and Gibbard [13]).

****A more complete survey of this field will be given elsewhere.

the competitive mechanism Hurwicz has shown that even in the case of a two-agent, two-commodity economy, the dimension of the competitive message space, in that case a two-dimensional space, does not permit the process to be one in which the outcomes come from an NNE of the derived message game. Imposing this as a requirement forces the message space to be at least three dimensional (Hurwicz [29]).*

REFERENCES

1. M. Aoki, "Increasing returns to scale and market mechanism," Technical Report No. 6, Institute for Mathematical Studies in the Social Sciences, Stanford University, 1967.

2. ———, "Two planning algorithms for an economy with public goods," Discussion Paper No. 029, Kyoto Institute for Economic Research, Kyoto University, 1970.

3. T. M. Apostol, *Mathematical Analysis*, Addison-Wesley, Reading, Mass., 1957.

4. K. Arrow, "An extension of the basic theorems of classical welfare economics" in J. Neyman (ed.), *Proceedings of the Second Berkeley Symposium on Mathematical Statistics and Probability*, University of California Press, Berkeley, 1951, pp. 507–532

5. K. J. Arrow and G. Debreu, "Existence of an equilibrium for a competitive economy," *Econometrica* **22** (1954), 265–290.

6. K. J. Arrow and L. Hurwicz, "Decentralization and computation in resource allocation," in R. W. Pfouts (ed.), *Essays in Economics and Econometrics*, University of North Carolina Press, Chapel Hill, 1960, pp. 34–104.

7. X. Calsamiglia, "On the possibility of informational decentralization in nonconvex environments," University of Minnesota, Ph.D. Thesis, 1975.

8. A. Camacho, "Externalities, optimality and informationally decentralized resource allocation processes," *International Economic Review*, **11** (1970), 318–327.

9. J. S. Chipman, "External economies of scale and competitive equilibrium," *The Quarterly Journal of Economics*, **LXXXIV** (August 1970).

10. G. Debreu, *Theory of Value*, Wiley and Sons, New York, 1959.

11. H. D. Dickinson, "Price formation in a Socialist community," *Economic Journal*, **XLIII** (December 1933).

12. J. H. Dreze and D. De La Vallee Poussin, "A tâtonnement process for guiding and financing an efficient production of public goods," Discussion Paper No. 6922, CORE, Univ. Cath. de Louvain, Belgium, 1969.

---

*D. Schmeidler and E. A. Pazner have also given formulations of the competitive process as non-cooperative games in unpublished papers.

13. A. Gibbard, "Manipulation of voting schemes: a general result," *Econometrica*, **41** (1973), 587–601.

14. T. Groves and J. Ledyard, "An incentive mechanism for efficient resource allocation in general equilibrium with public goods," Center for Mathematical Studies in Economics and Management Science, Northwestern University, Discussion Paper No. 119, 1974.

15. T. Groves and J. Ledyard, "The existence of an equilibrium under an optimal public goods allocation mechanism," manuscript, 1975.

16. R. Guesnerie, "Pareto optimality in non-convex economies," *Econometrica*, **43** (1975), No. 1, 1–29.

17. F. A. von Hayek, "The present state of the debate," in F. A. von Hayek, *Collectivist Economic Planning*, London, 1935, pp. 201–243.

18. ———, "The use of knowledge in society," *American Economic Review*, **35** (1945), 519–530. Reprinted in F. A. von Hayek, *Individualism and Economic Order*, The University of Chicago Press, Chicago, 1948.

19. G. M. Heal, "Planning without prices," *Review of Economic Studies*, **36** (1969), 346–362.

20. ———, "Planning, prices and increasing returns," *Review of Economic Studies*, **38** (1971), 281–294.

21. ———, *The Theory of Economic Planning*, North-Holland, Amsterdam, 1973.

22. H. Hotelling, "The general welfare in relation to problems of taxation and of railway and utility rates," *Econometrica*, **6** (1938), 242–269.

23. L. Hurwicz, "Optimality and informational efficiency in resource allocation processes," in Arrow, Karlin and Suppes (eds.), *Mathematical Methods in the Social Sciences 1959*, 1960, pp. 27–46.

24. ———, "On decentralizability in the presence of externatilities," paper presented at the San Francisco meeting of the Econometric Society (unpublished), 1966.

25. ———, "On the concept and possibility of informational decentralization," *American Economic Review*, **59** (1969), 513–534.

26. ———, "On informationally decentralized systems," in C. B. McGuire and R. Radner (eds.), *Decision and Organization*, Amsterdam, 1972, Chapter 14, pp. 1–29.

27. ———, "On the dimensional requirements of informationally decentralized Pareto-satisfactory processes," in the process of publication. Presented at the Conference Seminar on Decentralization, Northwestern University, February 1972.

28. ———, "On the existence of allocation systems whose manipulative Nash equilibria are Pareto-optimal," unpublished paper presented at 3rd World Congress of the Econometrica Society, Toronto, August 1975.

29. ———, "On informational requirements for non-wasteful resource allocation systems," unpublished manuscript, April 28, 1976.

30. L. Hurwicz, R. Radner, and S. Reiter, "A stochastic decentralized resource allocation process: part I," *Econometrica*, **43** (1975), 187–221, "Part II," *Econometrica*, **43** (1975), 363–393.

31. Hidei Kanemitsu, "On the stability of an adjustment process in non-convex environments," presented at the Second World Congress of the Econometric Society, England, September 1970, unpublished.

32. T. C. Koopmans, *Three Essays on the State of Economic Science*, McGraw-Hill, New York, 1957.

33. O. Lance, in B. E. Lippincott (ed.), *On the Economic Theory of Socialism*, University of Minnesota Press, Minneapolis, 1938.

34. J. O. Ledyard, "Resource allocation in unselfish environments," *American Economic Review*, **58** (1968), 227–237.

35. ———, "A convergent Pareto-satisfactory non-tatonnement adjustment process for a class of unselfish exchange environments," *Econometrica*, **39** (1971), 467–499.

36. A. P. Lerner, "Statistics and dynamics in socialist economics," *Econometrica*, **43** (1937), No. 1, 1–29.

37. E. Malinvaud, "Decentralized procedures for planning," in Bacharach and Malinvaud (eds.), *Activity Analysis in the Theory of Growth and Planning*, Macmillan, London, 1967, pp. 170–208.

38. K. Mount and S. Reiter, "The informational size of message spaces," *Journal of Economic Theory*, **8** (1974), 161–191.

39. K. Mount and S. Reiter, "Economic environments for which there are Pareto satisfactory mechanisms," Center for Mathematical Studies in Economics and Management Science, Northwestern University, Discussion Paper No. 124, (forthcoming in *Econometrica*), 1974.

40. Hiroaki Osana, "On the informational size of message spaces for resource allocation processes," presented April 1976 at the NBER Conference Seminar on Decentralization, Northwestern University, Evanston, Illinois.

41. S. Reiter, "The knowledge revealed by an allocation process and the informational size of the message space," *Journal of Economic Theory*, **8** (1974), 389–396.

42. ———, "Informational efficiency of iterative processes and the size of the message space," *Journal of Economic Theory*, **8** (1974), 193–205.

43. P. Samuelson, "The pure theory of public expenditures," *Review of Economics and Statistics*, **36** (1954), 387–389.

44. M. A. Satterthwaite, "Strategy-proofness and Arrow's conditions: existence and correspondence theorems for voting procedures and social welfare functions," *Journal of Economic Theory*, **10** (1975), 187–217.

45. H. Sonnenschein, "An axiomatic characterization of the price mechanism," *Econometrica*, **42** (1974) 425–434.

46. M. Walker, "On the informational size of message spaces," Economic Research Bureau, State University of New York, Stony Brook, Working Paper No. 146.

ON INFORMATIONAL DECENTRALIZATION AND EFFICIENCY IN RESOURCE ALLOCATION MECHANISMS[†]

Leonid Hurwicz

I. INTRODUCTION

This chapter is largely devoted to the study of certain informational properties of economic mechanisms.

Among informational properties of a mechanism, the focus is on the 'size' (often dimension) of the spaces of messages used for communication between units. Section II is devoted to the clarification of the concept of 'size' of the message space and to results

[†]Aid from a succession of National Science Foundation grants, most recently SES-8509547, is gratefully acknowledged. Opportunities and stimulation for this research were greatly enhanced by annual visits to the Stanford IMSSS, by the participation in the 1983/4 program of the Institute for Mathematics and its Applications, University of Minnesota, and by the visiting appointment at the California Institute of Technology during 1984/5 as a Sherman Fairchild Distinguished Scholar. The annual NBER/NSF-sponsored decentralization conferences have played a major role in stimulating and filtering many of the ideas reported in this paper.

specifying minimum size of a message space for a mechanism whose performance agrees with given goals. Section IV deals with analogous problems in situations where only approximate agreement is possible. Section III shows how, at least in certain cases, integration procedures can be used to 'derive' mechanisms whose performance agrees with specified goals. While other sections emphasize statics and the verification of equilibrium properties, Section V looks at the convergence properties of (dynamic) mechanisms. Game theoretic properties (hence incentive aspects) are ignored except in Sections VI and V.3.

I.1. Background. Contemporary writings on welfare economics, exemplified by Arrow, Debreu, Koopmans, and most recent textbooks on microeconomics, contain two basic theorems of welfare economics. The first of these states that competitive equilibrium allocations are Pareto-optimal; the second, that a Pareto-optimal allocation can be attained through competitive equilibria following a suitable redistribution of assets (endowments and profit shares). The validity of these assertions depends on the nature of the *environment*[†] (preferences, technologies, endowments): absence of externalities, indivisibilities, increasing returns, etc.[††] Related fundamental theorems deal with the existence, uniqueness, and stability of competitive equilibria.

The reasons for the economist's interest in these theorems are several. First, many regard the Pareto-optimality of allocations as a universal (and relatively noncontroversial) efficiency[†††] requirement, perhaps to be supplemented by postulates of fairness, etc.

[†] The term "environment," suggested by Jacob Marschak, corresponds to what is often simply called the "economy." However, the latter term is also used to mean the economic system (e.g., a "socialist economy"). To avoid confusion, we speak of the "environment" when referring to aspects that are usually taken as given, and of a "mechanism" when referring to rules of operation (regarded as subject to change and design).

[††] Externalities are ruled out in both theorems. Some of the other conditions (e.g., convexity) are only needed in the second. Environments satisfying the assumptions usually made in the welfare and existence theorems are sometimes called *classical*.

[†††] Of the resulting resource allocations.

the competitive mechanism is viewed as having important advantages in the spheres of incentives and information. The latter was emphasized in the Mises-Hayek-Lange-Lerner debate and will constitute the focus of our attention.

But the classical welfare economics theorems leave a number of issues open. First, how to deal with situations in nonclassical environments, e.g., in the presence of externalities or increasing returns. Here competitive equilibria may be nonoptimal or nonexistent. How does one look for alternative mechanisms which might fill the gap? But even in classical environments, there may be difficulties in supplementing (say, by taxes and subsidies) the competitive mechanism in such a way that not only optimality but also fairness of distribution is attained, and yet the informational and incentive advantages are not lost.

To study such questions we need to formalize the notions of resource allocation mechanisms, and their desired informational characteristics. The concept of a resource allocation mechanism should be broad enough to encompass not only competition, but other market and nonmarket (e.g., 'command') economies.

I.2. Resource allocation mechanisms. I.2.1. We think of a resource allocation mechanism as operating in time. It will be convenient here to think of time as discrete, $t = 0, 1, 2, \ldots$. An important distinction is that between tâtonnement and nontâtonnement processes. In the latter, actions are taken while adjustments are going on. We shall study the former, where actions are based on final (or: equilibrium) values. A tâtonnement process has two phases: message exchange, and choice of outcome. At each point in time, each participant emits a message, i.e., an element m_t^i from a set M^i (the ith agent's *language* or [individual] *message space*). Thus an observer watching the message exchange would see a (possibly infinite) matrix

$$\begin{bmatrix} m_0^1 \ldots m_0^n \\ m_1^1 \ldots m_1^n \\ \cdots \cdots \cdots \\ m_t^1 \ldots m_t^n \\ \cdots \cdots \cdots \end{bmatrix}$$

where n is the (finite) number of agents. The transition from the exchange of messages to actions (outcomes) can be modeled in different ways. The simplest would be a time limit, say some $T \geq 0$ such that the final message n-tuple, $m_T = (m_T^1, \ldots, m_T^n)$, constitutes the basis for a choice of actions (outcomes). This can be expressed through an *outcome function* h such that

$$a = h(m_T)$$

where $a \in A$, A is the class of possible actions (outcomes), and $m_T \in M^1 \times \cdots \times M^n$.

The finite time limit formulation is perhaps more realistic, but economists are more inclined to think in terms of equilibrium values. To define equilibrium, we postulate that the messages satisfy a system of temporally homogeneous difference equations of first order.[†] This is written as

$$m_{t+1}^i = F^i(m_t^1, \ldots, m_t^n; e), \quad i = 1, \ldots, n, \quad t = 0, 1, 2, \ldots . \quad (1)$$

F^i is called the *response function* of the ith agent. e stands for a description of the environment; i.e., $e \in E$ where E is the class of conceivable environments. We think of F^i as representing the rule by which the ith agent selects the message to be emitted at time $t + 1$ on the basis of such information as he/she has concerning the messages $m_t^1, \ldots, m_t^n$ and the environment e. (It is not assumed that each agent has complete information either about e or about the other agents' messages.)

More briefly, we may write (1) as

$$m_{t+1}^i = F^i(m_t; e), \quad i = 1, \ldots, n, \ t = 0, 1, 2, \ldots \quad (1')$$

or, even more briefly, as

$$m_{t+1} = F(m_t; e), \quad t = 0, 1, 2, \ldots, \quad (1'')$$

[†] We shall subsequently discuss possible generalizations of and alternatives to this model. For a stochastic counterpart, see Hurwicz, Radner, and Reiter [38] and Mitsui [57]. Temporally homogeneous difference equations of higher but finite order have static properties similar to those of first order.

where $m_\tau = (m_\tau^1, \ldots, m_\tau^n)$, $m_\tau^i \in M^i$, $\tau = 0, 1, \ldots$, and $F = (F^1, \ldots, F^n)$.

An *equilibrium* (*stationary*) *joint message*[†] $\overline{m} \in M^1 \times \cdots \times M^n$ is then defined by

$$\overline{m}^i = F^i(\overline{m}; e), \qquad i = 1, \ldots, n, \tag{2'}$$

i.e.,

$$\overline{m} = F(\overline{m}; e). \tag{2''}$$

Suppose that, for each i, M^i is an additive group, with the identity element 0_i. Defining the *equilibrium function* g^i by $g^i(m_1, \ldots, m_n; e) \equiv m_i - F^i(m_1, \ldots, m_n; e)$, we note that the system $(2')$ is equivalent to

$$g^i(\overline{m}; e) = 0_i, \qquad i = 1, \ldots, n. \tag{2'''}$$

Usually, we shall omit the subscript in 0_i.

Of course, such a stationary value may fail to exist. If it does exist it may or may not be unique. If stationary values do exist, one would hope that the system (1) would have some stability properties, either locally or globally. In Section V below we shall discuss some recent work devoted to the stability problem. In most of this paper, however, we shall concentrate on the static properties of the system.

If the system is in equilibrium, the stationary value $\overline{m}$ can serve as a basis for the choice of outcomes; i.e., the action a is chosen as

$$a = h(\overline{m}) \tag{3}$$

where $\overline{m}$ is a solution of (2) and $\overline{h}$ is an *outcome function*.[††]

[†] An *n*-tuple of individual messages is sometimes called a *joint message*, or even just a *message*. The set of possible joint messages is called a (*joint*) *message space*. In general, a message space need not be the Cartesian product of individual message spaces.

[††] In some cases, we shall consider mechanisms whose outcome function depends not only on the equilibrium message, but also on the agent's own characteristic, i.e., $a = h(m, e^i)$. Such an h is called a *parametric* outcome function, while $a = h(m)$ is called *nonparametric*. (See Section II.5 below.)

In this model a *mechanism* (in *response function form*) may be defined as a triple $(\underset{\sim}{M}, \underset{\sim}{F}, h)$ where $\underset{\sim}{M} = (M^1, \ldots, M^n)$ and $\underset{\sim}{F} = (F^1, \ldots, F^n)$.

Clearly, in the above model, $\overline{m} \in M^1 \times \cdots \times M^n$. However, when we confine ourselves to the static aspects of the mechanism, a slightly different, and analytically more convenient (although perhaps less natural) formulation can be adopted.

Let M be an arbitrary set, possibly but not necessarily of the form $M = M^1 \times \cdots \times M^n$, called the *message space*. For each agent i, define his (*individual*) *equilibrium correspondence* μ^i: $E \to \to M$.

An element $\overline{m} \in M$ is said to be an *equilibrium message* for the environment e if and only if

$$\overline{m} \in \mu^i(e) \quad \text{for all } i \in \{1, \ldots, n\}. \tag{4}$$

The earlier formulation is a special case where

$$M = M^1 \times \cdots \times M^n \tag{5.1}$$

(with $M^1, \ldots, M^n$ some given sets), and, for $m = (m^1, \ldots, m^n) \in M^1 \times \cdots \times M^n$,

$$m \in \mu^i(e) \Leftrightarrow m^i = F^i(m, e), \qquad i = 1, \ldots, n. \tag{5.2'}$$

When each M^i is an additive group we may define $G^i(m, e) \equiv m^i - F^i(m, e)$, so that

$$m \in \mu^i(e) \Leftrightarrow G^i(m, e) = 0, \qquad i = 1, \ldots, n. \tag{5.2''}$$

In this more general formulation,[†] the (joint) message space M need not be the Cartesian product of individual languages. A *mechanism* is then defined by the message space M, the n individual equilibrium correspondences μ^i: $E \to \to M$, $i = 1, \ldots, n$, and the outcome function h: $M \to A$. Briefly, a mechanism in *equi-*

[†] Due to Mount and Reiter [60].

librium correspondence form is denoted by $\pi = (M, \mu, h)$ where $\mu = (\mu^1, \ldots, \mu^n)$. In *equilibrium equation form*, a mechanism is defined by $(M, \underset{\sim}{G}, h)$ where $\underset{\sim}{G} = (G^1, \ldots, G^n)$.

One interpretation of this model can be visualized as follows. The participants are presented (say, on a display board) with a proposed message $m \in M$. The ith agent says "yes" if and only if $m \in \mu^i(e)$. m is declared an equilibrium message if and only if everyone says "yes." If $m \notin \mu^i(e)$, the ith agent says "no." If any "noes" are heard, a new message must be proposed, until one is found for which everyone says "yes." This interpretation is referred to as the *verification scenario*.

Given a mechanism (M, μ, h), we can define the *joint equilibrium correspondence* $\mu \colon E \to \to \underset{\sim}{M}$ by

$$\mu(e) = \bigcap_{i=1}^{n} \mu^i(e) \quad \text{for all } e \in E,$$

i.e.,

$$m \in \mu(e) \Leftrightarrow m \in \mu^i(e), \quad i \in \{1, \ldots, n\}.$$

In turn, we define the *performance* correspondence $\Phi_\pi \colon E \to \to A$ of the mechanism $\pi = (M, \underset{\sim}{\mu}, h)$ by

$$\Phi_\pi(e) = \{a \in A : a = h(m) \text{ and } m \in \mu(e) \text{ for some } m \in M\}$$

for any $e \in E$. We say that π is *decisive* on E if and only if $\Phi_\pi(e) \neq \varnothing$ for all $e \in E$.

The economist's desiderata can also be formulated as correspondences from E to A. For instance, the criterion of Pareto-optimality can be expressed as a correspondence $P \colon E \to \to A$ where $P(e)$ is the set of all outcomes that are Pareto-optimal in the environment e.[†]

[†] Let A be the set of feasible outcomes, and $\succeq_i$ the binary reflexive (weak preference) relation on A for person i. Let $e = (A, \{\succeq_i\}_{i=1}^{n})$. Then an element a in A is said to be Pareto-optimal for e if there does *not* exist an element a' in A such that: (1) $a' \succeq_i a$ for all $i \in \{1, \ldots, n\}$, and (2) $a' \succ_j a$ for some $j \in \{1, \ldots, n\}$. Here $a' \succ_j a$ means: $a' \succeq_j a$ but not $a \succeq_j a'$.

A mechanism π is said to be *nonwasteful* over the class E of environments, if, for every e in E, all values $\Phi_\pi(e)$ of the performance correspondence are Pareto-optimal for e; that is if $\Phi_\pi(e) \subseteq P(e)$ for all $e \in E$.

More generally, let $\Psi\colon E \to \to A$ be a social *goal correspondence*[†] expressing the desiderata, with $\Psi(e) \neq \varnothing$ for all $e \in E$. If a mechanism π is to be chosen, we want its performance correspondence Φ_π to be, in some sense, in agreement with the goal correspondence $\varnothing$. A modest requirement would be that

$$\Phi_\pi(e) \subseteq \Psi(e) \text{ for all } e \in E, \qquad (*)$$

and that π be decisive on E.

Would one require more, e.g., that

$$\Phi_\pi(e) = \Psi(e) \text{ for all } e \in E? \qquad (**)$$

Clearly not if Ψ is something as broad as the Pareto-criterion. On the other hand, if Ψ is single-valued and π decisive, then, of course, $(**)$ is equivalent to $(*)$. We shall say that π *realizes* Ψ on E if and only if π is decisive on E and $(*)$ holds.[††] π is said to *fully realize* Ψ on E if and only if π is decisive and $(**)$ holds.

A basic problem is how to go about designing mechanisms having suitable informational and incentive properties and realizing a prescribed choice correspondence. However, except for Section V.3, and VI, only informational aspects are discussed in the present paper.

I.2.2. *Message spaces.* So far the individual languages M^i and the joint message space M have been introduced as sets of arbitrary objects. There are at least three categories of languages and message spaces of special interest to the economist. First, there are

---

[†]Often called a social choice correspondence, a social choice rule, and sometimes a performance standard.

[††]We use the term "realize" to distinguish this requirement from the notion of "implementation" which takes into account incentives and involves a game-theoretic formulation. "Realization," as used here, is purely informational.

messages descriptive of the environment. Most frequently such a message provides information about its author's characteristic e^i (e.g., his/her preferences, endowments, or technology). These message spaces are used in direct revelation mechanisms (see Sections I.3 and III.1 below) and, partially, in parameter transfer processes (see Section III.1 below). Messages descriptive of all participants (i.e., profiles $(e^1, \ldots, e^n)$ of characteristics) are used in mechanisms implementing goal performance correspondences in Nash equilibria (see Section VI below). Such message spaces are very 'large' in the sense to be made precise in Section II below, typically infinite-dimensional. Relatively 'small' spaces are used in mechanisms realizing the Walrasian (competitive) correspondence (see Section II below); these are finite-dimensional Euclidean spaces.

A third category of message spaces uses, as a generic element m^i of the ith language M^i, a set A whose elements are 'net resource flow matrices.' In a pure exchange economy with n participants a *gross* resource flow matrix b is a square array $b = (b^{ij})_{i, j = 1, \ldots, n}$, where b^{ij} is an element of the commodity space $\mathcal{X}$, with b^{ij} representing the flow of goods from person j to person i. If $\mathcal{X}$ is an additive group, we define net trade $a^{ij} = b^{ij} - b^{ji}$. Thus the '*net resource flow matrix*' $a = (a^{ij})_{i, j = 1, \ldots, n}$ is skew symmetric, i.e., $a^{ij} + a^{ji} = 0_x$, $i, j = 1, \ldots, n$, where 0_x is the null element of $\mathcal{X}$. (See Hurwicz [27].) With various specifications of such resource flow language one can represent both perfect and imperfect markets and also various types of centralized ('command') economies. (See also Kanemitsu [48], [49].)

I.3. Decentralization. Returning to our first model of a mechanism, a response function F^i requires the agent to choose the next message m^i_{t+1} given the previous message $m^1_t, \ldots, m^n_t$ and the environment e. But we do not expect the agent to have complete knowledge of the environment. Rather, we think of each agent as initially having information only concerning his own individual *characteristic*[†] e^i, usually specified by his preferences R^i, initial

---

[†] We refer to such a situation as an *initial dispersion of information*. It need not be assumed that the agent has complete information concerning his own characteristic.

endowment ω^i and technology[†] T^i and written $e^i = (\omega^i, R^i, T^i)$. Denote by E^i the set of conceivable characteristics of the ith agent. We shall assume *independence* in the sense that $E = E^1 \times \cdots \times E^n$. Thus for any $e \in E$ we have $e = (e^1, \ldots, e^n)$, $e^i \in E^i$, $i \in \{1, \ldots, n\}$.

If we assume that, aside from messages received, the ith agent knows only his own characteristic e^i, we cannot require that his response depend on the e^j, $j \neq i$. Formally, we have[††]

$$F^i(m; \tilde{e}^1, \ldots, \tilde{e}^{i-1}, e^i, \tilde{e}^{i+1}, \ldots, \tilde{e}^n) =$$
$$F^i(m; \tilde{\tilde{e}}^1, \ldots, \tilde{\tilde{e}}^{i-1}, e^i, \tilde{\tilde{e}}^{i+1}, \ldots, \tilde{\tilde{e}}^n) \quad \text{for all } m, e^i, \tilde{e}^{)i(}, \tilde{\tilde{e}}^{)i(}.$$

Therefore, we may write

$$F^i(m; e^1, \ldots, e^n) \equiv f^i(m; e^i)$$

where $f^i: M^1 \times \cdots \times M^n \times E^i \to M^i$. Such a response function f^i is called *privacy-preserving*.[†††] In terms of the (M, μ, h) model, we call a joint equilibrium message correspondence $\underset{\sim}{\mu}$ *privacy-preserving* if and only if

$$\mu^i(\tilde{e}^1, \ldots, \tilde{e}^{i-1}, e^i, \tilde{e}^{i+1}, \ldots, \tilde{e}^n) = \mu^i(\tilde{\tilde{e}}^1, \ldots, \tilde{\tilde{e}}^{i-1}, e^i, \tilde{\tilde{e}}^{i+1}, \ldots \tilde{\tilde{e}}^n)$$

for all $e^i, \tilde{e}^{)i(}, \tilde{\tilde{e}}^{)i(}$. Without changing the symbol μ^i, we shall then write $\mu^i(e^i)$, so that now $\mu^i: E^i \to \to M$.[††††] Hence, using the above definition of μ, we have

$$\mu(e) = \bigcap_{i=1}^n \mu^i(e^i).$$

[†] We are *not*, at this point, assuming absence of externalities! For instance, T^i may be a *conditional* production function where productivity depends on others' activities. See Camacho [15].

[††] Where $)i($ stands for $(1, \ldots, i-1, i+1, \ldots, n)$.

[†††] One might also consider higher (but finite) order equation systems, say $m_t^i = F^i(m_t, \ldots, m_{t-p}; e^i)$ without introducing major new issues concerning the properties of equilibria. But infinite order (and not temporally homogenous) systems such as $m_{t+1}^i = F_t^i(m_t, \ldots, m_0; e^i)$ have radically different properties, even when each M^i is finite-dimensional Euclidean. (See Crémer [21], Calsamiglia [14], Hurwicz and Thomson [42].)

[††††] Whereas, previously, we had $\mu^i: E \to \to M$.

So far no restrictions have been imposed on the individual message spaces. In a class of mechanisms of particular interest, we set

$$\left.\begin{array}{l} M^i = E^i \\[2mm] f^i(m, e^i) = e^i \quad \text{for all} \quad (m, e^i) \end{array}\right\} i \in \{1, \ldots, n\}.$$

and

A mechanism with these properties is called a *direct revelation mechanism*. In effect, in the dynamic version of such a process, the ith agent sets

$$m^i_{t+1} = e^i$$

at all times; i.e., he/she repeatedly announces his/her characteristic. (Since $M^i = E^i$, such announcements are possible; the agent's language is sufficiently "rich.") In the Mount-Reiter formulation, we set $\mu^i(e^i) = \{e^i\} \times E^{)i(}$. In either case we clearly have

$$\overline{m} = (e^1, \ldots, e^n).$$

Hence, to realize a goal correspondence Ψ, it is sufficient to set

$$h(\overline{m}) = \psi(\overline{m})$$

where ψ is a selection from Ψ.[†] Obviously, this mechanism does realize Ψ because here the performance correspondence Φ_π is simply the function ψ.[††] However, such a mechanism, even though privacy-preserving, has the informational features of a centralized ('command') economy, since each agent communicates his characteristic and then, somewhere, the desired outcome is calculated. (On the plus side, the procedure converges in one step!)

[†] That is, $\psi \colon E \to A$ is a (single-valued) function, and $\psi(e) \in \Psi(e)$ for all $e \in E$.

[††] A direct revelation mechanism $\pi = (M, f, h)$ with $M^i = E^i$, $f^i(m, e^i) = e^i$, for all $i \in \{1, \ldots, n\}$, and h a selection from the goal correspondence Ψ is called *natural for* Ψ.

Something more than the privacy-preserving property is needed to express the notion of informational decentralization. This can be accomplished in various ways. Specifically, one may impose additional conditions either on the response functions (or, in the Mount-Reiter model, on the individual equilibrium correspondences) or on the message space, or both. The next section is devoted to certain aspects of the problem.[†]

II.   MEASURING THE INFORMATIONAL EFFICIENCY OF RESOURCE ALLOCATION MECHANISMS BY THEIR MESSAGE SPACE SIZE. MINIMALITY RESULTS

II.1.   Reasons for interest in message space size.   We have defined a (resource allocation) mechanism as an ordered triple $\pi = (\underset{\sim}{M}, \underset{\sim}{F}, h)$ where $\underset{\sim}{M}$ is the n-tuple of individual message spaces, $\underset{\sim}{F}$ the n-tuple of response functions, and h the outcome function. (When studying equilibrium properties, we may replace the response function n-tuple $\underset{\sim}{F}$ by the equilibrium function n-tuple $\underset{\sim}{G}$ or by the equilibrium correspondence μ, and the n-tuple $\underset{\sim}{M}$ by the message space $\mathscr{M}$.[††]) The informational efficiency of such a process can be looked at in a variety of ways. In general, it should measure the resources required to operate the system, the time it takes to arrive at reasonably correct answers, and the magnitude of errors it is likely to produce under given circumstances. The resources required will depend, other things being equal, on such factors as the fineness of distinctions called for in calculating the responses and the outcomes. Thus one natural concept of informational efficiency relates to the partitions induced by the response and outcome functions on the space of their arguments (see Hurwicz

[†] In Hurwicz [27] *informational decentralization* of those processes whose languages are sets of net resource flow matrices, is defined by requiring, in addition to the privacy-preserving property (then called 'externality'), also certain symmetry properties of the response functions and certain limitations on the permissible sets of such matrices.

[††] Which may, but in general need not, be the Cartesian product of individual message spaces.

[27]). Also, other things being equal, the resources required will increase with the number of variables the system contains. More specifically, let a typical element m of the message space $\mathcal{M}$ be a finite sequence of k numbers (some of which might be restricted to integers), say $m = (m_1, \ldots, m_k)$. We then say that the message space is k-dimensional, and we write dim $\mathcal{M} = k$. Other things being equal, one would expect that fewer resources will be required to operate the system when the dimension of the message space (i.e., the number of message variables) is smaller.

These considerations have led to a series of investigations designed to answer the following type of question: Given the desired performance of the system, what is the minimal dimension of the message space of a mechanism capable of realizing that performance in a specified class of environments?

The interest in size comparisons among message spaces is largely due to the following result, obtained in somewhat different forms by a number of writers.[†] The result, roughly speaking, is that, in pure exchange economies, a privacy-preserving mechanism realizing a Pareto-optimal interior-valued performance correspondence must use a message space of informational size not lower than that of a (static) version of the Walrasian process; the latter message space is a subset, with nonempty interior, of the Euclidean space of dimension $n \cdot (l - 1)$ where n is the number of agents and l the number of goods.[††]

Of course, a mechanism with minimal dimension of the message space may have more complex response or outcome functions; therefore, the total value (however defined) of resources needed to operate the system may be minimized by a mechanism whose message space dimension exceeds the possible minimum. Thus the study of minimal required dimension of the message space is analogous to the problem of finding the minimum required amount of one of several inputs used in a production process: the minimi-

---

[†] Mount and Reiter [58], [60], Hurwicz [29], Walker [90], [91], [92], Osana [71], Sato [80], Nayak [66].

[††] An analogous result concerning the Lindahl process in public goods economies was obtained by Sato [80].

zation of the cost of producing a given output will not, in general, call for the minimization of any given input. Nevertheless, the study of such minimal input requirements may be a first feasible step on the way to finding the efficient boundary of the production possibility set. A similar argument justifies the study of minimal dimensional requirements for message spaces. But such study is only a first step, and it is important to explore other aspects of resource needs, in particular the complexity of the mechanism.[†] But we shall not discuss this issue here.

The intuition leading to the desirability of minimizing the dimension of a message space whose elements are finite sequences of numbers is also relevant in other spaces. The more general idea is that the 'smaller' the message space, the better. However, the size of a message space cannot always be measured by its dimension. For some spaces there may not exist a natural definition of dimension. But even when it is possible to define its dimension, other properties may turn out to be important. In particular, even in systems with finite-dimensional message spaces, we shall see that continuity and smoothness properties of equilibrium correspondences are of crucial importance. These properties, however, depend not only on the algebraic features of the message space such as its dimension but also on the choice of topology. It, therefore, becomes natural to introduce topological factors in comparing message spaces.

II.2. Message space size concepts. When $\mathcal{M}$ is a (finite-dimensional) Euclidean space it is natural to define its size by its dimension, so that

$$\text{size } \mathcal{M} =_{\text{def}} \dim \mathcal{M}$$

The underlying idea is simply that the dimension of $\mathcal{M}$ represents the number of variables that must be observed (see Hurwicz [28]).

In many economic mechanisms $\mathcal{M}$ is not a finite-dimensional Euclidean space. For instance, $\mathcal{M}$ may be an infinite-dimensional

---

[†] See Futia [24], Mount and Reiter [63], Traub, et al [88].

space of all (classical) preference relations when the mechanism is one of direct revelation. [More precisely, in a direct revelation mechanism[†] in a pure exchange economy, with endowments and consumption sets assumed fixed and known to the designer, a typical element of $\mathcal{M}$ is of the form $(R^1, \ldots, R^n)$ where R^i is the ith agent's preference relation.] On the other hand $\mathcal{M}$ may be of the form

$$\mathcal{M} = Z \times \cdots \times Z$$

where Z is the set of all integers; this may occur when goods are indivisible or when measurements are rounded off to the closest integer. (See Hurwicz and Marschak [36] and [37].)

What is a natural extension of the concept of message space size in such cases? This question was first posed by Mount and Reiter in [58], [60] and the proposed solution was based on the topological properties of message spaces.

Let $\mathcal{M}'$ and $\mathcal{M}''$ be two topological message spaces. $\mathcal{M}'$ is said to have (informational) *Mount/Reiter size* at least as great as $\mathcal{M}''$ if and only if there exists a continuous surjection ("onto" function)

$$f: \mathcal{M}' \underset{\text{onto}}{\rightarrow} \mathcal{M}''$$

such that the inverse correspondence

$$f^{-1}: \mathcal{M}'' \rightarrow \rightarrow \mathcal{M}'$$

is locally threaded.[††] Following Osana [71] we then write

$$\mathcal{M}' \geq {}^{\text{MR}}\mathcal{M}''.$$

[†]See Section I.3 above.

[††]A correspondence $\phi: A \rightarrow \rightarrow B$ is said to be *locally threaded* if for every $a \in A$, there is an open neighborhood U in A of $\underline{a}$ and a continuous function $g: U \rightarrow B$ such that $g(a) \in \phi(a)$ for every $a' \in U$.

A surjective function f whose (lower) inverse f^{-1} is locally threaded is called *locally sectioned*.

The (lower) *inverse* of a correspondence $F: A \rightarrow \rightarrow B$ is the correspondence $F^{-1}: F[A] \rightarrow \rightarrow A$, defined by $F^{-1}(b) = \{a \in A: b \in F(a)\}$.

The binary relations $\geq^{MR}$ is reflexive and transitive (i.e., a preordering) but not necessarily total (i.e., not necessarily a *complete* preordering).[†] This relation has a number of intuitively appealing properties; in particular, for Euclidean spaces it agrees with ordering by dimension.[††] However, it was pointed out by Walker [90], [91], [92] that $\geq^{MR}$ also produces some paradoxes. In particular, it can happen that[†††] $\mathscr{M}' >^{MR} \mathscr{M}''$ even though $\mathscr{M}'$ is a topological subspace of $\mathscr{M}''$.[††††]

[†]See Debreu [22], p. 7.

[††]Thus, given two Euclidean spaces E^k, E^n with $k > n$ (resp. $k = n$), the Mount/Reiter (informational) size of E^k is strictly greater than (resp. equal to) that of E^n.

It is clear that $E^k \geq^{MR} E^n$ for $k > n$ because the projection from E^k to its (say) first n coordinates is the required continuous locally sectioned surjection. On the other hand there does not exist a *locally sectioned* continuous surjection from E^n to E^k. There are, of course, continuous surjections from E^n to E^k; these are the so-called Peano curves. But a Peano curve is not locally sectioned. For suppose f: $E^n \to E^k$ is a continuous locally sectioned surjection. Consider the inverse correspondence f^{-1}: $E^k \to \to E^n$. Since f is locally sectioned, f^{-1} is by definition locally threaded. Hence for every point x of E^k there exists a neighborhood U and a continuous function s: $U \to E^n$ such that, for every x' in U, $s(x')$ is in $f^{-1}(x')$. But s is a 1-1 function on U; in fact, by construction, $f(s(x')) = x'$ for all x' in U and $s(f(y')) = y'$ for all y' in $s[U]$. (See Mount and Reiter [60], Lemma 8, p. 173.) Since both f and s are continuous, s is a homeomorphism between U and $s[U]$. Hence (since U is homeomorphic with E^k) the space E^k is homeomorphic with $s[U]$. Now (as first shown by Brouwer [8]), the *topological* dimension of E^r is r. Also, a subspace of a space of topological dimension r is at most of topological dimension r (Hurewicz and Wallman [26], Th III.1, p. 26). So $s[U]$ is at most of topological dimension n while U has topological dimension k which is higher than n. Since topological dimension is a topological invariant, U and $s[U]$ cannot be homeomorphic. The preceding argument follows Mount and Reiter ([60], pp. 174–5).

[†††]$\mathscr{M}' >^{MR} \mathscr{M}''$ has the natural meaning: $\mathscr{M}' \geq^{MR} \mathscr{M}''$ but not $\mathscr{M}'' \geq^{MR} \mathscr{M}'$; i.e., it is the asymmetric part of $\geq^{MR}$.

[††††]For instance, we have $(0, 1) >^{MR} [0, 1]$, using relative Euclidean topology. (To have $[0, 1] \geq^{MR} (0, 1)$ it would be necessary to have a continuous surjection from $[0, 1]$ onto $(0, 1)$; but this is impossible because the first set is compact and the second is not. On the other hand, $(0, 1) \geq^{MR} [0, 1]$ because the following function f: $(0, 1) \to [0, 1]$ is a continuous locally sectioned surjection. The function is defined by: $f(x) = 2/3 + x$ for $0 < x \leq 1/3$; $f(x) = 2 - 3x$ for $1/3 \leq x \leq 2/3$; $f(x) = x - 2/3$ for $2/3 \leq x < 1$.)

To remedy such paradoxes, Walker suggested an alternative preordering relation. $\mathcal{M}'$ is said to have (informational) *Walker size* at least as great as $\mathcal{M}''$ (written here as $\mathcal{M}' \geq^W \mathcal{M}''$)[†] if and only if there exists some subspace $\mathcal{M}'_1$ of $\mathcal{M}'$ such that $\mathcal{M}'_1 \geq^{MR} \mathcal{M}''$.

We note the obvious relations:

(1) if $\mathcal{M}'$ is a topological subspace of $\mathcal{M}''$, then $\mathcal{M}' \leq^W \mathcal{M}''$;
(2) $\mathcal{M}' \geq^{MR} \mathcal{M}''$ implies $\mathcal{M}' \geq^W \mathcal{M}''$.[††]

We have mentioned earlier that the interest in size comparisons for message spaces is due to results showing that the Walrasian process has minimal size requirements among processes satisfying certain requirements. Now suppose that we have at our disposal two alternative message space size preorderings, denoted $\geq_1$ and $\geq_2$, such that $\geq_1$ implies $\geq_2$. We shall say that $\geq_1$ is *stronger* than $\geq_2$. Clearly, if the above result (message size minimality of the Walrasian process) is valid for the stronger preordering, it is *a fortiori* valid for the weaker one. Hence—*caeteris paribus*—the stronger the size preordering, the stronger the theorem. The Mount/Reiter preordering is stronger than the Walker preordering but it lacks the monotonicity with respect to subspaces, and this creates difficulties in establishing the minimality of the Walrasian message space (Walker [92]). These difficulties are removed, at least for the realization of the Walrasian performance correspondence, when the Walker size preordering is used (Walker [92]). But it turns out that the minimality results are also valid for a stronger size ordering, that of Fréchet (denoted $\geq^F$).

$\mathcal{M}'$ is said to have (informational) *Fréchet size* at least as great as $\mathcal{M}''$ (written $\mathcal{M}' \geq^F \mathcal{M}''$) if and only if there exists some subspace $\mathcal{M}'_1$ of $\mathcal{M}'$ such that $\mathcal{M}'_1$ is homeomorphic to $\mathcal{M}''$ (i.e., $\mathcal{M}''$ can be "embedded homeomorphically" in $\mathcal{M}'$.)[†††]

It is clear that $\geq^F$ has the monotonicity property with respect to subspaces and that for finite-dimensional Euclidean spaces $\geq^F$

[†] Walker uses the symbol $\geq^S$ (S for subspace). Osana writes $\geq^*$.

[††] In fact, as noted by Walker, $\geq^W$ is the smallest preordering satisfying (1) and (2).

[†††] Walker [90] also considered a local version of $\geq^F$, denoted $\geq^{LF}$.

is equivalent to $\geq^W$. (See Hurewicz and Wallman [26], p. 66, where the term used is 'Fréchet dimension-type,' and Walker [92], p. 369.) Note the statement in Walker [92], p. 375, to the effect that, for the validity of the Walrasian process minimality theorem, one cannot use preorderings stronger than the Fréchet preordering.

Of the writers following Mount and Reiter and Walker, Osana [71] uses the Walker preordering while Sato [80] and Nayak [65]–[70] use the Fréchet preordering. Sato's formally stated results refer to public goods economies and the size minimality of the Lindahl process, but they can be modified (as pointed out in Sato [80], p. 67) in an obvious way to apply to the pure Walrasian process problem. Such a modification strengthens the Osana result in two respects: the conclusion uses the stronger Fréchet ordering and the regularity conditions imposed on the equilibrium message correspondence are somewhat weaker. Nayak's result for pure exchange (which does not refer to Sato's work) is a slight strengthening of the 'modified Sato' result in that there is a further weakening of the regularity condition on the equilibrium message correspondence. In what follows we shall give results of somewhat greater generality.

For narrower classes of topological spaces (metric separable) it might be natural to utilize the dimension concepts discussed in Hurewicz and Wallman. For linear spaces (whether or not topological) one could define the size of the space in terms of its dimension, i.e., the cardinality of its Hamel base. (See Kelley and Namioka [51], p. 4.)

The above concepts, despite their generality and power, do not seem adequate for dealing with *discrete* spaces, e.g., spaces of the form

$$Z^{(n)} \equiv \underbrace{Z \times \cdots \times Z}_{n \text{ factors}}$$

where Z is the set of all integers.[†] In these cases an alternative preordering, based on Lipschitzian properties, has been suggested in Hurwicz and Marschak [36]. Its relationship to the Mount/Reiter and Walker concepts will be obvious from the following sketch.

[†] See, however, the (unpublished) Section IV, in Mount and Reiter [58].

Consider $x \in \mathbb{R}^m$, i.e., $x = (x_1, \ldots, x_m)$, $x_i \in \mathbb{R}$, $i \in \{1, \ldots, m\}$, and let $\|x\|$ denote its maximum norm:

$$\|x\| = \max\{|x_i|: i \in \{1, \ldots, m\}\}.^\dagger$$

In what follows each of the spaces $X, Y, A, B, \mathcal{M}', \mathcal{M}''$, is a subset of *finite-dimensional Euclidean space* $\mathbb{R}^k$ for some finite k. A function $f: X \to Y$ is said to be *Lipschitz-continuous* (or *Lipschitzian*) if and only if there exists $K > 0$ such that

$$\|f(x') - f(x'')\| \leqq K \cdot \|x' - x''\|$$
for all $x', x'' \in X$.

A function $g: A \to B$ is said to be *Lipschitz-sectioned* if and only if its inverse correspondence g^{-1} has a Lipschitzian selection, i.e., if and only if there exists a Lipschitzian function $s: g(A) \to A$ such that $s(b) \in g^{-1}(b)$ for all $b \in g(A)$.

We then say that $\mathcal{M}'$ has (informational) *Lipschitz size* at least as great as $\mathcal{M}''$ (written $\mathcal{M}' \geq^L \mathcal{M}''$) if and only if there exists a subset $\mathcal{M}'_1$ of $\mathcal{M}$ and a surjective function $g: \mathcal{M}'_1 \underset{\text{onto}}{\to} \mathcal{M}''$ which is Lipschitz sectioned.

Note that the concept of Lipschitz size uses more than just the topological properties of the message space. It has here been defined with the help of a norm, and could be similarly defined in any metric space. It appears that some uniformity structure is essential.

II.3. Minimality results. We shall now outline a strategy for obtaining minimality results of the type mentioned above.

Suppose we want to show that the message space $\mathcal{M}'$ is of minimal size for implementing a performance correspondence F over the class of environments E. Suppose that $\pi' = (\mathcal{M}', \mu', h')$ realizes F over E. We must then show that in any alternative process $\pi = (\mathcal{M}, \mu, h)$ realizing F over E, the size of $\mathcal{M}$ is at least

---

†Similar notation is used for other spaces, whose elements are finite sequences of reals.

as great as that of $\mathcal{M}'$. We then seek a subset E^* of E such that the lower inverse $(\mu|_{E^*})^{-1}$ of the correspondence $\mu|_{E^*}$ (i.e., of μ restricted to E^*) has the subset $\mu[E^*]$ of $\mathcal{M}$ as its domain and E^* as its range. Under a variety of regularity conditions on μ or its inverse, the size of the range must be less than or equal to that of the domain. Hence, when such regularity conditions are postulated, the size of $\mathcal{M}$ must be at least as great as that of E^*. In this manner one obtains a lower bound on the size of an acceptable message space. If furthermore one has been able to choose E^* so that the size of E^* equals that of $\mathcal{M}'$, it follows that the size of an acceptable message space must be at least as great as that of $\mathcal{M}'$. Denoting the size preordering by $\geq$, and the size equality by $\approx$, we have $\mathcal{M} \geq$ domain $[(\mu|_{E^*})^{-1}] \geq E^* \approx \mathcal{M}'$. Thus the minimality of the size of $\mathcal{M}'$ among mechanisms satisfying the regularity condition and realizing F over E^* will have been established.[†] The final step involves the transition from E^* to E. Intuitively it seems clear that a process realizing F over E cannot use a message space smaller than that needed to realize F over its subset E^*. But since topological properties are used, it is important to verify that E^* can be topologically embedded in E, with the relative topology for E^* being that used in the definition of regularity of μ. (See Osana [71], Theorem, p. 72; Sato [80], p. 59; Nayak [65].)

Given a performance correspondence F to be realized over the class of economies E, how does one go about finding a subset E^* such that the lower inverse $(\mu|_{E^*})^{-1}$ of the equilibrium correspondence restricted to E^* is necessarily single-valued, i.e., finding E^* such that the restricted correspondence $\mu|_{E^*}$ is injective? To lighten notation, we shall illustrate our procedure for the case of two agents.

We shall say that $E^* \subseteq E = E^1 \times E^2$ has the *uniqueness* property with respect to F on E if and only if: for any $e^* = (e^{*^1}, e^{*^2})$

[†]Of course, one should verify that μ' satisfies the postulated regularity conditions. If it had not been shown that μ' satisfies the postulated regularity conditions, and if no other mechanism is known realizing F over E with the same size message space, then we are only entitled to claim that the size of $\mathcal{M}'$ is a lower bound, but not necessarily a minimum among acceptable mechanisms.

in E^* and $e^{**} = (e^{**^1}, e^{**^2})$ in E^*, the condition

$$F(e^*) \cap F(e^{**^1}, e^{*^2}) \cap F(e^{*^1}, e^{**^2}) \neq \varnothing$$

implies

$$e^* = e^{**}.$$

When there are n agents, $n > 1$, the above condition becomes

$$F(e^*) \cap \left(\bigcap_{i=1}^{n} F(e^{**}, i/e^*) \right) \neq \varnothing$$

where

$$(e^{**}, i/e^*) = (e^{*^1}, \ldots, e^{*^{i-1}}, e^{**^i}, e^{*^{i+1}}, \ldots, e^{*^n}).$$

(See Hurwicz [31], Osana [71], Calsamiglia [10], Mount and Reiter [59]. In Mount and Reiter [60], the n-tuple $(e^{**}, i/e^*)$ is denoted by $e^{**} \otimes_i e^*$.)

SINGLE-VALUEDNESS (INJECTIVENESS)[†] LEMMA[††]. *Let* $(\mathcal{M}, \mu, h)$ *be a privacy-preserving process realizing* F *over* $E = E^1 \times E^2$.

Let $E^* \subseteq E$ *have the uniqueness property with respect to* F *on* E. *Then* μ *is injective, i.e., its inverse is single-valued.*

Proof. Let $m \in \mu(e^*)$ and $m \in \mu(e^{**})$ for some $e^*, e^{**} \in E^*$ and let $z = h(m)$. By the privacy-preserving property of the mechanism it follows that

$$m \in \mu^i(e^{*^i}) \quad i = 1, 2,$$
$$m \in \mu^i(e^{**^i}) \quad i = 1, 2,$$

[†]A correspondence $F: A \to\to B$ is *injective* if, for any $a', a'' \in A$, $F(a') \cap F(a'') \neq \varnothing$ implies $a' = a''$. (Hence the inverse F^{-1} of an injective correspondence is a (single-valued) function from $F[A]$ onto A.)

[††]For the sake of simplicity, we only state and prove this Lemma for $n = 2$, but it is valid for any $n > 1$. (See, e.g., Osana [71].)

and that

$$\mu^1(e^{*^1}) \cap \mu^2(e^{**^2}) = \mu(e^{*^1}, e^{**^2}).$$

Therefore,

$$m \in \mu(e^{*^1}, e^{**^2}),$$

and so

$$z = h(m) \in F(e^{*^1}, e^{**^2}).$$

Similarly,

$$m \in \mu(e^{**^1}, e^{*^2})$$

and so

$$z = h(m) \in F(e^{**^1}, e^{*^2}).$$

Thus

$$z \in F(e^*) \cap F(e^{*^1}, e^{**^2}) \cap F(e^{**^1}, e^{*^2}),$$

and so the hypothesis in the uniqueness property is satisfied (by z). Since the uniqueness property has been assumed, it follows that $e^* = e^{**}$. This proves the single-valuedness of $(\mu|_{E^*})^{-1}$.

PROPOSITION A. *A Cobb-Douglas class of pure exchange economies has the uniqueness property with regard to the interior-valued Pareto optimality performance-correspondence.*[†] We consider a class E^* of pure exchange economies with n agents, $n > 1$, and l goods, $l \geqq 1$. Every agent has the initial endowment $(1, \ldots, 1)$ and preferences representable by the utility function

$$u^i(z_1^i, \ldots, z_l^i) = \left(1 + z_1^i\right)^{a_1^i} \cdots \left(1 + z_l^i\right)^{a_l^i}$$

[†]See Mount and Reiter [60], Osana [71], and Hurwicz [31]. The latter treats only the special case where $n = 3$ and $l = 2$, and it assumes quadratic (rather than Cobb-Douglas) utility functions.

where $a_j^i > 0$ for all $i = 1, \ldots, n$ and all $j = 1, \ldots, l$, and, furthermore, for every $i = 1, \ldots, n$, it is assumed that $a_1^i + \cdots + a_l^i = 1$.
(Here the z_j^i are net trades.) For every $e \in E^*$, let $F(e)$ consist of
all net trade allocation matrices $\|z_j^i\|$ that are Pareto-optimal in e
and such that $z_j^i > -1$ for all i and all j.[†] The latter condition
rules out boundary optima, and hence, for every element z in $F(e)$,
$e \in E^*$, we have the familiar tangency (first-order necessary) conditions.

$$\lambda_i a_j^i u^i \left(1 + z_j^i\right)^{-1} = \mu_j \quad \text{all } i, j;$$

hence

$$\frac{b_{jk}^i}{b_{jk}^r} = \frac{1 + z_k^r}{1 + z_j^r} \cdot \frac{1 + z_j^i}{1 + z_k^i} \equiv q_{jk}^{ir}(z), \qquad \begin{array}{l} i, r = 1, \ldots, n \\ j, k = 1, \ldots, l \end{array}$$

where

$$b_{jk}^i = \frac{a_j^i}{a_k^i}.$$

Now suppose the hypothesis of the uniqueness property holds for
some interior Pareto-optimal $\bar{z}$, so that

$$\bar{z} \in F\left(e^{*^1}, \ldots, e^{*^n}\right), \qquad \bar{z} \in F\left(e^{**^1}, e^{*^2}, \ldots, e^{*^n}\right), \ldots,$$
$$\bar{z} \in F\left(e^{*^1}, \ldots, e^{*^{n-1}}, e^{**^n}\right).$$

Then for any $j, k \in \{1, \ldots, m\}$, we have, e.g.,

$$q_{jk}^{12}(\bar{z}) = \frac{b_{jk}^{*^1}}{b_{jk}^{*^2}} = \frac{b_{jk}^{**^1}}{b_{jk}^{*^2}}$$

[†] It has been pointed out by Professor M. K. Richter, Univ. of Minnesota, that the
conclusion is invalid if only the weak inequality $z_j^i \geqq -1$ is used, so that the 0
allocation (i.e., the net trade vector $(z_1^i, \ldots, z_l^i) = (-1, \ldots, -1)$) is admissible.

See the example in remark 1, Calsamiglia [11], pp. 19–20. As pointed out by
Calsamiglia (pp. 15 and 22) it is sufficient to postulate the nonextreme Pareto
correspondence which only rules out zero allocations, but does not rule out other
corner solutions.

hence

$$b_{jk}^{*^1} = b_{jk}^{**^1}.$$

Similarly we show that $b_{jk}^{*^i} = b_{jk}^{**^i}$ for all $i = 1, \ldots, n$, hence $b_{jk}^* = b_{jk}^{**}$. But then the condition $\sum_{j=1}^n a_j^i = 1$ implies $a^* = a^{**}$, q.e.d. (We require $\sum_{j=1}^n a_j^i = 1$ for reasons having to do with topological considerations discussed in Nayak [65].)

REMARK. Proposition A is not true for a one-agent economy ($n = 1$).

PROPOSITION B. *A Cobb-Douglas class of public goods economies has the uniqueness property with regard to the interior-valued Pareto optimality performance-correspondence.*

As shown in Sato [80], the situation in public goods economies is quite similar to that for pure exchange economies. In this economy, let there be l private goods, q public goods, and $n + 1$ agents, $n > 1$; namely, n consumers (indexed by $i = 1, \ldots, n$), and a single producer denoted by the subscript 0.[†]

[†] The following is a simple example, with $l = q = 1$, where the only private good (Z) is labor (in hours per day) and the only public good is a radio program braodcast (also in hours per day). The technology of producing the radio program is described by the input requirements function g; thus to produce ξ hours per day of the program requires $g(\xi)$ hours of labor per day. (So g is, in this example, the inverse of the production function.) We write this as $\zeta = g(\xi)$ where ξ is the amount produced of the public good and ζ the amount of input required to produce it. The ith consumer supplies z_i units of labors, so that $\zeta = \sum_{i=1}^n z_i$. By definition of a public good, the utilization of its services by one consumer does not interfere with the utilization by another, and no consumer can be excluded from listening or forced to pay for it. Thus, denoting by x_i the number of hours per day consumer i listens to the program, it is open to each consumer to choose as x_i any number between zero and ξ (the number of hours broadcast). I.e., $x_i \in [0, \xi]$ for $i \in \{1, \ldots, n\}$.

Let $u^i(z_i, x_i)$ be the ith consumer's utility function which is being maximized. Assuming, as is customary, that u^i is strictly increasing in x_i, we get $x_i = \xi$ for all $i \in \{1, \ldots, n\}$. (Admittedly, this assumption is somewhat unrealistic in the context of our example!) Furthermore, it is often assumed in models of economies with public goods that the input requirements function is linear; in our example, this

We now return to the general theory of minimality results. As indicated above, the *first phase* of our strategy consists in finding a set E^* having the uniqueness property with respect to the given performance criterion and such that its size equals that of the message space $\mathcal{M}'$ to be shown minimal. Once this has been accomplished we conclude (by the single-valuedness lemma) that,

---

means that $g(\xi) = k\xi$ for some fixed positive number k, so that $\sum_{i=1}^n z_i = k\xi$. Without loss of generality, the units of measurement of the public good can be so chosen that $k = 1$, so that $\sum_{i=1}^n z_i = \xi$. This is a frequent formulation in the literature of public goods.

Denote by $z_i = (z_{1i}, \ldots, z_{li})$ the net trade increment of private goods demanded by the ith consumer. Also let $\zeta = (\zeta_1, \ldots, \zeta_l)$ be the net supply of private goods by the producer, and let $x_1 = (x_{1i}, \ldots, x_{qi})$ denote the consumption vector of public goods by the ith consumer, while $\xi = (\xi_1, \ldots, \xi_q)$ denotes the production vector of public goods. Following Sato we call the vector $a_i = (z_i, x_i) \in \mathbb{R}^{l+q}$ an action of the ith consumer $(i = 1, \ldots, n)$ while the vector $a_0 = (\zeta, \xi) \in \mathbb{R}^{l+q}$ is the action of the producer. Finally the joint action vector is defined as

$$a = \left((a_i)_{i=1}^n, a_0 \right)$$
$$= \left(((z_i, x_i))_{i=1}^n, (\zeta, \xi) \right)$$

A joint action a is said to be consistent if and only if the aggregate consumers' demand equals the producer's supply, and if (as follows from the definition of a public good) the consumption of public goods by each consumer is equal to their total output. Thus we have

$$\sum_{i=1}^n z_i = \zeta,$$

and

$$x_i = \xi, \quad i = 1, \ldots, n.$$

A subclass E^* of such economies is defined by endowing the consumers with Cobb-Douglas utility functions and the producer with linear production functions and a positive endowment of production goods. It is then shown by Sato [80], pp. 61–66, that E^* has the uniqueness property with respect to the interior-valued Pareto optimal performance correspondence. The proof is analogous to that given above for pure exchange economies.

for a privacy preserving mechanism $(\mathcal{M}, \mu, h)$ realizing the given performance criterion, the inverse $(\mu|_{E*})^{-1}$ of the equilibrium correspondence restricted to $E*$ is single-valued; i.e., the restricted correspondence $\mu|_{E*}$ is injective. The *second phase* then is to show that, under certain regularity conditions, this implies that the required size of $\mathcal{M}$ is at least as great as that of $\mathcal{M}'$.

For reasons given above, the notion of size used will be that of Fréchet. [Recall that space A has Fréchet size at least as high as does B if and only if B can be homeomorphically embedded in A; this is written $A \geq {}^F B$.] Also, in this second phase we shall take as an assumption that $\mu|_{E*}$ is injective. But we must, of course, impose further restrictions on μ in order to conclude that $\mu[E*] \geq {}^F E*$. The nature of sufficient conditions implying such a size inequality is specified by the following fundamental topological lemma.

DEFINITION 1. A topological space X has the *similarity property* if and only if every open set V in X has a subset V' which, in the relative topology, is homeomorphic to X.

REMARK 1'. Any homeomorph of a finite-dimensional Euclidean space has the similarity property.

DEFINITION 2. A correspondence $F: X \to \to Y$ between two topological spaces is *spot-threaded* (with U as a *spot-domain*) if and only if there is an open set U in X and a continuous function (*spot selection*) $f: U \to Y$ such that $f(x) \in F(x)$ for all x in U.

REMARK 2'. The property of spot-threadedness was introduced and used, although not named, in Chander [16], p. 3 Cor. 1.2. Spot-threadedness is strictly weaker than local threadedness.

A TOPOLOGICAL LEMMA ON SIZE INEQUALITY. *Let S and T be topological spaces, with T having the similarity property. Let $\phi: T \to \to S$ be a spot-threaded injective correspondence with a spot-domain U. Then*

$$S \geq {}^F T$$

if either of the following two conditions is satisfied:

(a) *both S and T are Hausdorff and T is locally compact*; *or*

(b) *the inverse function* ϕ^{-1}: $\phi(T) \to T$ *is continuous on* $\phi(U)$.

REMARK. ϕ^{-1} is a function because ϕ is assumed injective.

Proof. (i) By the assumption of spot-threadedness there is an open set U in T and a continuous function f: $U \to S$ such that $f(t) \in \phi(t)$ for all t in U. This function is one-to-one because the correspondence ϕ is assumed injective.

(ii) We shall show below [in (iii)] that under our assumption there is a homeomorphism between an open subset V of U and $W = f(V)$, namely $f|_V$.[†] But then, by the similarity assumption, there is a subset V' of V which is homeomorphic to T. Write $W' = f(V')$. Then V' and W' are homeomorphic (with the homeomorphism $f|_{V'}$). Hence

$$W' \cong V' \cong T,$$

and so

$$W' \geq^F V' \geq^F T \qquad (*)$$

because, by the definition of $\geq^F$, $A \cong B$ implies $A \geq^F B$.

On the other hand, since $S \supseteq W'$, we have

$$S \geq^F W' \qquad (**)$$

because the Fréchet ordering $\geq^F$ is monotone with respect to set inclusion (in the relative topology). But the Fréchet ordering is transitive, so the relations $(*)$ and $(**)$ imply

$$S \geq^F T,$$

which is to be proved. It therefore remains to be shown that there exists an open subset V of U which is homeomorphic to its image $W = f(V)$.

[†]Since $f|_V$ is one-to-one and continuous, we shall have to show that its inverse $(f|_V)^{-1}$ is continuous.

(iii) The proof of existence of such V is divided into two parts.

(iii.a) Let condition (a) hold. I.e., T is locally compact Hausdorff and S is Hausdorff. By the local compactness and the Hausdorff property, there exists an open set V, $V \subseteq U$, whose closure $\overline{V}$ is compact. The restriction $f|_V \colon \overline{V} \to f(\overline{V})$ is a continuous one-to-one function from a compact space onto a Hausdorff space, hence a homeomorphism [Dugundji, [23] p. 226, Theorem 2.1(2)]. Hence this V and $W = f(V)$ have the desired properties.

(iii.b) Let condition (b) hold. Hence the function ϕ^{-1} is continuous on $f(U)$. Choose $V = U$ and define $W = f(U)$. Then $\phi^{-1}|_W \colon W \to V$ is a homeomorphism; it is bi-continuous by the condition (b) and the continuity of $f|_V$ which is its inverse. Again, V and W have the desired properties.

REMARK 1.   The preceding proof essentially follows the lines of those by Sato, Chander, and Nayak.

REMARK 2.   Sato [80], pp. 53–54 Lemmata 1 & 2, assumes ϕ to be *locally* threaded and the space T to be homeomorphic to a finite-dimensional Euclidean space. Our assumption on ϕ of *spot*-threadedness is strictly weaker. Our assumptions on T are satisfied by a homeomorph of a finite-dimensional Euclidean space, but are more general. This has been shown by Aizpurua and Manresa ([1], Example, p. 14) who have constructed the following non-Euclidean example.

Let J be an arbitrary infinite index set and let T be the Cartesian product $\prod_{\alpha \in J} X_\alpha$ where $X_\alpha = [0, 1]$, the closed unit interval, for all α. Aizpurua and Manresa have shown that, with $[0, 1]$ in the relative Euclidean topology, the space T—in the product topology—is locally compact Hausdorff and has the similarity property. Thus it satisfies the requirements of part (a) of the Lemma, but it is not homeomorphic to a subspace of a finite-dimensional Euclidean space.

REMARK 3.   Nayak ([66], Lemma 3 p. 13) assumes (the counterpart of) T to be a locally compact Hausdorff finite-dimensional vector space. (I interpret this as meaning a topological vector space, so that the operations of the addition and scalar multiplication are continuous. Actually, in the proof on p. 14 Nayak refers to an 'open ball,' which seems to imply a metric topology.) The proof (p. 14) uses the finite-dimensionality assumption to infer what we have called the similarity property.

A locally compact Hausdorff linear topological space is finite-dimensional. [Kelley and Namioka [51], p. 62] Furthermore, a finite-dimensional subspace of a linear topological Hausdorff space is topologically isomorphic to a finite-dimensional Euclidean space. [Kelley and Namioka, p. 59] (A topological isomorphism is a linear isomorphism which is also a homeomorphism; [51], p. 40.) Hence Nayak's assumptions on T are equivalent to those of Sato.

REMARK 4.   The role played by the assumption that the message space (here S) is Hausdorff was brought out by Walker [92]. Through an example derived from one constructed by Walker, Sato ([80] p. 54) shows that the Lemma is false when neither (a) nor (b) are assumed. Let both T and S be open unit intervals $(0, 1)$ and ϕ the identity map between them. I.e., $\phi(x) = x$ for all $0 < x < 1$. T has the usual Euclidean topology, but S has the cofinite topology: its proper closed subsets are precisely the finite subsets of the open unit interval. (See Walker [92], Ex. 1, p. 370.) $\phi: T \to S$ is injective and continuous, hence locally threaded. But S is not Hausdorff and ϕ^{-1} is not continuous, so neither (a) nor (b) is satisfied. No subspace of S is homeomorhic to T. Hence it is not the case that $S \geq^F T$, and so the conclusion of the Lemma fails to hold.

REMARK 5.   Osana's Remark ([71] p. 75) may be viewed as an application of assumption (a) with Hausdorff strengthened to Euclidean. Condition (b) appears in Osana's Theorem in the weaker form of lower hemi-continuity of ϕ^{-1}. (However, as pointed out by Sato, ([80] p. 55, ftn 15) the two conditions are equivalent when ϕ is injective; for in that case ϕ^{-1} is a function, and so hemi-continuity and continuity are equivalent.)

REMARK 6.   The assumption that the space T has the similarity property can be weakened, as shown by Aizpurua and Manresa [1], p. 2, who introduce two local versions of the similarity property, as follows. The space T is said to have the *weak local similarity property at an open subset U of T* iff there exist some $V \subseteq U$ which, in the relative topology, is homeomorphic to T. The space T is said to have the *strong local similarity property at an open subset U of T* iff every open subset $U' \subseteq U$ has a subset V' which, in the relative topology, is homeomorphic to T.

Using these concepts, Aizpurua and Manresa establish the following strengthening of the above Topological Lemma on size inequality:

Let S and T be topological spaces. Let $\phi: T \to \to S$ be a spot-threaded injective correspondence with a spot-domain V. Then

$$S \geq^F T$$

if either of the following two conditions is satisfied:

(a) both S and T are Hausdorff spaces, T is locally compact and it has the strong local similarity property at U; or

(b) the inverse function $\phi^{-1}: \phi(T) \to T$ is continuous on $\phi(U)$, and T has the weak local similarity property at U.

The proof is analogous to that of the Lemma above.

The above Topological Lemma on Size Inequality immediately yields the following

PROPOSITION 1. (i) Let E be a topological space of environments and $\pi = (\mathcal{M}, \mu, h)$ a mechanism on E. Let E^* be a subspace of E having the similarity property and let the restriction $\mu|_{E^*}$ of the equilibrium correspondence μ be injective and spot-threaded (with a spot domain $U \subseteq E^*$). Then

$$\mathcal{M} \geq^F E^*$$

if either of the following two conditions is satisfied:

(a) Both $\mathcal{M}$ and E^* are Hausdorff, and E^* is locally compact; or

(b) $(\mu|_{E^*})^{-1}$ is continuous on $\mu(U)$.

(ii) If the subspace E^* is homeomorphic to the Euclidean space of finite dimension K, the above conclusion becomes

$$\mathcal{M} \geq^F \mathbb{R}^K$$

Proof. M, E^*, and $\mu|_{E*}$ have, respectively, the properties postulated in the above Lemma for S, T, and ϕ. Hence the conclusion of the Lemma, that $S \geq^F T$ becomes $M \geq^F E^*$, which establishes part (i) of Proposition 1. Part (ii) follows from the fact that the Fréchet ordering $\geq^F$ is a topological invariant.

REMARK. If we restrict ourselves to Euclidean message spaces, Fréchet size corresponds to dimension, and so the conclusion of the above proposition becomes (as a special case of (a))

$$\dim \mathcal{M} \geqq \dim E^*.$$

In this case, moreover, one can use the Theorem 10-8, p. 258 in Apostol [2], to obtain the following alternative.

PROPOSITION 2. Let E be a topological space of environments and $\pi = (\mathcal{M}, \mu, h)$ a mechanism on E with finite-dimensional Euclidean $\mathcal{M}$. Let E^* be a subset of E such that $(\mu|_{E*})^{-1}$ is a Lipschitz continuous (single-valued) function on $\mu(E^*)$. Then

$$\dim \mathcal{M} \geqq \dim E^*.$$

(See Hurwicz [29], [31]; Chander [16], Theorem 2, p. 3.)

REMARK. The concepts of Proposition 1 are well defined in terms of topologies. On the other hand, the concept of Lipschitz continuity used in Proposition 2 requires that the message space be metric. The Lipschitzian property is useful in discrete spaces (e.g., sequences with integer-valued components; see Hurwicz and Marschak [36]).

REMARK. Note also that Proposition 2 imposes a regularity condition on μ^{-1} but no continuity restriction on μ itself.

REMARK.   Osana ([71], p. 67, footnote 5) gives an example of a function which is Lipschitz continuous but whose inverse is not locally threaded. In footnote 6, p. 67, he gives an example of a function which is not Lipschitz continuous but whose inverse is locally threaded. (It would be of interest to construct a function which is Lipschitz continuous but whose inverse is not spot-threaded.)

As a next stage, we state the following.

THEOREM 1.   (Using the uniqueness property to get injectiveness.) *Let E and $\mathcal{M}$ be topological spaces (of environments and messages respectively) and $\pi = (\mathcal{M}, \mu, h)$ a privacy-preserving mechanism realizing the performance correspondence F over E. Let E^* be a subspace of E having the uniqueness property with respect to F, and let $\mu|_{E^*}$ be spot-threaded on E^* with spot-domain $U \subseteq E^*$. Then*

$$\mathcal{M} \geqq {}^F E^*$$

if either of the following two conditions is satisfied:
   (a) (a.1) *$\mathcal{M}$ and E^* are both Hausdorff*
      (a.2) *and E^* is locally compact, or*
   (b) *$(\mu|_{E^*})^{-1}$ is continuous on $\mu(U)$.*

REMARK.   In his counterpart of condition (b), Nayak ([66], Theorem 2, p. 21) uses *partial* continuity. (For a definition of this concept see Kats and Slutsky [50].) Since hemicontinuous correspondences (whether upper or lower) are partially continuous, but not vice versa, Nayak's assumption of partial continuity constitutes a weakening of the condition in Sato ([80], Theorem 3, p. 67) which requires that $(\mu|_{E^*})^{-1}$ be either upper or lower hemicontinuous (unless the message space is Hausdorff).[†] However, because the uniqueness property implies the single-valuedness of $(\mu|_{E^*})^{-1}$,

---

[†]Sato's Theorem 3 applies to economies with public goods, but a corresponding pure exchange result could have been obtained with the help of Osana's proof of the uniqueness property.

partial continuity (as well as the two kinds of hemicontinuity) is equivalent to the continuity of the resulting function.

Proof. By the single-valuedness (injectivenes) lemma, $\mu|_{E^*}$ is injective. Hence the conclusion follows from Proposition 1.

We are now finally in a position to state the size minimality property of the Walrasian mechanism.

PROPOSITION C. *The Walrasian mechanism and its message space. In pure exchange economies with n participants, $n > 1$, and l commodities it is possible to implement the Walrasian correspondence with a message space of dimension $n \cdot (l - 1)$.*[†] Specifically, the message m^i of each participant $(i = 1, \ldots, n)$ is of the form $m^i = (m^i_1, \ldots, m^i_{l-1})$, $m^i_j \in \mathbb{R}$, so that a participant's language is $L = \mathbb{R}^{(l-1)}$ and the message space is $M = \mathbb{R}^{n(l-1)}$. The equilibrium equations for the process are given by[††]

$$\frac{u^k_j\left[\omega^k_1 + \overline{m}^k_1, \ldots, \omega^k_{l-1} + \overline{m}^k_{l-1}, \omega^k_l - \sum_{r=1}^{l-1} \overline{m}^n_r \overline{m}^k_r\right]}{u^k_l\left[\omega^k_1 + \overline{m}^k_1, \ldots, \omega^k_{l-1} + \overline{m}^k_{l-1}, \omega^k_l - \sum_{r=1}^{l-1} \overline{m}^n_r \overline{m}^k_r\right]} - \overline{m}^n_j = 0,$$

$$k = 1, \ldots, n-1$$
$$j = 1, \ldots, l-1 \quad (1_k)$$

[†] See Hurwicz [31], originally presented in 1972, for the special case $n = 2$, $l = 3$, and Mount and Reiter [58], [60] for the general formula.

[††] The meaning of these equations becomes more transparent if we consider the problem of maximizing the C^1 utility function u^i of the ith person, $i = 1, \ldots, n$, $n > 1$, as a function of his commodity 'bundle' $z^i = (z^i_1, \ldots, z^i_l)$ subject to the budget constraint $\sum_{q=1}^l P_q z^i_q = \sum_{q=1}^l P_q w^i_q$. (Here w_q is the amount of commodity q initially held by i, z^i_q is the amount of commodity q finally obtained by i, and P_q is the non-normalized price of commodity q.) Denoting by λ_i the ith Lagrange multiplier, we obtain the first order necessary conditions

$$u^i_q(z^i) = \lambda_i P_q \quad q = 1, \ldots, l \quad \text{and} \quad i = 1, \ldots, n.$$

and

$$\frac{u_j^n\left[\omega_1^n - \sum_{k=1}^{n-1} \overline{m}_1^k, \ldots, \omega_{l-1}^n - \sum_{k=1}^{n-1} \overline{m}_{l-1}^k, \omega_l^n + \sum_{k=1}^{n-1}\sum_{r=1}^{l-1} \overline{m}_r^n \overline{m}_r^k\right]}{u_l^n\left[\omega_1^n - \sum_{k=1}^{n-1} \overline{m}_1^k, \ldots, \omega_{l-1}^n - \sum_{k=1}^{n-1} \overline{m}_{l-1}^k, \omega_l^n + \sum_{k=1}^{n-1}\sum_{r=1}^{n-1} \overline{m}_r^n \overline{m}_r^k\right]}$$

$$- \overline{m}_j^n = 0, \qquad j = 1, \ldots, l-1 \tag{2}$$

where $u_j^k = \partial u^k/\partial x_j$ and $u^k(x_1, \ldots, x_l)$ is the kth agent's utility derived from holding the commodity bundle $(x_1, \ldots, x_l)$ and the bars over the message symbols indicate the stationary solution.

Assuming $u_l^i > 0$, $P_l > 0$, and writing $p_q = P_q/P_l$, these equations yield

$$\frac{u_j^i}{u_l^i} - p_j = 0 \quad j = 1, \ldots, l-1 \quad \text{and} \quad i = 1, \ldots, n. \tag{*}$$

(p_j is the normalized price of commodity j.)

Now define the net trade increment for person i in good q by $\xi_q^i = z_q^i - w_q^i$.

In terms of net trades the ith budget equation (in normalized prices) becomes $\sum_{q=1}^{l} p_q \xi_q^i = 0$, and so

$$z^i = \left(z_1^i, \ldots, z_l^i\right) = \left(w_1^i + \xi_1^i, \ldots, w_{l-1}^i + \xi_{l-1}^i, w_l - \sum_{r=1}^{l-1} p_r \xi_r^i\right). \tag{**}$$

With $\xi_r^k = \overline{m}_r^k$ and $p_r = \overline{m}_r^n$, (**) substituted into (*) for $i = 1, \ldots, n-1$ and $j = 1, \ldots, l-1$ yields equation (1_k) of the text. In (1_k), ω_g^i is written instead of w_g^i.

Now we further note that net trades must balance out to zero, i.e., $\sum_{i=1}^{n} \xi_q^i = 0$ for $q = 1, \ldots, l$. Therefore

$$z_q^n = w_q^n + \xi_q^n = w_q^n - \sum_{k=1}^{n-1} \xi_q^k \quad \text{for } q = 1, \ldots, l. \tag{***}$$

Also, using both the balance and budget equations, we get

$$z_l^n = w_l^n + \xi_l^n = w_l^n + \sum_{k=1}^{n-1} \xi_l^k = w_l^n - \sum_{k=1}^{n-1}\left(-\sum_{r=1}^{l-1} p_r \xi_r^i\right). \tag{****}$$

Through substitution into (*) for $i = n$ and $j = 1, \ldots, l-1$, equations (***) and (****) yield equation (2) of the text.

It is easily seen that the message vector m^n corresponds to the normalized Walrasian price vector $(p_1, \ldots, p_{1-1})$.

Clearly, the equilibrium message correspondences are defined by these equilibrium equations. Thus, for $k = 1, \ldots, n - 1$ the equilibrium correspondence μ^k is defined by

$$\mu^k(e^k) = \left\{ (\overline{m}^1, \ldots, \overline{m}^n) : \text{equation } (1_k) \text{ is satisfied} \right\}.$$

Similarly, the equilibrium message correspondence μ^n is given by

$$\mu^n(e^n) = \left\{ (\overline{m}^1, \ldots, \overline{m}^n) : \text{equation } (2) \text{ is satisfied} \right\}.$$

The outcome function h then is defined as follows in terms of the net increment vectors

$$\bar{\xi}^i = \left(\bar{\xi}^i_1, \ldots, \bar{\xi}^i_l \right), \quad i = 1, \ldots, n.$$

We set

$$\left(\xi^1, \ldots, \bar{\xi}^n \right) = h\left(\overline{m}^1, \ldots, \overline{m}^n \right)$$

where

$$\bar{\xi}^k_j = \overline{m}^k_j, \qquad k = 1, \ldots, n - 1; \qquad j = 1, \ldots, l - 1$$

$$\bar{\xi}^k_l = -\sum_{r=1}^{l-1} \overline{m}^n_r \overline{m}^k_r$$

$$\bar{\xi}^n_j = -\sum_{k=1}^{n-1} \overline{m}^k_j, \qquad j = 1, \ldots, l - 1$$

and

$$\bar{\xi}^n_l = \sum_{k=1}^{n-1} \sum_{r=1}^{l-1} \overline{m}^n_r \overline{m}^k_r.$$

It is easily verified that the balance equations

$$\sum_{i=1}^{n} \bar{\xi}_j^i = 0 \quad j = 1, \ldots, l$$

are satisfied. Also, writing $m^n = p$, where $m_j^n = p_j$ for $j = 1, \ldots, l - 1$, and $p_l = 1$, we find that the budget constraint is satisfied for all households, i.e.,

$$\bar{p} \cdot \bar{\xi}^i = 0 \qquad i = 1, \ldots, n.$$

Finally, with appropriate substitutions, the stationarity conditions are seen to be equivalent to

$$\frac{u_j^i(\omega^i + \bar{\xi}^i)}{u_l^i(\omega^i + \bar{\xi}^i)} - p_j = 0 \qquad \begin{array}{l} i = 1, \ldots, n \\ j = 1, \ldots, l. \end{array}$$

Thus they are again equivalent to the usual tangency conditions.

THEOREM 2. *Let E be a topological space of environments with $n > 1$ agents and $l \geq 1$ goods, containing as a subspace the Cobb-Douglas class of pure exchange economies E^C in its parametric-Euclidean topology, and let P^+ be the interior-valued Pareto performance correspondence on E. Let $\bar{\pi} = (\bar{\mathcal{M}}, \bar{\mu}, \bar{h})$ denote the Walrasian process of Proposition C where*

$$\dim \bar{\mathcal{M}} = n \cdot (l - 1), \qquad n > 1.$$

Let $\pi = (\mathcal{M}, \mu, h)$ be any mechanism realizing P^+ on E such that μ is spot-threaded on E^C and either (a) $\mathcal{M}$ is a Hausdorff space, or (b) $(\mu|_E C)^{-1}$ is partially continuous.
    Then

$$\mathcal{M} \geqslant^{\mathrm{F}} \bar{\mathcal{M}} \quad or, \ equivalently, \quad \mathcal{M} \geqslant^{\mathrm{F}} \mathbb{R}^{n \cdot (l-1)}$$

Proof. We have shown above (Proposition A, p. 259) that E^C has the uniqueness property with respect to P^+. Therefore, Theorem 1 is applicable, since the Euclidean space is Hausdorff locally compact and has the similarity property.

REMARK. Theorem 2, as well as Corollary 2 and Theorem 2*
below are not true for a one-agent economy ($n = 1$) where optimal
net trade is necessarily zero and P^+ is (initially) realized by a
mechanism with a one element M (so that dim $M = 0$), $g \equiv 0$,
$h \equiv 0$.

COROLLARY 2. *If the message space $\mathcal{M}$ is a subset of a finite
dimensional Euclidean space and if all other conditions of Theorem 2
are satisfied, then*

$$\dim \mathcal{M} \geqslant \dim \overline{\mathcal{M}} = n \cdot (l - 1).$$

THEOREM 2*. *Under the condition of Theorem 2, the message
space $\overline{\mathcal{M}} \subseteq \mathbb{R}^{n \cdot (l-1)}$ of the Walrasian process $\overline{\pi} = (\overline{\mathcal{M}}, \overline{\mu}, \overline{h})$ is of
minimal Fréchet size among processes realizing the interior-valued
Pareto correspondence P^+ over the class E^C with a spot-threaded
equilibrium correspondence.*[†]

Proof. By Theorem 2 and the results in Mount/Reiter, Osana,
Nayak, showing that the Walrasian mechanism has the required
property.

PROPOSITION D. *Lindahl mechanism and its message space.* In
this section we briefly sketch the Sato [80] version of the Lindahl
mechanism.[††] (For the description of the environment, see Proposition B above.) The first private good is used as numéraire, hence its
price equals unity. The message of this mechanism consists of the
vectors p, $(z_{*i})_{i=1}^{n}$, $(\pi_i)_{i=1}^{n}$, and ξ. [Here p_j is the price of the jth
private good, $j = 2, \ldots, l$; $z_{*i} = (z_{2i}, \ldots, z_{li})$, with z_{ji} the proposed exchange of good j by consumer i; $\pi_i = (\pi_{1i}, \ldots, \pi_{qi})$, with
π_{ri} the personalized price for consumer i of public good r; $\xi =
(\xi_1, \ldots, \xi_q)$, with ξ_r the proposed production of public good r.] It
is assumed that the budget constraints are binding for the agent;

[†] With the additional assumption of so-called individual rationality, Jordan [45]
shows that the Walrasian process is the only one having the minimal Fréchet size.

[††] I have specialized the Sato model to assume constant returns to scale; for that
reason profits are identically 0 in equilibrium, and therefore need not be taken into
consideration.

therefore each agent's demand for the first good is defined by prices and demand for other goods. It then turns out that:

PROPOSITION D. *The Lindahl process can be so defined as to require a Euclidean message space of dimension* $(n + 1) \cdot (l - 1) + 1$.

It will be seen in Theorems 2_p and 2_p^* below that any privacy-preserving mechanism which implements the interior Pareto correspondence and which satisfies certain regularity conditions on the class of Cobb-Douglas-linear environments described in Proposition B must be of Fréchet size not less than the Euclidean space of dimension $(n + 1) \cdot (l - 1) + 1$.

THEOREMS 2_p AND 2_p^*. *The corresponding* (*to Theorems* 2 *and* 2*) *results for public goods environments and the Lindahl mechanism.*

Proof. Using Proposition 2, the uniqueness property (Prop. B) (Sato, Nayak), and the fact that the Lindahl mechanism has the required properties (Prop. D) (Sato, Nayak).

THEOREM 3. *Let E be a topological space of environments containing as a subspace the Cobb-Douglas class of pure exchange economies* E^C *in its parametric-Euclidean topology, and let* P^+ *be the interior-valued Pareto performance correspondence on E. Let* $\bar{\pi} = (\overline{\mathscr{M}}, \bar{\mu}, \bar{h})$ *denote the Walrasian process of Proposition C where*

$$\dim \mathscr{M} = n \cdot (m - 1).$$

Let $\pi = (\mathscr{M}, \mu, h)$ *be any mechanism realizing* P^+ *on E such that* $\mathscr{M}$ *is a finite dimensional Euclidean space and* $(\mu|_{E^C})^{-1}$ *has a Lipschitzian selection. Then*

$$\dim \mathscr{M} \geqq \dim \overline{\mathscr{M}} = n \cdot (m - 1).$$

Proof. By Proposition 2, using the fact that E^C has the uniqueness property with respect to P^+ (see Proposition A, this section, above).

II.4. Nonconvex environments. The results discussed above refer to situations where the set having the uniqueness property is finite dimensional and there exists a nonwasteful[†] mechanism whose message space is of the same finite dimension. The theorems served to show that no lower dimension of the message space was possible.

There are, however, results showing that in certain (nonclassical) environments no nonwasteful processes exist with finite-dimensional message spaces. In view of previous theorems, it is sufficient to show that, for every finite k, there is a set E^*_{k+1} of dimension $k + 1$ having the uniqueness property with regard to the performance correspondence to be realized. This was done for certain nonconvex production economies in Hurwicz [31] and Calsamiglia [10]. In [10], Calsamiglia thus showed that for a certain class of environments involving nonconvex but monotone and smooth[††] production functions, there exists no nonwasteful process with finite-dimensional message space and a locally threaded equilibrium correspondence μ.

To gain an understanding of these results we must briefly review certain results of economic theory concerning the existence and Pareto-optimality of Walrasian ("competitive") equilibria in economies without public goods.[†††] First, under very mild restrictions on the environment (nonsatiation of preferences and absence of externalities), Walrasian equilibrium outcomes are Pareto-optimal. But more severe restrictions are imposed on the environment in order to guarantee the existence of Walrasian equilibria. (When these more severe restrictions are satisfied for an environment e, we refer to e as a 'classical' environment.) Among these restrictions are certain convexity properties of both preference relations and sets representing the production possibilities.

It is easy to construct examples of economies in which Walrasian equilibria do not exist because the convexity requirements are violated.

[†] See Section I.2 of the introduction for the definition of 'nonwasteful.'

[††] The production function in Hurwicz [31] lacked monotonicity and smoothness.

[†††] For details, see T. C. Koopmans [52], G. Debreu [22], Arrow and Hahn [7].

Now, in an economy with a finite number of (private) goods and a finite number of persons, the Walrasian process requires only a finite-dimensional message space.[†] Hence, when Walrasian equilibria do exist, while nonsatiation prevails and externalities are absent, we have available a nonwasteful mechanism using a finite-dimensional message space. But what if, because of nonconvexities, Walrasian equilibria fail to exist? Then, of course, the Walrasian mechanism is no longer available, but it is conceivable that some other informationally decentralized mechanism using a finite-dimensional message space might be found. Economists have, in fact, looked for such mechanisms, with marginal cost pricing as one candidate. But it turns out that for certain classes of environments violating the convexity requirements no informationally decentralized mechanism guaranteeing optimality and using a finite-dimensional message space can be designed.[††] We shall now describe a class of such environments.

Consider an economy consisting of two producers producing the same commodity Y and using the same input X. Denote by x_i the amount of input used by producer i, and by y_i that producer's output. The production function of the ith producer is denoted by Ψ_i, so that $y_i = \Psi_i(x_i)$, $i = 1, 2$. The total amount available of input is w, so that if all of it is used $x_1 + x_2 = w$. Assuming that Y is desired by consumers, optimality requires that the input be allocated between the two producers so as to maximize the total output. That is, it is desired to maximize $\Psi_1(x_1) + \Psi_2(w - x_1)$ with respect to x_1, subject to $x_1 \geqq 0$, $w - x_1 \geqq 0$. In this model, given w, an environment is defined by the two functions Ψ_i, $i = 1, 2$. That is, we may write $e = (\Psi_1, \Psi_2)$. If both Ψ_i's were concave, e would be classical and (with consumers satisfying the classical conditions) there would exist Walrasian equilibria. Both Hurwicz [31] and Calsamiglia [9] consider cases where not both Ψ_i's are concave. In particular Calsamiglia considers the case where Ψ_1 may be strictly convex (hence nonconcave) while Ψ_2 is concave.

[†] This was seen above for a pure exchange economy, but it is also true for an economy with production.

[††] In particular, marginal cost pricing would not guarantee optimality.

Assume $w = 1$ and define $\phi_2(x_1) \equiv \Psi_2(1 - x_1)$, so that we may write $e = (\Psi_1, \phi_2)$. Let now $\Psi_2(x_1)$ and $\phi_2(x_1)$ each be polynomials of degree N in x_1. More precisely, for $0 \le x_1 \le 1$, let

$$\Psi_1(x_1) = \sum_{n=1}^{N} e_{1n} x_1^n, \tag{1}$$

and

$$\phi_2(x_1) = \sum_{n=1}^{N} e_{2n} - \sum_{n=1}^{N} e_{2n} x_1^n, \tag{2}$$

with

$$e_{jn} \ge 0 \quad \text{for } j = 1, 2, \quad \text{and} \quad n = 1, \ldots, N, \tag{3}$$

and

$$\sum_{n=1}^{N} e_{1n} = 1, \quad e_{1n} = e_{2n} \quad \text{for all } n = 1, \ldots, N. \tag{4}$$

Let E_N be the class of all environments $e = (\Psi_1, \phi_2)$ satisfying conditions (1)–(4). Calsamiglia then shows that E_N has the uniqueness property for the above optimality criterion and that, for a locally threaded correspondence μ, the message space must be of dimension at least $N - 1$.

Consider now the class of environments $E = E^1 \times E^2$ where

$$E^1 = \left\{ \Psi_1 \in C^2(I) : \Psi_1(0) = 0, \Psi_1' \ge 0, \Psi_1'' \ge 0 \right\}$$
$$E^2 = \left\{ \phi_2 \in C^2(I) : \phi_2(1) = 0, \phi_2' \le 0, \phi_2'' \le 0 \right\}$$

where I is the unit interval and $C^2(I)$ is the class of all twice continuously differentiable functions on I. Clearly, $E_N \subseteq E$ for all finite N. Therefore

$$\dim M \ge N - 1 \quad \text{for all } N = 1, 2, \ldots, \text{ad inf.}$$

Clearly M cannot be finite-dimensional.[†]

[†]See Crémer [21] and Calsamiglia [14] concerning the possibility of using unbounded cumulative memory as an alternative to the use of an infinite-dimensional message space.

II.5. Parametric outcome functions. So far we have been dealing with outcome functions of the form

$$z = h(m)$$

where m is a point of the message space $\mathcal{M}$ and z is an element of the outcome space Z. In many economic applications it is natural to consider the outcome space Z as the Cartesian product

$$Z = Z^1 \times \cdots \times Z^n,$$

so that we may write

$$z = (z^1, \ldots, z^n)$$

where

$$z^i \in Z^i, \quad i = 1, \ldots, n.$$

In this case we have

$$h = (h^1, \ldots, h^n),$$

$h^i: \mathcal{M} \to Z^i$, $i = 1, \ldots, n$, and

$$z^i = h^i(m), \qquad i = 1, \ldots, n.$$

In such a situation we may imagine that the equilibrium message $\overline{m}$ is communicated to the participants and that each participant, knowing h^i, calculates his/her own z^i by evaluating $h^i(\overline{m})$. It then does no violence to the notion of privacy to suppose in this latter calculation that the participant might take into account his/her own characteristic. Thus the outcome function may be written as

$$z^i = h^i(m, e^i), \qquad i = 1, \ldots, n.$$

Such outcome functions were considered in Hurwicz [29 p. 310 ff]; in particular it was shown there (p. 313) that by admitting such "parametric"[†] outcome functions it may be possible to lower the required dimension of the message space.

[†] By contrast an outcome function of the form $h(m)$, i.e., independent of the characteristics, is called nonparametric.

Two recent contributions make use of parametric outcome functions (Calsamiglia [11] and Chander [17], [20]).

In Calsamiglia's paper (Sec. IV) it is shown that in certain contexts the use of parametric outcome functions can bring about "substantial savings in the channel capacity" required for a satisfactory performance. It turns out, however, that in three cases of particular interest to economists, the admission of parametric outcome functions does *not* lower the size requirements. Specifically, Calsamiglia shows that under assumptions similar to theorems used in the preceding section the size of the message space needed in pure exchange economies is at least as high as that of Euclidean space of dimension $n(l - 1)$. (The size comparison used in Calsamiglia's paper is that of Walker.) Similarly, it turns out that in a public goods economy of l goods, n consumers, and one producer, even with parametric outcome functions, the Walker-size of the message space must be at least as great as the Euclidean space of dimension $(n + 1)(l - 1) + 1$, in agreement with Sato's result.

Finally, there is an analogous result for economies involving nonconvexities: according to Calsamiglia, even with parametric outcome functions, no finite-dimensional Euclidean space is adequate.

Independently, Chander [17], [20] undertakes a systematic investigation of parametric processes, with applications to economies with production, in particular to what he calls the Taylor and Malinvaud-Taylor processes. He shows that the Taylor process has minimal dimensions among parametric processes; on the other hand, the Malinvaud-Taylor process is not of minimal dimension among parametric processes, even though it does have minimal dimension among nonparametric processes.

Both Calsamiglia and Chander carry out their analyses by introducing strengthened versions of the uniqueness property; in Chander, it is the "asymmetry property," in Calsamiglia, it is the "strong uniqueness property." (Chander's formulation follows Osana's extension of the uniqueness property. The (strong) uniqueness property is a special case of the Osana-Chander version when f in the Osana-Chander definition is the identity function.)

II.6. Proposed action mechanisms. Let $F: E \to \to Z$. Clearly, if $\pi = (M, \mu, h)$ fully realizes[†] F, it is necessary that $h(\mu(E)) \supseteq F(E)$. Hence, when μ and h have the usual smoothness properties, and M and Z are Euclidean, it must be that dim $M \geq$ dim $F(E)$. To simplify matters, suppose that $F(E) = Z$. Also assume that F is single-valued so that realization and full realization are equivalent. Suppose further that the message space is of the form $M = Z \times Q$, so that, for $m \in M$, we have $m = (z, q)$ where $z \in Z$ and $q \in Q$ is an "auxiliary variable," and that $h((z, q)) = z$ for all $(z, q) \in Z \times Q$.

Thus in the pure exchange Walrasian mechanism, the z's represent net trades while prices are the auxiliary variables. The previous minimality results show that, when realizing a Pareto-optimal F one cannot, in general, dispense with the auxiliary variables, since in a pure exchange economy dim $Z = l(n - 1)$ while the usual dimension of M was shown to be $n(l - 1)$.

But when it is possible to dispense with auxiliary variables (so that Q is a one-element set or $M = Z$), we speak of a *proposed action mechanism* (*process*)[††] since the elements of Z represent possible actions or outcomes.

For instance, for a pure exchange economy with $n = l = 2$, the Walrasian mechanism can be represented as a proposed action mechanism by specifying it as follows: (1) $M = \mathbb{R}^2 =$ the space of net trades $x^1 = (x_1^1, x_2^1)$ of agent 1; (2) $h(m) \equiv m$; (3) $g^1(m, u^1(\cdot), w^1) = 0$ if and only if m maximizes $u^1(x^1)$ on the budget set defined by the conditions $x^1 > -w^1$, and x^1 not above the "budget" line

$$\frac{x_2^1 - w_2^1}{x_1^1 - w_1^1} = \frac{w_2^1 - m_2}{w_1^1 - m_1}$$

going through the points $w^1 = (w_1^1, w_2^1)$ and $m = (m_1, m_2)$; (4) $g^2(m, u^2(\cdot), w^2)$ if and only if $-m$ maximizes $u^2(x^2)$ on the budget set defined by the conditions $x^2 \geq -w^2$, and x^2 not above

---

[†] See the definition on p. 245.

[††] See Section 2 in Hurwicz [29]; reprinted in Arrow and Hurwicz [6].

the "budget line"

$$\frac{x_2^2 - w_2^2}{x_1^2 - w_1^2} = \frac{w_2^2 + m_2}{w_1^2 + m_1}$$

going through the points $w^2 = (w_1^2, w_2^2)$ and $-m = (-m_1, -m_2)$. (w^i is the initial endowment of agent i.)

II.7. Convex economies with production.

The economists' interest in mechanism design has been to a considerable extent motivated by problems involving production decisions (witness marginal cost pricing proposals). In dealing with message space minimality, however, early studies were largely devoted to pure exchange models or economies with nonconvex (increasing returns) production possibility sets. As for classical economies with production (whose possibility sets are convex), Nayak [67] is the only systematic contribution I am aware of. Following the proof pattern described in Section II above, Nayak constructs a finite-parameter family E_1^* of classical environments with production, which has the uniqueness property with respect to the Pareto correspondence.

In E_1^* there are l goods, n consumers and m producers. In E_1^* each consumer has a Cobb-Douglas utility function whose exponents add up to 1, and a unit initial endowment vector. Hence each consumer is defined by $(l-1)$ parameters, a total of $(l-1) \cdot n$ parameters on consumption side. Each producer in E_1^* has a production possibility set defined by l parameters, a total of $l \cdot m$ parameters on production.[†] Thus an environment in E_1^* is defined by $(l-1)n + lm$ parameters. In fact, in the topology used by Nayak, E_1^* is homeomorphic to $\mathbb{R}^{(l-1)n+lm}$. Furthermore, E_1^* has the uniqueness property with respect to the Pareto correspondence. Under the usual regularity assumptions a lower bound on the

---

[†] Nayak's production function in E_1^* lives in what Koopmans called the Land of Cockaigne, i.e., they permit positive outputs with zero inputs (Nayak [67], p. 13), but it seems that they could be replaced by others of a more conventional nature without changing the number of free parameters or sacrificing other regularity features.

dimension of the message space is $(l - 1)n + lm$. On the other hand, Nayak shows that a "Walrasian equal (private) ownership"[†] mechanism defined on a superset E_1 of E_1^* uses a message space of dimension $(l - 1)n + lm$ and has a continuous equilibrium message correspondence.[††] Hence $(l - 1)n + lm$ is the minimal dimension of a message space in a smooth mechanism realizing the Pareto correspondence over a class E_1 of classical environments E_1 containing a class of E_1^* classical (hence convex) environments.

An instructive example of an activity analysis model with production was constructed by Arrow [3]. In this example there are two consumer goods, two primary factors, one consumer, three activity managers, and two resource managers. The proposed action vector may be written as $a \equiv ((r_{ij})_{i=1,2}, (x_j)_{j=1,2,3})$ where x_j is the level of activity j and r_{ij} the amount of resource i used in activity j. The technology of activity j is described by the relations $r_{ij} = \gamma_{ij}x_j$, known only to the respective activity managers. The

---

[†] 'Private ownership' means that the ith consumer's budget inequality is of the form $p \cdot z^i \leq \sum_{j=1}^n \theta_j^i \pi_j$ where π_j is the profit of the jth firm; here θ_j^i is interpreted as the ith consumer's share of ownership in the jth firm with profit π_j, so that $\sum_{i=1}^n \theta_j^i = 1$ for all $j = 1,\ldots, m$; z^i is the net trade vector of consumer i. By 'equal ownership' it is meant that $\theta_j^i = 1/m$ for all $i = 1,\ldots, n$ and all $j = 1,\ldots, m$.

In Nayak's formulation, private ownership seems to be included in the definitions of the classes of environments E_1^* and E_1. But in this writer's view it is more appropriate (and it strengthens the significance of the result) to regard private ownership not as a feature of the environments but rather as a property of the Walrasian mechanism used. Thus in our formulation, the result that $(l - 1)n + lm$ is a lower bound on the dimension of the message space is independent of institutional features such as private ownership of production units. The ownership feature only enters the description (or, more precisely, interpretation) of the Walrasian mechanism used to show that the above lower bound is in fact a minimum.

[††] The variables of the Walrasian mechanism are the consumers' net trade vectors $z^i \in \mathbb{R}^l$, $i = 1,\ldots, n$, the producers' net supply vectors $y^j \in \mathbb{R}^l$, $j = 1,\ldots, m$, and the price vector $p \in \mathbb{R}^l$, for a total of $l(n + m + 1)$ components. But the normalization of p, the balance equation $\sum_{i=1}^n z^i = \sum_{j=1}^m y^j$, and the budget equations subtract respectively 1, l, and $n - 1$ "degrees of freedom." (We subtract only $n - 1$ "degrees of freedom" for the n budget equations because the nth budget equation is implied by the others together with the balance equations.) The remaining number of "degrees of freedom" is $l(n + m + 1) - (1 + l + (n - 1)) = (l - 1)n + lm$.

initial resource endowments ρ_i are known only to the respective
resource managers. The utility function $U(z_1, z_2)$, where z_s is the
total consumption of consumer good s, is known only to the
consumer.

Arrow shows that there exists a *proposed action* privacy preserving process realizing the Pareto correspondence (here equivalent to
utility maximization subject to resource and technology constraints). Thus the dimension of the message space ($= \dim a$) is 9,
which under the above informational assumptions is minimal.

It may be noted that a message space of smaller dimension would
suffice if the three activities were under one manager in one firm
and if only the net inputs and outputs $(\Sigma_j r_{1j}, \Sigma_j r_{2j}, y_1, y_2)$—but not the separate activity levels—were regarded as
the unknown outcomes for the firm. In that case one could use the
above Walrasian mechanism with $n = m = 1$, $l = 4$, with the resulting dimension of the message space equal to $(4 - 1) \cdot 1 + 4 \cdot 1 = 7$.

III. DESIGNING MECHANISMS WITH A SPECIFIED GOAL
   PERFORMANCE FUNCTION

Traditionally, economists have studied the performance properties of given mechanisms. In the notation of Section I.2, they have
studied the performance correspondence Φ_π for a *given* mechanism
π, the most frequently studied mechanisms being market mechanisms of various types, especially Walrasian.[†]

In the present section, our approach is the reverse. We take as
given a specified performance correspondence, say F, and seek
mechanisms whose performance agrees with F. Thus here F is
given while π is the unknown. Section III shows, primarily in terms
of examples, how this can be accomplished by the integration of
differential equations. In simple cases a mechanism can be 'derived' from a given F by elementary integration processes (see

---

[†]It is important to distinguish a Walrasian *mechanism* from the Walrasian
performance correspondence. In fact we show that the Walrasian performance
correspondence can be realized by a non-Walrasian mechanism.

III.2.3 below). In general, we find it appropriate to use an analogue of the Frobenius Theorem and the tools of differential geometry[†] (see III.3.2–4 below).

III.1. Basic concepts. Given a privacy-preserving mechanism $\pi = (M, (\mu^i)_{i \in N}, h)$, $h: M \to Z$, on $E = X_{i \in N}E^i$, its *performance correspondence* $\Phi_\pi: E \to \to Z$ is defined by its value on $e \in E$ as

$$\Phi_\pi(e) = \{ z \in Z: m \in \mu(e) \text{ and } z = h(m) \text{ for some } m \in M \},$$

where $\mu(e) = \cap \mu^i(e^i)$, $e = (e^i)_{i \in N}$. (Here $N = \{1, \ldots, n\}$ is the set of participants, E^i the class of a priori admissible characteristics of person i, Z the set of conceivable outcomes; M is the message space, μ^i the ith equilibrium correspondence, and h the outcome function.)

We say that π *realizes*[††] a (goal) correspondence $F: E \to \to Z$ (on E) if and only if, for each $e \in E$,

(1) there exists $m \in M$ such that $m \in \mu(e)$;
and

(2) if $m \in \mu(e)$ and $z = h(m)$,
then

$$z \in F(e),$$

so that $\varnothing \neq \Phi_\pi(e) \subseteq F(e)$ for all e in E. If F is single-valued, this becomes $\Phi_\pi(e) = F(e)$ for all e in E. From now on we shall be assuming that the (goal) correspondence F to be realized has a smooth (C^2) selection. (In particular, if F is single-valued, it is a smooth (C^2) function.) Also, the response functions f^i and the

---

[†] The results reported in this section are largely based on a joint work with Reiter and Saari (see Hurwicz, Reiter, and Saari [39], [40], [41]). We owe a large debt of gratitude to Leonard Shapiro and Steven Williams for suggestions, improvements, and original ideas.

[††] We distinguish π realizing F from π implementing F. The latter expression involves game-theoretic concepts (see Section VI below), while the former does not.

Some authors use the two terms interchangeably. Our concept of realization is 'weak' in that we do not require $\Phi_\pi(E) = F(E)$. The latter equality corresponds to 'full' realization. But for single-valued F the two concepts coincide. The symbol F in this section is used in the same sense as Ψ (the goal correspondence) in Section I.2.1, p. 245.

equilibrium equation functions g^i are required to be smooth, and so is the outcome function h.

Every correspondence $F: E \to \to Z$ can be realized by the *direct revelation mechanism* in which (with X denoting the Cartesian product)

$$M = \underset{i \in N}{X} M^i; \qquad M^i = E^i, \qquad i \in N;$$
$$h = \text{a selection from } F,$$

and

$$\mu^i = \text{the identity function on } E^i, \qquad i \in N.$$

In response equation form this mechanism can be written as

$$\pi' = \left(M, (f^i)_{i \in N}, h \right)$$

where, as before,

$$M = \underset{i \in N}{X} M^i; \qquad M^i = E^i, \qquad i \in N,$$
$$h = \text{a selection from } F,$$

and, for every i,

$$f^i = \text{the identity function on } E^i.$$

Thus the response equations in (trivially) iterative form would be

$$m^i_{t+1} = e^i \quad \text{for all } i \in N, \quad \text{and} \quad t = 1, 2, \ldots.$$

Obviously, the equilibrium value $\overline{m}$ of such a message is

$$(\overline{m}^i)_{i \in N} = \overline{m} = e = (e^i)_{i \in N}; \qquad \overline{m}^i = e^i, \qquad i \in N.$$

An interpretation of such a mechanism is that each person verifies (or announces) his/her characteristic e^i, and the value $h(m) = h(e)$, $e = (e^1, \ldots, e^n)$, is then computed centrally. If F were single-valued (a function), then we would have $h = F$, i.e., $h(m) = F(m) = e$. Clearly this mechanism realizes F. When F is multivalued the outcome function h is chosen as a selection from F.

However, the direct revelation mechanism uses a message space $M = E$ of size that may be extremely large.[†] The question arises whether it is possible to realize F with a smaller message space.

A small saving on size is indeed possible through what is called a *parameter*[††] *transfer* process. For the case of single-valued F in response equation form, this mechanism can be written as follows:

$$M = \underset{i \in N}{X} M^i,$$

$$M^j = E^j \quad \text{for } j = 1, \ldots, n - 1,$$

$$M^n = Z,$$

$$f^j = \text{identity on } E^j \quad \text{for } j = 1, \ldots, n - 1,\text{[†††]}$$

$$f^n(m, e^n) \equiv F(m^1, \ldots, m^{n-1}, e^n), \qquad m = (m^1, \ldots, m^n),\text{[††††]}$$

$$h(m) \equiv m^n.$$

An interpretation is that persons other than n announce (verify) their characteristics to person n, who then calculates the performance function F using the messages of others.[†††††] This realizes F since here

$$h(m) = F(m^1, \ldots, m^{n-1}, e^n) = F(e^1, \ldots, e^n) = F(e).$$

However, even the parameter transfer process requires a huge message space $M = E^1 \times \cdots \times E^{n-1} \times Z$, especially when the E^j are infinite-dimensional.[*] Yet we know that there are important examples (e.g., for the Walrasian performance correspondence in

---

[†] In a typical economics problem, E is infinite-dimensional. E.g., E^i may be the class of all (smooth) quasi-concave utility functions on a given commodity space.

[††] This terminology arose in settings where e^j was defined by a parametric family of functions.

[†††] So that $m^j = e^j$ for $j = 1, \ldots, n - 1$.

[††††] So that $m^n = F(m^1, \ldots, m^{n-1}, e^n) = F(e^1, \ldots, e^{n-1}, e^n)$.

[†††††] In effect we assume that not only the designer, but also the agents know the function F.

[*] If the sets E^i, $i \in N$, are of unequal sizes, one obtains the smallest M by choosing n to be the person with the largest space of characteristics.

classical economies) where $F\colon E \to \to Z$ can be implemented with a finite-dimensional M even though E is infinite-dimensional.[†]

Our problem then is in general whether it is possible to realize a given goal correspondence F with a message space of size smaller than that required by a parameter transfer process, and—if it is possible—how to construct such a mechanism realizing F knowing only E, Z, and F.

We shall consider this problem in some detail for the case where E^i is finite-dimensional,[††] the outcome space Z is finite-dimensional Euclidean, and the goal correspondence F is single-valued, i.e., a function. We shall write

$$e^i = \Theta^i = \left(\Theta^i_1, \ldots, \Theta^i_{k_i} \right)$$

and

$$E^i = \Theta^i \subseteq \mathbb{R}^{k_i}, \qquad i \in N$$
$$\Theta = \Theta^1 \times \cdots \times \Theta^N \subseteq \mathbb{R}^K$$

where

$$K = \sum_{i \in N} k_i;$$

also

$$Z \subseteq \mathbb{R}^{k_0},$$

and all k_r, $r \in \{0\} \cup N$, are finite. We can now also write

$$F\colon \Theta \to Z.$$

[†] It should be noted, nevertheless, that direct revelation and parameter transfer has the dynamic merit of not requiring repeated iterations.

[††] E.g., a family of utility functions whose functional form is known to the designer (say, Cobb-Douglas), but whose parameters (finite in number) are known only to the respective agents.

In the special case where $\Theta^i = \mathbb{R}^{k_i}$, we have

$$F: \mathbb{R}^K \to \mathbb{R}^{k_0}.^\dagger$$

III.2.   Examples.   To clarify these concepts we first consider a simple but nontrivial class of cases where

$$N = 2, \quad k_i = 2 \quad \text{for } i = 1, 2, \quad k_0 = 1,$$

and each Θ^i is an open set in $\mathbb{R}^2$. Here $F: \mathbb{R}^4 \to \mathbb{R}$, and the parameter transfer process in response equation form†† is, say,

$$\begin{aligned} m^1 &= \theta^1, \\ m^2 &= F(m^1, \theta^2) \\ h(m^1, m^2) &\equiv m^2 \end{aligned}$$

with $M^1 = \mathbb{R}^2$, $M^2 = \mathbb{R}$. Hence dim $M = \dim(M^1 \times M^2) = 3$. (I.e., the response functions are $f^1(m, \theta^1) \equiv \theta^1$, $f^2(m, \theta^2) \equiv F(m^1, \theta^2)$, $m = (m^1, m^2)$.) The problem is (a) whether, or under what conditions, it is possible to realize a given $F: \mathbb{R}^4 \to \mathbb{R}$ with a message space M of dimension *less* than 3, and if so (b) how to construct such a mechanism given only the knowledge of the sets Θ^1, Θ^2 and of the function F.

We first consider question (a). It is easily seen that not all F's require a 3-dimensional message space. Suppose, for instance that F is additively separable in the two persons' parameter vectors, i.e.,

$$F(\theta^1, \theta^2) \equiv F^1(\theta^1) + F^2(\theta^2),$$

with F^i real-valued and smooth for $i = 1, 2$.

Such F can be realized with a two-dimensional message space through a *modified* parameter transfer process, stated in equi-

---

† By abuse of notation, we shall sometimes write $F: \mathbb{R}^K \to \mathbb{R}^{k_0}$ even though some $\Theta^i \subsetneqq \mathbb{R}^{k_i}$.

†† In equilibrium equation form, we have $g^1(m, \theta^1) \equiv m^1 - \theta^1$, $g^2(m, \theta^2) \equiv m^2 - F(m^1, \theta^2)$, $h(m^1, m^2) \equiv m^2$.

librium equation form as follows:

$$M = M^1 \times M^2,$$
$$M^i = \mathbb{R},$$
$$i = 1, 2,$$
$$g^1(m, \theta^1) \equiv m^1 - F^1(\theta^1),$$
$$g^2(m, \theta^2) \equiv m^2 - \left(m^1 + F^2(\theta^2)\right),$$
$$h(m) \equiv m^2,$$

where

$$m^i \in M^i, \qquad i = 1, 2, \quad \text{and} \quad m = (m^1, m^2).$$

Our interpretation is that person 1 verifies (announces) his value of the function $F^1(\theta^1)$ and person 2 calculates $F(\theta)$ by adding $F^2(\theta^2)$, which is known to him, to the communicated value $m^1 = F^1(\theta^1)$. (Recall that the function F is assumed known to the agents, as well as to the designer.)[†] On the other hand, there are smooth F's which cannot be realized with a message space of dimension lower than that used by the parameter transfer process. An example is the inner product, i.e.,

$$F(\theta) = \theta^1 \cdot \theta^2 = \sum_{r=1}^{k} \theta_r^1 \theta_r^2, \quad k = k_1 = k_2,$$

where we assume that each Θ^i contains the same nondegenerate open interval Λ in $\mathbb{R}^k$, and $\theta^1 \neq 0$ for $\theta^1 \in \Lambda$.

As shown in Hurwicz, Reiter, and Saari [39],[††] pp. 17–25, there exists a $(k + 1)$ dimensional set

$$\Theta^* = \left\{ \theta \in \Theta : \theta = (\theta^1, \theta^2), \theta^1 \neq 0, \frac{\theta_1^2}{\theta_1^1} > 0, \theta_s^1 = \theta_s^2 \text{ for } 1 < s \leq k \right\}$$
$$\cap (\Lambda \times \Lambda)$$

[†] In the more general case with arbitrary k_1, k_2, but $k_0 = 1$, if $F(\theta) = F^1(\theta^1) + F^2(\theta^2)$ with F^i real-valued smooth, we can still use M of dimension 2 whereas the parameter transfer process would require M of dimension $1 + \min(k_1, k_2)$.

[††] In what follows, references to Hurwicz, Reiter and Saari will be abbreviated as [HRS].

which has the uniqueness property[††] for the inner product F. Hence the inner product F requires dim $M \geqslant k + 1$, which is the dimension also required by the parameter transfer process. In particular, for $k_1 = k_2 = 2$, the inner product F requires a 3-dimensional message space, as does the parameter transfer process.

III.2.1. *A determinantal necessary condition for realizability.* There arises, therefore, the question whether one can find a test distinguishing between those F's which are like the inner product and require dim $M = 3$ and those F's that, like the additive separable one, can be realized with a message space of dimension 2 or less.

Clearly, one can get by with dim $M \leqslant 2$ if, for some i and j, we have $\partial F / \partial \theta_j^i \equiv 0$ on Θ. For in this case one may again use a modified parameter transfer process. For instance, suppose (without loss of generality) that $\dfrac{\partial F}{\partial \theta_2^1} \equiv 0$ on θ, i.e., $F(\theta) = \tilde{F}(\theta_1^1, \theta^2)$. Then $\tilde{F}$ can be realized by $M = \mathbb{R}^2$, with $g^1(m, \theta^1) \equiv m^1 - \theta_1^1, g^2 \equiv m^2 - \tilde{F}(m^1, \theta^2), h(m) \equiv m^2$. So, to avoid trivialities, we shall from now on assume that

$$\frac{\partial F}{\partial \theta_j^i} \neq 0 \quad \text{for all} \quad i = 1, 2, \qquad j = 1, 2$$

at all points of the parameter space Θ. (However, some of the results may be valid even without this restriction.)

It was shown in [HRS, 39], Lemma 1. p. V.3, that a necessary condition for the realizability of $F: \mathbb{R}^4 \to \mathbb{R}$ with dim $M \leqslant 2$ and a nonsingular Jacobian $(\partial g^i / \partial m_j)_{i, j = 1, 2}$, is that the bordered Hessian of F vanish, i.e., that

$$\begin{vmatrix} 0 & F_{b_1} & F_{b_2} \\ F_{a_1} & F_{a_1 b_1} & F_{a_1 b_2} \\ F_{a_2} & F_{a_2 b_1} & F_{a_2 b_2} \end{vmatrix} = 0 \quad \text{for all } (a, b), \qquad (*)$$

[††]See Section II.3 above.

where we write

$$\theta^1 = a = (a_1, a_2) \quad \text{and} \quad \theta^2 = b = (b_1, b_2).^\dagger$$

Note that this condition is in fact satisfied when some $F_{a_i} \equiv 0$ or some $F_{b_j} \equiv 0$. It is also satisfied by an additively separable F since then all the cross-derivatives vanish. On the other hand in the inner product case we have

$$\begin{vmatrix} 0 & a_1 & a_2 \\ b_1 & 1 & 0 \\ b_2 & 0 & 1 \end{vmatrix} = -b_1 a_1 + b_2(-a_2) = -a \cdot b \neq 0$$

at a point (a, b) where $a = b \neq 0$.

So we see again that the inner product performance function cannot be realized by a message space of dimension less than 3.

III.2.2. *Sufficient conditions for realizability.* Now suppose that there is given a smooth (C^2) performance function $F: \Theta \to \mathbb{R}, \Theta \subseteq \mathbb{R}^4$, with a vanishing bordered Hessian, i.e., such that equation (*) above is satisfied. Is it then possible to realize F on Θ with smooth equilibrium equation functions $g^i: M \times \Theta^i \to \mathbb{R}$, and a two-dimensional $M = \mathbb{R}$? The answer (see [HRS, 39] Theorem, p. V-13) is in the affirmative. Moreover, the proof is constructive, so that it reduces the problem of finding the mechanism to that of integrating a differential equation and inverting its solution.[††]

We state this result for the case where all partials of F are nonvanishing, since we have already seen how to realize F with vanishing partials by means of a two-dimensional M.

THEOREM. *Let $F: \Theta^1 \times \Theta^2 \to \mathbb{R}$ have nonvanishing first partial derivatives and let it satisfy equation (*) on Θ. Then there exist smooth functions G^1 and G^2 such that F is realized by (g^1, g^2, h, M)*

[†] In [HRS, 39] this condition has a different form but is equivalent.

[††] This theorem is a special case of more general results given below.

with

$$g^1(m, a) \equiv m_2 - G^1(m_1, a), \qquad a \in \Theta^1,$$
$$g^2(m, b) \equiv m_2 - G^2(m_1, b), \qquad b \in \Theta^2,$$
$$h(m) \equiv m_1,$$

and

$$M \equiv \mathbb{R}^2, \qquad m = (m_1, m_2), \qquad m_i \in \mathbb{R}, \qquad i = 1, 2.$$

We shall now sketch a proof of this theorem. First, we note that, with first partials of F nonvanishing, condition (*) is equivalent to

$$\frac{\partial}{\partial a_1} P(a, b) \bigg/ \frac{\partial}{\partial a_2} P(a, b) = F_{a_1}/F_{a_2} \quad \text{for all } (a, b) \in \Theta \quad (**)$$

where we write

$$P(a, b) =_{\text{def}} F_{b_1}(a, b)/F_{b_2}(a, b).$$

It can be shown ([HRS, 39] Lemma 2′, pp. V-10, 11) that condition (**) implies the existence of a smooth function $Q: \mathbb{R}^3 \to \mathbb{R}$ such that

$$P(a, b) = Q(F(a, b), b) \quad \text{for all } (a, b) \in \Theta. \quad (***)$$

In turn, a function $G^2: \mathbb{R} \times \mathbb{R}^2 \to \mathbb{R}$ is obtained as the solution of the partial differential equation

$$\frac{\partial G^2}{\partial b_1} - Q(m_1, b)\frac{\partial G^2}{\partial b_2} = 0, \qquad (+)$$

where $m_1 \in \mathbb{R}$.

To integrate this equation, consider the associated ordinary differential equation

$$\frac{db_2}{db_1} = -Q(m_1, b_1, b_2)$$

where m_1 may be viewed as a parameter. Its solution through (b_1^0, b_2^0) may be written as

$$b_2 = \beta\big(b_1; m_1; b_1^0; b_2^0\big).$$

Since Q is smooth, this can be uniquely smoothly solved for b_2^0, yielding, say,

$$b_2^0 = \phi\big(m_1, b\big)$$

where b_1^0 is assumed fixed and suppressed in notation, and ϕ is a solution of the partial differential equation $(+)$; i.e., $G^2(m_1, b) \equiv \phi(m_1, b)$. It is also to be noted that, under the conditions of the Theorem, $\partial G^2/\partial b_i \neq 0$, $i = 1, 2$. In turn, we obtain $G^1(m_1, a)$ as follows: Let $b_1 = B_1(m_1, a, b_2)$ be the solution for b_1 of the equation $m_1 = G(a, b)$. Define the function $R: \mathbb{R}^4 \to \mathbb{R}$ by

$$R\big(m_1, a, b_2\big) =_{\text{def}} G^2\big(m_1, B_1(m_1, a, b_2), b_2\big).$$

It can then be shown ([HRS, 39], Lemma 3, p. V-12) that conditions $(***)$ and $(+)$ imply

$$\partial R/\partial b_2 \equiv 0,$$

We can therefore define G^1 by

$$G^1\big(m_1, a\big) =_{\text{def}} R\big(m_1, a, b_2\big).$$

It may then be shown that $\partial G^1/\partial m_1 \neq \partial G^2/\partial m_1$ for all $m_1 \in R$, $(a, b) \in \Theta$.

Hence, in the equilibrium system

$$\begin{cases} g^1 \equiv m_2 - G^1(m_1, a) = 0, \\ g^2 \equiv m_2 - G^2(m_1, b) = 0, \end{cases} \qquad (++)$$

the Jacobian

$$\begin{pmatrix} \partial g^1/\partial m_1 & \partial g^1/\partial m_2 \\ \partial g^2/\partial m_1 & \partial g^2/\partial m_2 \end{pmatrix}$$

is nonsingular. We shall now show that, locally, the above g^1, g^2 in $(++)$, together with $h(m) \equiv m_1$, realize F.

Let (m, a, b) satisfy $(++)$. We must show that $m_1 = F(a, b)$. Now $(++)$ implies that $G^1(m_1, a) = G^2(m_1, b)$. But, by construction, $G^1(m, a) = G^2(m_1, B_1(m_1, a, b_2), b_2)$. Hence

$$G^2\big(m_1, B_1(m_1, a, b_2), b_2\big) = G^2(m_1, b).$$

Now suppose $m_1 \neq F(a, b)$. Then, since $b_1 = B_1(m_1, a_1, b_2)$ if and only if $m_1 = F(a, b)$, we have $B_1(m_1, a, b_2) \neq b_1$. That is,

$$G^2\big(m_1, b_1', b_2\big) = G^2\big(m_1, b_1, b_2\big)$$

for some $b_1' \neq b_1$. But, as noted above, $\partial G^2/\partial b_1 \neq 0$ everywhere, so G^2 must be strictly monotone with respect to b_1. Hence a contradiction.

III.2.3. *Explicit construction of a mechanism realizing a given goal performance function by elementary methods (an example).* We now give an explicit example of such an integration process.[†] Let the performance function be given by

$$F(a, b) = \frac{a_2 b_1 + a_1 b_2}{a_1 + b_1},$$

[†] This example is of interest for two reasons. It is related to the Walrasian performance in linear quadratic utility environments. Also, it shows that dim $M = 2$ is possible for F's that are not additively separable.

on the set

$$\Theta \subset \left\{ (a, b) \colon a_1 + b_1 \neq 0;\ a_i F_{a_i} \neq 0, \right.$$
$$\left. i = 1, 2;\ b_j F_{b_j} \neq 0,\ j = 1, 2 \right\}.$$

It can be verified that condition (*) is satisfied. We calculate

$$P(a, b) \equiv F_{b_1}/F_{b_2} = \frac{a_2 - b_2}{a_1 + b_1} = \frac{F(a, b) - b_2}{b_1},$$

so that the function Q in formula (***) of the proof is given by

$$Q(m_1, b) = \frac{m_1 - b_2}{b_1}.$$

The associated ordinary differential equation is therefore

$$\frac{db_2}{db_1} = \frac{b_2 - m_1}{b_1}.$$

Integrating by the method of separation of variables we get $b_2 - m_1 = b_1 c$. Solving for the value of b_2^0, we get

$$b_2^0 = m_1 + \frac{b_1^0}{b_1}(b_2 - m_1) = G^2(m_1, b).$$

In turn,

$$G^1(m_1, a) \equiv G^2(m_1, b)|_{b_1 = B_1(m_1, a, b_2)} = m_1 + b_1^0 \frac{m_1 - a_2}{a_1}.$$

At equilibrium, $m_2 = G^1(m_1, a) = G^2(m_1, b)$. Hence

$$m_1 + b_1^0 \frac{m_1 - a_2}{a_1} = m_1 + \frac{b_1^0}{b_1}(b_2 - m_1).$$

Solving for m_1 we then obtain

$$m_1 = \frac{a_1 b_2 + a_2 b_1}{a_1 + b_1},$$

i.e., $m_1 = F(a, b)$. Since $m_1 = h(m)$, this mechanism clearly realizes F over θ.

III.3. General theory of realization. In developing methods of dealing with more general situations than those discussed in the preceding section (arbitrary N, k_0, k_1, k_2), we focus on sets defined by the equilibrium relations.

We may start with the equilibrium equation form

$$g^i(m, \theta^i) = 0, \quad i \in N$$

where

$$M \subseteq \mathbb{R}^q, \quad \theta^i \in \Theta^i \subseteq \mathbb{R}^{k_i}, \quad g^i \colon M \times \Theta^i \to \mathbb{R}^{q_i}, \quad i \in N.$$

For each $i \in N$ and each $m \in M$, the ith equation of this system defines a set in the ith parameter space,

$$\mathscr{U}_m^i[g^i] = \{ \theta^i \in \Theta^i \colon g^i(m, \theta^i) = 0 \}.$$

If $g^i(m, \theta^i) = 0$ is equivalent to $m \in \mu^i(\theta^i)$, then we also have

$$\mathscr{U}_m^i[g^i] = \{ \theta^i \in \Theta^i \colon m \in \mu^i(\theta^i) \}.$$

We may note that if two different g^i functions generate the same equilibrium correspondence μ^i, then for each $m \in M$ the two g^i functions will also have the same set $\mathscr{U}_m^i$. However, there is a further invariance in the $\mathscr{U}_m^i$'s. Consider a map τ from the original space M to another message space M^*, written $m^* = \tau(m)$. Suppose there exists a function $g^{*i} \colon M^* \times \Theta^i \to \mathbb{R}^{q_i^*}$ such that

$$g^i(m, \theta^i) = 0 \quad \text{if and only if} \quad g^{*i}(\tau(m), \theta^i) = 0.$$

Then

$$\mathscr{U}^i_m[g^i] = \mathscr{U}^i_{\tau(m)}[g^{*i}].$$

III.3.1. *Example.* Let

$$M = \mathbb{R}^2, \quad m = (m_1, m_2), \quad i = 1, \quad \Theta^1 = \mathbb{R}^2,$$

and

$$g^1(m, \theta^1) \equiv m_1 + m_2 - \theta^1_1 - \theta^1_2.$$

Then

$$\mathscr{U}^1_m[g^1] = \left\{ \theta^1 \in \mathbb{R} : \theta^1_1 + \theta^1_2 = m_1 + m_2 \right\}.$$

Now let

$$M^* = \mathbb{R}, \quad \tau(m) = m_1 + m_2,$$

and

$$g^{*1} = m^* - \theta^1_1 - \theta^1_2.$$

We have

$$g^1(m, \theta^1) \equiv m_1 + m_2 - \theta^1_1 - \theta^1_2 = 0$$

if and only if

$$g^{*1}(\tau(m), \theta^1) \equiv (m_1 + m_2) - \theta^1_1 - \theta^1_2 = 0.$$

Clearly,

$$\mathscr{U}^1_{\tau(m)}[g^{*1}] = \mathscr{U}^1_m[g^1].$$

III.3.2. *General indexed and message-indexed product structures.*
More generally, consider two equilibrium systems $(g^1, \ldots, g^n, M)$
and $(g^{*1}, \ldots, g^{*n}, M)$ which have the same collection of $\mathscr{U}$-sets,
i.e.,

$$\left\{ \mathscr{U}_m^i[g^*] \right\}_{\substack{i \in N \\ m \in M}} = \left\{ \mathscr{U}_{m*}^i[g^{*i}] \right\}_{\substack{i \in N \\ m^* \in M^*}}.$$

Let F be a given goal (performance) function. Then F is realizable
through $(g^1, \ldots, g^n, M)$ if and only if it is realizable through
$(g^{*1}, \ldots, g^{*n}, M^*)$. (We say that $F: E \to Z$ is realizable through
$(g^1, \ldots, g^n, M)$ if and only if there exists an outcome function h
such that $(M, g^1, \ldots, g^n, h)$ realizes F.)

A necessary and sufficient condition that F be realizable through
$(g^1, \ldots, g^n, M)$ is that there exist a family $\{ M_c \}_{c \in F(E)}$ of subsets
of M such that

$$F^{-1}(c) = \bigcup_{m \in M_c} \left(\mathscr{U}^1[g^1] \times \cdots \times \mathscr{U}^1[g^n] \right) \text{ for each } c \in F(E). \quad (*)$$

In fact it suffices to define h so that $h(m) = c$ for all $m \in M_c$,
with arbitrary values assigned to $h(m)$ for $m \notin \bigcup_{c \in F(E)} M_c$.

Now consider a collection A of n-tuples $a = (a^1, \ldots, a^n)$ where
$a^i \subseteq \Theta^i$, $i \in N$, and write $\Pi a = a^1 \times \cdots \times a^n$. Also, write $\Pi A =
\{ \Pi a : a \in A \}$. In order that it be possible to construct, through the
elements of A, a mechanism realizing a given goal (performance)
function F, it is necessary and sufficient that there exist a set S, a
function $\phi: S \to \Pi A$, and a function $\psi: F(E) \to 2^S$ such that

$$F^{-1}(c) = \bigcup_{s \in \psi(c)} \phi(s) \quad \text{for all} \quad c \in F(E). \qquad (+)$$

The quadruple (A, S, ψ, ϕ) is called an *indexed product structure
for F on E* if and only if the preceding condition $(+)$ is satisfied.[†]
When S is the message space, we call this a *message-indexed
product structure for F on E*, abbreviated MPS.

[†] Note that the triple (A, ψ, ϕ) defines S as the domain of ϕ.

In turn, this is equivalent to the following condition:

for each $c \in F(E)$, there is a subset $A' \subseteq A$ such that
$$\bigcup_{a \in A'} \Pi a = F^{-1}(c). \qquad (++)$$

When $(++)$ is satisfied, an indexed product structure can be constructed as follows. Let

$$A_c^* = \left\{ A' \subseteq A: \bigcup_{a \in A'} \Pi a = F^{-1}(c) \right\},$$

$$S = \bigcup_{c \in F(E)} A_c^*,$$

$$\phi = \text{the identity function on } S,$$

and

$$\psi(c) = \bigcup \left\{ B \subseteq \Pi A_c^*: \bigcup_{\Pi a \in B} \Pi a = F^{-1}(c) \right\}.$$

Thus, on the one hand, whether a performance function is realizable through a given equilibrium system depends on whether its $\mathcal{U}$-sets satisfy condition $(*)$. On the other hand, given a family of sets satisfying condition $(++)$, one can index them (with some M) so that F is realizable through an equilibrium system, constructed from this family of sets so that the sets of this family are the $\mathcal{U}$-sets of the equilibrium system. Also, if two equilibrium systems have the same $\mathcal{U}$-sets, then, for any given performance function F, either F is realizable through both equilibrium systems or through neither.

These facts show that the family of $\mathcal{U}$-sets of an equilibrium system "distills" those of its features which are decisive for the realizability of various performance functions. It therefore becomes natural to study the problems of realizing given performance functions in relation to the properties of the families of $\mathcal{U}$-sets.

III.3.3. *Parameter-indexed product structures.* Consider a process π in μ-form, $\pi = (M, (\mu^i)_{i \in N}, h)$, realizing a given F with $\mu = \bigcap_{i \in N} \mu^i$ and μ single-valued. There is then a way of indexing the elements of the product structure of π which is of particular importance in what follows. Let $(\{\mathcal{U}^i\}_{m \in M}, i \in N\}$ be an MPS for F on E. We then re-index its sets by defining $U^i(\theta)$

$$U^i(\theta) = \mathcal{U}^i_{\mu(\theta)} \quad \text{for all } \theta \in \Theta \text{ and } i \in N.$$

In the notation of condition $(+)$ above, let $\Theta = S$ (the index set), and let ϕ be given by

$$\phi(\theta) = U^1(\theta) \times \cdots \times U^n(\theta)$$

where, as above,

$$U^i(\theta) = \mathcal{U}^i_{\mu(\theta)}.$$

Also, let

$$\psi(c) = \left\{ \tilde{\theta} \colon c = h(m) \text{ and } m \in \mu(\tilde{\theta}) \text{ for some } m \in M_c \right\}$$
$$= \left\{ \tilde{\theta} \colon \mu(\tilde{\theta}) \subseteq M_c \right\}.$$

Then the family $\{U^i(\theta)\}_{i \in N, \theta \in \Theta}$, together with the functions ϕ and ψ as just defined, constitutes an indexed product structure for F.

We shall now prove that $\theta \in \prod_i U^i(\theta)\prod$. First,

$$g^i(\mu(\theta), \theta^i) = 0, \forall i, \forall \theta,$$

because

$$m = \mu(\theta) \Leftrightarrow g^i(m, \theta^i) = 0, \forall i.$$

Hence

$$\theta^i \in \left\{ \tilde{\theta}^i \colon g^i(\mu(\theta), \tilde{\theta}^i) = 0 \right\} = \mathcal{U}^i_{\mu(\theta)} = U^i(\theta);$$

thus

$$\theta^i \in U^i(\theta),$$

and so

$$\theta \in \prod_i U^i(\theta).$$

The product structure $\{U^i(\theta), \theta \in \Theta\}_{i \in N}$ is called the *parameter-indexed product structure*, abbreviated as PPS.

Of particular interest is the case in which this product structure has certain differentiability properties.

Consider again a mechanism in equilibrium equation form,

$$\pi = \left(M, \left\{ g^i \right\}_{i \in N}, h \right), \quad M = \mathbb{R}^q, \quad q \le \sum k_i,$$

and for each i, let

$$g^i \colon M \times \Theta^i \to \mathbb{R}^{q_i}, \quad q_i \le k_i,$$

be a C^1 function such that the Jacobian

$$\frac{\partial g^i}{\partial \theta_1} \equiv \frac{\partial \left(g_1^i, \dots, g_{q_i}^i \right)}{\partial \left(\theta_{i1}, \dots, \theta_{i, k_i} \right)}$$

is of (maximal) rank q_i. Assume that π realizes a given performance function $F \colon \Pi \Theta^i \to \mathbb{R}^{k_0}$, $\Theta^i \subseteq \mathbb{R}^{k_i}$, all $i \in N$.

It can then be shown, using the Implicit Function Theorem, that dim $M \ge \Sigma_{i \in N} q_i$. Furthermore, the family $\left\{ \mathcal{U}_m^i [g^i] \right\}_{i \in N', m \in M}$, defined as above, constitutes a message-indexed product structure (MPS) for F, and each $\mathcal{U}_m^i$ is a differentiable manifold of constant (as m varies over M) dimension $k_i - q_i$.

Assume now that $\mu(\cdot)$ is a (single-valued) function on Θ. We can then construct the parameter-indexed product structure (PPS) corresponding to the above MPS by defining, for each $i \in N$ and $\theta \in \Theta$,

$$U^i(\theta) = \mathcal{U}_{\mu(\theta)}^i = \left\{ \tilde{\theta}_i \in \Theta^i \colon g^i \left(\mu(\theta), \tilde{\theta}_i \right) = 0 \right\}.$$

Since

$$g^i \left(\mu(\theta), \theta_i \right) = 0 \quad \text{for all } \theta \in \Theta.$$

we have

$$\theta \in \prod_{i \in N} U^i(\theta); \tag{a$'$}$$

$$\text{if } \tilde{\theta} \in \prod_{i \in N} U^i(\theta), \quad \text{then } U^i(\tilde{\theta}) = U^i(\theta) \quad \text{for each } i \in N, \tag{a$''$}$$

$$\prod_{i \in N} U^i(\theta) \subseteq F^{-1} \left(F(\theta) \right) \quad \text{for all } \theta \in \Theta. \tag{b}$$

Clearly, the family $\left\{ U^i(\theta) \right\}_{\substack{i \in N \\ \theta \in \Theta}}$ is a parameter-indexed product structure for F. Also

$$\text{for each } \theta \in \Theta, \ U^i(\theta) \text{ is a smooth } (C^1) \tag{c}$$
$$\text{submanifold of } \mathbb{R}^{k_i}, \text{ of dimension } k_i - q_i.$$

Now suppose furthermore that the Jacobian

$$\frac{\partial g}{\partial \mu} \equiv \frac{\partial\left(g_1^1, \ldots, g_{k_n}^n\right)}{\partial(m_1, \ldots, m_q)}$$

is of (maximal) rank q.

It can then be shown that $\dim M = \sum_{i \in N} q_i$. In this case the family $\{U^i(\theta)\}_{\substack{i \in N \\ \theta \in \Theta}}$ has an important additional property. To state it, define

$$\tilde{U}^i(\theta) \equiv \{\theta_1\} \times \cdots \times \{\theta_{i-1}\} \times U^i(\theta) \times \{\theta_{i+1}\} \times \cdots \times \{\theta_N\}.$$

Then

$$\text{for each } i, \text{ the family } \left\{\tilde{U}^i(\theta)\right\}_{\theta \in \Theta}, \tag{d}$$
$$\text{constitutes a } (k_i - q_i)\text{-dimensional foliation}^\dagger \text{ of } \Theta.$$

[†] Lawson [53], p. 370, defines a p-dimensional, class C^r *foliation* of an m-dimensional manifold M as a decomposition of M into a union of disjoint connected subsets $\{\mathscr{L}_\alpha\}_{\alpha \in A}$, called the *leaves* of the foliation, with the following property: every point in M has a neighborhood U and a system of local, class C^r coordinates $x = (x^1, \ldots, x^m): U \to \mathbb{R}^m$ such that for each leaf $\mathscr{L}_\alpha$, the components of $U \cap \mathscr{L}_\alpha$ are described by the equations $x^{p+1} = \text{constant}, \ldots, x^m = \text{constant}$.

Spivak [86], p. 264, defines a *foliation* of a C^∞ manifold M as a (usually disconnected) k-dimensional submanifold N of M if: (1) every point of M is in (some component of) N, and (2) if around every point $p \in M$ there is a coordinate system (x, U), with

$$x(U) = (-\varepsilon, \varepsilon) \times \cdots \times (-\varepsilon, \varepsilon),$$

such that the components of $N \cap U$ are the sets of the form

$$\left\{ q \in U \colon x^{k+1}(q) = a^{k+1}(q), \ldots, x^n(q) = a^n \right\},$$

and $|a^i| < \varepsilon$ for $i = k+1, \ldots, n$. Each component of N is called a *folium* or *leaf* of the foliation N.

Our use of the term 'foliation' corresponds to that in Spivak in that we also use the *cubic* coordinate system (see Warner [94], p. 5) by requiring that $x(U)$ be an open cube about the origin of $\mathbb{R}^n$, where n is the dimension of the manifold M.

A parameter-indexed product structure having the foliation property is called a *perfect* (parameter-indexed) product structure (abbreviated PPPS).

Formally, we have

DEFINITION. Given the smooth function $F: \Theta \to \mathbb{R}^{k_0}$, $\Theta = \prod_{i=1}^{n} \Theta \subseteq \prod_{i=1}^{n} \mathbb{R}^{k_i}$, the n families of connected sets $\{U^i\}$, $U^i \subseteq \mathbb{R}^{k_i}$, $i = 1, \ldots, n$, form a $\{\underline{k}; \underline{n}\} -$ *parameter-indexed perfect product structure*[†] for F (abbreviated as $\{\underline{k}; \underline{n}\}$-PPPS) if, for each $\Theta \in \prod_{i=1}^{n} \mathbb{R}^{k_i}$ and for each $i = 1, 2, \ldots, n$, there exists a unique member $U^i(\theta)$ of the family $\{U^i\}$ such that:

a') $\theta \in \prod_{i=1}^{n} U^i(\theta)$

a'') If $\tilde{\theta} \in \prod_{i=1}^{n} U^i(\theta)$, then
$U^i(\tilde{\theta}) = U^i(\theta)$ for each $i \in \{1, \ldots, n\}$.

b) $\prod_{j=1}^{n} U^j(\theta) \subseteq F^{-1}(F(\theta))$.

c) Each $U^i(\theta)$ is a smooth submanifold of $\mathbb{R}^{k_i}$ of dimension n_i.

d) For each i, the family $\{\tilde{U}^i(\theta)\}_{\theta \in \Theta}$, where[††]

$$\tilde{U}^i(\theta) \equiv \{\theta_1\} \times \cdots \times \{\theta_{i-1}\} \times U^i(\theta) \times \{\theta_{i+1}\} \times \cdots \times \{\theta_n\},$$

forms an n_i-dimensional foliation of Θ. (The n_i of this definition equals $k_i - q_i$ in our previous construction.)

This concept of foliation is used explicitly in Spivak's formulation ([86], p. 264) of the (global) Frobenius theorem. The same concept of foliation (with a cubic coordinate system), although not the term, is also used in Warner's formulation ([94], p. 42) of the local Frobenius theorem.

[†] Here $\{\underline{k}; \underline{n}\}$ is an abbreviation for $\{k_0, k_1, \ldots, k_n; n_1, \ldots, n_n\}$. (Note that n_n denotes the dimension of the manifold $U^n(\theta)$ in $\mathbb{R}^{k_n}$, i.e., in Θ^n where n is the number of participants.)

The term 'parameter-indexed' is used to distinguish this product structure from a 'message-indexed' product structure introduced in Def. 2 above. The term 'perfect' refers to the foliation property d) introduced in this definition.

[††] $\{\theta_i\}$ denotes the singleton consisting of $\theta_i \cdot \theta^{)i(} = (\theta_1, \ldots, \theta_{i-1}, \theta_{i+1}, \ldots, \theta_n)$.

III.3.4. *Necessary and sufficient conditions for the existence of a parameter-indexed product structure.* It turns out ([41], Theorem 6, necessity part) that if F has a $\{k; n\}$-PPPS, then there exist n smooth integrable distributions $D^1, \ldots, D^n$ in the tangent space $T(\prod_{j \in N} \Theta^j) = T(\prod_{j \in N} \mathbb{R}^{k_j})$ satisfying the following conditions:

i) For each $i \in \{1, \ldots, n\}$, D^i has dimension n_i. For each $\theta \in \prod_{j=1}^n \mathbb{R}^{k_j}$, $D^i(\theta)$ can be expressed as the Cartesian product of an n_i-dimensional linear subspace (say $\Delta^i(\theta)$) in $T_\theta \mathbb{R}^{k_i}$ and $\{0\}$, with 0, the origin of $\mathbb{R}^{\Sigma_{s \neq 1} k_s}$; more explicitly, $D^i(\theta) = \{0_{k_1}\} \times \cdots \times \{0_{k_{i-1}}\} \times \Delta^i(\theta) \times \{0_{k_{i+1}}\} \times \cdots \times \{0_{k_n}\}.$[†]

ii) $dF_\theta(v_i) = 0$ for each θ, each $i \in \{1, \ldots, n\}$, and each v_i in $\mathcal{D}_i(\theta)$.

iii) $D = D^1 \oplus D^2 \oplus \cdots \oplus D^n$ is an integrable distribution in $T(\prod_{j=1}^n \mathbb{R}^{k_j})$.[††]

The proof is constructive. For each i and θ, define $D^i(\theta) = T_\theta \tilde{U}^i(\theta)$, which makes $\tilde{U}^i(\theta)$ into an integral manifold through θ for D^i; thus the family $\{\tilde{U}^i(\theta)_{\theta \in \Theta}\}$ is the foliation of integral manifolds of the distribution D^i. For each θ, the set $\prod_{i \in N} U^i(\theta)$ turns out to be the integral manifold of the distribution D, defined as the direct sum of the D_i's.

But it is the converse of the preceding (i.e., [41], Theorem 6, sufficiency part) that is a basic result. If there exist n distributions D^i with the above properties, then F has a $[k; n]$ parameter indexed perfect product structure. In what follows we shall refer to Theorem 6 of [41] (both parts, necessity and sufficiency) as the Theorem.

[†] That is, for $n = 3$, $i = 1$, we have $D^1(\theta) = \Delta^1(\theta) \times \{0_{k_2}\} \times \{0_{k_3}\}$ where $\Delta^1(\theta)$ is an n_1-dimensional subspace of TR^{k_1} and 0_q is the origin of R^q.

For the sake of brevity, we sometimes write $D^i(\theta) = \Delta^i(\theta) \times 0_{)i(}$.

[††] That this direct sum is well defined is implied by the fact that for each θ, we have by condition (i) that, for $i \neq j$,

$$D^i(\theta) \cap D^j(\theta) = \{0\},$$

where 0 is the origin of $R^{\Sigma_{s=1}^n k_s}$.

Note that $\Delta^1(\theta) \times \cdots \times \Delta^n(\theta)$ can be identified with $D^1(\theta) \oplus \cdots \oplus D^n(\theta) = D(\theta)$.

The converse owes its importance to the fact that the distributions $D^1, \ldots, D^n$, can, at least in principle,[†] be constructed once F is given. Then the converse guarantees the existence of the corresponding PPPS from which (via the MPS) we can construct the equilibrium correspondence μ and the equilibrium equations. Thus it enables us to construct a mechanism given a performance function, which is our objective.

III.4.   *Using the general theory to construct a mechanism realizing the Walrasian performance function.*   Given a smooth performance function[††] $F: \prod_i R^{k_i} \to \mathbb{R}$, there are, as we know, various mechanisms which realize it, in particular the parameter transfer mechanism where

$$m = (m^1, \ldots, m^n),$$
$$g^j \equiv m^j - \theta^j, \quad m^j \in \mathbb{R}^{k_j}, \quad j = 1, \ldots, n-1$$
$$g^n \equiv M^n - F(m^1, \ldots, m^{n-1}, \theta^n), \qquad m^n \in \mathbb{R}$$
$$h(m) = m^n,$$

and agents are so numbered that

$$k_n \geq k_j \quad \text{for all} \quad j \in N.$$

Hence

$$q_n = 1, \quad q_j = k_j \quad \text{for } j = 1, \ldots, n-1,$$

and dim $M = 1 + \sum_{j=1}^{n-1} k_j$. We have seen that there are F's for which a lower dimension of the message space is impossible. But suppose it is known (or conjectured) that there exists a mechanism $\pi = (m, \{g^i\}_{i \in N}, h)$ with a message space of dimension less than $1 + \sum_{j=1}^{n-1} k_j$ and some specified values of the $q_i, i = 1, \ldots, n, \Sigma q_i = $ dim M. (Here the symbols g^i, h, and M represent entities different from those in the above parameter transfer mechanism!)

[†] This involves the integration of a system of partial differential equations.

[††] To simplify exposition we confine ourselves to the case $k_0 = 1$.

How do we go about constructing this mechanism, if it does exist, or determining that it does not exist if that is the case? We shall describe the procedure which will result either in showing that the mechanism of specified dimensions does not exist or (in principle!) in constructing it.

III.4.1.   *The Walrasian performance function and the price mechanism for a small economy.*   The first step involves the construction (or: attempt at construction) of the distributions $D^1, \ldots, D^n$, with D^i of dimension $k_i - q_i$, having the properties specified in the theorem. As an illustration of this construction process, we shall use that of the Walrasian performance function in a 2-person 2-good pure exchange economy (Edgeworth Box) with preferences representable by utility functions that are linear in one of the goods and quadratic in the other. We shall have here $n = 2$ and $k_1 = k_2 = 2$.

Denote the goods by X and Y and the traders by $i = 1, 2$. Let $u^i = \alpha_i X_i + (1/2)\beta_i X_i^2 + Y_i$, $x_i = X_i - \omega_i$, where X_i, Y_i are, respectively the total amounts of the goods X, Y in the hands of agent i, x_i is the net trade in good X for agent i, and ω_i the initial endowment of good X for agent i. Assume that the utility functions are strictly increasing within the Edgeworth Box. Writing $\gamma_i = \alpha_i + \beta_i \omega_i$, $i = 1, 2$, we obtain the Walrasian equilibrium equations

$$\gamma_i + \beta_i x_i = p, \qquad i = 1, 2$$
$$x_1 + x_2 = 0$$

Let the performance function F specify x_1 as a function of the parameters. Solving the above equations for x_1 we get

$$x_1 = \frac{\gamma_2 - \gamma_1}{\beta_1 + \beta_2},$$

(It will be assumed throughout that $\beta_1 + \beta_2 > 0$.) In terms of our general notation we have $\theta^i = (\theta^i_1, \theta^i_2) = (\beta_i, \gamma_i)$, $i = 1, 2$,

$$F(\theta) \equiv \frac{\theta^2_2 - \theta^1_2}{\theta^1_1 + \theta^2_1}.$$

Here again it will be convenient to simplify notation and write

$$\theta^1 = a = (a_1, a_2), \quad \theta^2 = b = (b_1, b_2),$$

with $\theta = (a, b)$ and

$$F(\theta) = F(a, b) \equiv \frac{b_2 - a_2}{a_1 + b_1}.$$

Clearly, the parameter transfer process will require a 3-dimensional message space, say with

$$g^1 = \begin{pmatrix} g^1 \\ g^2 \end{pmatrix} \equiv \begin{pmatrix} m^1_1 - a_1 \\ m^1_2 - a_2 \end{pmatrix},$$

$$g^2 \equiv m^2 - \frac{b_2 - m^1_2}{m^1_1 + b_1}$$

$$h(m) \equiv m^2,$$

with $m^1_1, m^1_2, m^2 \in \mathbb{R}$.

On the other hand, as economists we happen to know the customary price mechanism which can be reduced to

$$\gamma_1 + \beta_1 x_1 - p = 0$$
$$\gamma_2 - \beta_2 x_1 - p = 0.$$

This can be written as

$$m = (m_1, m_2), \quad m_i \in \mathbb{R}, \quad i = 1, 2,$$

as

$(*)$
$$\begin{cases} g^1 \equiv a_2 + a_1 m_1 - m_2 = 0 \\ g^2 \equiv b_2 - b_1 m_1 - m_2 = 0 \end{cases}$$
$$h(m) \equiv m_1 \quad (\text{i.e.,}^\dagger \ h = pr_1),$$

---

†In the following formula $h = pr_1$ means that $h(m)$ is the first component projection of $m = (m_1, m_2)$.

with

$$q_1 = q_2 = 1 \quad \text{and} \quad \dim M = 2.$$

We may note that (solving the equation system (*) for the m_i's) we have

(†)
$$\begin{cases} \mu^1(a, b) = \dfrac{b_2 - a_2}{a_1 + b_1}, \\[2mm] \mu^2(a, b) = \dfrac{a_2 b_1 + a_1 b_2}{a_1 + b_1}. \end{cases}$$

(The functions μ^i in this and the following sections are not to be confused with the correspondences μ^i in equations (5.2) of the Introduction.) Hence (by formula for $U^i(\cdot)$ in 3.3 p. 301)

(††)
$$\begin{cases} U^1(\bar{\theta}) = \mathcal{U}^1_{\mu(\bar{\theta})} = \left\{ a: a_2 + a_1 \mu^1(\bar{\theta}) - \mu^2(\bar{\theta}) = 0 \right\} \\[2mm] U^2(\bar{\theta}) = \mathcal{U}^2_{\mu(\bar{\theta})} = \left\{ b: b_2 - b_1 \mu^1(\bar{\theta}) - \mu^2(\bar{\theta}) = 0 \right\}. \end{cases}$$

After substitution into (††) of the values of $\mu^i(\bar{\theta})$ from (†) this yields

(†††)
$$\begin{cases} U^1(\bar{\theta}) = \left\{ a: \dfrac{a_2 - \bar{b}_2}{\bar{a}_2 - \bar{b}_2} = \dfrac{a_1 + \bar{b}_1}{\bar{a}_1 + \bar{b}_1} \right\} = \left\{ a: \dfrac{a_2 - \bar{a}_2}{\bar{a}_2 - \bar{b}_2} = \dfrac{a_1 - \bar{a}_1}{\bar{a}_1 + \bar{b}_1} \right\} \\[4mm] U^2(\bar{\theta}) = \left\{ b: \dfrac{b_2 - \bar{a}_2}{\bar{b}_2 - \bar{a}_2} = \dfrac{b_1 + \bar{a}_1}{\bar{a}_1 + \bar{b}_1} \right\} = \left\{ b: \dfrac{b_2 - \bar{b}_2}{\bar{b}_2 - \bar{a}_2} = \dfrac{b_1 - \bar{b}_1}{\bar{a}_1 + \bar{b}_1} \right\}. \end{cases}$$

III.4.2. *Finding the distributions and parameter-indexed product structures for a given goal performance function.* The preceding computation illustrates the procedure of obtaining the parameter-indexed product structure, here the family $\{U^1(\theta), U^2(\theta)\}_{\theta \in \Theta}$, when we know F *and* a mechanism. But the more interesting question is how we would have proceeded if we had known F and the fact that there exists some mechanisms with $q^1 = q^2 = 1$ and dim $M = 2$, but where we did *not* know the functions g^1, g^2, h.

We first seek the distributions D^1, D^2. In our example, this search is easy because it happens that the orthogonality condition (ii) of the Theorem completely determines the D^i. (In general, this would not be the case, and the search would be more complex.)

We first calculate the gradients F_a, F_b of the performance function F and their orthogonal complements $F_a^{\perp}$, $F_b^{\perp}$. Here,

$$F_a = \begin{pmatrix} F_{a_1} \\ F_{a_2} \end{pmatrix}, \qquad F_b = \begin{pmatrix} F_{b_1} \\ F_{b_2} \end{pmatrix}.$$

We find that

$$F_a = \begin{pmatrix} \dfrac{b_2 - a_2}{(a_1 + b_1)^2} \\ \dfrac{1}{a_1 + b_1} \end{pmatrix}, \qquad F_b = \begin{pmatrix} \dfrac{b_2 - a_2}{(a_1 + b_1)^2} \\ \dfrac{1}{a_1 + b_1} \end{pmatrix},$$

and that the orthogonal complements are, respectively,[†]

$$F_a^{\perp} = \left\langle \begin{pmatrix} a_1 + b_2 \\ b_2 - a_2 \end{pmatrix} \right\rangle, \qquad F_b^{\perp} = \left\langle \begin{pmatrix} a_1 + b_1 \\ b_2 - a_2 \end{pmatrix} \right\rangle.$$

Hence, by the orthogonality condition (ii) of the Theorem (HRS [39], Theorem 6; Section III.3.4 above),

$$D^1(a, b) = \{ \theta' \colon \theta' = (a_1', a_2', b_1', b_2'),$$
$$a_1' = -(a_1 + b_1), a_2' = b_2 - a_2, b_1' = b_2' = 0 \},$$
$$D^2(a, b) = \{ \theta'' \colon \theta'' = (a_1'', a_2'', b_1'', b_2''),$$
$$a_1'' = a_2'' = 0, b_1'' = a_1 + b_1, b_2'' = b_2 - a_2 \}.$$

[†] In the following formulae the symbol $\langle w \rangle$ denotes the linear space generated by w.

The system of (in this simple example, ordinary) differential equations corresponding to D^1 is

$$\frac{da_1}{ds} = -(a_1 + b_1), \qquad \frac{da_2}{ds} = b_2 - a_2, \qquad \frac{db_1}{ds} = \frac{db_2}{ds} = 0.$$

For initial values $(\bar{a}, \bar{b})$, elementary integration yields the solutions

$$a_1 + \bar{b}_1 = e^{-s}(\bar{a}_1 + \bar{b}_1), \qquad a_2 - \bar{b}_2 = e^{-s}(\bar{a}_2 - \bar{b}_2),$$
$$b_1 = \bar{b}_1, \qquad b_2 = \bar{b}_2.$$

By eliminating e^{-s} between the first two equations we obtain the formula for the integral manifold of D^1 through $(\bar{a}, \bar{b})$, to wit

$$\tilde{U}^1(\bar{a}, \bar{b}) = \left\{ (a, b) \colon \frac{a_1 + \bar{b}_1}{\bar{a}_1 + \bar{b}_1} = \frac{a_2 - \bar{b}_2}{\bar{a}_2 - \bar{b}_2}, \, b_1 = \bar{b}_1, b_2 = \bar{b}_2 \right\},$$

hence

$$U^1(\bar{a}, \bar{b}) = pr_a\tilde{U}^1(\bar{a}, \bar{b}) = \left\{ a \colon \frac{a_1 + \bar{b}_1}{\bar{a}_1 + \bar{b}_1} = \frac{a_2 - \bar{b}_2}{\bar{a}_2 - \bar{b}_2} \right\}.$$

(We note that this is the same formula as that obtained in (†††), Section III.4.1 above. But previously, we had obtained it from known g^1, g^2, while here it has been obtained on the basis of knowledge of F only, first using the orthogonality condition of the Theorem in Section III.3.4 to find the distributions D^1, D^2 and then integrating these distributions.)

Similarly, the system of differential equations corresponding to D^2 is

$$\frac{da_1}{dt} = 0, \qquad \frac{da_2}{dt} = 0, \qquad \frac{db_1}{dt} = a_1 + b_1, \qquad \frac{db_2}{dt} = b_2 - a_2.$$

This yields the solution through $(\bar{a}, \bar{b})$ as

$$a_1 = \bar{a}_1, \qquad a_2 = \bar{a}_2, \qquad b_1 + \bar{a}_1 = e^t(\bar{a}_1 + \bar{b}_1),$$
$$b_2 - \bar{a}_2 = e^t(\bar{b}_2 - \bar{a}_2).$$

After elimination of e^t and some algebraic manipulation, we see that the integral manifold of D^2 through $(\bar{a}, \bar{b})$ is

$$\tilde{U}^2(\bar{a}, \bar{b}) = \left\{ (a, b) \colon \frac{b_1 + \bar{a}_1}{\bar{b}_1 + \bar{a}_1} = \frac{b_2 - \bar{a}_2}{\bar{b}_2 - \bar{a}_2}, \, a_1 = \bar{a}_1, \, a_2 = \bar{a}_2 \right\}$$

and so

$$U^2(\bar{a}, \bar{b}) = pr_b \tilde{U}^2(\bar{a}, \bar{b}) = \left\{ b \colon \frac{b_1 + \bar{a}_1}{\bar{b}_1 + \bar{a}_1} = \frac{b_2 - \bar{a}_2}{\bar{b}_2 - \bar{a}_2} \right\},$$

again as obtained in (†††), Section III.4.1 above.

It may be verified that

$$U(\bar{a}, \bar{b}) \equiv U^1(\bar{a}, \bar{b}) \times U^2(\bar{a}, \bar{b})$$
$$= \left\{ (a, b) \colon \frac{a_1 + \bar{b}_1}{\bar{a}_1 + \bar{b}_1} = \frac{a_2 - \bar{b}_2}{\bar{a}_2 - \bar{b}_2}, \, \frac{b_1 + \bar{a}_1}{\bar{b}_1 + \bar{a}_1} = \frac{b_2 - \bar{a}_2}{\bar{b}_2 - \bar{a}_2} \right\}$$

is the integral manifold through $(\bar{a}, \bar{b})$ of $D \equiv D^1 \oplus D^2$.

III.4.3. *Constructing the equilibrium relations and the outcome function.* We have now found the parameter-indexed product structure, but we must still find a privacy preserving process—either in the form (μ^1, μ^2, h, M) or in the form (g^1, g^2, h, M). This is accomplished by taking advantage of the foliation property of the family of integral manifolds.

The elements of the message space to be constructed can be thought of as labeling the leaves (folia) of the foliation $\{U(\theta)\}_{\theta \in \Theta}$. A way of providing the labels is to find a manifold T in Θ that is transversal to the folia, and to use the coordinates of the one-point intersection $T \cap U(\theta)$ as the label for $U(\theta)$. It turns out that this provides a mapping defining the foliating coordinate system.

In our Walrasian performance quadratic utility example, one transversal manifold that can be used is the set

$$T = \{(a, b): a_1 = 0, b_2 = 0\}.$$

writing the integral manifold $U(\bar{\theta})$, $\bar{\theta} = (\bar{a}, \bar{b})$, as

$$U(\bar{\theta}) = \{(a, b,): G_1(a, \bar{\theta}) = 0, G_2(b, \bar{\theta}) = 0\},$$

we find the coordinates $\theta' \equiv (a', b')$ of the intersection $T \cap U(\bar{\theta})$ to be given by the equation system

$$G_1(a', \bar{\theta}) = 0, \qquad G_2(b', \bar{\theta}) = 0, \qquad a_1' = 0, \qquad b_2' = 0,$$

so that the coordinates a_2' and b_1' are respectively the solutions of $G_1(0, a_2' \bar{\theta}) = 0$ and $G_2(b_1', 0, \bar{\theta}) = 0$. In the parameter region where $\bar{a}_1 + \bar{b}_1 \neq 0$ and $\bar{a}_2 - \bar{b}_2 \neq 0$, these two (linear) equations have solutions which are unique, so that a_2' and b_1' are well-defined functions of $\bar{\theta}$, denoted respectively by $\sigma_1(\bar{\theta})$ and $\sigma_2(\bar{\theta})$. Explicitly,

$$a_2' \equiv \sigma_1(\bar{\theta}) = \frac{\bar{a}_1 \bar{b}_2 + \bar{a}_2 \bar{b}_1}{\bar{a}_1 + \bar{b}_1},$$

$$b_1' \equiv \sigma_2(\bar{\theta}) = \frac{\bar{a}_1 \bar{b}_2 + \bar{a}_2 \bar{b}_1}{\bar{a}_2 - \bar{b}_2}.^{\dagger}$$

---

†Geometrically, $\sigma_1(\bar{\theta})$ is the value of the a_2-intercept of the straight line (in a-space) representing the manifold $U^1(\bar{\theta})$ and given by the equation

$$\frac{a_2 - \bar{b}_2}{\bar{a}_2 - \bar{b}_2} = \frac{a_1 + \bar{b}_1}{\bar{a}_1 + \bar{b}_1}.$$

Similarly $\sigma_2(\bar{\theta})$ is the value of the b_1-intercept of the straight line (in b-space) representing the manifold $U^2(\bar{\theta})$ and given by the equation

$$\frac{\bar{a}_1 + b_1}{\bar{a}_1 + \bar{b}_1} = \frac{b_2 - \bar{a}_2}{\bar{b}_2 - \bar{a}_2}.$$

These functions can be used to express the U-sets and U^i-sets in a convenient form. It can be shown that, with $\theta = (a, b)$, and $\sigma(\theta) = (\sigma_1(\theta), \sigma_2(\theta))$,

$$U(\bar{\theta}) = \{(a, b): \sigma(\theta) = \sigma(\bar{\theta})\},$$
$$U^1(\bar{\theta}) = \{a: \sigma(a, \bar{b}) = \sigma(\bar{a}, \bar{b})\},$$
$$U^2(\bar{\theta}) = \{b: \sigma(\bar{a}, b) = \sigma(\bar{a}, \bar{b})\}.$$

Correspondingly, the integral manifold of D^1 and D^2 can respectively be written as

$$\tilde{U}^1(\bar{\theta}) = U^1(\bar{\theta}) \times \{\bar{b}\} = \{\theta: \sigma(\theta) = \sigma(\bar{\theta}), b = \bar{b}\}$$

and

$$\tilde{U}^2(\bar{\theta}) = \{\bar{a}\} \times U^2(\bar{\theta}) = \{\theta: \sigma(\theta) = \sigma(\bar{\theta}), a = \bar{a}\}.$$

But it can be shown that the two relations $\sigma(\theta) = \sigma(\bar{\theta})$, $b_2 = \bar{b}_2$ imply $b_1 = \bar{b}_1$; similarly the relations $\sigma(\theta) = \sigma(\bar{\theta})$, $a_1 = \bar{a}_1$ imply $a_2 = \bar{a}_2$. Hence, we may rewrite the preceding formulae as

$$\tilde{U}^1(\bar{\theta}) = \{\theta: \sigma(\theta) = \sigma(\bar{\theta}), b_2 = \bar{b}_2\}$$

and

$$\tilde{U}^2(\bar{\theta}) = \{\theta: \sigma(\theta) = \sigma(\bar{\theta}), a_1 = \bar{a}_1\}.$$

The latter form shows that the relations σ_1, σ_2 obtained in determining the intersection point $T \cap U(\bar{\theta})$ can be used to define a foliating ("rectifying") mapping ϕ such that, for any point θ^* in Θ, there is a coordinate system (ϕ, V) with the following properties:

(1) $\phi: \Theta \to \mathbb{R}^4$, $\phi = (\phi_1, \phi_2)$, $\phi_1 = (\phi_1^1, \phi_1^2)$, $\phi_2 = (\phi_2^1, \phi_2^2)$, $\phi_j^i: \Theta \to \mathbb{R}$;

(2) for some $\varepsilon > 0$, $\phi(V) = (-\varepsilon, \varepsilon) \times (-\varepsilon, \varepsilon) \times (-\varepsilon, \varepsilon) \times (-\varepsilon, \varepsilon)$;

(3) $\begin{cases} \tilde{U}^1(\theta) \cap V = \{\theta \in V: \phi_2(\theta) = \phi_2(\bar{\theta}), \phi_1^1(\theta) = \phi_1^1(\bar{\theta})\}, \\ \tilde{U}^2(\theta) \cap V = \{\theta \in V: \phi_1(\theta) = \phi_1(\bar{\theta}), \phi_2^1(\theta) = \phi_2^1(\bar{\theta})\}, \\ U(\theta) \cap V = \{\theta \in V: \phi_1^1(\theta) = \phi_1^1(\bar{\theta}), \phi_2^1(\theta) = \phi_2^1(\bar{\theta})\}. \end{cases}$

Thus ϕ effects the simultaneous "rectification" of the three systems of integral manifolds.[†] The mapping ϕ is defined by:

$$\begin{cases} \phi_i^1(\theta) \equiv \sigma_i(\theta), & i = 1, 2, \\ \phi_1^2(\theta) \equiv a_1, & \phi_2^2(\theta) \equiv b_2. \end{cases}$$

It may be verified that, except on a set of lower dimension in the parameter space, ϕ, has a nonsingular Jacobian, so that the inverse ϕ^{-1} exists. For a sufficiently small $\varepsilon > 0$, a neighborhood V of the coordinate system (V, ϕ) is defined by $V = \phi^{-1}((-\varepsilon, \varepsilon)^4)$.

The labeling provided by the coordinates (a_2', b_1') of the intersection provides a message space and equilibrium correspondences, to be denoted by $\tilde{\mu}^1(\theta) \equiv \sigma_2(\theta),$[†] $\tilde{\mu}^2(\theta) \equiv \sigma_1(\theta)$; i.e.,

$$\tilde{\mu}^1(a, b) = \frac{a_1 b_2 + a_2 b_1}{a_2 - b_2}, \quad \tilde{\mu}^2(a, b) = \frac{a_1 b_2 + a_2 b_1}{a_1 + b_1}.$$

We shall now show how the knowledge of the equilibrium correspondences $\tilde{\mu}^i$ enables us to construct the equilibrium equation function $\tilde{g}^i$ and the outcome function $\tilde{h}$.

Given the $\tilde{\mu}^i$ functions, with $\theta = (a, b)$, we have

$$\mathcal{U}_{\tilde{m}}^1 = \left\{ a: \exists b \text{ s.t. } \tilde{m}_i = \tilde{\mu}^i(\theta), i = 1, 2 \right\}$$

$$\mathcal{U}_{\tilde{m}}^2 = \left\{ b: \exists a \text{ s.t. } \tilde{m}_i = \tilde{\mu}^i(\theta), i = 1, 2 \right\}.$$

Since $\mathcal{U}_{\tilde{m}}^1$ is a 1-dimensional manifold, we require that the equations $m_i = \tilde{\mu}^i(\theta)$, $i = 1, 2$ which are linear in b_1, b_2 as the unknowns, should have a vanishing discriminant $\tilde{\Delta}_1$. This yields

$$\tilde{\Delta}_1 \equiv \tilde{m}_1 a_2 + \tilde{m}_1 \tilde{m}_2 + a_2 \tilde{m}_2 = 0.$$

Hence

$$\tilde{g}^1(\tilde{m}, a) \equiv -\tilde{m}_1 a_2 + \tilde{m}_1 \tilde{m}_2 + a_1 \tilde{m}_2.$$

[†] The idea of such simultaneous rectification and the related proofs are due to Steven Williams.

[†] Tildes are used here (and, similarly, below for $\tilde{m}_i$, $\tilde{g}^i$, $\tilde{h}$) to avoid confusion with the earlier construction of μ^i (and other symbols). Indices are reversed as between the σ's and the $\tilde{\mu}$'s to facilitate certain comparisons.

Similarly, since $\tilde{\mathcal{U}}_{\tilde{m}}^2$ is a 1-dimensional manifold, we require that the equations $\tilde{m}_i = \tilde{\mu}^i(a, b)$, $i = 1, 2$, which are linear in a_1, a_2 as the unknowns, have a vanishing discriminant

$$\tilde{\Delta}_2 \equiv -\tilde{m}_1 b_2 - b_1 \tilde{m}_2 + \tilde{m}_1 \tilde{m}_2 = 0,$$

so that

$$\tilde{g}^2(\tilde{m}, b) \equiv -\tilde{m}_1 b_2 - b_1 \tilde{m}_2 + \tilde{m}_1 \tilde{m}_2.$$

Finally, we construct the outcome function $\tilde{h}$ by using the above foliation mapping ϕ (defined on p. 315), here written as

$$\tilde{m}_1 = \tilde{\mu}^1(a, b) \equiv \frac{a_1 b_2 + a_2 b_1}{a_2 - b_2},$$

$$\tilde{m}_2 = \tilde{\mu}^2(a, b) \equiv \frac{a_1 b_2 + a_2 b_1}{a_1 + b_1},$$

$$v_1 = a_1,$$

$$v_2 = b_2.$$

For the mechanism being constructed to realize F, it is necessary that $h(m) = F(\phi^{-1}(m, v^*))$ for all m in M and some $v^* = (v_1^*, v_2^*)$. We choose $v^* = (0, 0)$, i.e., $a_1^* = 0$, $b_2^* = 0$, the values on the transversal T. Now (as given in Section III.4.1)

$$F(\theta) = \frac{b_2 - a_2}{a_1 + b_1},$$

i.e., it is determined by the four parameters a_1, a_2, b_1, b_2. We solve for these four parameters the system $\phi(\theta) = (\tilde{m}_1, \tilde{m}_2, 0, 0)$, i.e.,

$$\frac{a_1 b_2 + a_2 b_1}{a_2 - b_2} = \tilde{m}_1,$$

$$\frac{a_1 b_2 + a_2 b_1}{a_1 + b_1} = \tilde{m}_2,$$

$$a_1 = 0,$$

$$b_2 = 0.$$

This yields

$$\tilde{m}_1 = b_1,$$
$$\tilde{m}_2 = a_2,$$
$$a_1 = 0,$$
$$b_2 = 0,$$

i.e.,

$$\theta = (a_1, a_2, b_1, b_2) = \phi^{-1}(\tilde{m}, v^*) = (0, \tilde{m}_2, \tilde{m}_1, 0).$$

Hence

$$F(\theta) = F(\phi^{-1}(\tilde{m}, v^*)) = \left. \frac{b_2 - a_2}{a_1 + b_1} \right|_{\theta = (0, \tilde{m}_2, \tilde{m}_1, 0)} = \frac{0 - \tilde{m}_2}{0 + \tilde{m}_1},$$

and so

$$\tilde{h}(\tilde{m}) \equiv -\frac{\tilde{m}_2}{\tilde{m}_1}.$$

We may now verify directly that $(\tilde{g}^1, \tilde{g}^2, \tilde{h}, \tilde{M})$, with $\tilde{M} = \mathbb{R}^2$, does in fact realize F. Solving the equations $\tilde{g}^1(\tilde{m}, a) = 0$, $\tilde{g}^2(\tilde{m}, b) = 0$ obtained above we, of course, get

$$\tilde{m}_1 = \frac{a_1 b_2 + a_2 b_1}{a_2 - b_2}, \quad \tilde{m}_2 = \frac{a_1 b_2 + a_2 b_1}{a_1 + b_1}.$$

Hence,

$$h(\tilde{m}) \equiv -\frac{\tilde{m}_2}{\tilde{m}_1} = -\frac{(a_1 b_2 + a_2 b_1)/(a_1 + b_1)}{(a_1 b_2 + a_2 b_1)/(a_2 - b_2)}$$

$$= -\frac{a_2 - b_2}{a_1 + b_1} = F(a, b),$$

as given, for instance, in Section 4.1.

Comparing the formulae (†) for the μ^i in Sec. 4.1 with those for the $\tilde{\mu}^i$ in Sec. 4.3, we note that $\tilde{\mu}^2 = \mu^2$, while $\tilde{\mu}^1 \neq \mu^1$ where the μ^i were obtained from the "customary" Walrasian process discussed earlier; consequently the $\tilde{g}^i$-equations were also different from their usual Walrasian forms. This discrepancy is not surprising since the choice of a transversal manifold and of labeling is somewhat arbitrary. But would it have been possible to choose some mapping other than ϕ so as to get back to the original equations and the original μ^i's? The answer is "yes."

To accomplish this, however, we must use a different rectification mapping λ, namely, that defined by

$$\lambda_1^1(\theta) \equiv \frac{a_1 b_2 + a_2 b_1}{a_1 + b_1},$$

$$\lambda_1^2(\theta) \equiv a_1,$$

$$\lambda_2^1(\theta) \equiv \frac{b_2 - a_2}{a_1 + b_1},$$

$$\lambda_2^2(\theta) \equiv b_2.^\dagger$$

Denoting the messages by m_1, m_2 and following the same procedure as that followed previously to derive the $\tilde{\mu}^i$ and the $\tilde{g}^i$, we find the equations specifying the vanishing of the discriminants, and so obtain the equilibrium equations

$$g^1(a, m) \equiv a_1 m_1 - m_2 + a_2 = 0,$$

$$g^2(b, m) \equiv -b_1 m_1 - m_2 + b_2 = 0,$$

which are identical with those on p. 308 above.

It remains to construct the outcome function h. As previously, we must have $h(m) = F(\lambda^{-1}(m, v^*))$, where $\lambda(\theta) =$

$\dagger$ It may be noted that only λ_2^1 differs from ϕ_2^1 while $\lambda_j^i = \phi_j^i$ for other combinations of the indices $i, j \in \{1, 2\}$.

Geometrically, $\lambda_2^1(\bar{\theta})$ is the slope of the straight line representing $U^2(\bar{\theta})$ in the b-space.

(m_1, m_2, v_1^*, v_2^*), so that $\theta = (a_1, a_2, b_1, b_2) = \lambda^{-1}(m, v^*) = (v_1^*, m_2, m_1, v_2^*)$. But in this case things happen to be much simpler than previously, because by construction, $m_1 = \lambda_2^1(\theta) = \dfrac{b_2 - a_2}{a_1 + b_1}$.

Since $F(\theta) \equiv \dfrac{b_2 - a_2}{a_1 + b_1} \equiv \lambda_2^1(\theta)$, we see immediately that $h(m) \equiv m_1$, without going through the process of calculating all of λ^{-1} and regardless of the values chosen for v^*. Again, this outcome function is identical with the customary Walrasian one (see Section III.4.1 equations (*) above).

Clearly, with this outcome function h, and the above equilibrium functions g^1, g^2, we have reconstructed the usual Walrasian process. But the earlier construction (yielding $\tilde{h}, \tilde{g}^1, \tilde{h}^2$) shows, first of all, that there are alternative mechanisms realizing the Walrasian performance function $F \equiv \dfrac{b_2 - a_2}{a_1 + b_1}$, and also that one need not have prior knowledge of a mechanism realizing F to construct one.

III.5. Williams' Genericity Theorem. In Williams [97] it is shown that, among C^∞ smooth performance functions, those which cannot be realized by a message space smaller than that of parameter transfer are generic. More precisely, let $\Theta = \Theta^1 \times \cdots \times \Theta^n$, with Θ^i an open subset of $\mathbb{R}^{k_i}$ for each $i \in \{1, \ldots, n\}$. To be realized are smooth real-valued functions on Θ, where smooth means C^∞, i.e., continuous and continuously differentiable functions of class C^k for every positive integer k. The topology used is the Whitney C^∞ topology (see Golubitsky and Guillemin [25], p. 42). Because only local properties are involved, in considering functions defined at and near some point θ in Θ, two such functions are said to be *equivalent near θ* if they coincide on some neighborhood of θ. Such an equivalence class is called a *germ at θ*. The symbol $C_\theta^\infty(\Theta)$ denotes the space, in the Whitney C^∞ topology, of all germs of smooth real-valued functions on Θ. (See Golubitsky and Guillemin [25], p. 103.)

Let now $F: \Theta \to R$ be smooth and (privacy-preserving) realizable in a neighborhood Θ' of some $\bar{\theta} \in \Theta$ by a mechanism[†]

[†] In equilibrium equation form, see I.2, equation (5.2″).

$(M, \{g^i\}_{i \in N}, h)$ where M is Euclidean, and each g^i: $M \times \Theta^i \to R^{q_i}$ is smooth and 'nondegenerate' in that it satisfies the following condition:

$$\text{the functional matrix } \left. \frac{\partial g^i(m, \theta^i)}{\partial \theta_i} \right|_{\theta = \bar{\theta}_i}$$

has rank q_i for any m such that $g^i(m, \bar{\theta}^i) = 0$. It is furthermore assumed that, in the neighborhood Θ',

$$g^i(m, \theta^i) = 0, \qquad i = 1, \ldots, n$$

is uniquely solvable for $m \in M$. (It follows that dim $M = \sum_{i=1}^{n} q_i$.)

Williams' main result is that, for any $\bar{\theta} \in \Theta$ satisfying these conditions, there exists an open dense set Ω of $C_{\bar{\theta}}^{\infty}(\Theta)$ such that if a smooth real-valued F in Ω is realizable in the above manner, then there exists at most one index value, say j in $\{1, \ldots, n\}$ such that $q_i \neq k_j$. To put it the other way, it is necessarily the case that for some $j \in \{1, \ldots, n\}$ we have

$$q_s = k_s \quad \text{for all } s \in \{1, \ldots, j-1, j+1, \ldots, n\}.$$

In the most favorable case satisfying this condition, we have $q_j = 1$. Thus we have $n - 1$ sets of k_s equations of the form $g^s(m, \theta^s) = 0$, $s \neq j$, and one additional equation $g^j(m, \theta^j) = 0$ with g^j real-valued. But this is precisely the situation in the parameter transfer process where $m = (m^1, \ldots, m^n)$,

$$g^s(m, \theta^s) \equiv m^s - \theta^s, \qquad s \neq j$$

$$g^j(m, \theta^j) \equiv m^j - F(m^1, \ldots, m^{j-1}, \theta^j, m^{j+1}, \ldots, m^n),$$

with $m^s \in M^s$, dim $M^s = k^s$ for $s \neq j$, and $m^j \in M^j$, dim $M^j = 1$. Then, for $M = M^1 \times \cdots \times M^n$, one gets dim $M = \sum_{i=1}^{n} \dim M^i = 1 + \sum_{s \neq j} k_s$.

If one thinks of all C^{∞} smooth (goal) performance functions as equally likely to arise in economic applications, Williams' result is rather discouraging. It suggests that cases such as the inner product

(Section III.2), where parametric transfer is the best one can do, are typical while those like the Walrasian performance function in convex economies (Section III.4.1), where one can get by with a message space smaller than that of parameter transfer, are exceptional. Furthermore, since in economic models environments are typically assumed infinite dimensional, it would follow that, generically, a finite-dimensional message space is insufficient. Thus the situation exemplified by nonconvex economies discussed in Section II.4 would be the norm rather than an exception. But not all goal functions are of equal interest to the economist. In fact much of social choice theory deals with postulates to be satisfied by goal functions (e.g., Pareto optimality, individual rationality.) The question of genericity within narrower classes of performance functions defined by such postulates remains to be explored.

IV. APPROXIMATE REALIZATION IN DISCRETE SPACES

In practice the whole real axis is not available as a message space nor as the space for the determination of outcomes.[†] Hurwicz and T. Marschak have studied the consequences of assuming the choice of message spaces to be limited to discrete sets, while maintaining the assumption that the individual characteristics (here the individual parameter vectors θ^i) vary over the Euclidean continuum.

The following brief exposition will be limited to the problem of (approximate) realization of a real-valued performance function ϕ in a world with only two agents, i.e., $\theta = (\theta^1, \theta^2)$, $\phi: \Theta^1 \times \Theta^2 \to \mathbb{R}$.

Suppose first that, while $\phi(\Theta) \subseteq \mathbb{R}$ is a set containing an interval, the permissible outcome space X is that of integers, i.e., $X = \{ \ldots, -1, 0, 1, \ldots \}$.[†]

[†] This point was made very forcefully by Jacob Marschak at a 1976 session of the American Economic Association. His comments stimulated the work by Hurwicz and Thomas Marschak, part of which is being reported here. (See Hurwicz and Marschak [36], [37].)

[†] The analysis of the case where $X \equiv X_b = \{ \ldots, -2b, -b, 0, b, 2b, \ldots \}$, where b is a fixed positive real number, would be essentially the same. *Finite* outcome and message spaces have also been studied, but the results will not be discussed here.

Suppose that $\phi(\Theta)$ contains a neighborhood which includes a number of the form $n + \frac{1}{2}$, where n is an integer. Clearly, no matter what the mechanism, a lower bound on maximum error is $\frac{1}{2}$, i.e.,

$$\varepsilon(\mu, h, M, X; \Theta, \varphi) \underset{\text{def}}{=} \sup_{\theta \in \Theta} \sup_{m \in \mu(e)} |h(m) - \varphi(\theta)| \geq \frac{1}{2}.$$

Suppose now that we are constrained to use mechanisms whose message spaces are discrete, i.e., of the form

$$M^{(k)} = M_1 \times \cdots \times M_k \qquad (1 \leq k < \infty)$$

where

$$M_r \subseteq \{\ldots, -2b_r, -b_r, 0, b_r, 2b_r, \ldots\}$$

where $r = 1, \ldots, k$, and $b_r > 0$.

An interesting question is whether there exist mechanisms attaining the above lower bound of $\frac{1}{2}$. In fact, it has been shown that the answer is in the negative for any denumerably infinite (not merely discrete) message space. On the other hand, it turns out that under certain regularity conditions, it is possible to construct mechanisms, using discrete outcome and message spaces, whose errors $\varepsilon(\mu, h, M, X; \Theta, \phi)$ come arbitrarily close to the lower bound $\frac{1}{2}$.

As an example, we consider the familiar case of the two-agent two good economy with linear-quadratic utility functions. The usual equilibrium equations are

$$g^1(m, \theta^1) \equiv p + \beta_1 x - \theta_1 = 0,$$
$$g^2(m, \theta^2) \equiv p - \beta_2 x - \theta_2 = 0,$$
$$m = (p, x), \qquad p, x \in \{\ldots, -1, 0, 1, \ldots\},$$

where

$$\theta^1 = (\beta_1, \theta_1), \qquad \theta^2 = (\beta_2, \theta_2),$$

p is the price of good X, and x the net trade of agent 1. The performance function seeks the unique Pareto-optimal value of x, i.e.,

$$\phi(\theta^1, \theta^2) = \frac{\theta_1 - \theta_2}{\beta_1 + \beta_2}.$$

Thus, because complete accuracy is impossible in this case, we are in effect realizing the performance correspondence defined by

$$\Phi_\varepsilon(\theta) = \{ x \in x : |x - \phi(\theta)| \le \varepsilon \}.$$

In the light of previous comments, the best we can ask for with $X = \{ \ldots, -1, 0, 1, \ldots \}$ is that, for a specified $\varepsilon > 0$,

$$|x - \phi(\theta)| \le \frac{1}{2} + \varepsilon.$$

When the message space is discrete (i.e., p and x are limited to discrete sets described above), there will not, in general exist $m \in M$, such that

$$g^i(m, \theta^i) = 0, \qquad i = 1, 2.$$

So, again, we may only ask that, for some preassigned $\delta_i > 0$, $i = 1, 2$, the inequalities

$$|g^i(m, \theta^i)| \le \delta_i, \qquad i = 1, 2$$

be satisfied. (When $h(p, x) \equiv x$, we have what is called the approximate price mechanism.) This fits very naturally into the Mount-Reiter model, with the individual equilibrium message correspondence defined by

$$\mu^i(\theta^i) = \{ m \in M : |g^i(m, \theta^i)| \le \delta_i \},$$

and the joint equilibrium correspondence, as usual, by

$$\mu(\theta) = \mu^1(\theta^1) \cap \mu^2(\theta^2).$$

Now, as in the continuum-mechanism realization problem, a lower bound on the size of the required message space is obtained by finding a subset of the parameter space which has the *uniqueness property* with respect to the performance correspondence Φ_ε. It can be shown that such a subset is obtained as

$$\Theta_{\varepsilon\eta} = \Theta^1_{\varepsilon\eta} \times \Theta^2_{\varepsilon\eta}$$

where

$$\Theta^i_{\varepsilon\eta} = \left\{ \theta^i \in \Theta^i : \theta^i = (\beta_i, \theta_i),\ \beta_i = 1, \theta_i = n \cdot (4\varepsilon + \eta) \right.$$
$$\left. \text{for some } n \in \{0, 1, 2, \dots\} \right\}$$

for some $\eta > 0$. We note that $\Theta_{\varepsilon\eta}$ is isomorphic with N^2 where N is the set of all nonnegative integers.

In order to get the analogues of theorems previously obtained for continuum mechanisms, we now need a concept of ordering of discrete message spaces according to size. This is accomplished as follows. For $x = (x_1, \dots, x_m) \in \mathbb{R}^m$, write

$$\|x\| = \max\{|x_i| : i \in \{1, \dots, m\}\}.$$

DEFINITION 1. A (single-valued *function f*: $X \to Y$ is said to be *Lipschitzian* (or Lipschitz-continuous) iff there is a number $K > 0$ such that:

$$\|f(x') - f(x'')\| \le K \cdot \|x' - x''\| \quad \text{for all } x', x'' \in X.$$

This, of course, is the usual definition.

DEFINITION 2. A function g: $A \to B$ is said to be *Lipschitz-sectioned* iff the inverse correspondence has a Lipschitzian selection, i.e., iff there is a Lipschitzian function s: $g(A) \to A$ such that

$$s(b) \in g^{-1}(b) \quad \text{for all } b \in g(A).$$

EXAMPLE. The standard one-to-one mapping ϕ: $N \to N^2$, where $N = \{0, 1, 2, \dots\}$ is Lipschitzian (with $K = 1$), but it is not Lipschitz-sectioned.

DEFINITION 3. We shall say that the (informational) *Lipschitz size* of space A is at least as great as that of space B, written $A \geq^L B$ iff there is a surjective function $g: A' \underset{\text{onto}}{\to} B$ which is Lipschitz-sectioned, where A' is a subset of A.

We write $A >^L B$ to mean "$A \geq^L B$ but not $B \geq^L A$."

EXAMPLE. Clearly, $N^2 \geq^L N$. In fact, it can be shown that $N^2 >^L N$.

DEFINITION 4. A function $f: A \to B$ is said to be *pseudo-Lipschitzian* iff, for each $c > 0$, there is a number $K > 0$ such that for all $a', a'' \in A$ satisfying the inequality

$$\|a' - a''\| \geq c,$$

we have

$$\|f(a') - f(a'')\| \leq K \cdot \|a' - a''\|.$$

Note that a Lipschitzian function is pseudo-Lipschitzian. Also, if the domain A of f is discrete, then a pseudo-Lipschitzian function f is Lipschitzian. However, a pseudo-Lipschitzian function need not be continuous. (Consider $f(x) = [x]$, the largest integer not exceeding x.) Also, a continuous function need not be pseudo-Lipschitzian. (Consider $f(x) = x^2$, $x \in \mathbb{R}$).

The following result has been established:

PROPOSITION A. Let a privacy-preserving $\mu: \Theta \to M$ have a pseudo-Lipschitzian selection, and let the mechanism (M, μ, h) realize Φ_ε on a subset of Θ containing $\Theta_{\varepsilon\eta}$. Suppose that M, the message space, is known to be one of the following: $\{0\}, N, N^2, \ldots$. Then

$$M \geq^L N^2.$$

Furthermore, a mechanism of the type described above satisfies the conditions of Proposition A. We have:

PROPOSITION B. Let $(\varepsilon, \delta_1, \delta_2, \eta)$ be such that the above approximate price mechanism, with $M = Z \times Z$, $g^i \equiv p +$

$(-1)^{i+1}\beta_i x$, $h(p, x) = x$, covers $\Theta_{\varepsilon\eta}$, i.e.,

$$\mu(\theta) \neq \varnothing \quad \text{for all } \theta \in \Theta_{\varepsilon\eta}.$$

Then this mechanism is pseudo-Lipschitzian, and it realizes Φ_ε on

$$\{\theta \in \Theta : \beta_1 = \beta_2 = 1, \theta_1 \geq 0, \theta_2 \geq 0\}.$$

It is also possible to define a modified approximate price mechanism, by a rescaling of the variables, so that $\varepsilon > 0$ can be chosen arbitrarily small.[†]

V. STABILITY

Although our basic model (see Section I.2, eq. (1)) of a mechanism was dynamic[††] and formulated as a system of difference equations, most attention has been focused on the mechanism's equilibrium, i.e., static properties. More recently, however, there have been important contributions in the area of dynamics, centered on the question of the required dimension of the message space to achieve stability.[†††]

The basic finding is that, in general, if the minimum dimension of the message space required to (statically) realize a performance function is, say, $q(F)$, then a higher dimensionality than $q(F)$ is required to construct a mechanism which not only realizes F but is also stable.

V.1. Reiter's difference equation system example.
An instructive example was constructed by Reiter [77]. It involves the performance function

---

[†] Hurwicz and T. Marschak [36], Proposition C.

[††] In fact, what we now call a mechanism was originally called an 'adjustment process' (Hurwicz [27]).

[†††] The problem of speed of convergence and of the error remaining after a finite number of iterations does not seem to have been studied as yet.

$$F(\theta) = \frac{\theta_1^1 \theta_2^2 - \theta_2^1 \theta_1^2}{\theta_1^1 - \theta_1^2}, \quad \theta^i = (\theta_1^i, \theta_2^i), \quad \theta_j^i \in \mathbb{R}, \quad i, j = 1, 2,$$

over Θ such that $\theta_1^1 - \theta_1^2 \neq 0$. This performance function is closely related to those discussed in earlier sections and arises as the Walrasian outcome in linear-quadratic utility environments. This F can be realized by the mechanism (g^1, g^2, h, M) with

$$(+) \begin{cases} M = \mathbb{R}^2, \, m = (m_1, m_2), \\ \quad h(m) \equiv \quad m_1, \\ g^1(m, \theta^1) \equiv m_1 - \theta^1 m_2 - \theta^1, \\ g^2(m, \theta^2) \equiv m_1 - \theta^2 m_2 - \theta^2. \end{cases}$$

Corresponding to this static system, we can write a difference equation system, say

$$m_1(t+1) - m_1(t) = m_1(t) - \theta_1^1 m_2(t) - \theta_2^1,$$
$$m_2(t+1) - m_2(t) = m_1(t) - \theta_1^2 m_2(t) - \theta_2^2,$$

and check it for stability. But if it turned out unstable, this would not exclude the possibility that some alternative "dynamization" would stabilize it.

The question therefore would be whether there exist response functions f^1, f^2 such that

$$m_1 = f^1(m, \theta^1)$$
$$m_2 = f^2(m, \theta^2)$$

if and only if

$$g^1(m, \theta^1) = 0$$
$$g^2(m, \theta^2) = 0$$

and such that the difference equation system

$$m_1(t+1) = f^i(m(t), \theta^i), \quad i = 1, 2 \qquad (*)$$

is stable in some specified sense. Reiter [77] required that the system be locally asymptotically stable, in the sense that for initial values $m(0)$ sufficiently close to an equilibrium point, the solution function $m(t, m(0))$ should converge to this equilibrium point. He found that for any choice of f^1 and f^2 having continuous partial derivatives with respect to m_1 and m_2, there is an open subset of the parameter space Θ for which the above difference equation system (*) fails to be locally asymptotically stable.

This result showed that the dimension of the space here ($M = \mathbb{R}^2$) that is adequate for static realization may fail to be adequate for (asymptotic local) stable realization.

On the other hand, Reiter also constructed a process with a bigger message space ($M = \mathbb{R}^4$) for which a convergent process with the required equilibrium does exist. The following are the response equations of the convergent process:

$$
m_1^i(t + 1) = \frac{\theta_1^i}{1 + \left(\theta_1^i\right)^2}\left[\theta_1^i\left((1/2)\left(m_1^i(t) + m_2^1(t)\right.\right.\right.
$$
$$
\left.\left.\left. + m_1^2(t) + m_2^2(t)\right) - \theta_1^i\theta_2^i\right)\right] + \theta_2^i,
$$
$$
m_2^i(t + 1) = \frac{\theta_1^i}{1 + \left(\theta_1^i\right)^2}\left[(1/2)\left(m_1^i(t) + m_2^1(t) + m_1^2(t)\right.\right.
$$
$$
\left.\left. + m_2^2(t)\right) - \theta_1^i\theta_2^i\right], \qquad i = 1, 2.
$$

Thus, locally at least, it is not impossible in this case to dynamize the system in a stable way, but a bigger message space is required.

It is natural to ask whether the impossibility of stable dynamization is due to some exceptional features of the Reiter example or whether it represents a more general phenomenon.

This problem has been studied from several points of view, although subsequent work has dealt with dynamization in terms of ordinary differential (rather than difference) equations, say of the form

$$
\dot{m}_i = g^i(m, e^i), \quad i = 1, \ldots, n,
$$

where $\dot{m}_i = dm_i/dt$.

Also, in some cases (local) Lyapunov stability is required, in others both (local) Lyapunov and (local) asymptotic.

The Reiter example raised the question of stable dynamization of a particular static system, viz. (g^1, g^2, M) satisfying conditions $(+)$ above. Mount and Reiter [62], studied the problem of stable (in the sense of Lyapunov) dynamization separately for two kinds of situations: those with dim $M = 2$, and those with M of arbitrary dimension.

For the case dim $M = 2$, they admit a broad class of adjustment functions h^i: $M \times E \to M^i$ which are continuous in (m, e) and locally Lipschitzian in m, such that, in the neighborhood of the origin, the set of zeros of $h^i(i, e)$ is a submanifold, and a further regularity condition (Assumption 3) is postulated.[†] They then investigate the class of dynamic systems of the form

$$\dot{m}_i = h^i(m, e), \qquad i = 1, 2 \qquad (**)$$

for h^i satisfying the above conditions and having an equilibrium at a point $\overline{m}$ of the message space, i.e., such that

$$h^i(\overline{m}, e) = 0, \qquad i = 1, 2.$$

(This last requirement corresponds to the requirement in the Reiter example that the equilibria of the f-equations be the same as those of the given g-equations.) The main result is that, for dim $M = 2$, and given any $m \in M$, there does not exist a dynamic process of the form $(**)$, with the h^i satisfying the three assumptions, for which $\overline{m}$ is a locally stable equilibrium in the Lyapunov sense.

In their analysis of processes with dim $M \geq 2$, Mount and Reiter study those with a nonsingular linear part, and show that, again with an additional assumption, there will be a point in the parameter space Θ such that at least one of the eigenvalues is positive real; hence again (Lyapunov) instability arises. The implications of these

---

[†] The following system, closely related to the original Reiter example, is shown to satisfy all three conditions imposed on the adjustment functions: $h^1(m, \theta^1) \equiv \theta^1 - \theta_2^1 m_2 - m_1$, $h^2(m, \theta^2) \equiv \theta_1^2 - \theta_2^2 m_1 - m_2$. An example is also given where a locally stable process not satisfying Assumption 3 does exist.

findings are explored in Williams [95]. Williams notes a special feature of the Reiter example type situation giving rise to instability in the Mount and Reiter [62] theorem, viz. that at a certain point $e' = (e_1', e_2') \in E$ the determinant of the Jacobian

$$\left. \frac{\partial(g^1, g^2)}{\partial(m_1, m_2)} \right|_{e=e'}$$

changes sign. He then modifies the Reiter example somewhat to show that instabilities arise even without the singularity of the Jacobian. The example is as follows:

$$\dot{m}_1 = \theta_1^1 - \theta_2^1 m_1 - m_2$$
$$\dot{m}_2 = \theta_1^2 - m_1 - \theta_2^2 m_2$$

where $|\theta_2^i| < 1$, $i = 1, 2$, and hence $\partial g/\partial m = \theta^1\theta^2 - 1 < 0$, so $\partial g/\partial m$ never changes sign. Nevertheless, it is shown, instability is again necessarily present in any dynamization. Williams' Theorem 5 formulates general[†] conditions on the elements of the Jacobian $(\partial g^i/\partial m_j)_{i, j=1, 2}$ which result in instability of all dynamizations of the system $g^i(m, e^i) = 0$, $i = 1, 2$. In contrast to these "negative" results, Williams also obtains a positive result (Theorem 6) showing how, subject to certain conditions on the principal minors of the Jacobian $\left(\dfrac{\partial g^i}{\partial m_j} \right)$, there exists a diagonal matrix A such that the system $\dot{m} = A \cdot G$, where

$$G = \begin{bmatrix} g^1 \\ \vdots \\ g^n \end{bmatrix},$$

is locally stable. The important point is, of course, that in this class

---

[†]It is to be noted, however, that Williams assumes continuous differentiability, while Mount and Reiter only postulate continuity and a Lipschitzian property.

of cases the dimension of the message space need not be raised in the transition from static to stable dynamics. An example is given to show that a weakening of the hypotheses of Theorem 6 may result in destabilization.

V.2. General dynamic systems. Although the message adjustment model was largely inspired by the theory of Walrasian tâtonnement, models such as

$$m^i_{t+1} = f^i(m_t, e^i), \quad i = 1, \ldots, n,$$

or

$$\dot{m}^i = g^i(m, e^i), \quad i = 1, \ldots, n,$$

where i refers to an agent, do not specialize to the Walrasian tâtonnement system

$$\dot{p}_j = H_j(\phi_j(p)), \quad j = 1, \ldots, l,$$

where j refers to a commodity, $p = (p_1, \ldots, p_l)$ is the price vector, and ϕ^i is the aggregate excess demand function, say

$$\phi_j(p) \equiv \sum_{i=1}^{n} \phi^i_j(p), \quad j = 1, \ldots, l.$$

In particular, if one is interested in convergent alternatives to the standard Walrasian process, it is not obvious how to specify the requirement of privacy. This makes it difficult to integrate the contributions arising from the study of Walrasian tâtonnement with those generated by the study of abstractly formalized processes.

One way of reformulating the tâtonnement process is as follows. Introduce the quantity messages $z^i = (z^i_1, \ldots, z^i_l)$, $z = (z^1 \ldots, z^n)$, and construct the system

$$z^i = \phi^i(p, e^i), \quad i = 1, \ldots, n,$$

$$\dot{p}_j = H_j\left(\sum_{i=1}^{n} z^i\right), \quad j = 1, \ldots, l.$$

Here the privacy-preserving property is evident in the static part of
the system, whereas in our previous models, of the form $\dot{m}^i =
g^i(m, e^i)$, $i = 1, \ldots, n$, the dynamic equations are privacy preserv-
ing. However, it should be noted that if $m = (z, p)$ is the generic
message, the dynamic equation does not require any information
about the environment, hence formally it can be "operated" by any
agent. (In customary economic models, it is operated by an
auctioneer who need not have any information about the environment.)

Jordan [46] constructed a model general enough to encompass
both types of systems by introducing two types of messages: the
"control messages," one (denoted by c^i) for each agent, and "state
messages" m. The complete system is then written as

$$c^i = f^i(m, e^i), \qquad i = 1, \ldots, n$$

and

$$\dot{m}_j = \alpha_j(c, m), \qquad j = 1, \ldots, q.$$

where $q = \dim M$.

Clearly, the above version of the tâtonnement process is obtained by setting $c^i = z^i$, $m = p$, and $\alpha_j = H_j$. On the other hand
consider the special case where $q = n$ and, for each j there is a β_j
such that $\alpha_j(c_1, \ldots, c_n, m) = \beta_j(c_j, m)$ for all (c, m). Then

$$m_j = \beta_j(c_j, m) = \beta_j(f^j(m, e^j)) = g_j(m, e^j), \quad j = 1, \ldots, n,$$

which is the privacy-preserving abstract adjustment process form
used previously.[†]

Thus Jordan's model is more general than those previously
considered.[††] But as Jordan himself notes, the resulting differential
equation systems are not, in general, privacy preserving. The prime
example is the Walrasian tâtonnement process, even if we were to

---

[†] For a more general formulation, see Mount and Reiter [62], Lemma 2.
[††] Mount and Reiter introduce an even more general class of dynamic systems.

think of one agent adjusting the price of a good or group of goods,[†] since to adjust p_j according to the equation

$$\dot{p}_j = H^j\left(\sum_{i=1}^{n} \zeta_j^i(p, e^i) \right)$$

requires the knowledge of all e^i, $i = 1, \ldots, n$. However, suppose that (as is customary in microeconomics) we think of the adjustment as being carried out by an auctioneer (or various auctioneers for various goods) according to

$$\dot{p}_j = H^j\left(\sum_{i=1}^{n} z^i \right)$$

where the z^i are messages sent to the auctioneer by agent i based on his/her calculation of $z^i = \zeta^i(p, e^i)$, where ζ^i maximizes the ith agent's utility subject to the budget. Then the resulting system

$$z^i = \zeta^i(p, e^i), \quad i = 1, \ldots, n,$$

$$\dot{p}_j = M^j\left(\sum_{j=1}^{n} z^i \right), \quad j = 1, \ldots, l,$$

with the message space $Z \times P$ of dimension $nl + l$, is privacy-preserving.

Suppose that ζ is a C^2 function and that the matrix $D_p\zeta(p, e)$ is nonsingular. Then the so-called Newton's method system

$$\dot{p} = -\left(D_p\zeta(p, e) \right)^{-1}\zeta(p, e)$$

is locally stable.[††] To represent this process as privacy-preserving (with an auctioneer), we must introduce additional messages z_k^i

---

[†] The same is true of the Newton method.

[††] See Saari and Simon [79], Section 3, p. 1103. (Originally presented at the NBER Conf. Feb. 1976; Northwestern U., Discussion Paper No. 259, Nov. 1976.) For global stability see Smale [85] *Journal of Mathematical Economics* 3, pp. 107–120. "A Convergent Process of Price Adjustment and Global Newton Methods."

such that

$$z^i_{jk} = \frac{\partial \zeta^i_j(p, e^i)}{\partial p_k} \quad \left(\text{abbreviated as } \zeta^i_{jk}(p, e^i)\right).$$

Then the process may be written as

$$z^i_j = \zeta^i(p, e^i) \qquad i = 1, \ldots, n; \qquad j = 1, \ldots, l; \qquad h = 1, \ldots, l,$$
$$z^i_{ju} = \zeta^i_{jk}(p, e^i),$$
$$\dot{p} = -Bp,$$

where

$$p = (p_1, \ldots, p_l),$$
$$B = D^{-1},$$

and

$$D = \left(\begin{array}{ccc} z_{11} & \cdots & z_{1l} \\ \hline z_{l1} & \cdots & z_{ll} \end{array}\right),$$
$$z_{jk} = \sum_{i=1}^{n} z^i_{jk}.$$

Since this is a much greater message than that of the tâtonnement process, the question arises whether there might not exist an alternative process of a similar form with lower dimensional requirements. This question was studied by Saari and Simon [79] who considered the class of mechanisms of the form

$$\dot{p} = M(f(p), Df(p))$$

where M is smooth and $M(f(p), Df(p)) = 0$ if and only $f(p) = 0$.[†] (Because of normalization, we may here interpret l as the number of goods minus one, e.g., the number of non-numéraire goods.)

[†] I.e., the Walrasian equilibria are preserved.

Writing

$$M\left(z_1, \ldots, z_l; (z_{rs})_{\substack{r=1 \ldots, l \\ s=1 \ldots, l}}\right),$$

they then ask how many of these $l + l^2$ coordinates are "ignorable." (A coordinate z_{rs} is called ignorable if there exists a stable mechanism M for which $\partial M / \partial z_{rs} \equiv 0$; similarly for a coordinate z_j.)

Saari and Simon confine themselves to smooth mechanisms, satisfying nondegeneracy conditions: there exists at least one smooth excess demand function ζ^* and a zero p^* of ζ^* such that $DM_{f^*}(p^*)$ is nonsingular. (Here $M_f(p) =_{\text{def}} M(x; (z_{rs}))$, $x = f(p)$, $(z_{rs}) = Df(p)$.) A mechanism M is called a *local effective price mechanism* (abbreviated LEPM) if, for any smooth excess demand function ζ, any equilibrium price vector p (i.e., p such that $\zeta(p) = 0$) is an attractor[†] of the ODE system $\dot{p} = M(\zeta(p), D\zeta(p))$.

Part (b) of their main result is that for $l > 1$ (i.e., for an economy with 3 or more goods) M is not a LEPM if any coordinate z_{rs} is ignorable in the neighborhood of $z = 0$.[††] Saari and Simon also consider *global* stability properties. Here they require that, for some fixed open set V and almost all p^0 in V, the solutions of $\dot{p} = M(\zeta(p)), D(\zeta(p))$ through p^0 converge to *some* equilibrium point of ζ, i.e., to some $\bar{p}$ such that $\zeta(\bar{p}) = 0$.[†††] Mechanisms with this property are called *effective price mechanisms* (abbreviated EPM). When $l = 1$, it is known[††††] that $\dot{p} = \zeta(p)$ is an EPM (Saari and Simon [79], p. 1105, *Theorem*, part (a)).

[†] A locally asymptotically stable equilibrium point.

[††] A closely related result is found in Traub and Woźniakowski [87], especially Lemma 4.3 and Theorem 4.2; see also Traub and Woźniakowski [89], Section 7.5.

[†††] On the specified subset of V, this corresponds to the concept of global system stability in Arrow and Hurwicz [5], p. 524, or [6], p. 200.

Note that this requirement does not imply the local stability of all equilibrium points.

[††††] See Arrow and Hurwicz [5], Theorem 6, p. 541 (or [6], p. 214), and Arrow, Block, and Hurwicz [4], Section 6.3, p. 108 (or [6], p. 253).

It is shown in Smale [85] that the global Newton method is an EPM, with V chosen as some open neighborhood of the boundary of the price domain. But the Newton mechanism has no ignorable coordinates. Parts (c), (d), (e) of Saari and Simon [79] specify upper bounds on how many ignorable coordinates an EPM mechanism can have and where these coordinates can be located when there are three or more goods. These bounds are very severe. For instance, for $l = 2$ or 3 (i.e., when there are three or four goods), if M has two ignorable coordinates z_{ij} and z_{hk} with $i \neq h$ (i.e., in different rows), then M is not an EPM. More generally, when $l \geq 2$ (i.e., when there are three or more goods), and subject to a certain nondegeneracy condition, if z_{ij} and z_{hk} are ignorable coordinates for M in some neighborhood of $z = 0$, where $i \neq h$ and $j \neq k$ (i.e., when the ignorable coordinates are in different rows and columns of the Jacobian matrix), then M is not an EPM.

An example is given[†] with a whole column of ignorable entries. Also, an example is constructed[††] for a 3-good economy which is different from the Newton method (in fact, it requires no matrix inversion), has ignorable coordinates, and is locally convergent.

In Jordan [46], a closely related result is proved under somewhat weaker assumptions. In particular, his α_j functions are only required to be Lipschitzian. It should be noted, however, that Jordan requires structural stability for small perturbations of the environment as a part of the local stability concept. Also, Jordan requires that *all* equilibria be locally stable (both in the sense of Lyapunov and asymptotically). His model involves a decentralized control sector, which is not the case in Saari and Simon. And, finally, his informational requirements are formulated in terms of the dimension of the control space rather than in terms of ignorable coordinates.[†††]

It is interesting to compare the conclusions of Mount-Reiter and Jordan for the two-good, two-agent economy. Mount-Reiter has a

---

[†] Saari and Simon [79], pp. 1123–24.

[††] Ibid., [79] pp. 1124–25.

[†††] It may be possible to lower the dimension of the control (or message) space without permitting any coordinate to be ignorable.

weaker definition of stability and concludes that dim $M \geq 3$. Jordan's conclusion, with the stronger definition of stability, would be that dim $C \geq 4$.

V.3. Stability in Nash implementation. In Section VI of this paper we discuss the problem of constructing a (static) privacy-preserving mechanism realizing the Walrasian correspondence (or more generally, a Pareto-optimal correspondence) which at the same time implements this correspondence in (terms of) Nash equilibria.

When the mechanism is balanced and smooth, subject to certain regularity conditions, this cannot be accomplished for *two* agents.[†] When the number of agents is $n \geq 3$, smooth implementing balanced mechanisms do exist [73], [33].

In Jordan [47] the corresponding dynamic question is examined. His model permits the presence of an auctioneer,[††] and it assumes the outcome function (game form) to be C^1 and concave. It is then shown that there will be a failure of local stability for a specified (sufficiently rich) class of (pure exchange) environments.

It should be noted that Jordan's definition of local stability includes structural stability for small perturbations of the environment and requires that all equilibria be locally stable in both Lyapunov and asymptotic sense.

VI. INFORMATIONAL ASPECTS OF NASH IMPLEMENTATION OF PERFORMANCE CORRESPONDENCES

Let $E = E^1 \times \cdots \times E^n$ be a class of environments, with E^i the class of admissible characteristics for agent i, and Z the outcome space. A performance (social choice) correspondence is a correspondence $F: E \to \to Z$. For each agent i and each $e^i \in E^i$, there

---

[†]See [74] for the Walrasian correspondence and [43] for Pareto optimal correspondences.

[††]So it is a quasi-game in the sense of Hurwicz [34].

is defined a (reflexive) preference relation $R^i(e^i)$ on the space Z.[†]
Let S^i be a strategy space for the ith agent, $S = S^1 \times \cdots \times S^n$
and $h: S^1 \times \cdots \times S^n \to Z$ an outcome function (game form). A
Nash equilibrium for the game[††] $\Gamma_e = ((S^i, R^i(e^i)))_{i=1}^n, h)$ is defined as a list of strategies $s^* \in S$ such that, for each $i = 1, \ldots, n$,

$$h(s^*) R^i(e^i) h(s^{*1}, \ldots, s^{*i-1}, s^i, s^{*i+1}, \ldots, s^{*n})$$

for all $s^i \in S^i$. We say that $(S^1, \ldots, S^n, h)$ *Nash implements* the
correspondence F over E if and only if, for each $e \in E$,

(1)   the game $\Gamma_e = ((S^i, R^i(e^i))_{i=1}^n, h)$ has a Nash equilibrium;

and

(2)   if s^* is a Nash equilibrium of Γ_e, then $h(s^*) \in F(e)$.

Given an environment $e \in E$, there is a set $Z(e) \subseteq Z$ of feasible
outcomes. We shall assume that $F(e) \subseteq Z(e)$ for all $e \in E$. If it is
required that $h(s) \in Z(e)$ for each $e \in E$, the *implementation* is
said to be *feasible*.[†††] However, in the existing literature the
feasibility requirement is not always imposed. In pure exchange
models, the outcomes are allocations $z = (z^1, \ldots, z^n)$ where $z^i \in \mathbb{R}^l$
is a commodity bundle. Here each agent, in addition to the
preference relation $R^i(e^i)$, also has an initial endowment $\omega^i(e^i) \in$
$\mathbb{R}^l$ and a feasible consumption set $Z^i(e^i) \subseteq R$. The set of feasible
net trades for the ith agent is $\tilde{Z}^i(e^i) = \{\tilde{z}^i \in \mathbb{R}^l: \tilde{z}^i = z^i - \omega^i(e^i),$

[†] $z' \mathbb{R}^i(e^i) z''$ is interpreted as meaning that agent i, with characteristic e^i, likes z'
at least as well as he does z''.

[††] If $R^i(e^i)$ is represented by the utility function u^i, then the game Γ_e has the
real-valued payoff function $\phi^i = u^i \cdot h$ for all i.

[†††] By construction, the equilibrium outcome is always feasible since $h(s^*) \in$
$F(e) \subseteq Z(e)$.

$z^i \in Z^i(e^i)\}$; the set of jointly feasible net trades is

$$\tilde{Z}(e) = \left\{ (\tilde{z}^1, \ldots, \tilde{z}^n) \in \mathbb{R}^{ln} : \sum_{i=1}^{n} \tilde{z}^i = 0_l \quad \text{and} \quad \tilde{z}^i \in \tilde{Z}^i(e^i) \right.$$

$$\left. \text{for all } i = 1, \ldots, n \right\},$$

where 0_l is the origin of R^l.

A net trade outcome function is $\tilde{h}: S \to \mathbb{R}^{ln}$ is *balanced* if for all $s \in S$,

$$\tilde{h}(s) = (\tilde{h}^1(s), \ldots, \tilde{h}^n(s)), \quad \tilde{h}^i(s) \in R^l \quad \text{for all } i = 1, \ldots, n,$$

and

$$\sum_{i=1}^{n} \tilde{h}^i(s) = 0_l \quad \text{for all } s \in S.$$

(Note that this requirement holds out of equilibrium as well as in equilibrium.) Equivalently, in terms of finally available goods rather than net trades, h is said to be *balanced* on E if

$$h(s) = (h^1(s), \ldots, h^n(s)), \quad h^i(s) \in \mathbb{R}^l \quad \text{for all } i = 1, \ldots, n,$$

and for all $e \in E$ and $s \in S$, we have

$$\sum_{i=1}^{n} h^i(s) = \sum_{i=1}^{n} \omega^i(e^i).$$

A net trade outcome function $\tilde{h}$ is balanced without being feasible on E if

$$\sum_{s=1}^{n} \tilde{h}^i(s) = 0_l \quad \text{for all } s \in S$$

but, for some $e \in E$, some $s \in S$, and some $i = 1, \ldots, n$, it is the case that

$$\tilde{h}^i(s) \notin \tilde{Z}^i(e^i).^\dagger$$

We then say that $\tilde{h}$ is not individually feasible out of equilibrium. (Analogous definitions hold for economies with public goods and economies with production.)

In the literature of Nash implementation, the issue of feasibility is treated in a variety of ways. The Groves-Ledyard mechanism for Pareto-optimal Nash implementation in a public goods economy is balanced but not necessarily individually feasible (out of equilibrium). The same is true of the Schmeidler [81], [82] implementation of the Walrasian performance correspondence W and the Hurwicz [32] implementation of both the Walras correspondence W and the Lindahl correspondence $L.^{\dagger\dagger}$ On the other hand Maskin [55] showed how to construct feasible outcome functions implementing a broad class of performance provided the feasible set Z^* is fixed (i.e., the same for all $e \in E$) and known to the designer.††† In Hurwicz, Maskin, and Postlewaite [35] it is shown how to construct mechanisms with feasible outcome functions even when $Z(e)$ varies over E and is not known to the designer. However, these mechanisms use large strategy spaces. If F is single-valued, and Z^* fixed and known to the designer, the strategy space of each agent i is

$$S^i = E^1 \times \cdots \times E^n, \quad i = 1, \ldots, n.$$

Thus all agents have the same strategy space, namely the class of all *a priori* admissible profiles. So, for every agent i, an element of his strategy space is of the form

$$s^i = (e^1, \ldots, e^n).$$

This construction has been generalized by Williams in [96]. (When the feasibility conditions are fixed, this is equivalent to $S^i = (R^1, \ldots, R^n)$, a preference profile.) When F is not single-valued,

---

† Equivalently, if $h^i(s) \notin Z^i(e^i)$.

†† In the originally circulated 1976 version of Hurwicz [32], there were also outcome functions implementing W(resp. L) which were neither balanced, nor individually feasible out of equilibrium, but these were omitted from the published version.

††† See also Williams [96].

each S^i is of the form

$$S^i = E^1 \times \cdots \times E^n \times Z^*$$

where Z^* is the fixed *a priori* known feasible set; here an element $s^i \in S^i$ is of the form

$$s^i = (e^1, \ldots, e^n, z),$$

where it is required that $z \in F(e)$.[†]

When the feasible set is variable and not *a priori* known, we have strategy spaces of the form

$$S^i = E^1 \times \cdots \times E^n \times Z^i(\omega^i)$$

and

$$e^i = (\omega^i, R^i, Z^i).$$

These are of course, unreasonably large strategy spaces, but they appear in "algorithms" specifying how to construct game forms for a variety of F's. On the other hand, for specific performance correspondences (Walras, Lindahl), there are game forms with much smaller spaces. This is true for the feasible implementation of W when the feasible set is *a priori* known and fixed (Postlewaite and Wettstein [72]), and for the balanced (but not individually feasible out of equilibrium) implementation of W and L (Schmeidler [81], [82], Hurwicz [32]).

However, even in the latter cases the strategy spaces are bigger than the minimal dimension message spaces found in the theory of realization (as distinct from implementation) of performance correspondences, i.e., when behavior incentives need not be taken into account but smoothness and informational decentralization (privacy-preserving) are required.

This raises the question whether, or to what extent, it is possible to achieve implementation with strategy spaces of lower size (dimension) than those used in the above game forms.

[†] In more recent versions, the requirement $z \in F(e)$ is dropped.

The Williams approach is to develop a procedure for converting the realization of a given F into a feasible implementation when the feasible outcome set is fixed and known. The Maskin type "algorithm" converts a direct revelation realization mechanism whose individual message space M^i is E^i (so the joint message space is $M = M^1 \times \cdots \times M^n = E$) into a game form whose individual strategy space is $S^i = E^1 \times \cdots \times E^n = M$. By a similar conversion of a realization mechanism with a smaller message space M, Williams shows how under certain conditions, one can obtain a Nash implementation with correspondingly smaller individual strategy spaces, again using $S^i = M$ for each $i = 1, \ldots, n$.

An earlier line of attack has been to consider special categories of performance correspondences, especially those that are Pareto-optimal, and most particularly the Walras and Lindahl correspondences (W and L).

The implementation problem for such correspondences has been studied primarily in terms of outcome functions that are smooth and balanced (out of equilibrium) but not necessarily individually feasible out of equilibrium. The question has been (1) whether such an implementation is at all possible, and, if so (2) what is the minimal dimension of the strategy space usable for implementation.

In Hurwicz [30], it was shown that, in a 2-good, 2-person economy, Nash implementation of a Pareto-optimal correspondence cannot be implemented over a sufficiently rich class of environments with a message space of less than three dimensions when the outcome function is balanced, smooth (C^1) and concave. (Similar methods yield the corresponding result for Lindahl correspondences.)

Recently, Reichelstein [74] showed that in a 2-agent 2-good pure exchange economy the Walrasian correspondence cannot be implemented by balanced smooth outcome functions. Subsequently, Hurwicz and Weinberger [43] have found that in a 2-agent pure exchange economy no Pareto-optimal correspondence can be implemented by a smooth strictly concave outcome function.

Note, however, that smoothness is essential to the above results. In Hurwicz [33], a balanced (but not individually feasible) *discontinuous* mechanism was constructed for two-agent economies which implement W with individual strategy spaces whose typical elements are of the form $s^i = (p_i, z_i)$ where p_i is a price vector and z_i a commodity bundle, $p_i, z_i, \in \mathbb{R}^{l-1}$, $i = 1, 2$. For known and fixed feasible sets, Nash implementation with similar strategy spaces has been constructed in [35] and in Postlewaite and Wettstein [72], continuously in [72] but not in [35].

By contrast, when there are three or more agents, there is no difficulty[†] in constructing *smooth* concave balanced outcome functions implementing the Walrasian or Lindahl correspondences (Hurwicz [32], for both W and L, Walker [93] for L).

For $n \geq 3$, Walker [93] implements the Lindahl correspondence in a two good economy with a one-dimensional strategy space. This is obviously minimal. (The Hurwicz [32] message space is bigger.) For the Walrasian correspondence, with $n \geq 3$, the matter is more complicated and not yet completely solved. The results so far available are due to Reichelstein [73]. On the one hand, he has constructed a game form that, for $n \geq 3$, and any l, with

$$S_j = \mathbb{R}^{l-1} \quad \text{for } 1 \leq j \leq n - 1$$

implements the Walrasian correspondence on a large class of economies.

Hence dim $S = (n - 1)(l - 1) + 2(l - 1) = (n + 1)(l - 1)$. On the other hand, for $l = 2$, $n \geq 3$, he has shown that, for a sufficiently rich family of environments, implementation is impossible with a message space of lower dimension than that of the above mentioned game; i.e., for $n \geq 3$, $l = 2$, it is necessary that dim $S \geq (n + 1)(l - 1)$.

It will be noted that this lower bound is higher than the (purely informational) realization which only requires that dim $M \geq n(l - 1)$, and where a version of the Walrasian mechanism attains this lower bound (Mount and Reiter [60], Osana [71], Hurwicz [31]).

The above mentioned Reichelstein game form may be interpreted as having agents act as auctioneers for one another, but in a manner more efficient (though less symmetrical) than in Hurwicz [32].

[†] Provided we do not insist on individual feasibility.

Explicitly, the Reichelstein game form is as follows: Denote an element of S^n by $(s_n, p) \in \mathbb{R}^{l-1} \times p^{l-1}$, and an element of S^j, $1 \le j \le n-1$, by $s_j \in \mathbb{R}^{l-1}$. (Note that s_n is not the whole strategy of agent n.) s_i, $1 \le i \le n$, can be interpreted as a net trade proposal by agent i. Let good l be the numéraire. Let $g_i^j(s) \in R$, where i refers to the agent and j to the good, and let $G_i(s) = (g_i^1(s), \ldots, g_i^{l-1}(s))$, $i = 1, \ldots, n$. For each $s \in S$, the real-valued function $T(s)$ in the formula below is defined so as to make $\sum_{i=1}^n g_i^l(s) = 0$.

For any non-numéraire good j and any agent i,

$$g_i^j(s) = s_i^j - \sum_{k \ne i} s_k^j / (n-1).$$

For the numéraire good the matter is slightly more complicated. The numéraire outcomes are defined by the following relations:

$$g_1^l(s) = -p \cdot G_1(s),$$

$$g_r^l(s) = -\frac{p + s_1}{2} G_r(s) + T(S)/(n-2), 2 \le r \le n-1,$$

$$g_n^l(s) = -s_1 \cdot G_n(s) - (p - s_1)^2.$$

As mentioned above, the strategy space of this game form is of minimal dimension for $l = 2$. For $l > 2$, research is currently in progress.

Acknowledgements

For stimulation, fruitful new ideas, and moral support in work on problems dealt with in this paper I am in debt to Stanley Reiter, Northwestern University, to an extent greater than can be expressed in a footnote. Section III of this paper draws heavily on our joint work with Don Saari and utilizes important suggestions and unpublished notes by Leonard Shapiro, North Dakota State University, and Steven Williams, Northwestern University. Section IV is largely based on joint work with Thomas Marschak, University of California, Berkeley. Comments by my Minnesota colleague James Jordan have also been extremely helpful.

REFERENCES

1. J. Aizpurua and A. Manresa, "Two notes on Hurwicz's topological lemma," Discussion Paper No. 199, February 1984, Economics Resource Center, University of Minnesota.

2. T. Apostol, *Mathematical Analysis*, Addison-Wesley, Reading, Massachusetts, 1957, pp. 255–258 and pp. 396–398.

3. K. J. Arrow, Private communication. (Final exam in a course at Harvard University, Spring 1977, question no. 2, pp. 1, 3–5.)

4. K. J. Arrow, H. D. Block, and L. Hurwicz, "On the stability of the competitive equilibrium II," *Econometrica*, January 1959.

5. K. J. Arrow and L. Hurwicz, "On the stability of the competitive equilibrium I," *Econometrica*, October 1958.

6. K. J. Arrow and L. Hurwicz, *Studies in Resource Allocation Processes*, Cambridge University Press, 1977.

7. K. J. Arrow and F. Hahn, *General Competitive Analysis*, Holden-Day, San Francisco, 1971.

8. Brouwer, "Über den natürlichen Dimensionsbergriff," *Journ. F. Math.* **142** (1913), 146–152.

9. X. Calsamiglia, "On the dimension of the message space under non-convexities," W.P.16.76, Universitat Autònoma de Barcelona, Spain, January, 1977.

10. ———, "Decentralized resource allocation and increasing returns," *Journal of Economic Theory* **14** (1977), 263–283.

11. ———, "Decentralized planning and increasing returns: a further comment," Universitat Autònoma de Barcelona, Spain, January, 1981.

12. ———, "On the size of the message space under non-convexities," Discussion paper No. 81-150, Center for Economic Research, University of Minnesota, June, 1981.

13. ———, "Informational requirements of parametric resource allocation processes," Discussion Paper No. 81-149, Center for Economic Research, University of Minnesota, June, 1981.

14. ———, "On the size of the message space under non-convexities," *Journal of Mathematical Economics* **10** (1982), 197–203.

15. A. Camacho, "Externalities, optimality and informationally decentralized resource allocation processes," *International Economic Review* **11**, no. 2, (June 1970), 318–327.

16. P. Chander, "Dimension of Euclidean message spaces," Mimeo, Indian Statistical Institute, New Delhi, India, December, 1980.

17. ——, "Dimensional requirements of efficient processes," Mimeo, Indian Statistical Institute, New Delhi, India, February, 1981.

18. ——, "On the informational size of message spaces for efficient resource allocation processes," Mimeo, Indian Statistical Institute, New Delhi, India, July, 1982.

19. ——, "On the informational efficiency of the competitive resource allocation process," Mimeo, Indian Statistical Institute, New Delhi, India, July, 1982.

20. ——, "On the informational size of message spaces for efficient resource allocation processes," *Econometrica* **51** (1983), 919–938.

21. J. Crémer, "A comment on 'Decentralized planning and increasing returns'," *Journal of Economic Theory* **19** (1978), 217–221.

22. G. Debreu, *Theory of Value*, Wiley, New York, 1959.

23. J. Dugundji, *Topology*, Allyn and Bacon, Boston, 1966.

24. C. Futia, "The complexity of economic decision rules," *Journal of Mathematical Economics* **4** (1977), 289–299.

25. M. Golubitsky and V. Guillemin, *Stable Mappings and Their Singularities*, Springer-Verlag, New York, 1973.

26. W. Hurewicz and H. Wallman, *Dimension Theory*, Princeton University Press, 1948.

27. L. Hurwicz, "Optimality and informational efficiency in resource allocation processes," *Mathematical Methods in the Social Sciences*, edited by Kenneth J. Arrow, Samuel Karlin, and Patrick Suppes, Stanford University Press, 1960; also in: K. J. Arrow and T. Scitovsky, eds., *Readings in Welfare Economics*, Irwin, 1969.

28. ——, "On the concept and possibility of informational decentralization," *American Economic Review* **59** (1969).

29. ——, "On informationally decentralized systems," in *Decision and Organization Volume in Honor of Jacob Marschak*, edited by B. McGuire and R. Radner, North-Holland, Amsterdam, 1972.

30. ——, "On informational requirements for non-wasteful resource allocation systems," *Mathematical Models in Economics: Papers and Proceedings of a U.S.-U.S.S.R. Seminar, Moscow, 1976*, NBER, New York, 1978; also in: *Issues in Contemporary Microeconomics and Welfare*, edited by G. Feiwel, MacMillan, London, 1985.

31. ——, "On the dimensional requirements of informationally decentralized Pareto satisfactory processes," in *Studies in Resource Allocation Processes*, edited by K. J. Arrow and L. Hurwicz, Cambridge University Press, 1977.

32. ——, "Outcome functions yielding Walrasian and Lindahl allocations at Nash equilibrium points," *Review of Economic Studies* **XLVI** (2), 1979.

33. ——, "Balanced outcome functions yielding Walrasian and Lindahl allocations at Nash equilibrium points for two or more agents," *General Equilibrium, Growth, and Trade*, edited by J. Green and J. Scheinkman, Academic Press, 1979.

34. ——, "On allocations attainable through Nash equilibria," *Journal of Economic Theory* **21**, No. 1, 1979; also in: *Aggregation and Revelation of Preferences*, Chapter 22, edited by J.-J. Laffont, North-Holland, 1979.

35. L. Hurwicz, E. Maskin, and H. Postlewaite, "Feasible implementation of social choice correspondences by Nash equilibria," presented at 1980 Aix-en-Provence World Econometric Congress and IMSSS 1979 summer symposium.

36. L. Hurwicz, and T. Marschak, "Discrete allocation mechanisms: dimensional requirements for resource allocation mechanisms when desired outcomes are unbounded," *Journal of Complexity* **1**, 1985, 264–303.

37. L. Hurwicz, and T. Marschak, "Discrete allocation mechanisms, Part I: designing informationally efficient mechanisms when desired outcomes are bounded," *Working Papers in Economic Theory and Econometrics*, IP-322, Center for Research in Management Science, Institute of Business and Economic Research, University of California, Berkeley, May 1984.

38. L. Hurwicz, R. Radner, and S. Reiter, "A stochastic decentralized resource allocation process," *Econometrica* **43** (1975); Part I published in No. 2, March 1975; Part II published in No. 3, May 1975.

39. L. Hurwicz, R. Reiter, and D. Saari, "On constructing mechanisms with message spaces of minimal dimension for smooth performance functions," Mimeo, 1978.

40. L. Hurwicz, S. Reiter, and D. Saari, "On constructing an informationally decentralized process implementing a given performance function," presented at 1980 Aix-en-Provence, World Econometric Congress.

41. L. Hurwicz, S. Reiter, and D. Saari, "An explicit analysis of the case where each of the two agents has three parameters ($n = 2$, $k_1 = k_2 = 3$)," mimeo, 1980.

42. L. Hurwicz and W. Thomson, "Iterative planning procedures with a finite memory," Mimeo, May 1983, to appear in *International Journal of Development Planning*.

43. L. Hurwicz and H. Weinberger, "On smooth balanced Nash mechanisms which implement Pareto-optimal performance correspondence in pure exchange economies with two agents," Mimeo, University of Minnesota, 1984.

44. J. S. Jordan, "The competitive allocation process is informationally efficient uniquely," Discussion Paper No. 79–108, Center for Economic Research, University of Minnesota, February, 1979.

45. ——, "The competitive allocation process is informationally efficient uniquely," *Journal of Economic Theory* **28** (1982), 1–18.

46. ——, "The informational requirements of local stability in decentralized allocation mechanisms," Unpublished, University of Minnesota, May, 1982.

47. ——, "Instability in the implementation of Walrasian allocations," Institute for Mathematics and Its Applications, preprint # 91, University of Minnesota, August 1984.

48. H. Kanemitsu, "On the stability of the (metric) inertia greed process," Unpublished, Sophia University, Japan, June, 1970.

49. ——, "A stable non-tâtonnement adjustment process with production and consumption," Unpublished, Sophia University, Japan, October, 1976.

50. A. Kats and S. Slutsky "On partially continuous correspondences," *Journal of Economic Theory* **15** (1977), 376–380.

51. J. L. Kelley and I. Namioka (et al.), *Linear Topological Spaces*, Van Nostrand, Princeton, 1963, pp. 58–65.

52. T. C. Koopmans, *Three Essays on the State of Economic Science*, McGraw-Hill, New York, 1957.

53. H.B. Lawson, Jr., "Foliations," *Bulletin of the American Mathematical Society* **80**, no. 3 (May 1974), pp. 369–418.

54. D. Maleug, "The role of information in economics and in the economy," Conference notes taken by David Maleug, Unpublished, Northwestern University, Illinois, November, 1980.

55. E. Maskin, "Nash equilibrium and welfare optimality, Preliminary Version," Mimeo M.I.T., Cambridge, 1977.

56. C. B. McGuire and R. Radner (eds.), *Decision and Organization, A Volume in Honor of Jacob Marschak*, North Holland, Amsterdam, 1972, pp. 306–321.

57. T. Mitsui, "A stochastic adjustment process for non-convex and indecomposable environments," Mimeo, University of Minnesota, Minneapolis, 1981.

58. K. Mount and S. Reiter, "The informational size of message spaces," Discussion Paper No. 3, Center for Mathematical Studies in Economics and Management Science, Northwestern University, Illinois, June, 1972.

59. ———, "On the definition of informational size," Mimeo, December 1974.

60. ———, "The informational size of message spaces," *Journal of Economic Theory* **8** (1974), 161–192.

61. ———, "Economic environments for which there are Pareto satisfactory mechanisms," *Econometrica* **45** (1977), 821–842.

62. ———, "On the existence of a locally stable dynamic process with a statically minimal message space," Discussion Paper No. 550, Center for Mathematical Studies in Economics and Management Science, Northwestern University, Illinois, February, 1983.

63. ———, "Computational complexity of resource allocation mechanisms," mimeo, May 1983.

64. J. Munkres, *Topology, A First Course*, Prentice-Hall, Englewood Cliffs, New Jersey, 1975.

65. J. Nayak, "Imbedding requirements in the topologising of preferences," Research Paper No. 19, Churchill College, University of Cambridge, 1982.

66. ———, "The informational efficiency of the Walras process in pure exchange economies," Research Paper No. 20, Churchill College, University of Cambridge, 1982.

67. ———, "The informational efficiency of the Walras process in economies with production," Research Paper No. 21, Churchill College, University of Cambridge, 1982.

68. ———, "An informationally efficient process for economies with production non-convexities," Research Paper No. 22, Churchill College, University of Cambridge, 1982.

69. ———, "The informational efficiency of the Lindahl process in economies with public goods," Research Paper No. 23, Churchill College, University of Cambridge, 1982.

70. ———, "Informationally efficient processes for economies with externalities," Research Paper No. 24, Churchill College, University of Cambridge, 1982.

71. H. Osana, "On the informational size of message spaces for resource allocation processes," *Journal of Economic Theory* **17** (1978), 66–78.

72. A. Postlewaite, and D. Wettstein, "Implementing constrained Walrasian equilibria continuously," CARESS Working Paper # 83–24, August 1982, revised October 1983.

73. S. Reichelstein, "On the informational requirements for the implementation of social choice rules," Handout for the Decentralization Conference, Minneapolis, May 1982.

74. ———, "Smooth versus discontinuous mechanisms," *Economic Letters* **16** (1984), 239–242.

75. S. Reiter, "The knowledge revealed by an allocation process and the informational size of the message space," *Journal of Economic Theory* **8** (1974), 389–396.

76. ———, "Informational efficiency of iterative processes and the size of message spaces," *Journal of Economic Theory* **8** (1974), 193–205.

77. ———, "There is no adjustment process with two-dimensional message spaces for 'counter examples'," Mimeo, Northwestern University, Illinois, December, 1979.

78. M. K. Richter, "Informational efficiency and decentralization," Unpublished, University of Minnesota, 1980.

79. D. G. Saari, and C. P. Simon, "Effective price mechanisms, " *Econometrica* **46** (1978), 1097–1125.

80. F. Sato, "On the informational size of message spaces for resource allocation processes in economies with public goods," *Journal of Economic Theory* **24** (1981), 48–69.

81. D. Schmeidler, "A Remark on a Game Theoretic Interpretation of Walras Equilibria," mimeo, Minneapolis, University of Minnesota, 1976.

82. ———, "Walrasian analysis via strategic outcome functions," *Econometrica* **48** (1980), 1585–1594.

83. W. Sierpinski, *Cardinal and Ordinal Numbers*, Monografie Matematyczne, Vol. 34, Warsaw, 1958, pp. 66–69.

84. G. Simmons, "Continuous curves and the Hahn-Mazurkiewicz theorem," *Introduction to Topology and Modern Analysis*, McGraw-Hill, New York, 1963, pp. 341–343.

85. S. Smale, "A convergent process of price adjustment and global Newton methods," *Journal of Mathematical Economics* **3** (1976), 107–120.

86. M. Spivak, *A Comprehensive Introduction to Differential Geometry*, Vol. 1, Second Edition, Publish or Perish, Inc., Berkeley, 1979.

87. J. F. Traub and H. Woźniakowski, "Optimal linear information for the solution of non-linear operator equations," in *Algorithms and Complexity*, J.F. Traub, ed., 1976.

88. J. F. Traub, G. W. Wasilkowski, and H. Woźniakowski, *Information, Uncertainty, Complexity*, Addison-Wesley Publishing, Reading, Mass., 1983.
89. J. F. Traub and H. Woźniakowski, "Information and computation," in *Advances in Computers*, Vol. 23, edited by M. Yovits, Academic Press, 1984.
90. M. Walker, "On the informational size of message spaces," Working Paper No. 149, State University of New York, November, 1975.
91. ———, "On the informational size of message spaces," Unpublished, State University of New York, August, 1976.
92. ———, "On the informational size of message spaces," *Journal of Economic Theory* **15** (1977), 366–375.
93. ———, "A simple incentive compatible scheme for attaining Lindahl allocations," *Econometrica* **49** (1981), 65–71.
94. F. W. Warner, *Foundations of Differentiable Manifolds and Lie Groups*, Scott-Foresman and Co., Glenview, IL, 1971.
95. S. Williams, "Manipulating a message process to achieve stability," Mimeo, University of Minnesota, August 1983.
96. ———, "Realization and Nash implementation: two aspects of mechanism design," Institute for Mathematics and its Applications preprint # 69, University of Minnesota, May 1984.
97. ———, "Implementing a generic smooth function," Institute for Mathematics and its Applications preprint # 89, University of Minnesota, July 1984. (To appear in the *Journal of Mathematical Economics*.)
98. ———, "Necessary and sufficient conditions for existence of a locally stable process," Institute for Mathematics and its Applications preprint # 88, University of Minnesota, July 1984.

BEHAVIORAL MODELS OF STOCHASTIC CONTROL

Roy Radner

1. INTRODUCTION*

A manager in charge of several activities typically faces a problem of how to allocate his limited time and effort to their supervision and control. Given sufficient effort, a supervised activity tends to improve, whereas a neglected activity tends to deteriorate. Both of these tendencies are subject to stochastic disturbances, however, so that the results of managerial effort (or lack of it) cannot be predicted with certainty. A *behavior* of the manager is a rule that determines his allocation of effort among the activities at each date, as a function of the past history of his actions and the activities' performance.

Economists have generally used one of two theoretical approaches to explain a manager's behavior in such a situation. The

*This chapter is based on research supported in part by the National Science Foundation, and was written while the author was Taussig Professor of Economics at Harvard University. The subject matter of the chapter is based largely on Radner, [12], and Radner and Rothschild, [14]. The proofs have been entirely revised, however, to conform to the purpose of this volume.

first, and probably most common, is to describe or postulate the manager's preference ordering over all possible sequences of outcomes of the process, and to predict that the manager chooses an *optimal* behavior that maximizes his preference, or its expectation. A difficulty with this approach is that the resulting optimization problem may be extremely complex and difficult, indeed, so difficult that economic theorists themselves may be unable to solve it! In addition, it may be difficult to discover the manager's preferences, or the manager's behavior may reflect competing organizational goals that have not been resolved into a single overall preference ordering. Under these circumstances, the prediction of optimal behavior becomes impossible.

A second approach is to postulate commonly observed or plausible behaviors, and derive their properties. This is in the spirit of what Herbert Simon has called "bounded rationality," * and is the approach that will be exemplified in this chapter. The particular behaviors that will be examined here can also be viewed as simple servomechanisms such as are studied in the engineering/operations research theories of stochastic control.

In the first part of this chapter, we shall look at a model of how a manager might allocate effort to a single activity, without explicit regard to the performance of other activities. In this model, the manager's behavior is formally analogous to the operation of a thermostat. The manager devotes his effort to the activity until its performance reaches a prescribed level (the "upper setting" of the thermostat), and then turns his attention to other things until the performance of the activity first falls to or below a second prescribed level (the "lower setting"). At that time the manager again devotes his effort to improving the performance of the activity, etc. The upper prescribed setting may be interpreted as a level of "satisfactory" performance. (For this reason, such behavior is sometimes called *satisficing*.) The gap between the two settings is the magnitude of the decline below satisfactory performance that will trigger the manager's renewed effort to correct the "unsatisfactory" situation. Since the changes in performance are stochastic,

---

*See Simon, [17], and Chapter 8 of McGuire and Radner, [7].

there is no a priori guarantee that the thermostat process has any stability properties; indeed, there is no a priori guarantee that during an effort phase the level of performance will eventually reach the satisfactory level. Nevertheless, we shall give conditions under which the thermostat behavior of the manager, together with the performance of the activity, form an ergodic Markov chain, and we shall give an explicit formula for the long-run frequency of effort. In the special case in which performance can change by at most one unit per time period, we shall be able to give a more detailed account of the properties of the thermostat behavior, including the long-run average level of performance.

When we consider the behavior of the manager in allocating his effort among several activities, we must recognize that, if his total effort is limited (the usual case!), then the opportunity cost of an effort towards improving one activity is the neglect of others. A common managerial behavior is to devote effort only to those activities that are giving the most trouble, i.e. (with a suitable origin and scale for measuring the performance of each activity), to those activities that have the lowest level of performance at that date. We call this "putting out fires." This behavior has a number of remarkable asymptotic properties, which we derive in Section 6 (in the special case of two activities). In particular, the difference between the best and the worst activities is ergodic, and the long-run average rates of change of performance are the same for the two activities. A simple criterion can be given to determine whether this rate is positive or negative, and an equally simple formula can be given for the long-run allocation of effort between the two activities.

Putting out fires is related to the thermostat in the following way. If the manager is putting out fires, but we observe only his allocation of effort to a single activity, then it will appear as if he is using a thermostat with variable settings. Put another way, it will appear that what is a "satisfactory" level of performance for one activity changes over time; in fact, those satisfactory levels will be determined by the current levels of performance of the other activity (or activities).

Putting out fires has another property, which is important for a theory of bounded rationality: *the manager need have no knowledge of the parameters of the probability distributions of the relevant random variables in order to implement the behavior!* Nevertheless, the resulting performance has many "desirable" properties.

Models like the ones described in this chapter are just beginning to find their way into the economic theory literature. A probability model equivalent to putting-out-fires behavior has been used to develop a theory of cost-reducing innovations (Radner, [13]). Satisficing plays an important role in the models of stochastic equilibrium of Winter, [20], Nelson and Winter, [8], and Nelson, Winter, and Schuette, [9]. Stochastic search for improvement is a key element of a decentralized resource allocation process that converges to Pareto optimal allocations in the presence of non-convexities, as described in Hurwicz, Radner, and Reiter, [5]. Related stochastic adjustment processes for reaching the core of a game have been analyzed by Green [4] and Neuefeind [10].

Note on Mathematical Background. The probability theory needed for this chapter can all be found in Feller [2]. This includes an introductory knowledge of Markov chains with a countable state space. In particular, a measure-theoretic treatment of probability is not needed. The basic probabilistic material used concerns the first passage problem for sums of independent, identically distributed, integer-valued, bounded random variables. The required results are derived in Section 3. In addition, a special case of the ergodic theorem for Markov chains is needed in the second half of the chapter; this is derived in an appendix.

2. A CONSERVATIVE THERMOSTAT

Our first, and simplest, model describes the behavior of a manager who is supervising an activity during successive time periods, and who decides at the beginning of each period whether or not to allocate effort during the coming period to improving the operation of the activity. Let $U(t)$ denote a measure of performance of the activity during period t ($t = 0, 1, \ldots$). Suppose that the successive levels of performance are stochastic, so that the $U(t)$ are random variables. During a period in which the manager makes an effort to improve the activity, performance can be expected to increase, at least on the average, whereas during a period in which the manager makes no such effort, performance can be expected to decrease. We shall model this situation as follows. Let $\{X(t)\}$ and $\{Y(t)\}$ each be a sequence of independent and identically distributed random variables, with the two sequences mutually independent. Let the mean of $X(t)$ be negative and the mean of $Y(t)$ be positive, i.e.,

$$
\begin{aligned}
\mathscr{E}X(t) &= \xi < 0, \\
\mathscr{E}Y(t) &= \eta > 0.
\end{aligned}
\tag{1}
$$

If an improvement effort is made in period t, then the *increment* in performance is $Y(t)$, whereas if no such effort is made, the increment in performance is $X(t)$. Formally, let $a(t)$ denote the manager's allocation of improvement effort during period t, with $a(t) = 1$ denoting an effort, and $a(t) = 0$ denoting no effort. Then

$$
Z(t) \equiv U(t) - U(t-1) = a(t)Y(t) + \left[1 - a(t)\right]X(t). \tag{2}
$$

(Although in the present model $a(t)$ can take on only the values 0 or 1, the form of equation (2) suggests a more general model in which fractional allocations of effort would be possible; see Section 6 below.) We shall call $a(t)$ the manager's *action* at date t.

A *behavior* is a sequence of functions, A_t, that determine the manager's actions on the basis of past performance levels. Thus A_t is a function of $U(0), \ldots, U(t-1)$, and takes the values 0 or 1, and

$$
a(t) = A_t[U(0), \ldots, U(t-1)], \qquad t = 1, 2, \ldots \tag{3}
$$

We shall start by examining a very simple behavior, which is similar to that of a thermostat with fixed upper and lower settings, say α and β, respectively. If the initial performance level, $U(0)$, is less than α, then the manager makes an improvement effort until the first time that performance reaches or goes above α. At that time the manager ceases effort until the performance drops to or below β. The manager then renews his improvement effort until performance again reaches or goes above α, etc. If the initial performance level is at least α, then the manager starts with no effort, and proceeds as above. We shall call this the *conservative thermostat* behavior, with settings α and β ($\alpha > \beta$). Formally,

$$a(1) = \begin{Bmatrix} 0 \\ 1 \end{Bmatrix} \quad \text{according as} \quad U(0)\begin{Bmatrix} \geqq \\ < \end{Bmatrix}\alpha; \quad \text{for } t > 1,$$

$$\text{if} \quad a(t-1) = 0, \quad \text{then } a(t) = \begin{Bmatrix} 0 \\ 1 \end{Bmatrix} \quad \text{as} \quad U(t-1)\begin{Bmatrix} > \\ \leqq \end{Bmatrix}\beta,$$

$$\text{if} \quad a(t-1) = 1, \quad \text{then } a(t) = \begin{Bmatrix} 0 \\ 1 \end{Bmatrix} \quad \text{as} \quad U(t-1)\begin{Bmatrix} \geqq \\ < \end{Bmatrix}\alpha. \tag{4}$$

Given the manager's behavior, and the distributions of the random variables $X(t)$ and $Y(t)$, we shall be interested in the long-run properties of the sequence $\{U(t)\}$ of performance levels and the sequence $\{a(t)\}$ of actions. It is intuitively plausible that the performance levels would fluctuate indefinitely, spending most of the time "near" the interval $[\beta, \alpha]$. In this case, we would be interested in the long-run average level of performance, and the long-run relative frequency of periods in which an improvement effort is made. In order to proceed with a mathematical analysis, we shall of course have to make these notions more precise. In addition, certain prior questions will have to be answered. For example, if the process is in an "effort phase," with performance less than the upper setting α, is it sure that performance will eventually reach or exceed α? If so, is the expected time to reach α finite or infinite? How low can performance sink before reaching α? (Analogous questions arise for the "no effort" phase.)

In order to simplify the analysis, we shall make three additional assumptions about the random variables $X(t)$ and $Y(t)$: (1) they are integer-valued, (2) they are bounded, and (3) they take the values -1, 0, and $+1$ with positive probability. The last of these three will be called the *continuity* assumption. These three assumptions are essentially technical, in the sense that a more general treatment is possible, but would require more advanced mathematical methods. (For references, see the last section of this chapter.) Since these three properties are satisfied by both sequences $X(t)$ and $Y(t)$, they are also satisfied by the sequence $Z(t)$.

As an example, consider the case in which the random variables $X(t)$ and $Y(t)$ can take *only* the values -1, 0, and $+1$, with

$$\text{Prob}\{ X(t) = +1 \} = p_0, \qquad \text{Prob}\{ Y(t) = +1 \} = p_1,$$
$$\text{Prob}\{ X(t) = 0 \} = q_0, \qquad \text{Prob}\{ Y(t) = 0 \} = q_1, \qquad (5)$$
$$\text{Prob}\{ X(t) = -1 \} = r_0, \qquad \text{Prob}\{ Y(t) = -1 \} = r_1,$$
$$p_0 + q_0 + r_0 = p_1 + q_1 + r_1 = 1,$$

and all six probabilities are positive.

In this case, performance can change by at most one unit in any one time period, whether or not there is any improvement effort, and we have

$$\xi = \mathscr{E}X(t) = p_0 - r_0 < 0,$$
$$\eta = \mathscr{E}Y(t) = p_1 - r_1 > 0. \qquad (6)$$

For future reference, this special case will be called the *one-step example*.

To begin our analysis of the properties of the conservative thermostat, we first note that the sequence of pairs $[a(t), U(t)]$ is a Markov chain. The state space of this chain is the set of all pairs (a, u) in which a is 0 or 1 and u is an integer (positive, negative, or zero). Thus the state space is countably infinite. The transition probabilities are determined by condition (4), and if we make the convention that $a(0) = 1$, then the transition probabilities are stationary, i.e., independent of t. Because of the continuity assumption, every state can be reached from every other state (directly or indirectly), and so the Markov chain is irreducible. Furthermore, the continuity assumption also implies that every state is aperiodic. In an irreducible chain, all states are of the same type (Feller, [2], Chapter XV, Section 6), so that only three possibilities remain:

(i) all states are transient,
(ii) all states are null persistent,
(iii) all states are ergodic.*

---

*The terminology used here is that of Feller, [2], Chapter XV. Some authors use the term *recurrent* in place of *persistent*.

An irreducible chain whose states are ergodic is called an *ergodic chain*. We shall show that, in fact, the *conservative thermostat is ergodic*.

We shall use the following notation from Feller [2]. For two states j and k, let $f_{jk}^{(t)}$ denote the probability that, given that the chain starts in state j, the first (subsequent) entry into state k occurs at date t. Furthermore, define

$$f_{jk} \equiv \sum_{t=1}^{\infty} f_{jk}^{(t)},$$
$$\mu_j \equiv \sum_{t=1}^{\infty} t f_{jj}^{(t)}. \tag{7}$$

The number f_{jk} is the probability that, starting from state j, the chain will ever (subsequently) be in state k (at some date $t > 0$); recall that a state j is called *persistent* if $f_{jj} = 1$, and *transient* if $f_{jj} < 1$. For a persistent state j, the number μ_j is called the *mean recurrence time*; recall that a persistent state is called *null* if its mean recurrence time is infinite, and an aperiodic persistent state is called *ergodic* if its mean recurrence time is finite.

Since all of the states of our irreducible aperiodic chain are of the same type, to show that the chain is ergodic it suffices to show that a single state is ergodic, say the state $(1, \alpha)$. In other words, we want to show that, if the level performance is at the upper setting of the thermostat (α), and the manager has just been making an improvement effort, then the expected number of periods until the same situation arises again is finite.

Suppose then that the chain starts in state $(1, \alpha)$. In the next period there will be no improvement effort, and there will be no further improvement effort until the performance level reaches or falls below β. If and when this happens, there will then be an improvement effort until the performance level first reaches or exceeds α. Call this date the *first return to rest*, and denote it by R_1. Recall that the increments $Z(t)$ in performance are bounded, say by b, so that

$$|Z(t)| \le b, \qquad \text{with probability one.} \tag{8}$$

Therefore, at the first return to rest,

$$\alpha \leqq U(R_1) \leqq \alpha + b - 1. \tag{9}$$

Let $\mathcal{R}$ denote the set of states (a, u) such that $a = 1$ and $\alpha \leqq u \leqq \alpha + b - 1$; note that $\mathcal{R}$ is finite. What we have just shown is that at the first return to rest the state of the chain must be in $\mathcal{R}$, which of course contains the state $(1, \alpha)$.

We can now organize the proof that the state $(1, \alpha)$ is ergodic into two parts. Let us say that the set $\mathcal{R}$ is *positive recurrent* if, starting from any state in $\mathcal{R}$, with probability one the chain will eventually return to $\mathcal{R}$, and the expected time to return is finite. Suppose that we can show that the set $\mathcal{R}$ is positive recurrent, and let R_1, R_2, etc. be the successive dates at which the chain returns* to $\mathcal{R}$. At the dates $(R_n - 1)$ the chain must be in the (finite) set $\mathcal{R}'$ of states (a, u) such that $\alpha - b \leqq u < \alpha$. Hence if the set $\mathcal{R}$ is positive recurrent, then starting from any state in $\mathcal{R}$ the expected time to visit the set $\mathcal{R}'$ is finite. By the continuity assumption, starting from any state in $\mathcal{R}'$ there is a positive probability that the next return to $\mathcal{R}$ will be in the state $(1, \alpha)$; let p denote the minimum of these probabilities ($p > 0$ because $\mathcal{R}'$ is finite). Hence for each return to $\mathcal{R}$ the probability is at least p that the return will be in state $(1, \alpha)$. Therefore, the probability that the first return to the state $(1, \alpha)$ occurs on or before the date R_n is at least $1 - (1 - p)^n$, which tends to one as n increases without limit. It follows that, starting from any state in $\mathcal{R}$, the probability is one that the chain will eventually return to the state $(1, \alpha)$. In particular, the state $(1, \alpha)$ is persistent.

To show that the state $(1, \alpha)$ is ergodic, we need to show in addition that the expected time to return to it is finite. (We maintain our supposition that the set $\mathcal{R}$ is positive recurrent, a fact that we shall prove below.) Starting from state $(1, \alpha)$, let the first

---

*Note that if the chain is in $\mathcal{R}$ at date t, then it cannot be in $\mathcal{R}$ at date $t - 1$ or at date $t + 1$.

return to $(1, \alpha)$ occur at date R_N. We want to show that $\mathscr{E}R_N$ is finite. We can express $\mathscr{E}R_N$ as

$$\mathscr{E}R_N = \sum_{N=1}^{\infty} \mathscr{E}(R_n|N=n)\operatorname{Prob}(N=n). \quad (10)$$

For any states j and k in $\mathscr{R}$ define:

p_{jk} = the probability that, *starting* from j, the first return to $\mathscr{R}$ is in k;

m_j = the expected time to return to $\mathscr{R}$, starting from j;

m_{jk} = the conditional expected time to return to $\mathscr{R}$ from j, given that the first return to $\mathscr{R}$ is in k.

Then

$$m_j = \sum_{k \in \mathscr{R}} p_{jk} m_{jk}. \quad (11)$$

Since m_j is finite ($\mathscr{R}$ is positive recurrent), m_{jk} is finite for every k for which $p_{jk} > 0$. Define

$$m = \max\{m_{jk}: j, k \text{ in } \mathscr{R}, p_{jk} > 0\}; \quad (12)$$

then m is also finite, and

$$\mathscr{E}(R_N|N=n) \leq nm. \quad (13)$$

Therefore, combining (10) and (13),

$$\begin{aligned}
\mathscr{E}(R_N) &\leq m \sum_{n=1}^{\infty} n\operatorname{Prob}(N=n) \\
&= m \sum_{n=1}^{\infty} \operatorname{Prob}(N \geq n) \\
&\leq m \sum_{n=1}^{\infty} (1-p)^{n-1} \\
&= m\frac{1}{p} < \infty.
\end{aligned}$$

Thus we have completed the proof that, if $\mathscr{R}$ is positive recurrent, then the state $(1, \alpha)$ is ergodic, and therefore the conservative thermostat is ergodic.

We shall now see that the proof that $\mathscr{R}$ is positive recurrent can be reduced to a basic problem in probability theory, called the *first-passage problem* for sums of independent, identically distributed random variables. Let $\mathscr{S}$ denote the set of states (a, u) such that $a = 0$ and $\beta - b + 1 \leq u \leq \beta$. If the chain is in the set $\mathscr{R}$ at date t_0, then before it can return to $\mathscr{R}$ it must visit the set $\mathscr{S}$. The first visit to $\mathscr{S}$ after t_0 will occur at the first date $(t_0 + n)$ such that

$$X(t_0 + 1) + \cdots + X(t_0 + n) \leq \beta - U(t_0). \tag{14}$$

Call this date t_1. Similarly, the first return to the set $\mathscr{R}$ after t_0 will occur at the first date $(t_1 + n)$ such that

$$Y(t_1 + 1) + \cdots + Y(t_1 - n) \geq \alpha - U(t_1). \tag{15}$$

Call this date t_2. The set $\mathscr{R}$ will be positive recurrent if and only if the random variables $(t_1 - t_0)$ and $(t_2 - t_1)$ have finite expectations.

Thus we are led to study the following problem. Let $V(1)$, $V(2), \ldots$ be an infinite sequence of independent identically distributed random variables that are integer-valued and bounded, such that $\mathscr{E}V(t) \equiv V > 0$. Define the partial sums $S(t)$ by

$$S(t) = V(1) + \cdots + V(t). \tag{16}$$

For any positive integer c, define T_c by

$$T_c = \min\{t : S(t) \geq c\}, \tag{17}$$

with the understanding that T_c may be infinite. The "random variable" T_c is called the *first-passage time through c*. We want to show that the first-passage times have finite expectations. We shall study the first-passage time problem in the next section.

3. THE FIRST-PASSAGE PROBLEM

Recall that the first-passage problem concerns the behavior of the partial sums of a sequence $\{V(t)\}$ of independent identically distributed random variables, which we assume to be integer-valued and bounded. The *partial sums* are

$$S(t) \equiv V(1) + \cdots + V(t), \qquad (1)$$

and for any positive integer c the corresponding *first-passage time* is

$$T_c \equiv \min\{t: S(t) \geq c\}, \qquad (2)$$

where it is understood that T_c may be infinite. The event $\{T_c = n\}$ is equivalent to the event

$$\begin{cases} S(t) < c, & t = 1, \ldots, n - 1, \\ S(n) \geq c, \end{cases} \qquad (3)$$

and thus depends on the random variables $V(1), \ldots, V(n)$. For the purposes of this section, denote the probability of the event (3) by $\varphi_c(n)$, i.e.,

$$\varphi_c(n) = \text{Prob}\{T_c = n\}. \qquad (4)$$

For every N,

$$\varphi_c(1) + \cdots + \varphi_c(N) \leq 1; \qquad (5)$$

hence

$$\sum_{n=1}^{\infty} \varphi_c(n) \leq 1. \qquad (6)$$

The sum in (6) is the probability that T_c is finite, and

$$1 - \sum_{n=1}^{\infty} \varphi_c(n) \qquad (7)$$

is the probability that T_c is infinite, i.e., that $S(t) < c$ for all t. Note that the event "T is finite" depends on the entire sequence $\{V(t)\}$. In effect, we have *defined* the probability of this event as the limit of the sums in (5) as N increases without limit. Each sum (5) is the probability that T_c does not exceed N, which depends only on the first N variables $V(t)$. In this way, we avoid a general measure-theoretic treatment. See Feller, [2], Chapter VIII, Section 1.

If the probability that T_c is finite is 1, then we define its expectation, the *mean first-passage time*, by

$$\mathscr{E}T_c = \sum_{n=1}^{\infty} n\varphi_c(n), \tag{8}$$

which may be infinite.*

Our proof of the ergodicity of the conservative thermostat was based on the following important theorem about first-passage times, which we shall also need in subsequent sections of this chapter.

THEOREM. *If $\mathscr{E}V(t) \equiv v > 0$, then*

$$\mathrm{Prob}(T_c < \infty) = 1, \tag{9a}$$

and

$$\mathscr{E}T_c < \infty. \tag{9b}$$

Proof. Our proof of (9a) is based on the Strong Law of Large Numbers,** which states that

$$\lim_{t \to \infty} \frac{S(t)}{t} = v, \tag{10}$$

---

*Note that the terms in the infinite series (8) are all nonnegative, so the series either converges or diverges to plus infinity.

**See Feller, [2], Chapter X, Section 7.

with probability one. This means that, for every positive number h there is a random variable $\tilde{T}_h$ (which is finite with probability one) such that

$$\left| \frac{S(t)}{t} - v \right| \leq h \qquad \text{for } t \geq \tilde{T}_h. \tag{11}$$

In particular, take $h = v/2$; then (11) implies that

$$S(t) \geq \frac{tv}{2} \qquad \text{for } t \geq \tilde{T}_{v/2}. \tag{12}$$

Define $\tilde{T}$ to be the smallest integer that is greater than or equal to both $\tilde{T}_{v/2}$ and $2c/v$; then

$$S(t) \geq c \qquad \text{for } t \geq \tilde{T}. \tag{13}$$

Since $\tilde{T}$ is finite with probability one, we have proved (9a).

To prove (9b), consider the random variable $S(T_c)$, which is the partial sum of the random variables $V(t)$ just at the first-passage time. (Since T_c is finite, with probability 1, the random variable $S(T_c)$ is well defined.) If b is the bound on $V(t)$, then

$$c \leq S(T_c) \leq c + b - 1; \tag{14}$$

hence the expectation of $S(T_c)$ is finite. Define the "indicator variables" $I(t)$ by

$$I(t) = \begin{Bmatrix} 1 \\ 0 \end{Bmatrix} \quad \text{according as} \quad T_c \begin{Bmatrix} > \\ \leq \end{Bmatrix} t; \tag{15}$$

then

$$S(T_c) = \sum_{t=1}^{\infty} V(t) I(t-1)$$

$$\mathscr{E}S(T_c) = \mathscr{E}\left[\sum_{t=1}^{\infty} V(t) I(t-1) \right] \tag{16}$$

$$= \sum_{t=1}^{\infty} \mathscr{E}\left[V(t) I(t-1) \right].$$

(The interchange of the expectation and summation operations in (16) will be justified below.*) Consider a single term in the second line of (16). By the formula for iteration of expectation,**

$$
\begin{aligned}
\mathscr{E}[V(t)I(t-1)] \\
= \mathscr{E}[V(t)I(t-1)|I(t-1) = 1]\text{Prob}[I(t-1) = 1] \\
+ \mathscr{E}[V(t)I(t-1)|I(t-1) = 0]\text{Prob}[I(t-1) = 0] \\
= \mathscr{E}[V(t)|I(t-1) = 1]\text{Prob}[I(t-1) = 1].
\end{aligned}
$$

But the event "$I(t-1) = 1$" depends only on the random variables $V(1), \ldots, V(t-1)$, which are independent of $V(t)$. Hence

$$
\begin{aligned}
\mathscr{E}[V(t)|I(t-1) = 1] &= \mathscr{E}V(t) = v, \\
\mathscr{E}[V(t)I(t-1)] &= v\text{Prob}[I(t-1) = 1] \\
&= v\text{Prob}[T_c > t-1] \\
&= v\text{Prob}[T_c \geqq t],
\end{aligned}
$$

so that, by (16)

$$
\mathscr{E}S(T_c) = v \sum_{t=1}^{\infty} \text{Prob}(T_c \geqq t).
$$

Using the identity***

$$
\mathscr{E}T_c = \sum_{t=1}^{\infty} \text{Prob}(T_c \geqq t),
$$

we finally have

$$
\mathscr{E}S(T_c) = v\mathscr{E}T_c, \tag{17}
$$

---

*See Appendix 2.

**Feller, [2], Chapter IX, equation (2.9).

***For integer-valued random variables. This can be proved directly, or see Feller, [2], Chapter XI, Theorem 2.

or, since $v > 0$,

$$\mathscr{E}T_c = \frac{\mathscr{E}S(T_c)}{v}, \tag{18}$$

which completes the proof of (9b).

Equations (18) and (14) give us bounds on the mean first-passage time,

$$\frac{c}{v} \leqq \mathscr{E}T_c \leqq \frac{c + b - 1}{v}. \tag{19}$$

If the random variables $V(t)$ take on only the values -1, 0, and $+1$, then $b = 1$, and (19) gives us the exact expression $\mathscr{E}T_c = c/v$. This special case is, of course, the one that arises in the "one-step example" of the previous section.

In the analysis of the conservative thermostat, we would like to be able to calculate the long-run average level of performance. Since the thermostat alternates between "effort phases" $(a(t) = 1)$ and "rest phases" $(a(t) = 0)$, the long-run average performance should be a weighted average of the average performance in the two phases. This leads to the following question: In the first-passage time problem, what is the expected value of the sum of the partial sums $S(t)$ up to the time of first passage? In other words, we want to calculate the expected value of the sum

$$\tilde{S} \equiv S(1) + \cdots + S(T_c - 1). \tag{20}$$

We shall consider only the one-step example. We shall first solve this problem for the case $c = 1$. Let σ_1 denote $\tilde{S}$. We can express σ_1 as a weighted average of three conditional expectations corresponding to the three possible outcomes of the first trial:

$$\begin{aligned}
\sigma_1 \equiv \mathscr{E}\tilde{S} &= p\mathscr{E}\{\tilde{S}|V(1) = +1\} \\
&\quad + q\mathscr{E}\{\tilde{S}|V(1) = 0\} \\
&\quad + r\mathscr{E}\{\tilde{S}|V(1) = -1\}.
\end{aligned} \tag{21}$$

If $V(1) = +1$, then $\tilde{S} = 0$. If $V(1) = 0$, then

$$\tilde{S} = S(2) + \cdots + S(T_1 - 1),$$

and the conditional distribution of this last sum given that $V(1) = 0$ is the same as the unconditional distribution of $\tilde{S}$. Hence, if we denote

$$\sigma_2 \equiv \mathscr{E}\{\tilde{S}|V(1) = -1\},$$

then (21) becomes

$$\begin{aligned} \sigma_1 &= p \cdot 0 + q\sigma_1 + r\sigma_2 \\ &= q\sigma_1 + r\sigma_2. \end{aligned}$$

Solving this for σ_1 in terms of σ_2, and recalling that $q = 1 - p - r$, we get

$$\sigma_1 = \frac{r\sigma_2}{p + r}. \tag{22}$$

We can also relate σ_2 to σ_1 in another way; this will give us a second equation that we can solve together with (22). Suppose that $V(1) = -1$, and let T' be the first $t > 0$ such that $S(t) = 0$. Define

$$\begin{aligned} S'(t) &\equiv V(2) + \cdots + V(t), & 2 &\leq t \leq T', \\ S''(t) &\equiv V(T' + 1) + \cdots + V(t), & T' + 1 &\leq t \leq T_1. \end{aligned} \tag{23}$$

Keeping in mind that $V(1) = -1$, we have

$$\begin{aligned} S(1) &= -1 \\ S(t) &= -1 + S'(t), & 2 &\leq t < T', \\ S(T') &= 0, \\ S(t) &= S''(t), & T' + 1 &\leq t \leq T_1. \end{aligned} \tag{24}$$

Hence we can express $\tilde{S}$ as

$$\begin{aligned} \tilde{S} &= -1 + \sum_{t=2}^{T'-1} [-1 + S'(t)] + \sum_{t=T'+1}^{T_1-1} S''(t) \\ &= -(T' - 1) + \tilde{S}' + \tilde{S}'', \end{aligned} \tag{25}$$

where

$$\tilde{S}' \equiv S'(2) + \cdots + S'(T' - 1)$$
$$\tilde{S}'' \equiv S''(T' + 1) + \cdots + S''(T_1 - 1) \tag{26}$$

Now observe that, *conditional on* $V(1) = -1$,

(a) $(T' - 1)$ has the same distribution as the unconditional distribution of T_1, and

(b) $\tilde{S}'$ and S'' each have the same distribution as the unconditional distribution of $\tilde{S}$. $\tag{27}$

Recall that the mean of the first-passage time T_1 is

$$\mathscr{E}T_1 = \frac{1}{p - r} \tag{28}$$

(see (19) and the discussion that follows it). Therefore, putting together (25) through (28) we have our second equation relating σ_2 and σ_1:

$$\sigma_2 = -\frac{1}{p - r} + 2\sigma_1. \tag{29}$$

The solution of the pair of equations (22) and (29) for σ_1 is

$$\sigma_1 = -\frac{r}{(p - r)^2}. \tag{30}$$

This solves our problem for the case $c = 1$.

Consider now the general case of any positive c. Let T_m denote the first $t > 0$ such that $S(t) = m$, let $T_0 \equiv 0$, and $S(0) \equiv 0$. Define

$$\tilde{S}_m \equiv S(T_{m-1}) + \cdots + S(T_m - 1) - (T_m - T_{m-1})(m - 1),$$
$$m \geqq 1,$$
$$\tilde{S} = S(0) + \cdots + S(T_c - 1).$$

Then

$$\tilde{S} = \sum_{m=1}^{c} \left[\tilde{S}_m + (T_m - T_{m-1})(m - 1) \right]. \tag{31}$$

The $\tilde{S}_m$ are identically distributed with mean σ_1, and the $(T_m - T_{m-1})$ are identically distributed, with mean $1/(p - r)$. Hence, from the identity (31),

$$\mathcal{E}\tilde{S} = c\sigma_1 + \left(\frac{1}{p - r}\right)\left(\frac{c[c - 1]}{2}\right).$$

From this and (30) we finally obtain the expected total of the partial sums from $t = 1$ to $t = T_c - 1$:

$$\mathcal{E}\tilde{S} = -\frac{cr}{(p - r)^2} + \frac{c(c - 1)}{2(p - r)}. \tag{32}$$

Imagine now that the first-passage situation is repeated indefinitely, the successive trials being independent. Let $T_c^{(n)}$ denote the successive first-passage times, and $\tilde{S}^{(n)}$ denote the corresponding totals of the partial sums between first-passage times. The average partial sum for the first N "cycles" of first passages is

$$\bar{S}(t) = \left(\frac{1}{t}\right)[S(0) + \cdots + S(t - 1)], \tag{33}$$

where

$$t = T_c^{(1)} + \cdots + T_c^{(N)}. \tag{34}$$

We can thus write $\bar{S}(t)$ as

$$\begin{aligned}
\bar{S}(t) &= \frac{S(0) + \cdots + S(t - 1)}{T_c^{(1)} + \cdots + T_c^{(N)}} \\
&= \frac{\tilde{S}^{(1)} + \cdots + \tilde{S}^{(N)}}{T_c^{(1)} + \cdots + T_c^{(N)}} \\
&= \frac{\left(\dfrac{1}{N}\right)(\tilde{S}^{(1)} + \cdots + \tilde{S}^{(N)})}{\left(\dfrac{1}{N}\right)(T_c^{(1)} + \cdots + T_c^{(N)})}.
\end{aligned} \tag{35}$$

By the Strong Law of Large Numbers,* the numerator in the last line of (35) approaches $\mathscr{E}\tilde{S}^{(n)} = \sigma_1$, with probability 1, as N increases without limit, and the denominator correspondingly approaches $\mathscr{E}T_c^{(n)} = \mathscr{E}T_C$. Recall that

$$\mathscr{E}T_c = \frac{c}{p - r} \tag{36}$$

(see the discussion following (19)). Hence, dividing (32) by (36), we obtain the long-run average of the partial sums,

$$\lim_{N \to \infty} \bar{S}(t) = \frac{c - 1}{2} - \frac{r}{p - r}, \tag{37}$$

with probability 1, where t is related to N by (34).

4. THE ONE-STEP EXAMPLE

We shall now consider the one-step example of the conservative thermostat in more detail. Recall that in the one-step example performance can change by at most one unit in any one period; see equations (5) and (6) of Section 2.

We first calculate the expected length of time for the thermostat to go through a complete "cycle." Recall that the state of the thermostat is characterized by the pair (a, u), where a equals 1 or 0 according to whether there has or has not been an effort during the current period, and u is the resulting new level of performance (an integer). Given the current action a and the previous performance level u', the new performance level u will be $(u' + 1)$, u', or $(u' - 1)$, with probabilities p_a, r_a and q_a, respectively, where all these (six) probabilities are strictly positive, and $p_a + r_a + q_a = 1$ $(a = 0, 1)$. The transitions for the action a are deterministic, and are described by (4) of Section 2. The thermostat will alternate between "effort phases" $(a = 1)$ and "rest phases" $(a = 0)$. Each

---

*See Feller, [2], Chapter X, Section 7, especially p. 260.

rest phase ends when the thermostat reaches the state $(0, \beta)$, and each effort phase ends when the thermostat reaches the state $(1, \alpha)$, where β and α are the lower and upper settings of the thermostat, respectively. Note that in the one-step example the thermostat cannot "overshoot" these settings in one period. On the other hand, during an effort phase the level of performance may still fall indefinitely far below β before it next reaches α; similarly, during a rest phase performance may exceed α by any amount before it next falls to β. Because of the strict alternation of phases, we may take the end of a complete cycle to be either the state $(0, \beta)$ or the state $(1, \alpha)$. For our present purpose, it will be convenient to suppose that at date $t = 0$ the thermostat is in state $(0, \beta)$, and therefore about to start an effort phase.

During the effort phase, the successive increments in performance are the independent identically distributed random variables $Y(t)$, which have mean

$$\eta = p_1 - r_1 > 0. \tag{1}$$

If we denote by c the difference $(\alpha - \beta)$ between the upper and lower settings, then the expected time to reach the state $(1, \alpha)$ is*

$$\tau_1 \equiv \frac{c}{p_1 - r_1} = \frac{c}{\eta}. \tag{2}$$

Similarly, during the subsequent rest phase, the successive increments in performance are the independent identically distributed random variables $X(t)$, which have mean

$$\xi = p_0 - r_0 < 0. \tag{3}$$

To see the rest phase in terms of the first-passage problem we must reverse the performance scale and, in the notation of Section 3, take $V(t) = -X(t)$, $p = r_0$, $q = q_0$, $r = p_0$, and (again) $c = \alpha - \beta$. The expected time to reach the state $(0, \beta)$ from the state $(1, \alpha)$ is

---

*See equation (36) of Section 3.

thus seen to be

$$\tau_0 \equiv \frac{c}{r_0 - p_0} = \frac{c}{|\xi|}. \tag{4}$$

The expected time for a complete cycle is therefore

$$\tau \equiv \tau_1 + \tau_0 = c\left(\frac{1}{\eta} + \frac{1}{|\xi|}\right). \tag{5}$$

We can now easily calculate the long-run frequency of effort. Successive cycles are mutually independent. Let E_n denote the length of the n'th effort phase, and R_n the length of the n'th rest phase. The fraction of time spent on effort during the first N cycles is

$$\frac{E_1 + \cdots + E_N}{E_1 + R_1 + \cdots + E_N + R_N}. \tag{6}$$

By the Strong Law of Large Numbers,

$$\lim_{N \to \infty} \left(\frac{1}{N}\right)(E_1 + \cdots + E_N) = \mathscr{E}E_n = \tau_1$$

$$\lim_{N \to \infty} \left(\frac{1}{N}\right)(E_1 + R_1 + \cdots + E_N + R_N) = \mathscr{E}(E_n + R_n) \tag{7}$$

$$= \tau_1 + \tau_0.$$

Hence, dividing the numerator and the denominator of (6) each by N, and letting N increase without limit, we get

$$\lim_{N \to \infty} \frac{E_1 + \cdots + E_N}{E_1 + R_1 + \cdots + E_N + R_N} = \frac{\tau_1}{\tau_1 + \tau_0} \equiv \bar{a}. \tag{8}$$

From (2) and (4) we see that this long-run frequency of effort, $\bar{a}$, is equal to

$$\bar{a} = \cfrac{\cfrac{1}{\eta}}{\cfrac{1}{\eta} + \cfrac{1}{|\xi|}}, \tag{9}$$

which is independent of the thermostat settings!

Finally, we shall calculate the long-run average performance. For this purpose we can use formula (32) of Section 3 for the expected total of the partial sums in the first-passage problem. Suppose that the thermostat starts in state $(0, \beta)$ so that $U(0) = \beta$. In the notation of Section 3, take

$$V(t) = Y(t), \qquad p = p_1, \qquad q = q_1,$$
$$r = r_1, \qquad T_c = E_1, \qquad c = \alpha - \beta,$$
$$S(t) = U(t) - U(0) = U(t) - \beta.$$

Hence

$$\tilde{S} = [U(0) - \beta] + \cdots + [U(E_1 - 1) - \beta]$$
$$= U(0) + \cdots + U(E_1 - 1) - E_1\beta,$$

so that

$$U(0) + \cdots + U(E_1 - 1) = \tilde{S} + E_1\beta.$$
$$= \tilde{S} + T_c\beta. \tag{10}$$

Taking the expected value of (10), and using (26) and (30) of Section 3, we obtain

$$[U(0) + \cdots + U(E_1 - 1)] = \frac{c}{\eta}\left(-\frac{r_1}{\eta} + \frac{c-1}{2} + \beta\right) \tag{11}$$

as the expected total performance from date 0 up to (but not including) the end of the first effort phase. Similarly, at date $t = E_1$

the thermostat is in state $(1, \alpha)$, and to apply the first-passage analysis we reverse the performance scale and take

$$V(t) = -X(E_1 + t), \qquad p = r_0, \qquad q = q_0,$$
$$r = p_0, \qquad T_c = R_1, \quad c = \alpha - \beta,$$
$$S(t) = U(E_1) - U(E_1 + t) = \alpha - U(E_1 + t),$$

so that

$$\tilde{S} = [\alpha - U(E_1)] + \cdots + [\alpha - U(E_1 + R_1 - 1)]$$
$$= R_1\alpha - U(E_1) - \cdots - U(E_1 + R_1 - 1),$$
$$U(E_1) + \cdots + U(E_1 + R_1 - 1) = R_1\alpha - \tilde{S} = T_c\alpha - \tilde{S}.$$
$$\mathscr{E}[U(E_1) + \cdots + U(E_1 + R_1 - 1)] = \frac{c}{\xi}\left(\alpha + \frac{p_0}{|\xi|} - \frac{c - 1}{2}\right).$$
(12)

Adding (11) and (12) we get the expected total performance, $\mathscr{E}\tilde{U}$, over the complete cycle (including $t = 0$ but not $t = E_1 + R_1$):

$$\mathscr{E}\tilde{U} = \frac{c}{\eta}\left(\beta + \frac{c - 1}{2} - \frac{r_1}{\eta}\right)$$
$$+ \frac{c}{|\xi|}\left(\alpha - \frac{c - 1}{2} + \frac{p_0}{|\xi|}\right).$$
(13)

If we let $\gamma \equiv (\alpha + \beta)/2$, then we can rewrite (13) as

$$\mathscr{E}\tilde{U} = \frac{c}{\eta}\left(\gamma - \frac{1}{2} - \frac{r_1}{\eta}\right) + \frac{c}{|\xi|}\left(\gamma + \frac{1}{2} + \frac{p_0}{|\xi|}\right)$$
$$= \gamma c\left(\frac{1}{\eta} + \frac{1}{|\xi|}\right) + \frac{c}{|\xi|}\left(\frac{1}{2} + \frac{p_0}{|\xi|}\right) - \frac{c}{\eta}\left(\frac{1}{2} + \frac{r_1}{|\eta|}\right).$$
(14)

The expected length of a complete cycle has already been calculated in (5) above as

$$\mathscr{E}(E_1 + R_1) = c\left(\frac{1}{\eta} + \frac{1}{|\xi|}\right). \tag{15}$$

By an argument analogous to that used to derive (31) of Section 3 we can then conclude that *the long-run average performance, $\bar{u}$, of the thermostat* is the ratio of (14) to (15), namely,

$$\bar{u} \equiv \lim_{N \to \infty} \frac{U(0) + \cdots + U\left(\sum_{n=1}^{N} [E_n + R_n]\right)}{\sum_{n=1}^{N} [E_n + R_n]}$$

$$= \frac{\tilde{U}}{(E_1 + R_1)} \tag{16}$$

$$= \gamma + \frac{\left(\dfrac{1}{|\xi|}\right)\left(\dfrac{1}{2} + \dfrac{p_0}{|\xi|}\right) - \left(\dfrac{1}{\eta}\right)\left(\dfrac{1}{2} + \dfrac{r_1}{\eta}\right)}{\dfrac{1}{\eta} + \dfrac{1}{|\xi|}}.$$

Using the formula (9) for the long-run average frequency of effort, $\bar{a}$, we can simplify the formula for $\bar{u}$ to

$$\bar{u} = \gamma + (1 - \bar{a})\left(\frac{1}{2} + \frac{p_0}{|\xi|}\right) - \bar{a}\left(\frac{1}{2} + \frac{r_1}{\eta}\right). \tag{17}$$

Recall that γ is the midpoint between the upper and lower thermostat settings, and note that $(\bar{u} - \gamma)$ *is independent of the thermostat settings*!

To interpret the formula (17) for $\bar{u}$ more easily, we rewrite (9) as

$$\bar{a} = \frac{1}{1 + \dfrac{\eta}{|\xi|}};$$

also, recall that

$$\xi = p_0 - r_0 < 0,$$
$$\eta = p_1 - r_1 > 0.$$

Roughly speaking, η is the average rate per unit time at which performance increases during the effort phase, and $|\xi|$ is the corresponding rate of decrease of performance during the rest phase. The larger the ratio, $\eta/|\xi|$, of these two rates, the smaller is the long-run frequency of effort, $\bar{a}$, since *relatively* less time is needed to go from β to α (with effort) than to go from α to β (without effort).

If $p_0 = r_1$ and $r_0 = p_1$, then $\bar{a} = 1/2$ and $\bar{u} = \gamma$, i.e., long-run average performance will be half-way between the upper and lower settings. Suppose that p_0 and r_0 are fixed, and that p_1 is decreased and/or r_1 is increased. Then η and $\bar{a}$ will decrease and $\bar{u}$ will also decrease. During the effort phase performance may drift quite far below β before it finally reaches the upper setting α again. In the extreme case, as p_1 decreases to r_1 (with r_1 fixed), η approaches zero and $\bar{u}$ diverges to minus infinity. One can show that in the limit, with $p_1 = r_1$, the effort phase will be a null persistent Markov chain. With probability one the level of performance will eventually reach α, but the expected time to do so is infinite! Furthermore, fluctuations in performance very far below β will be sufficiently frequent so that the long-run average performance during the effort phase will be minus infinity.* Analogous considerations apply to the rest phase.

5. THE FREQUENCY OF EFFORT, THE RATE OF CHANGE OF PERFORMANCE, AND A STRONG LAW OF LARGE NUMBERS FOR GENERAL BEHAVIORS

Recall that in Section 2 we defined a general *behavior* as a sequence of functions, A_t, that determine the manager's action at

---

*See Feller, [2], Chapter XI, Section 3, and Chapter XIV, Sections 2 and 3, on the Gambler's Ruin Problem.

each date on the basis of past performance levels:

$$a(t) = A_t[U(0), \ldots, U(t-1)], \qquad t = 1, 2, \ldots .$$

In this section we shall show that, for any behavior, if the long-run average frequency of effort approaches a nonrandom number, say $\bar{a}$, then the long-run average rate of change of performance will also approach a nonrandom number, say $\bar{\zeta}$, and that these two limits are related by

$$\bar{\zeta} = \bar{a}\eta + (1 - \bar{a})\xi. \qquad (1)$$

As a byproduct of this proposition, we shall show that formula (9) in Section 4 for the long-run frequency of effort in the one-step example is also valid for the general conservative thermostat. We shall also apply the proposition in Section 6, on "putting out fires." In order to prove the proposition, we shall have to prove that a version of the Strong Law of Large Numbers is valid for the increments in performance, $Z(t)$, even though these increments are not independent and identically distributed.

Define

$$
\begin{aligned}
\bar{a} &= \lim_{t \to \infty} \frac{1}{t}[a(1) + \cdots + a(t)], \\
\bar{\zeta} &\equiv \lim_{t \to \infty} \frac{1}{t}[U(t) - U(0)],
\end{aligned}
\qquad (2)
$$

provided these limits exist. In principle, these limits could be random variables, but in our situation they will be nonrandom. Recall that the increments in performance are

$$Z(t) = a(t)Y(t) + [1 - a(t)]X(t).$$

It will be convenient to "center" our variables as follows:

$$
\begin{aligned}
x(t) &= X(t) - \xi, \qquad y(t) = Y(t) - \eta, \\
\zeta(t) &= a(t)\eta + [1 - a(t)]\xi, \\
z(t) &= Z(t) - \zeta(t) = a(t)y(t) + [1 - a(t)]x(t).
\end{aligned}
\qquad (3)
$$

It is clear that if $\bar{a}$ exists, then

$$\lim_{t \to \infty} \frac{1}{t} [\zeta(1) + \cdots + \zeta(t)] = \bar{a}\eta + (1 - \bar{a})\xi. \tag{4}$$

Hence, to prove that if $\bar{a}$ exists then the limit $\bar{\zeta}$ exists it is sufficient to prove that

$$\lim_{t \to \infty} \frac{1}{t} [z(1) + \cdots + z(t)] = 0. \tag{5}$$

In other words, if we define the partial sums $s(t)$ by

$$s(t) \equiv z(1) + \cdots + z(t), \tag{6}$$

we want to prove the following *Generalized Strong Law of Large Numbers*:

THEOREM.   *For any behavior*, $\displaystyle\lim_{t \to \infty} \frac{s(t)}{t} = 0$ *with probability one.*

In the course of the proof of the theorem it will be convenient to have a notation for the history of all the random variables up to and including date t; we shall call this history $H(t)$. Thus

$$H(t) = [x(1), y(1), x(2), y(2), \ldots, x(t), y(t)]. \tag{7}$$

We first prove a lemma about the variance of $s(t)$. Note that the expected values of $x(t)$ and $y(t)$, and hence $s(t)$, are zero. Denote the variances of $x(t)$ and $y(t)$, respectively by σ_0^2 and σ_1^2, and define

$$\bar{\sigma}_t^2 \equiv \mathscr{E}\sigma_{a(t)}^2. \tag{8}$$

LEMMA 1.   *The variance of $s(t)$ is given by*

$$\mathscr{E}[s(t)]^2 = \bar{\sigma}_1^2 + \cdots + \bar{\sigma}_t^2 \equiv w(t). \tag{9}$$

The proof of Lemma 1 is by induction. Consider first the case $t = 1$;

$$s(1) = z(1) = a(1)y(1) + [1 - a(1)]x(1).$$

$$\begin{aligned}\mathscr{E}[s(1)]^2 &= \mathscr{E}[y(1)]^2\text{Prob}[a(1) = 1] \\ &\quad + \mathscr{E}[x(1)]^2\text{Prob}[a(1) = 0] \\ &= \bar{\sigma}_1^2 = w(1).\end{aligned} \tag{10}$$

Now suppose that the lemma is true for $t = n$. From the definition (6) of $s(t)$,

$$[s(n + 1)]^2 = [s(n)]^2 + 2s(n)z(n + 1) + [z(n + 1)]^2. \tag{11}$$

We shall use the rule for the iteration of expectations,* to get

$$\mathscr{E}[s(n + 1)]^2 = \mathscr{E}\mathscr{E}\{[s(n + 1)]^2|H(n)\}. \tag{12}$$

Looking at the right-hand side of (11) we see that $s(n)$ is determined given $H(n)$, and that

$$\mathscr{E}\{z(n + 1)|H(n)\} = 0;$$

the last follows from (3). Thus the conditional expectation of (11) given $H(n)$ is

$$\mathscr{E}\{[s(n + 1)]^2|H(n)\} = [s(n)]^2 + \mathscr{E}\{[z(n + 1)]^2|H(n)\}. \tag{13}$$

Taking the expectation of both sides of (13) we get

$$\mathscr{E}[s(n + 1)]^2 = \mathscr{E}[s(n)]^2 + \mathscr{E}[z(n + 1)]^2. \tag{14}$$

By the same argument used for (10) we obtain

$$\mathscr{E}[z(n + 1)]^2 = \bar{\sigma}_n^2,$$

---

*Feller, [2], Chapter IX, equation (2.9).

which, with (14), completes the induction and the proof of the lemma.

The next lemma is a generalization of Kolmogorov's Inequality.*

LEMMA 2. *For any real number $r > 0$, and any date $t \geqq 1$, define the events E_k by*

$$[s(k)]^2 \geqq rw(t); \tag{15}$$

then the probability that none of the events $E_1, \ldots, E_t$ occurs is at least $1 - (1/r)$.

Proof. Let p denote the probability that at least one of the events $E_1, \ldots, E_t$ occurs. We want to show that p does not exceed $1/r$, or that $pr \leqq 1$. Define the indicator variables I_k by: I_k equals 1 if and only if k is the first date at which even E_k occurs; otherwise I_k equals 0. Also, define

$$I = I_1 + \cdots + I_t.$$

Note that at most one of the variables I_k is positive (unity), and hence that $I \leqq 1$ and

$$p = \text{Prob}(I = 1) = \mathscr{E}I. \tag{16}$$

We shall obtain the desired bound on pr in two steps.

First, for any date $k < t$ we write $s(t) = s(k) + s'(k)$ where

$$s'(k) \equiv z(k+1) + \cdots + z(t).$$

With this notation we can write

$$I_k[s(t)]^2 = I_k[s(k)]^2 + 2I_k s(k) s'(k) + I_k[s'(k)]^2. \tag{17}$$

---

*See Feller, [2], Chapter IX, Section 7. The proof of Lemma 2 is given in full here, for completeness, but it is an easy adaptation of Feller's proof, once one has Lemma 1. (Compare equations (7.9) and (7.10) of Feller, p. 235.)

Note that, given the history $H(k)$, $I(k)$ and $s(k)$ are determined, and

$$\mathscr{E}\{s'(k)|H(k)\} = 0.$$

Hence, taking the conditional expectation of (17) given $H(k)$ we get

$$\mathscr{E}\{I_k[s(t)]^2|H(k)\} = I_k[s(k)]^2 + I_k\mathscr{E}\{[s'(k)]^2|H(k)\} \geq I_k[s(k)]^2. \tag{18}$$

Taking the (unconditional) expectation of both sides of (18) we get

$$\mathscr{E}I_k[s(t)]^2 \geq \mathscr{E}I_k[s(k)]^2. \tag{19}$$

But, by definition of the event E_k,

$$I_k[s(k)]^2 \geq I_krw(t),$$

so that

$$\mathscr{E}I_k[s(k)]^2 \geq rw(t)\mathscr{E}I_k,$$

which, with (19), gives

$$\mathscr{E}I_k[s(t)]^2 \geq rw(t)\mathscr{E}I_k. \tag{20}$$

Summing the inequalities (20) for k from 1 to t:

$$\sum_{k=1}^t \mathscr{E}I_k[s(t)]^2 \geq rw(t)\sum_{k=1}^t \mathscr{E}I_k = rw(t)\mathscr{E}\sum_{k=1}^t I_k = rw(t)p. \tag{21}$$

Second, recalling that $I \leq 1$, we have, from Lemma 1,

$$w(t) = \mathscr{E}[s(t)]^2 \geq \mathscr{E}I[s(t)]^2 = \sum_{k=1}^t \mathscr{E}I_k[s(t)]^2. \tag{22}$$

Inequalities (21) and (22) together imply

$$w(t) \geqq rw(t)p. \tag{23}$$

The Continuity Assumption on the random variables $X(t)$ and $Y(t)$ guarantees that $w(t) > 0$, so that from (23) we get the desired inequality, $pr \leqq 1$, which completes the proof of the lemma.

We are now in a position to complete the proof of the theorem. We shall use an argument similar to that used to derive the Kolmogorov Criterion in the case of independent summands.* Let $\varepsilon > 0$ be given and let F_n denote the event that for some m with $2^{n-1} < m \leqq 2^n$

$$\frac{|s(m)|}{m} > \varepsilon. \tag{24}$$

We wish to show that only finitely many of the events F_n will occur, and for this it suffices to show that

$$\sum_{n=1}^{\infty} \mathrm{Prob}(F_n) < \infty, \tag{25}$$

by the first Borel-Cantelli Lemma.** Event F_n implies that, for some m with $2^{n-1} < m \leqq 2^n$

$$[s(m)]^2 > (\varepsilon m)^2 > (\varepsilon 2^{n-1})^2,$$

so that by Lemma 2, taking

$$t = 2^n, \qquad r = \frac{(\varepsilon 2^{n-1})^2}{w(2^n)},$$

---

*See Feller, [2], Chapter X, Section 7. The argument given here is modelled after Feller's demonstration, which uses Kolmogorov's Inequality. Essentially, Lemmas 1 and 2 above enable us to extend the standard argument, which is based on independence, with little modification.

**See Feller, [2], Chapter VIII, Section 3.

we have

$$\text{Prob}(F_n) \leqq \frac{w(2^n)}{(\varepsilon 2^{n-1})^2}.$$

Now using Lemma 1 to evaluate $w(2^n)$ we have

$$
\begin{aligned}
\sum_{n=1}^{\infty} \text{Prob}(F_n) &\leqq \sum_{n=1}^{\infty} \frac{\displaystyle\sum_{k=1}^{2^n} \bar{\sigma}_k^2}{(\varepsilon 2^{n-1})^2} \\
&= 4\varepsilon^{-2} \sum_{n=1}^{\infty} 2^{-2n} \sum_{k=1}^{2^n} \bar{\sigma}_k^2 \qquad (26) \\
&= 4\varepsilon^{-2} \sum_{k=1}^{\infty} \bar{\sigma}_k^2 \sum_{2^n \geqq k} 2^{-2n} \\
&\leqq 8\varepsilon^{-2} \sum_{k=1}^{\infty} \frac{\bar{\sigma}_k^2}{k^2}.
\end{aligned}
$$

But $\bar{\sigma}_k^2$ is no larger than $\max(\sigma_0^2, \sigma_1^2)$, so that the last sum on the right-hand side of (26) is finite. Hence the left-hand side of (26) is finite, which completes the proof of the theorem.

COROLLARY 1. *For any behavior in the performance process of Section 2, if*

$$\bar{a} \equiv \lim_{t \to \infty} \frac{1}{t}\big[a(1) + \cdots + a(t)\big]$$

exists with probability one (and is nonrandom), then

$$\bar{\zeta} \equiv \lim_{t \to \infty} \frac{1}{t}\big[U(t) - U(0)\big] = \bar{a}\eta + (1 - \bar{a})\xi, \qquad (27)$$

with probability one.

COROLLARY 2. *In the conservative thermostat, the long-run frequency of effort is*

$$\bar{a} = \frac{|\xi|}{|\xi| + \eta}. \tag{28}$$

(Note that this is the same formula as in the case of the one-step example.)

The proof of Corollary 2 is based on an important fact about ergodic Markov chains. Recall that in the conservative thermostat the sequence of pairs $[a(t), U(t)]$ is an ergodic Markov chain. By a well-known ergodic theorem,* the long-run frequency of states for which $a(t) = 1$ has a limit, $\bar{a}$. It follows from our Corollary 1 that $\bar{\zeta}$ also exists, and is given by (27). If $\bar{\zeta} > 0$, then $U(t)$ would diverge to $+\infty$, which would contradict the fact that every state is ergodic. Similarly, $\bar{\zeta}$ cannot be < 0. Hence $\bar{\zeta} = 0$, so we get the desired result by solving the equation $\bar{a}\eta + (1 - \bar{a})\xi = 0$.

6.   "PUTTING OUT FIRES"

A manager usually supervises more than one activity. For any given level of improvement effort per unit time, the opportunity cost of an improvement effort for one activity is the neglect of others. A common managerial behavior is to pay attention only to those activities that are giving the most trouble; this is colloquially called "putting out fires." We can easily adapt our model of Section 2 to describe this behavior in formal terms. Roughly speaking, we shall model each activity as a process like that studied in Section 2. At each date the manager must decide to which activity he will devote his improvement effort. In putting-out-fires (POF) behavior, the manager devotes his improvement effort to the activity that has the lowest level of performance. (Something has to be said, of course, about what to do in case of ties.)

---

*See the Appendix to this chapter, or Chung, [1], Section I.15, Theorem 2, p. 92. Unfortunately, this topic is not treated in Feller, [2].

In this section we shall study the asymptotic properties of POF behavior in the special case of two activities.* We shall see that the successive actions of the manager and the successive *differences* in performance between the two activities together form a Markov chain that is formally equivalent to the conservative thermostat of Section 2. This equivalence will provide an immediate proof that this Markov chain is ergodic. It will also enable us to give simple formulas for the long-run frequency of effort and the long-run average rate of change of performance for each of the two activities. Indeed, we shall see that these last two rates are the same; call this common rate r.

The successive actions of the manager and the successive levels of performance of the two activities also form a Markov chain. However, this Markov chain is not ergodic under POF behavior. If r is strictly positive, then this second Markov chain will be transient, and furthermore both performance levels will diverge to plus infinity, with probability one. We shall also see that in this case, for every prescribed probability p less than unity there is a level of performance, say B, such that, with probability at least p, neither activity's performance ever reaches or falls below B. In other words, if r is strictly positive, then with high probability "disastrously" low levels of performance can be avoided, provided that "disaster" is suitably defined.

We turn now to a formal description of our model. There are two activities; $U_i(t)$ denotes the level of performance of activity i at date t. The U_i-process for each activity has the properties of the U-process of Section 2, with parameters η_i and ξ_i. Furthermore, the sequence of pairs of random variables $[X_1(t), Y_1(t)]$ and the sequence of pairs $[X_2(t), Y_2(t)]$ are mutually independent. The allocation of the manager's effort will be denoted by the pair (a_1, a_2); $a_i(t)$ will equal 1 or 0 according to whether the manager does or does not devote effort to activity i at date t. To express the idea that the manager's supply of effort at any date is limited, we

---

*Almost everything that we shall prove about the case of two activities can be generalized to the case of more than two activities, but this generalization would require mathematical tools that are beyond the level set for this chapter. See Section 7 for the relevant references.

impose the constraint that the manager can devote effort to at most one activity at any one date, i.e.,

$$a_1(t) + a_2(t) \leq 1. \tag{1}$$

Putting-out-fires behavior (POF) is defined as follows:

(a)   If $a_1(t - 1) = 1$,   then
$$a_1(t) = \begin{Bmatrix} 1 \\ 0 \end{Bmatrix} \quad \text{as} \quad U_1(t - 1) \begin{Bmatrix} \leq \\ > \end{Bmatrix} U_2(t - 1).$$

(b)   If $a_1(t - 1) = 0$,   then
$$a_1(t) = \begin{Bmatrix} 1 \\ 0 \end{Bmatrix} \quad \text{as} \quad U_1(t - 1) \begin{Bmatrix} < \\ \geq \end{Bmatrix} U_2(t - 1). \tag{2}$$

(c) $a_2(t) = 1 - a_1(t).$

Notice that (a) and (b) provide for ties by stating that a change in the allocation of effort will not occur unless there is a strict reversal in the ranking of performance of the two activities. Also, by (c), the manager is always devoting his (full) effort to one of the two activities.

Let $D(t)$ denote the difference between the two performance levels;

$$D(t) = U_1(t) - U_2(t). \tag{3}$$

We can express POF behavior in terms of $D(t)$ as follows:

(a)   If $a_1(t - 1) = 1$,   then $a_1(t) = 1$ or 0 as
$$D(t - 1) < \text{or} \geq +1.$$

(b)   If $a_1(t - 1) = 0$,   then $a_1(t) = 1$ or 0 as
$$D(t - 1) \leq \text{or} > -1. \tag{4}$$

(c) $a_2(t) = 1 - a_1(t).$

With this description, it is clear that the successive pairs $[a_1(t), D(t)]$ form a Markov chain, since

$$D(t) - D(t - 1) = a_1(t)[Y_1(t) - X_2(t)]$$
$$+ [1 - a_1(t)][X_1(t) - Y_2(t)]. \tag{5}$$

Furthermore, *the Markov chain* $[a_1(t), D(t)]$ *is equivalent to a conservative thermostat.* The following relationships establish this equivalence:

$$a(t) = a_1(t),$$
$$Y(t) = Y_1(t) - X_2(t), \qquad \eta = \eta_1 - \xi_2 > 0,$$
$$X(t) = X_1(t) - Y_2(t), \qquad \xi = \xi_1 - \eta_2 < 0,$$
$$Z(t) = D(t) - D(t - 1),$$
$$U(t) = D(t),$$
$$\alpha = +1, \qquad \beta = -1.$$

(6)

We shall call the chain $[a_1(t), D(t)]$ the *centered POF chain.*

Applying the results of Section 2 we can immediately conclude that the centered POF chain is ergodic. Note that if each U_i-process satisfies the assumptions of Section 2, then so will the centered POF chain. On the other hand, the centered POF chain can never satisfy the conditions of the one-step example, even if each U_i-process does, so that we cannot use the special results of Section 4.

In the centered POF chain, the dates at which effort is devoted to improving activity 1 correspond to the "effort phases" of the equivalent conservative thermostat. Hence, by Corollary 2 of Section 5, equation (28), the long-run frequency effort on activity 1 is given by

$$\bar{a}_1 = \frac{|\xi_1 - \eta_2|}{|\xi_1 - \eta_2| + \eta_1 - \xi_2}$$
$$= \frac{(\eta_2 - \xi_1)}{(\eta_1 - \xi_1) + (\eta_2 - \xi_2)}.$$

(7)

The long-run frequency of effort on activity 2 is, of course, $\bar{a}_2 = 1 - \bar{a}_1$.

With (7), we can apply Corollary 1 of the theorem of Section 5, equation (27), to calculate the long-run average rate of change of performance per unit time, say r_i for activity i. One easily verifies that *these rates are the same for both activities*, and that

$$r_1 = r_2 \equiv r = \frac{\eta_1\eta_2 - \xi_1\xi_2}{(\eta_1 - \xi_1) + (\eta_2 - \xi_2)}. \tag{8}$$

We see from (8) that r is positive if and only if $\eta_1\eta_2 > \xi_1\xi_2$. (Recall that ξ_1 and ξ_2 are negative.) We might imagine that the more total effort the manager could expend per unit of time, the larger would be η_1 and η_2. Thus we might interpret the condition $r > 0$ as a criterion of whether or not the manager has a large enough (or an effective enough) supply of total effort to cause a long-run improvement in both activities.

From the identity $U_i(t) = t[U_i(t)/t]$ it is clear that if $r > 0$ then

$$\lim_{t \to \infty} U_i(t) = +\infty, \qquad i = 1, 2, \tag{9}$$

with probability one. It follows that the minimum of the two performance levels will also diverge to plus infinity, i.e., let

$$m(t) \equiv \min\{U_1(t), U_2(t)\};$$

then $r > 0$ implies that

$$\lim_{t \to \infty} m(t) = +\infty, \tag{10}$$

with probability one.

We shall now show that (10) implies that, *with probability close to one, $m(t)$ stays permanently above very low levels of performance (and hence so does each activity level).* A precise statement of this is: for every $h > 0$ there is a number $B(h)$ such that

$$\text{Prob}\{m(t) > B(h) \text{ for all } t\} \geqq 1 - h. \tag{11}$$

To prove (11), let us first restate (10). For every number n, there is some date T_n such that

$$m(t) \geqq n \qquad \text{for all } t \geqq T_n; \tag{12}$$

the date T_n is, of course, a random variable. By taking $n = m(0)$ we see that the random variable

$$M \equiv \min_t m(t)$$

is well defined (and finite), since

$$M = \min\{m(t): 0 \leq t \leq T_{m(0)}\}.$$

To complete the proof of (11), take $B(h)$ to satisfy

$$\text{Prob}\{M \leq B(h)\} \leq h.$$

It is interesting to contrast POF behavior with another behavior that has superficially similar properties. Recall that with POF behavior the long-run frequencies of effort on the two activities are $\bar{a}_1$ and $\bar{a}_2 = 1 - \bar{a}_1$; see equation (7). Suppose that the manager could divide his effort between the two activities in a single period, in arbitrary proportions. Consider a behavior in which the manager devotes a constant fraction, equal to $\bar{a}_i$, of his effort to activity i in each period; call this the *balanced constant proportions* (BCP) behavior. If the evolution of performance of each activity is still determined by equation (2) of Section 2 (an assumption!), then

$$Z_i(t) \equiv U_i(t) - U_i(t-1) = \bar{a}_i Y_i(t) + (1 - \bar{a}_i) X_i(t). \quad (13)$$

In this case, for each i the random variables $Z_i(t)$ are independent and identically distributed, and the two sequences are mutually independent. Furthermore, it is easy to verify that

$$\mathscr{E}Z_1(t) = \mathscr{E}Z_2(t) = r, \qquad \text{all } t, \quad (14)$$

where r is given by (8). By the Strong Law of Large Numbers for independent identically distributed random variables, it follows that, for each activity i,

$$\lim_{t \to \infty} \frac{1}{t}[U_i(t) - U_i(0)] = r, \quad (15)$$

with probability one. From this, it follows further that BCP behavior has properties (9)–(11), in common with POF.

On the other hand, let us examine the properties of $D(t)$, the difference between $U_1(t)$ and $U_2(t)$. The successive increments in $D(T)$ are

$$K(t) \equiv D(t) - D(t-1) = Z_1(t) - Z_2(t). \qquad (16)$$

The random variables $K(t)$ are independent and identically distributed, and from (14) and (16) we see that they have mean zero. Hence, given $D(0)$,

$$\mathscr{E}D(t) = 0$$

$$\text{Variance } D(t) = t\sigma_K^2, \qquad (17)$$

where σ_K^2 is the common variance of the increments $K(t)$. This means that as t gets large, the distribution of $D(t)$, given $D(0)$, becomes more and more dispersed; although the mean of $D(t)$ is zero, we can expect $D(t)$ to be far from zero at any particular date t in the distant future. In terms of performance, if $r > 0$ then under BCP behavior we can expect both activities to improve indefinitely as time goes on, at the same average rate, *but we can also expect them to wander farther and farther from each other in performance*. This is in contrast with the situation for POF behavior, in which $D(t)$ is ergodic.*

---

*Technically, under BCP behavior, $D(t)$ is a random walk with increments that have mean zero. One can show that, with our technical assumptions of Section 2, this random walk is a null persistent (null recurrent) Markov chain; see Kemeny, Snell, and Knapp, [6], p. 149. (For a derivation of this result in the special case of a one-step random walk, see Feller, [2], Chapters III and XIV. However, as was noted above, $D(t)$ cannot be a one-step random walk with our assumptions, so we cannot apply Feller's analysis.) This implies that $D(t)$ has no invariant probability distribution under BCP, whereas it does under POF, since $D(t)$ is ergodic under POF; see Feller, [2], Chapter XV, Section 7.

7. EXTENSIONS AND GENERALIZATIONS

In this section we shall briefly sketch or indicate some extensions and generalizations of the results derived in this chapter, and provide a corresponding guide to the literature on the subject.

First, the type of analysis we have seen here can be extended to other behaviors. In one such extension of the "thermostat" model, the settings of the thermostat are periodically adjusted as a function of previous performance, rather than being fixed. In the conservative thermostat, we may think of the upper setting, α, as a "level of aspiration" for the manager. A drop of $c = (\alpha - \beta)$ or more below this level triggers an effort by the manager to once again attain the aspiration level α. Suppose, however, that after a period of effort the manager actually surpasses the level α at date t, so that $U(t) > \alpha$. One could imagine that the manager, realizing now that the level $U(t)$ is possible, will reset α to equal $\alpha' \equiv U(t)$, and reset β to equal $\alpha' - c$. In particular, the next effort phase will be continued until performance reaches or exceeds α'. If at that date, say t', performance actually exceeds α', then α will be reset again, to equal $U(t')$, etc. We might call this behavior the *ambitious thermostat*.

Under the ambitious thermostat behavior, let V_n denote the performance level at the end of the n'th period of effort. The successive increments in V_n are independent and identically distributed, and are nonnegative. One can easily show that, if there is a positive probability of a performance increment greater than one during the effort phase, then there will be a positive probability that increments in V_n are (strictly) positive. In this case, the Strong Law of Large Numbers implies that the sequence V_n will diverge to plus infinity, with probability one. On the other hand, if successive increments in performance during the effort phase cannot exceed one, as in the one-step example, then the sequence V_n will be constant, and there will be no observable difference between the conservative and the ambitious thermostats.

Turning to the case of more than one activity, we first note that the results of Section 6 on putting-out-fires behavior can be extended to the situation in which there are more than two activities (see Radner and Rothschild, [14]). This extension seems to require more advanced mathematical methods, however, even without any relaxation of the assumptions about the underlying processes. A basic tool used by Radner and Rothschild is the theory of semi-martingales, and in particular a powerful inequality due to Freedman [3] concerning the distribution of first-passage times.*

Still within the context of our model of allocation of effort among several activities, one can consider behaviors other than putting out fires. For example, a radically different behavior is one that allocates all effort at any date to the best performing activity or activities. Following some colloquial practice, we might call such behavior *staying with a winner*. One can show that, under staying-with-a-winner behavior, the allocation of effort will eventually concentrate on a single activity, but which activity that will be cannot be predicted with certainty in advance. In other words, for some T and J all activity will be allocated to activity J from date T on, but T and J are random variables. The long-run average rate of change of performance of activity J will, of course, be $\eta_J > 0$, and the corresponding rate for each activity j other than J will be $\xi_j < 0$. In particular, the performance of activity J will diverge to plus infinity, and the performances of all other activities will diverge to minus infinity. Note that with positive probability the manager will eventually settle on an activity that has strictly less than the maximum η_j (provided these are not all equal). If the manager were trying by experimentation to guess the activity with the highest η_j, then he would face what is known in the statistical literature as the *two-armed bandit problem*. It is interesting that the asymptotic behavior of the *optimal* behavior in some two-armed bandit problems is identical to that of staying with a winner (see Rothschild, [15]). The above results on staying with a winner are proved in Radner and Rothschild, [14].]

In the probabilistic analysis used in this chapter, considerable use was made of the assumption that the random variables $X_j(t)$ and $Y_j(t)$ were independent. However, these independence assump-

---

*For an introduction to martingale theory for integer-valued random variables, see Kemeny, Snell, and Knapp, [6]. For a more advanced treatment, see Neveu, [11].

tions are much stronger than necessary. The key conditions that are needed concern the conditional expected values of the increments in performance given the allocation of effort. Let $H(t)$ denote the history of performance and allocation up through date t, let $a(t)$ denote the allocation of effort at date t, and let $Z_j(t)$ denote the increment in performance of activity j at date t. In this chapter we have assumed, among other things, that the random variables $Z_j(t)$ are integer-valued and bounded, that

$$\mathscr{E}\{Z_j(t)|H(t-1), a(t)\} = a_j(t)\eta_j + [1 - a_j(t)]\xi_j, \quad (1)$$

where η_j and ξ_j are fixed parameters with $\eta_j > 0, \xi_j < 0$, and also that

$$\text{given } H(t-1) \text{ and } a(t), Z_j(t) \text{ takes the values} \atop +1, 0, \text{ and } -1 \text{ with positive probability.} \quad (2)$$

With these conditions one can prove most of the results, or analogous ones, that were derived in this chapter.*

APPENDIX 1. AN ERGODIC THEOREM

Let $\{W(t), t = 0, 1, 2, \ldots\}$ be a Markov chain with a denumerable set of states, and let f be a function on the state space that takes only the values 1 and 0. We may think of f as indicating those states that are in a particular subset, say A, of the state space; namely, A is the set of states w for which $f(w) = 1$. Define

$$I(t) = f[W(t)], \atop s(t) = I(1) + \cdots + I(t). \quad (1)$$

The random variable $I(t)$ indicates whether or not the chain is in the set A at date t, and $s(t)$ equals the number of times the chain is in A from date 1 to date t. We suppose that the initial state, $W(0)$, is given (nonrandom).

---

*For results on thermostat behavior, see Radner, [12]. For results on putting out fires, see Rothschild, [16].

THEOREM.* *If the Markov chain $\{W(t)\}$ is ergodic, then with probability one the limit*

$$\lim_{t \to \infty} \frac{s(t)}{t} \equiv \bar{s} \qquad (2)$$

exists, is nonrandom, and is the same for all initial states $W(0)$.

We may interpret $\bar{s}$ as the long-run relative frequency with which the chain is in the set A.

To begin the proof of the theorem, let w^* be an arbitrary state of the chain, which will remain fixed throughout the proof. Let T_n denote the date of the n'th visit of the chain to state w^* (after date 0); i.e., T_n is the n'th date k (≥ 1) such that $W(k) = w^*$. Also, let $N(t)$ be the number of dates from 1 to t at which the chain is in state w^*. The general idea of the proof is to break up the evolution of the chain into successive "cycles" corresponding to the intervals of time between successive visits to the state w^*. We shall see that in a sense the cycles constitute a sequence of independent, replicated trials, to which we can apply the Strong Law of Large Numbers.

Define

$$s_n^* = I(T_n) + \cdots + I(T_{n+1} - 1) \qquad (3)$$

$$s'(t) = \begin{cases} I(1) + \cdots + I(T_1 - 1), & \text{if } T_1 = t, \\ 0, & \text{otherwise.} \end{cases} \qquad (4)$$

We can put upper and lower bounds on $s(t)$ as follows:

$$\sum_{n=1}^{N(t)-1} s_n^* \leq s(t) \leq s'(t) + \sum_{n=1}^{N(t)} s_n^*, \qquad (5)$$

where it is to be understood that a sum over an empty set is zero.

---

*The present theorem is a special case of a general ergodic theorem; see, for example, Chung, [1], Theorem 2 of Section I.15. See also the remarks at the end of this Appendix.

In (5) we are, of course, using the fact that the terms $I(t)$ are nonnegative. We shall show that we can apply the Strong Law of Large Numbers to the sums in (5), and that $s'(t)/t$ approaches zero as t gets large.

To study the sums in (5) we need a basic fact about Markov chains called the *strong Markov property*.

LEMMA 1. *For any state w_0, and any n, the conditional probability distribution of the random variables $W(T_n + 1), W(T_n + 2), \ldots$, given $W(0) = w_0$, is the same as the conditional distribution of the random variables $W(1), W(2), \ldots$, given $W(0) = w^*$.*

Lemma 1 is intuitively plausible, but one must be careful to notice that in the sequence following $W(T_n)$ the *dates* as well as the values of the variables are random. To write out the proof in full is a bit cumbersome, so we shall give the essential idea by proving that the conditional distribution of $W(T_1 + 1)$ given $W(0) = w_0$ is the same as the conditional distribution of $W(1)$ given $W(0) = w^*$.

For any $k \leq 1$ let $\mathscr{H}_k$ be the set of (finite) sequences $w_0, \ldots, w_k$ such that $w_k = w^*$ and $w_m \neq w^*$ for $1 \leq m < k$. Note that $T_1 = k$ if and only if $[W(0), \ldots, W(k)]$ is in $\mathscr{H}_k$. For the purpose of this proof, for any state w define p_w and p_w^* by

$$p_w \equiv \text{Prob}\{ W(T_1 + 1) = w | W(0) = w_0 \},$$
$$p_w^* \equiv \text{Prob}\{ W(1) = w | W(0) = w^* \}.$$

We wish to show that $p_w = p_w^*$. First observe that

$$p_w = \sum_{k \geq 1} \text{Prob}\{ W(k + 1) = w | T_1 = k, W(0) = w_0 \}$$
$$\times \text{Prob}\{ T_1 = k | W(0) = w_0 \} \qquad (6)$$
$$= \sum_{k} \sum_{H \in \mathscr{H}_k} \text{Prob}\{ W(k + 1) = w | H \} \text{Prob}\{ H | W(0) = w_0 \}.$$

By the definition of a Markov chain, for every k and every H in $\mathscr{H}_k$,

$$\text{Prob}\{ W(k + 1) = w | H \} = p_w^*.$$

Substitution of this in the second line of (6) gives

$$
\begin{aligned}
p_w &= p_w^* \sum_k \sum_{H \in \mathscr{H}_k} \text{Prob}\{ H | W(0) = w_0 \} \\
&= p_w^* \sum_k \text{Prob}\{ T_1 = k | W(0) = w_0 \}.
\end{aligned}
\tag{7}
$$

Since the chain is ergodic, T_1 is finite with probability one, so that the sum in the second line of (7) is unity. Hence $p_w = p_w^*$.

From Lemma 1 one easily verifies:

LEMMA 2. *The random variables s_n^* are independent and identically distributed.*

Lemma 2 and the Strong law of Large Numbers together give us

$$
\lim_{m \to \infty} \left(\frac{1}{m} \right) \sum_{n=1}^m s_n^* = \mathscr{E} s_n^*.
\tag{8}
$$

Since $0 \le I(t) \le 1$, $0 \le s_n^* \le T_{n+1} - T_n$. Since the chain is ergodic

$$
\mathscr{E}(T_{n+1} - T_n) < \infty,
$$

so that

$$
\mathscr{E} s_n^* < \infty.
\tag{9}
$$

Of course, $\mathscr{E} s_n^*$ is the same for all n.

Again, since the chain is ergodic, it will visit the state w^* infinitely often, so that

$$
\lim_{t \to \infty} N(t) = \infty.
\tag{10}
$$

Equations (8) and (10) together give us:

$$
\lim_{t \to \infty} \frac{\displaystyle\sum_{n=1}^{N(t)} s_n^*}{N(t)} = \mathscr{E} s_n^*.
\tag{11}
$$

Returning to (5), we make two observations. First $s'(t) \leqq T_1$, and T_1 is finite with probability one, so that, using (10) again,

$$\lim_{t \to \infty} \frac{s'(t)}{N(t)} = 0. \tag{12}$$

Second, again using (10), we have

$$\lim_{t \to \infty} \frac{N(t)}{N(t) - 1} = 1,$$

so that, from (11)

$$\lim_{t \to \infty} \frac{\sum_{n=1}^{N(t)-1} s_n^*}{N(t)} = \mathscr{E} s_n^*. \tag{13}$$

Putting together (5), (9), (11), (12), and (13), we have proved the basic result we need for our theorem:

LEMMA 3.   *With probability one*,

$$\lim_{t \to \infty} \frac{s(t)}{N(t)} = \mathscr{E} s_n^* < \infty. \tag{14}$$

As a special case of Lemma 3, take $f(w) = 1$ for all w; then $s(t) = t$, and

$$s_n^* = T_{n+1} - T_n \equiv \tau_n^*. \tag{15}$$

Here τ_n^* is the amount of time between the n'th and the $(n + 1)'$th visits to the state w^*. Lemma 3 now gives us

$$\lim_{t \to \infty} \frac{t}{N(t)} = \mathscr{E} \tau_n^* < \infty. \tag{16}$$

Since $\tau_n^* \geqq 1$, $\mathscr{E}\tau_n^* \geqq 1$. Hence dividing (14) by (16) we complete the proof of the Theorem with

$$\lim_{t \to \infty} \frac{s(t)}{t} = \frac{\mathscr{E}s_n^*}{\mathscr{E}\tau_n^*}. \tag{17}$$

A few remarks about the Theorem may be helpful. First, the Theorem shows that the limit $\bar{s}$ in (5) exists and is nonrandom. On the other hand, (17) gives us an explicit expression for $\bar{s}$, namely

$$\bar{s} = \frac{\mathscr{E}s_n^*}{\mathscr{E}\tau_n^*}, \tag{18}$$

which apparently depends on the choice of the state of w^*. However, the limit $\bar{s}$ in (5), if it exists at all, clearly is independent of the choice of w^*. This shows that *the ratio* $(\mathscr{E}s_n^*)/(\mathscr{E}\tau_n^*)$ *is the same for all states* w^*.

Second, recall that an ergodic Markov chain has a unique invariant probability distribution;* let $m(w)$ denote the invariant probability of the state w. Consider the special case in which $f(w^*) = 1$ and $f(w) = 0$ for $w \neq w^*$. In this case, $s(t)$ is the number of visits to w^* from date 1 to date t, and $s_n^* = 1$ for every n. Hence, from (18),

$$\bar{s} = \frac{1}{\mathscr{E}\tau_n^*}. \tag{19}$$

On the other hand, in an ergodic chain,

$$m(w^*) = \frac{1}{\mathscr{E}\tau_n^*}, \tag{20}$$

i.e., the invariant probability of w^* is the reciprocal of the mean

---

*See Feller, [2], Chapter XV, Section 7.

time b between visits* to w^*. Hence,

$$\bar{s} = m(w^*). \tag{21}$$

In other words, *the long-run relative frequency of visits to a single state is equal to the invariant probability of that state, with probability one.*

Equation (21) can be extended to the more general situation of our Theorem. Recall that f is the indicator function of a set A of states. One can show that

$$\bar{s} = \sum_{w \in A} m(w). \tag{22}$$

As a final generalization, let f be any function on the state space such that

$$\sum_{w} |f(w)| m(w) < \infty.$$

One can show** that, if the chain is ergodic, then

$$\lim_{t \to \infty} \frac{\sum_{k=1}^{t} f[W(t)]}{t} = \sum_{w} f(w) m(w),$$

with probability one. In other words, the long-run average of the value of the function on the chain equals the mean of the function under the invariant probability distribution.

APPENDIX 2. SUPPLEMENT TO THE FIRST-PASSAGE PROBLEM

The purpose of this appendix is to justify the interchange of expectation and summation operations in the infinite series (16) in Section 3. In the course of this argument we shall show that (if

---

*See Feller, [2], p. 393. One can also obtain this result from renewal theory, once one has demonstrated the Strong Markov Property of Lemma 1; see Feller, [2], Chapter XIII, Section 3.

**See Chung [1].

$V > 0$) the minimum of the partial sums $S(t)$ has a finite expectation. We shall maintain the notation and assumptions of Section 3. Define

$$S'(t) = \sum_{k=1}^{t} V(k)I(k-1). \tag{1}$$

We wish to prove:

PROPOSITION. $\lim_{t \to \infty} \mathscr{E}S'(t) = \mathscr{E}S(T_c)$.

Let $\mathscr{H}_t$ be the set of (finite) sequences $v_1, \ldots, v_t$ such that

$$\begin{aligned} v_1 + \cdots + v_k &< c \qquad \text{for } k < t, \\ v_1 + \cdots + v_t &\geq c, \tag{2} \\ |v_i| &\leq b. \end{aligned}$$

Thus $\mathscr{H}_t$ is the set of realizations of $V(1), \ldots, V(t)$ such that $T_c = t$. Define

$$\begin{aligned} \mathscr{H} &= \bigcup_{t \geq 1} \mathscr{H}_t, \\ \mathscr{F}_t &= \bigcup_{n > t} \mathscr{H}_n. \tag{3} \\ P(H) &= \text{Prob}\{[V(1), \ldots, V(t)] = H\}. \end{aligned}$$

The fact that T_c is finite with probability one implies that

$$\sum_{H \in \mathscr{H}} P(H) = 1.$$

Note that $\mathscr{H}$ is denumerable.

For $H = (v_1, \ldots, v_n)$ in $\mathscr{H}_n$ and $k \leq n$ define

$$\begin{aligned} s'(k, H) &= v_1 + \cdots + v_k, \\ s^*(H) &= \min_{k \leq n} s'(k, H), \tag{4} \\ s(H) &= v_1 + \cdots + v_n = s'(n, H). \end{aligned}$$

With this notation, we can write

$$\mathscr{E}S'(t) = \sum_{n \leq t} \sum_{H \in \mathscr{H}_n} s(H)P(H)$$

$$+ \sum_{H \in \mathscr{F}_t} s'(t, H)P(H), \qquad (5)$$

$$\mathscr{E}S(T_c) = \sum_{H \in \mathscr{H}} s(H)P(H). \qquad (6)$$

Subtracting (6) from (5) we have

$$\mathscr{E}S'(t) - \mathscr{E}S(T_c) = \sum_{H \in \mathscr{F}_t} s'(t, H)P(H)$$

$$- \sum_{H \in \mathscr{F}_t} s(H)P(H). \qquad (7)$$

Since $\mathscr{E}S(T_c)$ is finite, we know that the second sum in (7) converges to zero as t increases without limit. Hence, to prove the proposition it suffices to show that

$$\lim_{t \to \infty} \sum_{H \in \mathscr{F}_t} s'(t, H)P(H) = 0. \qquad (8)$$

Define

$$s^*(H) = \min_{k \leq n} s'(k, H), \qquad \text{for } H \text{ in } \mathscr{H}_n; \qquad (9)$$

then for $t < n$ and H in $\mathscr{H}_n$,

$$s^*(H) \leq s'(t, H) < c,$$

so that

$$\sum_{H \in \mathscr{F}_t} s^*(H)P(H) \leq \sum_{H \in \mathscr{F}_t} s'(t, H)P(H) \leq c \sum_{H \in \mathscr{F}_t} P(H). \quad (10)$$

The right-hand sum in (10) approaches zero as t increases without limit, and so will the left-hand sum if the random variable

$$S^* = \min_{t \le T_c} S(t) \tag{11}$$

has a finite expectation. Define the random variable S^{**} by

$$S^{**} = \min_{t} S(t),$$

and note that, with probability one,

$$-\infty < S^{**} \le S^* \le b. \tag{12}$$

Hence it suffices to prove the following:

LEMMA. S^{**} *has finite expectation.*

Recall that $|V(t)| \le b$. Since S^{**} is finite with probability one, there exists a number of $B > b$ such that

$$\text{Prob}\{ S(t) \le -B \text{ for some } t \} \le \tfrac{1}{2}. \tag{13}$$

Think of a sequence of "experiments" as follows: let N_1 be the first t, if any, such that $S(t) \le -B$; otherwise let $N_1 = +\infty$; if N_1 is finite, then let N_2 be the first $t > N_1$ such that $S(t) \le S(N_1) - B$, etc. By the Strong Markov Property (Lemma 1 of Appendix 1), if N_j is finite then

$$\text{Prob}\{ S(N_j + t) \le x - B \text{ for some } t | S(N_j) = x \}$$
$$\le \text{Prob}\{ S(t) \le -B \text{ for some } t \}. \tag{14}$$

Hence the probability that $N_1, \ldots, N_k$ are finite does not exceed 2^{-k}. Observe that, if N_{j+1} is finite,

$$-B - b < S(N_{j+1}) - S(N_j) \le -B.$$

Hence, if N_k is finite,

$$-k(B + b) < S(N_k) \le -kB.$$

It follows that

$$\text{Prob}\{ S^{**} \leqq -k(B+b) \} < \frac{1}{2^k}. \tag{15}$$

On the other hand,

$$S^{**} \leqq b. \tag{16}$$

Inequalities (15) and (16) together imply that $\mathscr{E}S^{**}$ is finite.

REFERENCES

1. K. L. Chung, *Markov Chains with Stationary Transition Probabilities*, Springer Verlag, New York, 2nd ed., 1967.
2. W. Feller, *An Introduction to Probability Theory and Its Applications*, Wiley, New York, 3rd ed., 1968.
3. D. Freedman, "Another note on the Borel-Cantelli lemma and the strong law," *Ann. Probability* 1 (1973), 910–925.
4. J. Green, "The stability of Edgeworth's recontracting process," *Econometrica* 42 (1974) 21–34.
5. L. Hurwicz, R. Radner and S. Reiter, "A stochastic decentralized resource allocation process: Parts I and II," *Econometrica* 43, (1975) 187–221, and 363–393.
6. J. G. Kemeny, J. L. Snell, and A. W. Knapp, *Denumerable Markov Chains*, Van Nostrand, Princeton, New Jersey, 1966.
7. C. B. McGuire and R. Radner (eds.), *Decision and Organization*, University of Minnesota Press, 2nd edition, 1986.
8. R. R. Nelson and S. G. Winter, *An Evolutionary Theory of Economic Change*, Harvard Univ. Press, Cambridge, MA, 1982.
9. R. R. Nelson, S. G. Winter and H. L. Schuette, "Technical change in an evolutionary model," *Quarterly J. Econ.* (1976), 90–118.
10. W. Neuefeind, "A stochastic bargaining process for *n*-person games," *J. of Mathematical Economics* 1 (1974), 175–191.
11. J. Neveu, *Discrete-Time Martingales*, North-Holland, Amsterdam, 1975.
12. R. Radner, "Satisficing," *J. of Math. Econ.* 2 (1975), 253–262.
13. R. Radner, "A behavioral model of cost reduction," *Bell J. of Economics and Management Science* 6 (1975), 196–215.
14. R. Radner and M. Rothschild, "On the allocation of effort," *J. Econ. Theory* 10 (1975), 358–376.
15. M. Rothschild, "A two-armed bandit theory of market pricing," *J. Econ. Theory* 9 (1974), 185–202.

16. ———, "Further notes on the allocation of effort," in T. Groves and R. Day (eds.), *Adaptive Economic Models*, Academic Press, New York, 1975, pp. 195–220.

17. H. A. Simon, "Theories of decision-making in economics and behavioral science," *American Economic Review* **49** (1959), 253–283.

18. ———, "Theories of bounded rationality," Chapter 8 in C. B. McGuire and R. Radner (eds.), [7].

19. F. Spitzer, *Principles of Random Walk*, Van Nostrand, Princeton, New Jersey, 1964.

20. S. G. Winter, "Satisficing, selection and the innovating remnant," *Quarter J. of Economics* **85** (1971), 237–261.

FOUR ASPECTS OF THE MATHEMATICAL THEORY OF ECONOMIC EQUILIBRIUM

Gerard Debreu*

The observed state of an economy can be viewed as an equilibrium resulting from the interaction of a large number of agents with partially conflicting interests. Taking this viewpoint, exactly one hundred years ago, Léon Walras presented in his *Eléments d'Economie Politique Pure* the first general mathematical analysis of this equilibrium problem. During the last four decades, Walrasian theory has given rise to several developments that require the use of basic concepts and results borrowed from diverse branches of mathematics. In this article, I propose to review four of them.

1. THE EXISTENCE OF ECONOMIC EQUILIBRIA

As soon as an equilibrium state is defined for a model of an economy, the fundamental question of its existence is raised. The first solution of this problem was provided by A. Wald ([36], [37],

---

*This chapter is a reprint of an article published some years ago.

[38]), and after a twenty-year interruption, research by a large number of authors has steadily extended the framework in which the existence of an equilibrium can be established. Although no work was done on the problem of existence of a Walrasian equilibrium from the early thirties to the early fifties, several contributions, which, later on, were to play a major role in the study of that problem, were made in related areas during that period. One of them was a lemma proved by J. von Neumann [28] in connection with his model of economic growth. This lemma was reformulated by S. Kakutani [21] as a fixed-point theorem which became the most powerful tool for proofs of existence in economics. Another contribution, due to J. Nash [27], was the first use of that tool in the solution of a problem of social equilibrium. For later reference we state Kakutani's theorem. Given two sets U and V, a *correspondence* ρ from U to V associates with every element $u \in U$, a nonempty subset $\rho(u)$ of V.

THEOREM. *If D is a nonempty, compact, convex subset of a Euclidean space, and ρ is a convex-valued, closed-graph correspondence from D to D, then there is d^* such that $d^* \in \rho(d^*)$.*

As a simple prototype of a Walrasian equilibrium problem, we now consider an exchange economy with l commodities, and a finite set A of consumers. The consumption of consumer $a \in A$ is described by a point x_a in R_+^l; the ith coordinate x_a^i of x_a being the quantity of the ith commodity that he consumes. A price system p is an l-list of strictly positive numbers, i.e., a point in $P = \text{Int } R_+^l$; the ith coordinate of p being the amount to be paid for one unit of the ith commodity. Thus the value of x_a relative to p is the inner product $p \cdot x_a$. Given the price vector $p \in P$, and his wealth $w \in L$, the set of strictly positive numbers, consumer a is constrained to satisfy the budget inequality $p \cdot x_a \leqq w$. Since multiplication of p and w by a strictly positive number has no effect on the behavior of consumers, we can normalize p, restricting it to the strictly positive part of the unit sphere $S = \{ p \in P \| \|p\| = 1 \}$. We postulate that, presented with the pair $(p, w) \in S \times L$, consumer a demands the consumption vector $f_a(p, w)$ in R_+^l, and that the demand function f_a is continuous. If that consumer is insatiable, f_a also satisfies

$$\text{for every } (p, w) \in S \times L, \qquad p \cdot f_a(p, w) = w. \qquad (1)$$

To complete the description of the economy $\mathscr{E}$, we specify for consumer a an initial endowment vector $e_a \in P$. Thus the characteristics of consumer a are the pair (f_a, e_a), and $\mathscr{E}$ is the list $((f_a, e_a))_{a \in A}$ of those pairs for $a \in A$. Consider now a price vector $p \in S$. The corresponding wealth of consumer a is $p \cdot e_a$; his demand is $f_a(p, p \cdot e_a)$. Therefore the excess demand of the economy is

$$F(p) = \sum_{a \in A} \left[f_a(p, p \cdot e_a) - e_a \right]$$

and p is an equilibrium price vector if and only if $F(p) = 0$. Because of (1), the function F from S to R^l satisfies

Walras' law. $\quad p \cdot F(p) = 0.$

Consequently, F is a continuous vector field on S, all of whose coordinates are bounded below. Finally, we make an assumption about the behavior of F near ∂S.

Boundary condition. If p_n in S tends to p_0 in ∂S, then $\{ F(p_n) \}$ is unbounded.

This condition expresses that every commodity is collectively desired. Here and below I freely make unnecessarily strong assumptions when they facilitate the exposition. Of the many variants of the existence theorem that have been proposed, I select the following statement by E. Dierker ([9], Section 8), some of whose antecedents were L. McKenzie [26], D. Gale [15], H. Nikaido [29], and K. Arrow and F. Hahn [3].

THEOREM. *If F is continuous, bounded below, and satisfies Walras' law and the boundary condition, then there is an equilibrium.*

We indicate the main ideas of a proof because they will recur in this section and in the next. Here it is most convenient

to normalize the price vector so that it belongs to the simplex
$\Pi = \{ p \in R^l_+ | \Sigma^l_{i=1} p^i = 1\}$.

Consider a price vector $p \notin \partial\Pi$ yielding an excess demand
$F(p) \neq 0$. According to a commonly held view of the role of
prices, a natural reaction of a price-setting agency to this disequi-
librium situation would be to select a new price vector so as to
make the excess demand $F(p)$ as expensive as possible, i.e., to
select
(K. Arrow and G. Debreu [2]) a price vector in the set

$$\mu(p) = \left\{ \pi \in \Pi | \pi \cdot F(p) = \max_{q \in \Pi} q \cdot F(p) \right\}.$$

When $p \in \partial\Pi$, the excess demand is not defined. In this case,
we let $\mu(p) = \{ \pi \in \Pi | \pi \cdot p = 0\}$.

By Kakutani's theorem, the correspondence μ from Π to Π has
a fixed point p^*. Obviously, $p^* \notin \partial\Pi$. But then $p^* \in \mu(p^*)$
implies $F(p^*) = 0$.

From the fact that $\mu(p)$ is always a face of Π one suspects
(rightly as we will see in the next section) that Kakutani's theorem
is too powerful a tool for this result. But such is not the case in the
general situation to which we will turn after having pointed out the
broad interpretation that the concept of commodity must be given.
In contemporary Walrasian theory, a commodity is defined as a
good or a service with specified physical characteristics, to be
delivered at a specified date, at a specified location, if (K. Arrow
[1]) a specified event occurs. Aside from this mere question of
interpretation of a concept, the model can be expanded so as to
include a finite set B of producers. Producer $b \in B$ chooses a
production vector y_b (whose positive coordinates correspond to
outputs, and negative coordinates to inputs) in his production set
Y_b, a nonempty subset of R^l, interpreted as the set of feasible
production vectors. When the price vector p is given, producer b
actually chooses his production vector in a nonempty subset $\psi_b(p)$
of Y_b. It is essential here, as it was not in the case of consumers, to
provide for situations in which p does not uniquely determine the
reaction of every producer, which may arise for instance if producer b maximizes his profit $p \cdot y_b$ in a cone Y_b with vertex 0

(constant returns to scale technology). In an economy with production, consumer a not only demands goods and services, but also supplies certain quantities of certain types of labor, which will appear as negative coordinates of his consumption vector x_a; this vector x_a is constrained to belong to his consumption set X_a, a given nonempty subset of R^l. A suitable extension of the concept of demand function covers this case. However, the wealth of a consumer is now the sum of the value of his endowment vector and of his shares of the profits of producers. In this manner an integrated model of consumption and production is obtained, in which a state of the economy is a list $((x_a)_{a \in A}, (y_b)_{b \in B}, p)$ of vectors of R^l, where, for every $a \in A$, $x_a \in X_a$; for every $b \in B$, $y_b \in Y_b$; and $p \in \Pi$. The problem of existence of an equilibrium for such an economy has often been reduced to a situation similar to that of the last theorem, the continuous excess demand function being replaced by an excess demand correspondence with a closed graph. Alternatively, it can be formulated in the following general terms, in the spirit of J. Nash [27]. The social system is composed of a finite set C of agents. For each $c \in C$, a set D_c of possible actions is given. Consequently, a state of the system is an element d of the product $D = \times_{c \in C} D_c$. We denote by $d_{C \setminus c}$ the list of actions obtained by deleting d_c from d. Given $d_{C \setminus c}$, i.e., the actions chosen by all the other agents, agent c reacts by choosing his own action in the set $\rho_c(d_{C \setminus c})$. The state d^* is an equilibrium if and only if, for every $c \in C$, $d_c^* \in \rho_c(d_{C \setminus c}^*)$. Thus, the reaction correspondence ρ from D to D being defined by $\rho(d) = \times_{c \in C} \rho_c(d_{C \setminus c})$, the state d^* is an equilibrium if and only if it is a fixed point of ρ. In the integrated economic model of consumption and production that we discussed, one of the agents is the impersonal market to which we assign the reaction correspondence μ introduced in the proof of the existence theorem.

Still broader interpretations and further extensions of the preceding model have been proposed. They include negative or zero prices, preference relations with weak properties instead of demand functions for consumers, measure spaces of agents, infinite-dimensional commodity spaces, monopolistic competition, public goods, redistribution of income, indivisible commodities, transaction costs,

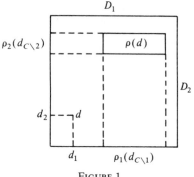

FIGURE 1

money, the use of nonstandard analysis, ... Since this extensive, and still rapidly growing, literature cannot be surveyed in detail here, I refer to the excellent account by K. Arrow and F. Hahn [3], to the books mentioned in the next sections, and to recent volumes of *Econometrica*, *Journal of Economic Theory*, and *Journal of Mathematical Economics*.

2. THE COMPUTATION OF ECONOMIC EQUILIBRIA

While the first proof of existence is forty years old, decisive steps towards an efficient algorithm for the computation of Walras equilibria were taken only during the last decade. In 1964, C. Lemke and J. Howson gave an effective procedure for the computation of an equilibrium of a non-zero-sum two-person game. H. Scarf [31], [32] then showed how a technique similar to that of C. Lemke and J. Howson could be used to compute an approximate Walras equilibrium, and proposed a general algorithm for the calculation of an approximate fixed point of a correspondence. This algorithm, which has revealed itself to be surprisingly efficient, had the drawback of not permitting a gradual improvement of the degree of approximation of the solution. An essential extension due to C. Eaves [12], [13], stimulated by a fixed-point theorem of F. Browder [7], overcame this difficulty.

Before presenting a version of the algorithm based on H. Scarf [32], and C. Eaves [13], we note that in the preceding proof of existence, we have actually associated with every point $p \in \Pi$ a set $\Lambda(p)$ of integers in $I = \{1, \ldots, l\}$, as follows.

$$\Lambda(p) = \left\{ i | F^i(p) = \max_j F^j(p) \right\} \quad \text{if } p \notin \partial\Pi,$$

$$= \left\{ i | p^i = 0 \right\} \quad \quad \quad \text{if } p \in \partial\Pi.$$

The point p^* is an equilibrium if and only if $\Lambda(p^*) = I$, in other words, if and only if it is in the intersection of the closed sets $E_i = \{ p | i \in \Lambda(p) \}$. Showing that this intersection is not empty would yield an existence proof in the manner of D. Gale [15].

We specify our terminology. By a simplex, we always mean a closed simplex, and, of course, similarly for a face of a simplex. A *facet* of an n-simplex is an $(n-1)$-face. For each $p \in \Pi$, select now a label $\lambda(p)$ in $\Lambda(p)$. A set M of points is said to be *completely labeled*, abbreviated to *c.l.*, if the set $\lambda(M)$ of its labels is I. The labeling λ is chosen so as to satisfy the following restrictions on $\partial\Pi$:

(α)   the set of vertices of Π is c.l.,
(β)   no facet of Π is c.l.[1]

The algorithm will yield a c.l. set of l points of Π whose diameter can be made arbitrarily small, and consequently a point of Π at which the value of F can be made arbitrarily small.

Let T be the part of R_+^l that is above Π, and $\mathcal{T}$ be a standard regular triangulation of T having for vertices the points of T with integral coordinates, used by H. Kuhn [23], [24], T. Hansen [17], and C. Eaves [12], and illustrated by the figure. (Other considerably more efficient triangulations of, or more appropriately pseudo-

---

[1] Here is a simple example of a labeling of $\partial\Pi$ satisfying those restrictions. Given $p \in \partial\Pi$, select any $\lambda(p)$ in $\Lambda(p)$ such that $\lambda(p) - 1 \pmod{l}$ is not in $\Lambda(p)$.

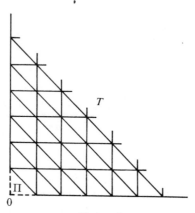

FIGURE 2

manifold structures on, T have been used, C. Eaves [12], [13].)
Give any point in T the same label as its projection from 0 into Π;
and say that two $(l-1)$-simplexes of $\mathscr{T}$ are *adjacent* if there is an
l-simplex of $\mathscr{T}$ of which they are facets. Consider now an $(l-1)$-
simplex s of $\mathscr{T}$ with c.l. vertices.

(i) If $s = \Pi$, s is a facet of exactly one l-simplex of $\mathscr{T}$; hence
there is exactly one $(l-1)$-simplex of $\mathscr{T}$ with c.l. vertices adjacent
to s.

(ii) If $s \neq \Pi$, because of (β), s is not in the boundary of T;
therefore s is a facet of exactly two l-simplexes of $\mathscr{T}$; hence there
are exactly two $(l-1)$-simplexes of $\mathscr{T}$ with c.l. vertices adjacent to s.

The algorithm starts from $s^0 = \Pi$. Take s^1 to be the unique
$(l-1)$-simplex of $\mathscr{T}$ with c.l. vertices adjacent to s^0. For $k > 0$,
take s^{k+1} to be the unique $(l-1)$-simplex of $\mathscr{T}$ with c.l. vertices
adjacent to s^k, and other than s^{k-1}. Clearly this algorithm
never returns to a previously used $(l-1)$-simplex and never
terminates. Given any integer n, after a finite number of steps, one
obtains an $(l-1)$-simplex with c.l. vertices above the hyperplane

$\{ p \in R^l | \Sigma_{i=1}^l p^i = n \}$. Projecting from 0 into Π, one obtains a sequence of c.l. sets of l points of Π whose diameter tends to 0 as n tends to $+\infty$.

An approximate fixed point (i.e., a point close to its image) of a continuous function from a finite-dimensional, nonempty, compact, convex set to itself can be obtained by a direct application of this algorithm. But in order to solve the analogous problem for a fixed point of a correspondence, and consequently, for a Walras equilibrium of an economy with production, H. Scarf and C. Eaves have used vector labels rather than the preceding integer labels. With every point p of Π, one now associates a suitably chosen vector $\lambda(p)$ in R^{l-1}, and one says that a set M of points of Π is c.l. if the origin of R^{l-1} belongs to the convex hull of $\lambda(M)$. As before, the labeling λ of Π is restricted to satisfy (α) and (β). The last two paragraphs can then be repeated word for word with the following single exception. Let σ be an l-simplex of $\mathscr{T}$, and s be a facet of σ with c.l. vertices. Denote by V_σ (resp. V_s) the set of vertices of σ (resp. of s). If $\lambda(V_\sigma)$ is in general position in R^{l-1}, then 0 is interior to the convex hull of $\lambda(V_s)$, and there is exactly one other facet of σ with c.l. vertices. However, if $\lambda(V_\sigma)$ is not in general position, a degenerate case where there are several other facets of σ with c.l. vertices may arise. An appropriate use of the lexic refinement of linear programming resolves this degeneracy. In this general form, the algorithm can indeed be directly applied to the computation of approximate Kakutani fixed points.

The simplicity of this algorithm is very appealing, but its most remarkable feature is its efficiency. Experience with several thousand examples has been reported, in particular in H. Scarf [32] and R. Wilmuth [40]. As a typical case of the version of the integer-labeling algorithm presented above (which uses an inefficient triangulation of T), let $l = 10$. To reach an elevation $n = 100$ in T, i.e., a triangulation of Π for which every edge is divided into 100 equal intervals, the number of iterations required rarely exceeds 2,000, and the computing time on an IBM 370 is usually less than 15 seconds. The number of vertices that are examined in the computation is therefore a small fraction of the number of vertices of the triangulation of Π at elevation 100.

The best general reference on the problem discussed in this section is H. Scarf [1973]. *Mathematical Programming* is a good bibliographical source for more recent developments.

3. REGULAR DIFFERENTIABLE ECONOMIES

The model $\mathscr{E} = ((f_a, e_a))_{a \in A}$ of an exchange economy presented at the beginning of Section 1 would provide a complete explanation of the observed state of that economy in the Walrasian framework if the set $E(\mathscr{E})$ of its equilibrium price vectors had exactly one element. However, this global uniqueness requirement has revealed itself to be excessively strong, and was replaced, in the last five years, by that of local uniqueness. Not only does one wish $E(\mathscr{E})$ to be discrete, one would also like the correspondence E to be continuous. Otherwise, the slightest error of observation on the data of the economy might lead to an entirely different set of predicted equilibria. This consideration, which is common in the study of physical systems, applies with even greater force to the study of social systems. Basic differential topology has provided simple and satisfactory answers to the two questions of discreteness of $E(\mathscr{E})$, and of continuity of E.

At first, we keep the list $f = (f_a)_{a \in A}$ of demand functions fixed, and we assume that each one of them is of class C^r ($r \geqq 1$). Thus an economy is identified with the point $e = (e_a)_{a \in A}$ in P^A. We denote by E the set of $(e, p) \in P^A \times S$ such that p is an equilibrium price vector for the economy e, and by $E(e)$ the set of equilibrium price vectors associated with a given e. The central importance of the manifold E, or of a related manifold of S. Smale [34], has been recognized by S. Smale [34] and Y. Balasko [5]. Recently Y. Balasko [6] has noticed the property of C^r-isomorphism to P^A.

THEOREM. *E is a C^r-submanifold of $P^A \times S$ of the same dimension as P^A. If for every $a \in A$ the range of f_a is contained in P, then E is C^r-isomorphic to P^A.*

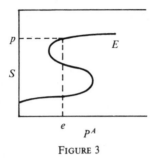

FIGURE 3

Now let π be the projection $P^A \times S \rightarrow P^A$, and $\tilde{\pi}$ be its restriction to the manifold E.

DEFINITION.   The economy $\mathscr{E} = (f, e)$ is *regular* if e is a regular value of $\tilde{\pi}$. It is *critical* if it is not regular.

By Sard's theorem, the set of critical e has Lebesgue measure zero. Suppose in addition we assume that every demand function f_a satisfies the

Strong boundary condition.   If (p_n, w_n) in $S \times L$ tends to (p_0, w_0) in $\partial S \times L$, then $\{f_a(p_n, w_n)\}$ is unbounded.

Then we readily obtain that $\tilde{\pi}$ is proper (Y. Balasko [6]). In this case the critical set is closed (relative to P^A). It is therefore negligible in a strong sense. As for economies in the regular set $\mathscr{R}$, the complement of the critical set, they are well behaved in the following sense. At $e \in \mathscr{R}$, the compact set $E(e) = \tilde{\pi}^{-1}(e)$ is discrete, therefore finite, and $\tilde{\pi}^{-1}$ is locally a C^r-diffeomorphism.

In order to prepare for the discussion of regular economies in the context of the next section, we note an equivalent definition (E. and H. Dierker [10]) of a critical point of the manifold E for $\tilde{\pi}$. Given e, let $F(p)$ be the excess demand associated with p, and denote by $\hat{F}(p)$ the projection of $F(p)$ into some fixed $(l - 1)$-dimensional coordinate subspace of R^l. Because of Walras' law, and because p is strictly positive, $F(p) = 0$ is equivalent to $\hat{F}(p) = 0$. Let then $J[\hat{F}(p)]$ be the Jacobian determinant of $\hat{F}$ at p. As Y. Balasko [6] shows, (e, p) is a critical point of $\tilde{\pi}$ if and only if $J[\hat{F}(p)] = 0$.

Since it is desirable to let demand functions vary as well as initial endowments (F. Delbaen [8], E. and H. Dierker [10]), we endow the set D of C^r demand functions $(r \geq 1)$ satisfying the strong boundary condition with the topology of uniform C^r-convergence.

An economy $\mathcal{E}$ is now defined as an element of $(D \times P)^A$, a regular element of the latter space being a pair (f, e) for which the Jacobian determinant introduced in the last paragraph is different from zero for every equilibrium price vector associated with (f, e). The regular set is then shown to be open and dense in $(D \times P)^A$. Another extension, by S. Smale [34], established the same two properties of the regular set in the context of utility functions with weak properties, rather than in the context of demand functions.

Still further generalizations, for instance, to cases where production is possible, have been obtained. E. Dierker [9] surveys a large part of the area covered in this section more leisurely than I did. Recent volumes of the three journals listed at the end of Section 1 are also relevant here.

4. THE CORE OF A LARGE ECONOMY

So far the discussion of consumer behavior has been in terms of demand functions. We now introduce for consumer a the more basic concept of a binary preference relation $\precsim_a$ on R^l_+, for which we read "$x \precsim_a y$" as "for agent a, commodity vector y is at least as desired as commodity vector x." The relation of strict preference "$x \prec_a y$" is defined by "$x \precsim_a y$ and not $y \precsim_a x$," and of indifference "$x \sim_a y$" by "$x \precsim_a y$ and $y \precsim_a x$." Similarly, for two vectors x, y in R^l we denote by "$x \leq y$" the relation "$y - x \in R^l_+$," by "$x < y$" the relation "$x \leq y$ and not $y \leq x$," and by "$x \lessdot y$" the relation "$y - x \in P$."

We assume that $\precsim_a$ is a complete preorder with a closed graph, and that it satisfies the monotony condition, $x < y$ implies $x \prec_a y$, expressing the desirability of all commodities for consumer a. The set of preference relations satisfying these assumptions is denoted by $\mathcal{P}$, and viewing an element of $\mathcal{P}$ as a closed subset of R^{2l}, we endow $\mathscr{P}$ with Hausdorff's [18] topology of closed convergence (Y. Kannai [22]).

The characteristics of consumer $a \in A$ are now a pair $(\precsim_a, e_a)$ of a preference relation in $\mathscr{P}$, and an endowment vector in R_+^l. Thus an exchange *economy* $\mathscr{E}$ is a function from A to $\mathscr{P} \times R_+^l$. The result of any exchange process in this economy is an *allocation*, i.e., a function x from A to R_+^l, that is *attainable* in the sense that $\Sigma_{a \in A} x_a = \Sigma_{a \in A} e_a$.

A proposed allocation x is *blocked* by a coalition E of consumers if

(i) $E \neq \varnothing$,

and the members of E can reallocate their own endowments among themselves so as to make every member of E better off, i.e., if

(ii)   there is an allocation y such that $\Sigma_{a \in E} y_a = \Sigma_{a \in E} e_a$ and, for every $a \in E$, $x_a \prec_a y_a$.

From this viewpoint, first taken by F. Edgeworth [14], only the unblocked attainable allocations are viable. The set of those allocations is the *core* $C(\mathscr{E})$ of the economy. The goal of this section is to relate the core to the equilibrium concept that underlies the analysis of the first three sections. Formally, we define a *Walras allocation* as an attainable allocation x for which there is a price system $p \in \Pi$ such that, for every $a \in A$, x_a is a greatest element for $\precsim_a$ of the budget set $\{z \in R_+^l | p \cdot z \leqq p \cdot e_a\}$.

The set of Walras allocations of $\mathscr{E}$ is denoted by $W(\mathscr{E})$. It satisfies the mathematically trivial but economically important relation $W(\mathscr{E}) \subset C(\mathscr{E})$.

Simple examples show that for small economies the second set is much larger than the first. However, F. Edgeworth [14] perceived that as the number of agents tends to $+\infty$ in such a way that each one of them becomes insignificant relative to their totality, the two sets tend to coincide. The conditions under which F. Edgeworth proved his limit theorem were very special. The first generalization was obtained by H. Scarf [30], after M. Shubik [33] had called attention to the connection between F. Edgeworth's "contract curve" and the game-theoretical concept of the core. The problem was then placed in its natural setting by R. Aumann [4]. The agents now form a positive measure space $(A, \mathcal{A}, \nu)$ such that $\nu(A) = 1$. The elements of $\mathcal{A}$ are the *coalitions*, and for $E \in \mathcal{A}$, $\nu(E)$ is interpreted as the fraction of the totality of agents in coalition E. Since the characteristics of an agent $a \in A$ are the pair $(\precsim_a, e_a)$, an *economy* $\mathcal{E}$ is defined (W. Hildenbrand [20]), as a measurable function from A to $\mathcal{P} \times R_+^l$ such that e is integrable. The definitions of an unblocked attainable allocation and of a Walras allocation are extended in an obvious fashion. As trivially as before $W(\mathcal{E}) \subset C(\mathcal{E})$. But in the case in which the space of agents is atomless, i.e., in which every agent is negligible, R. Aumann [4] has proved the

THEOREM. *If the economy $\mathcal{E}$ is atomless and $\int_A e \, d\nu \gg 0$, then* $W(\mathcal{E}) = C(\mathcal{E})$.

This remarkable result reconciles two fundamental and a priori very different equilibrium concepts. Its proof can be based (K. Vind [35]) on Lyapunov's theorem on the convexity of the range of an atomless finite-dimensional vector measure.

There remains to determine the extent to which the equality of the core and of the set of Walras allocations holds approximately for a finite economy with a large number of nearly insignificant agents. This program is the object of W. Hildenbrand [20], one of whose main results we now present.

Letting $K = \mathcal{P} \times R_+^l$ be the set of agents' characteristics, we introduce the basic concepts associated with the economy $\mathcal{E}$ that we need. The image measure $\mu = \nu \circ \mathcal{E}^{-1}$ of ν via $\mathcal{E}$ is a probability on K called the *characteristic distribution* of $\mathcal{E}$. Given an allocation x for $\mathcal{E}$ (i.e., an integrable function from A to R_+^l), consider the function γ_x from A to $K \times R_+^l$ defined by $\gamma_x(a) = (\mathcal{E}(a), x(a))$. The image measure $\nu \circ \gamma_x^{-1}$ of ν via γ_x is a probability on $K \times R_+^l$ called the *characteristic-consumption distribution* of x. We denote by $W_{\mathcal{D}}(\mathcal{E})$ the set of characteristic-consumption distributions of the Walras allocations of $\mathcal{E}$, and similarly by $C_{\mathcal{D}}(\mathcal{E})$ the set of characteristic-consumption distributions of the core allocations of $\mathcal{E}$. Finally, we formalize the idea of a competitive sequence of finite economies. $\#A_n$ will denote the number of agents of $\mathcal{E}_n$, μ_n the characteristic distribution of $\mathcal{E}_n$, and pr_2 the projection from K into R_+^l. The sequence $(\mathcal{E}_n)$ is *competitive* if

(i) $\#A_n \to +\infty$,
(ii) μ_n converges weakly to a limit μ,
(iii) $\int_K pr_2 \, d\mu_n \to \int_K pr_2 \, d\mu \geqslant 0$.

We denote by $\mathscr{E}^\mu$ the economy defined as the identity map from K, endowed with its Borel σ-field $\mathscr{B}(K)$, and the measure μ, to K. Then, endowing the set of probability measures on $K \times R_+^l$ with the topology of weak convergence, we obtain the theorem of W. Hildenbrand ([20], Chapter 3).

THEOREM. *If the sequence $(\mathscr{E}_n)$ is competitive, and U is a neighborhood of $W_\mathscr{D}(\mathscr{E}^\mu)$, then, for n large enough, $C_\mathscr{D}(\mathscr{E}_n) \subset U$.*

To go further, and to obtain full continuity results, as well as results on the rate of convergence of the core of $\mathscr{E}_n$, we need an extension (F. Delbaen [8], K. Hildenbrand [20], and H. Dierker [11]) of the concepts and of the propositions of Section 3 to the present context of a measure space of agents. Specifically, we place ourselves in the framework of H. Dierker [11]. In addition to being in $\mathscr{P}$, the preference relations of consumers are now assumed to satisfy the following conditions. For every point $x \in P$, the preference-or-indifference set $\{y \in P | x \precsim y\}$ is convex, and the indifference set $I(x) = \{y \in P | y \sim x\}$ is a C^2-hypersurface of P whose Gaussian curvature is everywhere nonzero, and whose closure relative to R^l is contained in P. Finally denoting by $g(x)$ the positive unit normal of $I(x)$ at the point x, we assume that g is C^1 on P. These conditions make it possible to identify the preference relation $\precsim$ with the C^1 vector field g on P. The set G of these vector fields is endowed with the topology of uniform C^1 convergence on compact subsets. $\mathscr{M}$ then denotes the set of characteristic distributions on $G \times P$ with compact support. The assumptions that we have made imply that every agent has a C^1 demand function. Therefore it is possible to define a *regular* element μ of $\mathscr{M}$ as a characteristic distribution μ in $\mathscr{M}$ such that the Jacobian determinant introduced in Section 3 is different from zero for every equilibrium price vector associated with μ. Having suitably topologized the set $\mathscr{M}$, one can give, in the manner of H. Dierker [11], general conditions under which the regular set is open and dense in $\mathscr{M}$.

In this framework, the following result on the rate of convergence of the core of an economy has recently been obtained (B. Grodal [16]) for the case in which the agents' characteristics belong to a compact subset Q of $G \times P$. For a finite set A, d^A denotes the metric defined on the set of functions from A to R^l by $d^A(x, y) = \text{Max}_{a \in A}\|x(a) - y(a)\|$, and $\delta^A(X, Y)$ denotes the associated Hausdorff distance of two compact sets X, Y of functions from A to R^l. In the statement of the theorem, $\mathcal{M}_Q$ denotes the set of characteristic distributions on Q with the topology of weak convergence.

THEOREM. *If Q is a compact subset of $G \times P$, and μ is a regular characteristic distribution on Q, then there are a neighborhood V of μ in $\mathcal{M}_Q$, and a real number k such that for every economy $\mathcal{E}$ with a finite set A of agents, and whose characteristic distribution belongs to V,*

$$\delta^A[C(\mathcal{E}), W(\mathcal{E})] \leq k/\#A.$$

Thus if $(\mathcal{E}_n)$ is a competitive sequence of economies on Q, and if the limit characteristic distribution is regular, then $\delta^A[C(\mathcal{E}_n), W(\mathcal{E}_n)]$ tends to 0 at least as fast as the inverse of the number of agents.

The basic reference for this section is W. Hildenbrand [20].

The analysis of Walras equilibria, of the core, and of their relationship has yielded valuable insights into the role of prices in an economy. But possibly of greater importance has been the recognition that the techniques used in that analysis are indispensable for the mathematical study of social systems: algebraic topology for the test of existence that mathematical models of social equilibrium must pass; differential topology for the more demanding tests of discreteness, and of continuity for the set of equilibria; combinatorial techniques for the computation of equilibria; and measure theory for the study of large sets of small agents.

The author gratefully acknowledges the support of the Miller Institute of the University of California, Berkeley, and of the National Science Foundation, and the comments of Birgit Grodal, Werner Hildenbrand, Andreu Mas-Colell, and Herbert Scarf.

REFERENCES

1. K. J. Arrow, "Le rôle des valeurs boursières pour la répartition la meilleure des risques," *Econométrie*, pp. 41–47; discussion, pp. 47–48, *Colloq. Internat. Centre National de la Recherche Scientifique*, no. 40 (Paris, 1952), Centre de la Recherche Scientifique, Paris, 1953; Translated in *Review of Economic Studies*, **31** (1964), 91–96. MR **16**, 943.

2. K. J. Arrow and G. Debreu, "Existence of an equilibrium for a competitive economy," *Econometrica*, **22** (1954), 265–290. MR **17**, 985.

3. K. J. Arrow and F. H. Hahn, *General Competitive Analysis*, Holden-Day, San Francisco, California, 1971.

4. R. J. Aumann, "Markets with a continuum of traders," *Econometrica*, **32** (1964), 39–50. MR **30**, #2908.

5. Y. Balasko, "On the graph of the Walras correspondence," *Econometrica*, **43** (1975), 907–912.

6. ———, "Some results on uniqueness and on stability of equilibrium in general equilibrium theory," *J. Math. Economics*, **2** (1975), 95–118.

7. F. E. Browder, "On continuity of fixed points under deformations of continuous mappings," *Summa Brasil. Mat.*, **4** (1960), 183–191. MR **24** #A543.

8. F. Delbaen, *Lower and upper semi-continuity of the Walras correspondence*, Doctoral Dissertation, Free University of Brussels, 1971.

9. E. Dierker, "Topological methods in Walrasian economics," *Lecture Notes in Economics and Mathematical Systems*, **92** (1974), Springer-Verlag, Berlin.

10. E. Dierker and H. Dierker, "On the local uniqueness of equilibria," *Econometrica*, **40** (1972), 867–881.

11. H. Dierker, "Smooth preferences and the regularity of equilibria," *J. Math. Economics*, **2** (1975), 43–62.

12. B. C. Eaves, "Homotopies for computation of fixed points," *Math. Programming*, **3** (1972), 1–22. MR **46** #3089.

13. ———, "Properly labeled simplexes," *Studies in Optimization*, MAA Studies in Mathematics, Vol. 10, G. B. Dantzig and B. C. Eaves, eds., Mathematical Association of America, 1974.

14. F. Y. Edgeworth, *Mathematical Psychics*, Paul Kegan, London, 1881.

15. D. Gale, "The law of supply and demand," *Math. Scand.*, **3** (1955), 155–169. MR **17**, 985.

16. B. Grodal, "The rate of convergence of the core for a purely competitive sequence of economies," *J. Math. Economics*, **2** (1975), 171–186.

17. T. Hansen, *On the approximation of a competitive equilibrium*, Ph.D. Dissertation, Yale University, New Haven, Connecticut, 1968.

18. F. Hausdorf, *Set Theory*, Chelsea, New York, 1957. MR **19**, 111.

19. K. Hildenbrand, "Finiteness of $\Pi(E)$ and continuity of Π," Appendix to Chapter 2 in W. Hildenbrand [20].

20. W. Hildenbrand, *Core and Equilibria of a Large Economy*, Princeton University Press, Princeton, New Jersey, 1974.

21. S. Kakutani, "A generalization of Brouwer's fixed point theorem," *Duke Math. J.*, **8** (1941), 457–459. MR **3**, 60.

22. Y. Kannai, "Continuity properties of the core of a market," *Econometrica*, **38** (1970), 791–815.

23. H. W. Kuhn, "Some combinatorial lemmas in topology," *IBM J. Res. Develop.*, **4** (1960), 518–524. MR **23** #A1358.

24. ——, "Simplicial approximation of fixed points," *Proc. Nat. Acad. Sci. U.S.A.*, **61** (1968), 1238–1242.

25. C. E. Lemke and J. T. Howson, Jr., "Equilibrium points of bimatrix games," *J. Soc. Indust. Appl. Math.*, **12** (1964), 413–423. MR **30** #3769.

26. L.W. McKenzie, "On equilibrium in Graham's model of world trade and other competitive systems," *Econometrica*, **22** (1954), 147–161.

27. J. Nash, "Equilibrium points in *n*-person games," *Proc. Nat. Acad. Sci. U.S.A.*, **36** (1950), 48–49. MR **11**, 192.

28. J. von Neumann, Über ein ökonomisches Gleichungssystem und eine Verallgemeinerung des Brouwerschen fixpunktsatzes," *Ergebnisse eines mathematischen Kolloquiums*, no. 8 (1937), 83–73; Translated in *Review of Economic Studies*, **13** (1945), 1–9.

29. H. Nikaido, "On the classical multilateral exchange problem," *Metroecon.*, **8** (1956), 135–145. MR **18**, 266.

30. H. Scarf, "An analysis of markets with a large number of participants," *Recent Advances in Game Theory*, Princeton University Conference Report, 1962.

31. ——, "The approximation of fixed points of a continuous mapping," *SIAM J. Appl. Math.*, **15** (1967), 1328–1343. MR **39** #3814.

32. ——, (with the collaboration of T. Hansen), *The Computation of Economic Equilibria*, Yale University Press, New Haven, Connecticut, 1973.

33. M. Shubik, "Edgeworth market games," *Contributions to the Theory of Games*, Vol. IV, Ann. of Math. Studies, no. 40, Princeton University Press, Princeton, New Jersey, 1959. MR **21** #2538.

34. S. Smale, "Global analysis and economics," IIA, *J. Math. Economics*, **1** (1974), 1–14.

35. K. Vind, "Edgeworth-allocations in an exchange economy with many traders," *Internat. Economic Rev.*, **5** (1964), 165–177.

36. A. Wald, "Über die eindeutige positive Lösbarkeit der neuen Produktionsgleichungen, *Ergebnisse eines mathematischen Kolloquiums*, **6** (1935), 12–20.

37. ——, "Über die Produktionsgleichungen der ökonomischen Wertlehre, *Ergebnisse eines mathematischen Kolloquiums*, **7** (1936), 1–6.

38. ——, "Über einige Gleichungssysteme der mathematischen Ökonomie, *Nationalökonomie*, **7** (1936), 637–670; Translated as "On some systems of equations of mathematical economics," *Econometrica*, **19** (1951), 368–503. MR **13**, 370.

39. L. Walras, *Eléments d'Economie Politique Pure*, Lausanne, Corbaz, 1874–1977; Translated as *Elements of Pure Economics*, Irwin, Homewood, Illinois, 1954.

40. R. J. Wilmuth, *The Computation of Fixed Points*, Ph.D. Dissertation, Stanford University, Stanford, California, 1973.

NAME INDEX

SUBJECT INDEX

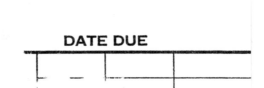

DATE DUE